Radio Free Dixie

Radio Free Dixie
Robert F. Williams & the Roots of Black Power

Timothy B. Tyson

The University of North Carolina Press   Chapel Hill & London

Publication of this work was aided by a generous
grant from the Z. Smith Reynolds Foundation.

The paper in this book meets the guidelines for
permanence and durability of the Committee on
Production Guidelines for Book Longevity of the
Council on Library Resources.

Library of Congress
Cataloging-in-Publication Data
Tyson, Timothy B.
Radio Free Dixie : Robert F. Williams and the
roots of Black power / by Timothy B. Tyson.
    p. cm.
Includes bibliographical references and index.
ISBN-13: 978-0-8078-2502-0 (cloth : alk. paper)
ISBN-10: 0-8078-2502-6 (cloth : alk. paper)
ISBN-13: 978-0-8078-4923-1 (pbk. : alk. paper)
ISBN-10: 0-8078-4923-5 (pbk. : alk. paper)
    1. Williams, Robert Franklin, 1925–   . 2. Afro-
American civil rights workers—North Carolina—
Monroe—Biography. 3. Civil rights workers—
North Carolina—Monroe—Biography. 4. Monroe
(N.C.)—Race relations. 5. Afro-Americans—Civil
rights—North Carolina—Monroe—History—20th
century. 6. Black power—United States—
History—20th century. 7. Radio Free Dixie
(Radio program)
    I. Title.
F264.M75T97   1999
975.6'755—dc21   99-11981
                        CIP

cloth 05   04   03   02   01   6   5   4   3   2

paper 10   09   08   07   06   10   9   8   7   6

For Perri

Contents

Introduction: On Trembling Earth, 1

Chapter 1. The Legacies, 4

Chapter 2. Wars for Democracy, 26

Chapter 3. I'd Rather Die and Go to Hell, 49

Chapter 4. The Kissing Case, 90

Chapter 5. Communist Front Shouts Kissing Case to the World, 102

Chapter 6. The Sissy Race of All Mankind, 137

Chapter 7. Crusaders, 189

Chapter 8. Cuba Libre, 220

Chapter 9. When Fire Breaks Out, 244

Chapter 10. Freedom Rider, 262

Conclusion: Radio Free Dixie, 287

Notes, 309

Bibliography, 361

Acknowledgments, 379

Index, 385

A section of illustrations follows page 165.

Radio Free Dixie

Introduction: On Trembling Earth

"The childhood of Southerners, white and colored," Lillian Smith wrote in 1949, "has been lived on trembling earth."[1] For one black boy in the small town of Monroe, North Carolina, the first tremor came on a warm September afternoon in 1936.

Emma Williams had sent her eleven-year-old son, Robert, to the post office downtown shortly after one of the regular Friday prayer meetings that met at her home. He was a thick-chested, round-faced, almost cherubic youngster with chestnut-brown skin and a ready smile. "What a Friend We Have in Jesus" still echoed in his ears as he walked from Boyte Street toward the railroad. As Robert crossed the gravel railroad bed, he met a black man walking the tracks, clutching a pint of whiskey and singing, "Trouble in mind, I'm blue / But I won't be blue always / Because the sun is gonna shine in my back door someday." The boy smiled to himself and headed on toward the courthouse square in the middle of Monroe, not suspecting that what he would witness there would shake his whole world.[2]

Walking down Main Street, Williams watched a white police officer accost an African American woman. The policeman, Jesse Alexander Helms Sr., an admirer once recalled, "had the sharpest shoe in town and he didn't mind using it." His son, U.S. Senator Jesse Helms, remembered "Big Jesse" as "a six-foot, two hundred pound gorilla—when he said 'smile,' I smiled."[3] Eleven-year-old Robert Williams looked on in terror as Big Jesse flattened the black woman with his huge fists, then "dragged her off to the nearby jailhouse, her dress up over her head, the same way that a cave man would club and drag his sexual prey." Williams recalled "her tortured screams as the flesh was ground away from the friction of the concrete." The memory of this violent spectacle and the laughter of white bystanders haunted him for decades. Perhaps the deferential way that the African American men on the street responded was even more deeply troubling. "The emasculated black men hung their heads in shame and hurried silently [away] from the cruelly bizarre sight," Williams recalled.[4]

Knowledge of such scenes was as commonplace as coffee cups in the American South that had recently helped to elect Franklin Delano Roosevelt. For the rest of his life, Robert Williams repeated this searing story to friends, readers, listeners, reporters, and historians. In the late 1950s, Williams used the story to help inspire African American domestic workers and military veterans of Monroe to build the most militant chapter of the National Association for the Advancement of Colored People (NAACP) in the United States. He preached it from street corner stepladders to eager crowds on 7th Avenue and 125th Street in Harlem and to Muslim congregants in Malcolm X's Temple Number 7. He bore witness to its brutality in labor halls and college auditoriums across the United States. It contributed to the fervor of his widely published debate with Martin Luther King Jr. in 1960 and fueled his hesitant bids for leadership in the black freedom struggle. Its merciless truths must have tightened in his fingers on the night in 1961 when he fled Ku Klux Klan terrorists and a Federal Bureau of Investigation (FBI) dragnet with his wife and two small children, a machine gun slung over one shoulder. Williams revisited the bitter memory on platforms that he shared with Fidel Castro, Ho Chi Minh, and Mao Zedong. He told it over "Radio Free Dixie," his regular program on Radio Havana from 1962 to 1965, and retold it from Hanoi in broadcasts directed to African American soldiers in Vietnam. It echoed from transistor radios in Watts and from gigantic speakers in Tiananmen Square. The childhood story opens the pages of his autobiography, "While God Lay Sleeping," which Williams completed just before his death on October 15, 1996.

To be sure, one moment in one life rarely changes history. But we can find distilled in the anguish of that eleven year old historical realities that shaped one of the South's most dynamic race rebels and thousands of other black insurgents: African American cultural resilience; white racial violence; the perilous intersection of race, gender, and sexualized brutality; the persistent national failure, a century after the fall of slavery, to enforce equal protection of the laws; and the physical and psychological necessity for African American self-defense. That moment marked Robert

Williams's life, and his life marked the African American freedom movement in the United States.

This is the story of one of the most influential African American radicals of a generation that toppled Jim Crow, created a new black sense of self, and forever altered the arc of American history. Robert F. Williams shadows these pages, a troubled intellectual, a fiery prophet, a courageous grassroots leader whose outbursts sometimes came back to haunt him, but the inner wellsprings of his mind and spirit are probably not to be found here. Though this is a biography, it is as much the story of a political movement—and a political moment—as it is the portrait of a political man. The life at its center is as important for the truths it reveals as for the things it accomplished.

The life of Robert Williams teaches us that the African American freedom movement had its origins in long-standing traditions of resistance to white supremacy. His story underlines the decisive racial significance of World War II. Both his victories and his defeats reveal the central importance of the Cold War to the African American freedom movement, giving black Southerners leverage to redeem or repudiate American democracy in the eyes of the world. Likewise, these struggles reveal the crucial impact of sexuality and gender in racial politics. His defiance—and that of thousands of other black activists—testifies to the fact that, throughout the "civil rights" era, black Southerners stood prepared to defend home and family by force. The life of Robert F. Williams illustrates that "the civil rights movement" and "the Black Power movement" emerged from the same soil, confronted the same predicaments, and reflected the same quest for African American freedom.

As if to dramatize the point, Rosa Parks, whose refusal to surrender a bus seat in Montgomery in 1955 had come to symbolize the nonviolent civil rights movement, mounted the pulpit of a church in Monroe, North Carolina, on October 22, 1996. The body of Robert F. Williams lay before her, dressed in a gray suit given to him by Mao Zedong, his casket draped in the red, black, and green Pan-African flag favored by the followers of Marcus Garvey. She was delighted, Rosa Parks told the hundreds of mourners, to find herself at the funeral of a black leader who had died peacefully in his bed. She told the congregation that she and those who walked alongside Martin Luther King Jr. in Alabama had "always admired Robert Williams for his courage and his commitment to freedom. The work that he did should go down in history and never be forgotten."[5]

1:
The Legacies

The sturdy frame house stood like a haven on a hill, two stories and seven rooms overlooking the dusty lane called Boyte Street that ran through the heart of "Newtown," a segregated shanty-town about a mile across the tracks from the business district of Monroe. On February 26, 1925, Emma Carter Williams gave birth to the fourth of five children born in that house and named him Robert.

Like the other houses in the neighborhood, the Williams homeplace had an outhouse in the back, fetid in the summer and frigid in the winter. Women born into slavery still tended vegetable gardens along the street where young "Rob" grew up. Smoke from the locomotives of the Seaboard Air Line Railway lingered over the clusters of wooden frame houses. On hot summer nights when the windows were open, the tinkling of a juke-joint piano drifted across the honeysuckle that climbed in the hollows. On Sunday mornings, gospel choirs lifted up anthems of redemption that echoed through the scrub oaks around Elizabeth Baptist Church. Most black families in Union County labored as sharecroppers or paid rent to white landlords, but thanks to John Williams's position as a boiler washer with the Seaboard Air Line, he and his wife, Emma Williams, were fortunate enough to own their home. "Seven of us, five children and my mother and father," Williams remembered, "and this house belonged to us."[1]

Monroe, the small Southern county seat where Robert Williams entered the world, was home to 6,100 people, of whom just under a third were black. Monroe was "a good town to grow up in," former mayor J. Raymond Shute recalled. Born in 1904, Shute descended from one of the town's leading white merchant families, traveled widely, and held liberal opinions. In the decades after World War II, he became an integrationist and one of Robert Williams's closest allies for a time. Eventually, not even his wealth and prominence would prevent white terrorists from firing guns into Ray Shute's house to punish him for his heresy. Still, Shute remembered the years before the war with warm nostalgia. "There were no social problems that were of any significance," the genial businessman recalled, "and no bustle and hustle of the larger city. Everybody knew everybody, and life was good."[2]

Monroe's most prominent white conservative, born in 1921, waxed even more nostalgic. "I don't believe I could ever be dissatisfied with Monroe," Jesse Helms wrote in one of his 1956 newspaper columns. "I shall always remember the shady streets, the quiet Sundays, the cotton wagons, the Fourth of July parades."[3] Helms cherished his first-grade teacher, "Miss Lura Heath, bless her heart," and called her "my favorite unreconstructed Confederate."[4] Miss Heath inculcated in her students views that originated with her father, "the Major," who had fought for the Confederacy and later decried the "trend toward socialism in this country" and "the political manipulation of minority groups." Helms would echo this political legacy in his columns that appeared in the journal of the White Citizens' Council, in his "Viewpoint" broadcasts on WRAL-TV, and finally from a seat in the U.S. Senate. Nostalgia for "the Lost Cause" and fondness for the memory of the mythic Old South were central to the political culture of white Monroe. "I shall never forget," Helms wrote, "the stream of school kids marching uptown to place flowers on the courthouse square monument on Confederate Memorial Day."[5]

White citizens who remembered Monroe in the 1920s, one journalist reported, could count "five churches, four Republicans, one pool hall and one whorehouse."[6] The town's two or three police officers carried keys to Coke Helms's restaurant on Main Street so that they could help themselves to a midnight snack and leave money on the counter.[7] White citizens who violated minor ordinances dropped by the office of the clerk of court "at their convenience" to plead guilty and pay their fines.[8] White children who lost a dog felt no compunction about calling the mayor, who did not consider impromptu marriage counseling beyond the scope of his duties.[9] The Chamber of Commerce claimed that Monroe's "lighting plant is one of the most efficient, and illuminates many blocks of white way" and even boasted that there were "seven miles of paved streets" in Monroe in 1925 and that certain of these were "paralleled by cement sidewalks." These sidewalks, like so many things in Monroe, did not extend to the black community.[10]

Dotted with small farms, more than half of which were operated by sharecroppers and tenant farmers, Union County had a population of 40,979 in 1930. The census that year officially recognized 10,048 inhabitants as descendants of the 1,982 slaves and 51 free blacks reported in the 1850 tally.[11] "Sweet Union," as North Carolina's Governor Thomas Bickett had dubbed his home county, rolled down across the peach orchards of the Piedmont just southeast of Charlotte. It jutted into one South Carolina county, Lancaster, bordered on another, Chesterfield, and almost touched a third, York. Union County's streams had been unsuitable for water power or navigation, and its sandy soil was not the best farmland. Gold mines that had played out before the Civil War promised much but delivered little. The Monroe Chamber of Commerce, hoping to attract outside investors, claimed in 1902 that cotton farmers in Union County frequently found gold, "pick[ing] up pure nuggets in the branches or on the hillsides."[12]

Most residents of Union County, black and white, continued to try to scratch a living from the earth, but few mentioned gathering gold or much of anything else in the process. By 1925, soil depletion, boll weevils, and plummeting prices had turned King Cotton into threadbare royalty all across the upper South.[13] "Ain't nothing but cotton," one black citizen reported, "but that was a slave thing, there wasn't no money in that." White farmers fared only a little better, even though many more of them owned the land they tilled. "The first and only year my wife and I farmed, we sold cotton for five and a half cents," recalled Claude Thomas, a white sharecropper in Union County. "We didn't make enough to pay the fertilizer bill and eat. I figured it out like this: wherever I would go, whatever I did, I couldn't make it any worse than this. Just working like convicts and not making a living."[14]

Like hundreds of other hard-pressed farmers in Union County, Claude Thomas ended up in a textile mill. By the time that Robert Williams was born, the Southern piedmont had surpassed New England as the world's leading producer of yarn and cloth.[15] Hundreds of white men, women, and children moved to houses on "Factory Hill" and labored in the mills. Despite long hours at low pay, these jobs "furnished almost the only refuge for the white laboring people of the South from the strong competition of cheap negro labor," one mill owner wrote. The powerful sexual taboo against bringing black men into contact with white women, he argued, made it "wrong to work negroes in association with white women and children." Except for a handful of janitorial jobs, the cotton mills remained lily white.[16]

The celebration of white supremacy by the mill owners did not prevent conflict. From 1919 to 1929, violent strikes pitted piedmont millworkers against their employers in conflicts that featured terrorism sponsored by the owners and what Raleigh *News and Observer* columnist Nell Battle Lewis called "lawlessness on the part of the law." Gun battles in nearby Gastonia killed both the chief of police and one of the local strike leaders. In Marion, "special deputies" opened fire on pickets, killing six strikers and wounding twenty-five more. Authorities arrested Fred Beal, the lead organizer for the National Textile Workers Union, and held him in the Monroe city jail.[17]

Though the millhands were white, mill owners and white politicians charged that Communists had targeted the cotton mills in order to advance their radical agenda of "race-mixing" and social overthrow. David Clark of the *Southern Textile Bulletin* wrote that "the Communists may harangue until judgement day, but they can never convince the cotton mill operators of the South that negroes are their equals." Though Clark spoke for the mill owners, his assessment provides what amounts to a tragic summary of Southern labor history. Karl Marx exaggerated only slightly when he claimed that these hardworking people had nothing to lose but their chains. The links that white supremacy had hammered into those chains bound white working people in Union County not only to their poverty but to an ineffably deep sense of themselves as white Southerners. The bloody history of race and class conflict in the piedmont made it clear that white supremacy and the bitter legacy of slavery divided workers far more powerfully than self-interest could unite them; it was a lesson that Robert Williams learned over and over again.[18]

The Williams family was more prosperous than many of the white families in Monroe, but still there were many hardships. When he was about two years old, little Rob contracted pneumonia. Dr. Hubert Creft, the local black physician, thought "that it was impossible for me to live," Williams remembered. "My mother refused to give up." Emma Williams moved the small iron bed out into the living room beside the fireplace and nursed her son night and day. After two weeks, according to family lore, Dr. Creft heard that the toddler was still alive and dropped by to see how this miracle had come to pass. Emma Williams told the physician that each time the little boy stopped breathing, "she would take me and shake me. And then she would start praying." Decades later, Williams only faintly remembered the rancid smell of castor oil and the apples that she fed him during his illness. But the vision of a mother's unrelenting love, burnished by her steadfast faithfulness to her family, shone brightly in his mind.[19]

Emma Williams was a deeply devout Christian and raised her children in the Elizabeth Baptist Church. The church infused Robert Williams with a powerful and distinctive Afro-Christianity whose spiritual essence remained long after he had parted ways with its cautious politics and conservative theology. "She always taught us to help people," Robert Williams said, "to give them whatever assistance we could, when people were hungry and homeless and that type of thing." The Elizabeth Baptist congregation provided a strong sense of community and a nurturing place for the Williams children to discover and display their talents. "We used to get up and recite speeches and verse," Robert recalled. He enjoyed the Easter egg hunts and covered-dish suppers and relished the music. "At revival meetings they would have all kinds of singing and people would get happy, and they would sing and shout," said Williams. He never forgot the power of this religious experience and the importance of this spiritual community in his early life.

But for Williams the black church rarely confronted the harsh realities of the Jim Crow South in a way that transcended the politics of accommodation. "This preacher would preach and start very emotional sermons, but didn't say a thing about racial problems," he reflected. Oversimplifying matters somewhat, he claimed that most black preachers "didn't dare speak against the white people because some of the white people contributed money to the churches." Williams never attempted to make the black church the cornerstone of his racial activism, not because he rejected its moral teachings but because, in his eyes, the church did not live up to its own professed ideals. Williams objected to racial injustice out of an African American spiritual sensibility, even though he usually did not articulate it in religious language and often inveighed against the church.[20]

"My father didn't go to church too much, only occasionally," Williams said. John Williams "would always say he was tired." Robert's favorite uncle, Charlie Williams, spoke more bluntly. "You niggers are always on your knees praying," Charlie would say, only half-jokingly. "If you believe in God, and God is so good, why don't you pray to God to free us?" Black folks in Monroe accused Charlie Williams of being an atheist, Robert said, "and then in a small town it wasn't considered the proper thing to be an atheist." Emma Williams "didn't like for me to be with him very much," said Robert. His Uncle Charlie jabbed at organized religion "in a joking way," Robert recalled, "but [Mother] took it very seriously. Plus the fact that he used to drink what they called 'home brew,' and she found out that he had been giving me some of it."[21]

If Uncle Charlie liked to pull a cork, he was a handsome and dapper iconoclast, sharp edged and clear eyed, with a penetrating gaze that flashed both insight and anger. A veteran of the First World War, Charlie Williams had come home disillusioned that the war to make the world safe for democracy had done nothing to expand democracy for the black citizens of Monroe. He attended college at Florida A&M and law school at Wilberforce University in Ohio. Setting aside the larger opportunities that might have opened for him outside the South, Charlie Williams came home to teach school in Monroe. "Rob's uncle was instrumental in this community," Annie Bell Cherry, a longtime family friend, remembered.[22]

Once when a federal agency was conducting typing tests for young women to work in Washington, D.C., Uncle Charlie apparently carted his typewriter and a female cousin to the place where the local tests were given. She had been very reluctant, the story goes, partly because she could not even type. The woman waited anxiously while she listened to Williams put up a fierce fight for her to take the test. "As they walked away," Robert said, "she asked him nervously, 'What if they had agreed for me to take the test? You know I can't type!' Charlie Williams laughed and told her, 'I knew they would not allow a Negro woman to take the test but it is just a matter of letting them know that at least we have enough sense to know our rights.' " Despite pious admonitions from his mother, Robert idolized his uncle and emulated his example. "Charlie was bad and just about like an outlaw," Robert remembered, "but he was also said to be very brilliant and people respected him for that." His nephew may have overestimated Charlie Williams's renegade qualities—after all, he managed to retain his job in a school system run by whites—but Robert's relationship to his favorite uncle had a lasting influence on him.[23]

Robert Williams's paternal grandmother, Ellen Isabel Williams, was an even more compelling presence in the boy's life. Born a slave in Union County in 1858, she lived only a few dozen yards down Boyte Street. Williams and his siblings were all expected to help their grandmother with chores, and she repaid them richly, not only with her heaping platters of fried chicken and mouth-watering pots of collard greens, but with her vivid stories of their family's past.

Light-skinned and quick-witted, Ellen Williams was the daughter of

"Grandma Honeycutt," of whom Robert's parents were reluctant to speak. "Susanna Honeycutt, slave, bore four children sired by Daniel Tomblin, her slave master," a family history reads. Though Tomblin also had a white wife and seven white children, he made no secret of his relationship with Susanna Honeycutt, whom her daughter, pointing to a cast-iron kettle, always described as "black as that pot." Tomblin and Honeycutt had two boys and two girls—Ellen, Mary, Frank, and Daniel—the last son named after their white father.[24] There is little evidence as to the nature of this relationship—whether it was consensual or coerced, or whether Susanna Honeycutt had worked some weary truce between love and necessity. If Daniel Tomblin regarded it as incongruous to keep his own children as slaves, there is no record of it. Certainly the arrangement was not unusual; Ella Belle Stitt, a slave woman born on the Green Ray plantation in Union County, remembered that "the Negro women were subject to the wills of the white men, and there was hardly any plantation around that you couldn't see that the owners had fathered some of the slaves."[25]

In truth, the Southern family tree had never been as straight as the Carolina pines. "Despite the daytime white abuse and hatred of our race," Robert recounted, "the darkness of night brought an influx of prowling white men in quest of black sex." The immense social prerogatives of white men tempted some to have illicit lovers and even whole families on the other side of the color line. The resulting relationships—and children—did little to threaten the hierarchies of race and gender; they were largely a matter for unspoken resentments among blacks and furtive whisperings between whites. "My grandmother, her father was white," Robert's older brother John Herman Williams recalled. "People knew that. Once when we went to Secrest's Drug Store, the druggist told my father, 'John, we're cousins, but don't tell anybody.' [White people] wouldn't let anybody know that. But a lot of [black] families were treated differently because the whites they knew were relatives."[26]

If blood ties could not bring white slaveholders to acknowledge the humanity of their mixed-race children, it is hardly surprising that neither time nor kinship could bridge the racial chasm in Union County with respect to the memory of slavery. White natives recalled slavery as a largely benign and even charitable institution. Whites viewed slavery as "paternalistic, sometimes harsh but for the most part benevolent," a white local historian wrote. William Henry Belk, who grew up on a cotton plantation and became the wealthiest New South merchant in North Carolina, remembered how his mother taught children to read. "She especially wanted the Negroes to know how to read the Bible," he recalled.[27]

The oral tradition in the black community reflected an entirely different world. Ella Bell Stitt, who later cooked for the Belk family, told of how her mother had come home from working in the fields to find that Mary Bell, her three-year-old daughter, was gone. When her mother asked the plantation mistress about the girl, Stitt recalled, "the white woman looked at her without changing her expression and told her, 'Your Missy got married and I gave her Mary Bell and some more niggers for a wedding present.' " When her mother could not stop crying, Stitt said, the mistress threatened to have her whipped. "Mother never saw Mary Bell again," Ella Bell Stitt reported. "She named all of us girls Bell, hoping that one of us would meet her someday and know each other by our names." For blacks, this was the historical knife-edge of slavery, the violent, soul-murdering institution that white citizens in Union County preferred to remember as the "first and only opportunity," one local white man wrote in 1959, for black people "to indulge in anything like civilized living."[28]

A red brick symbol of this war between black and white historical memory in Monroe still stands on the courthouse square at the center of town. The oldest building in Monroe, Town Hall is a proud landmark for white residents, depicted in civic memorabilia and featured in historical presentations.[29] For black citizens, however, the brick structure marks a different past. In 1847 John Medlin, a wealthy planter who owned more slaves than anyone else in Union County, fastened a logging chain around the neck of a rebellious slave and dragged him to death behind a wagon. Medlin hauled the body of his bondsman through the dusty streets for all to see. This kind of open violence was an affront even to white sensibilities, in part because it undermined the paternalist justification for slavery and thus weakened the South's "peculiar institution."[30] Authorities arrested Medlin for "felony and manslaughter," a capital crime. Although the offense mandated the death penalty, the judge imposed merely a substantial fine. Authorities used the money to launch the brick structure that housed the city government for almost a century.[31] When J. Raymond Shute, Monroe's leading white liberal for many decades, served as mayor, his office in Town Hall was "right on the street, clearly marked, with door wide open, weather permitting," he wrote, "accessible to all—white and colored, rich and poor—practically at any hour of the day." But for black citizens of Monroe, Town Hall would never be a point of historical pride or a symbol of democratic governance.[32]

Both pride and democracy, however, featured prominently in the stories that Ellen Williams told her grandchildren, especially the tales about Sikes Williams, her late husband, to whom Robert bore a notable physical—and many said temperamental—resemblance. "They all said I was just like him," Robert recalled. In 1875, at age sixteen, Ellen Williams had married the handsome and articulate nineteen year old who, like herself, had been born into slavery in Union County.[33] In defiance of North Carolina law, Sikes Williams had managed to learn to read and write even while he was a slave. After Emancipation, the former slave attended Biddle Institute in Charlotte, a black college known for its biblical and classical orientation and for leadership that rejected accommodation to white supremacy. Years later, Biddle became Johnson C. Smith University, a center of the black freedom movement in North Carolina a century after Emancipation.[34] Sikes and Ellen Williams lived not only as man and wife, but as professional colleagues; they both returned to Union County as schoolteachers to a generation of African Americans hungry for education. Broad-shouldered and heavy-set, with dark skin and a thick mustache, Sikes Williams grew to manhood amid the political tumult and white terror of Reconstruction and eventually joined the Republican Party.[35]

The piedmont region became the stronghold of the Republican Party in North Carolina after the Civil War. Founded in 1867 and led by liberated slaves and the white political heirs of Abraham Lincoln, this biracial coalition endorsed universal manhood suffrage, removed property require-ments for voting, and threatened to overturn long-standing local hierarchies. More than a quarter of the white men who voted in Union County in 1868 wagered their political futures on an alliance with black men that promised a more democratic society for all.[36] The conservative *Monroe Enquirer* derided white Republicans for their poverty, castigating them as "socialists and adventurers, who had lived among us without preferment or possessions of qualifications entitling them to it." These "agrarian and commune whites who exist in every community," the editors pointed out, shamelessly allied themselves with "a race of brutal savages and barbarians" who had been "lately emancipated from long years of hereditary slavery and immured in mental darkness."[37] The Democrats, also known as the Conservatives, derided the Republican coalition for "breaking down every vistige of honorable distinction and attempting to plant upon its ruin the unwise . . . doctrine of universal equality." Government, they argued, should remain in the hands of "virtue and property and intelligence" rather than being yielded to the power "of mere *numbers*."[38]

In order to recruit the same lower-class whites that they otherwise dismissed as rabble, Conservatives sought to drive a wedge between the races by attacking African Americans. They argued that "the negro, since his freedom[, has] become more savage and brutal." The rape of white women by black men, the *Monroe Enquirer* argued, was "a natural result of the political teachings" of the Republican Party. Democrats in Monroe insisted that "Social Equality and Rape" were the "natural offspring" of the Civil Rights Bill of 1875. "Radicals may squirm and twist," the editors declared just before the election of 1876, "but they cannot evade or deny the fact that Civil Rights naturally and inevitably leads to Social Equality." In Union County, Democrats loudly advocated "the reestablishment of the whipping post" because "the State has suffered as much from its abolishment as from any other cause." Headlines such as "LYNCH HIM!" and "BURNED AT THE STAKE" made it plain how far the Democratic Party in Monroe was willing to take the politics of white supremacy. "Every man must stand to his post," the *Monroe Enquirer* urged white men of Union County. "Shoot deserters on the spot."[39]

Confronted by a formidable enemy espousing a social vision far more democratic than their own, white Conservatives turned to violence to preserve the remnants of an antebellum social order rooted in white domination and aristocratic privilege. Nothing less than violence would restrain the political aspirations of African American activists and their white allies. The Ku Klux Klan murdered, maimed, or terrorized hundreds and possibly thousands of black and white citizens across the Republican piedmont between 1868 and 1872. In Rutherford County alone there were one hundred to two hundred whippings. Nightriders burned many of the schoolhouses built by former slaves and poor whites for whom education had become an important symbol of democratic aspirations. Klan terrorists frequently claimed that they were only punishing immoral sexual behavior between blacks and whites. This reflected a hypocrisy so rank that even the white observers choked on it; the Greensboro *Register* replied to this argument: "Why you know yourself that there isn't a mulatto child in town scarcely whose 'daddy' isn't a Ku Klux."[40] Mandy Coverson, who had been a slave in Union County, recalled that the Ku Klux Klan "done a heap of beatin' and chasin' folks out of the county" and that the struggle for political power "was mostly the cause of it."[41] Blacks sometimes fought back. Near Enfield, North Carolina, young black men organized a militia to defend their community against the Klan; they laid an ambush, and the white terrorists "got wind of it and stopped coming."[42]

White racial violence, electoral fraud, and divisions within the Republican Party brought the Democrats back into power in Union County and across the South in 1876. The Ku Klux Klan was "a political organization of the Conservative party, in the interest of the Conservative party," one Klansman declared. "It was understood," another Klan member added, "that on the night before the election the Ku Kluks would turn out *en masse* and visit the houses of the colored people" to let them know that "if [black citizens] went to election they would meet them on the way." In Union County, the Conservatives won 427 of 554 votes cast and celebrated with a "grand torchlight procession."[43]

By the mid-1870s, Conservative victories mounted across the South. The national Republican Party, long weary of the burden of protecting black Southerners, now left them to their own devices and to the dubious mercies of their former masters. "In short," crowed the *Charlotte Democrat* in 1876, "North Carolina is now a white man's state and white men intend to govern it hereafter."[44]

Terrorized and defrauded at the local level, and more or less abandoned by their own party at the national level, black Republicans in North Carolina concentrated on survival. "Some of the darkies over the county," the *Monroe Enquirer* observed with distinct satisfaction, "are really frightened, and think that 'freedom's up.'"[45] Conservative legislators allowed registrars to bar opposition voters, especially blacks and illiterate whites, on the flimsiest pretext. In Union County, the Democrats refused to count black ballots from 1876 to 1896.[46]

Only violence or its well-founded threat could enforce such a blatant repudiation of the U.S. Constitution. Arsonists torched the local AME Zion Church in 1877.[47] In 1881 one hundred of what the *Monroe Enquirer* called the "best citizens" of Union County seized Edmund Davis, a black man accused of raping a white woman, from the constable and announced that they would lynch him a few hours later. Observing that Davis had strangled for forty minutes before dying, the Democratic editors stated that the victim had been "justly and promptly hanged" before the mob, "satisfied that he was quite dead, dispersed, leaving him still hanging." There were no prosecutions.[48] Black residents scrambled to protect themselves from the same fate and to persist in their beleaguered hopes for democracy. "Many of my race," the Reverend A. B. Smyer, a black preacher in Monroe, wrote, "are becoming wonderfully stirred up about emigrating to Liberia," while "others have left their crops and what property they had and gone somewhere." Life had grown "very gloomy with us here," he acknowledged, "but God is still with us."[49]

But the expansive vision of freedom kindled in slavery and fanned to flame at Emancipation did not leave for Liberia. Nor did it desert North Carolina for Kansas or Indiana with the thousands of black citizens who struck out for a better life in the late 1870s and 1880s. Most black North Carolinians held fast to their roots, and many in the piedmont refused to relinquish the promise of interracial democracy that Reconstruction had held forth; it is true, of course, that their realistic political options were limited. "The only hope of our people," the *Messenger*, a black newspaper in nearby Charlotte, declared in 1883, "is to unite their forces with the liberal and progressive element among southern whites. There is a large class of these men," the editors continued, "who in their heart of hearts loath the dull despotism that hangs over their native section like a nightmare." This radical democratic vision would neither cringe nor compromise, but its authors asserted that if "these enlightened Southerners declare themselves in favor of free schools and a free ballot, simple justice and equal opportunities for all men, we will meet them halfway, whether they were abolitionists or slaveholders." Robert Williams was an heir to this outlook.[50]

Soon this prophetic vision of biracial democracy once again found white adherents in Monroe. In 1887 white tenant farmers, sharecroppers, and yeomen in Union County organized a farmers' alliance that challenged conservative merchants and planters and helped launch the Populist Party. "Fusion" between Populists and Republicans seized control of the state from the Democrats in 1894 and instituted sweeping democratic change. In Union County, electoral reforms gave black voters the balance of power between contending factions of whites. In 1896 fusionist campaign flyers, "To The Colored Voters of Union County," reminded African American voters that "two years ago the Republicans and Populists of North Carolina united and made one grand struggle for liberty" that defeated the Democratic Party and enabled blacks to vote again after two decades of disfranchisement. "THE CHAINS OF SERVITUDE ARE BROKEN," the county's second biracial political alliance proclaimed to its black constituents in 1896. "NOW NEVER LICK THE HAND THAT LASHED YOU."[51]

It is likely that Robert Williams's grandfather, the husband of Ellen Williams, himself born to the chains of servitude, posted or even wrote these campaign flyers. Sikes Williams became a Republican activist during the late nineteenth century and "traveled all over the county and the State making speeches and soliciting support for the Party."[52] Just as they had done when Sikes Williams was a young man, black Republicans again allied themselves with white working people who had organized on the basis of economic interest against the business-oriented "Bourbons" of the Democratic Party. Williams and another black man, Darling Thomas, obtained a printing press and published a small newspaper called the *People's Voice*. The broadside "was supposed to be a paper for dealing with the black people and against certain kinds of oppression," Robert Williams recalled. His grandfather "was called a radical," according to Williams, "and had a lot of trouble with the whites." Not surprisingly, Sikes Williams kept a loaded rifle close at hand to protect himself and his family from white vigilantes.[53]

In 1896 the biracial Populist-Republican alliance of which Sikes Williams was a part swept both the county and the state, taking the governor's mansion and seizing a 120-50 advantage in the legislature. Democrats did not win a single office in Monroe and Union County, nor did they retain any statewide office except their seats on the North Carolina Supreme Court.[54] Two years later, however, white conservatives unleashed the violent white supremacy campaigns of 1898. "Redshirt" terrorists attacked Republicans, Populists, and especially African Americans. White vigilantes broke up fusionist political rallies, whipped black leaders, and drove black voters from the polls. "Go to the polls tomorrow," Alfred Waddell, soon to be mayor of Wilmington, told white citizens there, "and if you find the negro out voting, tell him to leave the polls, and if he refuses, kill him, shoot him down in his tracks."[55] Just after the election, white mobs in Wilmington slaughtered black citizens in the streets and forced black public officials to resign at gunpoint. Across the state, "the party of white supremacy" seized power. In Monroe, Democrats elected to the state senate Thomas J. Jerome, author of *Ku Klux Klan No. 40*, a book that lauded as heroes the hooded terrorists of Reconstruction.[56] Democrats had again turned to violence, fraud, and disfranchisement to secure what *News and Observer* editor Josephus Daniels celebrated as "permanent good government by the party of the White Man."[57]

The national government's failure to intervene in North Carolina's bloody white supremacy revolt left black citizens to rely on their own ability to defend themselves. When the Democrats quickly moved to take the ballot from African Americans by constitutional amendment, white Populist newspapers abandoned even their own limited support for black rights. Biracial politics, they argued, had provoked so much fraud and violence that disfranchisement might be for the best. "If it will settle the Negro question and give political freedom to white people and guarantee them to vote as they please and have that vote counted," the editors of the *Times-Mercury* suggested, "Populists should vote for it." But "stopping [the Negro] from voting will not settle it," they added gravely. The only way to "do it humanely is to colonize him. We prefer this to killing them. One of the two will be done and that soon."[58]

The problem, according to Furnifold Simmons, one of the foremost architects of the white supremacy campaign, was the fragility of white racial solidarity. The future U.S. senator conceded that Democrats must realize that "the white people will not always stand together." What the party sought in 1900, another Democratic politician frankly stated, was "a good, square, honest law that will always give a good Democratic majority." Gubernatorial candidate Charles B. Aycock called whites who opposed the disfranchisement of black citizens in 1900 "public enemies" who deserved "the contempt of all mankind."[59] Three-quarters of the voters in Union County—by a margin of 2,396 to 822—supported the amendment to bar black voters. Disfranchisement passed across the state by a margin of 59 percent to 41 percent. "In North Carolina," the *Monroe Enquirer* wrote ten years afterward, "the negro has been removed from politics and every good citizen is glad of it." It would be six decades before a single white political leader in North Carolina would openly challenge this point of view.[60]

It is not clear how Sikes Williams responded to the crushing of interracial democracy in Monroe; a fire destroyed all but a handful of his voluminous personal papers. In the early days of the civil rights movement, however, an African American man who had "lived in Monroe for seventy-five years" recalled that "in all that time I have known just two real Negro men, one was Sikes Williams and the other," he continued, "is his grandson Robert F. Williams. I have felt the same as both of them, I suppose, but I was afraid to do or say anything about it."[61] In the thirty-five years after Emancipation, interracial politics had threatened entrenched power twice in the South and been turned back each time by violence and demagoguery. But traditions of interracial democracy and black liberation, born in the hopes and agonies of Reconstruction, persisted in African American communities.[62] Black Southerners developed an expansive vision of democracy in their effort to secure the fruits of emancipation. Into such a community Robert Williams was born.

Unlike his illustrious father, John Williams was no firebrand. Perhaps because of Sikes Williams's volatile career in racial politics or perhaps because times had grown so much harder for black North Carolinians after 1898, his son stepped carefully along the color line. He was a solid "race man," to be sure, but "very quiet, soft spoken," Robert recalled. John Williams did not neglect to instruct his children in the perils of race. "Me and my father used to talk about the race riots in Atlanta and different places," Robert remembered, "and the fact that at that time they had a series of brutal lynchings." In public, however, John Williams took care not to offend white people. "In fact," Robert recalled, "in later years whites in the community used to always tell me that I should be like my father, that he was a good man and he was a hard worker, and he never gave them any trouble."[63]

His father was not reckless, but neither was he a deferential soul or in any sense a pacifist. One night a black man came running through the streets of Newtown yelling "like a town crier," Robert said. "You niggers better stay in the house tonight because it's gonna be hell in this town," the man warned. Boyce Richardson, a black man from out in the country, had been sitting on the curb on Main Street eating watermelon with his small son, according to the story, and Chief of Police Elmsley Armfield walked up and kicked Richardson off the curb. Richardson whipped out a knife and nearly sliced the collar off the police chief's throat, threatening to kill him. White men seized Richardson, beat him, and threw him in jail. The word on the street was that a lynch mob was gathering for Boyce Richardson and that many other black citizens would be run out of town. That night, when it was time to go to work, John Williams collected his hat and his lunch and quietly slipped a pistol into the pocket of his overalls as he left the house. "He admonished us to stay in the house," Robert recalled. Whites who opposed lynching managed to prevent mob violence, but the streets remained "as deserted and silent as a cemetery." It was an atmosphere of racial terror all too familiar in the Monroe of Robert Williams's youth. "The older people, who had experienced the ferocity of racist violence unleashed in earlier years, exuded such fear that they unwittingly infected their children," Williams recalled. "To be so terrorized was to feel a chill deep inside me that made me feel numb and helpless." At the same time, he never forgot that his father dared to go out into that night, or that he carried a gun when he did so.[64]

As a boiler washer on the Seaboard Air Line, Robert Williams's father had a skilled position that made him one of the best-paid black men in Monroe. "They classified him as a boiler washer because that was as high as a black man could go," his son said. "They had a system on the railroad that the boiler maker had to be a white man [but] the white man could have a helper." According to Williams, "My father used to do all of the work and the white man was getting the money," even though the boiler maker "stayed drunk all the time. [The white man] would go into houses in the black community where they sold whisky, or bootleggers, and he would leave my father and another man to do the work."[65]

Despite racial discrimination, working for the railroad shielded the family from the worst indignities of dependence on local whites. "In fact," Robert explained, "the railroad had it arranged so that anybody who worked for the railroad could get credit anywhere in the town, so this was a form of prestige." Unlike most jobs available to blacks, railroad work provided employment that did not depend entirely on the local white power structure. Within the African American community, a position with the Seaboard afforded a man considerable status. "He was able to keep a family, to keep a home that he bought," Robert recounted. "He worked very hard." Nobody at the Williams house went hungry or lacked for clothing. Christmas morning might bring a brand-new red wagon or shiny new bicycles for the Williams children; a little boy's BB gun became a .22-caliber rifle as Robert grew older. "The fact that my father was working and had a pretty secure job," Williams remembered, "this gave us some insulation from some of the harshness and abuses that some black children experienced."[66]

When John Williams went to work at the railroad roundhouse in the evenings, he frequently took Robert along to keep him company. "At night they didn't have many people working there," his son said, "and he would show me all about the boiler and the trains." Young Robert Williams also observed the racial politics of the railroad yard. Black women walking from Newtown crossed the railroad yard on their way to work in the kitchens of white families. White workers using the washroom "would walk all around the place and in the yard nude. They would do that," according to black workers, "just so the black women would see them." According to Williams, white workers also liked to "talk about how they liked black women and which black women they had gone with." This was done as a deliberate humiliation, an expression of white dominance, he said, largely because whites "didn't want [blacks] to make as much money as the railroad was paying them." White workers acted this way, African American men felt, because "the only thing they had was their white authority, the power of their white skin."[67]

One of the railroad workers with "a notorious reputation for lauding his interracial exploits over Black men" was a much-hated white man from Georgia named Clarkston. On Saturday nights, like a number of white men, Clarkston would cruise his fancy automobile through a dark, isolated section of Newtown called "the Neck" or "Fourteen" to pick up a local black woman for sex. As a teenager, Williams organized several friends into a secret organization called X-32 "to make war on white philanderers who fancied Black women after dark." The boys of X-32 sewed white hoods to conceal their identities and "night after night we vainly patrolled the alleys and dark sectors of the streets hoping to catch him." One evening, as Clarkston's distinctive car rolled slowly into the Neck, Williams and his cohorts swooped down on the vehicle and unleashed a broadside of bricks and stones, smashing all of the car's windows and sending their enemy screeching off into the night. The boys fled and regrouped in the woods, where they rolled on the ground, pounding the earth "in a seizure of laughter and satisfaction." It was Williams's first direct confrontation with white supremacy, and he always remembered it with deep pleasure.[68]

The power of white skin in the Jim Crow South was both stark and subtle. White supremacy permeated daily life so deeply that most people could no more ponder it than a fish might discuss the wetness of water. Racial etiquette was at once bizarre, arbitrary, and nearly inviolable, inscribed in what W. E. B. Du Bois termed "the cake of custom." A white man who would never shake hands with a black man would refuse to permit anyone but a black man to shave his face, cut his hair, or give him a shampoo. A white man might share his bed with a black woman but never his table. Black breasts could suckle white babies, black hands would pat out biscuit dough for white mouths, but black heads must not try on a hat in a department store, lest it be rendered unfit for sale to white people. Black maids washed the bodies of the aged and infirm, but the uniforms that they were required to wear could never be laundered in the same washing machines that white people used. While it was permissible to call a favored black man "Uncle" or "Professor"—a mixture of affection and mockery—he must never hear the words "mister" or "sir." Black women were "girls" until they were old enough to be called "auntie," but they could never hear a white person, regardless of age, address them as "Mrs." or "Miss." Whites regarded black people as inherently lazy and shiftless, but when a white man said he had "worked like a nigger," he meant that he had engaged in dirty, back-breaking labor to the point of collapse. J. Ray Shute grew up in one of the finest white homes in Monroe but "spent nearly as much time in the home of our cook, who had boys my age." Shute and the black boys would "slip off and go swimming together," he remembered. "Never thought anything of it until after we got to school, and the teachers told us it was wrong."[69]

The racial views of the Almighty were well known to the white citizens of Monroe. "When I was a small boy, I was given to understand that the colored folks were our neighbors and must be treated as such," Fred Wolfe wrote in his column in the *Monroe Enquirer*. "But God made me white and them black," he added, "and He expected them to stay that way, and that each should have his own churches and schools." The natural world provided a frequent metaphor for race, with whites in effect placing blacks in a separate species. "Segregation is a fundamental law of nature," another white native wrote. "The mockingbirds and the robins lead separate and peaceful lives." "God did not create all men equal," Bunyan Simpson of Monroe declared. "If that is not true we would all be the same color."[70] James Y. Joyner, the North Carolina state superintendent of education, cautioned African American college students that any challenge to white supremacy would be "a violation of God's eternal laws as fixed as the stars." Joyner's remarks reflected the opinions of the leading white men in North Carolina. More than half of the county officials surveyed in 1933 believed that African Americans should receive either no education or none beyond seventh grade. Almost 80 percent agreed that blacks should not be permitted to vote, and nearly 15 percent even insisted that the descendants of slaves should not be allowed to own land.[71]

Political and social arrangements in the county reflected the triumph of white supremacy in 1898. Though Union County officials apparently began to permit a handful of favored blacks to register to vote during the 1920s, only twenty-two of the thousands of voting-age black citizens appeared on Union County voter rolls in 1934. This reflected what Governor Thomas Bickett, a native of Monroe, called "the unalterable determination of the whites to keep in their hands the reins of government."[72] Blacks represented 30 percent of Monroe's population but less than 1 percent of its homeowners. The African American community "turned segregation into 'congregation,'" but did so in ghettos owned by white landlords; authorities ignored housing codes when whites rented to blacks, and most of the houses in these areas were in terrible condition. City services that white citizens took for granted were unavailable to black taxpayers. "When I grew older," Ethel Azalea Johnson, who lived in the next block from the Williams family, said, "I noticed that all the streets where white people lived were paved, and had sidewalks, and in our section of town they were not." Black babies born in Union County Hospital shared the basement with dirty laundry and soiled bedpans; they died at a rate almost three times that of white infants.[73] There were almost no jobs for black people in Monroe beyond domestic service and menial labor. White newspapers in Monroe slung the word "nigger" freely and rarely printed anything about black citizens that did not reflect vicious stereotypes. "We were not treated as human beings," Williams recalled bitterly.[74]

As long as African Americans did not challenge these arrangements, racial peace prevailed. But beneath the green ivy of civility stood a stone wall of coercion. When Robert Williams was a small boy in the 1920s, Ku Klux Klan membership swelled into the millions across the United States. In North Carolina, Klan rolls grew to around 50,000 and included the state's "best people," according to the *News and Observer*'s Josephus Daniels.[75] Monroe newspapers estimated attendance at a nearby Klan rally in 1922 as "possibly exceeding 5,000." Klan terrorists stood ready to enforce white supremacy with gun, whip, razor, torch, and rope. Dissent was rare; the Klan gave a member of the Fayetteville board of aldermen ten days to leave town because "your continual abuse of our organization has become unbearable to us." The letter urged the white leader not to "let your nerve get you killed." The *Monroe Journal* denounced Klan violence—"if this is 100 per cent Americanism, we don't like it," the editors said—and also bemoaned the fact that decent people stood silent in the face of murder.[76] Lynch mobs in North Carolina murdered more than sixty blacks from 1900 to 1943. "It is not so much that christian people condone lynching," the editors explained, "as that they do not sufficiently oppose it."[77] Word of such outrages proved almost as compelling for young Robert Williams as the violence that he had seen. "Everybody in the black community used to talk about these lynchings," Williams said. Where a black man stood accused of raping a white woman, J. Ray Shute recalled, "quite often he'd be killed before the sheriff got to him."[78]

Violence, though frequently rationalized in terms of protecting white womanhood, often had political or economic motivations. Ethel Johnson remembered "the day a Negro minister was beaten with undressed planks by whites, because he tried to register [to vote.] The minister had to flee under cover of darkness and later had friends to sell his home."[79] Any African American bold enough to fight back found it necessary to flee the community. White dissenters could not speak their minds in peace. "Segregation was a way of life," said Ray House, principal of the white high school. "If we would have started a fight against it, somebody would have shot us." Forged in violence, inculcated by custom, and written into law, the racial caste system in Monroe seemed impregnable.[80]

Jim Crow, however, did not entirely define black life in the world where Robert grew up. The railroad tracks that hummed in steel harmony toward New Orleans, New York, and the Atlantic Ocean seemed to open Monroe to a much larger world. "It used to be a big deal," Robert reminisced, "that people who worked on the railroad got free passes to ride free." Robert's mother would take him shopping for the day in Charlotte, which seemed incredibly cosmopolitan. The legendary engineer, "Happy Day," would steam through Monroe. "He was the only engineer who could blow a tune on his train whistle," Robert recalled, "and he always when he passed through, he would wave to the people and strike up this song, 'Happy Days Are Here Again.' " (Some recalled that the engineer played the gospel song "Oh Happy Day"—he may have played both.) And then there was the steady stream of visitors. "In those days there used to be hoboes riding freight trains from the Deep South, trying to go North," he remembered. Among these were blues musicians who came to play at the neighborhood drink houses, for example.[81]

The blues coming from "Miss Sis" Polk's juke joint captured Williams's imagination at an early age. On hot summer nights, "barrel-house music engulfed the neighborhood like a dense fog," he recalled. As a young teenager, Robert Williams used to steal from bed, pretend to be headed for the outhouse, and then keep going. He "could hear the piano, hot and spicy, rolling out the blues." The 1920s and 1930s were the heyday of the Piedmont blues, at once party music and deep lament, hammered out on piano, guitar, harmonica, banjo, and washboard, slow dragging and high stepping in juke joints that nuzzled the railroad tracks from Atlanta to Durham.[82] "The down home blues" pouring out of Miss Sis's Place "drew me like a magnet," he wrote in his unpublished autobiography more than fifty years later.

The barrel house was filled to overflowing, and the boy stood among the crowd outside in the dark. "The aroma of fish frying drifted out of the kitchen window," Williams recalled, and finally the boy was able to climb up into the window frame and peer inside. A big, dark-skinned man hunched over the old upright in the corner, eyes closed, perspiration pouring off his face, "and pounded the keys of the piano as if all the adversities of his life were being transferred through his fingers." Washboard, guitar, and harmonica "complemented the piano and at times seemed to challenge its blue note." Mason jars of "stump-hole liquor" passed from hand to hand. Someone would call, "Mercy, mercy, mercy!" or cry out, "Let the good times roll!" The dancers swayed and grinded, belly to belly, turning the tired black bodies that white employers regarded as agricultural machinery into fountains of beauty, sensuality, pleasure, and community. Years later, it would occur to him that this apparent paradise provided merely "momentary escape to a sanctuary free from the white man's hatred that had created a black man's hell." But for the moment, he thought heaven had opened its windows, if not its doors, and bid him look in, if not enter. When he crawled back into his bed just before dawn, young Williams felt both satisfied and hungry, filled with "the impatience of a boy in a hurry to become a man."[83]

Robert Williams found his first real niche in the world of adults through the example of his grandmother. Ellen Williams "specialized in history," he recalled. Politics and the past consumed her thoughts. "She read *everything*," another grandchild recalled. So light skinned that she could be mistaken for a white woman, Ellen Williams taught her children to be proud of being black. Once a white insurance salesman, seeing her alone on her porch, stepped up and asked her whether they were the only white family in the neighborhood. "I am *not* white!" she spat, shooing the salesman from her door.[84] During the depression years, she would gather her grandchildren at her feet and read to them from newspapers, pausing to provide political commentary and tell stories about race and politics. "This is where I heard about Hitler," Robert recounted. "When Hitler was coming to power, she kept telling us the story about Germany and what was going on there." Hitler's genocide against the Jews became the central metaphor for evil in Williams's mind, and the clear necessity of stopping Hitler by any means necessary endured for him as an unanswerable challenge to pacifism.

In 1939 young Robert took a job delivering afternoon newspapers and made a place for himself among the circle of railroad men who met each day at Sam Roddy's store. Following his grandmother's lead, Robert became an interpreter of the news. "The *Charlotte News* gave me status and some money to boot," he recalled. Each day after his route, Robert would stop at the store on Winchester Street. "There was very little recreation and entertainment for black people, and respected railroad men didn't dare be caught coming out of a 'barrel house,'" he said. "They would get off from work and sit around and play checkers and discuss different things and just laugh and talk. Most of them could read and write but some couldn't, and the ones that could didn't know very much about the news." Between his reading and his grandmother's commentary, Williams kept himself so well informed about world events that the crowd at the store called him "the news man," he recalled, "and each day I would go and explain who Hitler was and Mussolini and what was taking place." This was Williams's first role as a political interpreter of the world, modeled after the example of his grandmother.[85]

In an article titled "Someday, I'm Going Back South" he wrote for the *Daily Worker* in 1949, Robert Williams remembered his grandmother as "my greatest friend."[86] Conceived by a slaveowner and his black concubine, born as chattel property, Ellen Williams cut her political teeth in the terrible violence of Reconstruction. She watched the democratic hopes that she and Sikes Williams had risked their lives to build dashed by disfranchisement. As her life waned, she saw Adolph Hitler rise to threaten the world with his vision of a master race, while the country that had taken the vote from her people in the name of white supremacy portrayed itself as the citadel of democracy. But she did not give up the embattled dream of freedom. Perhaps because Robert so strikingly resembled her handsome late husband, Ellen Williams would point to the iron printing press rusting in the barn and tell her grandson stories of the crusading editor's political exploits. The legacy that nurtured Robert Williams also instructed him in the hard realities of racial politics. Before she died, Ellen Williams carefully wrapped a gift that symbolized all that slavery and the struggle against racial oppression had taught her. She presented young Robert with the ancient rifle that had belonged to Sikes Williams.[87]

2:
Wars for
Democracy

Robert Williams had first learned about the rise of Adolph Hitler and his theories of a master race from his grandmother, but the sixteen year old had no idea how sharply the war in Europe would reshape his world. On December 7, 1941, he twisted the dial on the big wooden Atwater Kent radio console that his Uncle Charlie had left him after his death. Young Rob Williams loved to tune the short-wave on Saturday nights and hear the big bands cooking from the Cotton Club in Harlem. Most Sundays he tuned in the New York Philharmonic on CBS. But on this particular Sunday, a voice interrupted the orchestra to inform listeners that the Japanese had bombed Pearl Harbor. The United States was at war. In the kitchen, Emma Williams wiped her face on her apron in disbelief and sat down at the table. His mother, who had seen the young men return from what would soon be called the First World War "gassed and maimed forever," he wrote, "just shook her head, thinking of her three sons."[1]

Robert Williams's war years make him seem not so much typical as emblematic, almost a black Everyman. First he enrolled in a federal job training program, experienced racial discrimination and organized an effective protest. In 1942, at seventeen, Williams climbed aboard a segregated Greyhound bus and headed for Detroit, where the following summer he became caught up in one of the worst race riots in U.S. history before leaving for California to work in a shipyard. In his pilgrimages, Williams joined hundreds of thousands of other black Southerners who forever changed the landscape of American life by heading to the cities of the North and West. Drafted into the U.S. Army for eighteen months at the end of the war, both his agonies and his achievements transformed

Williams forever. By the time that Private Williams returned to North Carolina in 1946, his wartime collisions with white supremacy had altered forever his understanding of white people. "Before then, it appeared that they were so well-organized and so powerful," he recalled, "it seemed that they really might be superior. But then I found that they are a long ways from being superior." Even in the exercise of their power, Williams detected a fragility. "I also realized that they are afraid, and that they had certain weaknesses," he said, "and this is why they had to react so violently and so swiftly in stamping out anything that they figured to be contrary to their interest." Like many of his black compatriots, Williams came home unable to accommodate himself to the traditional racial etiquette that prevailed in the South.[2]

Williams's new resolve to resist white supremacy reflected a transformation that was not merely personal but marked a sea change in African American political life. At the national level, A. Philip Randolph and the Brotherhood of Sleeping Car Porters organized the all-black March on Washington Movement (MOWM). Threatening to bring thousands of black Americans to the nation's capital, Randolph forced President Franklin D. Roosevelt to issue Executive Order 8802, which banned racial discrimination in the defense industries and created the Fair Employment Practices Commission. A longtime socialist, Randolph adopted racial separatism when he found it tactically useful and rejected accommodationist politics: "One thing is certain," he declared in 1941, "and that is that if Negroes are going to get anything out of this National Defense, we must fight for it and fight with the gloves off." The MOWM fueled a mass-based black militancy "which had not surfaced since Garveyism," sociologist Lewis Killian writes, "and would not be seen again until the slogan 'Black Power' echoed through the land." Though Executive Order 8802 carried little power to enforce its provisions, the MOWM did "let the Negro masses speak," in Randolph's resonant phrase, and Roosevelt's decree carried symbolic weight as the first presidential order on civil rights since Reconstruction.[3]

If the MOWM seemed to foreshadow both civil rights and Black Power, it was because there was always less difference in the origins and in the objectives of these movements than most observers have recognized. One of the most important aspects of the MOWM, for example, was that its organizers excluded white people. C. C. Dellums of the Brotherhood of Sleeping Car Porters explained that the organizers remained "unalterably opposed to segregation" but indicated that winning black freedom required not only that black people overcome white resistance but also that they affirm a black sense of self. Randolph and his allies understood, Dellums continued, "that Negroes needed an example of Negroes doing something for themselves." A militant campaign organized by and for African Americans could have a galvanizing psychological effect, helping to create "faith by Negroes in Negroes," Randolph explained. Still, there was no hostility to whites per se. "We told our white friends over the country why this had to be a Negro march," said Dellums. "It had to be for the inspiration of Negroes yet unborn."[4] While Williams did not take part in these protests, their sense of political realism, their racial pride, and their eclectic black nationalism informed his politics.

The MOWM showcased the potential of mass-based black protest and independent black political action.[5] In a skit performed for an overflow crowd at an MOWM convention in Madison Square Garden in 1942, a black draftee told Selective Service officials, "I'll fight Hitler, Mussolini, and the Japs all at the same time, but I'm telling you I'll give those crackers down South the same damn medicine." The crowd of 18,000 thundered its approval.[6] But MOWM organizers also introduced thousands of African Americans to Gandhian nonviolent direct action, a protest technique that later symbolized the civil rights movement in the minds of many.[7] Randolph praised Mohandas Gandhi at the 1942 MOWM convention and predicted that "disciplined non-violent demonstrations" held the future of the freedom movement. At the 1943 MOWM convention in Chicago, Bayard Rustin and James Farmer, who had helped found the Congress of Racial Equality (CORE) the year before, spoke in favor of nonviolent direct action.[8] The only white speaker at the convention was E. Stanley Jones, an evangelist in India and a friend of Gandhi. Jones outlined a program titled "Non-violent Direct Action—What It Is and How It Can Be Applied to Racial Problems in America."[9] It is important to remember that the wartime movement that Randolph led foreshadowed the all-black militancy of Black Power that Robert Williams helped to inspire. Equally telling, however, is that the MOWM of the 1940s inspired the 1963 March on Washington, where Martin Luther King Jr. unfurled the interracial "dream" of racial equality.

The overarching political logic of the war against fascism rang in a global revolution in racial consciousness of which the African American freedom struggle must be seen as a part.[10] "The problem of the Negro in the United States is no longer a purely domestic question but has world significance," Randolph declared in 1943. "We have become the barometer of democracy to the colored peoples of the world."[11] It was Hitler, the NAACP's Roy Wilkins wrote in 1944, who "jammed our white people into their logically untenable position. Forced to oppose him for the sake of the life of the nation, they were jockeyed into declaring against his racial theories—publicly."[12] The Germans air-dropped leaflets in North Africa that depicted police brutality in Detroit; the Japanese highlighted Western white supremacy in propaganda to promote their "Greater East Asia Co-Prosperity Sphere."[13] The distance between democratic rhetoric and American reality—and that race relations in the United States had become a significant pawn in the international struggle—gave African American activists unprecedented new leverage. "We are living in the midst of perhaps the greatest revolution within human experience," black political organizer Osceola McKaine wrote from South Carolina in 1941. "Nothing, no nation, will be as it was before when the peace comes. . . . There is no such thing as the status quo."[14]

African Americans wielded these contradictions as weapons of war. Now the most influential black political figure in America, Randolph argued in 1943 that there was "no difference between Hitler of Germany and Talmadge of Georgia or Tojo of Japan and Bilbo of Mississippi."[15] The black press beat the drum for "Double V" campaigns beneath banners urging Americans to "Defeat Mussolini and Hitler by Enforcing the Constitution and Abolishing Jim Crow." Circulation of African American newspapers increased by 40 percent during the war.[16] Ella Baker, who set out "to place the NAACP and its program on the lips of all the people[,] . . . the uncouth MASSES included," became national director of branches in 1943.[17] NAACP membership grew nearly tenfold during the war, and the number of branches tripled, three-quarters of these in the South.[18] CORE pursued nonviolent direct action campaigns in northern cities that laid the groundwork for its important campaigns of the 1960s.[19] For black citizens across the country, the war years brought experiences and opportunities that made it easier to resist and harder to accept the contradictions of Jim Crow democracy. Having fought for their country, moreover, black veterans—not only Robert Williams but thousands like him—came home prepared to fight for their place in it.

Pauli Murray, who later served as Robert Williams's attorney, wrote in the November 1944 issue of The Crisis about a young man from North Carolina, William Raines, who "for months" urged students at Howard University to try what he called "the stool-sitting technique," a tactic that four students from North Carolina Agricultural and Technical College

(A&T) would make famous in the Greensboro sit-ins almost twenty years later and that Robert Williams would use in Monroe a few days afterward. "We'll take a seat on a lunch stool," Raines implored, "and if they don't serve us, we'll just sit there and read our books." Although Raines left Howard for the army, Murray explained, "his idea went on." Picketing local restaurants with signs that read, "We die together—why can't we eat together?" the NAACP youth chapter at Howard organized sit-ins that opened several restaurants in the District of Columbia and "led the way toward new and perhaps successful techniques to achieve first class citizenship," Murray wrote.[20]

African American activists in North Carolina first had to fight for "the right to fight." A white physician in Rocky Mount observed that about 80 percent of the black draftees in his community were rejected because "it seemed easier to say IV-F—and send the negro home—and close the case. The army had rather have them in munitions or anything but the army."[21] In Charlotte a black high school teacher with a master's degree from Columbia University accompanied four of his students to an army recruiting station in 1940 to get enlistment information. Told that the station was for "whites only," he pressed for an explanation. White soldiers beat the teacher severely, breaking his jaw.[22] Fighting for the right to face Hitler, however, was only part of the struggle. "We have to think of the home front whether we want to or not," one black North Carolinian argued. "No clear thinking Negro can long afford to ignore our Hitlers here in America."[23]

This logic reflected the thinking of black activists across North Carolina. From 1941 to 1945 the number of NAACP branches in the state more than doubled. "Our drives are all shaping up well in North Carolina," an NAACP organizer wrote to the national office in 1942. "In fact, they are progressing much better than anticipated."[24] Ella Baker persuaded branch presidents to create the North Carolina Conference of Branches in 1943. Fiery editor Louis Austin of the *Carolina Times* published a weekly wartime platform that demanded, among other things, an end to discrimination in the military and in the defense industries, "higher wages for domestic servants," the employment of "Negro policemen where Negroes are involved," equal access to the ballot box, and "better housing for Negroes."[25]

Black residents in Wilmington jammed city council meetings to demand that the city hire "Negro policemen [who] could be employed in the Negro districts of the city" and that "a place where Negroes might swim at [whites-only] Greenfield Lake be reserved, the place to be supervised by Negroes recommended by Negro citizens." Mayor Bruce Cameron promised small concessions but privately complained to Governor J. Melville Broughton that "the Negroes are ready and willing at all times to go en masse to the court house." The mayor begged Broughton to "tell them as long as you are governor the colored people will have to behave themselves."[26] But official proclamations did nothing to stem the statewide determination of black citizens to put an end to second-class citizenship. "Negroes are organizing all over the state to secure their rights," Roy Wilkins wrote after a wartime visit to North Carolina. "They are not frightened."[27]

The same cannot be said, however, of white North Carolinians, whose fears about the racial consequences of the war bordered on the paranoid. One widespread rumor, according to University of North Carolina sociologist Howard Odum, asserted that "the Negroes were buying up all the icepicks" in the state and "waiting for the first blackout to start an attack." Perhaps because these rumors resonated in the recesses of memory where slave insurrections and the mythical "black brutes" of Reconstruction once dwelled, white Southerners could not see the ludicrous humor in their image of a black guerilla army wielding icepicks in the dark, overrunning a state whose borders contained tens of thousands of white soldiers with machine guns and armored tanks. An only slightly more plausible murmur through the white grapevine had it that the state police had "raided a Negro church in which was found an arsenal of firearms and ammunition" intended for a black revolution. Less verifiable—and thus perhaps more chilling—was the rumor that black North Carolinians were mail-ordering massive amounts of munitions from the Sears, Roebuck catalog. Other gossip pressed the notion of "bump days" and "pushing clubs," which were thought to encourage blacks to nudge white pedestrians off sidewalks and streetcars.[28]

But the rumor that raced the fastest and the farthest among white people in the state, apparently, remained the classic story of the "Eleanor Clubs," a phantom conspiracy named after Eleanor Roosevelt, whose horrifying agenda, News and Observer publisher Frank Daniels claimed, featured "their aim of putting every white woman in her own kitchen by Christmas." The wellspring of the rumor, according to an FBI informant in Wilmington, was the fact "that where formerly Negroes earned ten or twelve dollars a week, they are now able to support their own homes without their wives doing domestic work in white homes" and hence "many white people have been of the opinion that Negroes 'were up to something' because they would not do domestic work."[29]

Not all white fears rested on rumor. In 1942 Jonathan Daniels, whom President Franklin D. Roosevelt had selected as his adviser on race relations, wrote to Lester B. Granger, head of the National Urban League, about his alarm at "the rising insistence of Negroes on their rights now" and "the rising tide of white feeling against the Negroes in the South and other sections." Daniels feared both "bloodshed at home" and "material for dangerous anti-American propaganda abroad." Black demands were "logically strong," he conceded: "If we are fighting for democracy and human freedom, it is logical to insist that our pretensions in the world be proved at home." But Daniels knew that racial feeling often transcended logic. His deepest anxiety was that "a dreadful solution" might emerge from the crucible of war: white Americans, he feared, "might resort to Fascist methods in the creation of a ruthless unity."[30]

In part, Jonathan Daniels's almost apocalyptic apprehension reflected the fact that his post in Washington required him to collect information pertaining to racial tensions across the country. But his anguish flowed also from a source closer to home and closer to heart. After years as editor, Jonathan Daniels had left the *News and Observer* to the management of his older brother, Frank Daniels, a leading figure in the state's Democratic Party, and had accepted a post as adviser to the president. In 1942 he received an angry letter from Frank attacking him for being "in with all the pinkeys and liberals tied up with advancement for the Negro race. The situation here in Raleigh regarding the feeling of the white people toward the more or less new ideas of negroes," Frank wrote, "is really alarming." If black Americans continue to "keep on insisting for more privileges," he said, "a worse condition is going to exist in North Carolina before very long than the period from 1895 to 1902, because white people just aren't going to stand for it." This sentiment required little explanation. Josephus Daniels, father of both men and still the elder statesman of the Democratic Party in North Carolina, had helped to orchestrate the violent white supremacy campaign at the turn of the century that had brought the party to power. If African Americans continued to press for "equality," Frank Daniels told his brother, "the white people are going to rise in arms and eliminate them from the national picture." Lest there be any confusion about his meaning, the publisher warned that black efforts for racial advancement were "going to mean that all of them that can read and write are going to be eliminated in the Hitler style."[31]

One of the closest white observers of wartime racial politics, Howard Odum, noted in 1943 that "a surprisingly large number of the ablest and best Negro leaders . . . had concluded sadly that it might be necessary to 'fight it out,' " and Odum observed "a growing hatred on the part of many Negroes for the whites."[32] From Birmingham, liberal activist Virginia Durr's father wrote to her that "all white people in Alabama are buying pistols and other ammunition in preparation for the race war which is coming."[33] A particular flash point was relations between black citizens and law enforcement officers, whom white citizens depended on to preserve racial etiquette: "The police can handle these bad eggs quite handily," one North Carolina editor wrote, "if the uplifters—i.e. social workers and those who think like them—don't barge in. A zoot-suiter should be no great problem."[34]

But the police were not always able to contain black anger over persistent police brutality. After white officers beat an unarmed black man to death on his front porch in Greenville in 1943, "a crowd of Negroes—men and women—assembled and threatened the officer," one of the policemen stated, until he brandished a pistol and promised to "drop them one by one," waving his gun at the protesters. In a separate incident, "several hundred Negroes at Grifton Saturday night attempted to storm the jail," the Carolina Times reported, "and prevent police officers from placing a Negro woman, Mrs. Rosa Lee Picott, in jail on a charge of being disorderly and creating a disturbance."[35] From Goldsboro, a local black leader wrote that the town was "a 'hot spot' due to the killing of a Negro by an officer" in the summer of 1945. "This is the first time that Negroes here are attempting to fight back."[36]

A few weeks later in Erwin, North Carolina, twenty-two black men signed a letter informing Governor Broughton of "the disturbment between the white and colored people, of this town." The men told Broughton that "we can't go up the street at night in peace, they are throwing rock at us and threating us with pistols and rifles." The black community would not endure much more abuse, they warned: "If something don't be done in the furture, evidently someone may be killed." Soon thereafter, Governor Broughton received a letter of explanation from Herbert Taylor, a leading white businessman in Erwin. He acknowledged white violence but discounted it as "just a case of some young fellows throwing rocks, following some very insolent remarks having been made by some colored men." The trouble was "nothing but the negroes taking advantage of conditions," Taylor protested, and "little by little easing into things the best they can, under their belief that 'they are as good as anybody else.' "[37]

On the same Sunday that Robert Williams had heard the radio announcement of the bombing of Pearl Harbor, German antiaircraft guns in North Africa killed a young man from North Carolina who had run off to become a flight sergeant in the Royal Canadian Air Force at the outbreak of the war in Europe. Frank Sutton was the first of more than 100 young men from Monroe to die in the war. "We immediately began working to get an Army camp here," the chair of the Union County Commission, J. Ray Shute, recalled. "I got them to name it for Frank Sutton."[38] Thousands of strangers poured into the small town, renting every available attic and tool shed; by 1943, 645 civilians and a revolving cast of thousands of Army trainees, black and white, swarmed over Monroe.[39] A rollicking red-light district sprang up after authorities legalized the sale of beer and wine. "Monroe enjoyed a prosperity not equaled by any of the surrounding cities," according to Shute. "Monroe boomed."[40]

Camp Sutton also placed great strains on Monroe, as black soldiers from all over the United States arrived at the training camp. One, a handsome, quick-witted young recruit from Texas named Albert E. Perry, later returned to Monroe and became one of Robert Williams's key lieutenants in the postwar black freedom struggle.[41] But many other black soldiers found Monroe considerably less hospitable. Like many training camps across the South, Camp Sutton experienced almost routine clashes between black soldiers and white police officers. "Every payday," E. Frederic Morrow, later the first African American presidential aide, recalled, "trucks and M.P. vans drove up to our area and dropped off the bloody, beaten hulks of [black] men who had run afoul of the lawmen in Monroe." The violence frequently seemed to carry a sexual subtext; white police beat African American soldiers, according to Morrow, because the black men were "thought to be rapists or 'social equality' seekers, and they had to be kept in their place."[42]

Social equality provided at least the rhetorical center of gravity in Southern racial politics during the war. White politicians denounced any manifestation of it; African American leaders denied any interest in it. "Social equality" was the euphemism of choice for the ancient taboo of sex between black men and white women. Virtually any self-assertion on the part of African Americans conjured images of "amalgamation" in the minds of white Southerners. In his *Race and Rumors of Race: Challenge to American Crisis*, published in 1943, Howard Odum pronounced this taboo "first and foremost" among white racial fears during the war. Racial hierarchy, "although it reflected the cumulative racial and economic heritage of the South," Odum wrote, "was primarily one of sex." Odum felt that this underlying reality barred most discussion of reform among black and white Southerners. "If it were not for the sex-caste foundation," he believed, "it might have been possible to make adjustments."[43]

Even in Chapel Hill, supposedly the enlightened seat of Southern liberalism, the sex-caste foundation perched atop pure dynamite. According to a War Department intelligence report titled "Commingling of Whites and Negroes at Chapel Hill, N.C.," the Reverend Charles M. Jones, a liberal Presbyterian minister, "entertained some members of the Navy Band (Negroes) at his church" on July 12, 1944, along with "some co-eds of the University of North Carolina (white, of course)." The local chief of police reported that "the coeds and negroes were seen walking side by side on the streets of Chapel Hill." A state highway patrol officer claimed that "Rev. Jones' daughter, who is about nineteen, had a date with one of the Negro members of the band on the same occasion and they were seen walking together in a lonely section of the campus late at night." Many members "refuse[d] to attend the church so long as the present minister remains," according to the report, but the Board of Trustees voted four to three to retain Jones. Among the board members who supported the minister were Dr. Frank Porter Graham, president of the university, and Dr. F. F. Bradshaw, dean of students. The chief of police later "talked with Mr. Bradshaw and pointed out to him the seriousness of the situation if Rev. Jones is not dismissed at once."[44]

This confounding obsession was not confined to the South or to the lower classes; it echoed in the corridors of power and the halls of Congress. FBI director J. Edgar Hoover wrote to the head of the Selective Services and warned that white women were endangered by the number of black men left at home.[45] White Mississippian David L. Cohn, in an effort to tell the nation "How The South Feels" from the pages of the *Atlantic Monthly* in 1944, called the racial clash in the South "at bottom a blood or sexual question."[46] Secretary of War Henry Stimson, a New Yorker with degrees from Harvard and Yale, denounced "radical leaders of the colored race" who intended, he charged, "to use the war for obtaining race equality and interracial marriages."[47] Governor Broughton noted that "the Constitution of North Carolina prevents intermarriage between the white and negro races" and claimed that "there is no sentiment on the part of either race to change this wise provision."[48] Only a few weeks earlier, however, the governor had decried "radical negro leaders" who "are seeking to use the war emergency to advance theories and philosophies which if carried to their ultimate conclusion would result only in a mongrel race."[49]

Black leaders found it necessary to navigate the treacherous political eddies that swirled around this issue of social equality. Many African American speakers, confronted with the intermarriage question, joked to the effect that "Well, I'm married already myself." But it was not a subject that could be easily laughed off. "It stirs Negroes to ironic laughter," Sterling Brown noted, but "on all levels they recognize that the white man's fear of intermarriage is deep-seated."[50] Six of the fourteen African American contributors to Rayford Logan's 1944 landmark collection, *What the Negro Wants*, considered social equality at some length. W. E. B. Du Bois's essay spends four pages on the issue, concluding that "there is no scientific reason why there should not be intermarriage between two human beings who happen to be of different race or color." But Gordon B. Hancock, a conservative black academician from Richmond, was more typical, arguing that "the social and economic advancement of the Negro has not resulted in greater intermarriage but definitely less."[51]

At the public celebration of the eightieth anniversary of the Emancipation Proclamation organized by black citizens of Monroe in 1943, a local black preacher promised that "political freedom" was the only goal of black Southerners. "Negroes do not want social equality," he assured listeners, but merely "to enter the professional fields upon the basis of educational and technical qualifications."[52] James Shepard, the conservative president of North Carolina College for Negroes in Durham, stated in a national radio address in 1944 that "Negroes do not seek social equality and have never sought it."[53] But across town at the *Carolina Times*, editor Louis E. Austin stated his own views with characteristic candor: "Social equality," Austin declared, "is the age-old scarecrow that is always brought out of the attic and dusted off to frighten the weak-minded whenever Negroes ask for better jobs, better wages, better schools, and other improvements." Besides, Austin noted dryly, "our streets are crowded with Negroes, the color of whose skin bears testimony to the fact that there are individuals in both races who have been engaging in the highest point of social equality."[54]

Louis Austin may have been the most prominent "radical agitator" in North Carolina during World War II, but he was not the only one. In 1941 sixteen-year-old Robert Williams had enrolled with his schoolmate Bennie Montgomery in a National Youth Administration (NYA) job training program near Monroe "because at that time they were just training youth for defense work and they were just beginning then because of the manpower shortage."[55] Here Williams organized the protest that launched his FBI subject file, marked "Security-C," meaning that the FBI thought he might be a Communist. The NYA "had meant for us to be training for stone masons," Williams recalled, but local officials "had the white boys, teaching them, [but] they had us digging stone." The indignity of drinking from segregated water buckets out of filthy Coca-Cola bottles was the last straw. "We decided to strike and we struck," he recalled. The burly young Williams kicked over the water bucket and led a mass walkout of the young black men; he and Montgomery recruited one of their high school teachers to help draft a complaint to the state NYA office. "The state came in and said they had to send us to a real trade school," Williams said.[56] He and Montgomery and several other friends then transferred to an NYA training program in Rocky Mount, North Carolina, where Robert learned to make machine tools. "Everybody who finished there was supposed to go to the Navy yard, work for the Navy, in the machine trade," he recalled. "But I told them that my brother lived in Detroit and he told me that I could get a job at Ford Motor Company in the defense plant."[57]

Robert Williams's growing racial militancy mirrored that of African Americans across wartime North Carolina, many of whom were newly minted soldiers, who defied Jim Crow every day. In fact, the War Department reported in 1943, there was "general unrest" among black troops all over the country and the imminent danger of revolt; "most Negro soldiers have secreted ammunition," one War Department memo stated.[58] White officials from the bus company that operated the Durham-Butner line complained that black soldiers from Camp Butner made it "utterly impossible" to enforce the segregation statutes. Clashes were common even though the legislature had amended the Jim Crow laws in 1939 to give bus drivers "police powers and authority to carry out the provisions of this section."[59] An African American captain at Camp Butner acknowledged that "our men tipped over a couple of buses because they had to wait while whites boarded first."[60] The chair of the State Utilities Board complained to Governor Broughton that "in spite of the [bus drivers'] efforts to control the [African American] passengers, in many instances it is beyond their power to do so." Local white editors argued that racial trouble in North Carolina "was not home grown" but attributable to outsiders who failed to "conduct themselves in an orderly manner and in keeping with the laws and customs of this section." State officials affirmed this view, blaming the troubles on "Northern negro soldiers at Camp Butner and Northern white officers who do not believe in our segregation laws and encourage the negro soldiers to break them."[61]

On April 3, 1943, that spirit of resistance exploded into a riot in the Hayti section of Durham, where many black soldiers from Camp Butner spent their free time. An argument about ration books turned into a brawl between an African American soldier and a white liquor store clerk. The clerk brandished a blackjack and the soldier drew a knife. Their violent scuffle spread into the streets, where white police and then hundreds of African American soldiers and local citizens joined the melee. Rioters hurled bricks, rocks, and hunks of cement, injuring a white bus driver and several policemen. Though local police tried to disperse the men with tear gas, the mob slashed tires, smashed windshields, and demolished store-fronts until machine gun trucks and military police units from Camp Butner finally restored order. "Durham is one of the worst places we have, due to the large negro population," one state official reported to the governor afterward. "We have already had some open trouble there and I apprehend that we will have more. It is a bad situation."[62]

If there was anywhere more tense than Durham, it was Detroit. Robert Williams moved to the Motor City in 1942 to live with his older brother Edward, whom the family called "Pete." His other brother John had already been drafted into an army artillery unit that ended up in Europe. Pete Williams worked in a defense plant and helped his younger brother land a job on the afternoon shift at Ford Motor Company's enormous River Rouge plant, "a sprawling complex that staggered my imagination. It was said to be the workplace of eighty thousand men and women." Long sheets of rolled steel, white with heat, rumbled down the conveyor belt toward Robert Williams, the youngest worker on the assembly line. It was hot, heavy work.[63] But as a defense worker, Williams recalled, "you could get an exemption from the military." The brothers made outstanding wages by Southern standards and lived in Conant Gardens, Detroit's wealthiest black neighborhood, "a pretty bourgeois, middle-class black community, all private homes," according to Robert Williams. In his spare time, Robert read every book he could get his hands on; he especially enjoyed the blues rhythms and barbed humor of Langston Hughes, relishing Hughes's couplet that expressed the central racial irony of the war: "You tell me that Hitler is a mighty bad man / He must have took lessons from the Ku Klux Klan." Despite Detroit's advantages, Williams found the city crowded, harsh, and impersonal. "I don't like the atmosphere of dog-eat-dog and each one is trying to survive and doesn't care how he survives and who is hurt and who is crushed," Williams said. "In our communities in the South we never had this type of thing."[64]

Williams had grown up rooted in a rural Southern black ethos that stressed the importance of family and community. Though it strongly encouraged individualism in many respects, Southern black culture tended to underline the common humanity and communal spirit of its people. Ella Baker, one of the decisive figures of the black freedom movement, described her own upbringing in rural North Carolina: "Where we lived there was no sense of social hierarchy in terms of those who have, having the right to look down upon, or evaluate as a lesser breed, those who didn't have." Like Williams, Baker "grew up hearing stories about slavery from her maternal grandmother, a light-skinned house slave, a daughter of the man who owned her." Baker's race pride and egalitarian politics, like Williams's, were exemplified in her legendary grandfather. It is hardly surprising that insurgent black Southerners like Williams became attracted to left-wing radical politics when they moved to northern cities; their "model of the Good Life was not derived from the lifestyle of middle-class whites," Charles Payne writes, "nor from any pre-cut ideological scheme, as it was for some of [their] Marxist acquaintances," but from an abiding respect for their own roots.[65]

Williams joined Local 600 of the United Automobile Workers of America, CIO, a militant interracial union that the FBI believed had Communists among the leadership; at that time, Local 600 had joined African American church and community group efforts to push for integration in all defense-related housing.[66] Demonstrations at the plant gate were common, and one FBI informant reported that "the chief aim of a number of Negroes" at the River Rouge plant "seemed to be to make life miserable for white people by making an issue of almost anything that might arise." Other left-wing groups such as the Socialist Workers Party (SWP), the FBI reported, "are extremely active in distributing pamphlets and other literature pertaining to the Negro situation" and "vie among themselves for Negro support."[67]

The Communist and socialist organizers Williams met in Detroit were "impressive to me," he recalled. "I wasn't interested in politics," he said, but "these things sounded quite good, the idea of equality, the denial of the power of one man to exploit another man, of equal justice, also the fact that men shouldn't be allowed to hog the money, or some men to hog the property, that it should be collectively owned." To Williams, this rhetoric rang more with the Sermon on the Mount and Negro spirituals than with *The Communist Manifesto* or "The Internationale." "I didn't think of them as communists from a political point of view," he said, "but saw them as what we considered friends, people who wanted to abolish racism." In Monroe, Williams had not known white people whose lofty ideas resonated with the best that his heritage had taught him. Though he never joined the Communist Party or any of the other left-wing sects competing for influence in the black community, Williams read the *Daily Worker* and attended demonstrations occasionally, especially when the rallies focused on "cases in the South" and when "they would have black people doing most of the speaking."[68]

Not that Williams found Detroit, generally speaking, to be a racially congenial environment. From 1940 to 1943, 50,000 African Americans and 450,000 other people poured into the city. Housing shortages, labor trouble, and race-baiting demagogues created a vicious climate that many observers warned could explode at any minute. Racial clashes in workplaces, schools, and parks; fistfights on trolleys and buses; and cross burnings throughout the city became everyday events. On April 13, 1943, a white foreman at the plant where Williams worked called a black worker "nigger," and the worker hit the foreman, fracturing his skull and killing him. One observer described the city as "a keg of powder with a short fuse." When the charge finally blew on June 20, 1943, Detroit's mayor told reporters, "I was taken by surprise only by the day it happened."[69]

Early that blistering hot afternoon, Robert, his brother Pete and Pete's wife, and another black couple set out for Belle Isle Amusement Park for a picnic. A 985-acre island in the Detroit River, Belle Isle had become popular among African Americans in Detroit in the years just before the war; it was convenient to Paradise Valley, the big eastside black ghetto, and was one of the few recreation areas open to black citizens. Thousands of whites still used Belle Isle, however, and there was open resentment about the black presence there. Many whites called it "Nigger Island." On June 20, about 100,000 people crowded the park in the 91 degree heat.[70] As evening fell, the Williams family started back across the Jefferson Street bridge, which was jammed with cars and pedestrians. Robert sat calmly in the back seat, smoking his pipe. "This was Sunday evening," Williams recounted, "so we thought it was just a traffic jam." Unbeknownst to them, however, small racial clashes on the island had spread to the bridge. White sailors from the nearby naval armory ran to join the fray, and soon hundreds of blacks and whites were fighting all over the bridge.[71]

Suddenly the Williamses' car was surrounded by the frenzied clashes. "We saw a lot of white sailors, and we saw one black man in the middle, and he was fighting, really fighting, to keep them off from him. . . . We were right at the edge of this big circle and they had him in the middle." The lone black figure kicked and twirled and swung his fists, trying desperately to escape from the white mob. "They were running this black guy," Pete Williams recalled, "and I said we might as well get out and fight." Robert was the only one in the car unarmed. "My brother had a knife and the other guy had a knife, and they asked me if I had anything and I said 'no,'" Robert remembered. "We got out of the car and I held that [tobacco] pipe like it may have been a gun, you see." A white woman on the edge of the mob yelled to the sailors, "There are some more niggers and they've got knives!" With the word "knives," Williams said, "the line just opened up. . . . They started falling back and this guy went right out of that hole. [The black man] didn't stop to say anything to us, we didn't see him anymore. We supposed he got away, but he had a long way to go on that bridge." The men got back in the car, still unaware of the magnitude of the violence around them. "We just thought it was one fight."[72]

As the line of cars began to lurch forward, it became clear that this was not an isolated scuffle. White sailors mobbed the car several times. Pete Williams asked his wife to drive and sat behind her with his knife out the left rear window. The other man sat up front and kept his knife out the right front window; Robert did the best he could with his hands. "All the way we had to fight to keep those people off the car. They were breaking windshields and then we knew that it was pretty serious," Robert said. At the mainland end of Jefferson Street bridge, they faced a white mob that police later estimated at 5,000 people. Gladys House, a black woman escorting a handicapped man across the bridge, described the scene. "We don't want any niggers on Belle Isle," the white men told House and her companion as they attacked. As she reached the end of the bridge, House was terrified to see "several hundred white people standing at the mainland entrance to the bridge, waiting to attack Negroes as they came along," she testified later.[73] "When we got to the end of the bridge," Robert Williams recalled, white sailors "were breaking out the windows of the cars of the black people, and the cops were standing there directing traffic like they didn't see it. We finally got out. And we thought it was over and went on home."[74]

The violence on the bridge from Belle Isle, however, was only the beginning of one of the worst race riots in U.S. history. Shortly after the Williams family made their escape through the mob, a young black man mounted the stage at the Forest Club, a popular black hangout in Paradise Valley, seized the microphone from the band leader, and told the crowd,

"There's a riot at Belle Isle. The whites have killed a colored lady and her baby. Thrown them over the bridge. Everybody come on." The rumor about the woman and her baby was not true, but thousands of African Americans raged through the streets, stoning white motorists and looting white businesses. White agitators spread similar rumors of outrage, many of which were sexual in nature, as white mobs rampaged on streetcars and set fire to black automobiles. Many white rioters traveled substantial distances from all-white communities, as one put it, "to kill us a nigger." White police ignored and sometimes encouraged white rioters; some became active participants in the violence. Every one of the seventeen citizens killed by police bullets was an African American. Two days of rioting left 38 people dead, 676 injured, and $2 million worth of property destroyed. State and local authorities across the country braced themselves for more of the same, with good reason. According to the Social Science Institute at Fisk University, groups of blacks and whites clashed at least 242 times in 47 cities in 1943 alone.[75]

After all the tumult in Detroit, Robert Williams was none too eager to stay there, even though he enjoyed living with his brother. In 1943 federal agencies cooperated with San Francisco Bay Area employers such as Kaiser Shipyards to recruit massive numbers of defense workers to California.[76] "They promised first class transportation, available housing and high wages for relocating," Williams wrote later. The prospect of seeing the West and making good money seemed to promise "a new life and a new world." Williams signed up along with several of his friends in Detroit. Just before they were scheduled to leave, however, the Kaiser recruiter called Williams to the state employment office, where he informed the young man that the machinists' union in California barred black workers. "I had heard communists say how these capitalists were the ones who were promoting racial discrimination," Williams recalled. Proud to be a member of Ford's radical Local 600, the idea of discrimination by a union rankled him all the more: "And it was supposed to be a liberal union."[77]

A navy recruiter in the same employment office was willing to hire Williams to work at the Mare Island Naval Yard in Port Chicago, California. Housing, meals, and a Pullman ticket across the country came with the job. Soon Williams was unpacking his suitcase in a dingy dormitory in a place that did not resemble the fantasies of the golden West that he had entertained. Nothing about California seemed to welcome him. Racial fights broke out in the dormitories, and the police were hard on black workers. His sinuses suddenly began to give him severe headaches.

After only three months in California, Williams boarded a bus for North Carolina.[78]

"Monroe, North Carolina was as dusty, hot and sooty as ever," he wrote many years later. But the Monroe that Robert Williams came home to in 1944 was quite different from the little town he had left only two years earlier.[79] Three gold teeth made a ghoulish display in the window of Langdon's Jewelry Store; a soldier from Monroe had mailed them to his mother from faraway Guadalcanal, where he had "kicked them out of a Jap mouth."[80] Wartime labor shortages pulled local white women into the job market in unprecedented numbers. The Monroe Enquirer ran stories such as "Truck Driving Job Farm Girl's Pride," which informed readers that one woman was "not much larger than a half-pint of cider, but she can handle a truck."[81] The Seaboard Air Line Railway hired black women to do the heavy, dirty work that black men had always done. German prisoners of war labored on local farms and ate their lunch in restaurants downtown where African American soldiers were not welcome.[82] A black sixth-grader at Winchester Street School named Mabel Robinson, whose energy and ingenuity would later prove decisive to Robert Williams, placed second among the town's schoolchildren in their drive to sell war savings stamps.[83]

Military training maneuvers staged in Union County and the arrival of Camp Sutton stimulated local business enormously and launched a watershed shift toward a manufacturing economy.[84] Camp Sutton had brought not only prosperity but thousands of strangers and their unfamiliar ways to Monroe. Dozens of private homes became boardinghouses overnight. "Every house was filled," J. Ray Shute remembered, "empty rooms, garage apartments."[85] Thousands of soldiers poured through the training facility, filling pockets with money and minds with apprehension. The bars and brothels that opened after Monroe legalized the sale of beer and wine in 1942 launched a battle between the Bible Belt and the balance sheet: "Our greed of money and pleasure," one Monroe native warned in 1942, "is going to eat our souls out." Preachers reproached the community for forsaking the time-honored observation of the Sabbath. "We remain in business until midnight and later to allow our soldiers to dissipate their much needed strength," another outraged citizen complained. "Some of us are out to make all we can off the soldiers when we should be giving them all that we can."[86]

The most glaring strains that wartime brought to social relations in Monroe, however, were around issues of race. Thousands of black soldiers from all over the country received training at Camp Sutton, bringing them into almost constant conflict with local segregation practices and white military authorities. Racial fights were practically a daily affair and larger clashes were commonplace. On September 22, 1943, according to a War Department investigation, "a disturbance occurred at the Negro Service Club at Camp Sutton which threatened to assume riot proportions" when white military police tried to arrest a black soldier for being absent without leave. A mob of black soldiers fought the MPs, and "shouts were heard from the colored soldiers that 'We may as well die here as over there.'" Authorities considered the affray not "evidence of a planned outbreak but rather further evidence of the volatile character of the general Negro situation."[87]

Roland Beasley, editor of the *Monroe Journal*, however, claimed that "though the Negro has in this country every right and opportunity that a white man has . . . the agitators are fanning the flames." Despite "white only" signs posted all over town and glaring racial inequalities of wealth and privilege, Beasley insisted that "no man can deny that the white majority is seeking honestly and earnestly" to achieve racial justice. Well known for his racial liberalism and a devoted admirer of socialist intellectual Henry George, Beasley argued that blacks sought "amalgamation"—the old "social equality" bugaboo. "The races are distinct and that fact may as well be recognized," Beasley declared from the editorial pages of the *Journal*. "The white race can amalgamate with the black only by committing suicide and any arrangement which tends to encourage amalgamation cannot be encouraged." While unwilling to endorse "mob violence, the Ku Klux Klan, or in any way cheating the Negro," the editor asserted that racial lines must be preserved inviolate. At bottom, Beasley maintained, the race "problem" was rooted in the underlying biological reality that justified white supremacy: "No one could doubt that upon the whole the white race is superior to the black." Anyone who might "suppose that the two races can mingle socially with restriction" and "have no race riots," the editor asserted, "is foolish."[88]

If race-mixing caused riots, as Beasley claimed, segregation apparently did little to prevent them, at least not in the wartime South. In late 1943 an intelligence report indicated that "colored soldiers . . . stationed at this post were gathering live ammunition for the purposes of retaliating against taxicab and bus drivers." When military authorities searched several black enlisted men from Camp Sutton, the inspection "resulted in the recovery of substantial amounts of ammunition" and other weapons.

Though authorities uncovered this particular insurgency, black resistance to ill treatment and racial discrimination persisted. In a letter to Jonathan Daniels, FBI director J. Edgar Hoover described a racial clash on February 8, 1944, in which "350 Negro soldiers from Camp Sutton resisted military police as well as civilian authorities," injuring several soldiers and police officers. Hoover blamed the fracas on "friction which has been existing between Negro soldiers and white officers." A few weeks later, the white commanding officer at Camp Sutton was "struck in the back of his head by a Negro private" with a bottle and "had to have stitches in his head." An informer among the black trainees reported "that the Negro enlisted men were planning a concerted program of insubordination."

Clashes between African Americans and white civilians were even more common. On April 25, 1944, the War Department reported, a white civilian employee at Camp Sutton attacked a thirteen-year-old black boy and threw him off a bridge into Richardson Creek. Though the white man apparently was not arrested, local police officers "seemed to move with great zeal and dispatch when they saw an opportunity to club a black soldier," Robert Williams wrote of his wartime stay in Monroe. At a local dive called the New York Cafe, Williams said, he witnessed a clash in which the white proprietor would not permit a black military policeman to enter, and the black MP faced down the owner by sticking a gun in his face.[89]

That same summer, four black soldiers from Camp Sutton walked into a cafe in nearby Concord, North Carolina, and asked to be served. "They were told that colored persons would not be served and they started to leave," a War Department investigator reported. "As they were leaving, a white patron also left and as he started out he shoved one of the Negroes telling him to get out of his way." The black soldier whipped out a knife and stabbed the white man. When the white counterman jumped into the fight, the soldier stabbed the second man as well, killing him. A white mob began to gather outside the cafe, but the black soldiers fled. "The soldiers made their getaway," the report stated, "but had the town's inhabitants caught them undoubtedly they would have been lynched."[90] John and Emma Williams began to think that Robert should not stay in Monroe.

Given their son's rebellious spirit, the Williams family feared that it was only a matter of time before young Robert got caught up in the escalating racial conflict, "an emotion felt by many black parents who dared to think of what white hate could do to their sons in Dixie," he wrote later. "Although my mother had been glad to see me return from so far away," he wrote, "I could tell that she was suffering some apprehension relative to my being there. . . . I am sure that my father concurred with her misgivings." Up North, they told him, his training as a machinist could open doors that would remain closed in the South for a long time to come. Enlisting two friends and singing "I'm Going to the Apple to Live on Lenox Avenue," Williams moved to Harlem, where he worked unloading freight barges on the waterfront. Within three months, however, Robert opened a letter from the draft board that ordered him to report for induction. Germany had fallen, but the Pacific war raged on and the invasion of Japan was expected to be bloody. He was going to fight, but whether he would battle the Empire of the Sun or the legions of Jim Crow was hard to say.[91]

As battles in North Carolina continued to rage, Robert Williams put on a uniform and entered his own private war. He reported for duty at Fort Bragg, North Carolina, on July 12, 1945, less than a month before the atomic bomb fell on Hiroshima. After about a week at Fort Bragg, Williams and his cohorts took a train to Camp Crowder, Missouri, by way of South Carolina, Alabama, and Tennessee. "They put us on a troop train," he recalled, "and they had the last two cars for the blacks, front of the train was all for whites." In South Carolina the white soldiers ate hot meals, "but they just gave us some sandwiches and we had to get back on the train." The next day in Birmingham, the women of the local Red Cross served doughnuts and coffee to white soldiers on the station platform. When Private Williams and his companions tried to get off in their crisp new uniforms, the white conductor accosted them. "You think you're going to have a white woman serve you doughnuts and coffee?" he demanded. "Not here you're not." One of the white officers ordered the black men to get back on the train.[92]

Despite the lack of coffee, Private Williams passed a "weary and sleepless night" as the train rolled through Tennessee and then on toward Missouri. "The incident at Birmingham had left a bitter imprint on my heart and soul." As the railway cars rumbled through the darkness, he could not help but ponder his ancestors riding in the bottom of a ship in "the anguish and brutal misery of the savage slave trade," Williams wrote later. He thought about his brother John, who had risked his life for the last two years fighting in an artillery unit in France, and his boyhood friend Bennie Montgomery, who recently had suffered a head wound at the Battle of the Bulge. "I wondered how a so-called civilized nation could do what America had done to us," he said, "then force us to go to the other side of the world in a supposed conflict to save 'democracy.'" It was an inauspicious start for a reluctant young soldier.[93]

His relationship with the U.S. Army did not improve very much over the next eighteen months. Lodged at Camp Crowder in a segregated cluster of dilapidated, tar-papered sheds that the black soldiers called "Shantytown," Williams knew that any bond of loyalty he might have felt for the army had been broken. The racial ironies of the war confronted him at every turn; training films depicted Japanese as "dark with bayonets and white teeth and white eyes so it looked like they were actually Negroes. I remember seeing a poster where the Japanese soldier was supposed to be trying to rape a white woman," Williams remembered. "I knew this was what they were accusing the black man of doing, see, and I knew it was based on racism."[94]

Williams did enjoy weapons training, however, and savored the heft of a .45 in his hand, the smell of gun oil, and the precision and power of military rifles. The only other bright spot was a creative writing course that he took at an army-sponsored off-duty school; he composed "mostly verse and articles about Southern life. Just about life in the South, and lynching." Looking back, he said, the writings seemed inconsequential; "just about what a liberal might do today—say how horrible this is that people would do this to each other, but never really get down to how you would change it." Williams himself had clearly begun to move far beyond liberal pieties.

"I decided that I just wasn't going to let any white man have that much authority over me," he said. Among black soldiers this defiant posture carried "a certain status," Williams recounted, "if you had enough nerve to stand up to a white officer and tell him what you felt." White officers seemed to think that "it was a form of arrogance for a black man not to be submissive," as Williams saw things, and he "felt it was my duty not to be what they tried to make me—a 'nigger.' They were not the masters to mold me—I had to mold myself."[95] His contempt for white authority soon earned him a three-month sentence in the stockade for insubordination; at the hearing, Williams said, "I told them that I was black, and that prison did not scare me because black men are born in prison. All they could do was put me in a smaller prison." In the brig, Williams remembered, he felt proud, "because of the fact that I was in there for resisting. They would have preferred to have me as a nigger than locked up, but I preferred to be locked up than to be what they considered a nigger."[96]

The army discharged Williams on November 27, 1946, for "convenience of the government" after he had served eighteen months, much of it passed in the brig for a variety of defiant acts. "Although he received an honorable discharge," his FBI file noted, "in the Army he was the subject of considerable controversy for failure to obey orders, disrespect towards an officer, and because he went absent without leave on several occasions."[97]

At twenty-one, Private Williams stepped down from a segregated Greyhound in Monroe wearing the uniform of a country he could not be quite sure was his own. His government-issue shoe leather scraped the same pavement where ten years earlier he had watched helplessly as Big Jesse Helms had beaten a black woman and dragged her off to jail. But he was no longer a frightened child. "The Negro soldier who returns from the far-flung battlefields of the world will be a lot different from the young man you knew," Captain Grant Reynolds declared to the NAACP's War Emergency Conference in 1944. Reynolds could have been describing Robert Williams himself: "He will be a man come of age. The Negro soldier expects a new definition of the American ideals of liberty, justice and equality to come out of the present war."[98]

Another soldier from North Carolina, the commander of a black veterans' organization in Winston-Salem, informed Governor Broughton that "there will have to be a change in the old form of Democracy that has been handed down to my group I mean the colored people. . . . If I could bear arms and shed blood for this Great Democracy my people should share in the spoils."[99] Williams would have had mixed feelings about whether "Great Democracy" was an appropriate description, but he knew that a change would have to come to his homeland, a change as deep and fundamental as the changes that he now felt within himself.

Just under six feet tall now, Williams weighed two hundred pounds and carried himself like a prizefighter. Handsome and rugged, at twenty-one he could build cars, hand-tool machine parts, handle a .50-caliber machine gun, and write a sonnet. He had lived in Detroit and Harlem, fought in a riot, joined a union, and read widely in American literature and history. Though his service in the army had been difficult for him, his experience had made him wise and his endurance had made him proud. Military training had given most black veterans "some feeling of security and self-assurance," he thought. "The Army indoctrination instilled in us what a virtue it was to fight for democracy and that we were fighting for democracy and upholding the Constitution. But most of all they taught us to use arms." Like thousands of other black veterans whom John Dittmer has characterized as "the shock troops of the modern civil rights movement," Robert Williams did not come home to pick cotton.[100]

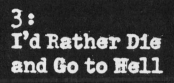

Robert Williams did not come home from the army to pick cotton, but his friend Bennie Montgomery did. He returned to the farm his father operated as a sharecropper for W. W. Mangum, a white landowner near Monroe. Montgomery had been Williams's classmate in high school and his companion at the NYA training camp where Williams led his first racial protest. When Williams moved to Detroit, Montgomery went into the army and fought the Germans in Europe. Badly wounded in the Battle of the Bulge, Montgomery "had a steel plate in his head," according to Williams, and "wasn't normal" anymore. Whether the injury had anything to do with what happened after Montgomery came home is difficult to say.

On Friday night, May 31, 1946, Bennie Montgomery drank too much and wrecked his father's car. Saturday was a regular workday on the Mangum place, but Montgomery asked the landlord for his wages at noon, explaining that he needed to go to Monroe and have his father's automobile repaired. Whatever may have been said, Montgomery apparently stepped outside the dance of deference that governed Southern race relations. Mangum kicked and slapped the young veteran, and a fistfight broke out between the two men, in the heat of which Montgomery whipped out a pocketknife and cut his employer's throat, killing the white man and showering himself with blood. According to Williams, the police found Montgomery "sitting in this little old restaurant drinking beer, still had the blood on his clothes and everything, sitting there drinking beer just as though nothing hadn't happened." The Ku Klux Klan wanted to lynch the black sharecropper, but state authorities whisked him away from the Monroe jail for safekeeping. Tried and convicted of murder, Bennie Montgomery was sitting on Death Row at Central Prison in Raleigh, North Carolina, when Williams returned home from the army. "Everybody was trying to get the governor to commute his death penalty," Williams said, "and the governor wouldn't do it, so they gassed him." Bennie Montgomery died in North Carolina's gas chamber at Central Prison on March 28, 1947.[1]

The state of North Carolina shipped Montgomery's body back to Monroe for burial. Robbed of their lynching, the local chapter of the Ku Klux Klan let it be known that the body belonged not to the Montgomery family but to "the invisible empire." The Klan threatened to kill the black funeral director unless he removed the U.S. flag atop the veteran's casket. "They was gonna come and take Bennie's body out and drag it up and down the street," J. W. McDow, another African American veteran, recalled. "I rather die and go to hell before I see that happen." A group of former soldiers met at Booker T. Perry's barbershop and made a battle plan. When the Klan motorcade pulled up in front of Harris Funeral Home, forty black men leveled their rifles, taking aim at the line of cars. Not a shot was fired; the Klansmen simply weighed their chances and then drove away.

While Booker T. Perry, a World War I veteran, orchestrated the defense of Bennie Montgomery's body, former U.S. Army private Robert F. Williams carried a rifle that night. So did three other men who would become key lieutenants in the "black militia" that Williams organized in Monroe ten years later, after leadership in the struggle had passed to a new generation. "That was one of the first incidents," Williams recalled, "that really started us to understanding that we had to resist, and that resistance could be effective if we resisted in groups, and if we resisted with guns."[2]

That resistance flowed from the black dream of freedom, a paradox born in bondage and sustained across almost a century of post-Emancipation travail. It was an expansive dream imagined in Baptist churches on Sunday mornings and enlarged in jerry-built juke joints on Saturday nights, celebrated in spirituals and blues and gospel songs, and preserved in stories and sermons and folktales. Hemmed in by law, custom, violence, and a pervasive ideology of black inferiority, this dream of freedom still glowed like banked coals beneath the ashes of political defeat. But World War II brought what Walter White, head of the NAACP, called "a rising wind" of racial possibility. After World War II, black activists found themselves in a radically altered political context that enabled them to fan old embers into flames.

The dream of freedom and the promise of factory jobs drew millions of black Southerners to the cities of the North and West during and after

World War II, giving African Americans startling new leverage at the ballot box. By 1948 black voters held the balance of power in the decisive battleground states of U.S. presidential politics. The combined electoral votes of only four Northern states—Illinois, New York, Michigan, and Pennsylvania—exceeded that of the entire South; in each of these states, the percentage of black voters exceeded the 1944 margin of victory or defeat.[3] "Although isolation of any single election factor risks presenting a false picture," historian David L. Lewis states, "the reality that Afro-American votes were now determinative in 16 non-South states with 2/8 electoral votes escaped no serious political strategist."[4]

This electoral calculus and the increasing tendency of the U.S. Supreme Court to rule in favor of African Americans—especially the 1944 *Smith v. Allwright* decision, which outlawed the "white primary" and thus eliminated the greatest legal barrier to black ballots—certainly raised black hopes.[5] Although whites across the region persistently and often violently obstructed their paths to the polls, the number of black registered voters in the South rose from 250,000 in 1944 to a million in 1952—from 5 percent of those eligible to 20 percent in only eight years. *Smith v. Allwright* provided a crucial political opening; Thurgood Marshall regarded it as a more important victory than *Brown v. Board of Education*.[6] But the ruling would have come to precious little without bold voter registration campaigns, most of which were led by returning World War II veterans determined to seize full citizenship.[7]

World War II not only changed the landscape of domestic politics but gave African Americans an unprecedented power to redeem or repudiate American democracy in the eyes of the world. The war crippled European colonialism and gave rise to the Cold War rivalry between the United States and the Soviet Union. Among the darker-skinned peoples of the Third World, the postwar competition between the superpowers was urgent largely in terms of their own racial and anticolonial concerns; thus the color caste system in the United States sometimes spoke louder than the nation's ringing rhetoric of democracy. "The division of opinion on many issues" in the newly created United Nations General Assembly, a State Department report conceded, "has sometimes tended to follow a color line, white against non-whites, with Russia seeking to be recognized as the champion of non-whites."[8]

The creation of the United Nations as a public forum gave not only the emerging nations of the Third World but black Americans themselves a powerful podium from which to address racial issues. "It is not Russia that threatens the United States so much as Mississippi," the NAACP declared in a 1947 petition to the United Nations, "not Stalin and Molotov but Bilbo and Rankin," in a reference to two of the Senate's most avid antiblack demagogues. The petition, which decried "the denial of human rights to minorities in the case of citizens of Negro descent in the United States," created an "international sensation," causing the NAACP's offices to be "flooded with requests for copies of the document" from nations "pleased to have documentary proof that the United States did not practice what it preached about freedom and democracy," according to Walter White.[9] The new understanding that international politics held the key to African American freedom marked "an historic moment in our struggle for equality," one black newspaper editor wrote to W. E. B. Du Bois, praising the NAACP petition. "Finally we are beginning to see that America can be answerable to the family of nations for its injustices to the Negro minority."[10]

Many elements of the federal government appeared to agree with the substance of the NAACP's assertion. "We cannot escape the fact that our civil rights record has become an issue in world politics," President Harry S. Truman's Committee on Civil Rights declared in 1947. "The world's press and radio are full of it. . . . Those with competing philosophies have stressed—and are shamelessly distorting—our shortcomings."[11] Secretary of State Dean Acheson wrote in 1952 that "racial discrimination in the United States remains a source of constant embarrassment to this Government in the day-to-day conduct of its foreign relations." The Justice Department filed a series of briefs in the cases leading up to the Supreme Court's *Brown v. Board of Education* decision that supported the NAACP's position in precisely those terms. "Racial discrimination furnishes grist for the Communist propaganda mills," the attorney general wrote to the Court, "and it raises doubts even among friendly nations as to the intensity of our devotion to the democratic faith."[12] Vice-President Richard Nixon spoke even more firmly on the subject: "Every act of discrimination or prejudice in the United States," he declared in 1954, "hurts America just as much as an espionage agent who turns over a weapon to a foreign country."[13] On May 17, 1954, when the Court finally struck down the "separate-but-equal" doctrine that had provided the legal foundation for segregation since 1896, the Voice of America broadcast the news across the planet in thirty-five languages within a matter of hours.[14] The decision eased but did not end the painfully contradictory positions of the United States. In 1958 Vice-President Nixon's point would be underscored when anti-American mobs in Venezuela stoned his motorcade, screaming, "What about Little Rock?"[15]

Momentous shifts in international and national politics thus transformed the strategic environment that confronted the activists of the postwar African American freedom movements. The migration of millions of rural black Southerners to places where they could vote; the political opportunities presented by World War II; the mechanization of Southern agriculture, which eliminated many "black jobs" in the rural South; and the emergence of the Cold War, among other things, forever altered the landscape of African American possibilities. But the postwar freedom movements were neither rising winds nor raging floods nor prairie fires, and the metaphors of meteorology can only obscure the origins of those struggles. Shifts in political economy can only produce those social movements that human beings are able to organize from the patterns of aspiration and belonging that have made them. Visionary black activists like Robert Williams read the new situation as best they could and then sought to redeem a democratic vision rooted in the living ingredients of their own history. Even the most startling structural changes would have meant little if black Southerners had not been willing to risk everything to challenge white supremacy.

Many individuals who fought Jim Crow in the years immediately following World War II were veterans like Robert Williams and the men who defended Bennie Montgomery's body at Harris Funeral Home in Monroe. "After a lot of the veterans came back you find more and more that militancy was growing," Williams remembered twenty years later. "If you will check some of the papers back then you will see where there were quite a lot of clashes."[16] In January 1946 one hundred African American veterans marched through the main streets of Birmingham, Alabama, wearing their uniforms and waving their discharge papers, demanding the right to register and vote; within a month, Birmingham police officers had killed as many as five black veterans.[17] On July 2, 1946, twenty-one-year-old Medgar Evers led a group of black veterans to the Decatur, Mississippi, courthouse to vote. Blocked by fifteen or twenty armed white men, the former soldiers went home, got their guns and came back, but decided not to fight when confronted a second time by the mob.[18] In Durham, North Carolina, black veterans led a 1946 registration campaign that lifted the black vote from "a doubtful 3,000" to "an effective 5,500" in only twelve days.[19] Across the South, returning black veterans organized NAACP chapters, sparked voter registration drives, and resisted attempts to reestablish the racial status quo.[20]

White Southerners, however, met black aspirations with a wave of racial violence. In Taylor County, Georgia, a sign nailed to the door of a local black church warned, "The first Negro to vote will never vote again." Maceo Snipes, a black World War II veteran, cast his first ballot soon thereafter. That night, four white men dragged him out of his house and shot him dead.[21] In Monroe, Georgia, state police and white terrorists murdered two black couples on a lonely road after one of the men, a World War II veteran, had clashed with his landlord. "Up until George went in the army, he was a good nigger," one of the murderers explained years after the lynching. "But when he came out, they thought they were as good as any white people."[22] Whether the ferocity reflected the trembling of a region hovering on the edge of historic change, or whether it was part of a systematic reassertion of white supremacy, the violence across the South immediately after the war produced dozens of dead, hundreds of injured, and thousands of terrified citizens for whom the protection of the law meant little or nothing. Walter White announced that black Southerners might be forced to take up arms to defend their lives.[23]

Insistence by whites that the color line be nailed firmly back in place, ironically, helped to forge a compelling sense of community among the African American soldiers who returned to Monroe along with Robert Williams. About 150 black veterans enrolled in a variety of segregated Veterans Administration programs that met at Winchester Avenue High School. Most of the men worked during the day and attended vocational classes in the evenings, receiving a monthly stipend check for their participation. After class, they stood around and swapped stories, developing a strong sense of themselves as a group. Robert Williams recalled that his classmates often "congregated in the local barbershop," where they developed "a tightly knit comraderie." Veterans also drew federal unemployment payments of $20 per week for fifty-two weeks or until they found a job. Williams and his friends called the program "the 52-20 club."[24]

"Veterans who were sustained by the 52-20 club had to report to the local unemployment office weekly," Williams recorded in his autobiography, "with a list of at least three places we had visited in quest of work." The office employees were all white, he said, and the veterans detected considerable resentment that black men received federal benefits. "We had a hard time because they did not want to give it to the black soldiers," he recalled. One white woman, in particular, "talked to what she called 'colorud' veterans as if we were no more than dogs." Her contempt for African Americans was a daily topic of conversation at Booker T. Perry's barbershop. The black men quietly avoided her whenever they could. But when she insisted that Williams accept a job that paid $18 a week—two dollars less than he received in veterans benefits—he refused, insisting that he was "not paying to work." She threatened to call Big Jesse Helms, the much-feared assistant chief of police, and have Williams thrown out of the office. "I told her to go ahead and call him," Williams said, offering himself to "call Washington and see if this is your money." The woman was furious. "The trouble with you nigra veterans," Williams remembered her snarling at him, "is that you think the world owes you a living!"[25]

Robert Williams was a member of the 52-20 club when he met a beautiful sixteen-year-old girl named Mabel Ola Robinson. "He came back from the Army," she recalled, "and his best friend had married my older sister. And so that's how we got together."[26] One night when Robert came to pick up his friend, young Mabel walked out and got in the back seat. "That's the first time that I remember seeing him. He was in a uniform," she remembered. "Handsome, strong, tall. He was just a strong, handsome, beautiful black man, you know." Robert recalls that he whispered a little too loudly to his friend, "Is that Snooky's little sister?" and that she had interrupted him firmly: "My *name* is Mabel." Robert mumbled something to the effect that he had thought she was still a little girl. "I'm no little girl," Mabel snapped. Before either of them knew what was happening, it became clear that she was telling the truth. Over the next five decades, Mabel became Robert's most important political ally, mother to their two sons, editor of his writings, and partner to this troubled activist and intellectual, sometimes at great price to herself but with an increasingly shared commitment to black liberation. Had Williams fallen in love with someone else, things could have gone very differently.[27]

Mabel Robinson was born on June 1, 1931, to a family that most black people in Union County considered quite fortunate. Her father, David Robinson, served as chauffeur to the Belk family, probably the wealthiest white family in North Carolina. Her mother, Emma Perry Robinson, worked for the Belks as a maid; Mabel was named after one of the Belk daughters. David Robinson died when Mabel was only two years old. "Before my father died, the Belk family had bought a house and said that my mother could have it for as long as she lived." According to a paternalistic arrangement designed to ensure that the loyal family retainer would remain tied to her employer, Emma Robinson could not legally sell the house, but her children would inherit it after she died. Mabel and her siblings dressed in the finest hand-me-downs that Belk money could buy, but she still remembers the humiliation that she felt when the matron of the Belk family would come to the house and lift her skirt to make sure she had clean underwear.[28]

Mabel's mother remarried, to a railroad man named Chalmers Barber, a union that "substantially upgraded our status," Mabel Williams said. Like Robert Williams's father, Barber worked for the Seaboard Air Line Railway and "made a pretty good living. We were one of the few people in our neighborhood who had an indoor bathtub and running water." They lived on "Quality Hill," an African American community three miles across town from Newtown, the other black section, where the Williams family lived. Mabel attended Winchester Avenue High School in Newtown, and the handsome former soldier began to walk her home each day and take her to dances at what had been the black service club at Camp Sutton. "I was about to turn sixteen in June and early on, before that birthday, I realized that this was the man I wanted to marry," Mabel recalled. "I was going to run away with him after my sixteenth birthday, was what I was thinking." On June 19, 1947, Robert and Mabel went to the preacher of the local Colored Methodist Episcopal Church, who pronounced them man and wife in his living room.[29]

Emma C. Williams, Robert's mother, was only forty-nine when she died of a sudden hemorrhage soon after the wedding; her death came as a great shock to Robert and his father.[30] The young couple moved in with John Williams in the house on Boyte Street where Robert had been born. "It didn't take long to realize that [Robert] wasn't normal," the bride remembered years later. She knew that he fought constantly with the bureaucrats at the local Veterans Administration. He wrote poetry, too, and seemed to find money to buy books even when they lacked things that she felt were far more necessary. Robert's passionate political views sometimes disturbed his young wife. "Having grown up in the South and being accustomed to the way it should be according to custom and tradition," she said later, "I could see what was happening when other people bucked the system—it would slap them down." Her fears and complaints "stemmed from the fact that he did not conform to what a black husband was supposed to be in those days."[31]

Mabel received crucial advice from her new father-in-law, whom she called "Daddy John." He cherished this lovely young woman who brightened his household. "He was very instrumental in helping me to understand Robert," she said. The widower was not the firebrand that his son was fast becoming; however, he accepted Robert's rebellious spirit, even as he tried "to protect him and get him to fit into the mold so that Robert would not become a victim—get killed," as Mabel Williams put it. At the same time, John Williams taught his new daughter-in-law about the family tradition of resistance to white supremacy. "He began to tell me about Robert's uncle, who was a great influence on Robert and who was Mr. Williams's brother," she recalled, "Uncle Charlie. And I began to realize that Robert wasn't just something that just popped up, that it was kind of an extension of something that had already been there in that family." She noticed, too, that even though the older man spoke calmly, John Williams himself carried on the Williams family heritage of defiance. "Daddy John always had a shotgun ready," she laughed. "Always the shotgun was there and it was always loaded and it was always at the door. And that was the tradition."[32]

Robert may not have been normal, but he was far from alone in his reluctance to accept white supremacy after the war. Elsewhere in Union County, black veterans who worked as garbage collectors in the town of Marshville organized a wildcat strike for higher wages, picketing without the support of any union. The mayor insisted that garbage work provided steady wages for which black men should be grateful; the town council threatened to hire young white men to replace the strikers. "They were just trying to discourage them," one local black woman recalled. "But don't no white dudes want to clean no streets and tote no garbage." In the end, whites would not take the jobs, blacks refused to cross the picket line, and the veterans won their raise.[33]

Black veterans who came back to labor as sharecroppers now pressed white landlords to permit them to sell their own cotton crop. This arrangement defied the long-standing practice of farming "on halves" and denied the landlord the customary opportunity to cheat the sharecroppers or bill them as he saw fit. James Rushing remembered his unshakable insistence that his white landlord "let me sell my own cotton, rather than let the white man sell it and bring me the money." Refused by the landlord, Rushing took matters into his own hands. During the night he picked every other row of the entire crop of cotton and sold it himself the following day. This ingenious act of defiance left no room for dispute that the halves had been equitably shared. Even so, it was an act that easily could have provoked a lynching in years past. Taken to court for picking his landlord's cotton, James Rushing was acquitted. "I didn't pick his cotton," he explained. "I picked mine. I left his in the fields."[34]

Black citizens of Union County pushed racial boundaries on several fronts. The Monroe NAACP chapter, founded during the war, swelled to 163 members in 1946. Branch president Edward Belton, a schoolteacher, led a campaign to urge the city to pave 4th Street in the Newtown area of Monroe. Robert Williams described the local chapter as "a social club" that was merely "having meetings and drinking tea and doing nothing."[35] In other communities, NAACP chapters were sometimes at the center of voter registration efforts. But if Williams's critique was uncharitable, it was probably not inaccurate; when Belton sought to organize an aggressive, door-to-door campaign to register black voters, he found it necessary to organize a separate organization, the Monroe–Union County Civic League, in which aggressive black veterans led the way. By 1950 there were approximately 250 black voters in Monroe, up from only 22 fifteen years earlier.[36] "I really think the blacks—especially those that were veterans—had a good point when they came back and said they were due their privileges," a local white historian of Monroe said four decades afterward. "They had been other places and seen it work differently."[37]

At the time, however, white North Carolinians viewed black self-assertion with considerable uneasiness. William I. Turner of Magnolia, North Carolina, wrote to the Raleigh *News and Observer* in 1946 to applaud the elections of Senators Theodore Bilbo of Mississippi and Herman Talmadge of Georgia, "who stand up and fight for our state rights." Returning black veterans were likely to present quite a challenge, Turner argued. "We will be needing [the Ku Klux Klan] back in the South again," he wrote. These sentiments spread like kudzu vine across the region; only weeks after V-J Day, a revived Ku Klux Klan torched a three-hundred-foot cross atop Georgia's Stone Mountain "just to let the niggers know the war is over and that the Klan is back on the market," according to one speaker.[38]

White Southerners feared that postwar political self-assertion by black men pointed toward underlying sexual desires for white women. These age-old fears reflected Reconstruction- and Fusion-era images of the "black beast" whose ravenous appetite for white women could only be deterred by violence.[39] The closer a black man got to a ballot box, black activists joked, the more he looked like a rapist. But it was not a laughing matter among whites. One eastern North Carolina editor mirrored widespread feelings among whites when he wrote in 1947,

The negro has been "up North," he has joined the Eleanor Clubs, he has heard of the activities of the northern-financed "Society for the Advancement of the Colored Race," he remembers that during the war he was allowed to eat and sleep with white men, he is conscious of a friendly federal government. . . . He has heard of the white preachers who advocated you and I being thrown with the negro socially, he has ideas that at last the colored man and woman is coming into his own and will soon be rulers of the land. So all in all why shouldn't he go out and take a white woman when he pleases?

Though there was nothing to confirm that sexual assaults of whatever description had increased, sensationalized rumors and reports of black men attacking white women convinced many white North Carolinians that there was literally an orchestrated "rape movement" afoot among black men in North Carolina.[40] Black-on-white sexual assaults "are being carried on throughout our state," one Rocky Mount woman wrote. "To my mind lynching is the proper thing."[41]

"Negroes are treating the women of this country as brutally as animals," the wife of the chief of police in Rich Square wrote in defense of an attempted lynching in 1947. "Until the Negroes are educated to the fact that they were brought here as servants and are not to be placed on a basis of equality with whites, I fear we shall have trouble."[42] Many angry whites agreed with another woman who claimed that "Yankee organizations and Southern 'liberals' are, in a measure, responsible for these crimes. Their continual harping on 'racial prejudice' and 'racial discrimination' lays the foundation for such acts of violence."[43] As the Cold War began to quicken, others blamed the unseen hands of Communism. "Although we have no evidence," one white woman wrote to the governor in 1947, "there are many of us who believe that this outbreak of crime is being suggested and encouraged by some outside element, some group who are trying to promote discord among us."[44]

While it was preposterous to suggest that Communist agents were somehow responsible for postwar racial tensions, racial violence in the South provided a steady source of raw material for Soviet propagandists. The brutality that had always undergirded white domination now combined with the international dynamics of the Cold War to create a curious but compelling political fulcrum for the national office of the NAACP. The 1947 lynching of Willie Earle, a black man accused of killing a cab driver in South Carolina, had "terrific news value," an NAACP attorney reported to

Thurgood Marshall. The attorney urged "serious consideration of a nationwide tour . . . using Mrs. Earle and this case as a drawing card, the appeals to be directed towards raising funds for the Association generally."[45] When an all-white jury set the self-confessed killers of Willie Earle free, the NAACP was quick to play the Cold War card: "I imagine that the front page news from America today in PRAVDA and IZVESTIA," Walter White declared on May 23, "is the story of the acquittal of the South Carolina lynchers, which makes America's protestations of its democracy hollow."[46]

That same day, Roy Wilkins received an urgent memo "that there has been a new lynching in Jackson, North Carolina." The report did not celebrate the violence but stressed the political opportunity it had created. Godwin Bush, a black veteran from Rich Square, North Carolina, who had been charged with attempted rape of a white woman, had been taken from his jail cell in nearby Jackson by a lynch mob. "If the report of the new lynching is true," the memo suggested, "we ought to strip our decks for a real fight."[47]

In Rich Square, the local black community was preparing for a different sort of fight. Captain Lester Jones of the North Carolina state highway patrol reported to Governor R. Gregg Cherry that local police had "informed me that the negro race, under the supervision of selected leaders, was organizing in different sections of the community and planning to march on Rich Square in mass formation about 9 P.M." Arriving at the scene, Jones discovered that "the women and children, or many of them in the Rich Square area, were being moved to nearby towns" and that both black and white men were arming themselves and returning to the small Southern hamlet. "I found that there was a possible chance of a riot and that possibly the negroes were organizing for such an attack." Noting that "forces of the Highway Patrol were being carefully checked" by African American sentries, Jones ordered eighty-five heavily armed patrolmen to Rich Square, after which "it was immediately noticed that all of the assemblies were being disbanded and the situation immediately became quiet."[48]

What no one, black or white, realized that night was that Godwin Bush was not dead. As headlines around the world announced his lynching, Bush was hiding in a swamp. The mob had dragged him from the jail and stuffed him into the back seat of a car, but the young black man had popped the door latch on the opposite side and rolled out of the moving vehicle. Scrambling to his feet and fleeing from the white men, who fired at him but missed, Bush outran several carloads of captors. He hid for two days until a black preacher helped him contact the FBI and arrange his surrender. The white woman whom he had allegedly assaulted then testified that Bush was not the man who had frightened her. According to "diplomatic circles," United Press International (UPI) reported, the Rich Square incident provided "excellent propaganda for Communist agents who have been decrying America's brand of 'freedom' and 'democracy.'" President Truman's Committee on Civil Rights called the attempted lynching "excellent propaganda ammunition for Communist agents" and further evidence that "our civil rights record has growing international implications."[49]

Few of the victims of the postwar white backlash in North Carolina were as lucky as Godwin Bush. In mid-August 1946 a white mob in Bailey, North Carolina, hunted down and summarily shot J. C. Farmer, a twenty-year-old African American veteran who had clashed with the local constable.[50] James Branch of Durham County, witness to another act of white terrorism, begged the national office of the NAACP in 1946 to prosecute "This Man That shoot down Those 4 peples." A Hendersonville member wrote in 1948 that "there is three Whites in Jail waiting trial for killing an ex G.I. man" and observed that NAACP membership increased in response to the slaying. "One of our young Negro citizens and World War II Veterans was murdered by a white filling station operator," the NAACP branch secretary reported. In Polk County the local NAACP branch requested literature "to hold an NAACP rally" after several sexual assaults against black women by white men in 1951. "With the Ku Klux Klan again on the march and our girls and women being insulted," the writer stated, "we need an active Branch here."[51]

The reborn Ku Klux Klan in the Carolinas, led by Grand Dragon Thomas Hamilton, launched a postwar reign of terror. In one notorious incident, about fifty Klansmen fired more than a hundred shots into a black home and whipped the woman of the house after accusing her and her husband of having sex with white people. In another attack, Hamilton and nine others kidnapped a pair of lovers, took them across the state line, and flogged them with a machine belt nailed to a pick handle. Dozens of kidnappings, shootings, and whippings resulted in felony indictments for more than sixty Klan members, including the chief of police of Tabor City. Hamilton, a thick-necked, cigar-chomping former wholesale grocer, bellowed at 5,000 people who attended a rally halfway between Tabor City and Whiteville: "Do you want some burr-headed nigra to come up on your porch and ask for the hand of your daughter in marriage?" Referring to the admission of black World War II veteran Floyd McKissick to the University of North Carolina law school in 1951, Hamilton told the crowd that the university had admitted black students and that "if I had a daughter, I would never let her darken its doors again." He warned that white ministers who advocated "mongrelization, which God never intended," were a particular threat. "If your preacher is telling you that," he ranted, "then he needs a special thermostat in hell to burn him with."[52]

It was not Klan terror, however, but the lack of good employment prospects in North Carolina that sent Robert Williams back to Detroit in 1948 after Mabel gave birth to their first son, Robert Jr., and Robert's GI benefits ran out. Like his father, Robert Williams was a skilled artisan, but jobs of that sort were scarce in Dixie. "If I had been able to make a living in the South," he recounted, "I never would have gone." Black workers "could make about three times in Detroit what you could make in Monroe," Robert said, "but a black person couldn't get the job in Monroe that you could in Detroit." During the day, Mabel attended Northwestern High School in Detroit while Robert kept the baby. At night Robert worked for the Cadillac Motor Company, buffing the gleaming chrome fins and bumpers that Americans wanted in those days. It appeared that the Williams family might join the millions of Southern migrants who settled permanently in the North.

At Cadillac, Robert rejoined militant Local 600 of the United Automobile Workers, CIO. Both the union local and the assembly line were "integrated completely," he recalled. The North was less segregated, though many places were informally off limits to African Americans, and at Cadillac it was obvious that "the higher you'd go the whiter it got," he observed. Despite the broader opportunities and decent wages, building cars did not satisfy Robert Williams. The noise of the factory gave him excruciating headaches; more importantly, he dreamed of being a writer and continued to compose poems and stories and to wrestle with questions of race, democracy, and economic justice. He also longed to go home and struggle for freedom in the footsteps of his grandmother, grandfather, and Uncle Charlie. In 1948 Williams voted for the first time, casting his ballot for Henry Wallace and the Progressive Party. A political wanderer along the edges of the American left, Williams often read the Detroit edition of the Communist Party's *Daily Worker*. "They used to have them in the washrooms," he recalled, "so I would read."[53]

In the spring of 1949, Robert submitted an extraordinary story to the Detroit *Daily Worker* titled, "Someday, I'm Going Back South." In this thinly fictionalized, poignant depiction of a black veteran's return to the small-town South, an employment officer asks, "So you're a high school graduate, a machinist by trade, a clerk typist in the Army and also trained as a telephone lineman?" When Williams's protagonist nods in the affirmative, the interviewer replies, "I'm sorry, boy, but they don't hire Negroes for this type of work down here." Moving to the North presented its own problems: "My family roots were buried deep in the soil of the South," Williams wrote. "I couldn't extract them and bury them somewhere else overnight." After the heartbreaking loss of his beloved "Grannie"—clearly a composite figure of Robert's mother and grandmother—the narrator buys a one-way ticket for the urban North. "But it wasn't a one-way journey," he vows. "It was one way of arming myself for a battle that someday I hoped to spearhead." Here Williams made both a prophecy and a promise: "Someday I would return, seasoned from the battle in the north and more efficient in the fight for the liberation of my people."[54]

Returning to the South was not, however, the dream of Mabel Williams's heart. "I was so happy to get out of North Carolina," she recounted. "I knew that if [Robert] stayed there he was going to end up in serious trouble." But Detroit brought troubles of its own. Robert "would have headaches so bad that when he would come home he could hardly even sleep," according to Mabel. It did not help that the young family lived in cramped quarters in a rooming house on McGraw Street. "We looked forward to the weekends when we could go over to Conant Gardens and visit with Pete and his family," she remembered.[55]

Even though Cadillac employed blacks, there was "a great amount of friction, there was a lot of racial consciousness," said Robert. By his account, the white power structure in Detroit encouraged racial enmity because it "resented the fact that blacks were coming in such great numbers" and "didn't want too much unity in the labor movement." Williams's refusal to passively accept gruff treatment from the managers at Cadillac caused problems. He "had a hard time with these people who had a fourth grade education and held a supervisor's position over him just because they were white," Mabel Williams recalled.[56] By mid-1949 the young family was back in Monroe; FBI reports hint at a racial incident on the shop floor: "In February 1949, he was discharged from his job with the Cadillac Motor Car Company in Detroit because of excessive absenteeism and threatening his supervisors with bodily harm." The first biographer of Robert Williams—an unnamed FBI agent—hit the nail on the head: "Wherever he has gone, Williams has constantly complained, both in the Army and at previous places of employment, that he has been discriminated against." That much, at least, was true.[57]

When Mabel and Robert moved back to Monroe, they found the post-war "red scare" had already gathered considerable force. To secure support for a global containment policy against the Soviet Union and an unprecedented commitment to foreign aid, President Truman sought to persuade Americans that the United States was under a massive, ideologically based assault on both its international aims and its internal security. With the Federal Employee Loyalty Program and the attorney general's list of subversive organizations in 1947, the Truman administration helped to legitimate the atmosphere of political inquisition that became known as McCarthyism.[58] In 1948 the Truman campaign aimed, in the words of its key strategist, "to identify [Henry Wallace] and isolate him in the public mind with the Communists."[59] Anticommunism in the South pointed straight at the race issue. When Henry Wallace toured North Carolina during the 1948 election campaign, violent mobs screaming the almost inseparable epithets of "communist!" and "nigger lover!" attacked Wallace and his entourage in Durham, Burlington, and Charlotte. Arriving in Monroe, Robert Williams could see that the editors of the *Monroe Journal* had discovered "the communist menace."[60]

More alarming was his discovery that the FBI apparently considered him a Communist menace. "I understand from some of the neighbors that the FBI had been in the community asking about me," said Williams. FBI agents told people in Monroe that he "had used communist words and slogans like 'freedom' and 'democracy' and 'justice,' " Williams reported. The agents "came into the community and the school and everywhere and they went around to people who had known me since I had grown up, but there was nothing for them to find."[61]

By the late 1940s many Americans equated support for racial equality with Communism. "FBI agents spotted white Communists by their ease and politeness around Negroes," historian Taylor Branch writes, "or by the simple fact that they socialized with Negroes at all."[62] The leading anticommunist demagogues in Congress—notably Martin Dies of Texas and John Rankin and James Eastland of Mississippi—were equally ferocious opponents of civil rights. "If someone insists there is discrimination against Negroes in this country, or that there is inequality of wealth," the chair of a Washington state investigative committee declared, "there is every reason to believe that person is a Communist." The head of a federal departmental loyalty board was more circumspect: "Of course, the fact that a person believes in racial equality doesn't *prove* that he's a Communist, but it certainly does make you look twice."[63]

The FBI witch-hunt was a less immediate concern than what Williams called "the matter of working and survival. Actually, I was trying to get ready to go to college." He worked odd jobs and ransacked college catalogs, looking for a place to use the two years of educational support owed him under the GI bill. Meanwhile, Mabel Williams completed her final months of high school at Winchester Avenue High School. In the fall of 1949 Robert enrolled in West Virginia State College in Charleston. "It had a reputation for its scholarship," he said, and "it had a course of creative writing which most of the black schools did not have." Mabel continued to live in the house on Boyte Street with Daddy John and little "Bobby," now two years old, while Robert lived in a dormitory in Charleston and traveled home on the bus every few weeks.[64]

West Virginia State College was a historically black school with an integrated faculty. The college "was one of the most militant schools," Robert recalled. "I didn't exactly understand what was going on, but I could see that they had nationalist tendencies." Its president, Dr. John W. Davis, was a longtime black activist. Williams "fell under the spell of Dr. Herman G. Canady and Dr. John W. Davis," he said, "who greatly enhanced my tendency towards black consciousness."[65]

Canady was a legendary professor of psychology, the son of a black minister from Guthrie, Oklahoma. Widely published on subjects such as the American caste system and the question of Negro intelligence, Canady had earned his Ph.D. from Northwestern in 1927 and had become chair of the Department of Psychology at West Virginia State College the following year. Dapper and energetic, the forty-eight-year-old professor preached like a prophet and ranted like a comedian. In one lecture Canady told his students, "Now look at you darkies, you are the descendants of the Uncle Tom slave niggers, the ones who survived—the real militants, the bad ones, didn't survive," Robert recalled. "You are the descendants of the submissive Africans, so this is why we have to be patient with you until we can get again the type of people who won't be submissive." When the sound of seniors practicing for graduation exercises interrupted one of Canady's lectures, Williams remembered, the professor thundered, "Listen to that noise! Do you hear those people! Those are DANGEROUS people—because a little bit of learning is a dangerous thing!"

Sometimes the young man from Monroe felt as though the professor were speaking to him alone. "We got all of these students here, most of it is a waste of time," Williams remembered Canady telling the class. "But if through this school we can get one Frederick Douglass, then we can consider this school worthwhile."[66]

It took little to convince Williams to prepare himself for leadership in the freedom struggle that increasingly occupied his thoughts. He wrote for the college newspaper and served on the staff of the Quill, the school's literary magazine. He avoided the overtures of fraternities and disdained the careerism of his classmates. "The fallacy is that most students are thinking, as they have been taught to think, of their personal careers, or becoming a third class aristocracy in a Jim Crowed world," he wrote during his college years.[67] Students at West Virginia State "were looking forward to Cadillacs and mink coats, and split-level homes, thinking about how much they could make in this or that field," he said later. Because of his open contempt for the profit motive and his outspoken personal style, Williams stated, "I was considered a radical." Robert received a great deal of affirmation and encouragement from the faculty for his writing and speaking ability; it was a time of growth for him. But after Mabel gave birth to another son, John Chalmers Williams, Robert moved back to North Carolina.[68]

In the summer of 1950 Williams enrolled at North Carolina College for Negroes in Durham, where he roomed with Cad Roddy, an old friend from Monroe. Here he met a Communist Party organizer named Junius Scales, a personable young white man from a wealthy textile family in Greensboro. Scales had joined the party in the early 1940s and was elected vice-president of the Southern Negro Youth Congress in 1946—the only white officer ever chosen. Scales had publicly announced his party membership in 1947. The red-hunters denounced him as a "nigger-loving commie" and eventually sentenced him to six years in prison under the Smith Act, a 1940 law prohibiting anyone "to teach and advocate" the overthrow of the U.S. government. Scales's sentence was the stiffest penalty in the history of that law, which the Supreme Court later found unconstitutional.[69] "He had some black fellows working with him, and they started bringing that literature onto the campus," Robert recounted. "I read The Communist Manifesto, a lot of the communist stuff, Lenin."[70]

Williams was not the only North Carolinian pondering Communism and race that year. The Democratic primary for U.S. Senate pitted Frank Porter Graham, the South's most prominent liberal, against Willis Smith, a conservative Raleigh attorney. Graham's supporters sought to capitalize on the saintly reputation that he had built as president of the University of

North Carolina. The Smith forces made race and communism the central issues of the campaign.

Young Jesse Helms wrote press releases and ad copy for the campaign. In a snappy phrase attributed to Helms, Smith flyers labeled UNC "the University of Negroes and Communists." One Smith ad stated, "We don't accuse Dr. Graham of being a Communist," and then went on to charge that Graham had been a member of eighteen groups cited by the House Un-American Activities Committee as "communist fronts." On May 27 the state gave Graham a 53,000-vote plurality, which fell barely short of an absolute majority and entitled Smith to ask for a runoff.

In the second primary, Smith aides—with young Helms in a decisive role—launched a raw, unscrupulous appeal to racial sentiment. Flyers asked, "Do you want Negroes working beside you and your wife and daughters?" Smith's followers circulated spurious postcards signed by "Walter Wite" of the "National Society for the Advancement of Colored People" that urged support for Graham. They raised the specter of social equality and miscegenation with lurid handbills featuring photographs of black soldiers dancing with white women. A broadside titled "WHITE PEOPLE WAKE UP" claimed that "Frank Graham favors mingling of the races." On June 24, Willis Smith beat Graham by 19,325 votes. "The election demonstrated clearly," the definitive history of the campaign states, "that North Carolina, in fact, had never been the liberal bastion on matters of race that writers had often portrayed." Louis Austin of the *Carolina Times* lamented in the wake of Graham's bitter defeat, "The torch of freedom has been snuffed out in North Carolina and there is a darkness all over the state."[71]

If Willis Smith's victory in 1950 symbolized the continuing triumph of white supremacy, Robert Williams had not forgotten his own countervailing political traditions. Mindful that his family's history had seen "previous generations of the same lineage pass from the carefree scene to the world's most serious business," Williams moved back to Monroe that fall and attended Johnson C. Smith College in Charlotte, "the school my grandfather, Sikes Williams, had gone to" after the fall of slavery.[72] The move allowed him to live with his wife and two young sons and eased their financial situation considerably. "It was a rugged daily commute from Monroe to Charlotte," he wrote later, "riding the back of the bus which the law and white culture required."[73]

The following year, soon after Williams arrived at Johnson C. Smith, a revealing legal case in North Carolina highlighted questions of race, sex,

Communism, and international politics and made a lasting impression on him. On June 4, 1951, authorities in Caswell County arrested a forty-two-year-old African American sharecropper named Mack Ingram for "assault on William Jean Boswell, white, female, aged 18, with intent to criminally assault her." Boswell claimed that Ingram "was looking at her in a leering manner" as she walked to a tobacco field carrying a hoe to her father. Officers noted that Ingram "did not lay hands on her," and even in Boswell's account, Ingram had never been closer than seventy-five feet. According to Ingram, he was walking to borrow a trailer from her father and had not even noticed that the person walking ahead of him in bib overalls was a female. Boswell ran, however, and her brother testified that she arrived at the field terrified and exhausted. Jailed without bond, Ingram, who had nine children, was sentenced to two years at hard labor for the reduced charge of "assault on a female."

The *Caswell Messenger* reported the following day that the Ingram case had "attained world-wide significance" after the Communist Party "plastered Europe and New York" with "prejudicial" accounts. "As soon as the propaganda hit England," the local newspaper reported, "the U.S. State Department began its rebuttal." State Department officials called twice "to get a court record of the case in order to combat Communist propaganda in Europe," the local solicitor reported. "The Reds are playing up the fact," the editors charged, "that the Negro never actually touched the girl." The case fed the spirit of the anticommunist witch-hunt in North Carolina, as editors of the *Caswell Messenger* wondered "what person or persons locally are feeding prejudiced information to the Communist Party" and observed that the State Bureau of Investigation (SBI) and the FBI "may be called in to ascertain if there are Communist Party members or persons with Communist leanings trying to disrupt peaceful race relations." Though the national office was initially reluctant to become involved in such a controversial case, the NAACP obtained power of attorney from Ingram in order to prevent "left wing" organizations from using the case for propaganda, its attorneys stated. After two years of appeals, the North Carolina Supreme Court finally dismissed the case against Mack Ingram. But Robert Williams would always remember the case as "a shameful and savage misappropriation of the [legal] machinery."[74]

Despite such distractions, Williams pursued his dream of becoming a writer while he was at Johnson C. Smith, publishing poems in half a dozen obscure journals and one remarkable article in *Freedom*, a newspaper published in New York by Paul Robeson. "N. Carolina College Youth Calls for a Militant Student Generation" drew on his experiences at the three colleges he had attended and on the deep hurt that the South's racial caste system had inflicted on him. His story appeared on the same page with an article by young Lorraine Hansberry, who would soon begin work on her classic play, *A Raisin in the Sun*. *Freedom* included a brief biographical sketch accompanied by a photograph of the twenty-seven-year-old Williams. "In the South," he wrote, "one is constantly reminded that he is a Negro and thus, must live in a third class world with a very slight hope of the ultimate expression of his human capacities." Williams lamented the "passive acceptance of a limited life" that he saw in his classmates and the fact that "many teachers are introducing a new version of Uncle Tomism which will surely leave its crippling marks upon the race." Black college students in the South "should be the most militant agitators for democracy in America today. They have nothing to lose and all to gain." Despite the apathy encouraged by many faculty members, Williams asserted, "there are a few militant Southern students determined to seek truth and justice." No doubt, he had his own dreams firmly in mind. "In them is the hope and strength of Negro liberation, the dignity of the Negro race."[75]

Soon afterward, the aspiring young writer met one of his literary heroes, Langston Hughes. "I was a student when he came to Johnson C. Smith in Charlotte for a lecture," Williams recalled years later. Hughes, who had relatives in Charlotte, took an interest in young Williams, who evidently made a considerable impression. Years afterward, the famed poet of the Harlem Renaissance sent Williams two hand-copied poems, "The Backlash Blues" and "Crowns and Garlands," as a New Year's greeting. "I only knew him as a student," Williams explained. "He thought I had promise as a writer."[76]

In 1953, just before he left Johnson C. Smith, Williams published a poem in the SWP newspaper, the *Militant*, that reflected both his potential as a poet and his passion for politics. "Go Awaken My People" reveals the political fervor and the international dimension that would be his trademarks in the years to come. This excerpt also suggests, as older activists sometimes joked in the 1960s, that the Black Power movement did not discover Africa:

> Go awaken my people from Texas to Virginia,
> Tell them of our glorious brothers in the colony of Kenya.
> Go tell my people that the dawn has come,
> Sound the trumpet, beat the drum!

Let the tyrant shudder, let the oppressor tremble at the thunder,
For the tide of humanity rises to sweep the despot under.
Go awaken my people wherever they sleep,
Tell them that we have a rendezvous that we must keep.

As the young poet's writings grew, however, his savings dwindled, and after a year at Johnson C. Smith there was no more money for schooling. "After my third year, my GI bill was out, so I came out," said Williams.[77]

Whether it was merely economics that sent him to the want ads or whether lingering uneasiness in his marriage may have played a part, Williams found a copy of the Sunday *New York Times* and saw an ad for metalworkers at an aircraft factory in Woodbridge, New Jersey. After taking the train from Charlotte, Williams landed a job at Curtiss Wrights Aeronautics. Leaving his wife and children in Monroe, Williams lived with his Aunt Estelle Williams on 117th Street in Harlem and commuted to work. Here he spent considerable time among a group of white radicals whom he met through friends. "Some were liberals, some were in the American Labor Party, some in the Communist Party, it was difficult to tell them apart," Williams commented. "A lot of these people were mixed up. I used to laugh when I heard J. Edgar Hoover talking about these people plotting and conspiring to overthrow the government. They used to sit around and drink cocktails on the wall-to-wall carpeting talking about the working class."

These would-be revolutionaries were eager to recruit Williams to their cause. "To them," he said, "a worker was something of a novelty. They saw this as a possibility that they would be able to have workers and intellectuals, this unity, black and white unity." Williams "sensed that they were trying to pull me into their group" and spent a lot of time in their company. His new white friends published some of Robert's verse in their youth magazine and offered Williams a scholarship to the Jefferson School of Social Science, the most famous and influential of the adult-education establishments by which the Communist Party USA sought to connect with politically committed members of the working class. "Robert was learning all the time," Mabel Williams said of those days. "He had affiliated with these leftists who were nurturing him, I'm sure they had to be [Communist Party members], and so he was going along with them because they were so supportive." But Williams attended only one class session at Jefferson School and never went back. Put off by their dismissal of Christianity as "mysticism" and by their insistence that the triumph of the working class would put an end to racism, Williams found their brand of Marxism implausible. "I was working in the factory and I wasn't interested in using my night time sitting [in] a class somewhere with these people who were talking about something that was far-fetched."

Some of the white radicals encouraged Williams to sublet their apartment in Yorkville on an all-white block of 88th Street between 3rd and 4th Avenues, where his family could join him. It was cheaper than Harlem, but the neighbors called him "nigger," banged on the ceiling, scratched his name off the mailbox, and blocked the doorway with trash cans. "We had a fuse box," Williams recounted, "and sometimes they would go and pull the switch at night," leaving him in the dark. Hostile telephone calls were routine. "Down South I had seen this kind of thing," he said, "but I didn't think it was so explosive and so intense in the North. . . . I began to realize that these people didn't want us among them North or South. . . . I always made sure to be quiet, to be polite to them and courteous, but that didn't make any difference." After Mabel Williams moved up from Monroe with the baby, she stayed indoors and kept their 9-mm Luger pistol close at hand. "He always told me, 'Just keep the doors locked. Don't answer the door,'" Mabel Williams remembered. "And I was there all day, for ten hours, afraid to go out. New York did not look so good to me. I really got scared and was glad when I left New York."[78]

Partly because he feared for their safety during the day, Williams moved his little family back to Monroe, where he found temporary work as a chauffeur. He tried to get a job as a machinist in Charlotte; though he knew that the FBI had been asking about him, Williams had no idea that agents secretly informed his prospective employers that he was a "security risk" and took pains to block his employment. Hearing that there was work at the Kodak plant in Rochester, New York, Williams traveled there by bus. "I walked that place inch by inch, and there was no job to be had," he said. Lacking even enough money to get home to Monroe, Williams found work at a migrant camp picking beans, cherries, and apples. Truckloads of black migrant workers from the Deep South poured into the camp "just like cattle," and the employer "had radio cars patrolling it," according to Williams. "I could never pick enough beans to make over $3 or $4 a day," he said, but he finally saved enough money for a bus ticket back to Monroe.[79]

As it turned out, perhaps he should have stayed in Monroe, but Williams ended up enduring an unhappy stint in the U.S. Marine Corps. Discouraged but determined, Williams had seen another newspaper advertisement for aircraft workers near Los Angeles. Selling many of his possessions to pay his way, he had set out alone in 1954, trying one more time to make a place for himself and his family outside the South. "While I was out there," he said, "I got stranded, my money was running out." Eventually he could not even afford the flophouse where he had landed. As he walked the streets alone in desperation, Williams saw the U.S. Marine Corps recruiting station. Terrified that he would end up among "those bums sleeping in doorways," Williams pondered his options. Three years in the Marine Corps, the recruiters told him, would afford him GI benefits to cover three more years of college. In the meantime, they showed Williams "courses that ran for 18 months for radio, writing for journalism. These courses were equivalent to university courses, so I figured this was going to be real good, plus I would get a chance to go to the east coast, which was closer to home." The recruiters promised him that the corps assigned enlistees according to their aptitude tests. "My testing showed an aptitude for information services," Williams said. "This meant that after my basic training, I would be sent to Quantico, Virginia"—only a long day's drive from his family—"and given college level training in journalism." His relationship with Mabel Williams had become tenuous. Without even conferring with his wife, who was still in Monroe with the two children, he signed the enlistment papers.[80]

This hasty decision turned out to be a serious mistake. For one thing, Mabel was furious when she heard what he had done. Williams did exceptionally well in basic training, however, after which he went home to Monroe for three weeks. At first, Mabel was cold to him. "After many days of frustrated overtures," he wrote later, "I finally reached a reconciliation with my estranged wife." He then took the train back to Camp Pendleton, California, where the rugged life suited him so well that he even entertained the notion of becoming a career marine. "This is the first time in my life I've been treated like an American," Williams wrote in his diary. This new world came crashing down, however, when Williams was summoned to the commander's office to receive his assignment: supply sergeant. Though the commander described it as "the best job in the Marine Corps," Williams was furious and stammered that he had been promised training in journalism and wanted to write. There were no black marines in information services, the base authorities bluntly informed him, and any further protests on his part would only land him in trouble.

"If I had been in possession of a hydrogen bomb, at that moment," Williams wrote later, "I would have sacrificed my life to explode it." He fired off letters of protest to Congressmen Charles Diggs of Michigan and Adam Clayton Powell of Harlem. On January 18, 1955, U.S. Naval Intelligence reported, "subject in a letter to the President of the United States expressed desire to renounce his citizenship and live in a country which would not let his family starve."

Williams dispatched another letter and a telegram to President Dwight Eisenhower, complaining bitterly of racial discrimination in the Marine Corps. Now he became the subject of an espionage investigation, "due to his expressing himself in a radical manner and constantly complaining of racial discrimination," the Naval Intelligence reports stated. "Mail cover revealed subject sent two letters and a telegram to the President of the U.S. between 30 Mar. and 13 Apr. 1955, sent a letter to NAACP Headquarters, Washington, D.C. and received two letters from members of the U.S. House of Representatives on 25 and 28 Apr," Naval Intelligence agents wrote. When Mabel came to visit him, agents broke into their quarters while they were at dinner, finding "no questionable literature in hotel room or luggage [but] furnished a list of names found in address book of subject's wife." His commanding officer arranged for Williams to be sent to Pickle Meadows, Nevada, where the military tested men and equipment at winter temperatures that fell to forty below zero. "You came into the Marines a ditch digger, and you are going out a ditch digger," an administrative officer told him. Williams soon found himself on a train bound for Monroe with an undesirable discharge and a smoldering bitterness. "He was real angry about what happened to him," Robert's older brother John Williams recalled, "and he became real militant."[81]

His experience with institutionalized racism in the Marine Corps left a scar, but one evening in those sixteen months gleamed brightly in his memory. On May 17, 1954, Williams was standing around a television set with a handful of other black soldiers when the news came that the U.S. Supreme Court had struck down the "separate but equal" doctrine and ruled that racial segregation had no place in law. Williams could only compare the "jubilation" he felt with what his slave ancestors must have experienced at Emancipation almost a century earlier. This time, he thought, there must be a new reconstruction that white violence could not overturn. "At last I felt that I was part of America and that I belonged," he wrote later. "That was what I had wanted, even as a child."[82]

When Williams returned to his hometown in 1955, he was saddened and bitter, but also hopeful about the meaning of the *Brown* decision. "I was sure that this was the beginning of a new era in American democracy," he recalled. Jonathan Daniels, editor of the Raleigh *News and Observer*, predicted that the Supreme Court decision "will be met in the South with the good sense and the good will of the people of both races in a manner which will serve the children and honor America." For a time it seemed as though white North Carolinians might accept the ruling as law and move on.[83]

In the absence of bold and progressive leadership, however, the forces of white supremacy soon rallied; the *Monroe Enquirer* observed that "threats" and "fulminations" dominated local discussions among whites in Union County. Arsonists dashed black hopes of transforming an abandoned white school into the first brick Negro school building in Union County; the *Monroe Enquirer* reported the arson without comment, explaining that the plans for the school "had met with opposition of residents of that area." Behind the virulent opposition to racial equality was the ever-present shadow of miscegenation that undergirded white determination to preserve segregation. The state's leading segregationist, I. Beverly Lake, denounced the *Brown* decision as an effort "to condition your children, even before they are old enough to be conscious of sex, to accept integration not only in the classroom but in the living room and the bedroom as well."[84]

Though Lake attacked him, Governor Luther H. Hodges, a former textile executive and a born bureaucrat, would never stand in the schoolhouse door and defy federal authorities in the style of George Wallace. "Rather," writes journalist Osha Gray Davidson, Hodges "would quietly appoint a committee to deliberate for eternity over exactly which door, and of what dimensions, would best facilitate the ingress and egress of all students. The style of a Wallace was different, but the result was the same." In fact, the sophistication that Hodges brought to the struggle against desegregation made him far more effective than most proponents of massive resistance. "It is my own feeling," Governor Hodges wrote privately in the spring of 1955, "that the decree of the Supreme Court will make no difference but that we can go ahead with our segregated schools as usual this fall."[85]

When Hodges did take a public stand late in the summer of 1955, his radio and television address lambasted the NAACP as "selfish and militant" for dividing North Carolinians into "camps of racial antagonism." He called for African American citizens to accept "voluntary segregation" as an alternative to closing the public schools or exposing children to the violent turmoil that desegregation would bring. "The white citizens of the state will resist integration strenuously, resourcefully, and with growing bitterness," Hodges told his audience. Even though he purported to offer a more reasoned alternative to Lake and other hard-line segregationists, Hodges shamelessly invoked the specter of interracial sexuality: the NAACP would have the black race "lose itself in another race" and "lose their identity in *complete merger*" with whites.[86]

The speech brought Hodges to "the pinnacle of his popularity since becoming governor," the *Monroe Enquirer* gleefully reported. "Reaction to his speech indicated that, for the present at least, he has become as great a champion of segregation as Beverly Lake himself." Paul Green, the University of North Carolina's Pulitzer Prize-winning playwright, wrote after the speech, "Luther Hodges has done tragic damage to this state, and when trouble boils up under him due to his stirring mainly he'll have no platform to stand on. He has put the white citizenry in an unfair moral position with himself as leader towards prejudice and passion."[87]

Hodges had succeeded in "pre-empting all attacks from conservatives and in creating a situation where anything he proposed—short of an outright endorsement of the Ku Klux Klan—could be portrayed as 'moderate,'" historian William H. Chafe has observed. His pupil assignment law, the Pearsall Plan, specified that there would be "no racial segregation by law" but mandated "assignment according to natural racial preference and the administrative determination of what is best for the child." It also made provision for local school boards to close public schools rather than integrate them and permitted state tuition grants for white children to attend segregated private schools.[88]

Segregationist lawyers agreed that, unlike more defiant measures adopted by legislatures across the South, the Pearsall Plan represented a strong and resilient barrier to integration.[89] The *Charlotte Observer* called it "North Carolina's bulwark against public school integration." Union County voted by a margin of almost eight to one in 1956 to endorse the pupil assignment measure, which passed by a four-to-one margin across the state. The *Monroe Enquirer* hailed it as "a plan guaranteeing that no child in the state will ever be required to attend a segregated school against its will." Even the local Ku Klux Klan strongly endorsed Hodges's Pearsall Plan, though reminding the thousands of white citizens who attended their rallies in Monroe that "if the Pearsall Plan doesn't work, the Smith and Wesson plan will."[90]

This is not to say that Hodges and his scheme had no conservative critics. Jesse Helms, director of the North Carolina Banking Association, outflanked the Klan on the right, arguing that "unless our Negro citizens submit more easily than we predict they will," North Carolina would be forced either to integrate the schools or to close them down. Governor Hodges agreed with the Communist-inspired NAACP, Helms charged, that "public schools must be maintained at any cost." Rather than risk the possibility of racial integration, Helms favored substituting "free choice private schools," calling public education "merely a habit" but "far from the only way to make education available to our people."[91]

Helms turned out to be mistaken, however, in his criticism of the Pearsall Plan's effectiveness at preserving school segregation. Ten years after *Brown*, only one in a hundred black children across the South attended a desegregated school. In North Carolina, thanks to Hodges's scheme, that figure was one in two hundred. The Pearsall Plan was a subtle and insidious defense of segregation that postponed meaningful school desegregation in North Carolina for more than ten years, even longer than in many states whose leadership chose to pursue "massive resistance" to the Supreme Court's edict.[92]

Not all whites in Monroe applauded the effort to circumvent compliance with the *Brown* decision. J. Ray Shute, former mayor and former chair of the Union County Board of Education, blasted Governor Hodges after his call for voluntary segregation. Shute could not be dismissed as an outside agitator or a Communist sympathizer. The Shute family had arrived in Monroe in 1856. By the turn of the century, cotton gins, brickyards, warehouses, and mercantile stores permitted J. Shute and Sons to "pay more taxes than any other person, firm, or corporation in Union county," according to a local history. J. Ray Shute, heir to this wealth, had been the central figure in Monroe's economic development during and after World War II, serving not only as mayor, leading industrial recruiter, and civic booster but as chair of the county commission.

After Hodges had issued his pitch for voluntary segregation, Shute wrote a rejoinder published in both the *Monroe Enquirer* and the *Charlotte News*. "I fully realize what a shock it is to many people that our Supreme Court has finally ruled that democracy must be practiced in fact as well as preached," Shute declared. "However, I feel that our state's chief executive should recommend ways and means of accomplishing democracy as a fact, rather than recommending ways and means to thwart the law of the land."[93]

Ray Shute became Robert Williams's closest white friend in Monroe. Even before Shute's attack on Hodges had appeared in the *Charlotte News*,

Williams had published letters to the editor in the same newspaper that he had delivered as a boy, condemning folks back home whose first reaction to *Brown* was to search for ways to evade it.[94] Shute and his friends read Williams's letters and asked around about the author. Booker T. Perry "told them that my grandfather was one of the first Negro teachers in that town, and I had a long history among rebels, and talent," Williams recalled. When Williams got back to Monroe from the Marine Corps, Shute invited him and several other black citizens to visit the small, mostly white Unitarian fellowship that had begun to meet at his home. Shute "had a swimming pool and everything there. He had his own art gallery that he had built up," Williams remembered, "relics from all over the world and things he had collected." Shute and his friends "were local white people [but] their attitude was different," Williams said. "Shute owned most of the buildings downtown. He didn't feel he had to be afraid." Shute and his family "would take me places. They were proud to show they weren't prejudiced." After a while, whites who read his letters to the editor, "local bigots," according to Williams, "said, 'That nigger is not writing those letters, that Ray Shute is writing those letters.'"[95]

Ray Shute and Robert Williams were not literary collaborators, but they did become personal friends and political allies after Williams returned from the Marine Corps in 1955. Douglas Aircraft in Charlotte hired Williams as a machinist, but FBI agents intervened and convinced his new employer to withdraw the job offer. Though Williams did not know the full extent of FBI interference with his employment prospects at the time, he wrote later that "it appeared that my government and my country had declared war on me." His frustration was shared by perhaps thousands of other American citizens at the time, many of whom were Communists, while others, like Williams, simply had aroused the suspicions of FBI red-hunters.[96] Shute persuaded a friend who owned a textile factory in a neighboring county to hire Williams as a security guard. To help with the commute, Shute also gave Williams a used car, a small, blue British Hillman that Williams loved. Williams decided to join the Unitarian fellowship. "I felt, well, if [the Shutes] can be this way, maybe the others can be this way, too. I never felt insulted among them. In fact, I spoke a number of times on Sunday. I had caddied for a number of them at the Country Club and they always acted like they were glad to see me." The interracial congregation "would have this big dinner and basket lunches and things," Williams recalled. "They invited black people out of the community, but still mostly whites came, some came from Charlotte and different places around their liberal community."[97]

Not only these new allies but the stirring news of the bus boycott in Montgomery, Alabama, boosted Williams's spirits. In a Sunday sermon delivered to his fellow Unitarians on March 25, 1956, Robert Williams hailed the ongoing Montgomery Bus Boycott, which had persisted for more than one hundred days at that point, and celebrated what he called "the patriots of passive revolution." Official measures to suppress the boycott, he argued, were both futile and unconstitutional: "Has an American no right to walk when to ride would degrade his dignity? Has our beloved Republic reached the stage that the jails have no room for criminals, because they are filled with liberty-loving citizens whose only crime is that their voices cry out for freedom?" His bitter collision with the Marine Corps had not dampened his commitment to equal rights for all under the U.S. Constitution. Nor had he abandoned the many elements in the American political tradition that he believed undergirded the struggle for black liberation. In fact, he was optimistic. The racial crisis in the South "is a difficult problem," he conceded, "but Americans are noted for being able to solve difficult problems." Invoking "the spirit of Concord, Lexington, and Valley Forge," Williams declared from the pulpit that "the liberty bell peals once more and the Stars and Stripes shall wave forever."[98]

Williams was not the only African American activist in Monroe who seemed invigorated by the *Brown* decision. Less than three months after the Supreme Court ruling, Edward Belton of the local NAACP appeared before the city council with a group of black citizens. The delegation asked the city to pave 4th Street, to repair several other streets, and to hire its first African American police officer.[99] The council finally agreed to pave 4th Street, the first street ever paved in the black community. Though they stalled for nearly a year, the council eventually agreed that Elgie Gray, "a taxi driver operating on Winchester Avenue, was by far the best applicant available" to join the police force. Mayor Fred Wilson agreed "that Gray would make a good colored policeman." Denied the use of a patrol car, Gray walked a beat in north Monroe for the first year, working "the juke joints and the piccolos," he said. When he arrested someone, the retired army sergeant would "handcuff them to a pole and then go make my call," Gray said. "I was told that I was not allowed to arrest a white person." Even so, Gray's appointment was a tangible victory. Not only did it promise to decrease police brutality, but the fact that it had come at the instigation of the black community fed the hopes for greater change.[100]

While the *Brown* decision encouraged black aspirations, it also fueled a volatile and far-reaching white reaction against the NAACP. Describing the aftermath of the Court's decision as "the dark period of socialist infiltration," an editorial in the *Monroe Enquirer* argued that the Supreme Court was "no longer a court of law, but a court of men, thereby having lost the respect of the people." An unspoken but forceful backlash in Monroe exerted heavy pressure on the black middle class. "If [white authorities] found out that a teacher was in the NAACP, the board would dismiss them," Mrs. M. G. Rorie recalled. Most blacks in Union County depended on local whites, one way or another, for their income, and any visible activism was sure to bring reprisals. White bank officials could deny loans, city officials could withhold building permits, and white employers could be counted on to dismiss "troublemakers."[101]

Sometimes reprisals went beyond the economic realm. Beginning in 1956, James "Catfish" Cole, a former carnival barker and Free Will Baptist tent evangelist from Marion, South Carolina, led an enormous Ku Klux Klan revival in the Carolina piedmont. The Reverend Mr. Cole hosted "The Free Will Hour" radio show on WFMO in Kinston, sold spurious diplomas from the "Southern Bible College," and whipped crowds into a frenzy with his fiery diatribes against race-mixing and Communism. In a series of twenty rallies beginning in late 1956—several in Monroe and a dozen within forty miles of Monroe—Cole revived the Ku Klux Klan, drawing crowds of as many as 15,000 whites to his speeches, according to local newspapers. The rabid rhetoric was not just empty talk; an Anti-Defamation League report in 1957 noted that "our study of the revived North Carolina Klan shows a growing tendency towards violence."[102] On November 18, 1957, Mr. and Mrs. Frank Clay, an African American couple in East Flat Rock, North Carolina, were found shot and slashed to death in their home after a series of telephone threats from callers claiming to represent the Klan; neighbors found a cross smoldering in their yard. Dynamite attacks on black activists in the area grew common, and lesser acts of terror became routine. "The echo of shots and dynamite blasts," the *Southern Patriot* said in a review of 1956, "has been almost continuous throughout the South."[103]

Charles McLean, NAACP field secretary for North Carolina, had written to the national office in 1953 that prominent local blacks in Monroe "were not enthusiastic about supporting the branch. I expect I will have to completely reorganize this branch before it becomes active again." Under the economic reprisals and physical intimidation that came after *Brown*, matters at the Monroe NAACP branch got even worse. The group dwindled to six members who then contemplated disbanding. "I became active," Robert Williams said, "at the behest of some of the local people in the NAACP, and I started to attend meetings." When the newest member strenuously objected to dissolving the branch, president Edward Belton nominated him to lead the chapter. "The [white] Southerners were coming down hard on the NAACP," Williams said, "and these old NAACP people who had been playing around on the prestige basis were getting economic pressure so that we [could not] fight. And they turned it over to me to die . . . so it would not die in their hands." The former leadership of the branch, with one or two exceptions, declined to participate after they elected Williams. "It is true that the middle-class blacks withdrew from the NAACP. Teachers did not feel that they could be involved in something this controversial and still keep a job," James Rushing recalled. "I was for the cause, but I didn't step out with them," Belton conceded. "They elected me president," Williams recalled with some derision, "and then they all left."[104]

Finding himself virtually a one-man NAACP chapter, Williams turned first to the black veterans with whom he had stood against the Klan that night in 1947 at Harris Funeral Home: Woodrow Wilson, B. J. Winfield, and John W. McDow. Another veteran, Dr. Albert E. Perry, had been an impatient member of the branch all along and remained to serve as vice-president. These core members were mostly independent entrepreneurs, staunch "race men," and fiercely loyal to Robert Williams. "He was the backbone," Walter Byrd, another member, recalled. "He was the only one who had the nerve to go out and do it. The rest of the people had jobs."[105]

One of Williams's first stops as NAACP president was the local poolroom. "I started to think of the possibility of getting some of these fellows to see if they would join," he recalled. "They were construction workers, some unemployed, and the kind of guys that you usually find in a poolroom." Williams tossed a stack of NAACP literature onto the green felt tabletop and silenced the clatter of the billiard balls. "I told them that I had been elected president of the NAACP and I was trying to get it reorganized, and that if we got it going, we were going to give these white people hell in this town." For a moment it was not clear to the pool hall crowd what this apparently crazy Negro wanted. "I told them that I wanted them to join and help," Williams recalled. The first response spoke volumes about their perception of the NAACP. "The guy said, 'Man, you mean to say *we* can join that thing?' I told him yes and I got six of them right there, signed them on the pool table. They had never been asked to join before because it was somewhat of a local black bourgeoisie thing and these people were looked down upon by these preachers and teachers and people who ran this thing."[106]

Williams painstakingly recruited from the pool halls, beauty parlors, street corners, and tenant farms of Union County, building a distinctive NAACP branch one member at a time. "In this section of the South today," Williams wrote to the national office in 1957, "many people are willing to support the NAACP financially but are in no position to expose themselves. For some people, public gatherings have become too open and I find it necessary to visit homes and appeal directly to individuals. I admit this is a slower process, but I'm sure that in the long run it will prove to be effective in more ways than one."[107] With the exception of Ethel Azalea Johnson, who served as secretary, all of the new officers were young black men and World War II veterans: Dr. Perry was chosen as vice-president and McDow served as treasurer.[108] The largest group among the new recruits, however, was African American women, most of whom worked as domestics. In part, many women joined because they trusted and respected Robert Williams, whose gracious manners and honest demeanor cast him credibly in the role of the devoted son. "I believe it was God's calling, that Rob Williams was sent here to save us. God sent somebody, just like He did in the Bible," Annie Belle Cherry recalled. But the crucial impetus came from the forceful commitment of the women themselves. "Women are pushing harder than the men," Mabel Williams told Anne Braden of the Southern Conference Educational Fund in 1959. "That is where our drive is coming from."[109]

From the beginning, the Monroe branch was "unique in the whole NAACP because of a working class composition and a leadership that was not middle class," Williams wrote. This was not entirely accurate; though Williams did not have an income that would qualify as "middle class," he lived in a house that his father owned outright, had been to college for three years, and published poetry in his spare time. Dr. Perry, in fact, was quite affluent and lived in a new brick home on the outskirts of the Newtown community. Several of the other male leaders were skilled tradesmen or independent contractors. Clearly, however, the rank-and-file membership drew upon social classes within the black community that the NAACP did not often reach. "We got some of the 'worst element' we could find," Williams recalled. "They had been abused, they had been mistreated, they had been in jail. It was easier to recruit those people because they really had suffered."[110]

With this grassroots approach, the branch grew almost daily. On the books, the Monroe NAACP went from 28 members in 1957 to 92 members the following year to 121 by late 1959. But national record books indicate that large numbers of the Monroe branch supporters declined to record memberships to avoid the perils of white reprisals. The Monroe branch needed to shield its members, NAACP records indicate, "for the purpose of protecting those who join the NAACP who do not want their names known so even [the national secretary] would not have the correct information." Within two years, Williams estimated the membership at roughly three hundred; two hundred seems a conservative tally. "The local branch of the national organization has rededicated itself to the cause of democracy and social justice in Union County, the state, and the nation," Williams announced in the *Monroe Enquirer*. "All citizens who believe in democracy, the rights of man, and brotherhood are urged to join and support the NAACP. This organization is open to all people, irrespective of race, who support the American cause as embodied in the United States Constitution."[111]

Williams was sincere in his openness to white participation in the freedom struggle. In fact, while he was reorganizing the Monroe NAACP, Williams remained active in the Unitarian fellowship and helped to found the Union County Council on Human Relations. In late 1955, quiet meetings between more than a dozen blacks and several whites took place at the Elizabeth Baptist Church, where Robert had been baptized as a boy. At Christmastime the members of this ad hoc group "curtailed their normal Christmas activities in order to work at a project which they hoped would give more lasting reality to the meaning of Christmas," their first press release stated. Hammering out a public statement, selecting a slate of officers, and agreeing to hold monthly meetings, the Union County Council on Human Relations announced its existence during "Brotherhood Week" in February 1956. The council elected Dr. A. E. Perry as president. J. Ray Shute agreed to serve as vice-president. Mabel Williams was chosen secretary, and Frances Cox became treasurer. Booker T. Perry, whose barbershop had been the meeting place for the black veterans who had faced down the Klan in 1947, served on the board.

Depending on this network of local leaders, the group hoped to help avert "tragic occurrences such as have already made their appearances in several Southern communities." The group asserted "that the time has come when the voice of moderation, of Christian ethics, of charity, love and understanding should be heard pleading for tolerance, democracy and orderly discussion of common problems." One purpose was simply to furnish "opportunities for discussion and fact-finding" among black and white citizens of goodwill. Assuring the public that "no effort will be made to reform society, to radically fight for immediate upheavals and revolutionary changes," the Human Relations Council promised to "promote equal opportunity for all citizens in employment, education, recreation and all other phases of community life." Stressing that it was "inter-denominational and inter-racial," the council appealed especially to "every minister in Union County" to help the group in its efforts. More than fifty people attended the first public meeting. Harry Golden, a Jewish liberal in Charlotte whose humorous and poignant writings would soon make him famous, sometimes attended. Golden characterized the whites involved as "liberals, 'do-gooders' here, some of them fine dedicated men and women, often fighting against racism at great risk to their social standing and means of livelihood."[112]

The consensus among well-meaning whites and blacks began to break down with the drowning death of a young black boy in a nearby lake in the summer of 1957. "Year after year, the summer months bring the same tragic story," Dr. Perry pleaded in a letter to the Parks and Recreation Commission in his capacity as president of the Human Relations Council. "The summer is young and yet tragic death has already cast its shadow over one of the county's many seemingly attractive swimming holes—a youngster has already lost his life." White children swam at the Monroe Country Club. Built in 1935 with $200,000 in federal funds from the Works Progress Administration (WPA) and $31,000 in local tax dollars, the Monroe Country Club offered league basketball, television, badminton, ping-pong, shuffleboard, volleyball, boxing lessons, "Teen Club Night" with "jukebox dancing," and group singing—all funded by city taxes and all closed to African American children. Every summer the city provided water safety instruction and swimming lessons for dozens of white youngsters.

The black children barred from these programs swam in isolated farm ponds, muddy creeks, and abandoned quarries—and they drowned all too frequently. "The weather is hot and the water is inviting. When there are no proper facilities available these conditions are invitations to death," Dr. Perry wrote. "The fact that most swimming-hole deaths involve Negroes is no accident." The Union County Council on Human Relations, though "wishing not to disrupt the racial harmony of the community," Perry told city officials, "requests that the Recreation Board make some provisions for supervised swimming pools for all its citizens. Must we wait for legal action to provide a solution to this problem?"[113]

It was clear that "the Monroe pool will not hold water in federal court," Williams joked, but it was equally clear that white citizens harbored deep and visceral objections to sharing the pool with black people. "Your attention is called to the ruling of the U.S. Supreme Court, November, 1955, outlawing segregation in recreation areas supported by public funds," Dr. Perry reminded the Parks and Recreation Commission a few days after his first letter. Only four days after he wrote on behalf of the interracial Human Relations Council, Perry wrote a second letter, this time as a representative of the Union County Civic League, an all-black organization. The swimming pool issue had instantly chased away their white allies.[114]

Mabel poked fun at her husband for being surprised. "White folks don't want you to sit beside them on the bus, Rob," she laughed. "You really think they're gonna let you jump in the water with them half-naked?" An all-black delegation including Dr. Perry, McDow, and attorney W. B. Nivens met with the commission that same day. "If Negroes 'pushed the issue,'" the commission told them, "the city would sell the facilities to 'private sources' who had already offered" to buy the pool and operate it as a segregated, members-only concession.[115]

Initially, the delegation had asked only that the city make some provision whereby black children could swim, even if it meant a "separate but equal" pool. "The City Council told us they did not have the money to build us a pool," Williams said. The delegation then suggested that perhaps the council could set aside two days a week for African American children to use the existing facility. One of the commissioners objected, according to Williams, "on the grounds that to allow Negroes to swim even once a week would be too expensive because the water would have to be changed after the colored people had used it." The chair of the commission, Harvey Morrison, assured the black delegation "that he would not recommend that Negroes be allowed to use the pool under any circumstances."[116]

Almost immediately, Dr. Perry and Robert Williams led a contingent of eight black youths with bathing suits and towels to the country club swimming pool, where they demanded to swim. Refused admission, they conducted a brief "stand-in" protest near the gate. The protesters repeated this process several times, "preparing the groundwork for possible court proceedings," Williams said. "We took the position that if they were too poor to afford dual facilities," he recounted, "then segregation was a luxury they could not afford. If they couldn't afford it, they had no business trying to have segregated facilities." Williams wrote to Kelly Alexander, head of the North Carolina Conference of Branches of the NAACP, to assure him that if the NAACP would support the case, "we are willing to prosecute it to the limit."[117]

When black activists pressed the issue of the swimming pool, white liberals backed off quickly; some undoubtedly felt authentic revulsion at the thought of interracial swimming, while others found the campaign impolitic and untimely. It became glaringly obvious that white liberals considered themselves the most appropriate strategists for the black freedom movement. Conceding that blacks in Monroe had been "prodded by Ku Kluxers," Harry Golden wrote that "the Negro leadership made several mistakes. Confronted with a major struggle in which they are backed by both morality and law"—Golden meant the campaign to desegregate the public schools—blacks in Monroe "sought instead to experiment with the crude emotions of a small Southern agricultural community."

White liberals believed the swimming pool campaign was a terrible political error. "There are projects which can be discussed, fought for, and won, like school integration," Golden said, but this was not one of them. Golden, close to both Alexander and the white liberals in Union County, criticized the crusade as "unwise and unrealistic." The specter of interracial sexuality "haunts every mention of the race question," the liberal man of letters believed, and he thought it "naive" to address an issue that touched so closely to the nerve. To Alexander, Golden complained about Robert Williams's "need for publicity" and his "stupid statement about that swimming pool. Let's fight this school battle first." Never did Golden or any of the white liberals show any sign of understanding that black children were dying because they had no safe place to swim.[118]

Harry Golden was right, however, about the "crude emotions" that the shadow of interracial sexuality could awaken in the white people of the area. Angry whites immediately drew up a petition "asking that local Negro integrationists be forced to leave Monroe," the Monroe Enquirer reported on November 11, 1957. "The petition is aimed at Robert F. Williams, president, and Dr. A. E. Perry, vice president of the Monroe NAACP." The petitioners asked that officials "with all deliberate speed and due process of law" order Perry and Williams "to leave and not return to the city of Monroe." Williams and Perry had "proven themselves unworthy of living in our City and County," it said, and white citizens could not tolerate "anyone that is connected with an organization like the NAACP who has as its officers people that are known Communist and trouble makers that are trying to overthrow the government of the United States by force, to live in our community and try to make as much trouble between the White and Negro Race as these two men have in the last two years." In one Saturday afternoon on the courthouse square, the petitioners collected almost 2,000 signatures.[119]

The effort to drive the NAACP out of Monroe went well beyond petitions. Catfish Cole's Ku Klux Klan took advantage of the apprehension around the swimming pool issue. It probably did not help matters that the Klan crusade coincided with the closure of several textile mills in the area, which pushed almost 5,000 white textile workers out of their jobs.[120] The day after Dr. Perry first approached the city council about the pool, 6,000 whites attended a Klan rally in nearby Salisbury. Thousands more attended five mass meetings held in Monroe over the next few weeks.

"A nigger who wants to go to a white swimming pool is not looking for a bath," Cole told a crowd of 2,000 on Highway 74 outside Monroe on August 8. "He is looking for a funeral." After each rally and cross burning, dozens of carloads of Klansmen rode through the black community, blowing their horns, throwing rocks and bottles, and firing pistol shots into the air. Chief of Police A. A. Mauney acknowledged to reporters that he led Ku Klux Klan motorcades through the black community, although he maintained that his squad car only accompanied the Klan to keep order. On several occasions, carloads of Klansmen fired shots into Dr. Perry's house.[121]

"Each time the Klan came on a raid they were led by police cars," Robert Williams said later. "We appealed to the President of the United States to have the Justice Department investigate the police. We appealed to Governor Luther Hodges. All of our appeals to constituted law were in vain." Some black preachers met with the city council and "pleaded with them to restrict the Klan from the colored community," Williams stated, but "the city fathers advised these cringing, begging Negro ministers that the Ku Klux Klan had constitutional rights to meet and organize in the same way as the NAACP."[122]

Williams, Perry, and others were deluged with death threats. Williams simply strapped on his .45 automatic, which was perfectly legal, and wore the pistol on errands to the post office and the courthouse, making it clear that anyone who acted on those threats did so at his own peril. Harry G. Boyte, a white liberal who lived in nearby Matthews, North Carolina, wrote to a friend that he had "personally observed on several occasions cars full of what appeared to be young white 'hoodlums' pass by Robert's house and fire guns as they passed." Although Williams and many others in the black community had always been armed and prepared to defend themselves, the enormous Ku Klux Klan revival in the Carolina piedmont in 1957 encouraged members of the Monroe NAACP to organize to defend their homes, families, and community.[123]

If the swimming pool campaign had put off the whites in the Union County Council on Human Relations, the necessity of what Robert Williams called "armed self-reliance" sent them scurrying. "As long as I was talking, just merely talking," Williams said, "I had lots of white liberal support, but when I actually started arming people and picking up guns, they said I had gone too far."[124]

In truth, there were other reasons for the collapse of interracial liberalism in Union County. Relatively few whites had shown up in the first place. "Most of the whites, being steeped in . . . racial prejudice," Mabel Williams wrote later, "not only did not participate, but they ostracized anyone who did. There seemed to be an organized effort against all who took part." The backlash "pretty much steamrollered over this group of liberals that was developing," her husband acknowledged later. Mabel Williams was sympathetic to the predicament of Ray Shute and the other white liberals who backed off when blacks prepared to fight back, but she did not hold them blameless. "It is now quite clear," she wrote bitterly in 1959, that "many people in Monroe posed as liberals for the sake of appearing lettered." The hope for interracial liberalism in Union County had flickered and died.[125]

At first, Dr. Perry more than Robert Williams became the central focus of white supremacist anger. The Klan blamed the resurgent NAACP on Perry, assumed that the physician financed the chapter, and objected to the fact that Perry was a Catholic. Albert Perry had grown up in Austin, Texas, but had come to Camp Sutton during World War II and fallen in love with a local young woman. In 1945 Perry finished college at nearby Johnson C. Smith College and then enrolled in Meharry Medical School in Nashville.[126] After Albert's residency in Winston-Salem, Bertha and Albert Perry moved back to her hometown, where Albert opened his own practice in 1950. Just before the *Brown* decision in 1954, the Perry family built a large, brick, split-level home on a hill over the highway at the edge of town, a house that many whites considered inappropriate for a black man.[127] Tall and elegant with wire-rimmed spectacles and a broad smile, Dr. Perry was adored by his clientele. "Whites didn't like him because he was so concerned about the welfare of poor blacks," B. J. Winfield said. "That's why they tried to kill him. And that's why I said I would die along with him."[128]

One night while Dr. Perry was at an NAACP meeting, Bertha Perry called and told him that the Ku Klux Klan had threatened to blow up their house. Even though death threats were hardly unusual among black activists, "most of the guys left the meeting and went home and got their guns and went to his house," Robert Williams recalled. Sipping coffee in Perry's garage with shotguns across their laps, the men agreed that defending their families was too important to do in haphazard fashion. "We started to really getting organized and setting up, digging foxholes and started getting up ammunition and training guys," Williams recalled. "In fact, we had started building our own rifle range, and we got our own M-1's and got our own Mausers and German semi-automatic rifles, and steel helmets. We had everything." About sixty men guarded the Perry house in rotating shifts, sleeping in the garage on cots next to the stacks of rifles and shotguns beside the washing machine. The women in the NAACP organized a "snowball system" for telephone alerts, since all of their families remained at risk.[129]

"Most important," Williams wrote, "we had a strong representation of veterans who were militant and didn't scare easily." This resolve, though genuine, may have contained a certain amount of bluster. In any case, Mabel Williams did not always share her husband's faith in their capacity to defend themselves. "Oh, God, we were afraid for our lives," she said of those times. "The kids were young, but they were both trained to use a gun. I remember nights when the four of us—me, Rob's father, and the two boys—we'd sit up all night with our guns, afraid someone would come kill us while Rob was at Dr. Perry's."[130]

On October 5, 1957, Catfish Cole's Ku Klux Klan held a huge rally near Monroe. After the rally, a large, heavily armed Klan motorcade roared out to Dr. Perry's place, firing their guns at the house and howling at the top of their lungs. The hooded terrorists met a hail of disciplined gunfire from Robert Williams and his men, who fired their weapons from behind sandbag fortifications and earthen entrenchments. Shooting low, they quickly turned the Klan raid into a complete rout. "[Police Chief] Mauney wouldn't stop them," B. J. Winfield said later, "and he knew they were coming, because he was in the Klan. When we started firing, they run. We run them out and they started just crying and going on." The Klan "hauled it and never did come back," Woodrow Wilson recalled. "The Klans was low-down people what would do dirty things. But if they found out that you would do dirty things, too, then they'd let you alone," he said. "We shot it out with the Klan and repelled their attack," Williams said, "and the Klan didn't have any more stomach for this type of fight. They stopped raiding our community."[131] The *Monroe Journal* blamed the Klan's "robed assemblies," calling the shootout "an uncivilized incident" that "should be sufficient grounds to outlaw such provocative assemblies in Union County." The following day, the Monroe city council held an emergency session and passed an ordinance banning Ku Klux Klan motorcades.[132]

Almost forty years later, B. J. Winfield, who fired back at the Klan that night, pondered what it had meant to stand up against white supremacy, even to the point of taking up arms. "The black man had been thinking it all the time, but too scared to say it, scared to do anything," he reflected. "Rob Williams, after he come out of service, we thought he was talking too much. But after we found out he was getting it from the big book—I mean, it was our rights—then we went with him. After we seen him do all these things and accomplish these things, we said, 'Well, he must know what he is talking about.' " Roy Crowder, who was just a teenager at the time, put it another way: "Back then, a lot of black people thought things would never get better—they had no hope. But Rob changed that. He gave us confidence to believe that things could get better if we stood up for ourselves."[133]

The night after Robert Williams and the Monroe NAACP drove Catfish Cole's Klan away from Dr. Perry's house, the black physician pulled his car into his driveway and found the police waiting with a warrant for his arrest on charges of "criminal abortion on a white woman." Although abortion was illegal in North Carolina in 1957, the statutes made no mention of race. The fact that newspapers and official documents invariably appended the phrase "on a white woman" suggests that the woman's race was considered highly relevant to the alleged crime. As though she were a fictional character created especially for the part of defiled white woman-hood, her name was Lilly Mae Rape.

An impoverished and illiterate twenty-five-year-old mother of four, Rape had once been a nurse's aide at the hospital where Perry worked. She claimed that she had come to Perry's clinic three times, pleading with him "to do something for me. I knew that I was going to lose my job," she stammered in court later, "and we couldn't afford another child." Unable to find a white doctor who would perform the abortion and "desperate" at her predicament, Rape went back to Perry, who told her that there was nothing he could do for her. "I called him a liar," she testified later. Perry advised her that it would be "dangerous," she claimed, but to "get up $75" and come back. When she returned on October 4, Rape swore, Perry reluctantly sterilized his instruments and performed the abortion. That night, sick with fever and frightened, Rape was admitted to Union County Memorial Hospital, where she apparently had a miscarriage. Almost immediately, she reported Perry to the police.[1]

Perry, a devout Catholic, acknowledged that Rape had come to his office late in the afternoon on three separate occasions, pleading for an abortion, but the physician maintained that he steadfastly had refused to accommodate her. The last time she came to see him, Perry stated, he had told Rape that there were "too many dangers" in a white woman even being in his office, reminded her that he had told her already not to come back, and demanded that she "get out." Never did she give him any money, he testified, nor did he perform any medical procedure. "I would have had to have been crazy to have done such an act in the face of all the animosity against me," Perry said later.[2] "I am Vice President of the local branch and it is because of this that I have been framed," the doctor wrote to NAACP executive secretary Roy Wilkins.[3]

Whatever occurred between Lillie Mae Rape and Dr. Perry made no difference in the minds of the black women of Union County. Word of the esteemed physician's arrest raced across the telephone lines and through the beauty parlors. Bertha Perry called B. J. Winfield and told him that they would need bail money. Robert Williams marched straight into the police station and demanded to know what bail had been set. "You can't get him," Chief of Police Mauney told Williams, referring to the fact that the magistrate had set bail at $7,500. Williams asked to use the telephone on the desk. "I called Mabel," Williams recounted, "and [Mauney] was standing there listening, and I said, 'Mabel, tell the boys I am in the police station and to get ready because we may have some action tonight.' And you should have seen that man's face."[4] Outside the station, dozens of angry African Americans, most of them women, filled the courthouse square. "Many were the nights when Dr. Perry risked his life against Klan threats to deliver a baby for a woman who didn't have a penny," Mabel Williams remembered fondly. It was time to return the favor.[5]

There was neither time nor need for Robert Williams to summon "the boys." From inside the station, Williams and the police chief heard tires squealing, motors racing, and the clamor of dozens of angry women. "Women came up with butcher knives, housewives with hatchets and shotguns and pistols," Robert Williams laughed years later.[6] "Within minutes," *Jet* magazine reported the next week, "an estimated 45–100 Negroes had rushed to the town square, crowded policemen out of the headquarters building, and confronted Police Chief Al Mauney." B. J. Winfield told the chief, "If they don't let him out, we are going to tear down the damn jailhouse." The black women demanded to see their beloved doctor alive and safe. "And when the chief seemed slow about arranging bail, and bringing the doctor up from the basement, where he was being held alone, the crowd got fidgety, surged against the doors, fingered their guns and knives until Perry was produced." The women who thronged the station cheered when the doctor walked upstairs under guard. Williams telephoned J. Ray Shute, who agreed to sign the $7,500 bond for Perry. The police soon released the physician into the arms of his family and friends, ending the drama for the moment.[7]

Almost a year later, as Perry's case ground on through the courts, an even more vivid local drama unfurled, dragging the little town of Monroe onto front pages around the world and further underlining the power of sexual issues in the racial politics of the segregation-era South. Accounts differed sharply. "The white—and official—version," wrote one white reporter, "is that the two Negro boys trapped the three white girls in a culvert and told them that the price of escape would be a kiss." Two of the girls, according to this rendition of events, managed to elude that levy. The third—a seven year old—either kissed or was kissed by Hanover Thompson. White sources asserted that one of the African American boys had held the girl while the other had kissed her or even tried to rape her. Local officials openly accused the boys of "molesting three white girls" and quietly suggested to reporters that what actually had occurred was a rape attempt. Governor Luther Hodges wrote to one critic that the boys "had assaulted three small white girls."[8]

The *Carolina Times*, the black newspaper published in Durham, touted separate eyewitness testimony that the girls, in a game, had sat voluntarily on the laps of black and white boys and kissed them playfully. The crisis in Monroe, editor Louis Austin wrote, had nothing to do with assault or delinquency. It stemmed from the embarrassment of white officials that the children had not yet learned "the unwritten law of white supremacy." That law, Austin observed, held "that white is right and that God is a respecter of persons and that He has made one race of men superior to another." In any case, Austin spat, "no one but a bunch of numbskulls with hearts full of the filthiest kind of dirt would attach any significance to what children of six to ten years of age do at play."[9]

David Ezell "Fuzzy" Simpson, eight, and James Hanover Grissom Thompson, ten, both black, remembered these events for the rest of their lives. In their accounts, the two playmates met a group of white children in a culvert below Harvard Street in a white section of Monroe. According to Simpson and Thompson, the pair saw some white boys playing and joined in their romp. "At first it was just boys playing," Thompson recalled thirty-five years later. "We was just running through the water with our feet at first, acting crazy like kids." A handful of white girls dawdled near the ditch. Gradually the two groups of children merged, and all but one or two of the white boys went home. One of the remaining boys suggested a kissing game in which each girl would sit on a boy's lap and kiss him, "like on TV or in the movies," ten-year-old Thompson told a white questioner soon afterward. According to the young boy, a white girl sat in both his lap and that of a white companion and kissed each of them.

Three decades later, Thompson could not be sure whether or not the children knew how deeply this "little peck on the jaw" violated the unspoken boundaries of race. But he suspected that he was strangely influenced by feelings of racial self-loathing that he had absorbed, almost without noticing them, from his world—perceptions about racial meaning that brought him to follow the lead of the white children regardless of the taboo. "Being a black kid growing up in that era," he speculated, "if the little white kids do something, you think it's right. That's what we were taught." Thompson knew Sissy Sutton, the girl who kissed him, fairly well; his grandmother, Angela Nixon, had worked as a maid for the Suttons for many years. "She tried to kiss David," Thompson remembered, "but I don't think David played. I know she kissed a white boy right in front of me and she kissed me."[10]

It is impossible to unravel precisely what took place among children playing in a deserted ditch on an autumn afternoon several decades distant. Memories falter, especially where childhood traumas intrude. Virtually all contemporary accounts—white and black, official and unofficial—shifted and shuffled "the facts" in reaction to a racially charged and politically perilous atmosphere. Both the defenders of the boys and the protectors of white supremacy in North Carolina launched massive public relations campaigns around the case.[11] Volatile reactions among their elders, too, probably shaped the accounts of all of the children. "As for the boys," reported George Weissman, who interviewed them soon afterward, "it was clear to us, when we saw them, that they felt from what had happened that they were caught up in some monstrous crime."[12]

Rarely has an event so small opened a window so large onto the life of a place and a people. The view from that window supports Gunnar Myrdal's 1944 observation that sex was "the principle around which the whole structure of segregation of the Negroes . . . [was] organized."[13] Sexuality, like violence, served as both pillar and signpost of the Southern social order. That order permitted white men in the South, by virtue of their position atop the caste system of race and gender, to take their liberties with black women, while black men and white women remained absolutely off-limits to one another; the much-traveled sexual backroad between the races was clearly marked "one-way."[14] Though black women were the most frequent victims of this bizarre arrangement, black men who dared to defy the code—and even a careless inflection of voice in addressing a white woman could constitute a violation—did so at the risk of death.

The murder of fourteen-year-old Emmett Till, butchered in Mississippi in 1955 for flirting with a white woman, drew the racial and sexual boundaries of the Jim Crow South in blood for the world to see. The sexual dynamic was not merely racial but signaled the whole shape of social power in the society. No black man could safely protect "his" women from any white man, while the black male who ventured across the color line represented not merely a threat to a particular white man but to white supremacy generally—and was likely to be dealt with as such.

At the same time, a legal system controlled by white men winked at sexual assaults on black women by men both black and white, since these attacks posed no threat to—indeed, they expressed and strengthened—the racial and sexual caste system of which they were a part.[15] "The rhetoric of protection—like the rape of black women," Jacquelyn Dowd Hall argues, "reflected a power struggle among men." Patriarchal control over women constituted an important part of the equation. "As absolutely inaccessible sexual property," states Hall, "white women became the most potent symbol of white male supremacy."[16] One fundamental truth shines through all accounts of the Monroe "kissing case," however seething or partisan: relations between black and white citizens in North Carolina were such that a single kiss between small children, stolen or shared across the color line, could cause the earth to tremble.

It was hardly unusual in the small towns of the segregated South for little children of both races to play together. The African American women who fried the chicken and tended the children in the homes of white families often brought their own little ones along, and games of cowboys-and-Indians or kick-the-can made for a certain sandlot equality. Though the residential sections of Monroe were segregated, black and white neighborhoods bordered one another, and children walked freely from one to the next, meeting, talking, and playing together. Only with the approach of puberty, when the natural openness and sensuality of children became freighted with sexual power, did such games pose a threat to the prevailing social order. "The racist," wrote Southern poet and essayist Wendell Berry, "fears that a child's honesty empowered by sex might turn in real and open affection toward members of the oppressed race, and so destroy the myth of that race's inferiority."[17]

The parents of Sissy Sutton heard about the kissing incident almost accidentally. Sissy's mother was only half-listening to the child later that same afternoon when she realized that what she had heard was not idle chatter but something that actually had happened to her daughter. Failing in her effort to restrain her emotions, Mrs. Sutton pressed the girl for details. When she heard that Sissy had kissed a black boy, "I was furious," she said. "I would have killed Hanover myself if I had the chance."[18] The parents of all three girls, according to the *Charlotte Observer*, were "hysterical," and one of them called the police.

The critical question was whether the police or the Suttons would find the two boys first. By several accounts, Mr. Sutton "armed himself, gathered friends, and went looking for the boys." Neighbors claimed that several white people with shotguns had raced to the Thompson house at 703 South Parker Street and threatened not only to kill the boys but to lynch their mothers. Mrs. Sutton, who made several public threats to kill the boys, admitted that she had been to the Thompson home that day but claimed that her intention was only to order Evelyn Thompson to get out of town, not to attack her. "When I had gotten in that afternoon," Mrs. Thompson recalled three decades later, "These people—that family—had been to my house with guns and said they were going to kill me."[19]

City officials recognized a mob in the making. Six carloads of police arrived at the Thompson house to forestall trouble.[20] Late that afternoon, a squad car spotted the youngsters pulling a red wagon loaded with soft drink bottles down Franklin Avenue, oblivious to their peril. "Both cops jumped out with their guns drawn," Thompson recalled. "They snatched us up and handcuffed us and threw us in the car." One of the police officers slapped Hanover Thompson and said, "We'll teach you little niggers not to kiss white girls." The boys were terrified. "When we got to the jail," Thompson recounted, "they drug us out of the car. They threw us down and then started beating us. Body punches, hitting us hard in the chest and calling us all kind of names."[21] "They threw us in these holding cells," Thompson said, "and they talked about how they was going to hang us and lynch us." Evelyn Thompson learned of her son's arrest from a neighbor's child. "A girl came down later in the afternoon and told me I better go get my children," she recalled, "because [the police] were beating them unmercifully in the bottom of one of the jail cells downtown." J. Hampton Price, the local juvenile court judge, reported that police had detained the boys for their own good "due to the feeling in the case."[22]

If the judge perhaps gave the police too much credit, he made a solid point about the reaction among white citizens. "The mothers were so frightened," their attorney said, "that for several nights they dared not sleep in their own houses but hid with neighbors."[23] Gunmen in passing cars fired dozens of shots into the Thompson home, and hooded terrorists burned a wooden cross on their lawn. A family member found Hanover Thompson's dog shot to death in the front yard. Both mothers were fired from their jobs as housekeepers. Evelyn Thompson's landlord served her with eviction papers two days after the kissing incident. The clamor of angry crowds outside the Monroe jail kept the boys in terror for their lives. "The Klan was all outside, trying to get in the jail, demonstrations, torches at night," according to Hanover Thompson. "People was out there trying to get in there to kill us."[24]

Robert Williams first heard about the kissing case from Mayor Fred Wilson, who called to enlist his help and advice. By Williams's account, the mayor wanted to know what the NAACP leader would advise him to do and suggested that perhaps Williams could arrange for the boys to be quietly spirited away from Monroe.[25] Williams instead rushed to the homes of the boys and found Newtown in a state of siege. "The whole neighborhood had been so terrorized," he later told a reporter for the *New York Post*, "that many people were afraid to turn their lights on at night. Others, including the boys' mothers, had stayed away from their home at night for fear that they might be lynched." Williams, his army .45 strapped to his belt, was the most obvious local ally for the mothers, who had known him for years, though not well, and he became their adviser and advocate. One of his first actions was to place the Thompson and Simpson homes under armed guard by the men of the Monroe NAACP.[26]

Though it is unlikely that most whites would have supported outright violence against the boys, many sympathized with the virulent reaction of the Suttons. If they did not support the Suttons, at any rate, they left no record of their dissent in the matter. Not even J. Ray Shute or any of the other white members of the Human Relations Council made any public statement in support of the boys. Those "decent and respectable white people" who may have disagreed with the prevailing tone of outrage, it seemed to Louis Austin, "have either been silenced or are afraid to speak out and halt the reign of terror now going on in their community against

Negroes." This state of coerced consensus reflected the depth of uneasiness and fear that issues of interracial sexuality aroused among white Southerners during the 1950s.[27]

Not surprisingly, the racial politics of rape reflected and focused the extraordinary power of the sexual taboo. Not only did white Southerners generally regard murder as an appropriate response to suggestions of sexual interest in white women on the part of black men. They also seemed to believe, as W. J. Cash put it, "that any assertion of any kind on the part of the Negro constituted in a perfectly real manner an attack on the Southern [white] woman."[28] White politicians in the South had long used rape as the central metaphor for any hint at alteration of the region's racial hierarchy; the 1959 report of the U.S. Civil Rights Commission, Senator Strom Thurmond charged, was an attempt by "the federal government [to] further *rape* the rights of the states." The continuous outpouring of such metaphors during the 1948 "Dixiecrat" revolt led by Thurmond prompted this response from W. E. B Du Bois: "The rape which your gentlemen have done against helpless black women in defiance of your own laws is written on the foreheads of millions of mulattoes, and written in ineffaceable blood."[29]

The double standard that prevailed in questions of sexuality and sexual violence was the subject of a letter from a white woman to the *Charlotte Observer* in 1959. "Our whole attitude has been that the violation of a Negro woman, while not condoned, of course, is not on the same plane of iniquity as the ravishing of a white woman," the writer charged.[30] In fact, a black man accused of the rape of a white woman in the South during the period from 1930 to 1976 was eighteen times more likely to be executed than a black man charged with the rape of a woman of his own race. "From all appearances," Louis Austin wrote in 1959, "the death penalty for that crime in this state was made 'for Negroes only.' " This, of course, was quite apart from the lingering possibility that a white mob would preempt the jury.[31]

Perhaps it was unusual for African American children eight and ten years of age to evoke what W. J. Cash called "the Southern rape complex."[32] The memory of the Till murder three years earlier hovered over Monroe, with hostile reporters quick to accuse Robert Williams of trying "to make another Emmett Till case out of this incident." One of Governor Hodges's advisers in the case privately remarked to the governor that "if Till had not made a pass at a white woman he would be alive today."[33] Still, the four-year age difference between Emmett Till and Hanover Thompson seemed to matter; a white woman from Greensboro who wrote to Governor Hodges on Christmas Eve to protest the cruelty of incarcerating the two boys over the holidays acknowledged that "if the boys were over twelve it would be a different story."[34] White sexual fears carry considerable weight in explaining the fierce reaction of white citizens to the kissing case. But the most immediate context for white sexual paranoia was the prospect of public school desegregation.

Governor Hodges hurried to the front of the movement to resist the *Brown* decision, partly by invoking the terrors of miscegenation.[35] This tactic was quite successful, resonating with the concerns of white citizens across the state. "What the white man fears and what the white man is fighting to prevent at any cost," one of the governor's editorial supporters wrote in 1955, "is the destruction of the purity of his race. He believes that integration would lead to miscegenation and there is some basis for his fears."[36] Many whites assumed that "race-mixing" in schools would lead to rampant interracial sexual activity and that the "death" of the white race might be inevitable. Mainstream conservative James J. Kilpatrick, whose national influence would persist well into the Ronald Reagan era, declared that white Southerners had every right "to preserve the predominately racial characteristics that have contributed to Western civilization over the past two thousand years." The *National Review* backed Kilpatrick, arguing that the white race was "entitled to take such measures as are necessary to prevail, politically and culturally, in areas where it does not predominate numerically." The murderers of Emmett Till could not have said it better.[37] "We can talk about it all we want to—justice, equality, all that sort of thing, talking," said one white man from western North Carolina, "but when we come right down to it, that's what it's all about: a nigger a-marrying your sister or your daughter."[38] James Baldwin, a shrewd observer of the dynamics at work, offered a timeless retort to this brand of muddled racial thinking. "You're not worried about me marrying *your* daughter," the black writer told a white segregationist who raised the matter of intermarriage. "You're worried about me marrying *your wife's* daughter. I've been marrying *your* daughter since the days of slavery."[39]

On October 17, 1958—less than two weeks before the kissing incident occurred—Robert and Mabel Williams had petitioned the local school board to transfer their sons to all-white East Elementary School, "now designated as a white school and excluding Negroes solely on racial grounds contrary to recent Supreme Court decisions and Amendment XIV of the United States Constitution," they wrote. The all-white school board intimidated black teachers, the Williams family charged, "to the extent that the American idea of intellectual freedom is a farce" in Union County. Black teachers held in racial subordination by white authorities "become agents of inferiority complexes, white supremacy, undemocratic and un-American traits." Their children, the Williamses insisted to the school board, were "not being properly educated for life in a democracy based upon the proposition that all men are created equal and that wholesome convictions of freedom are worth fighting for."

The Monroe Enquirer printed the entire text of the Williams family's letter to the school board.[40] No African American students had ever attempted to attend a white school in Monroe before the Williamses made their petition. White citizens in Monroe panicked at this challenge to racial etiquette, at least in part because of the sexual fears that accompanied their vision of where desegregation would lead. "If [black children] get into our rural schools and ride the buses with our white children," one woman wrote, "the Monroe 'kissing' incident is only a start of what we will have."[41]

In Monroe, opening white schools to black children was not even a matter for discussion. But there remained the question of what to do with the two small boys held in the basement of the Monroe jail. Chief of Police Mauney, Judge Price, and Mayor Wilson debated the matter, keeping Hanover Thompson and Fuzzy Simpson behind bars for the next six days without so much as a hearing. The authorities did not permit the boys to see parents, friends, or attorneys during this period. According to Thompson, jailers cruelly terrorized the youngsters. "Them people just beat us like they wanted to," he winced decades later. "They were trying to intimidate us by telling us the KKK was coming to kill us. They called us niggers, rapists, all kinds of names."[42]

The worst moment came on October 31 when white men draped in sheets stomped down the stairs into the basement cellblock. The two boys were convinced that the Ku Klux Klan had broken into the jail to lynch them. They knew little about the Klan, but they knew enough to be terrified. "I knew that they wore sheets over their head," Thompson recalled. "That they hated people. That they killed people." The boys screamed in horror. "We thought we was dead," said Thompson. "We thought we was going to die." The hooded men roared into a fit of laughter and shook off their sheets to reveal police uniforms. It had been their idea of a hilarious Halloween joke. More than thirty years later, the memory of that childhood terror still brought tears to Thompson's eyes.[43]

Police officials told Mrs. Thompson, Mrs. Simpson, and the local NAACP leadership that Fuzzy and Hanover were being held only for their protection and that there would be no charges against them. This was necessary, Judge Price repeated, "because of strong race tension resulting from the incident."[44] But not all observers agreed that the men who held these eight- and ten-year-old boys prisoner were preoccupied with their welfare. Indeed, since a local grand jury had only recently ruled that the Union County jail was "far below the standard" and had "no facilities to isolate delinquents from regular criminals, white or colored," it is easy to understand why the African American community concluded that the authorities did not care what evils might befall the children.[45] "It takes no sage to determine how much help a juvenile judge would be to two little Negro boys to whom he referred to twice in his testimony as 'niggers,'" Louis Austin snarled in the pages of the Carolina Times. "When [Judge Price] slammed them in jail and held them there for six days, he was giving them exactly the kind of help he felt they should have."[46]

On November 4, 1958, six days after taking the boys into custody, local authorities finally held a hearing, ostensibly to decide what would be done with Hanover Thompson and Fuzzy Simpson. Judge Price, however, had made his decision well in advance of the proceedings. As soon as the boys had been jailed, Price wrote to Blaine M. Madison, commissioner of the State Board of Corrections and Training, to ask whether the Morrison Training School in Hoffman could admit the two boys. When Madison replied that Morrison would take the boys as "emergency cases," the jurist immediately called a hearing. For Judge Price, the court session represented not an opportunity to hear the boys but simply an occasion to announce their punishment.[47]

"There were really two hearings," wrote Chester Davis, a reporter notably hostile to the two boys. "At 2 P.M. on Nov. 4 Judge Price heard the white girls and their parents. At 4 P.M. in the absence of any white parties to the case, he met with the two boys and their mothers."[48] According to Evelyn Thompson and Jennie Simpson, the judge twice referred to their sons as "niggers." Price claimed that the hearings had been "separate but equal."[49] The boys were not permitted legal counsel. The judge also barred Robert Williams from the courtroom. Nor were the boys allowed to confront their accuser; Sissy Sutton "wasn't even in court to identify them or give any testimony against them," said Williams. White defenders of the proceedings later argued that the mothers of the boys had not requested counsel, but another local woman "personally well acquainted with the parties concerned" explained to Governor Hodges that "the boys *were* refused counsel of law."[50]

Commissioner Madison argued that neither of the boys had been "held as a 'criminal' nor [was] the proceeding deemed a 'criminal prosecution or conviction.'" Other state officials, including the governor, attempted to persuade critics that the boys "as juveniles were not even convicted of a crime, under North Carolina law," and therefore did not require the legal rights generally extended to other defendants.[51]

But a written statement sent to Governor Hodges by J. Hampton Price on November 30 stated plainly that the boys "were tried for assault on three charges of assault and molesting three white girls."[52] On November 4, Price sentenced Hanover Thompson and Fuzzy Simpson to indeterminate terms in the Morrison Training School for Negroes in Hoffman, North Carolina. If they behaved well, Price told the boys, they might be released before they were twenty-one.[53]

On October 21, two weeks earlier, in Raleigh, the North Carolina Supreme Court had finally rejected Dr. Perry's last appeal and ordered the physician's imprisonment on charges of what the newspapers invariably called "criminal abortion on a white woman." On the night of the decision, Perry received a call from B. J. Winfield, a black sharecropper who lived in a rural area of Union County. For several years Winfield's daughter had suffered from chronic convulsions. Though Winfield could scarcely afford medical care, Perry had always accepted a sheaf of collard greens, a sack of sweet potatoes, or a jar of homemade honey in payment.

"He would speak for the poor black folks," Winfield said, "and it caused us to love him. You couldn't help but have love for a man like that." Hearing that the physician had been sentenced to five years in prison, Winfield rather bashfully asked Perry if he had any advice about diet or home remedies for his daughter. Perry insisted on driving far out into the darkened countryside to deliver some pills and dispense instructions. Afterward, as Perry left the house and made his way slowly through the darkness toward his automobile, the sharecropper could hear his soft voice wafting up the driveway: "Sometimes I feel like a motherless child / A long way from home." Winfield said later, "I couldn't keep from crying." When Dr. Perry got home, the state police were waiting to take him to prison.[54]

A week after J. Hampton Price suggested that the kissing case boys might well spend the rest of their childhoods in reform school, Judge J. Will Pless Jr. squinted out across a crowded courtroom some twenty-five miles from Monroe. "It's no crime to kiss a pretty girl," he declared. But he was not referring to the "crime" that Fuzzy Simpson and Hanover Thompson had committed. The pretty girl to whom the judge referred was a fifteen-year-old white girl who had been housed in the Gastonia jail as a delinquent. On at least one night during the girl's confinement, two white male adult prisoners slipped her a Coca-Cola bottle filled with moonshine whiskey smuggled into the facility by a trusty. The jailer then permitted the two men, both in their late twenties, to linger in her cell and, in her words, "romance" the young girl. The Raleigh News and Observer said rather lightly that the trio had "engaged in a little lovemaking."

When authorities got wind of these cellblock shenanigans, a local court convicted the male inmates of contributing to the delinquency of a minor. When the prisoners appealed the cases, however, Judge Pless did not weigh their sins so heavily. "If this court holds that a boy can't kiss a pretty girl," he grinned at the courtroom crowd, "I don't know what will happen to this country."[1]

Whatever acts were committed in that cell, whether consensual or coerced, lighthearted or sadistic, this case of kissing failed to ignite the fiery Christian sentiments of the Ku Klux Klan. If anyone suggested that the two men should be dragged from their jail cells and hanged from the highest tree in the county, the threat went unrecorded. Kisses stolen or exchanged in that cell posed no threat to a popular Southern governor's plausible national ambitions. This kissing case built no national reputations and aroused no global controversies. Neither the president of the United States nor the State Department expressed any concern that these kisses might undermine the foreign policy of the nation, nor did any of the lips involved smile from the pages of *Pravda*. But all of these things could have happened if the complexions of the two men in the young woman's jail cell had been darker. In the Monroe kissing case, all these things and more would come to pass. Such was the defining power of race in the United States in 1958.

From the outset, domestic racial politics had been a tiresome liability for the United States in its postwar struggle with the Soviet Union. The activists of the black freedom movement wielded these Cold War contradictions as weapons in their own struggle for democracy. God was not merely the God of love, Martin Luther King Jr. told the congregation at Holt Street Baptist Church on December 1, 1955, in his first public speech of the Montgomery Bus Boycott. "He's also the God that standeth before the nations and says, 'Be still and know that I am God—and if you don't obey Me I'm gonna break the backbone of your power—and cast you out of the arms of your national and international relationships.' " King reminded the growing movement that it was not enough to use love and "the tools of persuasion, but we've got to use the tools of coercion."[2]

King's forceful reference to the political fulcrum offered by the Cold War foreshadowed his overarching strategy for the black freedom movement. The strategy was not only King's, of course, but one that Robert Williams and most other leaders of the movement sought to employ in various ways. King elaborated on these dynamics seven years after Montgomery during the early 1963 planning sessions for the Birmingham campaign of the Southern Christian Leadership Conference (SCLC). "If [violence] comes," King observed, then "we will surface it for the world to see."[3] When the dogs and fire hoses directed by Public Safety Commissioner Eugene "Bull" Connor accommodated King's strategy, that is precisely what happened. Birmingham became the most triumphant campaign of the movement, and as the organizers celebrated their success, King unfurled his strategic vision for them. "The United States is concerned about its image," King told the throng at St. John's Church in Birmingham. "Mr. Kennedy is battling for the minds and the hearts of men in Asia and Africa, and they aren't gonna respect the United States of America if she deprives men and women of the basic rights of life because of the color of their skin."[4] It remains one of the enduring ironies of the movement that violence was so critical to the success of nonviolence.

Equally ironic was the fact that the threat posed by Communist totalitarianism finally afforded African Americans the political leverage to extract legal equality in the land of the free. Few African American activists grasped those dynamics more clearly or wielded them more skillfully than Robert Williams. By unveiling embarrassing American realities for an international audience—thus threatening to undermine the foreign policy goals of the United States at a critical moment—black Southerners forced reluctant federal authorities to intervene on their behalf. It was the power of international politics—first World War II but more decisively the Cold War—that shattered the Compromise of 1877, in which Northern Republicans and Southern Democrats had agreed to let the white South have its way on questions of race. During the decades after World War II, black Southerners found a strange, unpredictable, but potent ally in the anticommunist fevers that wracked America. "Because of the international situation," Williams explained, "the Federal government does not want racial incidents which draw the attention of the world to the situation in the South." The Cold War could make even a small place loom large for a moment in history.[5]

It was true, of course, that the defenders of the racial hierarchy in the South mixed a vicious pigment of anticommunism and white supremacy in order to smear most efforts at reform as part of a crimson conspiracy controlled from Moscow. Across the nation, anticommunism narrowed the political spectrum and subjected racial reformers in particular to charges of subversion and disloyalty.[6] The postwar red scare not only perpetrated grave injustices; it chased away many potential white allies of African American freedom movements across the country. In the Cold War world, however, overt white supremacy became an increasingly unaffordable embarrassment for the federal government.

For Governor Hodges, the kissing case not only embarrassed the nation but threatened to wreck his personal political agenda. The governor, one editor observed, "was greatly upset by the incident and the unfavorable world-wide publicity it gave Monroe and the state of North Carolina."[7] Hodges's family ties to Monroe made the notoriety of the case more galling. The governor's wife, Martha Blakeney Hodges, hailed from a prominent Monroe family, and their son, Luther Hodges Jr., had recently married a young woman from Monroe. The wedding, which took place at Monroe's First Baptist Church, was the biggest social event of 1958 for the town's white upper crust.[8]

A former textile executive, Hodges had entered politics in 1952 when he surprised political insiders by winning the lieutenant governorship. Acceding to the governor's mansion with the death of William Umstead in 1954, Hodges promoted his image as a New South governor by stressing racial moderation and economic expansion. "Industrialization, then, with all its advantages to the people and to the state, became the number one goal of my administration," Hodges wrote later.[9] Vermont Royster of the *Wall Street Journal* called Hodges "one of the best salesmen from the South that I have seen in a long time." The Raleigh-born editor admired Hodges for his energy and polish and observed that Hodges "looks good—like a governor ought to look."[10]

Hodges looked good to Northern Democrats in part because many feared another Dixiecrat bolt in the 1960 presidential campaign. One national columnist predicted that a regional clash among Democrats was "as inevitable as the nomination of Richard Nixon by the Republicans" and that "the result will likely be a bigger split than in 1948." More than a few Southern Democrats agreed that the national party had fallen into the hands of "Communists, communist sympathizers, and hypocritical do-gooders," in the words of one South Carolina official.[11]

Roughly half of the white Democrats in the South favored the formation of a second states' rights party should the national party nominate an integrationist in 1960.[12] At the same time, a significant shift of black ballots from the Democrats to the Republicans in 1956 gave the race question unprecedented political urgency for 1960.[13] Paul Butler, national chair of the Democratic Party, stated flatly in 1958 that party members opposed to a strong civil rights plank in the 1960 platform "are going to have to take political asylum where they can find it, either in the Republican Party or a third party." He made clear his view that any Democrat from below the Potomac "cannot, or should not, or will not be nominated for the Presidency." Senator Richard Russell of Georgia fired back that "this gang of phony liberals and party-wreckers have publicly advocated driving the South from the house of its fathers."[14]

To a national Democratic Party wracked by regional clashes over race, Hodges represented a new face with instant appeal. A talented New Southerner, moderate on questions of race, acceptable to Northern liberals, and attractive to business elements, he had played a critical diplomatic role at the 1956 national Democratic convention. By 1958, insiders routinely mentioned Hodges as a vice-presidential prospect. Both perennial aspirant Adlai Stevenson and front-runner John Kennedy touted Hodges's talent and sought the governor's endorsement, though Hodges first backed Lyndon Johnson for the 1960 presidential nomination. Senator Kennedy met with Hodges on January 15, 1959, in Charlotte and told reporters that Hodges was "held in high esteem all over the country" and "should add distinction to any Democratic ticket." In theory Hodges could provide both regional and ideological balance to a ticket topped by a Northeastern liberal without alienating key Northern constituencies.[15]

Though governor of a state whose tradition of anti-Catholic sentiment suggested rough sledding for a Kennedy ticket, Hodges not only would carry North Carolina into the Democratic column in 1960 but would stand among Kennedy's most effective Southern supporters. His efforts would be repaid with a post as secretary of commerce in the Kennedy administration.[16] Like Lyndon Johnson, the eventual vice-presidential nominee, Hodges was an ambitious and gifted Southerner whose national aspirations depended on his ability to step beyond the racial politics of his region.[17]

Dubbed an industrial pied piper by his promoters, Hodges crisscrossed the nation vaunting North Carolina's economic potential. His pitch for North Carolina featured minimal corporate tax rates, the lowest manufacturing wages in the nation, antiunion "right-to-work" laws, and the Research Triangle, which provided land and funds for industrial research in an area convenient to the University of North Carolina in Chapel Hill, North Carolina State University in Raleigh, and Duke University in Durham.[18] Hodges succeeded in drawing almost three hundred new factories to North Carolina between 1956 and 1958, nearly a quarter of the total new industrial plants created across the South during that period. Wages in the state, however, remained in the national cellar, and half of the state's industrial base remained concentrated in ten of its one hundred counties.[19]

Hodges nonetheless called his industrial development program "the North Carolina miracle" and linked its success to the state's progressive outlook on education and race relations. To white Southerners, Hodges touted his moderate racial policies in pragmatic segregationist terms; he criticized demagogues such as Orval Faubus and rejected the politics of "massive resistance," arguing that "the North Carolina way" offered a much more effective safeguard for segregation.[20]

The keystone of Hodges's national ambitions was his image as a moderate on questions of race. "To Luther Hodges," said a feature story in *Reader's Digest*, "the South's great tragedy is that it spends so much precious energy on racial issues." Nationally syndicated columnist Walter Winchell declared that Hodges was "blazing a bright new path through the forests of bigotry and ignorance."[21] The U.S. Information Agency (USIA) employed Hodges in its efforts to portray the country as racially progressive for audiences abroad. In a radio broadcast for the Voice of America in 1957, Hodges compared "our Negroes" to the "Laplanders" in the Scandinavian countries, noting that in each case "they are not educated and they do not have them in government." The proper tone was one of firm but generous paternal authority. The main obstacle to racial equality, as Hodges congenially described it, was that black Americans were ill prepared for citizenship. "If you have it in your heart to be good to people," Hodges explained, "you will bring them along as fast as they can take it." White Southerners, in his view, were the appropriate judges of when African Americans ought to regain the citizenship that had been taken from them after Reconstruction. "I feel that a great majority of the Southern people feel as I do," Hodges explained, "that although their personal feeling may be one thing, they want to obey the law. They want to see our Negroes come along rapidly."[22]

Hodges was not a venomous white supremacist in the mold of Governor George Wallace of Alabama or Senator James Eastland of Mississippi. He assumed, however, that black citizens should gratefully accept white leadership, and he demanded racial deference in return for his paternal generosity. One incident from 1955 reveals the limitations that Hodges brought to the racial crisis of the 1950s. Dedicating a new building at North Carolina A&T, a predominantly black institution in Greensboro, Hodges began to mispronounce the word "Negro" as "nigra." Offended, the students increasingly began to scrape their feet and cough until the governor, baffled but furious, was forced to stop his speech and ask whether he should continue. To a cringing letter of apology from A&T president F. D. Bluford, Hodges responded with one terse sentence: "I hereby acknowledge receipt of your communication of November 5 regarding the unfortunate incident at A&T College." Furious, Hodges then scrawled the following instruction to his secretary: "Maggie: Do not ack.[nowledge] letters from Negro students at A&T or *any other Negroes*." Hodges wrote to a friend that "I am through making speeches to colored people, certainly for the time being." His unspoken assumption throughout the stack of correspondence about this trifling incident was that the undifferentiated mass of African Americans in North Carolina was at fault for the lack of deference shown him by a handful of young people—an unimportant incident sparked by his own insensitivity.[23]

Despite his blindness with respect to African Americans themselves,

Governor Hodges was brilliant when it came to playing the politics of race. Trading on what historian William H. Chafe calls North Carolina's "progressive mystique," Hodges displayed a political range that permitted him to sing a duet of "Dixie" with Arkansas firebrand Orval Faubus in one breath and to denounce "extremists" in the next.[24] Coupled with his relentless pursuit of industrial expansion, Hodges's ability to define the political terrain on matters of race gave him a bright future. When headlines about the Monroe kissing case suddenly appeared on the front pages of newspapers all over the world in 1958, putting North Carolina in the unflattering glare of the spotlight, Luther Hodges had a great deal to lose.

The year before, *Business Week* had observed that Governor Hodges brought to the job "a sure-handed knowledge of public relations, especially in terms of gauging the public's reaction to a situation."[25] In the kissing case, however, this "businessman in the state house," as Hodges portrayed himself, was outdone by a poor black man twenty years his junior who had never held a white-collar job: Robert Williams.

Though Williams lacked Hodges's personal polish and public office, he had a less challenging audience; he was playing only to local black folks in Monroe, white liberals outside the South, and anti-American protesters around the world, all of whom were predisposed to accept his version of events. The governor was hobbled by the necessity of playing to two galleries at once—white voters in North Carolina and observers in the larger world—who tended to have different reactions to the case. The bare facts, too, were a comfort to Williams in a way that they could not be for Hodges; the state had, in fact, locked up two small children for the crime of a kiss, and official explanations rang hollow. By the time the governor could respond, Williams had set in motion what *Time* magazine would call a "rolling snowball" of worldwide publicity. "The kissing case, of course," a key Williams ally observed years later, "that was the case that got him in national and international attention."[26]

The first tremor of the eventual avalanche originated not with Williams but with Hanover Thompson's mother. Evelyn Thompson wrote to her daughter, Mary Lou Thompson, in Brooklyn, New York, to report that Hanover had been arrested for kissing a white child. Mary Lou Thompson sought advice on her brother's predicament from Larry J. Foster, an African American political leader in Brooklyn. Foster contacted Ted Poston, a heralded black writer for the *New York Post*. Poston called Harry Golden in Charlotte and Williams in Monroe to gather information. On November 3 the reporter published a hard-hitting front-page story in the *New York Post* on the kissing case, following up with another story on November 10.[27]

White officials in Monroe complained that Poston's story was "exaggerated and distorted" and, in a reference to Williams and his friends, "typical of the fulminations of one or more persons whose apparent aim is to inflame and engender racial discord in a peaceful community." A hostile white reporter, working hand-in-glove with the governor's office, criticized the Poston story as "a sob-sister sort of report that emphasized the kissing incident and overlooked the record of previous delinquency and the home background of the boys."[28]

Such reports hardly did justice to the realities of the situation. Monroe could scarcely be described as peaceful with Klan caravans rumbling through the streets, nor was it necessary for Williams or anybody else to engender racial discord under the circumstances. Whatever record of previous delinquency and home background—which remained matters of dispute—may have pertained, it was clear that the threatening aspects of the case had little to do with youthful mischief or family problems.[29] Even so, critics of the *New York Post*'s coverage of the kissing case had a point; Poston's story reflected the remarkable ability of Williams to shape press accounts for his own political ends.

As president of the Monroe branch of the NAACP, Williams turned first to his own organization to seek the release of the boys. Local members, loyal to Williams and politically mobilized and personally concerned about the children of their neighbors, stood eager to act. But at the state and national level, the NAACP effort faltered throughout November and December.

The head of the North Carolina chapter, Kelly Alexander, a conservative funeral home director from Charlotte, did not count himself among Williams's admirers. The fact that this was a "sex case," too, carried a special set of political risks. The NAACP had consistently distanced itself from issues of interracial sexuality, knowing that the deep-rooted taboo fueled white resistance to its goals. Alexander "said it would be better to leave it alone," Williams recalled, "they didn't want to get involved in it."[30]

The Reverend Reginald Hawkins, a Charlotte NAACP activist close to Alexander, explained years later, "You have got to understand the NAACP. It was a bourgeois organization. It did not want to deal with the underclass and such."[31] Williams contacted Roy Wilkins, executive secretary of the NAACP, who also declined to get involved. Larry Foster, active in the Brooklyn NAACP, followed up with Wilkins but found him completely uninterested. John Morsell of the national office tried to shift the blame onto Alexander, citing "failures of omission on the part of our state organization."[32]

Despite the initial failure of either the state or the national NAACP to assist his efforts, the branch president in Monroe became a determined one-man press office for the cause of freeing the Monroe boys. Throwing all of his energies into the campaign, Robert Williams issued press releases, called the television networks, hounded the national wire services, and sent yet another angry telegram to President Eisenhower. Though at first he had little success—the early November stories in the *New York Post* remained his central achievements for several weeks—Williams managed to sustain a slow trickle of newspaper coverage.

Uneasy state NAACP officials soon arrived in Monroe to suggest that perhaps the boys could be released quietly by clandestine contacts with Hodges via Harry Golden, who happened to be both an NAACP member and a friend to the governor. "Kelly [Alexander] and I went over because of the notoriety in the case. We met Rob and Dr. Perry and McDow and several other citizens," Hawkins recalled. "It wasn't until it broke national news that we got involved," Hawkins continued. "You have to understand, Kelly was taking his orders from Roy Wilkins. We had to get sanction from the national NAACP to get involved." Williams not only rejected as naive the notion that this back-channel approach might work; he also argued that it was unethical, since a private settlement would abandon the issues of racial injustice that gave the case its importance. The early days of the controversy witnessed the first wrangles of what would prove to be an extremely difficult relationship between the central office of the NAACP and the president of its Monroe chapter.[33]

Williams was hardly alone in his difficulties with the national NAACP. From the earliest days of the postwar freedom movement, some Southern black NAACP leaders wanted to move faster than the national office. This created uneasiness and antagonism between the Northern-based national office and its nearly all-black Southern branches.[34] The national office, though distant from the South, regarded itself as perfectly qualified to dictate political tactics and disregard local problems. Though it soon became commonplace to describe the NAACP as an overly cautious, politically conservative organization, it is important to distinguish between the local branches, which were the wellspring of many grassroots insurgencies, and the somewhat staid national office.

Many movement leaders across the region found it necessary to create independent local organizations to mobilize their constituencies and move beyond the narrow, bureaucratic orientation of the national NAACP. In Montgomery, E. D. Nixon ruled the local NAACP, but he and his allies founded the Montgomery Improvement Association rather than run the bus boycott through the NAACP. In Tallahassee, the Reverend C. K. Steele, president of the local NAACP, organized the Inter-Civic Council for that city's Montgomery-inspired bus boycott in 1956. Ironically, the NAACP was both too conservative and too controversial, since white supremacists had succeeded in firmly nailing the words "Communist-inspired" in front of "NAACP" in the minds of many white Southerners. In Birmingham, for example, the Alabama Christian Movement for Human Rights was born because state authorities virtually outlawed the state NAACP as an organization. The independent new protest organizations attracted large numbers of black Southerners, in part because they gave their members roles in decision making and local action.[35] In Monroe, Williams and his allies persisted as a chapter of the NAACP, but in late 1958 they decided to pursue the kissing case under the aegis of the Committee to Combat Racial Injustice (CCRI).

The controversial nature of the kissing case and the cautious style of the national office of the NAACP made the CCRI necessary for black activists in Monroe. In a certain sense, however, the CCRI was not simply another local organization like the Montgomery Improvement Association. Instead it was in part a front for the SWP a thousand miles north of Monroe in New York City. The SWP was a small Trotskyite organization with several hundred members. The history of the SWP and the CCRI presents a lesson in both the achievements and the limitations of the American left with respect to race. Founded in 1938 as a Trotskyite splinter group from the Communist Party USA, the SWP spent a decade underestimating the centrality of race in American politics. Like the rest of the Old Left, the SWP viewed white supremacy as a tragic symptom of the class struggle, a symptom that would disappear with the triumph of the working class. The SWP exhibited such a "canned, doctrinaire approach," one black socialist wrote, that it "appealed only to the mesmerized faithful." Under the intermittent influence of West Indian intellectual C. L. R. James, however, in the late 1940s the SWP began to envision that proponents of socialism and of black liberation might help one another to succeed as equal partners.[36]

In 1956 another African American member of the SWP, Claude De-Bruce, took up where James left off with an essay, "On the Negro Question," that attacked white Marxists for continuing to subordinate the black struggle to the class struggle and for their failures in "recruitment of Negroes into the party." The NAACP, DeBruce argued, was the appropriate "Negro organ of struggle," marred only by the fact that its national leadership represented "a privileged caste whose material interest is tied to the capitalist class, in spite of their contradiction of being discriminated against because they are Negroes." The NAACP should not be abandoned, however, DeBruce argued, but transformed from within so that it could "project a program in the interest of the mass of Negroes."[37] The 1957 convention of the SWP not only affirmed DeBruce's views but proclaimed the need for an independent African American political leadership—preferably one that also had ties to the NAACP—"to determine the program" for themselves and "to make it theirs."[38] Thus when Williams emerged from the black South in 1958, the SWP furnished a network of seasoned activists who stood poised to assist him on his own terms, an arrangement that suited the independent-minded Williams very well. If the CCRI was in some sense a front, it would be closer to the truth to say that the committee gave Williams free access to a small but energetic network of activists outside Monroe.

After the Poston story on the kissing case appeared in the *New York Post*, Conrad Lynn called Williams from New York City and offered to help with the case. A veteran activist and lawyer for the Emergency Civil Liberties Union, Lynn had faced white mobs in North Carolina during the 1947 Journey of Reconciliation, when pacifists from the Fellowship of Reconciliation and CORE rode into the South on buses to test the Supreme Court's 1946 *Morgan v. Virginia* ruling that segregation laws could not interfere with interstate travel.[39] Lynn's legal acumen, political savvy, and oratorical power would become long-standing assets to Robert Williams. In the immediate sense, however, his contacts with the SWP proved most useful.

Lynn arrived in Monroe on November 4, 1958, accompanied by George Weissman, an SWP activist who had contracted with the *Nation* to write a story on the kissing case. Weissman also wanted to meet Robert Williams to weigh the possibility that here might be the independent Southern black leadership that the party envisioned. "As soon as we reached Monroe, before I contacted anyone else," Lynn recalled, "I made an appointment with Juvenile Court Judge Hampton Price." This meeting took place in Price's office, Lynn said, "a cramped cubicle that smelled of mothballs and featured a Confederate flag." According to Lynn, Price explained that he had held "separate but equal hearings," first meeting with the white parents and children and that afterwards he had "summoned the two

nigger mothers and had the children brought up from the county jail."
Politely but firmly, Lynn recounted, Judge Price declined to alter the sentences and "advised me to go back to New York and stop interfering with local affairs."[40]

White conservatives habitually blamed outside interference for any evidence of racial dissent, but even in Monroe there was no solid wall of white consensus. Though most white dissidents remained silent, even in the face of absurd cruelties such as those presented by the kissing case, one local white woman wrote to Governor Hodges and spoke with passion and candor: "I live among these people, visit in their homes and go to the same clubs with them." Many white women in Monroe, she claimed, objected to what had happened to the children. "I know at least a dozen mothers and housewives like myself, who live within three blocks of me. We are all seething with indignation and protest," she wrote, "against these outrages that occur." Monroe had become "a hornet's nest of hate" and a "haven for the KKK," she claimed, due to "a small group of white people" who seek to "prove their superiority by trying to punish every negro they come in contact with." In this case, she continued, "their drastic mistake was when they started to pick on little children—that decent people will never stand for, regardless of color." She closed her letter with a challenge: "Do you have enough courage to handle this town?" Her own answer, however, was not a resounding affirmative; the woman appears not to have signed her real name.[41]

Not surprisingly, then, "outside agitators" such as Lynn played a significant role in Monroe, though the movement drew its fundamental strength from local black traditions of struggle. After meeting the mothers of the two boys, Lynn took Weissman to visit Hanover Thompson and Fuzzy Simpson at the reformatory in Hoffman. The two men were "the first persons to do so—since their arrest their mothers saw them only at the trial and not privately—and we got their side of the story," Weissman wrote to E. D. Nixon.[42]

On November 12, Lynn returned to Monroe to represent Evelyn Thompson in an eviction proceeding.[43] Strolling from Boyte Street to the hearing with a crowd of black people, Lynn realized that African Americans in Monroe walked in the street rather than on the sidewalk. It was part of the unspoken racial etiquette of segregation that blacks kept the sidewalks clear for white people. "There was no law against it," Lynn wrote later. "Walking in the street was simply part of their heritage, a heritage they never questioned."[44]

What happened in the courthouse defied the folkways of racial deference. "The NAACP officers, the mother, a delegation of Negro citizens
crowded the Justice of the Peace's office," Weissman wrote to the Reverend C. K. Steele in Tallahassee. "Lynn showed that the eviction order was
grossly defective from a legalistic point of view. The Justice of the Peace
hemmed and hawed, telephoned, and finally threw the conviction out.
This small victory was a great morale builder."[45] According to the attorney,
he and Robert Williams led the happy throng onto the sidewalk as they
walked back to Newtown. "An old black woman came forward, her eyes
agleam with defiance," in Lynn's account of the scene. "They came in
two's and three's, and finally all of them were on the sidewalk. By the time
we reached Williams's home on Boyte Street we were singing the stirring
words of a Negro spiritual."[46] The concrete sidewalk still became a dirt
path when they reached the black community, of course, but the old song
beckoned them toward a new day in Monroe.

On December 11 the *Monroe Enquirer* noted that "several new faces
were in town yesterday, investigating and checking recent happenings in
Union County." These included "Conrad J. Lynn, Negro attorney from
New York City," and "*The Nation*'s reporter Weissman." Robert Williams,
John McDow, and Dr. Albert Perry "were overjoyed by our coming down to
Monroe and our offer to organize some help," Weissman wrote from
Monroe. "They have been fighting the whole thing on their own and
Williams confided that they were beginning to get the feeling that they
were about at the end of their rope."[47]

Williams was not bound for the end of his rope or anyone else's, but he
was delighted to accept help from the SWP. He had no interest, however,
in easing the party's recruitment problems among African Americans.
"They knew I wasn't going to join any political party," he recounted,
"because I had made that plain." Williams knew something about white
leftists from his days in Detroit and Harlem and remained wary. If the SWP
sincerely sought independent black leadership, they certainly found it in
Monroe. "I wasn't interested in [the SWP] because I could see that they
weren't fully committed to the liberation of black people in America,"
recounted Williams. "They were thinking primarily about white workers—
[race] was incidental to the main problem of the working class." Though
the relationship would continue, Williams engaged the SWP on his own
terms. If the white leftists of the SWP met Williams's low expectations,
he exceeded their highest hopes. SWP reports from Monroe noted that

"Weissman confirmed our impression of Williams as a fighter from the top of his head to the tip of his toes."[48]

While Weissman and Lynn explored the situation in Monroe, Louis Austin at the *Carolina Times* published a blistering editorial on December 6 that highlighted the failure of established civil rights organizations in Union County, especially with regard to the Perry abortion case, and urged that "the NAACP or some other organization organize a committee for Dr. Perry's defense."[49] Williams, Lynn, and Weissman "decided after reading the editorial to go see L. E. Austin" in Durham, by Weissman's account. "We met him in his office last Thursday," he wrote, "and decided then to form a Committee To Combat Racial Injustice." Though Weissman did not say so, it seems likely that the SWP had already hoped to start a new organization. The party's report on Monroe noted that "Williams agreed to the formation of the committee and to functioning as chairman," as though this committee had been envisioned all along.[50]

Regardless of their politics, the four men who gathered in Austin's office in Durham that Thursday afternoon had little disagreement about the predicament of the black freedom movement in the South. Since the NAACP's victory in *Brown v. Board of Education* in 1954 and the triumph of the Montgomery Bus Boycott in 1956, school desegregation had proceeded with no speed and little deliberation. In the wake of those victories, white terrorism and political repression had swept the South, and several state legislatures had virtually outlawed the NAACP. The *New York Times* reported a higher number of civil rights demonstrations per year in 1946–48 than in 1957–59. President Eisenhower's decision to dispatch federal troops to protect black schoolchildren from mobs in Little Rock in 1957 may have heartened some black Southerners, but it fanned segregationists to white-hot fury.[51]

Under these circumstances, the national officers of the NAACP, reviled across the South as Communist-inspired insurrectionists, had neither the capacity nor the inclination to build a mass movement in the South. The NAACP leadership refused to endorse the nonviolent, direct action methods that Martin Luther King Jr. advocated. And yet King himself was not in an aggressive posture. The SCLC had "no machinery, no staff except me," acting director Ella Baker recalled, noting that her "office" was often a pocketful of change and a telephone booth.[52] Deadlocked with white supremacy, the freedom movement in late 1958 needed a more energetic, broad-based organization to organize help "where the NAACP or other established organizations are not furnishing aid."[53] It should muster support from the left and the labor movement, the founders of the CCRI thought, but take its direction from black Southerners. Williams, Austin, Lynn, and Weissman drew up a list of four other activists who they thought shared their perspective and could bring solid political sense and strong organizing ability. The names were Ella Baker, Carl Braden, the Reverend C. K. Steele, and E. D. Nixon.[54]

Like Williams, Baker, who grew up in Littleton, North Carolina, just after the turn of the century, drew her radical vision from the egalitarian culture and race pride of the rural black South. She had grown up under the influence of formerly enslaved grandparents who had labored long for racial and community uplift. Baker had served as the NAACP's national director of branches during World War II and had poured her matchless energies into the "spadework" that she hoped would make the NAACP into a mass movement.

Abandoning that effort in 1946 because of the stubborn bureaucratic and hierarchical orientation of the national office, Baker continued to support the struggle in the South and to explore "ways to develop the idea of a mass-based Southern organization as a counter-balance to the NAACP," according to historian Charles Payne.[55] She was probably the most effective and influential organizer in the black freedom struggle. Hired by Martin Luther King Jr. as acting director of the SCLC in 1957, Baker still entertained hopes that the organization would transcend its "pulpit mentality" and its lack of direction. On December 11, 1958, Lynn called her from Monroe to invite her to join the CCRI. "Conrad spoke to her," according to Weissman, "but she held off until she could see how things would shape up."[56]

That same evening Weissman called E. D. Nixon. "A Negro railroad porter with fists as big as eggplants and a coal-black face," as Taylor Branch describes him, Nixon was a movement legend and an adept organizer like Baker who could have been an enormous asset to the CCRI.[57] Trained as an organizer in the Brotherhood of Sleeping Car Porters, head of the Alabama state NAACP, and the leading activist in Montgomery from the 1930s to the 1950s, Nixon had recognized talent in a young preacher named King and did as much as any other individual to launch the Montgomery Bus Boycott. His ties to the labor movement and the American left, in particular, were critical in making the boycott a national event.[58] "In Robert Williams," Weissman wrote to Nixon a few days later, "I see a younger edition of the very same kind of leadership represented by you—

militant, and with a working-class orientation. Williams, too, has a trade union background."[59]

Despite the well-crafted appeal, Nixon declined to enlist with the CCRI, writing a bitter and passionate letter to Weissman that speaks volumes about the personal agonies that the politics of celebrity could inflict. "For 25 years I have been working in this feel to help bring freedom to un-freed people," Nixon wrote. "I have organize over 15 organizations including the Montgomery Improvement Association, and it was I who found Rev. King." Now everyone had forgotten him, Nixon said, and would only listen to King: "as a spokesman he is very good but no one man can do this job, but when people give all recognition to one because of his academic training and forge[t] other who do not have that kind of training but are making a worth while contribution to the cumity that make it hard." After a quarter-century of organizing, Nixon complained, "you can hardly find a project in Montgomery that I did not start it but after it got going I have been left out of the picture." Nixon was crushed to "have spent long hours and thousand of my own money to bring about these things that now exist and each time I be push in the background, frankly I do not care to be hurt any more." He wrote, "I just want to be let alone now." It was a sobering reflection not only on Nixon's tragic personal situation but on the narrow, media-driven vision of leadership that already had begun to take hold in the movement.[60]

The calls to Carl Braden and C. K. Steele were more successful. Braden was a white radical newspaperman who, along with his wife, Anne Braden, represented the Southern Conference Educational Fund, through which they remained among the most dedicated and well-connected activists in the South. The Reverend Mr. Steele, a small black man of large courage, was both friend and colleague to Martin Luther King Jr.[61] By the end of the first evening the CCRI had a solid core of Weissman, who had volunteered to be secretary-treasurer and offered six months of his labor; Lynn, who would serve as general counsel; Williams, who would chair the committee; Dr. Perry, who would be vice-president; and Braden and Steele, who would use their contacts to help build the organization. Beyond this, Lynn and Weissman obtained permission to use the names of the Reverend Fred Shuttlesworth, Dr. E. Franklin Frazier, Virginia Durr, and Norman Mailer on their first letterhead. The CCRI announced its founding at a press conference in New York City on December 19, 1958.[62]

The organizers of the CCRI shared a hope that the lever of worldwide publicity and the fulcrum of Cold War politics would lift them to victory, both in winning the release of the boys and in advancing the African American freedom movement in the South. "Before leaving," Weissman wrote to Austin, "Conrad and I talked with Harry Golden in Charlotte." Golden, whose book *Only in America* had recently become a national best-seller, was "about to commence a syndicated column in 20 papers next month," Weissman reported. "He will take up the case of the two little boys in his second column and asked us to send him all the data on the case."

In a remark that revealed both the volatile nature of sexual issues in racial politics and the limited political horizons of even the best white liberals, Golden also told Weissman and Lynn "what a loss Dr. Perry would be to the struggle," referring to Perry's travails over the abortion charges. He added that "we can't touch that kind of case down here," underlining Golden's belief that sexual issues too volatile even to address lay beneath the racial crisis in the South. More important than their conversation with Golden, as it turned out, was the contact the two men made with Joyce Egginton, a reporter for the *London News-Chronicle*, which had a European circulation of 1.5 million copies.[63]

The British public, always hungry for further evidence of American hypocrisy, apparently enjoyed reading about the racial contradictions in their former colony that made high-toned claims to moral leadership of "the free world." In late November the *News-Chronicle* flew Egginton across the Atlantic to report on Monroe. "Dr. Perry and his wife, Bertha, met me at the [Charlotte] airport some thirty miles away," she said. Certain mundane aspects of racial reality in the South became immediately apparent. Though it was lunchtime and they were all hungry, Egginton was white, and "there was no restaurant for hundreds of miles where the three of us would be allowed to eat together." They drove to the Perry home, where Bertha Perry fried chicken for them. That afternoon Dr. Perry took the risk of driving this white female reporter to the reformatory in Hoffman where the two boys were being held. Egginton posed as a social worker, and they smuggled a small camera secreted in a basket of fruit into the facility. The reporter got her story—with pictures. Back in Monroe, she charmed Mayor Fred Wilson into granting an interview. "The first thing was a British reporter who interrogated me then," Wilson recalled years later. "It seemed like she had the story all made up. She made us sound like a bunch of bigots."[64]

Indeed her article did just that, although the mayor might have conceded that Monroe had given her no shortage of raw material. The front page of the *London News-Chronicle* on December 15, 1958, featured a large photograph of Hanover Thompson and Fuzzy Simpson in the reformatory, and the story was accompanied by an emotionally charged article on the Monroe kissing case and a blistering front-page editorial. The story hit front pages all over Europe and thrust Monroe onto the international stage. Coverage in the United States appeared from coast to coast—outside the old Confederacy. Front pages in Italy featured large, sympathy-inducing photographs of the two boys under headlines such as "He Will Grow Up in Jail." News organizations in Germany, France, Belgium, the Netherlands, Spain, the Soviet Union, and China focused on Monroe. Demonstrators besieged the American embassy in London, and others followed suit across the Continent. The *Monroe Enquirer* did not mention the case until a month had passed, and then its first article on the matter rather awkwardly acknowledged that the incident had already drawn "international publicity." In the Communist bloc, the press seized upon the story as compelling proof that American democracy was a sham. The rolling snowball began to gather momentum.[65]

In the wake of the publicity spurred by the story in the *London News-Chronicle*, the Eisenhower administration felt compelled to respond to the unanswered telegram that Williams had sent to the president a month earlier. The unhappy task of reply fell to E. Frederic Morrow, the first African American presidential aide in U.S. history. Morrow, who remembered Monroe as a racist "hellhole" from his days at Camp Sutton during World War II, also knew firsthand the absurd but explosive dynamics of race and sexuality. Staff women in the Eisenhower White House "were under strict orders to enter and leave his office in pairs, so as to allay suspicions of sexual misconduct."[66] At the end of Reconstruction, moreover, Fred Morrow's grandfather, John Samuel Morrow, had been driven from North Carolina by the Ku Klux Klan for teaching former slaves to read and write. Almost a century later, Morrow had to tell Robert Williams that the White House "deplored" the sentencing of the two little boys but could do nothing to free them. "I pointed out," Morrow reported, "that this was outside the jurisdiction of the President's office, since it was a purely local matter."[67]

By the end of 1958, however, hundreds of thousands of people around the world had expressed their conviction that the events in Monroe were more than a "local matter." Activists formed protest committees in at least eight European countries and Canada. Outraged citizens demonstrated in front of American embassies across the globe. Prominent intellectuals and leading clerics voiced their objections to the State Department. According to Conrad Lynn, Eleanor Roosevelt begged President Eisenhower to intervene. Petitions bearing tens of thousands of signatures rained onto the desks of American officials at home and abroad. John Shure, head of the USIA at The Hague, reported receiving more than 11,000 letters even though "the response does not appear to have been organized." Even First Lady Mamie Eisenhower became the object of a letter-writing campaign. The flood of international correspondence to Raleigh eventually forced Governor Hodges to enlist a team of translators from the University of North Carolina to help manage his responses.[68]

The campaign to free the black youngsters was, of course, organized, though it was not the far-flung Communist conspiracy described by Hodges and his public relations team. Perhaps because Clare Boothe Luce, wife of publisher Henry R. Luce, was keenly aware—as she wrote to Martin Luther King Jr.—of how European Communists "pointed to events in our South to prove that American democracy was a 'capitalistic myth,'" *Time* magazine in early 1959 featured "The Rolling Snowball," a story that focused on the efforts of Stephanns Saris, a Rotterdam headwaiter moved by the plight of the Monroe boys. Saris, who volunteered part time at a Catholic boys' club, wrote to high school students across the Netherlands asking for letters of protest. In a single week he collected more than 12,000 missives. But Saris hardly saw this as an opportunity to damage the position of the United States in its Cold War rivalry with the Eastern bloc. "This is a case between two good neighbors living on the same side of the street," Saris snapped when Dutch Communists offered to join his crusade. "Go to your own neighbor, the Soviet Union, and mind your own dirty business over there."[69]

White officials in North Carolina complained that they could not deflect the "distorted" and "unfair" allegations put forward by civil rights activists because state and local authorities were restricted legally from making public the juvenile court records of the two boys. By the time these qualms were brushed aside, officials moaned, the state's reputation had been irreparably damaged. "Truth arrived in the Monroe 'kissing case' like a firetruck from the next county," the Lancaster, South Carolina, *News* commiserated with its neighbors to the north, "too late to do any good. The whole world outside the South is now convinced that North Carolina law sent two little Negro boys to prison for long terms for daring to kiss three little white girls."[70] As events soon revealed, however, white officials were constrained more by their own political tactics than by any legal or moral obligation toward the incarcerated juveniles. The case itself defined the clash of maneuver; white officials, with a wide range of options and a potential public relations millstone around their necks, kept quiet at first. Silence made sense because, to the whole world outside the South, the bare facts of the case represented an indictment of North Carolina.

The silence of white officials paralleled that of the state and national NAACP, which remained detached from the case because of a somewhat different dilemma. In the late 1950s the NAACP was under attack from all directions. Senator James Eastland charged that the NAACP was "heavily infiltrated" with Communists, and Senator A. Willis Robertson of Virginia accused the organization of collaborating with Communists "to destroy our form of government."[71] In North Carolina, state legislators threatened to follow the lead of Alabama and require the NAACP to disclose its membership lists—tantamount, under the circumstances, to banning the group.[72] For these Dixie demagogues, "amalgamation" and "Communism" were almost synonymous. The NAACP found itself facing the smear charges of "race-mixing" and "Communist subversion" over and over again. Ironically, after pushing W. E. B. Du Bois out of the NAACP a decade earlier, Roy Wilkins and Thurgood Marshall had made anticommunism the hallmark of their leadership, but they still suffered these smears.[73]

The kissing case raised both questions. This was obviously a "sex case," but leaders of the state conference of the NAACP not only believed that Williams was the "direct antithesis of all that our fine organization has stood for," Reginald Hawkins wrote to Kelly Alexander, but also that he was an agent of the Communist Party—the "tool of an organization that we want no parts of."[74] In the 1950s, such accusations could create, in Robert Penn Warren's memorable phrase, "a one-man leper colony." Many Americans regarded the red infection as incurable and contagious with the slightest contact. Given that most white Southerners already regarded the NAACP as the virus of international Communism, it is not surprising that these men would recoil from any such taint. "If we ever get identified with communism," Kelly Alexander said, "the Ku Klux Klan and the White [Citizens'] Councils will pick up the charge that we are 'reds' and use it like a club to beat us to death."[75]

At the same time, when the kissing case began to echo around the world, the publicity soon reached such proportions that the NAACP could not withdraw from the case without damaging itself among its rank-and-file constituents in the South. Nor could its leadership resist the opportunities to tap the case's fund-raising potential. After the front-page story in the London News-Chronicle, the national office ordered Alexander to re-solve his "personality conflicts" with Williams and help get the boys re-leased. "I pointed out to him," said Gloster Current, national director of branches, "that this entire situation can be very embarrassing to the Asso-ciation unless something is done."[76]

Predictably enough, the day after the News-Chronicle made the kissing case front-page news around the world, Alexander came to Robert Wil-liams to try to broker a deal. "Tell Conrad that Kelly Alexander came by last night about midnight and asked if I would attend a state level meeting Saturday at 12 noon in Charlotte (Dec. 20)," Williams wrote to George Weissman. "He has heard about the Committee and some of the local people are giving him hell. He sounded more like a TOM than ever."[77]

Alexander, a graduate of Tuskegee Institute, had founded the Charlotte branch of the NAACP in 1940 and had carefully forged ties with virtually every well-known African American political leader of the postwar period. Considered "fundamentally reasonable" by white moderates in Charlotte, Alexander displayed a cautious political style and conservative social out-look that neatly coincided with that of Roy Wilkins at the national office. "Kelly had no independent position," one NAACP insider explained.[78]

Stung by criticisms that he had fumbled the case, Alexander sought to undermine Williams's already poor relationship with the national office. He reported to Wilkins that "there is question among the solid citizens of Monroe as to the effectiveness of [Williams] as NAACP president," sug-gesting that Williams represented only lower-class and rural elements in the black community. "This is nothing unusual for NAACP leadership on a local level in small communities," Alexander explained. "The solid cit-izens won't participate and this leaves the opportunity for personalities that Mr. Williams represents to gain control of the branch." According to Williams, however, the impoverished blacks to whom Alexander referred "were looked down upon by these teachers and preachers and people who ran this thing. They didn't want people like that in there."[79]

Alexander was right, of course, in stating that Williams found his strongest supporters among the black poor of Union County, but soon Williams would move to enlarge his constituency greatly. During a series of breakneck tours beginning in late December, Williams delivered his strident saga of "this social jungle called Dixie" to civic groups, labor unions, NAACP chapters, student organizations, and church congrega-tions in New York, Chicago, Cleveland, Detroit, and several smaller cities of the Northeast and Midwest.[80] "He made a great impression, I am told,"

Weissman reported during the tour. " 'Electrified' his audiences is the way one letter put it." Radio and television interviews enlarged his audiences nearly everywhere he went. Protest letters poured into Governor Hodges's office at an astounding rate from the cities where Williams spoke. These fund-raising and publicity trips introduced Williams to activists and organizations across the country. With every appearance, Williams was "more enthusiastic about the possibilities than ever," Weissman wrote. "Everywhere," complained the *Monroe Enquirer*, "his subject was the same as he has carried far and wide—Monroe's so-called 'kissing case.' "[81]

Relations between Williams and the national NAACP office continued to be strained, but efforts were made to reach some understanding. Alexander insisted that Williams "did not want the NAACP to handle the case" and had "turned his back on the one organization that is responsible for him being in the spotlight today." Acknowledging that matters had spun out of his control, Alexander assured Wilkins on December 26 that "the inability of the state conference to secure the case will not, to my way of thinking, harm the activities of the NAACP in North Carolina." Alexander arranged for Wilkins and other top NAACP officials to meet with Williams and Lynn four days later on December 30. A letter from Wilkins to Lynn the following day formalized their understanding: "The NAACP, through its national and state conference," Wilkins wrote, "would assume responsibility for the Thompson and Simpson cases, including relocation [of the families] in a new community." The CCRI, Wilkins explained to the attorney, would "organiz[e] a great protest movement by publicizing the facts of the kissing case" and continue its efforts to "aid other victims of racial injustice in Union County." The accord helped the NAACP recoup only part of its political losses. Editors at the *Amsterdam News* in New York, for example, applauded the fact that the national office of the NAACP "has finally agreed to throw its weight behind the fight to free two little Negro boys who are being held in jail in North Carolina because one of them was kissed by a white girl" but reminded readers of the "shocking refusal and failure" of the NAACP to "go to the immediate aid of these children."[82]

As the "rolling snowball" of national and international news coverage continued to gather momentum, white officials in North Carolina cast aside any regard for the welfare of the two boys and sought to label them and their families as "incorrigible" degenerates. The governor's office aimed a whisper campaign at the North Carolina press and designed a "retail" response to individual critics, the purpose of which was to redefine the kissing incident as an assault on white womanhood. Officials in

Monroe and Raleigh both began to suggest to reporters, off the record, that what had actually occurred was a vicious rape attempt. Robert E. Giles, the governor's administrative aide, responded to the many letters of protest that "the two Negro boys in question were charged with, and proved, molesting a young white girl." Hodges himself wrote to one critic that the boys "had assaulted three small white girls." Even though no such reports existed, Hodges claimed that "official reports of welfare agencies" proved that the families of the boys were "quite disgraceful." "Of course," Hodges added sanctimoniously, "two young children should not be blamed for the fact that they have a shiftless and irresponsible family."[83] The U.S. State Department picked up the charges. John Shure of the USIA told the European press that the boys came from "anti-social families" and that "stripped of its emotionalism, distortion and heated exchanges," Monroe's "much publicized 'kissing incident' essentially becomes a question of the rehabilitation of two problem boys and their families."[84]

Unable to stem the tide of press coverage with attacks on the two boys, the authorities took aim at the news reports themselves. Hodges charged that newspaper accounts were "patently and viciously incorrect," constituted "pure propaganda on the part of the NAACP," and were "prompted not by a genuine interest in the welfare of the young boys themselves but by a very selfish motive on the part of some people who want to gain notoriety on the race question."[85] North Carolina's white newspapers echoed the blasts from the governor's office, aiming their own barrage across familiar battle lines of race, region, and ideology. The Charlotte Observer charged that the New York Post, which had covered the case heavily, was a "tabloid" that was "creating more injustice than it is discovering."[86] The Fayetteville Observer hailed Hodges as "a one-man Anti-defamation League to defend the good name of the people of North Carolina against the slanders and untruths being spread abroad in belittlement of North Carolina justice and customs" and denounced "the deliberate politico-communistic lies being circulated" by Yankee editors.[87] The Winston-Salem Journal and Sentinel, too, blamed the furor on "editing in Northern press rooms" and "the Communist and race press." The News and Observer in Raleigh, ever the loyal Democratic Party organ, backed state and local officials to the hilt: "All that has happened," wrote the editors, "is that two tiny miscreants . . . have been put in a training school where they will get better care and discipline than they were getting at home."[88]

By early January, both Hodges and the national office of the NAACP had incurred enough political damage that both began to seek a quiet resolution to the case. First, Hodges ordered Blaine Madison, the commissioner of the Board of Corrections and Training, to issue a statement that outlined the conditions under which the children could be released. The boys could go home, Madison said on January 2, when "the conduct of the [children] is such as to justify the conclusion that [they] will not, if released, be unruly, disobedient to parents, and wayward." Local welfare personnel, Madison continued, must establish "that the famil[ies] will not neglect [the boys] and will give reasonable protection, guidance, and home care for [the children]." Madison added that progress for the children had been good and that he hoped that "their family conditions can be improved to the extent that release can be granted as soon as possible." The implication was that the boys could be released under the congenial fiction that the state had detained them out of concern for their welfare. At the same time, Madison openly acknowledged that he made his statement because "the NAACP plans legal action to obtain release of the two young Negro boys."[89]

The Hodges administration maintained both that it hoped to relinquish the boys to their families at the earliest moment because of their progress at Morrison Training School for Negroes and that pressure from the NAACP was the reason for their release—in the same press conference. This posture was vintage Luther Hodges—a central claim to honest, capable, businesslike government accompanied by a heartfelt gesture to his right flank.[90] Hodges offered the NAACP hierarchy the opportunity to solve its own problems by accepting the credit—or, from the point of view of the white voters that Hodges courted, the blame—for the victory of a pressure campaign that the NAACP's leadership had yet to endorse publicly. Robert Williams saw through the emerging politics clearly and blasted Madison's statement as a "further attempt by the officials of North Carolina to whitewash the racist reason for the imprisonment of these two boys and to obscure and distort the facts."[91]

In fact, it was the CCRI rather than the NAACP that sought legal action, in part because "we had reason to believe there was a move afoot [by NAACP officials] to reach a deal with Hodges," Weissman wrote. In this emerging arrangement, he explained, "the parents would be put in new houses in Charlotte and declared 'rehabilitated' whereupon the Governor would free the kids on the basis that they were being held solely until there was a suitable home atmosphere for them." According to Williams, Kelly Alexander came to him and indicated that "Harry Golden had been talking to the governor" and that "they wanted the thing dropped" and that the NAACP should simply "leave the thing along and let it quietly die away and soon the boys will be released." With the families relocated to Charlotte, Alexander suggested, "nobody will know the difference" whether the boys were in training school or at home. "The parents of the little girl will be satisfied because they have been sent away," he reportedly explained, and "they will be let out and nobody will know it."[92]

While the two boys endured training school, their families faced an ongoing barrage of threats, reprisals, and eviction notices. Both Evelyn Thompson and Jennie Simpson lost all of their cleaning jobs in Monroe.[93] "Mrs. Thompson must be out of her house by Jan. 24 or back in court," Williams wrote. "They just won't let her rest." Governor Hodges defended the "rights of the landlord to refuse to continue to rent to [the mothers]" but privately bemoaned the fact that the evictions were "adding fuel to the propaganda which has been greatly exploited on this whole case." He asked his attorney general, Malcolm Seawell, to explain his political situation to local authorities in Monroe.[94] NAACP officials, meanwhile, paid for the families of the two boys to move from their community in Monroe to Double Oaks Apartments in Charlotte, which Kelly Alexander, one of the owners, claimed "pioneered in better housing for Negroes." The families did not want to move but had little choice. "Mrs. Thompson had to be coaxed to accept the new home," NAACP field secretary Charles McLean wrote to the national office. "She said she enjoyed being with the crowds [in Monroe] rather than the relatively quiet atmosphere of the 'Double Oaks' area."[95]

The class condescension of the NAACP officials in Charlotte was unbearable for Thompson and Simpson. The two mothers called Williams in mid-January and "accused Alexander and [McLean] of being rude to them, humiliating them, etc.," George Weissman reported. The mothers complained to Weissman that McLean "took them to the super-market to buy them $8 worth of food but refused to allow them to choose but directed what should be bought." Jennie Simpson felt "so humiliated in front of the curious that she ran out" of the grocery store. "Both resent the local press publicity about being 'rehabilitated,'" Weissman wrote. The treatment of the two women infuriated Williams. "These NAACP officials have no understanding of these people," he complained bitterly, "no sympathy for them, they are middle-class and just want the NAACP to be a collection agency."[96]

To forestall any quiet arrangement between the NAACP and Governor

Hodges, Conrad Lynn and Robert Williams obtained a court order for a habeas corpus hearing for the two boys to be held January 12, 1959, before Judge Walter Johnston Jr. in Wadesboro, North Carolina, about half an hour's drive from Monroe. Noting that the hearing had been brought about "largely from the efforts of one man, Robert Williams," the *News and Observer* chirped sunnily that the hearing "should clear the racially-charged atmosphere surrounding Monroe's celebrated kissing case." Governor Hodges, noting that the writ of habeas corpus "naturally involves the state," dispatched Seawell to handle the case personally. Hodges also sent his "segregation specialist," Ralph Moody, to assist the attorney general. The State of North Carolina planned to defend itself.[97]

Attorney General Seawell, a tall, bespectacled man of Scottish ancestry and fiery temperament, was poised to announce his candidacy for governor. Seawell had carved out an appealing public image as an independent-minded, homegrown moderate in front-page battles against the Ku Klux Klan, organized labor, and the American Civil Liberties Union. His strongest opponent would be Terry Sanford, both the Democratic machine candidate and a superbly gifted campaigner with unshakable support among the state's minority of black and liberal voters. The other candidate would be North Carolina's most articulate segregationist, Dr. I. Beverly Lake. Though Seawell had promise, one veteran political observer remarked, he had "first stepped into rough ground as attorney general when he said, in no uncertain terms, that the Supreme Court's school decision in 1954 is the law of the land and must be obeyed." White voters perceived Seawell as soft on race, and he had no hope of taking votes from Sanford among voters who might appreciate such a stance.[98]

In short, Seawell needed to take a sharp right turn in public. With Williams as his foil and a horde of reporters as his audience, the hearing in Wadesboro was his golden opportunity. Though the purpose of the hearing was to review the legal procedures that had sent the two boys to reform school, Seawell had a different agenda. "No sooner had the hearing begun," Gloster Current reported to Roy Wilkins, "than Seawell announced, 'I want Robert Franklin Williams on the witness stand.'"[99]

Judge Johnston ordered Williams to the witness stand. Due to the deplorable "storm of publicity from civil rights advocates and newspapers surrounding this case," intoned the judge, "the people should be given a full explanation of it." Conrad Lynn examined Williams, who related how Mayor Fred Wilson had called him on the telephone and told him that the boys were in jail for "assault and molesting three white females." He had "attempted to work out a plan with the mothers to move the children from racially charged Monroe," Williams testified, but Judge Price barred him from the hearing and sentenced the boys to reform school without permitting Williams even to obtain an attorney for the boys.[100]

With his chief quarry before him, Attorney General Seawell first sought to establish that Williams had not even known the children prior to this case and had no interest in them beyond his political ends. This line of inquiry was undercut somewhat when he asked how long Williams had known their mothers and Williams replied, "off and on all of my life." Seawell, who wanted to talk about the CCRI, asked Williams if he "had any official position with any organization" that prompted his interest in the two boys. "I am a member of the Unitarian Fellowship For Social Justice," he answered. "I am a member of the National Rifle Association"—here the judge interrupted: "R-i-f-l-e?" Williams nodded dutifully and added with mock solemnity, "And I consider myself a member of the American Red Cross." Knowing exactly what Seawell was fishing for, however, and not wishing to appear reluctant, Williams stated, "I am a member of the Committee to Combat Racial Injustice."[101]

Seawell wasted little time in maligning the fledgling organization as conspiratorial and unpatriotic. "Do you know Carl Braden?" he demanded. Williams conceded that he had heard of Braden, though they had never met. Braden's name was on the CCRI letterhead as a member of the board of directors, a fact Seawell wasted no time in establishing. Notorious among right-wing Southerners, Braden's devoted activism was frequently cited as proof that Communists directed the black freedom movement. Carl and Anne Braden had worked at the Louisville *Courier-Journal*, one of the South's more liberal white newspapers. In 1954 the Bradens bought a house in a white suburb of Louisville and then sold it to Andrew Wade, a black friend. Soon afterward, someone bombed the house. Because of left-wing publications found in their home, the Bradens and several of their local allies were charged with sedition, which carried a potential penalty of twenty-one years in prison in Kentucky. Though he dropped the charges against the other defendants, the commonwealth attorney in Louisville charged that Carl Braden was "a dedicated Communist" who had bombed his own house to cause racial conflict. The judge sentenced Braden to fifteen years in prison, of which he served eighteen months before winning his release. At the time of the hearing in Wadesboro, Braden was under indictment for contempt of Congress because of his refusal to name names before the House Un-American Activities Committee in early 1958.[102] "I'll ask you," Seawell demanded, "if in the year 1954 in Louisville, Kentucky, if Carl Braden wasn't charged with and convicted of the crime of sedition and received a sentence of fifteen years in prison and a five thousand dollar fine?"

Williams replied that he had heard "that Carl Braden had a lot of trouble in Louisville because he sold a house to a Negro in a white community." Seawell could not let that assessment stand. "You have knowledge of the fact [that] he, himself, was convicted of blowing up that house to create racial prejudice out in Louisville," the attorney general said, "and that's what he was convicted of?" Williams demurred. Seawell began to badger his witness angrily: "You don't know that?" Fuming, Williams would not answer. "You're not mad, are you?" the attorney general demanded. Sensing that he might get Williams to lose his temper, Seawell brought up the case of Dr. Perry, who had been taken to prison only recently. "I'll ask you if you don't know as a fact that [Dr. Perry] is under sentence to the State Prison in this state for a sentence of two to three years for performing an abortion?"

"I know he was framed," Williams shot back. "He was framed in the very beginning, because the state didn't take an interest in the Ku Klux Klan when they were after him and tried to run him away from his home." Shocked at the NAACP president's lack of deference, the attorney general asked pointedly when Williams had last seen the boys. "Did you go there Christmas?" he asked. "Did you go there January first?" Williams said that he had not. "You were up in New York, weren't you?" Seawell snarled, with an inflection that suggested that being in New York was in itself a matter for extreme suspicion. Exasperated, Williams lost his temper and began to make what Gloster Current described as "rash and irresponsible statements." Raising his voice, Williams stated, "I went to New York to solicit funds to bring democracy to this social jungle called Dixie!" Seawell fired back, "This Dixie you call a social jungle."

Conrad Lynn then summoned J. Hampton Price, the juvenile court judge who had sent the two boys to Morrison Training School. The attorney established through Price's testimony that the authorities had issued warrants for the arrest and prosecution of the two boys on assault charges, that they had held the boys in the county jail, and that Judge Price had not recorded any of the prior offenses alleged against the boys in the juvenile records as required by law. On cross-examination, Ralph Moody used the Monroe police blotter and the testimony of Judge Price to demonstrate that the two boys had, in fact, been caught in a string of petty thefts prior to the kissing incident—stealing a case of potato chips, breaking into a cracker machine and eating the contents, and stealing ham from someone's kitchen table. Price testified, too, that the families of the two boys were unfit. "I found out that the mother [of Hanover Thompson] was away from home practically all of the time in the day, and most of the time in the night, too," he said. By this time, eight-year-old Fuzzy Simpson had fallen asleep, his head resting on Hanover Thompson's shoulder.[103]

"J. Hampton Price yelled at [Evelyn Thompson]," Ted Poston wrote in the *New York Post*, "though it was stricken from the record, 'I heard some of her children are illegitimate, since her husband deserted her.'" Price also said that he had heard that Thompson "secreted another nigger girl from me when she couldn't be found to be sent up for violating probation." To the charges that she neglected her children, Evelyn Thompson had a ready answer for the newspaper reporter. "Well, I had five children to feed and I took day work where and when I could get it." She acknowledged that her son had not been perfect. "They say that Hanover stole a piece of ham from a lady's kitchen," Thompson told Poston. "I don't know—maybe he did. We were all so hungry most of the time."[104]

Several thorny exchanges ensued in which the attorney general suggested that the CCRI was exploiting the case to raise money, and Conrad Lynn argued that the boys' civil rights had been violated. Judge Walter Johnston upheld the original verdict of the juvenile court on the grounds that the court had committed Hanover Thompson and Fuzzy Simpson as juvenile delinquents, not sentenced them as criminals, and that the usual constitutional protections did not apply. "Now, if these boys had been sentenced to prison, or if their record showed that they had been found guilty of a criminal offense, then this court would not have any hesitancy whatever in setting aside their imprisonment," Johnston explained.[105]

Fuzzy Simpson awoke from his nap and, when he realized that the judge was sending him back to Morrison Training School, broke into loud sobs and buried his face in his mother's dress as they walked from the courtroom. Hanover Thompson tried to remain stoic, but in the hallway he began to cry and clutched for his own mother. In front of the courthouse, at the feet of a twenty-foot statue of a Confederate soldier with fixed bayonet, Superintendent P. R. Brown gently disengaged the two boys from their mothers and led them to a state patrol car.[106]

Though the setback in court sent the boys back to training school, it did not stop Robert Williams. "We must *start* our Committee rolling at full steam," Williams wrote a few days later. "I believe that it is really needed and that it can develop into a great thing."[107] Williams set out almost immediately on another whirlwind round of speaking engagements. In Cleveland, Williams made speeches before the Amalgamated Meat Cutters and Butcher Workmen and two other large labor groups and "made a big hit with the unionists," Weissman reported. "Dining car leaders held a luncheon for him at which some 25 union officials from all trades were present." Williams spoke on the radio twice in Cleveland, appeared on local television, and claimed that he "got more newspaper coverage than the mayor of West Berlin who was also in town." One meat cutter wrote, "We've been waiting for an organization that will fight—this is it." Another butcher, a native of Georgia, called Williams's speeches "a new 'noise' from the South, and I feel sort of proud to say I'm from the South."[108]

"In Chicago," Weissman wrote, "he made a tremendous impression on a shoe workers local—they want him back." The centerpiece of the trip was Williams's appearance alongside Sammy Davis Jr. before an enormous crowd at the Packinghouse Workers Hall in Chicago, speaking on "Negro History, Africa, the Rebel South and America's Future—Full Equality of Negroes or Collapse." In Michigan, Williams spoke to overflow crowds at churches, Democratic Party gatherings, labor unions, student organizations, and NAACP chapters, making at least twenty public speeches during one visit.[109] The mass meeting in New Rochelle, New York, "was the most successful yet," Weissman estimated; "750 attended; in addition to local expenses and $100 travel expenses, the collection yielded $293 for the CCRI and a like sum for the Union County NAACP." The Monroe Enquirer complained bitterly but accurately that Robert Williams "rode from obscurity to international attention on the back of the infamous 'kissing case.' "[110]

As protest letters continued to pour into Governor Hodges's office, he seemed perplexed. "I honestly don't know what you can do to keep propaganda groups from taking over a thing of this character," he told reporters. The main problem, Hodges claimed, was that juvenile law and common decency prevented him from releasing the boys' records to the public.[111] In fact, Hodges had already released their records, regardless of law or decency, and was preparing to do so yet again. The FBI soon volunteered its services in the governor's efforts to stop Williams. O. L. Richardson, former Speaker of the North Carolina House of Representatives and Hodges's closest political ally in Monroe, was chosen as conduit between the bureau and the governor. In a letter marked "PERSONAL AND CONFIDENTIAL," Richardson informed Hodges that "Robert L. Williams has been under investigation by the F.B.I. for a considerable period of time"—in fact, though he did not say so, since Williams was sixteen— "and that they have a large dossier on him. You would have access to this information if you desire." Richardson recommended that Hodges meet with an agent from the FBI's Charlotte office because "it may be necessary for the State to defend its position in the future."[112]

Hodges wasted no time. The governor launched a frenzied public relations campaign, calling on political cronies, advertising executives, and the FBI for resources and advice. "An opportunity such as this to give the NAACP a taste of its own medicine does not come along every day," one of his advisers wrote, urging Hodges to "pour it on—you will place the whole Confederacy in your debt." Another collaborator suggested that "by hitting directly at the Communist connection we might convince some people of the insincerity of these protests." Hodges seemed particularly concerned about the toll that the case might have taken on his industrial recruitment efforts. "May I suggest sounding out *U.S. News and World Report*?" one of his professional advisers wrote, observing that the editors were sympathetic to Hodges's own views on "the race problem." The adviser went on to say that "a report in its pages on the Monroe case would set the record straight for the benefit of a top-level readership, no doubt including potential investors in North Carolina."[113]

The *U.S. News and World Report* idea did not pan out, but Hodges found a formidable ally in Chester Davis, a former FBI agent now working as a journalist. Despite his claim that he had been handicapped by his reluctance to make juvenile delinquency records public, Hodges opened his office files to Davis, who took the posture of a journalist while he participated actively in Hodges's well-organized public relations campaign. Working hand in glove with Hodges, Davis produced a set of scurrilous articles—"Communist Front Shouts 'Kissing Case' to World," and "Press in North Gives Distorted Versions"—which expanded and amplified charges that Hodges had been making all along. "On the evidence, both direct and circumstantial," Davis opened his first article, "[the CCRI] is a Communist-directed front." Davis, of course, provided no direct evidence whatsoever, and his strongest circumstantial proof was that Conrad Lynn once had defended clients accused of violating the Smith Act. By this standard, of course, one might have proven that some of the most prestigious law firms in the country were Communist conspiracies. Ironically, the only leftist group that actually lurked behind the scenes, the SWP, went entirely unmentioned.[114]

Davis also attacked the financial integrity of the CCRI, repeating a wildly inaccurate assertion by Kelly Alexander that the committee had raised "at least $15,000 as of now" and that "the NAACP and the Simpson and Thompson families have not received one dime from the committee." Alexander did not mention, of course, that the NAACP had agreed to cover the expenses for the two families as part of its arrangement with the CCRI. Nor did he mention that the NAACP itself was holding fund-raisers around the case. It was not true, for that matter, that the families had received no money from the committee, although George Weissman pointed out that "since we agreed at our conference at the end of December that the NAACP would take over relocation and support of the mothers we were unable to (and never did) ask contributions for their support." In fact, Jennie Simpson and Evelyn Thompson wrote to the CCRI "to thank you for the money you sent beginning with the money for Christmas presents and then the checks you sent to help us with living expenses." Weissman, who was the only person authorized to write checks for the CCRI, kept impeccable financial records, but Davis made no effort to contact the organization before making this reckless attack. "The books of the committee are irreproachable," Weissman truthfully observed in a letter to Louis Austin, "receipt book, checkbook, all petty cash expenditures supported by vouchers."[115]

Moreover, Davis also resorted to invidious racial stereotypes in a series of personal attacks on Hanover Thompson and Fuzzy Simpson, their families, and many of their political allies, even though he did not attempt to interview them himself. The *Journal and Sentinel* articles listed nine minor acts of delinquency that, according to "police records," the two boys had committed. Davis also retailed second- and third-hand gossip to claim that both mothers were sexually promiscuous, and he made the vicious and unattributed charge that Evelyn Thompson had "a reputation for using her daughters in prostitution." Dr. Perry came under attack for his "criminal abortion on a white woman." Robert Williams was "overly aggressive, very extreme in his statements, and inclined to consider himself a martyr in the fight for racial justice." Louis Austin of the *Carolina Times* was an "often vitriolic spokesman for equal rights for Negroes." Conrad Lynn, Davis wrote, had many connections to the Communist Party, and Carl Braden was a Communist Party operative.[116]

Privately, Chester Davis admitted in a remarkable correspondence with Carl Braden—whom he had referred to as "a dedicated Communist"—that "in reporting Communist infiltration in the race movement I may be guilty of witch-hunting." Certain aspects of his articles "could be unfair," but "the central theme of my piece was valid" because "Communism is a real and present threat," Davis wrote. "I don't care how idealistic your motives are." Whether the organization was actually part of a Communist conspiracy or not, "your Committee To Combat Racial Injustice served no purpose other than that of a propaganda tub," Davis told Braden. Whatever the rights and wrongs of the matter, Davis mused further, "there is, I think, a certain pre-ordained tragedy in the fact that we, as individuals, do as we do because, being what we are, we can do no other way."[117]

Governor Hodges, hardly a fatalist himself, was delighted with Davis's articles. "This is the most complete and accurate newspaper account of this case that anyone has had," the governor wrote to Reed Surratt, the editor of the *Journal and Sentinel*, "and I am personally grateful for the careful attention he gave it." Another adviser to Hodges, a professional advertising executive, urged that copies of the articles as well as official reports from the commissioner of corrections and Judge J. Hampton Price "be circulated to key editors and executives of the New York dailies, news magazines, columnists, radio-TV commentators, wire services, etc.—the point being to advertise the smear within the trade. It might run up a big printing bill," the advertising man told Hodges, "but I believe in the present state of affairs it would be money well spent." The cost of the campaign was defrayed by editor Surratt, who provided thousands of free reprints to Hodges.[118] The governor's aides packed the reprints in slick press packets and dispatched them not only to news outlets but to thousands of citizens around the world. "The Governor of North Carolina," George Weissman wrote to Louis Austin, "is mailing reprints of these out to every person who ever wrote him on the kissing case—and that is quite a few."[119]

On February 13, Evelyn Thompson was shocked to see Superintendent P. R. Brown of the Morrison Training School standing at the door of her new apartment with her ten-year-old son and two social workers. The boys themselves did not know they were going home until early that morning when they were ordered to pack all their things. "The boys are happy, the mothers are happy," Mabel Williams wrote, "everybody is rejoicing though some eyes are still wet." That afternoon, Commissioner of Corrections Blaine M. Madison announced that the two families "are now located in a good neighborhood" in Charlotte and that reports from the Mecklenburg County Department of Social Services revealed "that the home situation has been improved and conditional release of the boys is justified at this time." Governor Hodges rather disingenuously acted as though this decision had been taken by others. "I have been informed today by Mr. Madison," he told reporters, "that the two boys have been returned to their mothers who have now established new homes since moving from Monroe to Charlotte. I am glad, of course," he continued, "that the home situations have improved to the extent that the boys can be given a conditional release. I hope that the mothers of these two boys will meet their responsibilities as mothers."[120]

Success has many fathers, it is said, while failure remains an orphan. Many people hurried to claim political paternity when Hodges finally released the two boys. Years later, Conrad Lynn explained that he had finally called Eleanor Roosevelt and told her the whole heart-rending story. "And then Eleanor Roosevelt began to cry," Lynn wrote. "That same day she called President Dwight Eisenhower." In Lynn's account, the president then called Governor Hodges and persuaded him to release the boys.[121] Harry Golden, never a particularly humble character, claimed that he himself had persuaded Hodges to release the two boys, an assertion that Kelly Alexander affirmed. "The NAACP had asked Harry Golden to intercede in this matter for the sake of the children," Alexander explained, emphasizing his own role: "Golden talked with me over the telephone." The New York Post, joining the scramble for credit, attributed the victory to "worldwide protests against state officials after the Post broke the story."[122]

There was some truth to each of these explanations. Lynn was an entertaining but unreliable storyteller; he probably did talk to Eleanor Roosevelt, but there is no evidence to confirm that she acted on the boys' behalf. It is true that Golden met Governor Hodges for breakfast the day before the children were released; undoubtedly they talked about the case.[123] Certainly the Post covered the story as closely as any other newspaper. The award for cynicism, however, must go to Roy Wilkins, who at first refused to intervene in the case and then later did a fair amount to obstruct Williams's fervent publicity campaign. "This case has become known throughout the world," he wrote, "primarily because of NAACP action and because of publicity in the foreign and domestic press."[124]

Robert Williams had finished a six-day speaking tour in Cleveland and was headed for Chicago when he got a telephone call from George Weissman in New York telling him that the boys were free. Without any reference to his own efforts, Williams told the Chicago Daily News that the release was "a great moral victory" and credited "pressure exerted on the governor, Luther H. Hodges, and the U.S. State Department by world opinion."[125] Back in Monroe, the kissing case victory won Williams great admiration and respect among his supporters. "Rob tells me that whereas previously he personally signed up all the new branch members," Weissman reported, "he got a letter announcing 20 new memberships in the Monroe branch last week." It had all been quite a remarkable success, Weissman observed. Robert Williams "has some audacious plans," he wrote, "which I think are feasible. Indeed, the more I see of him the more I think that he has the potentiality of becoming a *real* leader in the Negro struggle."[126]

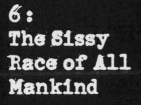

6:
The Sissy
Race of All
Mankind

The rout of Catfish Cole's bedsheet brigade by the Monroe NAACP on October 5, 1957, crushed the evangelist's aspiration to unite the Ku Klux Klan in the Carolinas under his charismatic leadership. His manly honor in tatters, Cole retreated from Union County to Robeson County in southeastern North Carolina to rebuild his following. "Both counties," one observer noted, "were Catfish Cole's territory."[1] In Robeson County, which had a history of strong support for the Klan, Cole hoped to rally his forces in a population divided almost evenly among African Americans, whites, and Lumbee Indians. "There's about 30,000 half-breeds in Robeson County and we are going to have a cross burning and scare them up," Cole announced. Asked whether he intended to use violence to stop the race-mixing in Robeson County, Cole replied that the guns his Klansmen carried "speak for themselves, and if they don't, they will." On January 13, 1958, the Klan burned a cross on the lawn of an Indian woman in the town of St. Pauls as "a warning" because, Cole claimed, she was "having an affair" with a white man.[2] The cross burnings continued, with the former carnival barker ranting at each gathering about the terrible evils of "mongrelization," the loose morals of Lumbee women, and the manly duties of white men "to fight [America's] enemies anywhere, anytime."[3] As one visitor to Monroe later wrote to a friend, "Cole was in a particular mad dog fury" because of rumors that Ava Gardner, eastern North Carolina's own homegrown movie star, was having a Hollywood affair with Sammy Davis Jr., whom Cole contemptuously referred to as "that one-eyed nigger."[4]

The climax of the Klan's Robeson County campaign was to be a heavily armed rally on January 18, 1958, near the small town of Maxton, at which,

Cole predicted, 5,000 Klansmen would remind Indians of "their place" in the racial order. "He said that, did he?" asked Simeon Oxendine, who had flown more than thirty missions against the Germans in World War II and now headed the Lumbee chapter of the Veterans of Foreign Wars. "Well, we'll just wait and see."[5]

Cole's references to Lumbee women were particularly galling. Robeson County sheriff Malcolm McLeod visited the grand wizard at his South Carolina home and "told him that his life would be in danger if he came to Maxton and made the same speech he'd been making." That Friday night, as a few dozen Klansmen gathered in a roadside field in darkness lit only by a single hanging bulb powered by a portable generator, more than five hundred Lumbee men assembled across the road with rifles and shotguns. The Lumbees fanned out across the highway to encircle the Klansmen. When Cole began to speak, a Lumbee dashed up and smashed the light with his rifle barrel. Hundreds of Indians let out a thunderous whoop and fired their weapons repeatedly into the air. Only four people were injured, none seriously; all but one were apparently hit by falling bullets. The Klansmen dropped their guns and scrambled for their cars, abandoning the unlit cross, their public address system, and an array of KKK paraphernalia. Magnanimous in victory, the Lumbees allowed the white supremacists to escape. The war party even helped push Cole's Cadillac out of the ditch where his wife, Carolyn, had driven in her panic. The grand wizard himself had abandoned "white womanhood" and fled on foot into the swamps. Laughing, the Lumbees set fire to the cross, hanged Catfish Cole in effigy, and had a rollicking victory bash. Draped in captured Klan regalia, they celebrated into the night. "If the Negroes had done something like this a long time ago, we wouldn't be bothered with the KKK," Oxendine said in a remark that kept his Lumbee troops clearly on a side of the color line different from that of African Americans.[6]

African Americans had, of course, given the hooded order a similar send-off in Monroe only a few weeks earlier, but white newspapers had ignored the Monroe NAACP's clash with the Ku Klux Klan.[7] The white press had a field day, however, with the Lumbee rout of the Klan. The cover of *Life* magazine featured a playful photograph of a beaming Oxendine wrapped in a confiscated Ku Klux Klan banner. Alabama's Governor "Big Jim" Folsom wired congratulations to the tribe and joked that he "hope[d] the Indians continue to beat the paleface."[8] "Did you notice," a columnist for the *New York Herald Tribune* asked readers, "how the Indians scalped the Ku Klux Klan?" From New York to New Mexico, amused editors sneered that "the Ku Klux Klan took on a tougher enemy than it had counted upon when it tried to scare the Indians" and asserted that "the Ku Klux Klan will be nothing but a bad joke for years to come," an observation that was much easier to make from a distance.[9] Closer to home, in tribute to the Lumbees the Raleigh *News and Observer* published an epic poem, "The Battle of Maxton," that hailed their triumph. The *Chapel Hill News Leader* declared the Lumbee victory "worthy to stand in the textbooks alongside the battles of Moores's Creek Bridge and King's Mountain," two noted North Carolina contests of the American Revolution.[10]

The white press "played up the Indian-Klan fight," Williams explained, because "the Indians are a tiny minority and people could afford to laugh at the incident as a sentimental joke—but no one wanted Negroes to get the impression that this was an accepted way to deal with the Klan."[11] In some respects, too, the lighthearted way that the white press covered the Lumbee uprising served to release tension in a South that trembled uncomfortably close to the edge of race war.

Luther Hodges took seriously Cole's threats to return to Robeson County with thousands of armed Klansmen. The governor had the political sophistication to understand that the organized white terror of the Klan represented as much a threat to the racial status quo as a defense of it. Hodges issued a four-page denunciation of the Klan.[12] The State of North Carolina indicted Cole on charges of "inciting to riot," on the grounds that he had called the Klan together "with the common intent to preach racial discrimination"—a charge that might well have been applied to several of Hodges's own press conferences. The state attorney general's office even suggested that the existence of the Ku Klux Klan itself, with its "tirade of hate," might be illegal. "Ku Klux Klan Wizard James W. Cole, who once attracted thousands to meetings here in Union County," the *Monroe Enquirer* reported, "heard himself sentenced to 18 to 24 months on the roads."[13] Cole served more than a year in prison as a result of the fiasco with the Lumbees. "You are being persecuted because of your devotion to our Lord Jesus Christ and your loyalty to America and the great White Race and America," notorious racial terrorist J. B. Stoner wrote to him. Klan organizers in Monroe sent Cole cigarettes and money and wrote to him regularly to remind him that "we have not forgotten you."[14]

Both the Lumbee triumph over the Klan and the national reaction to it—especially when compared with the reaction to any show of force by black citizens—revealed a great deal about the racial, sexual, and gender politics from which these events emerged. The Lumbee victory was a perfect display of both physical courage and manly restraint. They had taken up their guns, defended the honor of their women, and defeated the foe decisively; yet they had maintained sufficient composure that no one had been killed. In a society in which manhood constituted the most powerful metaphor for citizenship and even for human volition itself, the Lumbees became men, the Klan lost face, and the world applauded.

But there was more at stake than manhood alone; like so much else in Jim Crow society, manhood had been powerfully and poisonously racialized. The Lumbees, whose tribal identity had long been challenged by white enemies who accused them of being partly black, pursued their own agenda with respect to race and gender. In a society that had denied manly prerogatives to black men for centuries, the Lumbees sought to become not just men but *white* men, in a symbolic sense. More to the point, they had become *not black*. "The Lumbees routed the Klan to maintain their STATUS, a status they guard with tremendous zeal," Harry Golden thought. Their goal, Golden observed with considerable insight, was to avoid being "identified with the Negro race. The Ku Klux gangsters are dedicated to the project of 'scaring Negroes,' and the Indians were anxious to disassociate themselves from that category."[15] The Ku Klux Klan recognized the racial meaning of the claim that the Lumbee made with their guns. In a mass mailing titled "Dear Fellow Patriot," Carolyn Cole explained the incident to their supporters: her husband had been attacked by "kinky-haired Indians," she said, making the point that the Lumbee claim to whiteness should not be accepted.[16]

In the Jim Crow South, the protection of women and the projection of violence both reflected and created the architecture of social hierarchy. Men often used sexuality and violence to announce and contest relations of property and power.[17] In a world that lacked healthier conceptions of male identity, violence in the defense of womanhood did much to define both whiteness and manhood. An incident at a hotel bar in Winston-Salem, North Carolina, in 1959 was revealing. When a black male hotel employee asked a white female bartender to light his cigarette, a white patron protested, "I wouldn't ask one of your lady folks to light a cigarette for me," and then stabbed the black man to death.[18] White men were free to keep black women as mistresses, and white rapists often attacked black women with impunity; but a ten-year-old black boy risked his life by kissing a white girl in a game. For the Lumbees, defending the honor of their women was a claim to white manhood or, at least, an avowal that they were *not* to be regarded as black men.

Robert Williams felt the force of these complex racial and sexual dynamics in the core of his being. White violence against black women, he insisted, was not just an attack on the women but "a challenge to our manhood, especially to veterans, who had been trained to fight." The fact that white economic reprisals made it hard for him to support his family may have deepened his personal feelings; providing for one's family, he insisted, was a necessary but not sufficient expression of manhood. "Big cars, fine clothes, big houses, and college degrees won't make a Negro a respected being called a MAN," he declared on the first page of the first issue of The Crusader, the newsletter that the Monroe NAACP launched in 1959.[19] Williams denounced the "emasculated men" who preached non-violence while white mobs beat their wives and daughters.[20] "When we passively submit to these barbaric injustices," he raged, "we most surely can be called the 'sissy race' of all mankind."[21]

For black men as well as white men, the rhetoric of protecting women was an integral part of the politics of controlling women.[22] Black women prepared food, worked the telephones, and delivered the weekly newsletters, Robert Williams acknowledged, although it was not easy for the men to confine black women to these roles. When Williams and the other black veterans organized self-defense networks, he said, black women insisted that the men teach them to shoot. "They had volunteered," Williams recalled, "and they wanted to fight. But we kept them out of most of it."[23] In fact, black men did not successfully keep black women confined to what they saw as appropriate roles. The women both deployed gender stereotypes in assertive ways—demanding of black men, in effect, "Why aren't you protecting us?"—and defied such stereotypes through their own daily assertions. The crowd of armed black women who rushed into the Monroe police station after Dr. Perry's arrest was only the most dramatic demonstration of those assertions. Black women who worked as domestics played crucial roles as gatherers of intelligence, spying on employers who assumed their loyalty or unimportance. The fact that black women in Monroe frequently placed race and family ahead of their own problems with gender inequities did not mean that they were unaware of them. "Black women are relegated to the bottom of the scale," Mabel Williams wrote in The Crusader. "They are the least respected and the most exploited."[24]

Even so, black women as well as black men transmitted lessons about what black manhood should mean. Ethel Azalea Johnson helped write and distribute The Crusader. In her column, "Did You Know?" Johnson told the story of "my old school teacher [who] had pointed out to us from the classroom window, and said 'there it stand, the tree they hung [Andrew] Crawford on, look at it but never forget that he was hung for trying to be a man.' "[25] Williams's own grandmother Ellen Williams had hammered home this sense of embattled manly duty to her favorite grandson when he was only a young boy. Another black woman, Ella Belle "Mama" Stitt, who was, like Ellen Williams, born into slavery, lived next door to the Williams family. Mabel Williams recorded Mama Stitt's recollections, and the Williamses' two small sons, John and Bobby, performed daily household chores for their century-old neighbor.[26] Thus Robert Williams and the men of the Monroe NAACP considered their obligations "to come to the defense of our women" not as an abstract rhetorical commitment to black patriarchy but as a deep and daily personal responsibility.[27] The freedom movement in the South did not make itself out of pristine and idealized human relationships, but from the living resources of black Southern culture; the point here is neither to celebrate nor to denigrate black patriarchy, but to understand its social context.

There was a dimension to the protection of "their" women, however, that had as much to do with the identities of the African-American men of Monroe as it did with the security of their mothers, wives, sisters, and daughters. Rural Southerners, black and white, grew up in a world where differences were often settled in a direct and violent manner. Scholarly depictions of "that part of the United States lying below the Smith and Wesson line" illustrate that the white South reserved a special place for violence, be it rowdy fistfights, romantic duels, military warfare, or lynch mob murder.[28]

Yet the black South, too, had its own sense of honor, violence, and manhood, and a code that black men observed and black women sometimes used to their own ends. Largely unable to defend their honor against white men, black men frequently turned on one another. "Cutting scrapes" and juke-joint shootings were common among working-class black men in the South, and so long as the violence occurred only between blacks, a white editor complained in 1958, North Carolina's judges and juries often regarded the crime "as though it had occurred among a family of rabbits."[29] Black men in Monroe "are ready to fight at the drop of a hat—each other, I mean," Azalea Johnson liked to joke, suggesting that it would be considerably more manly of them to fight for black liberation.[30] Though Southern violence carried widely varied social meanings—depending mostly on who was being violent to whom—on all sides of the color line, willingness to defend one's honor was considered tantamount to manhood.

Black nationalism was heavily gendered. "We must protect our most valuable property—our women," the Nation of Islam's banners read. But contestations of a notion of manhood that excluded black men did not start or stop with black nationalists. In fact, given the extent to which nonviolence contradicted commonly held notions of manhood, it is not surprising that the foot soldiers in Martin Luther King's nonviolent armies frequently carried placards reading, "I *AM* a man."[31]

In the late spring of 1959, two news stories from other parts of the South gripped black America and revealed that black Southerners were far from committed to nonviolence. Both incidents underlined themes of violence, manhood, and the protection of women. One was the notorious lynching of Mack Charles Parker, a twenty-three-year-old black man accused of raping a white woman in Poplarville, Mississippi. Parker had been dragged from his unguarded cell on the night of April 25 and murdered by a mob that somehow had obtained the keys. A federal inquiry later revealed that the lynch mob included "at least one town official and a white clergyman." On May 4, the FBI located Parker's almost unrecognizable body floating in the nearby Pearl River. Although federal agents were able to identify the killers, the state declined to press charges, and the FBI dropped the case.[32] Williams used the tragedy as an opportunity to comment on the efficacy of nonviolence, speculating bitterly that the lynch mob would have been considerably less confident had Parker been permitted to keep a shotgun in his jail cell.[33] When NAACP field secretary Medgar Evers heard about the Parker lynching, he told his wife, Myrlie Evers, "I'd like to get a gun and start shooting." Even though Evers recognized that open armed struggle in the Delta would have been suicidal, many black activists across the region shared his bitter sentiments.[34]

The other agonizing news story during the spring of 1959 was the terrifying ordeal of four young black college students at Florida A&M University in Tallahassee. On May 1, four young white men with guns and knives interrupted two black couples parked on a lonely road after a college dance. The drunken assailants, who had vowed to "go out and get some nigger pussy," one of them testified later, forced the two eighteen-year-old black men to kneel while they tore at the women's formal gowns and discussed which one they should gang-rape.[35] One woman managed to break free and run away; the attackers pressed a switchblade to the throat of the other woman and drove her to a secluded spot. Slapping the young woman repeatedly, they told her she would "never get back home" unless she cooperated. The white men took turns raping her until daybreak approached, then tied her with a leather belt, gagged her with a baby diaper, and forced her to lie on the floor of the car. A sheriff's deputy spotted their brand-new blue Chevrolet around 4:30 A.M., and after a lengthy high-speed chase, deputies found the African American sophomore trembling, bloody, and incoherent in the back seat.[36] Her physical injuries alone required hospital treatment for five days. During the trial of her assailants, their attorney badgered the woman for an hour in an effort to make her admit that she had enjoyed her torture. "Didn't you derive pleasure from that?" he shouted at her again and again. "Didn't you?"[37] Students at Florida A&M at first planned an armed march in response but were persuaded to organize a "passive resistance" sit-in on the Monday after the kidnapping. Not everyone was sold on the nonviolent approach, however. When CORE organizers visited the campus later that year, they reported that many Florida A&M students lost interest in the group when informed that the basic foundation of CORE was nonviolence.[38]

These outrages fed a growing anger and militancy in the black South from which black college students would soon organize the massive sit-in movement that swept the region eight months later, after four members of a North Carolina NAACP Youth Council launched the Greensboro sit-ins.[39] In 1959, however, it was far from clear what would arise from these stirrings. After NAACP attorneys toppled the legal foundations of segregation in the *Brown v. Board of Education* victory of 1954, great hopes gushed forth among black Southerners, but no clear and immediate next step presented itself. The Supreme Court's lofty declarations would not enforce themselves. The murder of fourteen-year-old Emmett Till soon afterward and the acquittal of his murderers, who promptly confessed for *Look* magazine, did nothing to suggest that legal measures would be sufficient.[40] The NAACP, moreover, suffered enormous legal and extralegal pressure from its adversaries while it lacked the ability or even much inclination to mobilize people in large numbers. No clear strategy or leadership beckoned even after the triumph of the Montgomery Bus Boycott in 1955–56. The national office of the NAACP remained either "unwilling to become involved in mass action," Louis Lomax wrote in 1962, or unable to "decide what, if any, role it should play in the mass action movement."[41]

Local branches began both to pressure the impassive national organization and to hammer out their own bold approaches. Impatience with the NAACP hierarchy could be seen especially among the young. An NAACP

Youth Council in Durham, North Carolina, held a campaign of sit-ins at bus stations, parks, and hotels that culminated in the arrests of six activists at the Royal Ice Cream bar in 1957. Between 1957 and 1960, at least sixteen cities across the South witnessed such sit-ins. The emergence of newly independent nations in sub-Saharan Africa, beginning with Ghana in 1957, helped to fuel the impatience of African Americans. "At the rate things are going," James Baldwin lamented, "all of Africa will be free before we can get a lousy cup of coffee."[42] As the decade turned, the NAACP would lose by default the black students who would soon become "the most militant agitators for democracy in America," as Robert Williams had predicted in 1951. "Our parents had the NAACP," Cleveland Sellers of the Student Nonviolent Coordinating Committee (SNCC) would remember of black Southern youth in the late 1950s. "We needed something more. As far as we were concerned, the NAACP's approach was too slow, too courteous, too deferential and too ineffectual." But the decisive shift that the massive sit-in movement and the birth of SNCC in Raleigh would announce in 1960 was still over the horizon when the Parker lynching and the Tallahassee rape case confronted black Southerners.[43]

At the fevered height of this historical moment, local events vaulted Robert F. Williams once more into the national spotlight. The kissing case already had won Williams notoriety as a bold and passionate voice for African American liberation. His public challenge to the framework of the Cold War questioned America's claim as a beacon of freedom to the world. Less well known was the fact that many of his new allies—including Malcolm X—had begun to raise money to buy military carbines, machine guns, and dynamite for the Monroe NAACP.[44] On May 5, with the brutal lynching of Mack Parker and the terrifying rape case in Tallahassee emblazoned on front pages across the country, Robert Williams accompanied a crowd of black women to the Union County courthouse.

Brodus F. Shaw, a white railroad engineer, stood charged with assault on an African American cleaning woman at the Hotel Monroe. On a Saturday morning, Georgia Davis White called to another maid about whether or not the linen had been changed in one of the rooms. Shaw had emerged from his room in his underwear and shouted, "Why the hell are you disturbing my sleep?" He then struck White in the face with his fist and kicked her down a flight of stairs into the hotel lobby. After Dr. Perry released White from the hospital, Williams accompanied her to the courthouse to file charges. Even so, it was very difficult to convince the authorities to issue a warrant for the attacker's arrest. "Shaw, who said the maid ignored a 'Do Not Disturb' sign," reported the *Monroe Enquirer*, "was released on $100 bond."[45]

The following day, Constable Frank Gulledge arrested the assault victim, Georgia White, for allegedly failing to report her wages for temporary work over a six-day period in 1957 at the Monroe Poultry Company—a total of $4.00—to the Union County Employment Security Commission when she applied for unemployment compensation two years earlier. Williams called the charges "part of a pattern of intimidation against Negroes here," noting that "when a Negro charges a white person, there usually comes a counter-charge seeking to discredit the Negro complainant." State employment officials defended the prosecution as "routine," even though they had opened the office on Saturday and Sunday in order to prepare the warrant.[46] A few weeks later, a judge in Monroe ruled that the state's evidence against White—an endorsed check—had been forged. "The Judge had Mrs. White write her name six times on a plain sheet of paper," Dr. Perry wrote to a friend, and "acquitted Mrs. White on the grounds that the endorsement was not in her handwriting."[47]

After the vicious attack on White and the official complicity in reprisals against her, Williams said, "a lot of the Negro women wanted to get together and lynch that white man." Louis Austin knew that the situation in Monroe was perilous and addressed it in a column titled "Faith of Our Fathers in Monroe" published in the *Carolina Times*: "It will take strength to keep a cool head after a man has struck a woman of your race with his fist and kicked her down a flight of stairs simply because she talked too loud and disturbed his sleep," he wrote, framing his argument in the language of manhood. "It will take strength to keep a cool head while attempts are being maliciously made to prosecute the woman for swearing out a warrant against her assailant."[48]

The revenge case against Georgia White, fabricated by local officials of the North Carolina Employment Security Commission, was not the primary way in which the power of the state arrayed itself against this battered black cleaning woman. The SBI and the North Carolina attorney general's office secretly provided free investigative services to her attacker's defense attorney, O. L. Richardson, the same politician who was funneling information about Robert Williams from the FBI to Governor Hodges.[49] The FBI, apparently through a wiretap on Williams's telephone, monitored the local NAACP branch president's contact with the press.[50] Local officials feared, according to the *Monroe Enquirer*, that Williams would somehow turn the case into "another cause celebre for exploitation by the

CCRI and the NAACP." The kissing case had been such an overwhelming embarrassment that paranoia prevailed in official circles. "There is no information," SBI director Walter Anderson assured Shaw's attorney, "that the Communist Party has become interested in the case. We were unable to learn anything at all."[51]

The assault charges against Shaw came to trial on the same day that Lewis Medlin, a white mechanic, stood before the court in Monroe accused of assault with intent to rape. Mary Ruth Reed, a twenty-five-year-old black woman, "testified that Medlin came to the small sharecropper's cabin while her husband was at work and tried to rape her in the presence of her five children." Several months pregnant at the time of the assault, Reed fled across a plowed field with her youngest child in her arms. Medlin caught her, knocked her down, and beat her with his fists until her screams caught the attention of a white neighbor, who called the police. Medlin admitted that he had gone to Reed's house but denied that he had tried to rape her. He had drunk a glass of whisky in the car, Medlin explained, and "felt dizzy" at the time of the events.[52] After Medlin's arrest, Reed said, a friend of Medlin's came by and offered her $100 to drop the charges. "After my husband and I said we were going through with it," she told Ted Poston of the New York Post, "we received threats that we would be forced to move out of our sharecropper's house and my husband J.C. would be fired from his job in town. They said my children were going to starve to death."

Legal delays and daily threats discouraged the Reed family in the months prior to Medlin's trial, but they persisted in pursuing a legal solution. "He's probably not guilty of what he's charged with," Recorder's Court Judge J. Emmett Griffin announced to reporters several weeks before Medlin came to trial. "He was drunk, and may be guilty of assault on a female. But it was not aggravated assault."[53] This rather injudicious declaration by the judge prompted members of the Monroe NAACP to urge that the new machine guns and dynamite be tried out on Medlin prior to any legal proceedings. The brothers of Mary Ruth Reed "wanted to go and blow his house up," Williams recalled, and several of the women in the NAACP "wanted to go and machine gun his house," using the new machine guns that Julian Mayfield had brought to Monroe. According to Williams, he dismissed all such suggestions. "For your information," Williams explained over the telephone to Roy Wilkins at the national NAACP office, "I told them that this matter would be handled through the law and the NAACP would help and the Committee To Combat Racial

Injustice would help. We would be as bad as the white people if we resorted to violence."[54]

On May 5, 1959, the two cases that would force Williams to reconsider this position came to court. Shaw, the white railroad engineer who had attacked White, stood charged with assault on a female. Medlin, the white mechanic who had assaulted Reed, faced charges of aggravated assault with intent to rape. Governor Hodges, wary of bad publicity after the kissing case, "sent a solicitor to Monroe to tell the machine they couldn't just dismiss the [Reed] case," George Weissman wrote to Carl Braden. "Judge told Williams as much after the hearing."[55] The CCRI paid two attorneys, a local black lawyer and a white attorney from New York City, to assist with the prosecution.[56] Even so, Judge Walter Johnston, the same judge who had rejected the boys' plea for freedom in the kissing case, dropped the assault charges against Shaw even though he refused to show up for his court appearance.[57]

During Medlin's trial, defense attorney Richardson pleaded that his client was not guilty because he had been merely "drunk and having a little fun" at the time of the assault. As Mary Ruth Reed took the stand to testify about her terrifying ordeal, the *New York Post* reported, several of the white jurors laughed out loud. Reed's white neighbor, Mrs. Joe Griffin, corroborated the black woman's account of the attack, swearing that she had seen the white man attack Reed, that the black woman had fled to her neighbor's door, trembling and bleeding, children in tow, wearing only one shoe, her clothes badly torn.[58] Richardson countered this evidence by having Medlin's wife sit next to him at the defense table and by appealing to the sentiments of the jurors with respect to gender and race. "Your Honor, ladies and gentlemen of the jury," he reportedly said, "you see this pure white woman, this pure flower of life, God's greatest gift to man, this is [Lewis Medlin's] wife. This white woman is the pure flower of life, one of God's lovely creatures. And, do you think he would have left this pure flower, God's greatest gift," he said, then gesturing toward the victim, "for that?" Mary Ruth Reed began to cry uncontrollably. Richardson "made it appear as if the Afro-American woman were actually on trial," Robert Williams wrote later. After forty-five minutes of deliberation, the jury foreman announced that twelve white men had found Medlin not guilty.[59]

"The black women in the court made such an outcry," Williams recalled, "that the judge had to send Medlin out the rear door." The women then turned on Robert Williams and bitterly shamed him for failing to provide for their protection. If it had not been for you, he remembered them saying, this man would have been punished. In voices that must have evoked the memory of his grandmother, the black women castigated the courts for betraying them and Williams for being naive enough to let it happen. The women "said I was responsible for this man not being punished," Williams testified later, "and I had opened the floodgates on them, and what was I going to do, and now what was I going to say." The fact was, Williams conceded, "that I had kept the black men in the community from killing this man." The anger of these women "made me realize that this was the last straw, that we didn't have as much protection as a dog down there, and the Government didn't care about us." White Americans were proud of the American tradition of armed resistance to tyranny, Williams argued, "and I thought we had the same right to protect ourselves, to defend our women and children." The impotent fury of the moment resonated deeply in Robert Williams's mind. Perhaps it echoed in the bitter hollow where more than twenty years earlier a ten-year-old black boy, helpless to intervene, had watched Big Jesse Helms batter a black woman to the sidewalk and drag her bleeding body to jail. At this burning moment of anger and shame, Robert Williams turned to the UPI reporters who were present and declared that it was time to "meet violence with violence."[60]

Teletype machines across the nation soon clicked out his words:

We must be willing to kill if necessary. We cannot take these people who do us injustice to the court and it becomes necessary to punish them ourselves. In the future we are going to have to try and convict these people on the spot. [These court decisions] open the way to real violence. We cannot rely on the law. We get no justice under the present system. If we feel that injustice is done, we must right then and there on the spot be prepared to inflict punishment on these people. I feel this is the only way of survival. Since the federal government will not bring a halt to lynching in the South and since the so-called courts lynch our people legally, if it's necessary to stop lynching with lynching, then we must be willing to resort to that method.

Williams's fervent tirade set in motion a political firestorm that the editors of the *Carolina Times* later called "the biggest civil rights story of 1959."[61]

Banner headlines flagged his angry words as "symbols of a new militancy among young Negroes of the South."[62] "N.A.A.C.P. Leader Urges Violence," headlines in the *New York Times* announced. The Jackson, Mississippi, *State-Times* captioned the story "Negro Calls for Lynch of Whites." Thomas Waring, the fiery editor of the Charleston *News and Courier*, blamed this "bloodthirsty remark" squarely on the national office: "Hatred is the stock in trade of the NAACP. High officials of the organization may speak in cultivated accents and dress like Wall Street lawyers," Waring charged, "but they are engaged in a revolutionary enterprise."[63] When the words "meet violence with violence" arrived by courier at national NAACP headquarters in New York, Roy Wilkins immediately telephoned Robert Williams and recorded their conversation.

In some respects, the men on either end of the telephone line were as far apart as New York and Monroe, but other things united them. Both were the proud and angry grandsons of former slaves. Both were integrationists with first-rate political minds. Wilkins and Williams were sincere democrats, albeit with some autocratic personal tendencies, who believed deeply in the promise of the U.S. Constitution. In the wake of the lynching and the rape, Wilkins acknowledged years later, "there were limits to how much could be endured." Not only in Monroe but across the South the NAACP "found it hard to keep feelings in some of our branches from boiling over." Wilkins also conceded in his memoirs that "like Williams, I believe in self-defense."[64] But in 1959 class differences, philosophical disagreements, and personal animosity set the two men on different courses. "What we are trying to find out," Wilkins inquired icily, "is about the accuracy—whether or not the newspaper men quoted you correctly. You threatened to meet violence with violence. Is this right?"

Williams not only stood by his statement but informed an incredulous Wilkins that he would be saying the same thing in front of television cameras that very afternoon. "The TV people are coming here to my office to get films," Williams said. "I suppose it will be some national company, newsreel." Wilkins was furious. "Is that from the Monroe station?" the executive director asked nervously, his hopes of containing this potential political disaster fading. Any such hopes evaporated with Williams's reply: "One station was from California, one from Chicago, and one from Detroit. That's what I said and I am going to tell them this on the nation-wide pick-up. I am just about sick of this racial injustice down here." He also informed Wilkins that already he had taped half a dozen telephone interviews with radio stations across the country earlier that day.

"You know, of course," the fuming chieftain of the NAACP snorted into the receiver, "that it is not the policy of the NAACP to advocate meeting lynching with lynching. You are going to make it clear that you are not speaking for the NAACP?" Even as he uttered these words, Wilkins realized that there was little hope of conveying such distinctions to the news media, much less the general public. "Mr. Williams," he added, "in all these news stories, you are identified as president of the Union County chapter of the NAACP. You cannot, of course, separate this in public, the newspapers will label you with the NAACP."

Williams was unsympathetic. "They can't very well say that the national NAACP has been involved," he snapped. "You people are just interested in a few Negroes, not the masses of Negroes. Your office has not been interested in our welfare before now and I don't see why you take an interest now." The executive director made one last plea that Williams try to separate himself from the NAACP. "The point we are getting at, of course," Wilkins repeated, "is that it is not the policy of the national organization"—but Robert Williams interrupted. "This is not an organization speaking," he said sharply. "I am giving my opinion and the opinion of other people I know—people in the community and the feelings of the community. I am speaking for Robert Williams. I will do my best to clarify it." There the conversation ended, but the controversy had only begun.[65]

Before the day was over, Wilkins dispatched a telegram to Williams suspending the branch president from his post as an official of the NAACP "pending consideration of your status by the Board of Directors at its meeting May 11."[66] The national office virtually controlled the board of directors of the NAACP. If this was the forum in which Williams's fate would be determined, it was pointless for him to defend himself.[67] Even so, Williams wired back his intention to fight: "Acknowledge telegram informing me of suspension and board of directors meeting May 11th. Shall attend with counsel." In a parting gesture of defiance, he closed his telegram, "Robert F. Williams, President Union County NAACP."[68]

The following day, Williams appeared at a press conference in New York City to attempt to explain what he had meant by "meet violence with violence." He took special care to disavow his reference to lynching and fend off any suggestion that he favored military strikes against whites. "I do not mean that Negroes should go out and attempt to get revenge for mistreatments or injustice," Williams insisted, "but it is clear that there is no Fourteenth or Fifteenth Amendment[,] no court protection of Negroes' rights here, and Negroes have to defend themselves on the spot when they are attacked by whites." In his many interviews with radio and TV stations, Williams reiterated the point that he was "not advocating lynching" and that he had intended only to say that African Americans must defend their homes and families when attacked by terrorists.[69]

In public, Wilkins tried to put the best face possible on Williams's controversial outbursts and even expressed a limited sympathy for the duress under which Williams had spoken out. "The NAACP does not and has never in its history advocated the use of violence," Wilkins's initial press release read. "At the same time, it must be recognized that the mood of Negro citizens from one end of the nation to the other is one of bitterness and anger over the lynching in Poplarville, Mississippi, April 25, and over numerous instances of injustice meted out to Negroes by the courts in certain sections of the South." Wilkins's worst fears proved unjustified; most of the news stories about Williams's incendiary remarks framed the story as a clash between the Monroe firebrand and the national office. The executive director carefully repudiated "any pro-lynching statement by any one of our officers regardless of provocation," and the controversy showed signs of fading.[70]

Privately, the animosity became more personal. Wilkins mocked the branch president as "Lancelot of Monroe." In a letter to black newspaper publisher P. L. Prattis, Wilkins sought to persuade Prattis that, in fact, Williams did favor aggressive violence. "Since the dispute arose, Williams and his claque have sought to fashion this into one of the right to self-defense," Wilkins wrote. "He did not resort to this happy turn, calculated to obfuscate the people-at-large and win their ready sympathy until he was questioned closely by New York reporters at a press conference he called," Wilkins continued. "Their persistent inquiries finally got through to him and he perceived that he was in dire need of a more reasonable and respectable facade." Wilkins dismissed the man from Monroe as "a tragic sort of stubbornly resentful David, convinced that the Light and the Call have struck him and him only of all the prophets and crusaders on this question down through the decades." "In 1958," Wilkins sneered, Williams "was handed the Revelation which came long ago to Denmark Vesey," referring to the Charleston, South Carolina, carpenter who had plotted an unsuccessful slave revolt in 1822, "but for Williams there is no Vesey nor any others in between." Wilkins freely conceded, however, that Williams reflected rather than challenged the mood of black America in 1958. "The thought of using violence has been in the minds of Negroes," Wilkins conceded. "We know this a good deal better than Mr. Williams."[71]

Wilkins expressed the truth, in the sense that the brutal realities and frustrated hopes of the late 1950s drove many black Southerners to ponder both defensive and sometimes even retaliatory violence. NAACP field secretary Medgar Evers, who in 1953 named his first child after Kenyan revolutionary leader Jomo Kenyatta, "thought long and hard about the idea of Negroes engaging in guerilla warfare in the Delta," Charles Payne has written.[72] But violent resistance to white terrorism was not simply a matter of speculation or fantasy. The Reverend J. A. Delaine, whose activism in Clarendon County, South Carolina, became part of the NAACP's *Brown v. Board of Education* case, blazed away at white terrorists who fired on his home.[73] Williams was not even the first NAACP leader to defend himself with automatic weapons. When Thurgood Marshall of the NAACP Legal Defense Fund came to Birmingham in 1955, he slept at the home of NAACP attorney Arthur Shores, while black men with machine guns patrolled the sidewalk in front of the house.[74] Amzie Moore of Cleveland, Mississippi, the most important local role model for Bob Moses and SNCC, carried a gun "like most politically active Blacks in the Delta," Payne observes. "His home was well armed and at night the area around his house may have been the best lit spot in Cleveland."[75] Prominent NAACP activist Daisy Bates, who had been instrumental in the desegregation of Little Rock's Central High School in 1957, wrote to Thurgood Marshall in 1959 that she and her husband "keep 'Old Betsy' well-oiled and the guards are always on the alert."[76] In Northampton County, North Carolina, the NAACP branch encouraged its members to carry guns to all NAACP meetings. "All blacks in the community were armed," one member reported; "this was necessary." The Ku Klux Klan, in fact, was driven out of Roper, North Carolina, by armed NAACP members, the state conference secretary of the NAACP recalled.[77] The black South in the late 1950s did not hover on the edge of guerilla warfare, but the tactics Robert Williams advocated—"armed self-reliance," as he put it—were already widely practiced.

The fact that many black Southerners already were prepared to meet violence with violence does not mean, however, that it was popular or prudent for Williams to proclaim that fact from the front page of the *New York Times*. His brash declaration alienated many of his allies, some of whom made the good point that it was the political effect of such remarks, not their practical or philosophical merit, that concerned them. "What [Williams] has got to learn to do," Carl Braden pointed out to George Weissman, "is to think how a statement that he gives to UPI in Charlotte is going to sound elsewhere. The way his statement was distorted by the press, people have a twisted impression of his position." Not all of Williams's political supporters were so gracious. In fact, Louis Austin argued that Williams's declaration "drives from his side every law abiding and respectable citizen of North Carolina." Austin denounced any "so-called Negro leader who endorses resorting to lawlessness or violence as a means of securing justice."[78]

Ironically, the white newspaper across town from Louis Austin's *Carolina Times*, the *Durham Morning Herald*, was less hostile to Williams than the black editor was. Noting that the NAACP's record of opposing violence is "unquestioned," the *Herald*'s editors argued that the suspension of Robert Williams "raised serious doubts about the nature of the organization. Is the NAACP a voluntary organization in which the members choose their own officials, or is it an organization whose locals are controlled from headquarters?" The white editors took Wilkins rather severely to task for suspending Williams. Any continuation of the suspension, the *Herald* asserted, "will lend support to the charge of many critics of the NAACP that it is not truly representative of the Negro but imposes the will and wishes of a few on the race."[79]

Several black editors supported Williams without endorsing his incendiary rhetoric. Louis Lautier of the Baltimore *Afro-American* accused Roy Wilkins of "engaging in semantics" and called any harmful effects of Williams's declaration "remote or speculative." Citing the recent Lumbee defeat of the Klan in Maxton, Lautier argued that Williams "merely implies that colored people should defend themselves if and when violence is directed at them." The NAACP, "instead of hearing charges against Mr. Williams, should hear charges against Mr. Wilkins for abuse of authority." In Little Rock, Daisy and L. C. Bates of the *Arkansas State Press* acknowledged the widespread discussions of self-defense and nonviolence but declined to say whether they supported Williams or Wilkins. "We do know," they wrote, "that at times it is pretty hard to suppress certain feelings, when all around you, you see only hate." Acknowledging that violence solved few human problems, the Little Rock editors conceded that "nonviolence never saved George Lee in Belzoni, Miss., or Emmett Till, nor Mack Parker at Poplarville, Miss." "Since the question is one of such magnitude, and is already under discussion by members of the National Board of Directors of the [NAACP]," they equivocated, "it would be far better to let an opinion come from that august body."[80] This was not the kind of resounding support that Wilkins had in mind.

In preparation for the May 11 board meeting that was scheduled to rule on the issue of Williams's suspension, Kelly Alexander, a member of the national board of directors, organized a wave of telegrams from local

NAACP officials in support of Wilkins. This was largely an exercise in obedience; most of the forty telegrams were identically worded form letters. But half a dozen North Carolina NAACP officials, wary of crossing the national office but reluctant to condemn Williams, simply stated, "We uphold the Constitution of the NAACP and are advising you to act accordingly."[81] From Monroe came word from Ethel Azalea Johnson and the board of directors of the local NAACP: "We request that Robert F. Williams remain our president. In his recent statement he reflected the views of members and non-members in our community."[82] Much to Alexander's consternation, Daisy Bates, one of the most well known and glamorous NAACP activists in the country after her role in Little Rock, refused to send a telegram of support or even to attend the board meeting.[83] Wilkins decided to postpone resolution of the Williams matter until the June 8 board meeting, confident that by then he would have matters firmly in hand.

The NAACP's decision to destroy the growing influence of Robert Williams involved some rather unsavory chores, which tell us as much about the nature of American racial politics in the late 1950s as they do about the character of either the NAACP or its leaders. On June 4, 1959, Thurgood Marshall arranged a meeting with agents of the New York office of the FBI "in connection with his efforts to combat communist attempts to infiltrate the NAACP," as the FBI put it. The future U.S. Supreme Court justice informed them that Robert Williams had been suspended from the NAACP "due to his actions in connection with the defense of two Negro children who were sent to a North Carolina Training School for allowing white girls to kiss them." Williams should be investigated, Marshall allegedly told them, because he "will seek to arouse the people in the North Carolina area to take action which could become violent and cause racial unrest and tension." Marshall was, the FBI report stated, "afraid of people agitating on such matters in the South since race tension can be easily aroused, especially during the summer months. Mr. Marshall added that he believes [supporters of Robert Williams] will be used as a pressure group within the NAACP and that the matter of [Williams's 'meet violence with violence'] statement might possibly become an issue at the forthcoming National Convention of the NAACP to be held on July 13–19, 1959." Marshall suggested that the FBI not only should investigate Williams, but "that the Attorney General of North Carolina might have information concerning the persons who donated money to aid the CCRI and if contacted he believes the Attorney General would be willing to furnish this information to the Bureau."[84]

In 1957, Marshall's own FBI file reveals, Marshall had asked the FBI for information about the alleged Communist infiltration of civil rights groups, promising "that no one would know where he got the information." It would be simplistic, however, to dismiss Marshall as a red-baiting snitch lending his wholehearted efforts to the McCarthyite repression that plagued American politics in the 1950s. Marshall's relations with the FBI had not always been so cordial. After Marshall complained that the bureau refused to investigate racial violence in the South in the 1940s, J. Edgar Hoover condemned Marshall's "obvious hostility" toward the FBI. Hoover wielded such awesome and unchecked power by the late 1950s, however, that it was inevitable and necessary that the NAACP deal with him. The FBI was notably hostile to civil rights groups, and Hoover unquestionably had the power to make or break reputations. The FBI had opened an active file on Williams—classified "Security-C," meaning Communist—almost twenty years earlier. Given Williams's regular appearances in the newspapers in connection with white leftists and black liberation, a man of Marshall's political dexterity knew that the FBI watched Robert Williams.[85] Any information that the attorney general of North Carolina had about Williams and his allies could not help the FBI, since it had come from the FBI in the first place. In a sense, then, Marshall's appeal to the FBI could perhaps be understood as the political equivalent of throwing a dead body out of a life raft in order to distract the sharks. "Marshall may have been trying to protect the NAACP from the kind of attacks that the FBI directed at other groups by convincing Hoover that they were part of the fight against communism," Alex Charns, a noted legal scholar, suggests.[86] On the other hand, Marshall's entreaty coincided exactly with the NAACP's coordinated campaign to crush Williams politically. Perhaps the body Marshall threw out of the raft still had a pulse and Marshall considered Williams a serious threat to the NAACP, one to be stopped at any cost.

Marshall had reason to be cautious. The controversy revealed considerable support for the views of the Monroe branch president. The Brooklyn, New York, branch of the NAACP wired Wilkins to protest the "illegal and arbitrary removal from office of Robert F. Williams for expressing sentiments to which we subscribe." The Flint, Michigan, branch passed a resolution to the national board that celebrated Williams for having "won sympathy and respect for the NAACP across our land," opposed "the drastic action" of suspending him, and demanded "his immediate reinstatement."[87] A number of trade unionists and black activists wrote to the national office to defend Williams's right to speak his mind without intimidation. Others defended the substance of his statement. "I share his views one million per cent and so do many more of our members and non-members, too," one member wrote to Wilkins. "The white race have used force for many hundreds of years and they are the only free race on earth. . . . Why can't we do like the Indians did down in [North] Carolina last year?"[88] James Benjamine, an NAACP attorney in Bakersfield, California, wired back to "strongly urge that the Board of Directors rescind Wilkins action" and to insist that the NAACP demand for "the Southern people a republican representative form of government so that self defense will not be necessary."[89]

It is important to distinguish between the national office of the NAACP, where Williams was a pariah, and the local branches, where many of the rank and file defended their homes as a matter of course and agreed with Williams. Even some of the local NAACP officials who had dutifully complied with Alexander's request for telegrams of support did not agree that Williams was a menace. N. L. Gregg, an executive at the North Carolina Mutual Life Insurance Company, had signed a perfunctory telegram but replied privately to Alexander: "As for Williams, I felt once that he was a great deal of trouble but some people have changed my thinking." Williams was actually "doing the NAACP a great favor in that his position and the action of the National office is selling the NAACP to more Southern whites than ever before. A few fools like Williams could cause the state a lot of trouble if they got out of hand," Gregg wrote. Whites would win any armed confrontation, he conceded, but this would never be necessary because "you know as well as I do that they don't want any uprising in this country." With the threat of violence, the insurance executive argued, the white-controlled courts would be more responsive to NAACP litigation. "Believe it or not," Gregg told Alexander, "there are many people who feel that the position Williams took is the one all of us should take."[90]

In an article for the Baltimore *Afro-American* titled "There's Nothing New about It," John McCray, editor of the *Columbia Lighthouse and Informer* and veteran organizer of several decades of freedom struggles in South Carolina, did not applaud Williams's position but sought to place it in historical context. He argued that "the outspoken gentleman said nothing which is strange or new to the ears of those who have been in touch with civic and racial efforts in the South. For at least the forty years that I can recall," McCray pointed out, "there have been many methods suggested for forcing the southern white people to behave themselves and do right, methods which are more drastic and aggressive than those of United States law." Surveying the white violence that had "forged the Civil War, blood-spattered the Reconstruction era, [and] spawned the Ku Klux Klan, [and] the lynch mob," and noting that white Southerners at the moment sanctioned "different sorts of terrorisms, which range from bombings, shootings, and plain murdering to the economic reprisals of the White Citizens Council," the aging warrior observed that "while it is rare that one of their leaders lapses into a statement of the sort attributed to Mr. Williams, there is daily talk among colored people of returning violence for violence." Across "the length and breadth of the South today," McCray stated, "thousands of our people have secured 'protection' in their homes, mostly with the intent to repel night riders who, years ago, were terrors to their forebears." While the editor acknowledged the rising tide of black resistance, he also made it clear that armed self-defense had deep roots in the black South, citing many examples. In the end, McCray believed, even violence that seemed justified should be avoided because it rarely solved anything and because "a minority group cannot hope to win in campaigns of violence." One older black woman, according to McCray, told him, "We don't make ourselves better by getting in the same mud the other fellow's wallowing in."[91]

Not all black women agreed, however, that armed resistance to terrorists was demeaning or that Robert Williams had made a mistake. One woman from New York City wrote to the *Amsterdam News* during the NAACP controversy and mocked "the Negro men of America" for being "mice." Military service did not confer manhood, she argued: "You just went because the white man told you to go. When are you going to learn that you went to war so that the white man could keep *his* freedom?" If a black man in the South so much as looks at a white woman, she argued, "white men take the law into their own hands. Our Negro men stand by and let the white men do anything they want to our women." African American women had little reason to respect their menfolk, she complained bitterly: "You will never have your freedom until you learn to stand up and fight for it. You expect us women to respect you. Why should we?" The writer framed the controversy around Williams as a gender issue in the black community: "I am taking sides with Mr. Robert Williams," she said. "To fight violence with violence now is to show that Negro men are not mice." Throwing down the gauntlet of manhood, she taunted the national office of the NAACP for their failures to protect black women.

Real men, the black woman insisted, would not act this way. "If the NAACP men are afraid to do the job," she jeered, "why don't they move over and let the Negro women do the job?"[92]

With the rank and file thus divided and the national office accused of being unmanly, Daisy Bates was the one political prize that Roy Wilkins could not afford to lose. Wilkins had no intention of going into this battle without the support of the most prominent black woman in the freedom movement. Unfortunately for Wilkins, Bates was also one of his chief critics. Moreover, the heroine of Little Rock spoke frequently throughout the country and often made the point that she carried a pistol and knew how to use it. Only recently Bates had praised the mother of Elizabeth Eckford, the black girl who had faced mobs at Central High School alone, for having "the courage of Harriet Tubman" after Mrs. Eckford told her husband to "go to town and buy me a gun with plenty of bullets." When she saw the Bible and the gun side by side on Eckford's table, Bates said, "I looked at the Bible and I looked at the gun, and [Mrs. Eckford] smiled, 'Yes, the Bible is old, but the gun is new. God said wait as well as pray.'"[93] Bates's repeated exhortations on self-defense, however, did not constitute the political crisis that Robert Williams's statement seemed to present. In a world where manhood and violence were so intertwined, the fact that she was a woman muted the perceived threat. In any case, Wilkins needed help from Bates and was determined to have it whatever the cost.

Wilkins knew that the Bates family was under considerable financial pressure in Little Rock because of white economic reprisals in response to their civil rights activities. On May 19, 1959, Wilkins contacted Bates and "promised that the organization would supplement our income at $600 per month until December 31, 1959," as she reminded him later.[94] Two days later, after Wilkins cut the deal with Bates, Kelly Alexander wrote to her to explain that the organization was "very serious about soliciting your support for the position taken by Roy Wilkins." Scolding her for not having attended the earlier board meeting and for failing to send a telegram of support, Alexander demanded her "utmost cooperation to put a stop to Mr. Robert Williams by taking him out of a position to continue his office for personal advancement and violation of the policy of the NAACP. Your presence at the June Board meeting is essential and needed."[95]

Whether by coincidence or because he understood the gender politics at work, Robert Williams appeared before the June 8 board meeting with two female attorneys. One of them, Pauli Murray, an accomplished civil rights attorney and writer, had grown up in North Carolina and had attempted unsuccessfully in 1938 to become the first African American to enter graduate school at the University of North Carolina.[96] "I would recommend that the NAACP not condone violence," Murray told the board. But it was important, she insisted, to remember the context of Robert Williams's original statement as well as his qualified restatement of his views. "I think that the statement [Williams] made on May 5 was made in anger," Murray argued, "and there was provocation—the same day that Mack Parker's body was found, and the same day the co-ed in Florida was raped, the same day the President of the United States of America said he would not call for stronger civil rights legislation. Violence," she reminded board members, "was the order of the day." In a press release beforehand, Williams had defended his loyalty to the NAACP. "The NAACP is the best organization we have," he stated, and "Negroes should stay in it as I am trying to do and strive to make it better." During the hearing, Williams addressed the board in person, making it clear that he did not support retaliatory violence but merely immediate self-defense under attack. Since this was the NAACP's official position, the clash might well have ended there.[97]

But Roy Wilkins was intent on the public humiliation of this belligerent upstart. Not surprisingly, the board voted to support Wilkins and sustain the suspension. Williams called the vote "a betrayal of the gallant Negroes who are struggling for first class citizenship in the South" and "a maneuver on the part of the national board to avoid elections. They know I would be reelected."[98] Williams saw the clash as rooted in the class pretensions of the NAACP elite. National officials "said that I was a source of embarrassment to them," Williams recalled, "and that all I had was this rag-tag group of ignorant niggers."[99] The board referred Wilkins's action against Williams to the national committee on branches scheduled to convene at the fiftieth-anniversary convention of the NAACP in New York City in July. The stage was set for what amounted to a political show trial.[100]

The NAACP gathered in New York City in the summer of 1959 to celebrate half a century of steady statecraft on behalf of African Americans. At its fiftieth birthday the NAACP could look back with satisfaction at a remarkable series of legal victories and savor its status as the most important civil rights organization in the United States. Yet "the fifteen hundred delegates who gathered in New York's Coliseum were troubled," observed black journalist Louis Lomax; "there were deep rumblings of discontent." A showdown was in the works, and Roy Wilkins knew he was not the only one who sought this confrontation. "The lefties hope to use the Williams case in support of their long-time basic strategy," Wilkins wrote to a friend, "to assault the organizational structure of the NAACP as undemocratic and discredit the national leadership as being out of touch with the aspirations of the membership." Few of the "lefties" organizing against the shrewd conservative leader could have stated their own objectives more succinctly.[101]

Conrad Lynn, himself active in the New York Conference of Branches, circulated "a draft of a militant program to be pushed at the National Convention in New York." The report documented "the growth of lawless violence against Negroes in the South" and proposed that the convention lift Williams's suspension in order to "reaffirm the right and duty of Negroes in those areas of the South where no law protects them to defend themselves." It also blasted "red-baiting of the advocates of full citizenship for all Americans, including members of the National Board of the NAACP," and demanded all NAACP officials cease "to give aid and comfort to our enemies by resorting in their public statements to this same tactic." Lynn had drafted the other provisions of the program to win support among black working people, calling for extension of the minimum wage to domestic workers and for new laws making it a federal offense to discriminate against military veterans or to deny welfare benefits to anyone because of race. Lynn claimed that the program already had "the pledged support of a majority of the delegates of the New York metropolitan area branches."[102]

Whether or not Lynn was right about support for the "militant program," he gauged correctly that many of the convention delegates were unhappy with the NAACP hierarchy. The specific issue for most, however, was the continued refusal of the NAACP to endorse the tactics of nonviolent direct action. More than three years earlier, the Montgomery Bus Boycott and a profoundly stirring young preacher named King had emerged from the South. But Roy Wilkins saw Martin Luther King Jr. as a clear threat to his own position atop the civil rights pyramid. Wilkins "made it clear," David Garrow has written, that the NAACP leadership "had grave doubts about whether nonviolent mass resistance in the Montgomery style could really add much to the pursuit of civil rights."[103] John Morsell, Wilkins's chief assistant, argued in 1960 that the NAACP, because of its devotion to the rule of law, "can hardly advocate or condone a policy of civil disobedience." To endorse nonviolent direct action, he said, would constitute "a complete abandonment of the entire philosophy of operation which has sustained us for 51 years." The NAACP, Morsell declared, "will not advocate this procedure and we will not instruct our people to adopt it."[104]

Large numbers of the delegates, however, believed that it was high time for the calcified NAACP leadership to endorse the bold tactics that NAACP Youth Councils across the South were copying from King and the newly formed SCLC. Ironically, the greater the distance that opened between the NAACP hierarchy and its African American constituency, the more critical its respectable image among whites became as a political asset. For his part, King was eager to avoid any collision with Wilkins.[105] The flap over Robert Williams and his vow to "meet violence with violence" therefore made it possible, perhaps even necessary, for Wilkins and King to postpone their own political rivalry and join forces against the man from Monroe.

The lefties who backed Williams lacked the single-minded coordination of the national office, and many blurred the issues at stake. "The rebel delegates took to the floor in the name of the Williams cause," Lomax reported, "and, through muddy thinking, allowed the leadership of the convention to make the Williams case *the* issue." King himself preferred that any decisive confrontation over his leadership and philosophy take place in an arena that Wilkins did not operate as a personal fiefdom. Thus Wilkins was able skillfully to maneuver the rank-and-file and mass-action questions into the solitary, narrow issue of whether or not Robert Williams should be allowed to keep his post as an NAACP official. Confused delegates, Lomax noted, "somehow equated the Williams issue with mass action, and assumed that by corraling a rousing floor vote against the dismissal of Williams they would inspire the executive board to pay more attention to the rank and file."[106]

With the issue thus framed to his advantage, Wilkins cashed in his abundant political chits and twisted every available arm. Governor Nelson Rockefeller set the necessary tone of respectability with his speech on the opening night of the convention. The New York Republican declared that "segregation is on the way out in America" and celebrated "the kind of leadership the NAACP has given in this great struggle for civil rights." In an unmistakable reference to the Williams case, Rockefeller congratulated the delegates for having made "no appeal to violence" and for "rejecting retaliation against terror." In keeping with the leadership's whispered attempt to link Robert Williams to a red conspiracy, Rockefeller praised the NAACP for having "repulsed the threat of communism to invade your ranks." After the governor's speech, the convention chair announced that the matter of Robert Williams would be presented to the entire convention in the fifth session by the Resolutions Committee.[107]

Wilkins's strategy continued with a pamphlet, titled *The Single Issue in the Robert Williams Case*, distributed to every delegate. "There is no issue of self-defense," the four-page broadside claimed, and "there is no issue of free speech." The only issue at stake, it continued, is "mob action versus the orderly legal, legislative and educational procedures the NAACP has successfully pursued for half a century." The pamphlet narrowed the point of contention to one phrase of Williams's initial outburst. "No charges have been brought against Mr. Williams for his second-thought remarks," the leaflet argued. "The charges are based on his call for aggressive, premeditated violence. Lynching is never defensive."[108] Had this been the single issue, of course, not even Williams himself would have opposed his own suspension, since he had explicitly disavowed these remarks the day after he had uttered them.

When the question of Williams's suspension at last reached the floor of the convention, "the national office not only controlled the platform," one reporter wrote, "they subjected the Williams forces to a heavy bombardment from the NAACP's big guns." Forty speakers one after another denounced Robert Williams and supported Roy Wilkins's action against the Monroe leader. Martin Luther King Jr. offered his unequalled eloquence, arguing that violence by black Americans "would be the greatest tragedy that could befall us" because it would give "our oppressors . . . an opportunity to wipe out many innocent Negroes." Jackie Robinson, the second-baseman who had broken through professional baseball's color barrier, lent his enormous prestige to Wilkins's cause. Even so, the Wilkins team almost failed to turn their well-coached double play against Robert Williams.[109]

The fragility of Wilkins's position became clear when Williams strode down the aisle to make his plea. His force of personality made up for any lack of social polish. "There is no Fourteenth Amendment in that social jungle called Dixie," he declared. "There is no equal protection under the law." He had been angry, they all knew; trials had beset him, but he had never advocated lynching, he told them. But if the black men of Poplarville, Mississippi, had banded together to guard the jail the night that Mack Parker was lynched, Williams asked, would that have hurt the cause of justice? If the young black men who escorted the coed who was raped in Tallahassee had been able to defend her, Williams reminded them, such action would have been justified "even though it meant that they themselves or the white rapists were killed." "Please," he beseeched the assembly, "I ask you not to come crawling to these whites on your hands and knees and make me a sacrificial lamb."

And there the pleading stopped. He paused for a moment. Perhaps the spirit of his grandfather Sikes Williams, the former slave who had fought for interracial democracy and wielded a rifle against white terrorists, welled up within him. Perhaps it was the voice of his grandmother, who had passed that rifle down to him, that spoke through him. "We as men should stand up as men and protect our women and children," he said firmly. "I am a man and I will walk upright as a man should." His sonorous baritone rose almost to a roar. "I WILL NOT CRAWL!" When Williams left the podium, some experienced political observers thought—or perhaps merely hoped—that Wilkins was about to be embarrassed.[110]

Lomax called it "a desperation move" when "the NAACP leadership called in Mrs. Daisy Bates, then riding high as the heroine of Little Rock." But Lomax was wrong. Wilkins, veteran of many such wars, hardly left his political fate to chance. As Wilkins knew she would, Bates brought matchless symbolic appeal to this confrontation. Not only did she possess glamour, eloquence, and a reputation for integrity, but as a black woman, her voice would undercut Williams's visceral appeal for her protection. It was well known, moreover, that the Bates home in Little Rock had been the object of ceaseless attacks by carloads of trigger-happy white thugs. Bates herself knew how to handle a gun and was rumored to have taken shots at the nightriders. Mounting the podium, Bates denounced Williams for betraying the ideals of nonviolence and for endangering the success of the movement. Her impassioned speech overshadowed even King and Robinson. Bates turned the insurgent tide and sealed the vote against Williams. Because of Wilkins's "unit rule," in which the majority in each of the NAACP's seven regions determined the entire region's votes, the tally showed a vote of 781-0 to uphold the suspension of Robert Williams. A better assessment of the balance of power was reflected in the fact that Williams and his supporters were able to force the adoption of a statement endorsing the right of black people to defend themselves against terrorists: "We do not deny, but reaffirm the right of individual and collective self-defense against unlawful assaults."[111]

The convention concluded, and the delegates returned to their homes. Daisy Bates arrived back in Little Rock to confront a crisis that underlined the tragic miscalculation of the NAACP's suppression of Williams and his strategy of self-defense. "Shortly after I arrived home," she recalled, "a bomb made of several sticks of dynamite was hurled at our house."[112] Sitting up to guard the house with a .45 automatic—the same type of weapon that Williams carried in Monroe—Bates dispatched a telegram to the U.S. attorney general recounting the many attacks on her family. "Incendiary bombs have been thrown at our home from automobiles," she wrote. "Three KKK crosses have been burned on our lawn. Fire has been set to the house on two occasions." Her windows were smashed so often, she told him, that "steel screens had to be made to cover the front windows." But it came as no surprise to Williams when he heard that Bates found more desperate measures necessary. "We have been compelled to employ private guards," she told the attorney general.[113]

"I am sorry to hear that the white racists have decided to step up their campaign of violence against you," Williams wrote to Bates a couple of weeks later. But it was anger at her hypocrisy more than sympathy at her plight that inspired his letter. "I deeply regret that you took the position you did on my suspension," Williams wrote. "It is obvious that if you are to remain in Little Rock you will have to resort to the method I was suspended for advocating."[114]

Sikes Williams, born a slave in Union County, was a Republican activist during the late nineteenth century and edited a local newpaper called the *People's Voice*. In it he declared to black voters, THE CHAINS OF SERVITUDE ARE BROKEN. NOW NEVER LICK THE HAND THAT LASHED YOU. Robert Williams grew up on stories of his grandfather's political exploits. "They all said I was just like him," Williams recalled. Courtesy of John Herman Williams.

Robert's "Uncle Charlie," Charles Williams, taught school in Monroe and "was instrumental in this community," according to Annie Bell Cherry. A veteran of World War I, Charles Williams challenged racial boundaries in the South and was a pivotal influence on young Robert. Courtesy of John Herman Williams.

Robert Williams was born in the Williams family homeplace at 410 Boyte Street, in the "Newtown" section of Monroe. While most families in the neighborhood rented from whites, the Williams family owned their home. Courtesy of John Herman Williams.

While Robert looked for wartime work in Detroit and California, Mabel operated a day care center in Monroe. Courtesy of John Herman Williams.

Eighteen-year-old Robert F. Williams joined his brothers in Detroit, where he fought in the riot of 1943. Here he and his brother join several other men in a Detroit nightspot. Robert is second from the left. John Herman Williams is fourth from the left. Courtesy of John Herman Williams.

Unidentified African American man in front of "white only" laundromat, Monroe, 1961. Courtesy of John Herman Williams.

Private First Class Robert F. Williams, U.S. Marine Corps, 1954.
Courtesy of John Herman Williams.

"Catfish" Cole in defeat. In 1956 and 1957 Cole organized Klan rallies near
Monroe with crowds estimated by local newspapers at up to 12,000. When the
Monroe NAACP repelled an attack by Cole's Klansmen with gunfire in late 1957,
the city council banned Klan motorcades. Courtesy of James W. Cole Papers,
Joyner Library, East Carolina University.

Left to right: Robert's siblings, John Herman Williams, Lorraine G. Williams,
and Edward S. "Pete" Williams, with Dr. Albert E. Perry Jr., vice-president of the
Monroe branch of the NAACP, with some of the weapons the branch used to
defend Dr. Perry's house in 1957. Courtesy of John Herman Williams.

Left to right: Edward S. "Pete" Williams, Robert F. Williams, John Herman Williams (*crouching*), and Dr. Albert E. Perry Jr. at a meeting of the Monroe, N.C., NAACP in 1957. Courtesy of John Herman Williams.

"My strength cometh from the Lord." Robert Williams's siblings (*standing, left to right*), John Herman Williams, Lorraine Williams, and Edward S. "Pete" Williams; his two sons, John Chalmers Williams (*standing at left*) and Robert F. Williams Jr. (*seated at right*); and his father, John Williams (*middle*). Unidentified girl in the foreground. Courtesy of John Herman Williams.

In 1958 a judge in Monroe sentenced James Hanover Thompson, ten, and David E. "Fuzzy" Simpson, eight, to reform school for kissing a white playmate in a game. Williams launched a publicity campaign that made the "kissing case" front-page news around the world. Here Thompson and his mother are reunited briefly at the habeas corpus hearing in Wadesboro, N.C., in early 1959. Courtesy of State Historical Society of Wisconsin.

The Week's Conversation Piece

The NAACP controversy over Williams's vow to "meet violence with violence" created the biggest civil rights story of 1959. This cartoon appeared in the Baltimore *Afro-American* on May 23, 1959. Courtesy of Baltimore *Afro-American*.

Left to right: Mabel R. Williams, Robert F. Williams, Lorraine G. Williams, and Edward S. "Pete" Williams in the 1950s. Courtesy of John Herman Williams.

An interracial group of Freedom Riders, sponsored by CORE and the SCLC and led by James Forman, soon to head SNCC, came to Monroe in August 1961 to organize a campaign of nonviolent protest. Courtesy of John Herman Williams.

After a long day of picketing in August 1961, members of the Monroe Nonviolent Action Committee have a beer with Robert's brother John Herman Williams. The white man on the right is one of the Freedom Riders. Richard Crowder and Harold Reape (*fourth and fifth from left, respectively*) were charged with kidnapping several days later. Courtesy of John Herman Williams.

(*opposite*)During his first trip to Cuba in 1960, Williams grew a Castro-style beard. Courtesy of John Herman Williams.

Through *The Crusader* and Robert Williams's speaking tours, activists in Monroe persuaded people from all over the country to send food, clothing, and other relief to the poor in Union County. Here local supporters of Robert Williams unload one of the trucks. Courtesy of John Herman Williams.

One of the Freedom Riders with a sign referring to the fact that white police and white bystanders arrested and assaulted demonstrators who tried to take photographs in Monroe. Courtesy of John Herman Williams.

Genoa Culbertson Marsh, a young Williams supporter, picketing during the
summer of 1961, a period that Williams later called "a savage struggle for survival."
Photo by Declan Haun, courtesy of Declan Haun family.

Mrs. Crowder, a neighbor, was a staunch supporter of Robert F. Williams. After Williams fled for Cuba, investigators found a number of semiautomatic rifles hidden in the walls of her home. Courtesy of John Herman Williams.

Left to right: Richard Crowder, Mae Mallory, and Harold Reape were charged with kidnapping and spent time in prison as a result of the clashes on August 28, 1961. Courtesy of John Herman Williams.

The segregated swimming pool at the Monroe Country Club. The city of Monroe abandoned the pool rather than permit black citizens to use it. Many local African Americans still consider the pool an unacknowledged monument to Robert F. Williams. Courtesy of John Herman Williams.

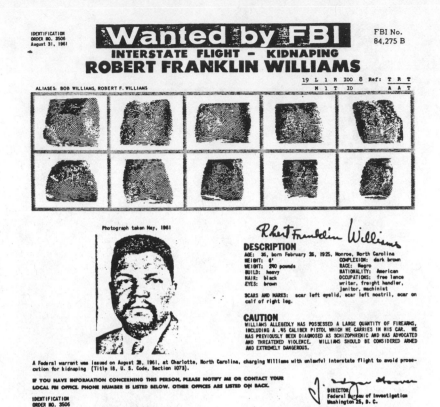

Wanted by FBI

INTERSTATE FLIGHT — KIDNAPING
ROBERT FRANKLIN WILLIAMS

FBI No.
84,275 B

ALIASES: BOB WILLIAMS, ROBERT F. WILLIAMS

19 L 1 R IOO 8 Ref: T R T
M 1 T IO A A T

Photograph taken May, 1961

DESCRIPTION

AGE: 35, born February 26, 1925, Monroe, North Carolina
HEIGHT: 6'
WEIGHT: 200 pounds
BUILD: heavy
HAIR: black
EYES: brown
COMPLEXION: dark brown
RACE: Negro
NATIONALITY: American
OCCUPATIONS: free lance writer, freight handler, janitor, machinist
SCARS AND MARKS: scar left eyelid, scar left nostril, scar on calf of right leg.

CAUTION

WILLIAMS ALLEGEDLY HAS POSSESSED A LARGE QUANTITY OF FIREARMS, INCLUDING A .45 CALIBER PISTOL WHICH HE CARRIES IN HIS CAR. HE HAS PREVIOUSLY BEEN DIAGNOSED AS SCHIZOPHRENIC AND HAS ADVOCATED AND THREATENED VIOLENCE. WILLIAMS SHOULD BE CONSIDERED ARMED AND EXTREMELY DANGEROUS.

A Federal warrant was issued on August 28, 1961, at Charlotte, North Carolina, charging Williams with unlawful interstate flight to avoid prosecution for kidnaping (Title 18, U. S. Code, Section 1073).

IF YOU HAVE INFORMATION CONCERNING THIS PERSON, PLEASE NOTIFY ME OR CONTACT YOUR LOCAL FBI OFFICE. PHONE NUMBER IS LISTED BELOW. OTHER OFFICES ARE LISTED ON BACK.

IDENTIFICATION
ORDER NO. 3506

DIRECTOR
Federal Bureau of Investigation
Washington 25, D. C.

The FBI falsely reported that Williams, who had escaped their dragnet, was "diagnosed as schizophrenic." Calling him "armed and extremely dangerous," FBI agents also fabricated the scars described on the poster. Robert F. Williams FBI Subject File, courtesy of Robert F. Williams.

A gleeful Robert F. Williams enjoys a Cuban cigar in celebration of his safe passage to Havana after escaping from a massive FBI dragnet in 1961. Courtesy of John Herman Williams.

Robert F. Williams teaches Mabel Williams, his wife, to use a pistol given to him
by Fidel Castro in Havana in 1961. Four months earlier she had held off Monroe police
officers with a .12-gauge shotgun when they came to arrest her husband. Courtesy of
John Herman Williams.

Mao Zedong autographs Robert Williams's copy of *The Quotations of Chairman Mao* in Beijing, China, 1966. Courtesy of John Herman Williams.

The Chinese government treated the Williams family as distinguished guests, providing them with an extended tour of the country and producing a full-length film of their journey, *Robert Williams in China*. Courtesy of John Herman Williams.

TWA and the U.S. State Department scheduled a special $20,000 flight from London to return Robert Williams to the United States. Courtesy of John Herman Williams.

Robert and Mabel Williams at a 1969 press conference.
Courtesy of John Herman Williams.

Robert F. Williams revisits Monroe Country Club in the mid-1970s.
Courtesy of John Herman Williams.

Robert and Mabel Williams, September 2, 1996, at their home in Baldwin, Michigan. They had been married for forty-nine years. Williams died a few weeks later, surrounded by his family. Courtesy of John Herman Williams.

Rosa Parks (*center*) arriving for Robert Williams's funeral. In her eulogy, Parks said that she and those who had marched with Martin Luther King Jr. in Alabama had always admired Robert Williams "for his courage and his dedication to freedom. The work that he did should go down in history and never be forgotten." Courtesy of John Herman Williams.

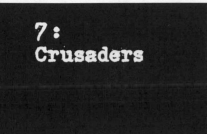

7:
Crusaders

"Mae, turn on the radio," her neighbor called out. "There's something on WLIB that you would be interested in." Mae Mallory, a thirty-two-year-old African American woman, dark-skinned and heavyset, turned the dial on her radio and heard a voice that changed her life forever. As a young girl growing up in a black ghetto in Macon, Georgia, Willie Mae Mallory had tried to roller-skate on a freshly blacktopped hill in a white neighborhood—the streets where she lived were not paved. White children blocked her path, and "a fight ensued and I fought back," Mallory recalled. "I took off my skates and I bloodied their heads." Another time, a white girl slapped Willie Mae and sent her home crying; Mallory's mother told her to go back and hit the white girl "or I wasn't going back into that house. And the girl's mother called the police." A series of similar clashes landed young Mallory on a train bound for New York City, where she lived with several other family members in her grandmother's one-room apartment in Brooklyn. "My mother could see I wasn't going to make it so good in the South," she recalled.

In the North, Mallory's festering rage collided with a string of employers, the welfare bureaucracy, and the city school board. During the early 1950s, Mallory joined the Communist Party, in part as a reaction to domestic anticommunism, which puzzled her greatly. "Every time I raised a question of better wages, better working conditions, and equality for black people," she said, "somebody would tell me that was communist. Then when I would pick up the newspaper, all I could hear was [Senator Joseph] McCarthy accusing somebody of being a communist." It appeared to Mallory that "the communists were the only ones who wanted these good things and here was somebody who wanted to put them in jail. So I decided I better seek out the communists." Impressed at first, Mallory joined the party. But soon she discovered that the organization's genuine commitment to interracialism was not matched by a deep understanding of African American life or a demonstrable ability to deliver on their manifestos for black liberation. "I could see that they didn't have the answers," Mallory remembered, "and the whole bottom of my world just fell out."

Disillusioned with the Communists, Mallory wandered through the various black nationalist circles of Harlem in the mid-1950s. "I went to the nationalist movement just to listen," she said, "and they talked a real militant thing but nobody did anything, you know. They didn't have any answers and the men had contempt for the women." Mallory decided to "set out on my own, to work with this group and with that group and the other group."[1]

According to a history of Harlem politics and culture, Mallory became "a prominent Harlem resident and community activist and part of a group known as the Harlem Mothers who brought a desegregation case against the school system along with eight other mothers and won the case."[2] As the freedom movement began to quicken in the late 1950s, the broad-shouldered black woman would watch with great interest but always held herself back. "I knew that I couldn't follow any discipline of a nonviolent demonstration," Mallory said later. "So I never bothered to go out on any of the picket lines or anything."[3]

In the summer of 1959, however, her Harlem neighbor called out to Mallory and she turned on the radio to hear Robert Williams tell the NAACP convention that black men needed to stand up, defend their homes and families, and treat black women with respect. Virtually no one had stood up for Mae Mallory or treated her with respect, so far as she was concerned. "So I heard it and I said, 'My God, you know, this is only right,'" she recalled. "So instead of going to work that day, I got up and went in the streets and organized some support for Robert Williams, a man that I had never met." After the NAACP upheld Williams's suspension, Mallory and her political allies "decided that, well, we'll all join his chapter." Mallory and her friends began to raise money in Harlem to support Williams.[4] Two years later, Mallory would find herself huddled in Robert Williams's house in Monroe, clutching a machine gun and wondering whether anyone there would live through the night.

Like Mae Mallory, black activists in the late 1950s cast about for weapons in the fight against white supremacy and struggled to give real meaning to victories already formally won. The Supreme Court's *Brown* decision inspired mostly opposition; across the South, historian Adam Fairclough has written, the decision "unleashed a wave of racism that reached hysterical proportions, drowning out the voices of moderation and compromise."[5] In the years to come, the reactionary politicians that massive resistance produced would become the unwitting accomplices of Martin Luther King Jr. and his SCLC organizers. White violence was an indispensable element in the street-theater morality plays that helped win passage of the Civil Rights Act of 1964 and the Voting Rights Act of 1965.[6] In the late 1950s, however, these dramatic victories certainly did not seem inevitable.

In the long run, too, the meaning of these policy achievements cannot be divorced from the freedom movement's creation of a new black sense of self, anchored in age-old traditions of struggle but generating new possibilities of individual self-respect and collective aspiration. Indigenous activism, rooted in race pride and citizenship traditions, made it possible for black men and women to win concrete victories that then fed that sense of African American pride and democratic self-assertion. When national organizations such as the NAACP and SCLC finally won federal legislation, it was left to ordinary black citizens to render those laws meaningful on the local level. As James Edward McCoy, an African American leader in Oxford, North Carolina, tartly observed of the measures regarding public accommodations, "Somebody still had to walk in there and get kicked in the ass."[7]

In 1959 and early 1960, amid an atmosphere of political stalemate and white intransigence, Robert Williams moved both to strengthen the local movement in Monroe and to reach out to a national audience with speeches, writings, and broadcasts. His message was neither racially separatist nor rigidly ideological. Though Williams underlined the fact that "both sides in the freedom movement are bi-racial," his emerging philosophy reinvigorated many elements of the black nationalist tradition whose forceful emergence in the mid-1960s would become known as Black Power.[8] Williams stressed black economic advancement, black pride, black culture, independent black political action, and what he referred to as armed self-reliance. He connected the Southern freedom struggle with the anticolonialism of the emerging Third World, especially African nations. In the late 1950s, when other integrationists focused on bus boycotts and voter registration, Williams insisted on addressing persistent black poverty: "We must consider that in Montgomery, where Negroes are riding in the front of buses," he said, "there are also Negroes who are starving."[9] His approach was practical, eclectic, and improvisational. There must be "flexibility in the freedom struggle," he argued, and tactics must emerge from the urgent realities of the confrontation itself.[10] At the core of his appeal, however, stood his calls for absolute equality under a fully enforced U.S. Constitution, backed by an uncompromising resistance to white supremacy.[11]

At the same time, a growing controversy over violence and nonviolence arose within the black freedom movement, revealed by Williams's censure by the national NAACP but spurred by the brutal realities that confronted the movement across the South. When Williams issued his call for self-defense, Martin Luther King Jr. and many other prominent activists seem to have realized how deeply such words resonated among their constituents. Just as Wilkins had found it necessary to do battle with "Lancelot of Monroe," King soon took the field against Robert Williams. In a published written debate, the minister not only felt compelled to embrace self-defense himself but also to caricature Williams's views in an effort to stem his influence. More than King's considerable persuasive skills, the sudden emergence of the student movement after the Greensboro sit-ins on February 1, 1960, temporarily set aside the debate over violence and nonviolence and gave the battalions of nonviolent direct action their compelling historical moment.

When we look back at history, however, it is important to resist the temptation to view all events as part of an inexorable chain of causality leading inevitably to the present. Nonviolent direct action was a fortunate but certainly not an inevitable course of strategy. Nor did it have deep roots in Southern black culture. Though nonviolence was compatible with the distinctive Afro-Christianity of the black South, it was not interchangeable with it. To understand its full-blown emergence with the sit-in movement in the spring of 1960, we must understand what nonviolence was and what it was not. We must understand, too, that for most black Southerners nonviolence was a tactical opportunity rather than a philosophical imperative. Thus we must reconsider that time before the sit-ins swept the South, before the founding of SNCC, before the Freedom Riders rolled through Dixie, before Albany and Birmingham and Selma etched their mark on human history, and before the dream of Martin Luther King Jr. captured the moral imagination of the world, when the course of events still might have gone quite differently.

In the wake of his showdown with the national office of the NAACP in the summer of 1959, Williams returned home determined to push the freedom struggle forward in Monroe and across the country. Although he had achieved notable success at using the press to his advantage in the kissing case, Williams realized that even the black press could not be relied on to support the bold strokes that were needed to break the racial stalemate. "My militant philosophy had evoked the enmity of most of the so-called black establishment," Williams wrote later.[12] His potential adversaries, moreover, could snipe at him from any number of prominent podiums in American culture. Roy Wilkins, for example, not only commanded considerable influence in editorial offices around the country, but he could pillory Williams in the pages of The Crisis.

And so Robert Williams, like his grandfather before him, became an editor and publisher. On July 26, 1959, the Williams family launched The Crusader Weekly Newsletter. Like Williams's entire career, The Crusader was an expression of homegrown black Southern radicalism that emerged from local black traditions and communities of resistance but took on international political implications. "I felt like we needed a way to get out our own side, our own story," Robert Williams said.

"What we were trying to do was actually to counteract Roy Wilkins and The Crisis," Williams explained.[13] According to Mabel Williams, however, the decision to start The Crusader was not entirely a response to the NAACP controversy. A year earlier, in the summer of 1958, she later wrote, Mabel, her husband, and Ethel Azalea Johnson first discussed founding a newspaper. "The three of us sat on the front porch discussing local happenings and world affairs," Mabel Williams wrote. "The conversation as usual drifted to our pet subjects: how the white press slanted and distorted facts of incidents regarding Negroes, and our great need for a news media that would be able to tell the whole story." The friends agreed that they should try to start a publication of their own, but they could not imagine how the necessary funds could be raised. "The next few days found us in and out of office machine companies, trying to find a bargain in a mimeographing machine and supplies with an installment plan," she wrote. But it would take more than a year before they could act on their plans, and in the end it was the impending collision with the national office of the NAACP that made The Crusader both necessary and possible.[14]

About two weeks after Mae Mallory heard Robert Williams on the radio defending himself against the national office of the NAACP, FBI agents reported to J. Edgar Hoover that Williams had "recently begun selling a weekly newsletter known as The Crusader on the streets of Monroe." Local informants provided copies of the first four issues, and agents noted that it "consist[ed] of approximately four letter-size mimeographed pages."[15] It was rough-hewn but passionate journalism, and the front page boasted a hand-sketched castle logo. "None of us knew much about mimeographing at first," Mabel wrote, "as evidenced in our first issue; nevertheless, we were proud and happy over it, and bought books on mimeographing so as to try and improve as we went along. We had only purchased enough supplies to last us a few weeks," she continued, "and with no more money to buy supplies we went with our Newsletter to the local people, who gladly paid their dime to read it."[16] By the time the civil rights establishment had crushed Robert Williams at the 1959 NAACP convention, the Monroe activists had painstakingly rolled three issues of The Crusader off the new hand-operated mimeograph machine. Copies circulated in the corridors at the convention and throughout the streets of Harlem, FBI agents noted.[17] "People who expect the Union County Branch of the NAACP to die are going to be disappointed," The Crusader declared after Williams went down to defeat at the convention. "THE UNION COUNTY BRANCH HAS WON THE RESPECT OF THE ENTIRE WORLD."[18]

From the start, the banner mission of The Crusader remained "ADVANCING THE CAUSE OF RACE PRIDE AND FREEDOM." Its title fittingly echoed the late Cyril V. Briggs, Harlem organizer of the left-wing African Black Brotherhood, whose newspaper of the same name had issued a "Declaration of War on the Ku Klux Klan" in 1921, as the Klan rose to heights of national power and political influence. "With the murderer clutching at our throats," Briggs wrote in the hooded order's heyday, "we can ill afford to choose our weapons, but must defend ourselves with what lies nearest whether that be poison, fire, or what." Williams chose his newsletter's title in honor of Briggs, whom he had heard about many years earlier, probably during his stay in Harlem.[19]

Robert Williams served as editor, while Mabel Williams worked as circulation manager and wrote an occasional African American history column titled "Looking Back." She also proved talented at sketching hilarious and often brilliant editorial cartoons. One early drawing showed an angry mouse chasing a startled cat and yelling, "I tol' ya you'd push me too far one of these days!"[20] Azalea Johnson managed the newsletter's finances and wrote a marvelous weekly column called "Did You Know?" From the very first issue, The Crusader took an uncompromising stand against white supremacy and black accommodationism. "We know the Uncle Toms will scream loud and long, but they have a vested interest in the oppression of our people," the first issue declared. "We know there can be no progress without friction, so we won't expect smooth sailing. We are in the field now and surely the battle cometh." From the outset, even the advertisements slammed segregation: "Why stand on the streets to eat when you can enjoy a delicious meal in Leo's Grill sitting down?"[21]

The Crusader linked its local readers to African American history and to broader worlds of politics and culture. An article by Mabel Williams on black women in South Africa's antiapartheid movement, for instance, connected caste and sex in that country to the lives of women in Monroe.[22] *The Crusader* celebrated the music of Billie Holiday and Louis Armstrong at the same time that it touted performances by Monroe's own Taylor Gospel Singers and the Five Trumpets of Wingate.[23] Mabel Williams wrote a one-page history of Harriet Tubman and the Underground Railroad but also published slave stories she collected from Mama Stitt, her hundred-year-old next-door neighbor.[24] One issue featured historical accounts of slave insurrections drawn from the work of Herbert Aptheker. Alongside Nat Turner and Denmark Vesey, however, stood an admiring profile of Monroe's own George H. Rushing Sr., a retired tradesman and schoolteacher whose patient, steady work as an independent artisan and voting-rights activist offered a local model to the young.[25]

At first the newsletter depended strictly on local readers and NAACP volunteers; friends helped run off copies, fold and stack them, and deliver the papers to the surrounding countryside. Black children hawked the newsletter on street corners. For Mabel Williams and her women friends, "a usual Saturday" meant driving to dozens of places within a thirty-mile radius of Monroe, delivering *The Crusader* to supporters in Wadesboro, Peachland, Polkton, Marshville, and Wingate. They drove "for hours, canvassing from door to door, chatting with the people and walking for miles."[26] This was one way, in fact, that the women kept the NAACP chapter growing, starting 1959 with 92 dues-paying members but expanding to 121 official members by October. In a period when NAACP chapters across the South dwindled dramatically, the Monroe branch thrived. "People know that they can call in the middle of the night and I'll help them," Mabel Williams told Anne Braden in 1959. "We've been under attack by everybody and we're still growing."[27]

What started as an NAACP branch newsletter quickly reached a small national audience. "We operated on this [purely local] basis for about a month when we decided to do some promotional mailing," Mabel Williams recounted. "Robert had acquired many friends through his traveling and speaking," she observed, "and after his statement that Negroes would have to 'meet violence with violence,' many more people with the same opinion had written to him. To these, and many more whom we believed wanted to hear the truth, went The Crusader. The response was good and we started receiving subscriptions." The success of the sample mailings surprised them, yielding first hundreds and soon a couple thousand subscribers across the country.[28]

Looking at The Crusader with the historian's privilege of hindsight, it is striking how the newsletter defies the conventional narrative of the black freedom movement that begins with civil rights and ends with Black Power. In fact, virtually all of the elements that we have come to associate with the Black Power movement that gained national attention after 1965—anticolonial internationalism, black pride, economic nationalism, cultural politics, and armed self-defense—resonated in these pages as early as 1959. "Through The Crusader, we became the first civil rights group to advocate a policy stressing Afro-American unity with the struggling liberation forces of Latin America, Asia and Africa," Robert Williams wrote some years later. "We steadfastly maintained, in the face of vigorous opposition from white liberals and the black bourgeoisie, that our struggle for black liberation in imperialist America was part and parcel of the international struggle."[29]

Africa seemed to echo from every page of The Crusader, frequently in expressions of international solidarity but often as a display of black self-affirmation, an emphasis that mirrored the Marcus Garvey movement of the 1920s. "Did you know," Azalea Johnson asked her readers, that "the Black people of Africa have race pride and want their race to remain black; that Blacks feel mighty good in their own company and are fighting to redeem their country for themselves?"[30] In the first issue, Mabel Williams sketched a cartoon depicting a young African man dressed in a business suit and tie, returning to Africa after his education in the United States, his suitcase bedecked with university pennants. Protruding from the graduate's back pocket was a newspaper with headlines about rape and lynching in the United States. Throwing his arms around his father, who wore African garb and carried a spear, the young man declared, "My father, you don't know how happy I am to be back home away from those savages." In an accompanying article, Robert Williams added, "We like to think of Africa as the land of savages and jungles, but there are not many jungles more savage than this section of America called Dixie."[31] While this recognition of African heritage does not fit the popular image of either the small-town South or the 1950s, black intellectual Harold Cruse observed in 1968, at the heyday of Black Power's discovery of Africa, that "the awareness of Africa was never as scarce among black people as many present-day experts make out."[32]

Like the Garveyites who preceded him and the Black Power advocates who followed him, Robert Williams stressed economic development, but he hit segregation just as hard. *The Crusader* persistently managed to blend these issues. Mabel Williams noted that the Union County Industrial Development Commission, though supported with tax dollars from black as well as white citizens, recruited firms that respected the local color line and hired only white skilled workers. The industrial commission bragged in its literature about the extensive vocational training available to high school students in Union County, she pointed out, even though "the Negro students of Union County do not receive this type of training."[33]

Azalea Johnson's "Did You Know?" column urged readers to spend their money with black entrepreneurs or with white businesses that employed black workers. "Since the 'good white folks' here are determined to keep us out of employment in Union County," she wrote, "we should be just as determined in where we spend our money."[34] When local white employers proved willing to hire black working people, however, *The Crusader* was quick to acknowledge and reward them. "The local THRIFTY FOOD STORE is the first Monroe store to lower the color bar and hire Negro youths," Robert Williams announced in 1960. "This should be a cue for people of color to buy at THRIFTY."[35]

Unlike either the Garveyites or the supporters of the Black Power movement, Williams remained an integrationist and was never reluctant to acknowledge the contributions of white supporters. "The struggle for human rights is a moral struggle, actually, not just a struggle of black against white and vice versa," he wrote. "Both sides of the human rights struggle are integrated," Williams pointed out. He freely acknowledged that a few African Americans supported segregation. "Most of these are either ill-informed or mercenary crumb snatchers," he argued. "In any event," Williams insisted, "the strange case of Jim Crow justice cannot be stereotyped with a label of black and white. All Negroes are not enlightened enough to be integrationists and all whites are not stupid enough to be segregationists."[36]

Williams was similarly evenhanded regarding the role of organized religion. Quotations from the Bible adorned every copy of *The Crusader*, and "Church News" was a regular feature. Both Mabel Williams's "Looking Back" features and Azalea Johnson's "Did You Know?" columns revealed deep and sincere Christian commitments. Even so, Robert Williams frequently mounted blistering attacks on black ministers—"brown-nosing vampires," he once charged—"who judge the worth of Christian individuals on the basis of real estate holdings."[37] At the same time, when local black ministers complained to white authorities in the fall of 1959 about a man in Monroe who accosted black women on back streets and tried to make them "dance" by shooting near their feet, Williams congratulated "the ministers who have come to the defense of our women who were the victims of the mad white gun slinger."[38] Though Williams saved his most brutal invective for white segregationists who claimed to be Christians, he recognized the sacrifices that white Christians across the South made every day. "Today many white ministers are being driven from their pulpits because of moral stands based upon the teachings of Christ that stress brotherhood free from racial bigotry," he wrote. "White teachers are being barred from Southern classrooms because they dare teach American principles of democracy."[39]

Williams was fond of unleashing the kind of red-white-and-blue rhetoric that white citizens relished at Fourth of July celebrations, but he typically deployed it for purposes that few white people dared to support—armed resistance to white terrorism, for example. "Tom Paine, Washington, Jefferson, and Patrick Henry were all honorable men," he wrote, "who are supposed to represent the true spirit of America. These noble men advocated violence as a vehicle of liberation. They are not considered wild-eyed, bloodthirsty fanatics by a long shot." Almost all white men and boys owned guns in Monroe; shooting clubs, firearms training, and hunting season were all part of daily life. Military service and the willingness to defend home and family were universally admired among white Southerners. The attitude of white liberals toward violence, Williams pointed out, depended a great deal on the color of the perpetrators and the victims. "One of the quickest ways for an Afro-American to lose some of his white friends is to advocate self-defense against white racist savages," he wrote in The Crusader in 1960. "Our belief in this principle has cost us some of our phoney white friends, however, we have also gained some true ones."[40]

Not all of Williams's white liberal friends deserted him, even in Union County. Harry G. Boyte, a liberal activist in nearby Matthews, retained his warm respect for Williams despite their disagreements about tactics. Boyte, who later became the first white staff member of the SCLC, considered Williams a serious political threat to the success of nonviolent direct action.[41] But he knew from firsthand experience that his friend was not a vicious or reckless person. "I was always convinced that Robert never would have initiated any violence," Boyte wrote, "although I felt that he did, indeed, feel an obligation to be prepared to defend his home and family as well as his neighbors." Boyte, a native of Union County— the street that the Williams family lived on was named after his great-grandfather—acknowledged that "a real onslaught of violence" by whites there remained an ever-present possibility.[42] Sitting in a swing on his own front porch, Williams told Boyte, "We don't want bloodshed. But we will not avoid it if they force it upon us."[43]

If concerns and emphases that in the mid-1960s would be considered aspects of the Black Power movement were already reflected in *The Crusader* in the late 1950s and early 1960s, one of the main sources was Azalea Johnson. Johnson supported herself by selling insurance to black people in Monroe, a job that introduced her to many black citizens and permitted her the independence to pursue her community activism with less fear of white economic reprisals. Her regular "Did You Know?" column, which she wrote from 1959 to 1961, showcased a mind deeply enmeshed in the freedom struggle and expanding with every passing day. In the early columns, the question—"Did You Know?"—would be followed by nuggets collected from J. A. Rogers's *100 Amazing Facts about the Negro*, a format that no doubt eased a fledgling writer's task.[44] Within a few months, however, Johnson was producing increasingly confident and graceful essays whose central theme was a fiery Christian vision of racial and social justice. Azalea Johnson chose her pen name shrewdly, calling herself "Asa Lee," which was how black people in Monroe pronounced her first name. This ruse allowed friends to know exactly who was writing but made it more difficult for enemies to find her.

Black pride, historical understanding, and sharp insights into the subtle social and psychological dynamics of race marked Johnson's writings throughout her stint with *The Crusader*. "What is wrong with being born black?" Azalea Johnson demanded to know. "Did not God make me in His own image?"[45] Her explanation was historical and mirrored Marcus Garvey's earlier assertion that "the world has made being black a crime." Like Garvey, Johnson was intent on making it a virtue.[46] "This brainwashing scheme starts in early childhood when children first learn to talk," she wrote. "They are taught that a black cat is a bad-luck cat; black Friday was a terrible day in America," she continued. "Blackmail is a bad crime and white means pure, good, spotless and Caucasian people." Azalea Johnson found a leading dictionary, she said, that defined "black" as "Negro, dirty, filthy."[47] But there was no need for African Americans to be "ignorantly ashamed" of their color, Johnson maintained. "The Bible really originated in Ancient Egypt," she wrote, "where the population, according to Herodotus and Aristotle, was black."[48]

Christianity was both a source of personal strength and a language of political struggle for Johnson. Her weekly column always closed with a passage from Psalms or Proverbs, and her own writing often rang with the cadence of the King James Bible: "I stretch forth my hands to Thee," she prayed in print, "they are black hands, O Lord, but surely Thou doeth not hold that against me, for they are the hands that Thou didst give me." Like her slave forebears who adopted the Christianity of their masters and molded it into a distinctive Afro-Christian theology of liberation, Johnson wielded her faith like a weapon: "I have often wondered how the white people can read the words of our Lord and sing the sacred hymns of Zion, and not allow any of the words to penetrate deeply enough into their hearts to cause them to treat the Negro people right."[49]

She was almost as hard on the black church as she was on white Christians. "The [black] church proclaims that 'all things are possible through God,' and yet our ministers are acting like God's powers are limited and the white man is the supreme being," she wrote.[50] While God did make all things possible, in her view, Johnson refused to "believe that He is coming down here in Monroe and sit-in at lunch counters or enroll our children in integrated schools, or apply for jobs in industrial plants for us." Irate at local clergymen for not supporting the civil rights movement, Johnson eventually declared that "most of the preachers here should be given a one-way ticket out of Monroe."[51]

Johnson supported integration in schools and public accommodations but had no illusions that the fall of barriers in those spheres would end the racial chasm in American life. She criticized "near-sighted" black leaders for pursuing integration, "which is fine," she said, "BUT they should be turning hell over to secure jobs for the Afro-American worker. Seek ye first the jobs," she argued, echoing the voice of the Scriptures and the views of Booker T. Washington, "and all these other things will be added unto you."[52] Johnson always kept her eyes on economics, assailing white businesses that would not employ blacks, attacking the local welfare bureaucracy for barring eligible blacks from government aid, and advising African Americans to "teach their children to patronize members of their own race or whites who are free of prejudice."[53]

The link between local poverty, white supremacy, and black illiteracy was clear to Johnson, who had great faith in the power of education. Children "who can't go to school because they don't have decent shoes and clothing" ended up illiterate, with minds "shackled to the babblings of others," Johnson wrote. Black children used the raggedy, cast-off books discarded by white schools, attended classes in buildings that lacked basic equipment, and abandoned their education to pick cotton at harvesttime. When black children turned ten, Johnson wrote, white welfare authorities would "advise the parent to take them out of school to work, to boost the family income." Many black workers labored in an undocumented realm of marginal employment, performing day labor for small amounts of cash. These jobs were "off the books," and hence white employers were not required to observe minimum-wage laws. The domestic jobs available to black women paid from $10 to $15 for a full week's work, and many black men had to take jobs outside their communities and commute. Under crushing financial burdens, sometimes black families kept older children out of school to babysit for younger siblings. "Committees have gone before the local all-white school board, about employing a [black] truant officer," Johnson wrote, but white school authorities "aren't going to pay someone to MAKE Afro-Americans go to school. They don't care if you never learn anything." Illiteracy among black citizens bolstered a sense of white superiority and undermined black assertiveness, she observed, and "that way [whites] can keep the black race subservient to them."[54]

Johnson and the other activists who clustered around Robert Williams were not the only black crusaders who challenged the boundaries of segregation in Monroe. Dr. H. H. Creft Jr. launched a campaign to open the municipally owned Monroe Country Club to all citizens. When Creft and other black professional men showed up with their golf clubs at the city's golf course, dumbstruck city officials permitted them to play. "The Crusader bows to the courageous Negroes who integrated the local golf course," Robert Williams congratulated them. "The golf course is now added to the library [as an example] of local integration without incident."[55] Soon thereafter, however, the black physician showed up with out-of-town guests—a privilege white members routinely enjoyed—and found himself accosted by the course "pro" and screaming, cursing members of the all-white city recreation board. Although the black foursome ignored the white men and finished their round of golf, soon afterward Creft petitioned the city unsuccessfully to extend membership to all citizens.[56] Only in America, Williams snorted, was it possible that "two doctors, a successful businessman, and a college student would not be considered good enough to play golf on the same course with rednecked crackers."[57]

While it was one thing to permit a black doctor to play on the golf course, provided he did not get "uppity" and act like a regular member, the white authorities in Monroe were not about to permit African American citizens to join the Monroe Country Club. This would have meant granting black children access to the swimming pool, of course, a goal that Williams and his NAACP branch continued to pursue in 1960 for the fourth consecutive summer. "Will Negroes be barred from their tax-supported lily-white swimming pool again this summer?" asked Azalea Johnson. "The national office of the NAACP has issued a statement that they will support all Negroes who attack segregation with peaceful demonstrations." The strategy now, apparently, was to establish the best possible grounds for an NAACP-sponsored lawsuit. "It is now left to us Negroes to start a peaceful demonstration to the swimming pool," Johnson continued, "but let us not stop at recreation—jobs, to me, are more important, education comes next."[58] It appears that Williams was actually a more enthusiastic integrationist than Azalea Johnson and many other blacks in Monroe.

On August 18, 1960, the Monroe Enquirer reported that "a small group of Negro boys, led by Robert F. Williams, NAACP head, was denied admission to the Monroe Country Club Pool Tuesday afternoon. Williams, who has led similar groups to the pool, told a news service that his next step would be court action."[59] Between August 14 and August 21, Williams and a number of black young people sought entrance on three separate occasions to the otherwise public swimming pool. Williams told newspaper reporters that he "wanted to be sure that we had a clear-cut case legally and that we were turned away on the basis of race." Each time, local whites gathered menacingly and recreation officials refused to admit the black children. The protesters were called "niggers" and were "threatened with violence," according to Williams, and the manager refused to let them swim. "One white woman threatened to slap one of us," Williams told the UPI stringer from Charlotte. "I told her that if she did it, it'd be the last person she ever slapped on this earth." Not only were whites in Monroe unwilling to obey the law, Williams complained, but they "do not even intend to adhere to the 'separate but equal' doctrine. The city of Monroe deserves an Oscar for stupidity in race relations."[60]

While Williams and the Monroe NAACP pushed forward the local freedom struggle, they reached out to connect their efforts with allies across the nation. The immediate goal was to organize Union County's poor blacks by furnishing the economic relief that the local welfare bureaucracy denied them. "We not only struggled for integration," Robert Williams recalled, "we were very conscious of the fact that there was a need for raising the economic level of the poor people." Azalea Johnson reminded readers in the fall of 1960 that "many Afro-American pre-school-age children can be seen on the streets, ragged and barefooted."[61]

In part through *The Crusader* and in part through political networks he had built during the kissing case and during his collision with the national office of the NAACP, Williams solicited support for CARE—the Crusaders Association for Relief and Enlightenment. According to *The Crusader*, "40 women have organized here to distribute the C.A.R.E. packages" that soon poured in by the truckload from "people of all races from all over America to the needy of Monroe and Union County."[62] The Good Samaritan Club of Los Angeles sent twenty-one boxes of new and used clothing and $300 in cash that first year.[63] The SWP, Conrad Lynn claimed, dispatched "a caravan of trucks" with food and clothing for the women of CARE to distribute among the poor. By the end of 1960, relief packages arrived almost daily, and the women of CARE kept busy passing out clothes, shoes, and canned goods among the poor of Union County. The women not only funneled aid from all over the country but undertook local projects that both raised money and celebrated Southern black culture. "Chitterling dinners will be on, Saturday, January 21, from 11:30 AM until ?" *The Crusader* announced in early 1961. "Plates will be delivered in the city. Call AT3-2776 or contact any member of C.A.R.E."[64]

In Harlem, Ora Mae Mobley (Robert Williams's first cousin), Mae Mallory, and others organized a support group for the Monroe crusaders. "Our little group decided that, well, we'll all join his chapter," Mallory recounted. "We called ourselves 'the Crusader Family,' because he put out a little pamphlet at that time called *The Crusader*," she continued. "We decided, let's send people *The Crusader* for Christmas instead of Christmas cards because this is a greater message, you know, than Hallmark." Audley "Queen Mother" Moore, a central figure in both Communist and nationalist political circles in Harlem from the 1920s to the 1970s, rallied the support teams for Robert Williams.[65] Williams dispatched bundles of *The Crusader* to his Harlem supporters, who "would seal it, distribute it, and pass out copies to spread to other people." Robert and Mabel Williams visited New York City regularly and took folks from Monroe with them.

"We developed quite a friendship at that time," Mae Mallory remembered, "Rob Williams, his wife, Mrs. Johnson, the other members of the Crusader Family, and myself."[66]

In 1959 and 1960 Williams tended his Harlem ties assiduously. He was bound for New York City on February 12, 1960, he told George Weissman of the SWP, but could not stay at Weissman's Manhattan apartment as he often had in the past. "The friends in Harlem want me to stay there while in N.Y.—then, too, I guess it'll be good for contacts."[67] Williams became a regular visitor to Louis Michaux's National Memorial African Bookstore on 7th Avenue off 125th Street, "the House of Common Sense and the Home of Proper Propaganda," its awning sign proclaimed. Michaux welcomed Williams to the platform the bookstore provided for the legendary Harlem street speakers of the day, which included, among others, Malcolm X, Adam Clayton Powell, Carlos Cooks, and Edward "Pork Chop" Davis.[68]

Williams found ready support among black intellectuals in Harlem, especially Julian Mayfield and a circle of friends that included John Hendrik Clarke, John Oliver Killens, Ossie Davis, Ruby Dee, Shirley Graham Du Bois, and other "nationalist oriented individuals from Harlem," in Harold Cruse's assessment, "not to speak of certain writers with muddled views on integrationism and nationalism. They all saw something in Monroe that did not actually exist—an immediately revolutionary situation." Cruse, who would later publish his classic *The Crisis of the Negro Intellectual*, considered himself an authority on which developments in African American politics were truly "revolutionary" in their approach; in retrospect, his acerbic observations seem more divisive than instructive. Regardless of whether Cruse's measure of Monroe's possibilities or Williams's magnetism was accurate, however, clearly the NAACP president from Union County had a strong appeal among black radicals of various stripes. "In the North," Cruse wrote, "the bulk of Williams's supporters in the young generation were nationalists. Neither Clarke nor Mayfield, however, belonged to this group, and even [LeRoi] Jones had not yet fully arrived [as a black nationalist]."[69]

Harlem radicals supported Robert Williams with guns and money. Julian Mayfield and John Hendrik Clarke, a prominent black writer and historian from Harlem, came to Union County in early December 1960 with a truckload of clothes and weapons for the Monroe insurgents.[70] "We had weapons that people had bought and sent in from the North and different places, mostly from Harlem," Williams recalled.[71] Mayfield found that "black people there in Monroe carried themselves with a pride and a dignity that I could not find matched nowhere else." What Williams called "armed self-reliance," Mayfield observed, "was the dominant philosophy of black people in this county." Though Mayfield found Monroe itself "dreary" and even "ugly" in appearance, the town's African American citizens astounded him with their happy determination and racial pride. "This is before we had the slogan 'black is beautiful' or anything like that," Mayfield laughed, "and I just fell in love with the town and kept going back."[72] Years later, Mayfield wrote an unpublished autobiography in which he disclosed that "a famous black writer made touch with gangsters in New Jersey and bought me two sub-machine guns which I took to Monroe." Williams may not have been the best-known black activist in the United States, but he was probably the best armed.[73]

The most notable of Williams's contacts among the Harlem nationalists was Malcolm X, minister at the Nation of Islam's Temple Number 7. "I spoke in the Muslim temple when Malcolm X was the minister at 116th Street," Williams recounted in 1968. "Every time I used to go to New York he would invite me to speak." Williams first met Malcolm X in 1958 and was deeply impressed; according to Williams, Malcolm collected funds to support the movement in Monroe. The charismatic Muslim minister persisted in "bringing me into the temple and raising money to support me, and they were giving me money every time I would go to the temple," Williams said. Malcolm X would tell his congregation "that 'our brother is here from North Carolina, and he is the only fighting man that we got and we have to help him so he can stay down there,'" Williams recalled. In later years, Malcolm claimed that Williams "was just a couple of years ahead of his time."[74]

The FBI took note of the alliance. In 1959 J. Edgar Hoover warned his Charlotte, North Carolina, office about Robert Williams's "recent activities in connection with the Nation of Islam at New York" and ordered that a file be opened with respect to Williams and the Nation of Islam. "I was the only leader of the NAACP who could have associated with all kinds of people—the nationalists and all," Williams recalled. "I was the only one from the NAACP who could go down in Harlem and stand on a ladder on a corner and speak there."[75]

These new contacts among the nationalists did not necessarily diminish his ties to the white left. "Even if I stay up in Harlem," Williams reassured George Weissman, "I'm sure I'll see a great deal of you while I am there." Williams reached out across the spectrum of American dissidents during this period, with particular success among the New York intellectual left. Williams received support from James Baldwin and many other black intellectuals and artists. Conrad Lynn organized black and white leftist writers such as Weissman, Truman Nelson, Lonnie Cross, and John Hendrik Clarke into the Coordinating Committee for Southern Relief in 1960 to help raise money for Williams. Neither a nationalist, a Marxist, nor a liberal, exactly, the NAACP leader from Monroe reached out to potential allies in all these camps while remaining committed to equal rights for all under the U.S. Constitution.[76]

As he had in Monroe, Williams courted a broad circle of friends in New York City and made allies who subscribed to a wide variety of ideologies. Never doctrinaire, Williams considered the idea of a separate black nation unworkable and was never a nationalist "to the point that I would exclude whites or that I would discriminate against whites or that I would be prejudiced toward whites."[77] His socially conservative streak mirrored certain Muslim doctrines, and he agreed with them on the necessity of self-defense but regarded their religion as a hindrance. The problem with Communists in general, Williams insisted, was that Marxism did not let them put race first. Their formulaic insistence that class struggle preceded all other matters prevented Communists from understanding the range and complexity of African American historical experiences.

White liberals had the same problem for different reasons. "The traditional white liberal leadership in civil rights organizations, and even white radicals," said Williams, "generally cannot understand what our struggle is and how we feel about it. They have always made our struggle secondary."[78] To Williams, "flexibility" and "armed self-reliance" were more compelling than nonviolence, in part because of the unpredictable and specific day-to-day demands of building local movements, in part because he believed that self-defense would help avert violence, but in large measure because of the primary necessity of building African American manhood and self-respect. "A man cannot have human dignity if he allows himself to be abused," Williams wrote, "to allow his wife and children to be attacked, refusing to defend them and himself on the basis that he's so pious, so self-righteous, that it would demean his personality if he fought back."[79]

Williams's mix-and-match skepticism about the various strains of communism, nationalism, and nonviolence did not mean that blacks should separate themselves from either the nonviolent movement or their many dependable allies among white Americans, especially the white left.

"I never would have been able to remain in the South as long as I did if it had not been for the support that I got from some white people in the North," Williams acknowledged. Williams steadfastly ignored the inevitable charge that he or his leftist allies were pawns of Moscow.[80] "We have been accused of being communists," *The Crusader* declared on its second birthday, "this is not true. We have been accused of being Muslims. We are not. We have been accused of being black racists," Williams continued, "this is not true. We have been accused of being agitators, to this charge WE PLEAD GUILTY!" The Monroe contingent, Williams maintained, were simply homegrown "radicals dedicated to the cause of freedom without compromise."[81]

The eclectic Williams took his friends where he could find them, courting the Nation of Islam but retaining his ties to the SWP and other Trotskyite groups. Beginning in November 1958, *The Militant*, the SWP's weekly newspaper, published dozens of articles about Williams and the struggle in Monroe—twenty-five articles on the kissing case alone. If the black nationalists in Harlem overestimated Monroe's importance, as Cruse claimed, the SWP trotted right alongside. *The Militant's* attention to Monroe dwarfed its coverage of many important developments for the American left in 1958 and 1959, including the Cuban revolution, the anticolonial uprising in the Belgian Congo, or even the surging African American freedom movements in Mississippi, Florida, and Alabama.[82]

Not only did Robert Williams have strong ideas of his own, but he was not afraid of other people with strong ideas. In 1959 Carey McWilliams, editor of the left-liberal weekly *The Nation*, asked Williams to consider writing for the magazine and requested a subscription to *The Crusader*.[83] "I think you are the most dynamic rebel in America today," radical activist Slim Brundage of Chicago wrote to Williams.[84] Despite his vow to meet violence with violence, in the spring of 1960 Williams took five African American students from Monroe to nonviolent direct action workshops sponsored by the American Friends Service Committee in Chapel Hill.[85] In the fall Robert and Mabel accompanied Azalea Johnson and several other women from Monroe to a week-long workshop at the Highlander Folk School in Tennessee.[86]

Searching for allies, Williams undertook two speaking tours through the South during the fall of 1960, carrying *The Crusader*, its staff, and his fiery message of armed self-reliance and eclectic radicalism with him. In South Carolina he addressed black audiences in Columbia, Greenville, and Charleston; in Georgia, he spoke to NAACP chapters in Savannah, Macon, and Atlanta. He delivered another speech to receptive black citizens in Jacksonville, Florida. "I was confronted with this new wonderful spirit rising throughout Dixie—this determination to break the chains of bondage and the spirit of valor of a people who just a few years ago were submissive peons," Williams wrote later.[87] In Savannah, Williams found a militant NAACP chapter with solid financial backing from local black business and labor leaders. One black union leader, Williams recounted, stood up and told the Savannah NAACP "that I was right when I said that 'we must meet violence with violence.'" Following Williams's speech in Atlanta, "a university professor was energetic about the new militant spirit on the part of the masses and very hopeful that new militant leadership will replace the old Uncle Toms." On the whole, Williams reported, "all signs point to increased resistance" to white supremacy, but "our struggle now is disorganized and merely a network of pockets of resistance. There must be an effective media of communication before we can have efficient, concerted mass action." This was the new, enlarged mission of *The Crusader*: "to be the voice of a united people charging Jim Crow in his last stand."[88]

Williams's growing network of supporters never remotely threatened to vault him to a position of nationally recognized leadership in the freedom movement comparable to that of Martin Luther King Jr. or Roy Wilkins. His estrangement from the national office of the NAACP and his alienation from the black church left him no institutional base among black Southerners, even though he spoke their language in a powerful idiom. Williams articulated black anger with considerable force and even humor, but the black freedom movement had more gifted orators. Nor could Williams muster the money to field teams of organizers like those that soon would be employed by the SCLC and SNCC. White liberals were hardly prepared to endorse a program that included armed resistance. Building a militant black movement "was a long, slow process, too long for the short time in which a well-heeled Gandhist movement could confuse and demoralize our people," Williams lamented later, as he watched the Black Power movement catch fire too late for him to lead it.[89]

In the period from 1959 to 1961, however, the FBI remained uneasy about his mounting influence. "Williams has traveled extensively throughout the United States and has associated himself with numerous organizations," J. Edgar Hoover wrote to the Charlotte office of the FBI, among them many NAACP branches, CORE, the Nation of Islam, the SWP, and his Harlem boosters. "In his travels, Williams has made speeches before numerous local chapters of these groups or met with local representatives." The FBI's files on Williams, the report continued, "reflect numerous instances where groups in various sections of the country have proclaimed and demonstrated their sympathies with Williams and have sent him money."[90]

The FBI actively sought to keep Williams unemployed, a campaign that FBI agents diligently recorded in his subject file. Local whites, too, applied economic pressure in whatever ways they could. "They were hoping to really starve me out," Williams said, "but actually what they did was to make me a full-time professional agitator." Money, though much too little, dribbled in from all over the country. His brothers, John and Pete, who lived in Detroit, had good jobs and helped him out regularly. "Pete's the one who gave him money to arm himself," John Herman Williams recalled. "Pete said, 'If you're going to do this, you've got to be prepared,'" and gave Robert Williams a substantial sum of money for guns and ammunition. There were other relatives whose support for Robert Williams helped to keep his family afloat. "We had an aunt who was worse than Robert," John Williams said. "Aunt Cora [Bass], she was really on his side. She was really a fighter." In Monroe, Williams could count on his close friends to provide steady and considerable financial support, and many local people gave him small sums. His tastes were not expensive, and his house belonged to the family free and clear. Neither local adversaries nor the FBI managed to sink Williams financially, no matter how much they abhorred his influence.[91]

Not only J. Edgar Hoover's FBI but Martin Luther King Jr.'s SCLC watched the growing influence of Robert Williams with apprehension. "The idea of striking back appeals to human nature," Harry Boyte wrote in 1961, after he had become an aide to King. Self-defense "meets a steady response among the downtrodden, grass roots of the southern Negro population. Although most national Negro publications officially support non-violence," Boyte continued, "even among their staff members there are many who secretly support a policy of retaliation." For several years Williams had "succeeded in reaching these grass roots," according to Boyte, and "exercised great influence in Union County and beyond because of his militant position and refusal to submit to intimidation." Boyte believed that "through his newsletter, The Crusader," Williams's philosophy was "very far-reaching and poses a real threat to more peaceful and non-violent methods of solving our problems."[92] It is important to remember that when Boyte wrote these words, nonviolent direct action had only barely been tried. The SCLC still drifted almost aimlessly, the NAACP still viewed King as a threat, and the mass of African Americans generally ignored the initiatives of both the NAACP and the SCLC.[93] Shortly after *The Crusader* began to spread its confrontational appeals, the first biography of Martin Luther King Jr. appeared, a glowing portrait written by L. D. Reddick, a member of the SCLC's board of directors. The book was titled *Crusader without Violence*. It is not clear that the title was a rejoinder to Williams, but it certainly situated the book within a lively and important public discussion that now welled up within the movement.[94]

"The great debate in the integration movement in recent months has been the question of violence vs. nonviolence, as instruments of social change," Anne Braden wrote in early 1960. "The nonviolent way was brought dramatically to the public consciousness by the successful Montgomery bus protest of 1955–56. This debate, long smoldering under the surface, was precipitated last spring when Robert Williams, Negro leader of Monroe, N.C., made his much publicized statement that Negroes must 'meet violence with violence.' "[95] Editor of the *Southern Patriot*, a movement newsletter sponsored by the Southern Conference Educational Fund, Braden observed the internal politics of the movement with considerable clarity. Her husband, Carl Braden, had resigned from the CCRI after the 1959 NAACP controversy. "Frankly," Carl Braden wrote to George Weissman, "I incline more to the King philosophy than to the Williams philosophy."[96]

As veteran leftists, the Bradens certainly recognized the deep class dimensions of the 1959–60 debate over nonviolence. In the late 1950s and early 1960s, Dr. King remained loyal to his roots in the black upper classes and played a decisive role in the struggle of the traditional leadership to maintain control over the blossoming and sometimes unruly black freedom movement. The controversy over nonviolence demonstrated the persistence of these class divisions. During the SCLC's long campaign in Albany, Georgia, for example, poor black youths stoned police cars while King and others struggled to control the black underclass that, though uninvited, had joined the protest.[97] In Birmingham, King and his organizers worked the taverns and pool halls, attempting unsuccessfully to prevent lower-class blacks from pelting the police with rocks and bottles.[98] Looking back on the 1959–60 dispute during the height of the 1963 Birmingham crisis, Anne Braden knew that black violence was "much more widespread than it was in 1960" and observed that "where retaliatory violence has erupted, it has been among those who have little to gain from the original limited goals of the nonviolent integration movement. It has been among the poor and the disinherited, the unemployed and the un-trained, who care little about the right to eat in a restaurant because they hardly have enough to buy beans for their own table."[99] Torn between her class sympathies and her racial politics, Braden sided with King but pointed out that the debate over nonviolence in the Southern freedom struggle reflected "much misunderstanding of both positions."[100]

Both nonviolence and armed struggle resonated in the history of the black South. The tradition of armed self-defense, rooted in the unforgetta-ble experiences of slave resistance and Reconstruction militancy, had sur-vived what historian Rayford Whittingham Logan called "the nadir" of African American life at the turn of the century. After an 1892 triple lynch-ing in Memphis, black editor Ida B. Wells "determined to sell my life as dearly as possible" and urged other black Southerners to do the same. "A Winchester rifle should have a place of honor in every home," Wells wrote. "When the white man . . . knows he runs as great a risk of biting the dust every time his Afro-American victim does, he would have a greater respect for Afro-American life."[101] In 1901, W. A. Pledger of the *Atlanta Age* told the Afro-American Press Association that many whites "are afraid to lynch us where they know the black man is standing behind the door with a Winchester. But they arrest us and then attack us defenseless in jail and lynch us." When white mobs raged through the street of Atlanta in 1906, W. E. B. Du Bois hastened home to defend his wife and family. "I bought a Winchester double-barreled shotgun and two dozen rounds of shells filled with buckshot," he wrote later. "If a white mob had stepped on the cam-pus where I lived I would without hesitation have sprayed their guts over the grass." Even Robert Moton, president of Tuskegee Institute, prepared to defend Booker T. Washington's legacy with shotguns when Tuskegee was menaced by the Ku Klux Klan in the 1920s.[102] In the 1930s, black Communist Harry Haywood saw "a small arsenal" when he attended a Share Croppers' Union meeting in Dadeville, Alabama. "There were guns of all kinds," he recalled, "shotguns, rifles and pistols. Sharecroppers were coming to the meeting armed." Thirty years later, when SNCC orga-nizers came to Lowndes County, Alabama, black farmers showed up for meetings armed and ready. One black sharecropper told Stokely Car-michael, "You turn the other cheek, and you'll get handed half what you're sitting on." Robert Williams grew up in this tradition, and he was not the only one.[103]

This sensibility was not foreign to Martin Luther King Jr. or to other members of his generation of black Southerners. In 1955 a black women's newsletter published in Jackson, Mississippi, announced that since "no law enforcement body in ignorant Miss. will protect any Negro who had membership in the NAACP, . . . the Negro must protect himself." The editors warned "the white hoodlums who are now parading around the premises" that the editors were "protected by armed guard."[104] Dr. T. R. M. Howard, an affluent African American physician and political activist in Mound Bayou, Mississippi, wrote to the national office of the NAACP in 1955 that "we have had all kinds of threats, so much so that we have found it necessary to see that our house is under the proper kind of protection twenty-four hours a day."[105] The Reverend Glenn Smiley, who visited King's home on behalf of the pacifist Fellowship of Reconciliation in 1956, as the Montgomery Bus Boycott was taking hold, wrote back that "the place is an arsenal" and that men with guns guarded King's home. In a history of American nonviolence written by Staughton Lynd, not one of the twenty-seven entries listed prior to the emergence of Dr. King reflects either Southern or African American origins.[106]

No one, not even Dr. King, was more closely identified with the principal of pure philosophical nonviolence than SNCC leader Bob Moses. From the beginning, however, SNCC organizers knew better than to push nonviolence on reluctant black Southerners. "In terms of the organizing," SNCC's Charles Cobb observed, "you didn't go to these towns and somehow enter into a discussion of violence and nonviolence." When white terrorists attacked the home of Hartman Turnbow, a local black farmer and SNCC stalwart in Holmes County, Mississippi, Cobb recalled, Turnbow "pushed his family out the back door and grabbed the rifle off the wall and started shooting. And his explanation was simply that 'I was not being,' as he said, 'non-nonviolent, I was protecting my wife and family.'"[107] Even Bob Moses acknowledged how deeply his pacifist convictions violated the mores of the black South. "Self-defense is so deeply engrained in rural Southern America," Moses told SNCC volunteers in 1964, "that we as a small group can't effect it. It's not contradictory for a farmer to say he's nonviolent and also to pledge to shoot a marauder's head off."[108]

Unlike nonviolence, the roots of a distinctive Afro-Christianity reached as deep as the racial bondage under which that faith was forged. Gathering in the dark woods and slave cabins of the South, enslaved Africans had transfigured the Christianity thrust upon them by their masters, creating a theology of liberation that affirmed their humanity and undermined their oppression.[109] Gandhi's ideas about nonviolent direct action had been circulating among the black intelligentsia since the 1930s and reached a much broader audience during A. Philip Randolph's MOWM during World War II. Bayard Rustin, one of the key links between the MOWM and the emerging black freedom movement, helped teach King about non-violent direct action. What King did with Gandhian nonviolence, however, was not unlike what his slave forebears had done with Christianity. He adapted rather than adopted it, articulating nonviolence in the language of the black church and grafting it onto the most compelling cultural tradition of the black South.[110]

Williams, in fact, gently explained his differences with King in terms of both King's theological training and his own military experiences. "This is why I never criticized Dr. King very much on his tactics, just the fact that he said violence would demean a person and reduce him to the level of the enemy," Williams observed. "Well, I didn't go along with that, but he was trained in a school of divinity so it would only be natural. . . . My training had a military background."[111] A prince in America's black elite and a "Morehouse man" bearing a doctorate of religion from Boston University, King carried the banner for nonviolence with a passionate spiritual grace that few could match. In late 1959 and early 1960, King came after Robert Williams.

Before he took on King, the man from Monroe confronted other crusaders for nonviolence. In a series of public debates in New York City on October 1, 1959, Robert Williams and Conrad Lynn faced Bayard Rustin, David Dellinger, and A. J. Muste. Muste was the elder statesman of American pacifism. Earlier that year he had been arrested at age seventy-four after he climbed a fence to trespass at a nuclear missile site in Omaha, Nebraska. Rustin had organized the 1947 Journey of Reconciliation in which black and white activists—including Conrad Lynn, ironically—boarded southbound buses to test the Supreme Court's ruling that segregation laws were unconstitutional in interstate commerce. Rustin narrowly escaped a Chapel Hill lynch mob and served several weeks on a North Carolina chain gang. An adviser to Dr. King during the Montgomery Bus Boycott, Rustin helped to organize the SCLC and remained one of King's closest counselors. Dellinger, a leading pacifist editor and activist, was a Yale graduate who had studied at Oxford, Yale Divinity School, and Union Theological Seminary.[112]

"Nonviolence is a powerful weapon in the struggle against social evil," Williams conceded to the pacifists. "It represents the ultimate step in revolution against intolerable oppression, a type of struggle wherein man may make war without debasing himself." The problem as Williams presented it, however, was that nonviolence depended on the conscience of the adversary; rattlesnakes, he observed, were immune to such appeals, as were many Southern white supremacists. "When Hitler's tyranny threatened the world, we did not hear very much about how immoral it is to meet violence with violence," Williams argued. "Even the Christian church was willing to 'Praise the Lord and Pass The Ammunition,' and by doing so we all stayed free." Williams noted, too, that Gandhi's old ally, Prime Minister Jawaharlal Nehru of India, had recently threatened violent resistance to Chinese aggression. "It does one's heart a little good," Williams quoted Nehru as having said, "to speak in a proud, defiant language." George Weissman wrote to Carl Braden in Louisville that Williams had drawn "a large audience to his debate with the pacifists at Community Church here and handled himself very well."[113]

In a widely reprinted debate first published in *Liberation* magazine in September and October 1959, Williams advocated armed self-reliance while Martin Luther King Jr. explained the social organization of nonviolence.[114] Williams recounted his optimistic return to civilian life in Monroe after the Supreme Court's decision in 1954. "The hope I had for Negro liberation faltered," he said, when "acts of violence and words and deeds of hate and spite rose from every quarter." Among the well-armed white population, Williams asserted, "there is open defiance to law and order throughout the South today." Where law had broken down, only self-defense could deter the attacks of white terrorists who commit violence in the service of their own sincere beliefs and time-honored prerogatives. "Nonviolence is a very potent weapon when the opponent is civilized," Williams stated, "but nonviolence is no repellent for a sadist."

Avoiding philosophical abstractions, the Monroe NAACP leader recapitulated the now-familiar tales of white supremacist outrages in Union County over just the last few years: Ku Klux Klan rallies attended by thousands, Klan raids led by police cars, gun battles in black neighborhoods, brisk acquittals of white men whose attacks on African American women they scarcely bothered to deny, and white terrorism that abated only when black men with guns protected their community from the nightriders. "I daresay that if Mack Parker had had an automatic shotgun at his disposal," Williams wrote of the black man lynched in Mississippi that spring, "he could have served as a great deterrent against lynching." Williams expressed "great respect for the pacifist" but declared that he himself was not a pacifist and that he could "safely say that most of my people are not."

Rather than submit to violence, "Negroes must be willing to defend themselves, their women, their children and their homes," he asserted. "Nowhere in the annals of history does the record show a people delivered from bondage by patience alone."

King's lofty essay, "The Social Organization of Nonviolence," acknowledged that the civil rights movement had "reached a stage of profound crisis." The Supreme Court's 1954 *Brown v. Board of Education* ruling and the triumph in Montgomery had yielded only small tokens, elaborate evasions, and widespread terrorism. African Americans were frustrated, he said, and their "current calls for violence" reflected "a confused, anger-motivated drive to strike back violently, to inflict damage," and were "punitive, not radical or constructive."

"It is unfortunately true that however the Negro acts, his struggle will not be free of violence initiated by his enemies," King acknowledged. Only three paths presented themselves. One could practice "pure nonviolence," King said, but this method "could not readily attract large masses, for it requires extraordinary discipline and courage." A position that encompassed legitimate self-defense was the only practical stance. "Violence exercised merely in self-defense," King conceded, "all societies, from the most primitive to the most cultured and civilized, accept as moral and legal. The principle of self-defense, even involving weapons and bloodshed, has never been condemned, even by Gandhi." Clearly, King the politician located his constituents in this position. "When the Negro uses force in self-defense," King continued, "he does not forfeit support—he may even win it, by the courage and self-respect it reflects." The third and entirely unacceptable position, King continued, "is the advocacy of violence as a tool of advancement, organized as in warfare, deliberately and consciously." Here, then, was the pale beyond which King sought to cast his adversary. "Mr. Robert Williams would have us believe that there is no collective and practical alternative," King insisted. "He argues that we must be cringing and submissive or take up arms. There are other meaningful alternatives." In any case, King asserted, "there is more power in socially organized masses on the march than there is in guns in the hands of a few desperate men."

In fact, King explained, "in Mr. Williams's own community of Monroe, North Carolina, a striking example of collective community action won a significant victory without use of arms or threats of violence. When the police incarcerated a Negro doctor unjustly, the aroused people of Monroe marched to the police station, crowded into its hall and corridors, and refused to leave until their colleague was released." Neither side, in King's account, "attempted to unleash violence." Fortunately for King, the debate was not face to face. Williams had been present at the jailhouse and could have affirmed, as *Jet* reported in its account of Dr. Perry's abortion arrest, that the black crowd was armed with guns and knives and threatened to tear down the building. Williams might well have noted, too, as King did not, that because whites controlled the legal machinery, Perry was sitting in a North Carolina prison as King celebrated the purportedly nonviolent achievement of his alleged freedom.

There were several other ways in which the King-Williams debate was stacked against Williams. *Liberation* was a pacifist publication edited by David Dellinger. Bayard Rustin and A. J. Muste were both closely affiliated with *Liberation*. In fact, it is possible that Rustin actually drafted King's essay; he had written at least one other piece for *Liberation* under King's byline.[115] Dellinger was an earnest admirer of Dr. King and a committed pacifist; his editorial format required Williams to write first and then permitted King to respond at length and at leisure.

These advantages, coupled with the minister's formidable eloquence, enabled King essentially to invent his own Robert Williams, a black Geronimo plotting bloody raids against the white man. He then responded to *that* Robert Williams rather than to the calm but defiant man who had spoken. Williams, lacking the polish of theological training and combative in his tone, left himself vulnerable to such distortions. It is crucial to note, however, that the philosophical position from which King centered his argument—preferring nonviolence but endorsing the principle of self-defense, even involving weapons and bloodshed—was in fact the same position that Williams had taken. Under any circumstances, Williams was no match for King in a debate. But the fact that King felt that he had to address Williams's challenge, and then sought to occupy the same ground on which Williams took his stand, was telling. Julian Bond, then a student activist in Atlanta, recalled reading the debate and "believing that Williams had gotten the better of it" and "that Williams was not the figure King and others depicted." (In 1960 Bond helped found SNCC, and in 1998 he was named head of the NAACP.)[116]

Anne Braden, herself committed to nonviolence and to Dr. King's leadership, reprinted the debate in the January 1960 issue of the *Southern Patriot*, noting the confusion among freedom movement activists with respect to both King and Williams. No one disputes the right to defend home and family, she said. "What the nonviolent movement says is that the weapons of social change should be nonviolent." But neither is it fair, she pointed out, to call the issue "a question of aggressive violence by Negroes to attack white people. Williams has never advocated this. What he believes is that an armed Negro community becomes a deterrent to violent white attacks and thus may lessen violence ultimately." Williams merely articulated "what many people feel," Braden observed, "and what many more people will express unless change comes rapidly."[117]

Actions speak louder than words, and it was African American college students in North Carolina whose boldness pushed aside these arguments among their elders. On February 1, 1960, 4 students from North Carolina Agricultural and Technical College in Greensboro walked into Woolworth's Department Store at about 4:30 in the afternoon, sat down at a segregated lunch counter, and asked to be served. Denied service, the young black men kept their seats until the counter closed. The following day, 23 classmates joined them at the counter. The next day, there were 66; the day after, 100; and on the fifth day, 1,000 students marched through downtown Greensboro to demand equality. Within two months, the sit-ins had spread to fifty-four towns and cities across nine states of the old Confederacy.[118] In April, Ella Baker convened a conference at Shaw University in Raleigh at which she helped give birth to SNCC. SNCC rang in an aggressive, student-led phase of the freedom movement that shattered the uneasy racial stalemate that had hovered over the South since 1954. As Williams had predicted back in 1951, black college students with little to lose and a world to gain had become the most militant force in the freedom movement.[119]

On March 1, one month after the first sit-ins in Greensboro, Williams led about a dozen black youths into Gamble's Drug Store in downtown Monroe. By this time, the sit-in movement had spread to dozens of cities across the South. "We became the thirteenth town in North Carolina to start sit-in demonstrations," Williams stated. Taking seats on the lunch counter stools, they asked to be served. Like hundreds of his colleagues across the South, the manager decided to close the lunch counter.[120]

After ten minutes, the group got up and walked to nearby Jones Drug Store, where they again sat down and asked to order food and drink. "They had tried us once before," the manager, W. R. May, recalled, "but I had locked the doors before they got in."[121] May told Williams that he did not serve black people sitting down and asked the group to leave. "They wouldn't leave so I got my coat and left the store to get a warrant," the manager stated.[122] One of the owners, Doland Jones, negotiated with

Williams while May was gone and apparently persuaded the protesters to leave the building. Williams returned moments later to buy a pack of cigarettes, according to Jones, and the police arrested him on the sidewalk as he departed.[123]

The arrest of Robert Williams did not stop the sit-in campaign in Monroe. Released from jail, Williams rejoined his young followers, and they renewed their nonviolent protests against lunch counter segregation, developing their own unique tactics. Moving unpredictably from one establishment to another in downtown Monroe, the black protesters kept white merchants off balance. With four drugstores in downtown Monroe and other lunch counters, it was hard to stop them. "Clusters of white spectators gathered on sidewalks watching the Negroes move from one store to another," the *Charlotte Observer* reported. "The Negroes remained in each store only a short time, usually until the management closed the counters."

Leading a passive resistance campaign, Williams still managed to sound like a warrior. "We're using hit-and-run tactics," he told reporters. "They never know when we're coming or when we're going to leave. That way we hope to wear them down." At Easter, the student protesters asked townspeople to refrain from holiday shopping in downtown Monroe to support the sit-ins.[124] "Did you know," Azalea Johnson wrote in a column after Williams's trial, "that after the manager of Jones Drug Store here made the statement in court, 'We don't serve niggers,' Afro-Americans who respect themselves don't go in Jones Drug Store?"[125] *The Crusader* called for boycotts against businesses hostile to blacks and took credit for the fact that Jones Drug Store went out of business the following year. Secrest Drug Store, still in downtown Monroe more than thirty years later, simply removed all the stools from its lunch counter and served everyone standing. "It was more for business reasons," A. M. Secrest recalled, "than for any great moral thing."[126]

When Williams's trespassing charges came before the court on May 10, an all-white jury sentenced him to thirty days at hard labor or a $50 fine and a two-year suspended sentence with a "good behavior" stipulation that would have blocked his participation in civil rights demonstrations.[127] "I had a 'nigra's' chance," Williams wrote the following week, "and in a southern kangaroo court a 'nigra's' got about as much chance as a pegleg man in a rump-kicking contest." His attorneys immediately filed for appeal, but Williams was briefly jailed anyway. "Even though two men were waiting to go my bond," Williams joked, "the state had to take the dangerous stool sitter bandit into custody while the lawyers prepared the necessary legal papers." Forced into a double line of prisoners and marched under guard down Main Street in handcuffs, Williams counted himself "honored," he said. "I had never felt prouder in my life."[128]

The subsequent series of legal appeals, which went all the way to the North Carolina Supreme Court, lasted for months, during which the sit-in movement in Monroe never let up. The main difference between the sit-ins in Monroe and those that swept the South during the same period, according to Williams, was "not a single demonstrator was even spat upon during our sit-ins." Sit-in participants elsewhere were stabbed, beaten, and fumigated; they had cigarettes ground out on their skin and ketchup and sugar poured on their heads.[129] "We had less violence because we'd shown the willingness and readiness to fight and defend ourselves," Williams said, perhaps overlooking differences between North Carolina and the Deep South. "We appeared as people with strength, and it was to the mutual advantage of all parties concerned that peaceful relations be maintained." The sit-ins continued all spring and into the summer and flared from time to time for the next year, sometimes organized by young people who had little connection to Williams and sometimes led by the stool-sitter bandit himself. "They were always doing something," the manager of Jones Drug Store recalled. "It's a wonder somebody didn't kill him."[130]

8 :
Cuba Libre

When Fidel Castro came to Harlem and lived at the Hotel Theresa for several days in the autumn of 1960, he met with Nikita Khrushchev of the Soviet Union, Gamal Abdel Nasser of Egypt, Jawaharlal Nehru of India, Malcolm X, and Robert F. Williams. The two men had struck up a friendship when Williams had traveled to Cuba earlier that year. When the Cuban leader played the race card in Harlem in this master stroke of international diplomacy, it was logical that he turned to Williams. "The man largely responsible for Castro's interest in American Negroes," syndicated newspaper columnist Drew Pearson charged, "is Robert F. Williams of Monroe, N.C."[1]

It was a long way from Monroe to Havana, but Williams was not the first native of Monroe to make the trek. Jesse Helms, a future U.S. senator, enjoyed a cruise to Havana in 1956 as the new director of the North Carolina Banking Association.[2] With the cooperation of military dictator Fulgencio Batista, who had overthrown the Cuban government in 1952, U.S. corporations and organized crime had turned Cuba into an American brothel. The Caribbean island was "where respectable North Americans went to gamble without restraint," historian Van Gosse observes, "to see live sex shows of the most inventive character, to indulge without fear of discovery in whoring with partners of either sex, to drink and eat cheaply, to be waited on hand and foot—all in an environment as close at hand as Miami and completely geared to servicing their tastes."[3] The comprehensive array of vice brought in millions of dollars every month; by the mid-1950s, 300,000 U.S. tourists vacationed in Cuba annually. "My fellow countrymen reeled through the streets, picking up fourteen-year-old Cuban girls and tossing coins to make men scramble in the gutter," historian Arthur M. Schlesinger Jr. observed. "One wondered how any Cuban—on the basis of this evidence—could regard the United States with anything but hatred."[4]

Anti-American sentiment in Cuba helped the guerilla army led by Castro. When a general strike by hundreds of thousands of Cubans forced Batista to flee on January 1, 1959, public opinion in the United States greeted the Cuban revolution with considerable sympathy. The most popular hosts on U.S. television, Jack Paar and Ed Sullivan, both flew to Havana to interview the man whom *Life* magazine depicted as the "bearded rebel scholar" in its cover story on Castro. Edward R. Murrow's "Person to Person" news program featured a lovable Castro and his young son in their pajamas with a puppy. "The undergraduates were delighted," Schlesinger wrote of the revolutionary leader's visit to Harvard in 1959. "They saw in him, I think, the hipster who, in the era of the Organization Man, had joyfully defied the system, summoned a dozen friends and overturned a government of wicked old men." On the mainland, the news media celebrated the departure of Batista and the victory of Castro as a triumph of humanity and democracy over tyranny and corruption, as the expression of a uniquely American brand of manly courage.[5]

Not surprisingly, Robert Williams detected a kindred spirit in the youth, vigor, and playful machismo of Castro, who had led an armed insurrection in a country whose own history was marked by slavery and whose social order was marred by racial hierarchy. "Even before the Fair Play for Cuba Committee was formed," Julian Mayfield wrote to the committee's members in 1961, "Robert F. Williams was telling the truth about Cuba in his outspoken and courageous newsletter."[6] *The Crusader* at first described Castro as "colored" and portrayed the revolution favorably, helping to insert the Cuban revolution into African American political dialogue.

This was not an unusual response among African American activists and politicians. Adam Clayton Powell, one of only two black members of Congress, flew to Cuba two weeks after Batista fled and stood alongside Castro at a huge rally in Havana. Powell praised the revolution for putting a decisive end to Cuban segregation, called for U.S. aid for the fledgling regime, and contrasted Castro's commitment to immediate racial equality with the sputtering gradualism of racial reform in the United States.

The black press followed suit. Noting the black aides and military officers around Castro, the Baltimore *Afro-American* declared in February

1959 that "every white man who cuffs, beats, deprives and abuses even the lowest colored person" should beware, because Castro had proven "that it is possible for the tables to be turned." The newspaper's magazine section showcased Gabino Ulacia, "Castro's Right Hand Man," who told reporters that he wished Arkansas governor Orval Faubus would come to Havana, where "he get good example of democracy. Maybe, he stop making war on children." *Ebony*'s April issue hailed the exploits of black revolutionary *comandante* Juan Almeida Bosque and claimed that Castro's vow to bring racial justice to Cuba had won Almeida's allegiance. "The colored American should take a good look at the Cuban Revolution," Mayfield wrote. "The important lesson in the Cuban experience is that social change need not wait on the patient education of white supremacists." That was the dream that Cuba kindled in Robert Williams's heart. "It was clear from the first days that Afro-Cubans were part of the Cuban Revolution on a basis of complete equality," he wrote. "A Negro, for example, was head of the Cuban armed forces and no one could hide that fact from us here in America."[7]

Williams was far from alone in his enthusiasm. President Dwight D. Eisenhower noted in his memoirs that "admiration for Castro died slowly throughout the year 1959." But many Americans remained receptive to *fidelismo*. Castro barnstormed the United States in the spring of 1960, touring Mount Vernon and the Jefferson Memorial in an effort to link his triumphant insurgency with an earlier generation of American revolutionaries. Twenty thousand admirers showed up to cheer him at New York City's Penn Station, and 40,000 more rallied in Central Park. "I think he is a good young man who has made some mistakes," former president Truman said at the end of July, "but who seems to want to do the right thing for the Cuban people." By the end of the year, however, the executions of many former Batista officials and the prospect of far-reaching economic reforms that would damage American business interests had begun to alienate opinion makers in the United States. The honeymoon had been brief, and the Central Intelligence Agency (CIA) launched plans to murder Castro—with the help of American gangsters who wanted their casinos and brothels back—and to overthrow the new Cuban government.[8]

African Americans were much slower to turn away from Castro when charges of "communist penetration" began to fly. "Remember," radical black journalist William Worthy fired back, "the White Citizens Councils and the seggies charge that the NAACP is Communist, when it isn't." The new Cuban government noted the political potential and the economic promise offered by an African American middle class with dollars to spend and few places to spend them. Castro's regime engaged the services of Rowe-Louis-Fischer-Lockhart, Inc., a New York advertising agency in which former heavyweight champion Joe Louis was a partner. "They had given [Louis] a contract to make Cuba a kind of black playground," Williams recalled. "Where else can an American Negro go for a winter vacation?" their ads asked, highlighting the sunny beaches and exotic nightclubs in Cuba where "you will be treated as a first-class citizen." Joe Louis and seventy-one others, including the publishers of the *Chicago Defender*, the *Philadelphia Tribune*, and the *Ohio Sentinel*, traveled to Cuba in an interracial group and appeared on U.S. television partying at the Havana Hilton on New Year's Eve. "The Brown Bomber" and his wife sat at the head table with Fidel Castro. By the time the travel season of 1960 began, however, the former heavyweight champion found himself pummeled by the mainstream white press, pressured by the Internal Revenue Service, and forced to repudiate the contract, even though the United States still recognized the Cuban government and many white-owned corporations continued to do business on the island. The hostility to the Cuban revolution among most "Cold War liberals" in the United States made it clear that domestic anticommunism entailed an unquestioning acceptance of U.S. foreign policy.[9]

Some liberals continued to admire the Cuban revolution after it became officially unfashionable. Robert Taber, a CBS reporter whose respect for Castro was based on his face-to-face experience in Cuba, wrote an article defending the revolution for *The Nation* in early 1960. Alan Sagner, an affluent reform Democrat from New Jersey, called Taber to suggest that they make an effort to refute some of "the propaganda with which we are being deluged," as Taber wrote to a friend the following month. Joined by Taber's CBS coworkers Ed Haddad and Richard Gibson, the only African American on the CBS staff, this handful of friends organized the Fair Play for Cuba Committee that spring.

Their first objective was to recruit a group of prominent intellectuals and activists to publish an advertisement in the *New York Times* explaining "what is *really* happening in Cuba" and calling for a fair hearing for the revolution. The thirty founding members included Jean-Paul Sartre, Simone de Beauvoir, Norman Mailer, and Truman Capote, but almost a third were African Americans. The black founders included novelists James Baldwin, John Oliver Killens, and Julian Mayfield; journalists William Worthy and Richard Gibson; historian John Hendrik Clarke; and Robert

Williams. Almost the entire black contingent was drawn from among Williams's nationalist supporters in Harlem.[10]

His support for the Fair Play for Cuba Committee, Williams said, was "one of the main reasons I got invited to Cuba." Richard Gibson called Williams early in the summer of 1960 and invited him to travel to the island. Williams published a piece in The Crusader titled "Why I Am Going to Cuba" just before his departure. "I gather from reading that Cuba, before the advent of Castro, was a racist 'republic' with a Jim Crow system that approximated that of our democratic state of Alabama. I hear that Jim Crow is passe there now," Williams stated. "I want to see Cuba for myself because I cannot accept the reports of the respectable American press which has proven itself a galvanized conductor of lies here when reporting incidents involving Negroes. . . . It is hard to believe that Cuba is worse than Mississippi."

Williams left North Carolina on June 9, 1960, and enjoyed a "bon voyage reception" hosted by the "Crusader Family" in New York City two days later. Williams flew to Havana with Gibson and toured the country at the host government's expense, meeting Castro and most of the other important figures in the new Cuban government. Marian Anderson, the famed African American contralto, sang "I Been 'Buked and I Been Scorned" in Havana as a guest of Castro during Williams's stay. Williams found post-revolutionary Cuba as inspirational as the spirituals. "I had never been to Cuba before and didn't have any kind of relationship with anybody in Cuba," he recalled. "But I was very much impressed with what they were trying to do there, especially the race issue in Cuba. The Black Cubans were benefitting quite a bit from the revolution." Wearing a new straw hat and the beginnings of a Castro-style beard, Williams strolled at his ease in the streets of Havana, where his color was no hindrance, following his curiosity without a tour guide. There were no "white only" signs to affront him. For the first time in years, Williams did not need to worry about his personal safety. A postcard from Havana to SWP organizer Berta Green spoke volumes: "Really enjoying the only freedom I have ever known."[11]

Williams became an overnight celebrity in Cuba. "He was a national hero in Cuba," recalled Amiri Baraka (then LeRoi Jones), who visited Cuba with Williams soon afterward. Williams and Castro "frequently appeared together on television" and developed "a warm friendship," Julian Mayfield wrote later. "After my television appearance on channel 2 of Revolución, a two-page spread in Bohemia magazine, coverage in every Cuban paper and radio," Williams boasted when he returned to Monroe, "I became as well known throughout the island as I am here in Union County. People on the street stopped to shake my hand." During his visit, Williams helped to put together a special issue of the weekly Cuban literary magazine *Lunes de Revolución*, on "Los Negros en USA," which featured work by James Baldwin, Langston Hughes, Harold Cruse, LeRoi Jones, John Hendrik Clarke, and Alice Childress. Telling photographs linked the African American struggle with the Cuban revolution. Pictures of white mobs in Little Rock carrying signs proclaiming "Race Mixing Is Communism," for example, were captioned "Los racistas son tambien anticommunistas" (the racists are also anticommunists). According to Mayfield, the camaraderie between Castro and the Monroe NAACP president was rooted both in personal respect and "mutual advantages: the Cuban leader was furnished with a gold mine of propaganda material to use in his clash with the Eisenhower administration, and Williams had a platform from which he could speak and be heard around the world."[12]

Not everyone liked what they heard. "Williams has appeared on Cuban television," a front-page story in the *New York Times* complained, "telling of violence and discrimination against Negroes in the United States." The FBI and the CIA took careful notes. Williams "almost came to blows," he told readers, with an American reporter in Havana who "said I had no business talking about the race problem over here and that I should do my talking at home. He said that they had recorded my whole two-hour television interview but that they were not going to send any stories out on me." Williams, who had attacked the U.S. press for its reluctance to report on racial issues, observed that "they never allow the Negroes' side of a story to be told, and then they squawk to high heaven when the Negro finds any audience who is willing to listen to our side."

Another U.S. journalist confronted him and "asked me if I would be willing to give up my American citizenship," Williams wrote later. "He seemed stunned when I answered by saying that as an Afro-American I had never had American citizenship." But Williams's best political counterpunch came at the expense of Congressman Charles Bennett of Florida, who during Williams's stay called for U.S. military intervention to guarantee "free elections" on the island. "As an oppressed American Negro now enjoying the greatest freedom of my life in democratic revolutionary Cuba," Williams told reporters, "I would like to remind Mr. Bennett that many Negroes have been without free elections for almost 200 years now."[13]

The racially integrated schools in Cuba made a deep impression on

Williams, who was still trying to get his children transferred to a white school in Monroe. From Havana he informed reporters for the *Chicago Defender* that Cuba provided "democratic, integrated education" for children of all races. By contrast, he said, his family in Monroe had "little hope that democracy and justice will be extended our children by the so-called white Christian gentlemen of the alleged Free World." After touring Ciudad Libertad, a Batista military base that the Castro regime had turned into a school, Williams said that his "indoctrination by the American Jim Crow educational system" had left him with "no concept of how much a government can do for the education of the poor."[14] When Williams called his family and his friends in Monroe on June 13, 1960, he told them, "I wish every American Negro could visit Cuba and see what it really means to be treated as a first-class citizen."[15]

Williams had first met Fidel Castro one day when the Cuban leader happened to be walking through the lobby of his tour group's hotel. Someone "ran over and told him that there were some Americans, some black Americans here," Williams recalled. "He came over and started shaking my hand and said that he had read about me in the press and everything and how he admired my position and appreciated my support of Cuba."[16] The stream of freedom movement activists through Havana that would become routine remained a welcome novelty in 1960. "Because I was from the South of the United States," Williams wrote in his memoirs thirty years later, "Fidel took a special interest in me." According to Carlos Moore, an Afro-Cuban who knew both Castro and Williams in 1960, Williams's visit had attracted the close attention of both Castro and Major Manuel Pineira Losado, the head of Cuban intelligence, who decided that the recruitment of black Americans should be a political priority and that Williams would be their vehicle. "Before the close of that summer," Moore writes, "the militant civil rights leader was invited back to Cuba. This time, however, he went as Fidel Castro's personal guest."[17]

If he could not simply stay, the Cuban leader pleaded with Williams, he could at least return to Cuba for the anniversary celebration of the July 26, 1953, revolt in Oriente province that marked the beginning of Castro's efforts to overthrow the Batista regime. Williams flew home, repacked his suitcase, and returned to New York City, where he led a troupe of African American intellectuals, writers, and activists organized by Richard Gibson of the Fair Play for Cuba Committee to see Cuba for themselves. Hence Williams enjoyed a second trip to Cuba that same summer, spending a total of about six weeks on the island. The nucleus of this second delegation, according to John Hendrik Clarke, consisted of the contributors to the special issue of *Lunes de Revolución* that Robert Williams had edited during his first trip to Cuba. Langston Hughes, James Baldwin, Alice Childress, and John Oliver Killens had been scheduled to come along, but each backed out at the last minute. "Before we left New York City," Clarke wrote, Williams "told me that no experience in his lifetime had impressed him more profoundly than the Cuban Revolution."[18]

Another member of the delegation, young writer Amiri Baraka, published an essay about the trip, "Cuba Libre," that signaled his transformation from a largely apolitical "beat" poet living in Greenwich Village to a major figure in the Black Arts movement.[19] Baraka recalled that "I only got to go because Langston [Hughes] didn't go, and this guy Richard Gibson called me up and said, 'You wanna go?' " The trip to Cuba "blew my mind; I was never the same again," a change in which Robert Williams played a crucial part. "You have to understand, Robert Williams changed my whole life," Baraka said flatly.[20]

In Baraka's understanding of the trip, "the Cuban government wanted [black intellectuals] to get a look and spread the word. Relations with the new Cuba and the U.S. had not gotten outright funky, but they were getting that way," he recalled. "The U.S. [government] could dig a Batista, their boy, but Fidel Castro was making noises like a democrat and you know they can't abide that shit." Baraka first met Williams at the airport in New York City, where he joined writer Harold Cruse, novelist Sarah Wright and her husband, painter Ed Clark, and several black journalists and activists. Harlem historian John Hendrik Clarke, the son of an Alabama sharecropper who had carried his dream of owning farmland to his grave, came to see whether the Cuban land reform program would improve "the lives of people in Cuba whose hopes and dreams are similar to those of my father." Julian Mayfield and his wife, Ana Livia Codero, M.D., met the group in Havana. The person who made the biggest impression on Baraka was Robert Williams. "He was wearing a big straw hat like a campesino (Cuban farmer) when I met him, with a wisp of beard," Baraka wrote. "He was a big man, maybe six feet three inches and about 240 pounds, imposing, strong-looking. One never doubted that, aroused, Rob could be a mean mf."[21]

At the Hotel Presidente in Havana, the black writers smoked cigars and drank rum, relishing the romance of revolution and the opportunity to talk politics far into the night. Mayfield, too, first encountered Robert Williams during the trip. A novelist who had worked as a journalist in New York City and Puerto Rico for a number of years, Mayfield was not an easy man to impress. But he had never met anyone like Robert Williams. "Night after night on the balcony of the Presidente Hotel, I asked him every tough question I could think of, and Williams never ducked one of them," Mayfield said. "He came across like the homespun and probably apocryphal portrait we have of Abraham Lincoln: simple, straightforward, and too good to be true."

Mayfield had followed Williams's political career and tried to bait him during one of their long evenings in Havana. "I think now that what sold me on Robert Williams was the answer to a question I asked, long after we both should have been in bed." The hardbitten journalist acknowledged that Williams had "had a good shot for your money. You've shaken up the NAACP with your self-defense stand and made a lot of Negroes think for the first time. You and Fidel are close buddies and from Havana you have a platform to broadcast to the world." But, Mayfield continued, "back home you don't have a political base." He jabbed, pressing hard. "All the money is on Martin Luther King. So what do you want now?" Williams pondered the question for only a moment, Mayfield remembered, "and then said in that slow, sometimes maddening North Carolina drawl, 'I just want to be free, that's all. And I will be.' "[22]

More intoxicating than any amount of the finest Cuban rum was the sense of freedom and the euphoria of fame that Williams enjoyed on his trips to Cuba. "I hung out with Rob Williams one day," Baraka wrote in his *Autobiography of LeRoi Jones,* "and everywhere he went people in the street cheered him. The Cubans had made his confrontations with the Klan and *yanqui racismo* known to people throughout the island, even though in the U.S. they tried to play it down." Williams's picture appeared in Cuban newspapers, and he was besieged by reporters seeking interviews on Cuban television and radio. "In most of the interviews," Baraka wrote in "Cuba Libre," Williams "put down the present administration of the U.S. very violently for its aberrant foreign policy and its hypocritical attitude on what is called 'the Negro question.' " When he and Williams visited the Office of Agrarian Reform, Baraka observed, the pistol-packing soldier typing at the front desk spun around in his chair "and let us have all thirty-two teeth. He recognized Robert Williams immediately and shook his hand vigorously." At the editorial offices of a Cuban magazine, the staff huddled around Williams to ask about North American politics.

"He impressed all of Cuba with the force of his personality," Baraka wrote. Strolling through old Havana with a pearl-handled pistol on his hip and a broad smile on his face, his barrel-shaped body parting the admiring crowds, the winning impression that Williams made on revolutionary Cuba was entirely mutual. "On the streets of Cuba," Williams wrote upon his return to North Carolina, "I learned for the first time in my life what it feels like to be respected as a fellow human being and to be accepted in the human race."[23]

Robert's sense of euphoria was interrupted on July 23 when he received word from Mabel in Monroe that the Ku Klux Klan had threatened to dynamite their home. There had been a large Klan rally in Union County that night, his wife said. Afterward an anonymous caller had told Mabel that Klan dynamite bombs would kill her and their two sons as "punishment to the father for backing the Cuban revolution," the *Monroe Enquirer* reported.[24] "It scared me to death," Mabel Williams remembered. The caller referred to her husband as "that communist nigger," she said.[25] Police chief A. A. Mauney made light of the matter and refused to respond. "This threat was a source of great concern to me because I was not there to defend them," Robert Williams recalled. In Havana, Williams decided to "escalate the situation to a point where the U.S. Government would have some special incentive to protect my family." He grabbed a Cuban news reporter, enlisted Amiri Baraka, and stomped to the American embassy in a rage.

"Rob, with me trailing along with him, went to see the U.S. ambassador," Baraka wrote later. "Rob was wearing a shoulder holster and his language was so hot you could hear him through the door." Williams demanded that the embassy contact federal officials in North Carolina to protect his family. Baraka heard him bellow, "If the U.S. government don't protect them, then I got people there who will!"[26] The ambassador "didn't seem to give too much credence to my story," Williams recounted, "until I told him that if anything should happen to my family that I would kill Americans in Havana and that he would be the first to go." Baraka, who recalled that "my heart went up in my throat," was almost speechless at the scene. "He told the ambassador, 'Either you call Washington, call whoever you call, and stop that [Klan attack], or I'm gonna blow your head off right here, because you know ain't nothing gon' stop me because we're in Cuba. These people love me outside. Fidel Castro is in power, you understand, and ain't nothing gonna happen except you gon' be dead.'" When Robert called home later that night, Mabel Williams told him that there was a police car dutifully patrolling Boyte Street. "Robert was a great man and I always had great respect for him," Baraka remembered, "but after that Cuban incident I was in awe of him because I had never seen nothing like that."[27]

On the evening of July 25, assured by his comrades-in-arms in the Monroe NAACP that his family was safe, Williams led the African American delegation into what John Hendrik Clarke called "the happy bedlam of the Central Terminus in Havana." Here they waited in an overflow crowd for a slow train to the mountains of Oriente province where Castro's band had launched its rebellion. Along the way, townspeople gathered to greet the lumbering cars rattling eastward down the rails. "From the joyful noise outside the windows, it seemed as if the entire population of the town had assembled to salute the delegations journeying to the July 26th celebration in the Sierra Maestra," Clarke wrote. "Cubans of every color from blonde white to jet black were participating in absolute equality and with the same show of enthusiasm. The sight of Robert Williams waving from the train," Clarke noted, "accelerated the demonstration. His forthright endorsement of the Cuban Revolution during his last visit had made him an accepted friend of the Cuban people." They rolled on through the night, sleeping in their seats, and woke up to the songs of the Mexican delegation and a breakfast of strong coffee and tomato juice. "We joined our voices in songs of freedom and struggle," Williams wrote later, and "I experienced a sensation that mere words cannot convey." Despite their euphoria, July 26 was a blistering hot day, and the bleary-eyed travelers left the train and climbed the last winding leg of the journey among thousands of celebrants, "a surging sea of people," Clarke said.[28]

"We were caught up in a revolutionary outpouring of thousands upon thousands of people making their way up the mountain roads to the shrine of the Revolution," Harold Cruse remembered, "under the hottest sun-drenching any of us Americans had probably ever experienced." But the suffocating heat could not stifle the enchantment that began to well up inside the visitors. Even Cruse, older than most of them and often cynical, admitted that it was difficult to remain a skeptic. The historic moment "had lifted us out of the anonymity of lonely struggle in the United States to the glorified rank of visiting dignitaries." A beautiful young woman ran up to Baraka and kissed him hard, exclaiming, "un americano, un americano." Photographers darted along behind Williams, snapping pictures as he led the delegation through the throng. Little girls in brown uniforms and red berets greeted the African Americans with armfuls of flowers.

Armed rebel soldiers led them to the official platform, where they "reached the outstretched and welcoming hand of Premier Fidel Castro,"

Clarke wrote soon afterward. "He greeted Robert F. Williams first and expressed his pleasure at seeing him in Cuba again." The African American delegation also shook hands with a grinning Juan Almeida Bosque and the legendary Che Guevara. When Castro overheard one of the women in their party complaining of thirst, the leader stopped his conversation and brought her a glass of water himself. "This very human gesture of consideration, coming from a busy revolutionist now engrossed in rebuilding his nation," Clarke said, "told me more about the character of Fidel Castro than the small mountain of newspaper articles that I have already read about him." The ensuing speech by the bearded head of state, which lasted several hours, was interrupted by a brisk, refreshing rainstorm and lengthy chants of "venceremos, venceremos" and "Fidel, Fidel, Fidel." Even though they were drenched to the skin, nothing could dampen the crowd's euphoria.[29] "At the end of our tour," Williams wrote later, "Fidel suggested to me that I remain in Cuba. He said the Cuban people liked me. I explained to him that I wanted to remain in the South," Williams said, but that "I could foresee the possibility of my having to leave the South eventually."[30]

Not surprisingly, the first issues of The Crusader published after Williams returned to Monroe trumpeted the triumphs of the Cuban revolution. For Williams, the experience in Oriente provided a kind of Pentecostal revelation that left him nearly at a loss for words:

> For what can one say of a glory that mankind has never before approximated? . . . I simply say that I have seen the face of Cuba . . . in the beauty and happiness of her sons and daughters who made a pilgrimage to the Sierra Maestra to hear the modern version of the Sermon on the Mount . . . on the happy face of a little boy who helped his father prepare a pig for the feast . . . on the humanitarian face of a little girl who stood by the side of the road and stretched forth a glass of water to the weary travelers . . . in the clean faces of the little boys in uniform who seemed so proud and confident of the future.

The Cuban patriots had created overnight "one of the greatest democracies in the world today," he declared, "the great social miracle of the twentieth century." Under a crude, homemade, but unmistakably clear drawing of the bearded leader of Cuba, The Crusader's caption read, "Fidel Castro: Spirit of Christ."[31]

It is hardly surprising that his weeks in Cuba made so deep an impression on Williams. He certainly was not alone. His friend and ally Conrad

Lynn, who visited Cuba separately that year, found the "euphoria of revolution" hard to resist. "I carried so much back with me," Amiri Baraka wrote of his trip with Williams, "that I was never the same again."[32] When Baraka came home, he later said, "I was turned *completely* around and began to go on a really aggressive attack as far as politics was concerned." Williams, too, noted that he himself had "returned full of enthusiasm for struggle." When he got home from Cuba, Williams took a Cuban flag that Castro had given him and ran it up the flagpole in his backyard, where it flapped in the breeze just beneath Old Glory.[33]

But his reaction to the Cuban journey went deeper than flag waving or political resolve. As hardened as Williams tried to seem, the daily injuries that Jim Crow heaped on him at home hurt the proud man deeply; the honor that Cubans lavished on him was balm to his soul. All of his life, Williams had dreamed of being recognized as a writer; in Havana he passed his evenings in the company of accomplished poets, playwrights, novelists, and journalists who took him quite seriously. He had often been ignored at home, but the declarations for racial equality that Williams hurled from Cuba seemed to echo throughout the world. From boyhood he had yearned to lead his people in a gallant struggle for liberty. All of Cuba lauded him as a visiting revolutionary hero, and Fidel Castro, the swashbuckling guerilla leader turned head of state, called him friend.

Perhaps most important was the sense of hope that soared within him. What he had sought to test in Cuba, Williams said, was the argument common among both segregationists and liberals in the United States— "that governments cannot stamp out racial inequality" and "that social justice must wait for a change of heart on the part of bigots."[34] The bigots that Williams had known did not seem to be walking any Damascus road with respect to the issue of race. If the country was becoming more liberal, it was not evident in Union County, North Carolina. Yet despair was an unaffordable luxury. The imperative to preserve hope may have rendered Williams unable to discern what he would later see so clearly: that socialism was no magical cure for white supremacy. In 1960, however, Williams needed to believe that "the Castro government has wiped out Jim Crow" and that "all Cubans regardless of race are given an opportunity of equality." His walk through the Sierra Maestra, the mountaintop cradle of the Cuban revolution, he wrote, had been "a pilgrimage to the shrine of hope."[35]

Williams soon saw Castro again, not in Cuba but in the United States. The Cuban leader flew to New York City on September 18, 1960, to address the fifteenth session of the United Nations General Assembly. The Shelburne Hotel in Manhattan, where Cuban diplomats usually stayed, demanded thousands of dollars in cash in advance. Castro refused, calling the manager a "gangster." New York's tabloid press, meanwhile, portrayed the bearded *fidelistas* as uncouth primitives, spreading unsubstantiated rumors that they killed, plucked, and cooked chickens in their rooms at the Shelburne and extinguished cigars on the expensive carpets. Nor were the Cubans permitted to travel freely in the United States: "Robert Williams' invitation to his friend Fidel Castro to visit Monroe might have been accepted (in view of recent events)," the *Monroe Enquirer* taunted, "if the dictator was not barred from leaving Manhattan." Castro threatened to pitch tents outside the United Nations in protest, but apparently members of the Fair Play for Cuba Committee had a better idea. The following night, the entire Cuban delegation moved to the Hotel Theresa in the heart of Harlem at 125th Street and 7th Avenue.[36]

Several hours before Castro came to Harlem, the telephone rang at the home of Sarah Elizabeth Wright, a novelist who had just returned from her trip to Cuba with Robert Williams. Many of Williams's most vocal supporters in Harlem—Clarke, Killens, and a dozen others—had gathered in her apartment for a meeting of the Harlem Writers Guild Workshop. The news that Castro was on his way to the Theresa sent them bolting from their chairs. "Immediately, we scrambled for our coats and headed uptown to cheer Fidel, to make sure no harm befell him," Wright recalled. "We climbed into taxis, jumped out in front of the Hotel Theresa into a mass of humanity buffeted by a driving rain." Gazing up, they could see crowds crammed onto rooftops and thousands of heads leaning out windows. "Some 2000 brown New Yorkers stood in the rain Monday night waiting for Cuba's Premier Fidel Castro to arrive at Harlem's famous old Hotel Theresa," the *New York Citizen-Call* reported. "To Harlem's oppressed ghetto dwellers, Castro was that bearded revolutionary who had thrown the nation's rascals out and who had told white America to go to hell." About midnight, Castro arrived wearing his trademark green fatigues, waved to the crowds, and ducked inside the hotel. Declining to speak with the mainstream press, Castro allowed two black reporters and a photographer to enter his suite, where he met with Malcolm X, who walked in out of the downpour in his black trenchcoat. "I think you will find the people in Harlem are not so addicted to the propaganda they put out downtown," Malcolm told Castro. "No one knows the master better than his servants."[37] If the move to the Theresa was "grand demagoguery," as North

Carolina's Senator Sam Ervin claimed, it was also global political theater on a grand scale.[38]

"To say that Harlem was flattered was to put it mildly," the *Pittsburgh Courier* observed. "She didn't give a continental as to whether the move of Castro to 'uptown' was a smashing propaganda victory for the Cubans." But it certainly was that. "The blood of Fidel Castro is proud like that of his colored ancestors," the editors of the *Afro-American* wrote. "He refuses to accept an inferior status, either for himself or for his country." For the next ten days, crowds thronged the Hotel Theresa day and night. In order to take full advantage of the political opportunity, Castro sent for the head of his army, Juan Almeida Bosque—syndicated newspaper columnist Drew Pearson called him a "full-blooded Negro"—who paraded through the streets of Harlem and posed on the hotel balcony with Castro to the applause of thousands of black citizens. The *New York Times* ran a photograph of Cuban foreign minister Raul Roa eating a hotdog at Chock-Full-o'-Nuts, a Harlem landmark, and observed that "Castro has earned considerable respect for his demonstrative opposition to racial discrimination."

A steady procession of international dignitaries and political leaders, including Khrushchev of the Soviet Union, Nasser of Egypt, and Nehru of India, strolled through Harlem in high-profile visits to Castro at the Hotel Theresa. Visitors from the United States included L. Joseph Overton of the Harlem NAACP, Malcolm X, and Robert Williams. Williams not only conferred with Castro privately but attended a grand reception for the Cuban delegation sponsored by the Fair Play for Cuba Committee. In attendance was his old friend and literary hero, Langston Hughes, as well as C. Wright Mills, Allen Ginsberg, I. F. Stone, Henri Cartier-Bresson, Amiri Baraka, and many others whose names would soon be familiar in the New Left, the black freedom movement, or the arts. Richard Gibson presented Castro with a bust of Abraham Lincoln, "from one liberator to another," he ad-libbed. Castro had pulled off a "master stroke" in Harlem, Conrad Lynn observed. Even the conservative Jackie Robinson, who came to the Hotel Theresa to denounce Castro's "propaganda," had to concede that the visit did "give Harlem a real lift—a sense of pride."[39]

Castro's grand gesture, columnist Pearson explained to the nation, was "part of a carefully calculated move to hit the United States where the Communist world considers us weak—with our Negro population." That was not far from the heart of it, though Castro was not yet aligned with the Soviet Union. "Castro's Harlem performance was not merely a propaganda stunt," Carlos Moore writes, "but a major tactical victory on at least three fronts." First, it strengthened Castro at home. The Cuban government quickly proclaimed "Solidarity Week with the Negro Peoples of the United States," and the "discrimination against Fidel" made Afro-Cubans feel that their young leader knew firsthand the injustice that they had experienced their entire lives. Second, though most blacks in the United States did not become *fidelistas*, African Americans did realize that racial progress in Cuba outstripped any reforms that white political leaders in the United States seemed likely to accept. Castro would be welcome in Harlem for decades to come. Third, and perhaps most important, the leaders of the new emerging states of Africa now saw Castro in a new and more favorable light, as Cuba was able to use its vaunted racial egalitarianism to strengthen its relations with the emerging nonaligned states and undermine the legitimacy of the United States by raising the race issue in an international context. The political gains for the Cuban revolution from the Harlem spectacle, both short- and long-term, were incalculable. And the man that Pearson and many others credited or blamed for all of this was Robert F. Williams.[40]

In mid-1960 the Fair Play for Cuba Committee decided to showcase Williams. Williams made the connection between the Cuban revolution and black liberation much more sharply than sunny beaches beyond the reach of Jim Crow or even the drama of Castro-comes-to-Harlem. In the fall of 1960 Williams repeatedly underlined Cuba's racial achievements during a series of speaking engagements for Fair Play. Eager to keep the committee away from anyone associated with the Communist Party USA and wishing to expand its national efforts, Robert Taber, Fair Play's founder and guiding light, struck a deal with Berta Green and other leaders in the SWP. The SWP, of course, had been a booster for Williams since the days of the kissing case. Green, a devoted organizer for the SWP, had become the most important Fair Play organizer in New York. Taber agreed that the SWP would furnish Green and three full-time traveling organizers for the East, the Midwest, and the West Coast. The SWP remained eager to promote Williams's leadership. The other important organizational element in the remarkable growth of Fair Play over the next year was Castro's appeal among African American activists—such as Richard Gibson, William Worthy, Julian Mayfield, John Hendrik Clarke, and Amiri Baraka—at the forefront of an emerging black nationalism. Williams was clearly the political icon of choice in these circles as well. In a few months, this combination of SWP activism, black nationalist revival, and the first stirrings of the New Left would expand the Fair Play for Cuba Committee from

2,000 subscribers to the *Fair Play* bulletin and three local chapters to a national organization of 7,000 members in twenty-seven adult chapters and forty student councils. In the fall of 1960, Taber traveled to Monroe to recruit Williams as a national speaker for Fair Play. As he had during the kissing case, Williams seized this opportunity to let the word go forth about a new day in Dixie.[41]

Taber attempted "to make Rob a revolutionary hero," Richard Gibson, the first secretary of the New York branch of Fair Play and later acting executive secretary, jeered a decade later. "I have always said that Rob was a simple black man thrown onto the stage of world history by pure accident. Unfortunately, he was unable to sustain the role we cast him in."[42] There may be some kernel of truth in Gibson's assessment. Williams never planned to be an international political celebrity. Gibson's imperious dismissal, however, overlooks the personal vision of Williams, the political role of American socialists, and the largely unexamined reawakening of black nationalism in late 1950s. In any case, Williams had his own agenda, and those who succeeded in using him for their purposes were few. Baraka, whose devotion to Williams reflected the renewal of black nationalism, claimed Williams as a nationalist and argued that Williams only made alliances with white leftists when it served his own agenda. This was true, for the most part. Mabel Williams, however, said that "many of these political people, these Trotskyists, as we found out, became our personal friends and helped us a great deal when we really needed it later." As usual, Robert Williams resisted ideological straitjackets and displayed a politics that was both personal and pragmatic.[43]

Fair Play first attempted to organize more trips to Cuba. As more U.S. citizens saw revolutionary Cuba firsthand, the committee's reasoning went, the American government would find it harder to crack down on Cuba. "You can spend a whole week in the luxurious Habana Riviera!" Williams told readers of *The Crusader*. Despite the low subsidized package prices, Fair Play had to postpone the first proposed tour from October 22 to October 29 after prospective black tourists began to receive anonymous threats. "Anybody who goes on the tour to Cuba is pretty sure of losing his job," Williams reported sadly. "At least that's what the people are being told." Williams, though he had no job to lose, reported receiving both threats and offers of bribes. Berta Green, in fact, had already been fired from her post with a pharmaceutical firm. Another Cuba tour finally proceeded, just after Christmas; then, soon after New Year's, the Kennedy administration closed off all travel to Cuba.

On November 17, 1960, Williams was the featured speaker at a large Fair Play rally in Harlem, which by now was political home turf for the man from Monroe. William Worthy of the Baltimore *Afro-American* and Daniel Watt of the Liberation Committee for Africa also addressed the crowd.[44] This was only the first of many speeches Williams made for Fair Play. His address at the New York Trade Show Building on February 9, 1961, launched another national tour for the militant NAACP branch president. Williams's New York speeches connected black nationalism with Pan-African internationalism in a way that pointed straight toward Black Power. Looking back on those days, Amiri Baraka goes so far as to say that these were "the same movement. It was an anti-imperialist movement, a movement against foreign domination and against national oppression. And I think all of us—Stokely [Carmichael] too—had been influenced by that."[45] Malcolm X formulated the point more succinctly at a Harlem rally protesting the U.S. foreign policy that had led to the assassination of Patrice Lumumba in the Congo: "You can't understand what is going on in Mississippi if you can't understand what is going on in the Congo."[46]

Williams delivered his final speech of the New York tour at a Harlem street rally on the evening of February 14. His fiery rhetoric helped to inspire one of the most tumultuous and telling moments in the early days of this anticolonial black nationalist revival.[47] The next morning, as Williams left to speak in Michigan, Mae Mallory, Calvin Hicks, Amiri Baraka, Carlos Moore, Maya Angelou, Carlos Cooks, Max Roach, Abby Lincoln, and many of Williams's other Harlem supporters joined demonstrators at the United Nations to protest the murder of Lumumba. This was not just "a handful of Stalinist-corrupted provocateurs," James Baldwin wrote soon afterward, adding that he "had intended to be there myself." Mallory, whom Lynn called "a very physical woman, a block of granite," pushed her way into the Security Council chambers. When one of the guards grabbed her, Mallory said, she whipped off one shoe and "cracked his head with my shoe heel. Then I wrapped my fist in the necktie of another guard." Baraka wrote later that "Mae put up a terrific battle and the police were sorry they ever put their hands on her. It took several of them to subdue her."[48]

The fighting spread into the streets, where angry black demonstrators hurled rocks and snowballs at guards. The New York Police Department dispatched thirty mounted officers to disperse the protesters, but the clashes continued as hundreds marched toward Times Square shouting, "Congo, sí! Yankee, no!" When the mounted police finally broke up the march, the demonstrators regrouped in front of the Hotel Theresa in Harlem. President Kennedy responded with a statement reaffirming U.S. support for the United Nations. Mainstream journalists, most notably James Reston of the *New York Times*, painted the protests as a Soviet-directed display of propaganda, even though most of the groups involved had no Marxist ties and some of the nationalist groups refused to associate with Communists.[49] "What I find appalling—and really dangerous," James Baldwin replied, "is the American assumption that the Negro is so contented with his lot here that only the cynical agents of a foreign power can rouse him to protest."[50]

Robert Williams needed no prodding from *Pravda* to persist in his speeches for Fair Play. It is not surprising that many of the venues were the same ones he had barnstormed during the kissing case two years earlier, since Trotskyite organizers orchestrated both efforts. From February 15 to February 19, Williams spoke in Michigan, at the University of Michigan in Ann Arbor, the Friday Night Forum and the Greater King Solomon Baptist Church in Detroit, and a labor hall in Flint. "We had a good meeting here for Williams last week," one student in Ann Arbor wrote, "with about 300 people turning out." On February 23 Williams addressed an overflow crowd at the Packinghouse Workers Hall in Chicago. Everywhere he spoke, Williams handed out copies of *The Crusader*, enrolled subscribers, and expanded his thick address book of contacts.[51]

On March 4 Williams inspired another riot when he opened his West Coast tour with an explosive appearance at a Fair Play rally in Los Angeles. Armed anti-Castro demonstrators, aided by Young Conservatives, rushed the podium. Fistfights erupted, and gunshots echoed inside the hall when plainclothes police officers intervened and arrested six of the attackers, one of them after a protracted gun battle. A week later, Williams addressed eight hundred people at Norse Auditorium in San Francisco. Students at the University of Washington in Seattle organized their "first big public meeting . . . around Williams." At the University of Colorado and at the University of British Columbia in Vancouver, students responded enthusiastically. The John Dewey Society and the university's NAACP chapter cosponsored a Williams speech at Yale. At the University of Minnesota, Young Americans for Freedom and the College Republican Club picketed Williams's appearance before a crowd of several hundred students. Winifred Chelstrom, a student, thought that "the pickets helped our meeting," first by their announcement that they would picket, then by creating such a spectacle that the local television station "picked up the meeting and telecast it," she wrote. "Williams gave a top-notch talk."[52]

A few years later, the New Left would be able to call hundreds of thousands into the streets to protest U.S. foreign policy; Fair Play at its height in the spring of 1961 could only deliver a few thousand. By the standards of that day, when any protest against U.S. foreign policy was risky and unusual, Fair Play made remarkable strides, attracting thousands of members and building a national network of local chapters in a matter of months. The magnitude of Fair Play's achievement can be measured in part by the degree to which it stunned and appalled its adversaries. "It is a little bit shocking to know that even at Carleton College there is a forty-member Fair Play for Cuba Committee," the president of the University of Minnesota Republican Club complained that spring, even though Carleton "is a high-class institution with only people from the higher economic brackets attending." The newsletter of the Young Americans for Freedom lamented in 1961 that "the Fair Play for Cuba Committee has made deep inroads into the political life of colleges in all parts of the country."[53]

With Williams delivering his fiery speeches, SWP organizers working behind the scenes, and a new generation of college students responding to fresh political and cultural currents from many directions—including the black freedom movement, rock and roll, and the peace movement—Fair Play was able to grow at a remarkable rate, stirring the straw of these newly radicalized young liberals into the clay of the Old Left to produce some of the important building blocks of the New Left. Though Williams would have mixed feelings about the results and Cuba eventually would disappoint him, his days with Fair Play brought him readers and friends from Vancouver to Long Island. Soon after the Kennedy administration launched its ill-fated invasion of Cuba at the Bay of Pigs on April 17, 1961, *The Crusader* announced that the newsletter's vastly expanded circulation now made it "next to impossible to produce manually. We appeal to our friends everywhere to contribute to our drive to raise funds to purchase automatic electronic equipment."[54]

The national office of the NAACP, which had tried so hard to crush Williams politically, was horrified to see its Union County branch president parading across the country as an advocate for Castro. In early April 1961, as planning for the "covert" invasion of Cuba by CIA-sponsored forces was becoming an open secret, Gloster Current wrote a desperate letter to Williams. Fair Play "advertising identified you as an NAACP leader," Current argued, and was therefore "confusing to the public as it relates to a controversial regime with which our government is fundamentally in disagreement." He insisted that Williams "resign from your affiliation with the NAACP." Current warned that Williams would find himself "used as just another pawn" in the struggle between Cuba and the United States and disparaged the sincerity of Cuban attempts to win African American support, asking Williams "how the Negro tourist would feel in Cuba at the constant chants of 'Cuba, sí, Yankee, no!'" Reminding Williams of the risks he was taking, the national official asked Williams, "Does not the example of Paul Robeson show you the dangers and mistakes of the road which you seem to be choosing?"

The Monroe branch president fired back that it was curious why anyone would ask whether he was offended at the sound of "Cuba, sí, Yankee, no" when no one had ever asked him "how it feels to constantly face 'white only' signs" in his own hometown. Nor had anyone "asked me how it feels to be marched under guard with felons along a public street for sitting on a 'white only' stool." For that matter, Williams continued, Paul Robeson's life was not so much a cautionary tale as commendable proof "that all black men are not for sale for thirty pieces of silver. He has lit a candle that many of the new generation will follow."[55]

A few days after Williams's sharp exchange with Current, thousands of members of that new generation attended at least 134 protest demonstrations across the country, organized in the wake of news that CIA-sponsored Cuban exiles had launched a catastrophically unsuccessful invasion of Cuba at a place called Playa de Girón, the Bay of Pigs. The invasion sparked public protests unprecedented during the Cold War with respect to U.S. foreign policy. Thousands rallied in Union Square in New York City to denounce the debacle. Acrimonious debates exploded among liberals. Graduate students at Harvard wired their former professor Arthur M. Schlesinger Jr., now President Kennedy's court intellectual, with a brutally sarcastic reference to Schlesinger's pronouncements during the 1960 presidential election: NIXON OR KENNEDY? DOES IT MAKE ANY DIFFERENCE? The ailing C. Wright Mills, who would leave his own mark on a generation of young radicals, sent a telegram to a huge demonstration in San Francisco: SORRY I CANNOT BE WITH YOU. WERE I PHYSICALLY ABLE TO DO SO, I WOULD AT THIS MOMENT BE FIGHTING ALONGSIDE FIDEL CASTRO. At this moment, Van Gosse writes, alongside the burgeoning black freedom struggle in the South, "a new U.S. left was making itself."[56]

Most Americans, however, rallied around the flag in the aftermath of the bungled invasion. When his secretary handed him a new Gallup poll indicating an 82 percent support rating, President Kennedy joked, "It's just like Eisenhower. The worse I do, the more popular I get." From North Carolina, however, Robert Williams taunted liberals who so pressed "the Negro" to abstain from violence, even in self-defense. "Kennedy is talking global war," Williams charged. "Where are all the so-called pacifists at this great hour of tragedy? Where are all the Martin Luther Kings who lecture poor, downtrodden Afro-Americans on 'the power of nonviolence and love'?"[57]

Sharper than his indignation was his magnificent sense of humor. Williams dispatched an open telegram to Adlai Stevenson, U.S. ambassador to the United Nations, whose public lies about the Bay of Pigs marked an embarrassing low point in his public career. Stevenson had dutifully repeated a stream of falsehoods about the U.S. posture toward Cuba, claiming that Cuba had been attacked by its own army, and was finally reduced to arguing that the failure of the assault proved that the United States had not staged it. Cuban foreign minister Raul Roa read aloud the telegram from Robert Williams to Ambassador Stevenson on the floor of the United Nations during the angry debate on April 20 when it was still unclear what would come of the invasion:

PLEASE CONVEY TO MR. ADLAI STEVENSON: NOW THAT THE UNITED STATES HAS PROCLAIMED SUPPORT FOR PEOPLE WILLING TO REBEL AGAINST OPPRESSION, OPPRESSED NEGROES OF THE SOUTH URGENTLY REQUEST TANKS, ARTILLERY, BOMBS, MONEY AND THE USE OF AMERICAN AIRFIELDS AND WHITE MERCENARIES TO CRUSH THE RACIST TYRANTS WHO HAVE BETRAYED THE AMERICAN REVOLUTION AND CIVIL WAR. WE ALSO REQUEST PRAYERS FOR THIS UNDERTAKING.

Robert F. Williams
410 Boyte Street
Monroe, NC

"I would like to ask Mr. Stevenson," the Cuban foreign minister elaborated angrily, "what would happen if the government of the United States, which claims to be the champion of democracy, dared to arm not only the Negroes of the cotton fields of the South, but the Negroes right here in Harlem?" The roaring laughter from the African and Asian delegates and Stevenson's red-faced anger signaled a diplomatic victory for Castro nearly as decisive as his military triumph at the Bay of Pigs.[58] Stevenson complained in a top-secret telegram to Secretary of State Dean Rusk that he could not understand why, if the U.S. government could not prevent the Bay of Pigs invasion from occurring at all, its ambassador "could not have been warned and provided prepared material with which to defend the U.S." against this ridicule.[59]

If Kennedy officials found Williams's mocking telegram to Stevenson less amusing than Williams did, they cannot have been pleased with his more sober response in the Baltimore *Afro-American* two days later and in the *New York Post* and several other newspapers over the next week. "Cuba—A Declaration of Conscience by Afro-Americans" was a full-page ad signed by Williams and many of his black allies. "Because we have known oppression, because we have suffered more than other Americans, because we are still fighting for our own liberation from tyranny, we Afro-Americans have the right and the duty to raise our voices in protest against the forces of oppression that now seek to crush a free people linked to us by the bonds of blood and a common heritage," it read. "Afro-Americans, don't be fooled—the enemies of the Cubans are our enemies, the Jim Crow bosses of this land where we are still denied our rights."[60] The Harlem nationalists who signed the declaration—John Hendrik Clarke, Amiri Baraka, Julian Mayfield, Daniel Watt, and Richard Gibson—were all affiliated with the Fair Play for Cuba Committee, as was reporter William Worthy of the *Afro-American*. Robert Maynard was a talented journalist who would later become a nationally syndicated columnist. Maya Angelou and Ossie Davis were important figures in the arts. Attorney Conrad Lynn, of course, was a longtime Williams supporter. John W. McDow from Monroe, who had struggled alongside Williams since 1946, also signed the declaration, as did Dr. W. E. B. Du Bois and his wife, Shirley Graham. Such a statement by leading black American intellectuals and activists on behalf of a foreign power was without precedent. "The most important signatory of the black 'Declaration' was Robert Williams, who had been personally in touch with Castro," historian Carlos Moore observes. "His popularity among U.S. Blacks at its height, Williams summoned black America to Castro's rescue," Moore argues.[61] But Castro would need more powerful allies than embattled African Americans. The use of force, intended to drive Castro away from the Soviet Union, ironically, provoked the diplomatic disaster that it was intended to prevent—namely, the installation of Soviet missiles in Cuba that would threaten a nuclear holocaust in the fall of 1962.[62]

The spring of 1961 marked an upsurge in both the international Cold War and African American freedom struggles across the United States. An ever-strengthening spirit of defiance among African Americans, especially the young, threatened to bypass the established civil rights leadership. On May 17, the seventh anniversary of their auspicious victory in *Brown v. Board*, the NAACP leadership roped off 7th Avenue in front of the Hotel Theresa for a celebration, perhaps seeking to mark the Harlem landmark as something other than a monument to Castro's diplomatic savvy.

Roy Wilkins, Daisy Bates, Clarence Mitchell, and other NAACP notables waited on the wooden dais erected for the occasion. Unnoticed by those elevated on the platform, Robert Williams stood quietly near the rear of the enormous crowd. Unfortunately for the official speakers, Williams now probably had, in absolute numbers, more friends and admirers in Harlem than he did in Monroe. When Wilkins rose to speak, the crowd got loud and hostile, drowning out his remarks. "Wilkins, the main speaker, had to stop for several minutes because he could not be heard above the shouts of the hecklers asking for [Robert] Williams," one wire service reported. "Wilkins finally was hooted down and was struck by an egg." Daisy Bates, whom Wilkins virtually had bribed to denounce Williams two years earlier, rose to defend Wilkins. Williams got his full measure of revenge, however. Large numbers of what the white press referred to as "agitators" shouted Bates down with chants of "We want Williams! We want Williams!" and refused to let her speak. Attempts by the band to drown out the crowd by playing "The Star-Spangled Banner" were fruitless, and eventually NAACP officials located Williams among the throng.

"We're going to let you speak," Gloster Current reportedly growled at Williams, "but we don't want no shit out of you." When Williams wheeled to leave without speaking, the NAACP officials virtually had to beg him to take the podium. "Williams was called to the rostrum and the heckling stopped as he began," wire service reports stated. "He had been ousted in 1959, he said, because 'I advocated Afro-American men should defend their women and children. I am tired of being oppressed,' Williams told Harlem, 'and I am going to meet violence with violence. It is better to live just thirty seconds, walking upright in human dignity, than to live a thousand years crawling at the feet of our oppressors!'" As he stepped back from the microphone, the crowd surged forward and hoisted Williams on their shoulders, lofting him back among their number high in the air. As soon as his supporters carried him from the podium, the crowd resumed its heckling of the NAACP leaders. "The band played 'The Star-Spangled Banner' for a second time," one of the national wire services reported, "in a futile attempt to restore order."[63]

9 :
When Fire
Breaks Out

If loud renditions of "The Star-Spangled Banner" could have maintained order, no doubt the Kennedy administration would have marched military bands across the South. Instead, it was the music of the black freedom movement that rang throughout the region in the spring of 1961. Like many other activists and citizens, Robert Williams watched with apprehension and excitement as one of the most dramatic and important episodes of the Southern freedom struggle unfolded. On May 4, seven blacks and six whites sponsored by CORE set out from Washington, D.C., on buses bound for New Orleans, determined to test the U.S. Supreme Court's 1960 decision in *Boynton v. Virginia*, which prohibited segregation in interstate travel facilities.[1]

The Freedom Rides of 1961 echoed CORE's 1947 Journey of Reconciliation, which had ended because of mob violence in North Carolina. Williams had heard stories about the earlier trip from Conrad Lynn, his attorney, who had participated in the 1947 test as had several of those who rode the buses southward in 1961. The Freedom Riders, schooled in Gandhian nonviolence—"outside agitators" almost by definition—expected to be met with violence this time, too. Justice Department officials feared vicious reactions among whites alarmed by the "ultimate southern taboo" of white women and black men sitting together on buses. "Most of the bus stations," historian Taylor Branch observes in a charming aside, "were located in parts of town where the Supreme Court and Gandhi were seldom discussed." In truth, people discussed these matters all over town, but workaday folk in the South in 1961 knew full well that neither the Supreme Court nor Gandhi could keep heads from cracking and blood from flowing when someone pushed against the boundaries of white supremacy.[2]

The Freedom Riders got their first taste of blood in a nasty scuffle in Rock Hill, South Carolina, thirty miles southwest of Monroe. But on Sunday, May 14, at the bus station in Anniston, Alabama, the rolling battalions of nonviolence rode into a mob of angry white men bearing bats, clubs, and knives. "This is Alabama, you black bastards," one of the attackers yelled. "Come on out and integrate."[3] As the mob surged around the buses and began slashing the tires, the bus driver sped away down Highway 78. Fifty carloads of Klan assailants burned rubber in pursuit. When the leaking tires forced the bus to the roadside, the mob smashed the windows with an ax and someone tossed a firebomb into the back of the bus. Pressed by the fire and smoke into the hands of the mob, the Freedom Riders were beaten until Alabama state troopers arrived and fired warning shots into the air. The following day, much to the dismay of President Kennedy, front pages around the world featured a photograph of the abandoned bus in flames.[4]

The brave riders obtained a new bus and rolled on, but Birmingham made Anniston seem almost hospitable by comparison. Public Safety Commissioner Bull Connor's police agreed to give the Ku Klux Klan fifteen unmolested minutes in which to beat the Freedom Riders. Police officers also telephoned the Klan at the Greyhound terminal to let them know that the first bus would arrive at the Trailways station instead. Despite detailed knowledge of these arrangements, the FBI neither protected nor warned the travelers. Beaten bloody with iron bars, lead pipes, brass knuckles, and baseball bats, most of the original Freedom Riders left the crusade and flew to New Orleans, but reinforcements organized by Diane Nash from the Nashville student movement slipped into Birmingham to carry the crusade to Montgomery.[5]

Stymied for several days by Bull Connor and the reluctant bus companies, the fresh troops finally rode toward Montgomery on May 20. In Montgomery, Police Commissioner L. B. Sullivan stated that he had "no intention of standing guard for a bunch of trouble makers coming into our city to make trouble."[6] Not surprisingly, Klansmen savagely beat several of the incoming integrationists at the Montgomery bus station.[7] When he heard that the Freedom Riders were besieged by white mobs, Martin Luther King Jr. flew into town to try to calm the situation.

White mobs trapped King, the Freedom Riders, and many members of the black community inside First Baptist Church. After several hours, as the raging white mob tried to storm the church, angry black men in the congregation began slipping out of the pews and pulling pistols and knives from their coat pockets. Heated whispers flew in the church foyer as some of the men told the preachers that they did not intend to let the mob kill or injure their loved ones without a fight, church or no church. King pleaded with Robert Kennedy on the telephone to send federal agents to intervene. "If they don't get here immediately," the minister told the attorney general, "we are going to have a bloody confrontation." Federal marshals finally rescued the congregation, and in the morning the Alabama National Guard escorted the group out of the church.[8]

For two days afterward, the Freedom Riders implored King to join them on the buses bound for Mississippi. Diane Nash, the bold and astute young leader from Nashville, confronted King point-blank. King could set an example of leadership, she urged him, that would hold nonviolence up for the nation to see. King agreed with Nash but said that he was not sure that he could go; he was on probation, he said. "I'm on probation, and I'm going," one student said. "Me, too," another added. King grew defensive, even angry. Paul Brooks, a young black seminarian from American Baptist Theological Seminary who had been jailed in Birmingham with the first busload of Nashville reinforcements, was deeply disillusioned. Brooks said later that he wished King had simply admitted that he was afraid. "I would have respected him more," Brooks stated.[9]

Brooks had begun to stay in touch with Robert Williams by telephone, which explains why Dr. King quickly received a bitter telegram from Monroe, North Carolina: "The cause of human decency and black liberation demands that you physically ride the buses with our gallant Freedom Riders. No sincere leader asks his followers to make sacrifices that he himself will not make. You are a phony. Gandhi was always in the forefront, suffering with his people. If you are the leader of this nonviolent movement, lead the way by example."

The telegram was a cheap shot, but Williams spoke for more than a few activists. He was even harder on King in his editorials for *The Crusader*. "One of the greatest disappointments to come out of the current 'Freedom Rider' campaign," he wrote, "is the news that Rev. Martin Luther King has declined field leadership to become a glorified verbal field director of some sort." Williams charged that "the white man's great limelight has given [King] too much to risk in an all-out struggle for liberation." The students launched the Freedom Rides, Williams said, and "King rushed to the scene to capture the ready-made glory." When the students asked King to join the rides, however, the minister offered only excuses. According to Williams, some of the SNCC and CORE youth called Williams in Monroe to complain that King "wants to ride the wave of publicity, but not the buses." Williams accused the minister of seeking to benefit from the sufferings of others. This was not quite fair. The Freedom Rides were a CORE project, and had King impetuously climbed aboard the buses, he probably would have been accused of trying to upstage James Farmer. But those politics meant little to Williams. King "had threatened to fill up the jails," he scoffed, but "of course, he meant with persons other than himself."[10]

Many of the students felt abandoned at the station by the messiah of Montgomery, but they boarded the buses and headed for Jackson, where by secret prearrangement between President Kennedy and Governor Ross Barnett, they were hustled briskly into the Mississippi prison system.[11] Brigadier General T. S. Birdsong of the Mississippi Highway Patrol claimed that the Freedom Rides were "directed, inspired and planned by known communists." Birdsong charged that 202 American students had been to Havana, where Soviet agents met with them "to teach the students how to make sit-ins, walk-ins, kneel-ins and Freedom Rides." He cited two Fair Play members among the Freedom Riders as proof that the protesters were "Communist-backed pawns."[12]

As if to add support to such assertions, Attorney General Robert Kennedy complained that their decision to remain in jail made "good propaganda for America's enemies." The Kennedy brothers had opposed the Freedom Rides as "an unnecessary burden" to U.S. foreign policy, compounding the disaster at the Bay of Pigs and complicating President Kennedy's upcoming summit meetings with Soviet premier Nikita Khrushchev and French president Charles de Gaulle. The protests would "discredit" the United States, the attorney general stated, at a point when "continual international publicity about ugly race riots in the South would send the leader of the free world into European palaces with mud on his shoes."[13]

Robert Kennedy was correct that the summer of 1961 was both a momentous time in the world and a tumultuous time across the South. In Monroe, Robert Williams wrote later, that summer was "a savage struggle for survival." The Ku Klux Klan crept back up out of hiding, to the consternation of respectable white citizens who feared the "attempts of the Ku Klux Klan to gain a foothold in Union County" would, in the words of the *Monroe Journal*'s white editor, pose a "threat to the reputation of Monroe."[14] Blacks harbored fears more serious than the town's reputation.

Among ordinary white citizens, uneasiness about Communist subversion and black insurrection swelled toward paranoia. "Many people in Monroe are interested in the John Birch Society," the *Monroe Enquirer* said in May, referring to the right-wing organization whose leader had recently called President Eisenhower a conscious agent of the international Communist conspiracy. An early June column published in the newspaper tied the Freedom Rides to the Bay of Pigs, charging that a "mighty left-wing pressure campaign" sought to take advantage of "the collapse of the Cuban invasion." The column urged Congress to "consider the timing of the 'Freedom Rides' into the South," seeing "clear" connections between antinuclear demonstrations in Scotland, protest letters to President Kennedy from Harvard faculty, a proposal by University of Colorado scientists to meet with "Red Chinese" colleagues, and the "revolutionary designs against this region." The Justice Department itself, the *Enquirer* alleged, was part of a vast Communist web conspiring "to tear down the constitutional form of government created by our forefathers."[15]

The right-wing resurgence in Monroe sometimes seemed out of tune with the rest of the state. With the ascendance of Terry Sanford to the governorship of North Carolina in 1960, it may have appeared that the voters of North Carolina were choosing the path of enlightened liberalism over that of racial backlash. In his Democratic primary victory over I. Beverly Lake, the state's most vociferous segregationist, Sanford had stayed away from the word "integration," a term that in 1960, he explained years afterward, carried explosive sexual connotations. "You could hardly talk about the thing rationally in those days," he said. "That would have been stupid." Alone among Southern governors, however, Sanford preached the gospel of jobs and education as solutions to the region's ills. The handsome attorney spoke in a lilting drawl that harnessed Southern history in the service of a new vision. The South, he declared, would "rise again and march again," but this time "it will make the march not with bayonets, but with textbooks. We will not be firing on Fort Sumter but on the dungeons of ignorance."[16] In hindsight, Governor Sanford was probably the most racially progressive Southern politician of his generation. But the last thing Sanford needed in 1960, as he tried to coax a fearful and potentially violent white South to follow him, was Robert Williams. And Williams, for his part, had had his fill of white liberals. The prospects for dialogue were limited from the outset.

"There was no question that we were going to have a very difficult time of it," Sanford recalled. "I realized then that this was a turning point in the history of North Carolina and the South and the country."[17] Early in 1961 he met with the cautious leadership of the Durham Committee on Negro Affairs and the timid liberals of the North Carolina Council on Human Relations, but he did not reply to requests from state NAACP head Kelly Alexander for a meeting after his inauguration in January. The NAACP was still considered radical and even Communist-inspired by most white Carolinians.

By June, however, it was clear to Sanford that Monroe was a time bomb ticking under all of his hopes for orderly racial progress. Sanford dispatched "a racially mixed committee, representing the Governor," Alexander reported, whose "objective was to get the state NAACP to use its influence to relieve some of the pressure on rapidly developing racial tension in Monroe, N.C." Even to Alexander, a gradualist far less militant than Williams, it seemed too little and too late. "Their plan was not acceptable to us because it aimed its correctional efforts at the Negroes only," he reported to Roy Wilkins in the national office. "We refused to cooperate." Alexander "pointed out that as early as January and before, there was generally known to be potentially explosive racial tension growing in Monroe."[18]

Not just in Monroe, however, but all across the South communities trembled at the edge of exploding into violence. In the spring of 1960, the sit-ins had assailed segregation; in 1961, the Freedom Rides rolled through Dixie. Bloodshed seemed almost inevitable. In Trinity, North Carolina, for example, a cotton mill and furniture factory town of about a hundred families, "five or six white boys beat a colored boy, not severely," according to state highway patrol reports. Local blacks, however, stated that "two colored youths had been severely beaten" and that thirteen-year-old Eugene Brown had been badly injured by a carload of whites while playing in his driveway. Two days later, half a dozen young blacks sought service at a local white cafe. The manager, Robert Parrish, "refused and told them to go around to the back," state investigators reported, and the young black men threatened revenge.

That evening, Parrish left the cafe with five friends and at least one firearm. "A crowd of Negroes, estimated from eighteen to twenty-five, were waiting outside the cafe," the officers reported. In the ensuing brawl, Parrish fired his pistol once, someone took it from him, and someone else fired a shotgun. Police came and confiscated "numerous knives and heavy tools" from the brawlers, many of whom were injured. Parrish himself disappeared, and "the rumor began circulating that the Negroes had kidnapped him and a large crowd of whites began gathering." The high-way patrol dispersed the mob and found Parrish under the porch of a nearby house.

The following night, dozens of angry whites reassembled, "some KKK members mingling with the crowd," state investigators observed, and began stoning passing cars driven by blacks. The white mob attempted to burn a nearby black school, an effort that the sheriff managed to interrupt without making a single arrest. "Several anonymous telephone calls were received by the State Highway Patrol and the Sheriff's Department to the effect that after midnight the Negroes would 'catch Hell,'" state investigators reported. Local African Americans prepared to defend themselves against the expected Klan rampage, a fact that did not escape the attention of the state highway patrol. Cars driven by blacks "into and through the Trinity area are being stopped and searched by police," *The Crusader* stated, assertions confirmed by state investigative reports. "The police are looking for arms and ammunition reportedly flowing into the community for purposes of self-defense."[19]

Events in Union County were even more alarming. The Sanford administration soon lost all hope of defusing the mounting racial crisis there. In early June the Ku Klux Klan burned a cross near Marshville, a Klan stronghold just outside Monroe. Besieged by death threats, Robert Williams sought reinforcements. "On June 14, 1961," Conrad Lynn noted, "a number of us met with Robert Williams in New York City to discuss the growing armed violence against blacks in Union County." Ossie Davis, Julian Mayfield, Calvin Hicks, Amiri Baraka, Ora Mae Mobley, and Mae Mallory attended the council in Harlem. Lynn's minutes of the meeting reveal much about the mood of the moment and offer a shorthand for what would become known several years later as Black Power:

> Robert Williams presented the situation in the South. Afro-Americans are beginning to believe that the whites will never consent to integration. The tactics of nonviolence in sit-ins, freedom rides, etc. has proved useful but has to be backed up with forceful self-defense as in Charlotte, Jacksonville, Montgomery. . . . Martin L. King trying to derail revolutionary upsurge.
>
> Ora Mae Mobley urged that we not forget the international context. . . . Ossie Davis threw out the analysis that the economic dilemma was the heart of the American crisis.
>
> Mae Mallory supports the view that we must hold ourselves separate

for struggle. Muslims and black nationalists seek basic stake in the economy. The role of unions.

Cal Hicks proposes political party. Others say it should at first be limited to Afro-Americans.

Four days after the meeting, Williams and his friends in Monroe launched "a determined campaign against the racist officials of the City of Monroe to secure swimming facilities for Afro-Americans." The Harlem contingent openly began raising money to buy rifles for the Monroe NAACP chapter. The watchword for the summer, Williams declared, would be "TOTAL STRUGGLE AT THE POOL."[20]

Since 1956 the Monroe Country Club had been an important site of struggle for the freedom movement in Monroe. As noted earlier, the club was a handsome facility built with tax dollars and WPA labor during the New Deal; it furnished white children with free swimming lessons, while black children swam in farm ponds and local creeks, where they often drowned. Whenever Williams and his allies went to the pool to test the segregation policy, "they would put up a sign that the pool was closed, even though white people were in the pool swimming," he said.

On Sunday afternoon, June 18, 1961, Williams led a dozen black teenagers to the pool to protest. Some black parents forbade their children to join the march; Williams himself, though he permitted his own children to picket, feared for their safety. As a result of earlier protests, Monroe authorities had promised to build a separate pool for African Americans when they found the money. By 1961 the city had a large financial surplus, black leaders noted, and still had made no movement toward building another facility. "Maybe they REALLY want integration at the pool," Azalea Johnson joked in her column. It was the fourth consecutive summer that young blacks had come to plod back and forth in the hot sun with their homemade signs. "The plackards carried by the colored people," the state highway patrol noted, "were 'Jim Crow Law,' and 'Monroe Is A Disgrace To America.'" One of the black teenagers carried a sign that read, "We Don't Want to Integrate, We Want Our Own Pool"; this was not Robert Williams's position on the issue, but he did not dictate the content of the signs.[21]

For three days the small band picketed at the pool without incident, though a growing number of young white men gathered sullenly in the parking lot and hurled insults. On Thursday, June 22, some of the whites showed up with guns and began firing them in the air; the chief of police sat in his squad car nearby and puffed on a cigar. The pool manager announced that the pool would close indefinitely due to a "broken chlorinator." Williams and his young insurgents, sure that the pool would reopen the minute that they discontinued their protests, persisted until late in the afternoon. "We have given the City Council until tomorrow (Friday) to answer our ultimatum to provide us with a pool in our section of town or integrate the present city pool," Williams told reporters whom he had summoned to the scene. There would be no respite from the heat or the protests, he said, until something was done. "If the pool is closed Friday, we'll keep coming back until it's reopened, and then we'll jump in, if our demands are not met." That white people were scared to touch water that had been fouled by black bodies was insulting, of course, but it could also be useful.[22]

"After picketing closed the 'white only' pool (tax supported)," Azalea Johnson wrote in her column, "it was reported that the 'K.K.K. will ride tonight.' But the supposed-to-be-scared Afro-Americans," she taunted, searched everywhere "for the used-to-be-dreaded Klan but could find none!"[23] The next morning, however, when Williams's threat of a "wade-in" appeared in the *Charlotte Observer*, more than a hundred angry white people gathered at the pool. They spent the afternoon watching Williams and about ten young blacks walk back and forth in the gravel with signs reading, "I must serve in the Army, why can't I swim?" and "We Demand Democracy in the United States." Chief of Police Mauney and Officer Jake Elliott watched from their squad car. Don Keziah, reportedly the head of the local Ku Klux Klan, came close and, spewing streams of profanity, loudly threatened to kill the first "nigger" who tried to "wade-in." Young whites yelled "communist nigger," "Castro," and "Fidel" from across the parking lot. Then the gunfire started again.

"About 3 P.M. the picketers sought relief from the hot sun in a shaded picnic area just south of the pool," the *Charlotte Observer* reported. "While they were there, what sounded like several distant rifle shots" split the summer air. "You could hear the bullets whistling in the trees," Williams said afterward. When Williams ran over to Chief Mauney's squad car to insist that he protect the black children, Mauney told him to move the group out of the "white only" picnic area. Threatening to call the Justice Department in Washington, Williams dashed over to his blue 1953 Hillman and sprayed gravel as he headed for the nearest telephone, taking one of the teenage boys, Albert Rorie, with him. Johnson, Mabel Williams, and Richard Crowder followed in a separate vehicle.[24]

As he sped down the Highway 74 bypass toward town, Williams "noticed a 1955 light blue De Soto following me. I did not think too much about it," he said. "I just thought he was following too close." About five hundred yards before they passed the state highway patrol station, the De Soto suddenly rammed his tiny Hillman hard from behind, backed off, and then rammed it again. On the second impact, which caused the front seat of the Hillman to slip off its tracks and collapse, the bumpers of the two cars locked. Williams tried his brakes, but the heavy De Soto sped up, pushing the tiny import up the highway at a speed approaching seventy miles an hour. Williams then tried to speed up, hoping to pull away. The driver of the De Soto, whom Williams now recognized as Bynum Griffin, a local Pontiac dealer, swerved back and forth, apparently trying to run Williams off the road. They skidded past the highway patrol station at high speed, with Williams and the women who were following both laying on their horns in an effort to attract attention. Williams yelled to Rorie to reach under the seat and hand him his carbine, but the small Italian rifle was wedged tightly under the fallen front seat. Finally the bumpers wrenched apart, and Williams "was able to run my car off the road into a shallow ditch without turning over."[25]

Returning quickly to the pool, Williams drove straight up to Chief Mauney, handed him the license plate number of the De Soto, and demanded that he arrest Bynum Griffin. "Standing a few feet from the car, with the back end all smashed in and oil running out of the damaged wheels and brake drums," Williams wrote later, "the police chief said, 'I don't see anything, Williams, I don't see anything at all. How can I arrest a man when there is nothing wrong with your car?'" Don Gray, a reporter for the *Charlotte Observer*, walked over with a pad and began jotting down a description of the back of Williams's automobile, noting that the trunk was smashed. "I saw your car when you left for town a little while ago," Gray offered, "this must have just happened." Under press scrutiny, Chief Mauney grudgingly agreed to swear out a warrant. Later at the police station, however, Williams charged, the police chief said, "Mr. Griffin didn't ram your car because I asked him, and he said he didn't do it."[26]

That night, Williams told FBI agents, "nothing happened, but we did get ten or twelve anonymous local telephone calls saying they were going to kill me, put gasoline on me, and that Negro pickets better not show up at the pool any more." Rather than return to the pool on Saturday, Williams dispatched a telegram to Attorney General Robert F. Kennedy and drove to Charlotte to plead with the FBI to protect the protesters. "Robert had a rather naive faith in the federal government in those days," Julian Mayfield recalled. "He kept the federal government informed of everything that was going on." After giving his report, Williams told the FBI agents that he could not wait for it to be transcribed so that he could sign it; it was not safe, he said, for him to drive through Union County after dark. Two agents brought the statement to his house on Boyte Street the following day, making careful notes about the number of firearms and his souvenirs from Cuba. Not surprisingly, Williams's radical politics were far more interesting to the FBI than his personal safety.[27]

The following day, Sunday, Williams and a group of teenagers including Richard Crowder, Frank Houston, J. D. Blount, and Lillian and Geraldine Redfern piled into several cars and headed for the Monroe Country Club about 12:30 in the afternoon. They picketed and picnicked, once again resting in the shade of the "white only" picnic area as police officers and hostile young white men glared and yelled obscenities. The whites launched a picket of their own, as several of the young men marched in front of the black picket line with their own signs, one of which read, "Birds Don't Mix, Why Should We." As the heat of the day approached, the crowd of angry whites at the pool grew to several hundred who police officers said "merely seemed to be curious." Police Chief Mauney told FBI agents, they reported, that "every available means were being used including members of the North Carolina State Highway Patrol, Union County Sheriff's Office, local constables, and his entire police force to afford Williams protection," but that he could not ensure the NAACP leader's safety because "tension was high in Union County."[28]

That local authorities either could not or would not protect Williams soon became apparent. About two in the afternoon, Robert Williams climbed into his familiar blue Hillman, its trunk still dented from the attempt on his life the day before, and went into town with sixteen-year-old J. D. Blount and seventeen-year-old Richard Crowder to pick up another teenager, Jay Vann Covington. Williams carried the Italian carbine, a 9-mm German Luger pistol, and a U.S. Army .45 automatic. The four protesters headed back toward the pool, a police car following close behind. As they approached the intersection of Highway 74 and Highway 601, commonly known as Hilltop, Williams noticed hundreds of white people milling near a drive-in restaurant. A white 1949 Ford stock car was parked on the left side of the road. The old clunker had all the glass removed, demolition-derby style, and a white teenager was perched behind the wheel. As the Hillman came closer, the junked Ford revved its engine and careened toward the highway. Williams swerved to miss it, but the Ford glanced off the front of the Hillman, shattering the left headlight and spinning both cars into the ditch.[29]

· "The man who was driving the stock car got out of the car with a baseball bat," Williams wrote later, "and started walking toward us and he was saying, 'Nigger, what did you hit me for?' "[30] Williams said nothing. "Monroe Police Cpt. Jake Elliott, Sgt. M. S. Nivens, [and] Policeman Jerry Helms watched from the pool as Robert Williams stopped on highway," the state highway patrol's report on the "minor accident" stated. "The Policemen got into a Police car, drove approximately 300 yards, got out of the Police car, and observed Robert Williams sitting under the wheel of his car with a rifle in plain view."[31] The furious crowd of whites surged toward the cars, screaming obscenities, throwing rocks, and looking like a lynch mob. Williams told Crowder to pass him the Italian carbine. "I gave Richard my Luger and handed Jay Vann Covington, the other teenager, my Army .45 pistol," Williams recalled. "I instructed the students to watch me and not to shoot unless they saw me shoot." He stood up in the door and shifted the bolt to slide a round into the chamber, unaware that Crowder had already cocked a bullet into the chamber. As Williams pulled the bolt back, the long, unfired eight-millimeter shell popped into the air and fell on the ground, where the nearest members of the mob stopped and stared at it as if it were a poisonous snake. An older man standing on the shoulder of the road "started screaming and crying like a baby," Williams said later. " 'God damn, God damn, what is this God damn country coming to that the niggers have got guns, the niggers are armed and the police can't even arrest them!' " Williams reflected later that "the old man saw his way of life slipping away right before his eyes." Violence, Williams observed, "was their last great bulwark, and without its effectiveness white supremacy was gone with the wind."[32]

One of the policemen ran up to Williams and ordered him to surrender the rifle. When the officer grabbed for it, however, Williams "pushed the carbine broadside into his chest, forcing him backwards, then aimed it straight into his face." He was not about to surrender to a mob, Williams told the officer. Another policeman approached from the far side of the car and started to draw his revolver from its holster. Jay Vann Covington, from the passenger's side of the front seat, stuck his pistol into the officer's face, cocked it, and told him to put the gun away or he would blow the man's brains out. Covington, the state highway patrol report indicated tersely, "displayed a .45 automatic pistol. No arrest was made.

The Police allowed Williams to proceed on to the pool for his picketing or demonstrations."[33]

Williams realized he had had a close call, and he was shaken considerably. He reported all of these events to the Charlotte office of the FBI. Bureau investigations of the two attempts on Williams's life that week generally confirmed his accounts, though without any enthusiasm for addressing the situation. "Corroborative information was also furnished indicating that the local authorities were present at the swimming pool on both occasions," the FBI memorandum noted. Williams stated "that he had sent telegrams today to President Kennedy and the Justice Department requesting the federal government protect his rights to protest and picket the pool at Monroe, North Carolina and to afford equal protection under the law," agents reported. "Williams became quite violent when advised by interviewing agents that FBI could not afford private citizens protection but that this responsibility [was that of] local authorities." Williams, desperate and furious, probably tried to frighten the authorities into protecting him. "Made statement that unless afforded protection he was going to have to kill white people and when he started shooting would kill all the white people he could including babies in the cradle." As Williams probably anticipated, the FBI agents passed these threats on to Police Chief Mauney.[34]

That night, Williams told FBI agents the following day, he "and some men in my neighborhood built some barricades around my home and in my neighborhood and armed ourselves with weapons and Molotov cocktails to defend our community against a threatened invasion by the Ku Klux Klan."[35] The Klan did not risk riding past large numbers of black sentries huddled behind sandbag fortifications with military rifles and perhaps even the widely rumored machine guns.

But FBI investigative reports indicated scattered racial violence against isolated black citizens all over town. White men pulled a black man named Willie Strand out of his car at an intersection and dragged him into the woods. A witness called Williams, who called the Associated Press stringer in Charleston, who called the Monroe Police Department, who found Strand badly beaten. Williams dispatched guards to protect Strand's house. Several young white men beat and robbed Robert Barret, a black man walking near the intersection of Highway 74 and Franklin Street. Another black man, accosted by two carloads of whites, was said to have pulled a pistol and shot six times, sending his assailants skidding off into the night. These reports of violence were collected by FBI agents from unnamed local sources other than Robert Williams.[36]

The white political elite in Monroe detested Robert Williams, resented the intrusions of federal and state agents, but realized that overt white violence undermined their political position. "We just closed the pool and drained it," Mayor Fred Wilson said. The city council immediately passed a picketing ordinance limiting the number of pickets to ten, restricting the size of signs, barring any "inflammatory" message on them, banning firearms at any such gatherings, and authorizing counterdemonstrations at each protest.[37] Some white leaders tried to persuade angry local whites to ignore the swimming pool demonstrations. White mobs and Ku Klux Klan attacks were "only presenting to the world an utterly false impression," the editor of the Monroe Journal complained the day after the near-riot at Hilltop. The "danger at the swimming pool is not to the protestors but to the reputation of Monroe." Williams and the integration movement were the ones who gained from white violence, the Journal said, because "injurious and threatening agitators can only thrive on an audience, the more violent and abusive the better for the cause which they espouse." The best way to block the movement, the editor urged, was to "let the picketers picket the public pool in unruffled peace and complete solitude."[38]

Law enforcement officials in Monroe, on the other hand, sought to disarm Williams and to diminish what little police protection his forces were getting. On June 28, Sheriff D. S. Griffin and Police Chief Mauney met with state highway patrol officials, city attorneys, and the local solicitor. "Chief Mauney and Sheriff Griffin," the state highway patrol reported, "advised that they did not see the necessity of having Patrol personnel remain in the pool vicinity." The state troopers would comply with this local request, the director informed Hugh Cannon, Governor Sanford's top aide, but felt that they should maintain a "riot squad" nearby and "a quantity of gas on hand" all the same. The city officials called the meeting to "attempt to obtain a restraining order . . . which would prohibit Robert Williams from carrying fire arms on or about his person," the patrol reported. City attorneys agreed to search the North Carolina gun laws for some provision that might be applied to deny Williams the right to bear arms. State highway patrol officials believed the protests would continue "until such time as the City Council meets with Robert Williams as he has requested and arrives at a solution to his demands, along the lines of equal rights and/or intergration of the swimming pool," but conceded that

Monroe city officials remained intransigent. "This meeting appears at this time unlikely to occur."[39]

Alarmed at the situation, Governor Sanford sent John R. Larkins, an African American state official whom he called "a great friend of mine," to investigate the growing trouble in Monroe. Larkins, a devoted racial accommodationist, held a post at the state Department of Public Welfare, where he had his own Jim Crow office. "He had an office off somewhere," Governor Sanford recalled, "they didn't have him up in the same building." Larkins drove from Raleigh on June 28 to investigate the racial situation in Monroe and to meet with Williams. First he went to Charlotte and spoke to Kelly Alexander and Reginald Hawkins, Williams's enemies in the NAACP, who expressed the view that Williams "is not interested in securing justice through legal channels but rabble rousing and seeking publicity. Alexander does not believe that [Williams] has as much local influence and support as he would lead people to believe." In Monroe, however, "three Negroes—one a cab driver," apparently selected at random, all expressed support for Williams and told Larkins that recently "they had seen a number of white men with guns showing out of their car windows riding through town."

Larkins found the notorious NAACP leader "wearing a dark blue beret, dark lumber jacket, checked sport shirt, bluish-gray slacks, and chukka boots. A large pistol was strapped to his right side and a rifle slung over his left shoulder." Williams seemed "quite elated that someone from Raleigh would be interested enough to try to get the Negro's side," Larkins told Sanford. "Two attempts have been made on his life and no attempt has been made to arrest and convict guilty persons." The black emissary asked Williams what had caused the recent confrontations and how threatening he considered the situation to be. Williams blamed "white refusal to share WPA-built, tax-supported municipal pool or supply one for Negroes now or sometime in the future." Williams emphasized that blacks could not depend on the police or the courts in Union County. "All through the conference," Larkins said, Williams "stated that there was no law and order in Monroe and Negroes were not protected from violence." Unless the men who had tried to kill him were arrested soon, Larkins said Williams told him, he would "picket the Court House with placards about injustice." This was their right, Williams claimed, and if anyone tried to deny them the right to protest, "he and his followers will fight until the city is bathed in blood." It was Larkins's opinion, though Williams denied it, that the Monroe NAACP leader might be "hoping to be attacked so that they could have a war and destroy the town. He claimed that he has a large following of Negroes who are well-armed." Larkins hurried back to Raleigh to file his report quickly, he told the governor, "so that you would have some type of record for action if it were needed."[40]

Saturday, June 29, the day after Larkins left Monroe, Robert Williams drove his blue Hillman all over Union County delivering stacks of *The Crusader* to their supporters while Mabel did housework and kept the children. Police Chief Mauney followed him in a squad car for much of the day. On his way home for supper, Williams saw another police car fall in behind them, then swing out to his left and pass, then slide over and force the blue Hillman to the right shoulder of the road. His taillights were improper, the officer told Williams, and he was under arrest. Williams protested that it was not yet dark, but the two police officers insisted that he was under arrest and that he must follow them downtown. Williams suspected that they were planning to kill him. "Rob told me that he knew that if he went to the police station, that was it," Mabel Williams recalled. He agreed to go and followed the two police cars down Fairley Avenue toward downtown, but when they crossed Boyte Street, the Hillman darted away and raced toward home. He roared into the driveway and slid behind the house, spraying a cloud of dust and gravel.

Mabel Williams ran to the back door. "I heard all these tires squeaking and squealing, and wondered what in the world was going on," she said. "I thought it was the Klan coming. So I grabbed the gun and said, 'This is it.'" Nine-year-old John was right behind her; he would always remember his pretty, slender mother standing in the back door holding that heavy .12-gauge shotgun. When Mabel opened the door and raised the shotgun, she saw her husband frantically trying to untie their German shepherd, Little Rock. "The police came up behind him with their guns drawn," she recalled. "And I just put that gun on them and said, 'What is going on?'" When the police said that Robert was under arrest, Mabel Williams stammered, "Do you have a warrant?" When they said that they did not have one, the trembling young woman insisted, "Well, you better get out of here until you get one."

Mabel suggested sharply that rather than arresting Robert for having broken taillights, they should arrest the white man who rammed the car and broke them trying to kill her husband. By that time, Robert had stepped around his wife and grabbed another rifle from inside. "You better get out of here," Mabel Williams repeated. The two white police officers put away their pistols and quickly got back into their cars. "I was scared and nervous and I am sure they saw that," she remembered. "And they knew that I was going to shoot them. They got in the cars and took off again, tires squealing. And they never did come back."

Williams quickly called John McDow, Woodrow Wilson, and several other members of the Monroe NAACP, who spread the word, armed themselves, and hurried to Boyte Street. He also telephoned Ted Poston of the *New York Post*, a call monitored by the FBI, whose agents noted that Williams "furnished information to [Poston] seeking publicity" and that he was "barricaded in his house with 25 guards." State highway patrol investigators commented that, while it was true that no one had looked into Williams's complaint about the damage to his car, "perhaps it would be unwise to send members of the Highway Patrol to Williams' residence in an effort to obtain the necessary evidence."[41]

In the weeks that followed, racial conflict continued in Monroe. One night a carload of white teenagers dashed a bucket of white paint into the face of an African American woman walking down the roadside, injuring her eyes. A few nights later, several white men jumped a black man as he tried to enter a cafe; he knocked one unconscious and hurt several of the others before fleeing himself. The reports came almost daily. "An Afro-American was dragged from his car and flogged by a white mob," Williams reported. "Another man of color was found beaten and unconscious in a rural community," he wrote. "One Afro-American was slightly injured and his wife was slightly injured when white men threw a bottle through his car window."

Death threats were a daily affair. One night in mid-July someone fired three shots into Williams's house from a distance. Williams "was later told that some white men in a car had been chased away from our community. I assume they were members of the Ku Klux Klan." In early August four white men roared by Williams's house in a blue and white 1958 Pontiac and fired two shots. Azalea Johnson's column hinted that the notorious machine guns had been put to effective use: "Did you know that the car load of whites who fired shots on Boyte Street recently received such a quick, almost spontaneous retaliatory firing, with much heavier artillery," she asked her readers, "that they haven't ventured another visit?" FBI reports indicated that "racial tension continues to be high in Monroe, North Carolina, the scene of a series of disturbances centering around the activities of Robert Franklin Williams."[42]

In truth, Williams was not the only racial agitator at work in Union County. White hostility to black demands mounted even faster than black impatience. Some whites expressed that enmity openly, with the apparent confidence that they spoke for their community. A few whites let their guns speak for them. Apart from defending his home and community against attackers, Williams adhered to the law; for all his vows to meet violence with violence, Williams never struck out at his white antagonists. "I keep an armed guard on my house at night," he warned newspaper reporters, "and if anyone attacks my house, the City of Monroe is going to see a blood bath."

But his enemies never had to sit up nights wondering if he would bomb their homes. Even when he monitored Klan gatherings with armed black men, Williams kept his distance and his cool. By midsummer, though, his nerves began to fray under the pressure. White terrorists persisted; no one on the far side of the color line uttered a word of disapproval that Williams could hear. Even Ray Shute and the small circle of Unitarians kept their distance. "Two carloads of white men passed down Boyte Street Thursday night and fired three shots from a car window," Williams wrote in the middle of July. "These antics meet the approval of the entire white population here at the present time," he concluded. "However," he added in a mysterious word of warning, "*when fire breaks out*, there is no telling where it will end."[43]

10: Freedom Rider

Even as Williams's apocalyptic warning hovered over Monroe, the ferment stirred by the Freedom Rides lingered. Debates over violence and nonviolence continued to rage within the movement. In the discussion, Robert Williams became "a figure of growing importance," who for many appeared to "symbolize the alternative to both tactical nonviolence and nonviolence as a way of life," according to James Forman of SNCC. The younger insurgents of the South tended to be "critical of the adults and nonviolence in general, and certain leaders in particular"—Martin Luther King Jr. first among them, Forman recalled. At a Nashville workshop attended by many individuals who would become key organizers for SNCC, "the level of discussion impressed me; people talked of revolution as necessary to end segregation."[1]

Most of the younger generation seemed to regard nonviolence not as a sacred principle or an end in itself, but as a tactical position of uncertain promise. Paul Brooks, one of the Freedom Riders who had challenged Dr. King to join them on the CORE buses, urged Forman to come with him on a trip to see Williams. On their way, they stopped to consult with Ella Baker in Atlanta, who encouraged them to go to Monroe and see what was happening for themselves. Williams "was in danger, isolated, with little support from America's black community," Forman wrote, and they wanted to help him if they could. Brooks obtained a letter from the SCLC office, according to Forman and Williams, that said he was "on an investigative trip for Dr. Martin Luther King."[2]

Thomas Jefferson once described the race question as "a fire-bell in the night," a metaphor of considerable immediacy for a plantation owner in a world where gin houses and tobacco barns mysteriously caught fire and prompted panics over abolitionist-inspired slave arson.[3] As Paul Brooks and James Forman—members of an organization whose official historian called them "the new abolitionists"—made their way toward Monroe, a series of calamitous fires illuminated what many people thought Williams must have meant when he had predicted that "when fire breaks out, there is no telling where it will end."

Just after 10:00 P.M. on July 26, 1961, flames soared through the roof of the Monroe Hardware Company's warehouse on Burke Street and lit up the night sky. "When we saw this," Fire Chief Jesse A. Helms Sr. said, "we immediately called out a second shift of 20 stand-by men." Forty fire-fighters pumped 400,000 gallons of water but lost the battle; property damage totaled $125,000. Two nights later, an unknown person or persons torched the Union Supply warehouse on East Windsor Street about 2:30 in the morning, a $50,000 loss.

Police held three young black men for questioning, but while they were in custody, an arsonist hurled a Coca-Cola bottle filled with gasoline and stoppered with a rag through the back window of the Monroe Seed Cleaning Company on Morgan Mill Road. Luckily for the owners, the flames licked through stacks of bulging burlap sacks that then spilled enough dry grass seed to suffocate the blaze before it spread.

About 1:45 the following morning, the crew on a freight train rolling into Monroe saw flames in the window of the Seaboard depot and stopped the blaze before it took the building. The railroad workers heard the fire engines and thought help was on the way, but the trucks were bound for the L&M Trading Company on Morgan Mill Road. Firebombs gutted the store in an almost simultaneous attack.

The next night, unknown arsonists completely destroyed the Monroe Fiber Mills, a small plant that prepared cotton waste for use in mattresses, and badly damaged the Downbeat Club, a night spot owned by a black schoolteacher who had written a letter to the Baltimore *Afro-American* urging readers to stop sending guns to Williams. These were the sixth and seventh acts of arson in five days. Authorities estimated total property damage at about $218,000.

Meanwhile, false alarms poured in at all hours; many directed fire trucks to Williams's house at 410 Boyte Street. That address was also the central focus of white suspicions about the arson campaign. "It seemed to frustrate them no end to always find me at home during the fires that flared in the night," Williams wrote. By the time that James Forman and

Paul Brooks arrived in Monroe, white residents of Union County were in a state of near panic.[4]

"I arrived in Monroe last Saturday," Forman reported to the Southern Conference Educational Fund and the National Freedom Council, "accompanied by Paul Brooks, who had a letter indicating he is on an investigating mission for the S.C.L.C." The pair heard loud gunfire near Williams's house on their first night in Monroe. Williams's burly and reliable lieutenant, Woodrow Wilson, told of being shot at by a carload of whites on Boyte Street a week earlier, and Forman interviewed several other witnesses to incidents of white terrorism. Forman had a political conversation with Williams about "the difference in connotation between meeting violence with violence and self-defense. It is the latter that they are doing," Forman reported, "a right guaranteed in the Constitution and practiced by many other civil rights fighters."

Forman sent back an emphatically favorable report on local leadership. "Robert Williams has certain values all civil rights leaders ought to have," Forman stated: "love for the common and poor man, an awareness that one Negro in an important position does not constitute progress for the race, and a recognition that leaders ought not to ask of others what they are not willing to do themselves." Forman concluded that the "growing support for Williams throughout the South" reflected the fact that "the Negro is becoming impatient and he is not always going to turn the other cheek." After four days in Monroe, Forman and Brooks went back to Jackson to recruit some of the Freedom Riders being released from prison to launch a support campaign for Robert Williams.[5]

The new Freedom Riders rolled into the Charlotte bus station on August 17. Janet Boyte, who helped care for the Freedom Riders during their stay in Union County, called them "eager and undisciplined." She and her husband, Harry Boyte, who reported regularly to the SCLC, opened their farmhouse in Matthews to the seventeen young men, all but two of whom were white. To the liberal Boytes, they "were typical of the off-beat, dedicated, impetuous young Americans who participated in the early rides and marches." Less sympathetic observers termed them "beatnik types," and the Monroe Enquirer referred to them as "imported self-styled bums." At the Justice Department, Burke Marshall's notes from conversations with CORE leaders indicated that two of the youths, Price Chatham and Kenneth Shilman, had attempted "fasting until death" in Parchman Farm Penitentiary—Chatham, in fact, did fast for twenty-four days—and that another young man bound for Monroe was "nutty." Certainly their bohemian style seemed out of place in Monroe. James Hinkel, the city manager, maintained thirty years later that "they were communists—right from Cuba."[6]

The Freedom Riders were not from Cuba but from cities and towns across the country from Minneapolis to Nashville to Brooklyn. Not one of them, with the exception of Brooks and Forman, who had met him only recently, knew Williams personally. They were idealistic youth "filled with zeal to carry their witness [of nonviolence] to the hamlets of the South," Anne Braden wrote. Forman, who would soon become the executive director of SNCC, wanted foremost "to form an organization of young people who would work full time in the South." He envisioned extending "the Monroe project" across the region, organizing "teams of 10 or 12 young people who could spend their summers in rural communities, attempting to develop nonviolent movements for justice, holding workshops and participating with local people in nonviolent action."

The motives of the mission to Monroe were as motley as its membership. The *Charlotte Observer* reported that Ed Kale, one of the spokespersons for the group, announced that "the trip to Monroe was 'designed to affect a reconciliation' between supporters and opponents of NAACP leader Robert Williams." Clearly, however, some of the Freedom Riders considered themselves philosophical if not personal adversaries, come to prove that Williams was wrong about nonviolence. "We have been friends with Mr. Williams," Joseph McDonald, a student at Nassau Community College in New York, said, "but we have no real connection with him because he believes in the defensive violence technique. That is to say, he would defend his home." John Lowery, whom close friends described as an anguished idealist, announced upon his arrival that "I believe Mr. Robert F. Williams to be potentially the most dangerous person in America." Lowery, the son of a wealthy New York family, had come to turn "the violence of two armed camps" toward nonviolence and social justice. "If the fight for civil rights is to continue to use nonviolence, we must be successful here," William Mahoney, a leader of the Nonviolent Action Group at Howard University, declared to reporters. "What happens here will determine the course taken in many other communities throughout the South."[7]

Williams had a similar—and likewise mixed—understanding of the stakes. "The Freedom Riders came at my invitation as president of the Union County branch of the National Association for the Advancement of Colored People," Williams wrote two years later. "Because I advocated a politics of self-defense," he said, "the Freedom Riders wanted to show me the power of nonviolence and love as taught by Gandhi." Despite their differences, it was plain even at the time that Williams embraced their efforts. "If you are a Freedom Fighter or a Freedom Rider," he declared in *The Crusader*, "Ride, Fly or Walk to Monroe, the Angola of America, and help us in this noble undertaking for human dignity."

Williams welcomed the Freedom Riders, opening not only his home but the pages of *The Crusader* and the doors of his community to the forces of nonviolence. When local activists bristled at the notion of pacifists joining their ranks, Williams took great pains to "convince them that we had to give the freedom riders a chance" and that "people from all over the world would be watching to see what happens here."[8] As both local activists and outside agitators implicitly and sometimes explicitly acknowledged, there was a confrontational aspect to this dialogue between advocates of armed self-reliance and proponents of nonviolent direct action. The Freedom Riders "are my friends," Williams wrote to William Worthy, "even though I am not a pacifist and don't believe their philosophy will work with conscienceless racists." He admired the young insurgents and was glad for them to try their hand in Monroe, in part because he was confident that his methods would soon make sense to them. The Freedom Riders "were supposed to be undermining me," Williams recalled. "But I knew they were going to fail in there because I knew those crackers, man, I knew them like a book." Williams saw the arrival of the advocates of nonviolence "as a challenge," he said, "but I also saw it as an opportunity to show that what King and them were preaching was bullshit."[9]

If most of the outside agitators had a different philosophical approach, they certainly did not roll in with their own agenda and try to supplant the aspirations of the black community. Joining with local young people, they established the Monroe Nonviolent Action Committee with Richard Crowder, a black youth who lived on Boyte Street and was close to Williams, as chair. Their stated objectives reflected the ten-point program endorsed by the Monroe NAACP. Dr. Perry, recently released from prison but still forbidden to practice medicine in Union County, did not let his legal problems deter him from exercising his rights. He signed the ten-point program along with Robert Williams and J. W. McDow and helped present these demands to the Monroe board of aldermen a few days before the Freedom Riders arrived. Among other things, the petition called for nondiscriminatory hiring in local factories; the extension of "the same privileges, courtesies and consideration given to whites" by the local welfare bureaucracy; and "the construction of a swimming pool in the Winchester Avenue area of Monroe." Though the petition made no mention of whether the pool in the black neighborhood would be officially integrated, it demanded the removal of "all signs in the city of Monroe designating one area for colored and another for whites." The desegregation of the city schools "no later than 1962" and the employment of black citizens "in skilled or supervisory positions in the city government" were also required.

The Monroe Nonviolent Action Committee asked everyone involved to "take an oath, swearing to adhere to pacifist principles," Williams said. While he and many of his followers refused to take any such oath, all agreed that the planned demonstrations downtown would take place under strict nonviolent discipline, that those not committed to nonviolence should avoid the demonstrations, and that the black community must continue to protect itself as necessary. This did not preclude close cooperation. "Many black people volunteered their homes for housing them," Williams recalled, and "women in the neighborhood volunteered food and cooking." They rented an empty cottage two doors down from Williams and dubbed it "Freedom House." Grateful for their assistance and supportive of their objectives, black folks in Newtown welcomed the Freedom Riders but stuck to their guns.[10]

The Freedom Riders were not the only outsiders who came to Monroe in late August. Constance Lever, a twenty-year-old student at the London School of Economics, arrived by bus from California, where she had been visiting relatives. A bookish antiapartheid activist with horn-rimmed glasses, Lever "did not know Mr. Williams and had not read his paper" but came to Monroe out of both curiosity and commitment. "When she came in on the bus," the Monroe Enquirer reported, "she inquired the direction of Boyte Street and then took off afoot, pushing her luggage on a wheel mechanism. Miss Lever was next seen in the vicinity of the Union county jail protesting the arrest of Rev. Paul Brooks, of the Southern Christian Leadership Council, on a traffic count."

Lever wrote soon afterward that she "immediately liked and respected" Robert Williams, "a big bearded man with a love of justice burning in his heart" in whose home she was welcomed immediately. "He has written poetry and music," Lever observed, noting that the family library included "books on every subject from religion and logic to psychology and biology." Lever found Williams and his neighbors "proud people who react to trouble with laughter and swearing and singing. They speak of the Klan not with bated breath but with mockery; of the police with indignation, not fear. Some of them refused apologetically to join the pickets outside the courthouse, knowing they could not take a blow without returning it or listen to insults in silence."[11]

Among those who would never enlist in the armies of nonviolence was broad-shouldered and dark-skinned Mae Mallory, who came to Monroe on a moment's notice because she expected that, with the Freedom Riders in town, "Mabel could use my help with the household chores." Julian Mayfield had jumped into his red Nash Rambler and headed for Monroe, stopping to pick up Mallory. The Rambler rolled southward, Mallory and Mayfield laughing uproariously on a beautiful summer afternoon. Arriving at the house on Boyte Street, they found that "things had heated up in Monroe since my last trip," Mayfield recalled. "Dr. King's nonviolent followers had descended on Newtown to convince Williams that there was a better way to achieve civil rights than through self-defense."

Racial tension was thick. When Mayfield gave John Lowery a ride across town, "a car filled with white boys" pulled up beside them. One of the boys yelled, "Hey, New York nigger, what are you doing here?" and sideswiped the Rambler on the bridge over the railroad tracks. "Driving alongside, they rammed the car again, harder this time," the black novelist said, "and I look[ed] out over that more than 100-foot drop. I grab[bed] the .38 pistol on the seat beside me." Lowery clutched Mayfield's arm and yelled, "No, Julian, that's not the way!" Mayfield was incredulous. He jerked his arm away from Lowery and backhanded him across the face. He then cocked and pointed the .38-caliber pistol "across my left arm out of the window straight into the faces of the laughing boys. I shout[ed]: 'I came to see your mother, motherfucker!' Their smiles disappear[ed]." Mayfield suspected that his attackers had "been misled by the New York license plates and the white boy sitting beside me. They thought I was one of Dr. King's people." Just then gunfire rang out from behind the assailants. Woodrow Wilson, ever on the alert, had been following the two cars and fired his pistol into the air over their heads. The carload of young white men veered quickly away.[12]

The Monroe Nonviolent Action Committee launched its campaign on Monday, August 21, sending ten demonstrators to picket at the courthouse square with signs that read "Justice" and "Freedom for All." Six white Freedom Riders, three young black men from Monroe, and Constance Lever paraded on the west side of the square, "carrying signs and observing recent picketing rules adopted by the Monroe city council," the Enquirer noted. "Police were on duty along the lines of march and a small number of people watched the group."[13]

The following day, both the growing crowd and Monroe police showed increasing hostility. Richard Griswold, a white photographer from Brooklyn, was arrested for "interfering with a police officer" when he snapped a photograph of a white onlooker hitting protester Paul Dietrich while police ignored the assault altogether. Police officers arrested three picketers for walking slightly closer to one another than the fifteen feet stipulated in the recently adopted city ordinance. Signs carried by white counterdemonstrators—"Robert Williams and his half-breed niggers go home," for example—did not seem to police officers to violate the ordinance's ban on "inflammatory language" for picket signs. Nor did police intervene when white bystanders spat on Constance Lever again and again. On Wednesday, however, police did arrest nineteen-year-old Jerry Anderson of Monroe for beating Daniel Thompson of Cleveland, Ohio, as he left the courthouse square. But a ten-year-old black boy who had been on the picket line, Prentice Robinson, was accosted by three young white men "who stomped him in town and almost killed him and put him in the hospital," Robert Williams said, apparently because his assailants mistakenly believed that he was Robert Williams's son. Despite the presence of several witnesses, the police made no arrests.[14]

In response to the violence, the Monroe Nonviolent Action Committee decided to target the fire station and the dentist office of Mayor Fred Wilson instead of the courthouse. At the fire station, Chief Jesse A. Helms Sr. chased the demonstrators off public property by pointing a pistol at them and threatening to shoot; the picketers moved to the sidewalk in front of Mayor Wilson's office. Wilson responded by having a city work crew come and break up the sidewalk with pneumatic drills and pickaxes, preparing to pour new concrete, so that the picketers had no place to walk.[15] The following day, when the demonstrators moved back to the courthouse, city employees fogged them with insecticide. A sniper shot picketer Ed Bromberg, a former student at Columbia University, with a lead pellet from a high-powered pump-action air rifle. "Luckily, he wasn't seriously injured," John Lowery said. "A band-aid, some antiseptic and he was back on the line in 20 minutes—placard, battle-scar and all. By the end of the day, all of us had been roughed up."[16]

The following day was Saturday, and with many local whites off work, the crowd around the courthouse square swelled into the hundreds. By 11:00 A.M. the state highway patrol reported that "a large crowd" confronted a band of about twenty protesters. "No trouble was experienced until 12:35 P.M. when a white man attacked one of the pickets and was immediately arrested," officers noted. Ten minutes later, police arrested two of the protesters for "failing to comply with city ordinance requiring pickets to remain a certain distance from each other," the highway patrol observed. "At 3:50 P.M., one of the colored pickets and a white male of Monroe became involved in a fight on the picket line," the report stated. Both men "were immediately arrested and brought to the Police Department where a large crowd gathered." The angry mob, which accused the police of being "nigger lovers" because of their halfhearted efforts to protect the protesters, alarmed Police Chief Mauney sufficiently that he requested that the state highway patrol rush over a squad of officers in riot gear to help disperse the crowd.[17]

James Forman, chosen by the group to make emergency decisions during the protests, asked for a police escort to help the marchers make their way back to Newtown. "The two police did start out with us," John Lowery said later, "but so did the whole damn town and, somehow, the cops got lost in the crowd." The marchers made their way through the hostile throng, singing "We Shall Overcome" and "We Shall Not Be Moved" as the mob yelled obscenities, "so between us we made quite a din," Lowery recalled. "As we passed one house in a white section, a woman came running out, yelling at us and brandishing a small kitchen knife. Young and agile, we managed to get out of her way, but she came pretty close to slashing some of us. The gentleman of the house joined her and started throwing soda bottles at us." As they walked "along Winchester Street headed for Boyte," Forman said, "car after car of whites passed—some loaded with guns, some with occupants throwing stones at us, all hurling insults and threats."

As the march neared Newtown, fights broke out along the line, and two of Williams's followers who had joined the nonviolent march broke discipline. They snatched "one guy who had been particularly obscene out of his car," Lowery recalled, "and roughed him up a little." Local blacks began to throw rocks at some of the cars, and pacifist Daniel Thompson ran in front of one car to try and stop the rock-throwers from hurting the driver. Thompson, who had been in the Jackson, Mississippi, jail for several weeks, "proved to be an individualistic and undisciplined person whose actions brought down a lot of criticism on the Freedom Riders as a group," by Forman's account. Saturday's racial clashes ended abruptly when a black man stepped out onto the porch of a nearby house with a rifle and fired several shots into the air, sending the whites fleeing back toward downtown Monroe.[18]

After the violent atmosphere calmed a little, Robert Williams reluctantly greeted a rather odd white visitor who suddenly appeared in his front yard. In 1961, future U.S. senator Jesse Helms, whose father had chased the Freedom Riders away from the fire station with a pistol, had become a political commentator for WRAL-TV in Raleigh. His strident editorials assailed the civil rights movement and denounced the federal government five nights a week, launching his long political career as a lightning rod of racial backlash and virulent anticommunism. Helms once asked his viewers, for example, "why so many editors are so hostile to the Klan but so apologetic for racial extremists on the other side." By "extremists," Helms meant people like Martin Luther King Jr., for example. "No court has declared that the Klan is in violation of any statute law on the books," Helms insisted.

Home in Monroe visiting his parents, the tall, bespectacled Helms bravely walked up to Williams's house alone with a camera. There were thirty or forty Negroes there, Helms recalled, and a handful of young whites. "Williams submitted to the interview grudgingly," Helms wrote later, "and answered few of the questions put to him." Williams was "hostile, often belligerent," Helms said, but "allowed his picture to be taken despite the threatening objections of a mob of militants gathered around him in the yard of his home in Monroe." Helms confronted Williams on the central question in his mind: "Are you a communist?" According to Helms, the NAACP leader replied only, "It's none of your business what I belong to," and "I don't want to discuss that." What Williams recalled best was their parting exchange. Helms shook his head and wondered, Williams said, why the son of a nice man like John Williams had become such a racial agitator. "Your father was a good man," Helms said, "he never gave us any trouble." Williams snapped back, "That's why I've got to. Because my father never did."[19]

Helms almost certainly saw more of the militants at First Baptist Church the next morning. Later that Saturday night, the Monroe Nonviolent Action Committee decided to attend white churches in interracial groups Sunday morning and to picket at the courthouse in the afternoon. According to Williams, he "was opposed to the Sunday demonstrations, because all the [white] millhands would be out of work and they'd start to drink and they'd be out looking for adventure." Weekend demonstrations had proved too dangerous, he said, because "every cracker and his brother will be free on Sunday." James Forman remembered their discussion quite differently. According to Forman, Williams "was in favor of the plan. 'We can't stop now,' he said excitedly. 'Things are hot but we have to make them hotter.' I did not agree with him," Forman wrote, "but if he felt that this was necessary, then I was willing to help him with the picketing."[20]

Whatever Williams's actual position, Sunday was "a beautiful day," John Lowery recalled, and "racially-mixed delegations" attended many of Monroe's white churches, "planning either to attend or kneel-in outside." The *Monroe Enquirer* reported that "two Negroes and a white man attended First Baptist Church and a Negro and a white man were seated at St. Luke's Lutheran Church." In an affront to the most deeply held taboo in the white South, "a white woman and a Negro man attended services at Central Methodist Church," the newspaper reported. There was no sign of danger or even opposition. "In fact," as Lowery put it, "we were received rather warmly everywhere. In most churches, the minister greeted us personally after the service and invited us to return the following week. Back in New-town," he recounted, "after we had a chance to exchange stories, we were pretty pleased with ourselves at this apparent victory, and set out for the courthouse and our picketing, not fully understanding the situation."[21]

When the Monroe Nonviolent Action Committee arrived downtown "for our afternoon stroll," Lowery said, "thousands of people were already there—apparently waiting for us." Crowd estimates ranged from 2,000 to 5,000 persons by the end of the afternoon, only 26 of whom were associated with the demonstrators.[22] Confederate flags waved above the angry throng, and signs proclaimed, "Open Season on Coons" and "Death to All Niggers and Nigger Lovers." Constance Lever drew particularly vicious jeering from whites who accused her of being interested in interracial sex rather than interracial democracy. It appeared that the Klan had decided to attend in large numbers; observers on all sides later noted the presence of dozens of cars bearing South Carolina and Georgia plates and filled with belligerent white men. "A number of young blacks from Newtown came on the scene," Forman wrote. "They did not picket and did not wish to join us. They stood across the street from the courthouse, and a crowd of whites began to threaten them. It was an annoying problem," according to Forman, "for they had no protection—they were not armed and they were not picketers, who, for the moment, had the protection of the police."

The demonstrators had arranged for a group of black cab drivers to pick them up at exactly 4:30 but had not counted on the presence of Williams's young supporters. Five minutes before the cabs arrived, the seething crowd surged toward them. Forman decided to put the young blacks who were not demonstrators into the four cabs that had just arrived and asked the drivers to come back for the rest of the Freedom Riders, hoping that the police would protect them. Moments later, however, the mob closed in on Heath Rush, a young white man from New Hampshire, and began beating him unmercifully. Just as Woodrow Wilson's car pulled up, other whites in the crowd turned their rage toward Constance Lever. Wilson had "wanted to see what was going on," he said later, and had brought several armed black men along for protection.

Forman hurriedly asked Wilson to take Lever to safety, but as he trundled her into the front passenger's seat, the white mob exploded. Officer J. W. Rushing yelled at Forman and Wilson, "You ain't going to put no white woman in a car with a bunch of niggers!" Captain Jake Elliot yelled at Officer Rushing to let the car proceed, but Rushing snapped back that there were guns inside and waved two other police officers over to the car. One cop grabbed an automatic shotgun out of the back seat and handed it to a young white man in the crowd, who cocked a round into the chamber and pushed the barrel straight into James Forman's face. "Nigger, stay away from that car," the white man told Forman. "If you move one step I am going to blow your black brains back to Africa."

Forman, surrounded by thousands of furious whites yelling, "Kill him! Kill him! Kill the nigger!" felt certain that this was his "moment of death." The angry faces before him "want[ed] blood; a nigger's blood, a black man's blood on a hot Sunday afternoon in Monroe, North Carolina," Forman wrote later, noting that he felt strangely cool but utterly terrified. He saw a man moving toward him with a long knife, Forman said, "holding it low." A black man, a white woman, an angry mob, and a gleaming blade—Forman felt a surge of horror and fear at the inescapable thought that he might be castrated.

He pressed Lever into the front seat of the car and turned to climb in after her, but the young white man with the shotgun brought the barrel down hard across Forman's head, splitting his scalp. "Out comes the blood, gushing like a volcano in eruption," Forman recalled, "another blow, more red blood down my face, into my ear, past my nose, across my chin, onto my dirty white shirt, blood, blood, coming from my head and more blood." The bright red flood "poured down his face," Constance Lever recalled, "and onto his shirt and my blouse. It was horrible." Unable to control the mob as it surged around the car, the white police officers jumped in with them and drove away—three white cops, four black men, and a white woman—jammed into one car and careening at high speed through hundreds of angry whites yelling for blood.[23]

"At the sight of blood, the crowd turned into a mob," John Lowery wrote. "It went on for about 20 minutes. Everyone was beaten up." The terrified and injured demonstrators eventually herded into the police station for protection, where officers arrested all twenty-six of them for inciting a riot. Even inside the station, Heath Rush recalled, "one man from the mob stood beside me, pressed a cigarette against my skin and then hauled off and gave me a tremendous punch on the jaw." The police did not arrest Rush's attacker and, in fact, arrested only half a dozen local whites all afternoon.[24]

From inside the police station, the battered activists could hear gunfire. State highway patrol records indicated "dozens of other small fights in progress at the time the shooting occurred, involving both white and colored people." Gun battles between black and white citizens and police officers raged between downtown Monroe and Newtown. Julian Mayfield, fleeing back toward Boyte Street in his car, saw a line of white men, some in police uniforms, along the overpass. They were firing downhill at blacks fleeing through some freight cars and across the railroad tracks. At Williams's house, Mayfield joined a group of armed black men who ran out to provide cover for those escaping. "My guess is that we were about a thousand yards apart," Mayfield wrote in his memoirs, "and we must all have been lousy shots because, as far as I know, only one white policeman on the overpass was hit by a bullet."[25]

At the Monroe city jail, police threw photographer Richard Griswold into a basement cell with a burly white prisoner named Howard J. Stack. Under indictment for passing bad checks, Stack was violent and mentally unstable. His father, storekeeper Floyd Stack, had been shot in the head and chest by a sixteen-year-old black youth in a botched robbery three years earlier. According to Griswold, as soon as he entered the cell, Stack "hit me in the face until I was bleeding from my nose and mouth." When he fell to the floor, Griswold said, Stack "started kicking me in the head and ribs. He threatened to kill me and I believe that he would have if an officer hadn't brought another Freedom Rider to an adjoining cell." Kenneth Shilman, the other Freedom Rider, said later that Griswold was "bleeding from the eyes, his nose broken, face covered with blood." He was so bloody, in fact, that Shilman did not recognize his friend until Griswold moaned his name. Stack later swore in writing that Monroe police officers had promised that "if I would by force assualt one of the freedom riders Griswould they would see I went free of my charges. This beating I did in the bottom cell of the Union county jail." Police Chief Mauney told reporters that the jail was so noisy that officers had not heard the screams from the basement.[26]

Horror stories from the jail and the courthouse, some authentic and others exaggerated, and rumors of mass slaughter and white rampage raced through the black community with the dozens of blacks fleeing the downtown area. According to Mae Mallory, who stayed at Williams's house because of her refusal to submit to nonviolent discipline, "people rushed in from downtown all agitated and said that all hell had broken loose downtown and white folks were trying to kill the blacks and the blacks were killing the whites and that blacks that were hurt were thrown in jail, they weren't given any medical attention."

Williams tried to insist that the growing mass of African Americans gathering around his house stay put, but he found it hard to control everyone. At least four of Williams's supporters—Cull Jordan, J. W. McDow, Jimmy Covington, and Albert Rorie—armed themselves with several pistols, a .12-gauge shotgun, and a semiautomatic military carbine and drove downtown to try to rescue the picketers. Rounding a corner on foot, the men ran into two police officers, Jerry Helms and J. W. Rushing, who hurried toward them with their service revolvers drawn. The police apparently fired at the four black men as they fled, and a furious gun battle ensued in which Officer Rushing fell with a bullet in his thigh. The black men ran back to Newtown on foot as several police officers traded shots with them, but no one else was hit.[27]

More than thirty highway patrolmen and about twenty police officers were unable to subdue the white mobs that raged in the downtown streets. After two hours the local commander called his superior in Raleigh and urgently pleaded for "extra ammunition, gas, and also requested that he order 15 additional men." Gangs of young white men accosted blacks throughout the community. A large number of black churchgoers returning from a Baptist revival meeting out of town had no idea that violence was sweeping Monroe. "There were lots of blacks stranded across town who had to walk back through downtown without having any idea of what was going on," Mayor Fred Wilson acknowledged years later. Newspapers reported open fighting in the streets until 10:00 that night, and the *Monroe Journal* reported that the courthouse square was "alive with people until well after midnight." Carloads of Klan terrorists roared through Union County all night, attacking blacks and even some whites known to have liberal leanings. "In regard to Ray Shute, the former mayor of Monroe," Harry Boyte wrote to a friend, "some 15 bullets were shot into the home of Mr. Shute, who lives in a privileged white section of the community. My understanding is that the shots were fired at Mr. Shute's residence because he was acquainted with Williams." Several carloads of white men sped through Newtown exchanging gunfire with black residents.[28]

While "police slowly, deliberately patrolled every dark nook and alley in town, notably in the Negro neighborhoods," the *Monroe Journal* reported, rumors of bloody racial battles and coming Klan battalions raced through black Monroe and the outlying rural areas. "Black people for miles around flocked into Newtown for protection," John Lowery, who had escaped the mobs downtown and made his way back to Boyte Street, wrote later. "Rob, too, expected the Klan to ride." Hundreds of blacks milled in the street in front of Williams's house, all of them angry and many of them armed. "Their friends and relatives had been beaten up and unjustly arrested," Lowery observed. "It was feared the jailed people would not live out the night. Some wanted to go into town, storm the jailhouse, and free their people." Williams recalled one of his neighbors, "a good church woman, gentle and kind," and how he had seen "that woman come through with a hatchet, tears just streaming down her face, and she said 'We ought to kill every white person in this town and just burn it to the ground.' " Williams tried to cool the crowd and keep people from leaving the neighborhood, Lowery said, but "had a difficult time controlling them."[29]

The many members of the Monroe NAACP at the scene responded to Williams in a disciplined, well-organized fashion. He ordered barricades built at either end of Boyte Street and posted several other young men as sentries; they climbed with rifles into trees along Winchester Avenue. Williams carefully unpacked two machine guns, loaded them, and walked briskly into the backyard, where he fired a quick burst from each weapon to make sure both were in working order. He placed these firearms on the front porch under the care of two of his teenaged assistants, Albert Rorie and Howard Williams. Two more young lieutenants, Harold Reape and Richard Crowder, stood guard with rifles on the porch of the Crowder home across the street. Williams's sons, Bobby and John, carefully stacked dozens of other rifles in the Williams living room. Robert unearthed a case of dynamite he had buried underneath his dog Little Rock's doghouse, prepared fuses, and distributed sticks of the dynamite to men whose judgment he trusted. Soon they had set up what Williams considered an effective defense perimeter along the edges of the property.[30]

When Williams felt that his forces were as ready as they were likely to get, he stood on his front porch and called to the crowd of armed and angry black people in the street, waving them to come closer and listen. Darkness was coming, he said, and nightfall would bring more trouble. It was important to remain in the community and protect one another from white terrorists. "They'll come in here burning your homes, raping your women, and killing your children," Williams told his neighbors. "The weapons that you have are not to kill people with—killing is wrong," he declared. "Your guns are to protect your families—to stop them from being killed," he said. "Let the Klan ride, but if they try to do wrong against you, stop them. If we're ever going to win this fight, we've got to have a clean record. Stay here, my friends, you're needed most here, stay and protect your homes." John Lowery, standing about twenty feet from Williams, remembered being "amazed at the greatness of this man, at his calm assuredness."[31]

Mabel Williams, meanwhile, worked the telephone, trying to prevent all of the defensive preparations from becoming necessary. "Early on that eventful Sunday evening," Janet Boyte wrote soon afterward, "Harry received a telephone call from Mabel Williams, telling him of the outbreak of violence, begging him to get state troopers or some sort of help into Monroe before bloodshed became wide and terrible." Boyte called his friend Dr. Sidney Freeman in Charlotte, who did "contact some state officials and report that troopers were already in route to Monroe." At 5:30 that afternoon, Burke Marshall, a key troubleshooter from the civil rights division of the Justice Department, telephoned Mayor Fred Wilson. Governor Terry Sanford's office had kept a close surveillance on Williams and needed little prodding from either federal authorities or Williams to intervene.[32]

Sanford suspected that Williams might be "deliberately trying to provoke an assault on himself." The governor was well aware that the Monroe NAACP, as he said later, "had all those guns," and he understood, of course, that there were also whites who might precipitate a confrontation. From his perspective, Sanford said later, "the question was how to get that fly," meaning Williams, "out of the soup, without messing up the soup and without killing the fly."[33] State troopers armed with submachine guns set up roadblocks all around the outskirts of Newtown and tried to prevent all whites from entering the area near Williams's house. Williams, of course, had barricaded Boyte Street himself, and the highway patrol kept a respectful distance from Williams's forces. "All those state troopers," Williams said later, "they did not come after me that night. They came to keep the whites away from there. Because they knew that we were going to wipe them out. . . . We had that thing set up so nobody would have escaped from there."[34]

It is clear, however, that neither Williams nor the state highway patrol had managed to barricade all of the streets leading into Newtown. As dusk began to settle over the community, about two hundred black people and a handful of white protesters milled about on Boyte Street, talking and laughing in worried tones and checking their weapons and ammunition. News reports of the violence in Monroe had spread to other parts of the country, and Robert Williams was on the telephone almost constantly. "People were calling about their children," he recalled, "what had happened to their sons and daughters."[35]

Around six o'clock, however, someone outside yelled, "Here they come!" A lone black automobile drove slowly up the block, weaving slightly. Two white residents of nearby Marshville, Charles Bruce Stegall and his wife, Mabel Stegall, had accidentally driven straight into the angry throng. Many in the crowd believed that they had seen the same automobile downtown the day before bearing a huge banner that proclaimed, "Open Season on Coons." The crowd of angry blacks, with Mae Mallory in the lead, surrounded the car and pulled the befuddled white couple out. "We were just surrounded by these niggers, and we couldn't move," Mabel Stegall recalled. "There were hundreds of niggers there, and they were armed, they were ready for war. I think they must have been expecting a bunch of white folks to come over through there and they was going to wipe them out."[36]

Several people in the crowd began to yell that the white people should be killed, while others vehemently disagreed and still others were simply furious and upset. The Stegalls did not help themselves much by their response. "We have colored people here on our place, and in our house every day, and my husband works them over at the mill, and we always treat them like we are supposed to, and then to go up there and have them treat us like that and wouldn't listen to a word we said," Mabel Stegall recounted. "That's what I tried to tell them that Sunday—how we love the colored people." Mae Mallory recalled that Bruce Stegall seemed drunk. "He was saying all the wrong things: 'What's the matter with you niggers? How come all you niggers are out here in the street? Whatcha pointing those guns at me for? I likes niggers, I works niggers, niggers cooks something good to eat'—all these stupid things that a patronizing racist would say." The Stegalls, like most white Southerners, felt at ease with their black neighbors only in paternalistic relationships of black deference and white supremacy. Their only other easily imaginable cross-racial encounters evoked frightening images of black savagery. "It was terrible," Mrs. Stegall said later. "They were like a bunch of wild animals."[37]

Robert Williams "heard this rumbling out on the street," he said afterward, "and people were screaming for me to come out of the house." Hanging up the telephone, he hurried outside. The people in the street "had this white couple and they had them surrounded," he recalled, "and they were screaming to kill them, and they really would have killed them. I had to fight the crowd because they were closing in on them and crying. Some—even men crying, 'kill them,' " Williams said. "I wasn't about to let them kill them in my yard." He "started fighting the crowd away from them," Williams said, and made it clear that he would not permit violence against the Stegalls.[38]

"Williams, he made out like he wanted to let us go," Mabel Stegall told reporters. "He acted like he wanted to be nice to us." Mrs. Stegall begged Williams to escort them out of the black community. "I said, 'Look, lady, I didn't bring you in here and I'm not going to take you out,' " Williams recalled. "You're free to leave any time you get ready." When someone called Williams back into the house, the anxious Stegalls followed him. "When I started in to the telephone," Williams said, Mabel Stegall "was pressing right up against my back." Her husband "was pressing right up against her."[39]

Mae Mallory took the terrified couple into a front bedroom, where they perched on the side of the bed. John Lowery noticed their car still sitting in the middle of the street and drove it to the curb, an act that later netted him a three-to-five-year prison sentence for kidnapping.

While Williams stayed on the telephone, talking to his informants around the county and his allies around the country, Mallory took charge of the Stegalls. Even Mabel Williams acknowledged that Mallory was a "bitter" woman, and Robert Williams and others had been forced to confront her several times about her rash temper. A few days earlier, Woodrow Wilson said, Mallory had declared that "she had a machine gun and said somebody was going to get killed since she was in Monroe. I told her we didn't want to kill anyone," Wilson recalled. "That was the stupidest thing I ever heard of and I talked to her good." Robert Williams had kept a close eye on her throughout that Sunday, and at one point Williams "chased me back in the house," Mallory said, "and came back into the kitchen to reprimand me" when she had seemed bent on violence. "This Mae Mallory was one of the main leaders and she was giving out orders and she held a gun on me," Mabel Stegall said a few months later. "We didn't have nothing, and we couldn't do nothing but beg, which I did, and she told me that she didn't want to hear my sob story," Stegall recounted. "All her nasty remarks she made, Mae Mallory ought to be strung up, and if she ever come up to Union County she might get just that."[40]

The central concern on Boyte Street was the fate of the protesters who remained in jail. There were tales of the withholding of medical care for the injured and of violence against the prisoners, some of which were evidently true. "I was informed by others, escaping from the riot scene," Robert Williams said, "that Negroes who needed medical attention were being locked in jail by police. I called the police station and asked for possible bond for the injured. It was denied." Soon afterward, according to Williams, Police Chief Mauney called him back. "He said, 'Robert, you have caused a lot of race trouble in this town, now state troopers are coming and in 30 minutes you'll be hanging in the Court House Square,'" Williams testified. Williams conceded that he may have threatened to march on the jail if the prisoners did not receive medical attention. Mauney reported to the highway patrol, however, that Williams had threatened "that unless the pickets were released, that Stegall and his wife would be killed at the end of a thirty-minute period." Both versions of the story agree that Williams permitted Bruce Stegall to speak to the chief of police. According to Mae Mallory, they heard the police chief advise Stegall "to get out from there because he was going to wipe out that whole nest of niggers."[41]

James Forman, when he eventually was taken to the hospital by police, apparently heard something about a "hostage situation" over the squad car's radio; this suggests that police at least believed the Stegalls were held captive. At the same time, however, police reports indicate that Chief Mauney was not even convinced that Stegall was at Williams's house. Rather than negotiate or intervene, Mauney ordered officers to "proceed to Marshville where Stegall resides in an effort to locate him" in order to "verify the story concerning Mr. Stegall and his wife." By the time that Deputy Sheriff Dutton contacted the Stegalls' grown children, the Stegalls had already left Boyte Street and driven their car to Marshville to the home of their son. Their wrong turn into trouble, if that is what it was, had cost them about two hours.[42] As they drove out of Newtown, the couple spoke with two police officers. They made no complaint but instead indicated that they were on their way home. "At the time, I was not even thinking about being kidnapped," Mabel Stegall said later. "The papers, the publicity and all that stuff is what brought in that kidnapping mess."[43]

While the Stegalls were in the house on Boyte Street, they told a deputy sheriff later that night, "they heard what sounded like about 50 shots . . . as a car passed down the street." Several carloads of white terrorists rolled past the barricades and roared down Boyte Street early that evening. "They made some quick passes," Williams said. One of the teenaged sentries confessed under police grilling afterward that he had been on the Crowder family's porch across the street when Richard Crowder and Harold Reape fired their rifles at a passing car. He also acknowledged that he had been on Williams's porch when someone emptied the machine gun at a passing car filled with gun-toting white men. Still another group of nightriders raced through later, "and some white guys fired a pistol out of the car," Robert Williams recalled. As the attacking car fled, about ten black men ran out and "formed a line across the street, and they had tracer bullets, and you could see those bullets going into the back of that car. . . . If nobody got killed that was one of the greatest miracles in history," Williams recalled. "Those crackers were really burning some rubber."[44]

As these sporadic assaults continued, Williams received telephone reports from black residents of Union County who had seen highway patrol, Ku Klux Klan, or National Guard caravans pouring into Monroe. Someone else told him that the governor of Alabama had offered to send troops to North Carolina. Surrounded by state troopers with machine guns and under persistent attacks by roving bands of armed white men, Williams pondered Police Chief Mauney's promise to see him hanging in the courthouse square. "I took this threat seriously, in light of the fact that four attempts had been made on my life within the two month period before that," Williams testified later.

"At this point Rob Williams had to make a decision," Julian Mayfield wrote. If Williams had stayed and fought, Mayfield believed, it likely would have led to a violent confrontation and the "certain slaughter of large numbers of people." Even Williams recognized the limits of armed struggle under the circumstances that prevailed in the Jim Crow South. While the Monroe NAACP could crush any attack by the Ku Klux Klan, Williams thought, "when you got state and federal governments and other states volunteering to send troops, that's a different situation." Though he considered staying in Monroe, Williams said, "I thought it would get a lot of people killed and I didn't want that to happen." Williams also may have worried about the legal consequences of firing on his attackers with machine guns. "I didn't want those racist dogs to have the satisfaction of legally lynching me," he wrote to Dr. Perry a few weeks later. From New York, Williams believed, he could unleash another of his patented propaganda storms before returning to Monroe in a week or two.[45]

The Williams family's escape from Monroe has been shrouded in mystery for decades. Some black residents still offer to show visitors where Fidel Castro's helicopters landed to spirit his friend away to Cuba. Others describe how a black funeral director from Charlotte used one of his hearses to slip Williams out of Monroe in a casket. The Boyte family in Matthews confessed later that "Williams, his wife and children eluded the police through our house, escaping into the woods in back, although none of us were home at the time," although this does not appear to have been their actual avenue of escape. For many years, Williams himself remained reluctant to reveal his path of flight, explaining that he had pledged to protect many people who had helped his family avoid capture. But in his unpublished autobiography and the unpublished autobiography of Julian Mayfield, much of the story finally unfolds.[46]

Sometime earlier, Williams had dispatched Julian Mayfield to Dr. Perry's house on the other side of Newtown. "At about six o'clock," Mayfield recalled, "Williams telephoned to say that if he didn't leave Monroe there would be a bloodbath." They already had arranged to meet at a designated point on Second Street near the American Legion Hut if there were an emergency. Robert Williams set out on foot wearing a dark beret and leading Mabel Williams, Mae Mallory, and his two small sons. He carried two pistols—his army .45 and the 9-mm Luger—a light rifle, and one of the machine guns slung over his shoulder. "I had about five or six hundred rounds of ammunition," he recalled. Just as they were leaving, a young woman called out from the house "that Reverend Martin Luther King was on the telephone and wanted to speak to me," Williams wrote. "I told her to ask him what the hell did he want at this late date and to tell him it was too late to talk now."

They walked across the land, avoiding the police roadblocks that ringed the black community. "The problem was that these cruisers were so close together, they were trying to prevent anybody from going out of the block and anybody from going in," Williams said. "At first," he went on to say, "I decided that if we couldn't get out I was going to have to shoot my way out, but finally we got a break, an interval, and the next car was about a block away. We ran across the street into the other side of the alley, and we were able to go down to the highway." They passed John McDow's house on their way and spoke to him briefly as he hurriedly buried some guns, then walked on to meet Julian Mayfield on Second Street. "In my good old Rambler we sped northward out of Union County," Mayfield recalled.[47]

With four adults and two children wedged into the small red car, the fugitives kept to back roads and byways as they drove north. Just over North Carolina's border with Virginia, they stopped on the roadside, removed the firing pins from the rifle and the machine gun to render them harmless, and threw them into a creek along with most of the ammunition. Through Virginia, Maryland, Pennsylvania, and New Jersey they rolled, all the way to New York City. When they arrived in Harlem the next morning, Williams wrote, "the Monroe incident and the fact that there was an all-points bulletin out for me was dominating the news."[48]

The many connections that Williams had made with the SWP and the Fair Play for Cuba Committee now meshed into a modern-day Underground Railroad for him and his family.[49] The children stayed with a couple who did not even know who they were, merely that they were fleeing the South, while Robert and Mabel hid with a Jewish doctor and his African American wife on Long Island. Most of the people who harbored the Williamses were "leftwingers," Mayfield wrote, "a few had once been communists, though none had ever been a Communist Party leader. Black, white and Chinese, they risked all by giving money, shelter and lodging when Williams was hottest."[50]

The FBI soon announced that Williams was wanted for interstate flight to avoid kidnapping charges. Wanted posters claimed that Williams "should be considered armed and extremely dangerous" and falsely stated that he had been "diagnosed as schizophrenic." The FBI also fabricated the existence of scars on his nose, eyelid, and right leg. William Worthy called these sinister distortions "a modern, euphemistic variation, in this case, of the familiar southern theme of 'the crazy nigger.'" A fearful Robert Williams considered the wording of the bulletin "tantamount to a 'shoot on sight' order."[51]

Law enforcement authorities combed the country for Williams and his family. "All divisions must continue to press the investigation to locate and apprehend Williams," J. Edgar Hoover ordered his agents. "All leads must receive immediate attention." Twenty FBI agents ransacked the little town of Monroe. In the walls of black homes, in the caskets at a Charlotte funeral home, and in various caches on Boyte Street they found pistols, rifles, machine guns, helmets, thousands of rounds of ammunition, and even a case of dynamite hidden beneath Little Rock's doghouse, but they did not find Robert Williams.[52] One local man assured FBI agents "that he does not believe ROBERT WILLIAMS would be taken alive" and that "if ROBERT WILLIAMS had not publicly exhibited a show of firearms in the Monroe, North Carolina area, that he would not be alive today." Numerous black people in both Monroe and Harlem told investigators "that Williams and his wife are in the South soliciting recruits to return to Monroe." Dr. Perry wrote to Williams from Monroe that he had "told them and I truly hoped so, that you were in this area and preparing to liberate Union County Negroes forcefully." While many of his allies surrendered their weapons and even turned in their friends under the pressure, their devotion to Robert Williams did not seem to waver: "Subject has become something of a 'John Brown' to Negroes around Monroe and they will do anything for him," an FBI agent reported to Hoover.[53]

The fact that "many of Williams's associates are subjects of security cases" should not deter FBI agents from "thorough interviews with them in this matter," Hoover ordered his men, instructing them to warn interviewees of the laws pertaining to harboring a fugitive. When FBI gumshoes arrived at the home of W. E. B. Du Bois, Shirley Graham Du Bois wrote later, the agents only left "after uttering dire threats of what would happen to us if we gave any 'aid or shelter to an escaping criminal.' " By that time, she wrote, she and Dr. Du Bois already "knew that Robert Williams was safe in Canada."[54]

Their hosts on Long Island had helped Robert and Mabel slip across the border to Canada. In Toronto they stayed together for about six weeks in the home of Vernal and Anne Olsen, a white socialist couple whom Robert had met when he was traveling with the Fair Play for Cuba Committee. "One day the *Toronto Globe and Mail* published a huge picture of me on its front page with an article stating that the U.S. government had asked Canada to arrest and extradite me," he wrote. Unnerved when the Royal Canadian Mounted Police joined the hunt for them, the runaways decided it would be safer to hide separately. "Members from the Socialist Party moved me to Nova Scotia," Robert said, "an ideal location because of a sizable Black population there" and because judges in French Canada, they believed, would be less likely to extradite him to Jim Crow justice. Nova Scotia, moreover, had a refueling stop for planes bound for Cuba.[55]

Soon after the Williamses thanked the Olsens for their hospitality and departed in separate directions, FBI and Royal Canadian agents raided the apartment and warned the white couple, "That man hasn't got a chance. We'll send him back to the States in a pine box."[56] Fortunately for Robert

Williams, he had resourceful allies. "The next week I was told by my Canadian friends that the Cubans knew that I was there and that they were working on a plan to get me safely to Cuba," he wrote.

Friends transported Robert Williams to the airport at Gander on New-foundland Island, where he was instructed to wait in a men's room near the runway. After what seemed like an eternity, a black man entered the restroom and asked him, in an unmistakable Afro-Cuban accent, if he was Robert Williams. "I will remain here," the black man said, ducking into the stall. "You join the group for Cuba." As the extremely anxious Williams walked up to a group of Cubans chatting nearby, a beautiful woman he had never seen before greeted him warmly and then "leaned on me and held onto my arm as if we might have been lovers," Williams recounted. "She and I walked arm in arm through the security gate as the guard recounted the number of passengers who re-entered the plane." Later Williams learned that his sly escort was the wife of Juan Almeida Bosque, the legendary Afro-Cuban commander of Fidel Castro's army.[57]

The escape of Robert Williams to Cuba "came as no surprise," Justice Department officials declared, since he "has been a Communist sympathizer and an outspoken advocate of Fidel Castro." The Justice Department falsely asserted that Williams had once sought asylum in the Soviet Union and reminded reporters that he was "considered by the Federal Bureau of Investigation to be extremely dangerous."[58] The real danger, FBI Director Hoover believed, was not so much Williams and his much-vaunted guns as what the fugitive might do "in the nature of propaganda against the United States." The FBI director saw Williams, his "subversive" ties, and the cataclysm in Monroe not merely as political threats, but as a chance to discredit the growing African American freedom movement. "We should watch developments on this," he wrote to Kenneth O'Donnell, special assistant to President Kennedy, stressing the political opportunity created by "a situation where left-wing elements are closely tied in with integration problems with the added element of violence."[59]

Although it would be a long time before FBI agents arrested Robert Williams, it took J. Edgar Hoover only a few weeks to hear from the fugitive family, who soon reunited in Havana. On Friday evenings at 11:00, listeners from Key West to Seattle tuned in to "Radio Free Dixie," an hour of the latest jazz, soul, and rock and roll; news coverage of the black freedom movement; and Robert Williams's fiery invective against white supremacy.

As the decade of the 1960s raced forward, Robert and Mabel Williams spoke to a culture in which their message of defiance was increasingly resonant. Like their slave ancestors "who defied and baffled the brutal slavemaster with the musical code of the spirituals," Mabel Williams explained to listeners in 1966, the new "rock and roll musicians are becoming the epic poets of the Afro-American revolt." With what aficionados called "freedom jazz" dancing behind her voice, she praised "the most solid and hep of the rock and roll artists" for their thinly veiled appeals to "unity, protest, and resistance. These new cats are no slackers. We are tuned to their wavelength and we dig them plenty." Curtis Mayfield's inspirational "Keep on Pushing," Nina Simone's blistering "Mississippi Goddamn," or the ineffable moan of Sam Cooke's "A Change Is Gonna Come" would follow, underlining her point. Often Mabel would read from the works of their old friend Langston Hughes, usually the humorous musings of "Jess B. Semple." Whenever the band struck up a rousing chorus of "Dixie," listeners could anticipate the familiar voice of Robert Williams delivering another ringing denunciation of "rump-licking Uncle Toms" and "Ku Klux Klan savages," closing with his customary cry for "FREEDOM, FREEDOM NOW OR DEATH!" Mabel Williams punctuated each segment of the eclectic program with a signature voiceover: "Radio Free Dixie invites you to listen to the free voice of the South. Stay with us for music, news, and commentary by Robert F. Williams," she would intone. "You are tuned to Radio Free Dixie, from Havana Cuba, where integration is an accomplished fact."[60]

Conclusion: Radio Free Dixie

"On the past few consecutive Friday evenings at 11:00," FBI agents reported to Director Hoover in 1963, "an English language program emanating from the facilities of a Havana, Cuba radio station has been broadcast for a period of approximately one and one-half hours. The English language announcer introduces the program as 'Radio Free Dixie.'" The broadcast, "narrated by Robert F. Williams," exhibited "a very strong signal which undoubtedly can be heard very clearly throughout the southern states." Reminding Hoover that state authorities in Alabama had complained about the program, the agents noted that Radio Free Dixie was "directed to the Negroes in the southern part of the United States, calling upon the oppressed Negroes to rise and free themselves." In fact, the program drew listener mail from the coast of Washington State to the ghettoes of Los Angeles to the shores of Lake Huron. "People here report hearing both you and Rob over the radio," Conrad Lynn wrote to Mabel Williams during a visit to Monroe. "Albert Perry said you sounded good." Radio Free Dixie "came in on my little transistor here on the east end of Long Island," one listener wrote to Robert Williams, "loud and clear." The music, the listener wrote, was remarkable. Most stations "do not care or dare to broadcast the new music our musicians are really playing today and our people's hearts are beating to, because the new music is for freedom."[1]

"Originally," Robert Williams said, "I was broadcasting 50,000 watts, which could be heard all the way up to Saskatchewan, Canada." Despite its range, Radio Free Dixie "was aimed at the South, primarily," he recounted, "because the black people in the South didn't have any voice. This was really the first true radio where the black people could say what they want to say and they didn't have to worry about sponsors, they didn't have to worry about censors."[2] Mabel Williams sometimes read editorials by the Reverend Albert B. Cleage Jr., who in the late 1960s became the leading voice of a new black nationalist theology. Robert churned out slashing new editorials for every program, mining his stack of old *Crusaders* for material but always following the latest developments in the South.

Radio Free Dixie was both innovative and rooted in African American cultural traditions. Leadbelly wailed "The Bourgeois Blues," and Joe Turner moaned of "Careless Love." Abby Lincoln and Max Roach laid out their "Freedom Now Suite," whose evocations of African memory and African American struggle reflected an emerging movement among jazz musicians seeking to test limits both artistic and political.[3]

Friends such as Amiri Baraka, Richard Gibson, Conrad Lynn, and William Worthy as well as listeners around the country sent Williams hundreds of phonograph records for the show. "Keep the jazz and blues flying and dig RFD," Williams closed a letter of thanks to Baraka. Radio Free Dixie featured Minister Louis X of the Nation of Islam—one day he would be better known as Louis Farrakhan—crooning "Look at My Chains."[4] The show highlighted the anthems of the Southern movement—the SNCC Freedom Singers rolling out "Oh, Freedom" and "Ain't Gonna Let Nobody Turn Me Around." But Williams's innovative use of jazz was the show's musical cutting edge. "I did some experiments with some of Max Roach's stuff," he said, "and Ornette Coleman, he was producing this new type of way-out jazz."

Williams used the new jazz in an effort to create "a new psychological concept of propaganda" by combining "the type of music people could feel, that would motivate them." He envisioned "something similar to what is used in the churches—the 'sanctified church,' there is a certain emotion that people reach." Williams mixed music with news about racial violence in Albany, Georgia, or voter registration campaigns in McComb, Mississippi, coverage culled from clippings that readers would send and from a wide array of magazines and newspapers funneled through the Olsens in Toronto.[5] Even after CIA jamming and Cuban censorship eventually hobbled Radio Free Dixie, WBAI in New York City and KPFA Radio in Berkeley, California, often rebroadcast the tapes. Bootleg copies circulated in Watts and Harlem: "Every time I play my copy," one listener wrote from Los Angeles in 1962, "I let someone else make another recording. That way more people will hear the story of Monroe."[6]

Even more powerful than the 50,000 watts that Cuba had loaned Williams was the storytelling tradition that the South had given him outright. In 1962 Williams unraveled his tales from Dixie for Marc Schliefer, a white American leftist who came to Havana and taped their sessions. The two men and Mabel polished the transcripts into *Negroes with Guns*, and Marzani and Munsell, a left-wing publishing house in New York, issued the slender volume. Though hastily produced, *Negroes with Guns* became one of the classic documents of the black freedom struggle. Williams opened his book with a question: "Why do I speak to you from exile?" His story was his answer. Williams told what had happened in Monroe and called upon African Americans to "create a black militancy of our own. We must direct our own struggle."

Even so, Williams was quick to point out that he owed his life to white friends and allies and that "there are white people who are willing to give us aid without strings attached." Though he ardently supported the right of self-defense, *Negroes with Guns* called for the continued pressure of nonviolent direct action. "My only difference with Dr. King is that I believe in flexibility in the freedom struggle," Williams said. Those who sought to create a more democratic society, he insisted, must not lapse into "dogmatism" of any kind. Williams also pointed out that he was neither a communist nor strictly a black nationalist—at least "not to the point that I would exclude whites"—and called himself instead an "inter-nationalist." The book reprinted Dr. King's 1959 rejoinder to Williams, "The Social Organization of Nonviolence." The writer for the *Detroit Free Press* who claimed in 1969 that the book "laid the groundwork for the Black Power movement" probably overstated its impact. But *Negroes with Guns* became the single most important influence on Huey P. Newton, one of the founders of the Black Panther Party for Self-Defense in Oakland, California, and remained a bible of militance to a generation of young African American revolutionaries.[7]

Other media spread the message. A play based on *Negroes with Guns*, Frank Greenwood's *If We Must Live*, ran in the Watts area of Los Angeles from July to December 1965 to eager crowds and enthusiastic reviews. "We appeared in Watts and really shook up and inspired the brothers out there," Greenwood wrote to Williams. In August 1965 an uprising in Watts killed at least 34 people, injured approximately 1,000 others, destroyed $200 million worth of property, and required 16,000 law enforcement agents to subdue. Many far-right observers, overstating their evidence and overlooking local realities, blamed Williams's influence in Los Angeles for the destruction.[8]

More peacefully, Pete Seeger performed his "Ballad of Monroe" all over the country during the 1960s folk revival: "Robert Williams was a leader, a giant of a man," the leftist troubadour sang.[9] After the bombing of the 16th Street Baptist Church in Birmingham in 1963, Mao Zedong issued a ringing statement of "support for the American Negroes in their struggle against racial discrimination and for freedom and equal rights," a lengthy declaration inspired, Mao said, by the influence of "Mr. Robert Williams, the former President of the Monroe, North Carolina, chapter of the National Association for the Advancement of Colored People."[10]

What expanded Williams's influence the most was probably his decision to revive The Crusader, which he and Mabel Williams published as a monthly newsletter from Havana. A Cuban printing shop volunteered staff time, and the Olsens in Toronto agreed to serve as a bulk distribution point.[11] "We must get more Crusaders into the deep South and elsewhere," Williams wrote to Max Stanford, who had organized dozens of followers of Robert Williams into the Revolutionary Action Movement in 1963. "I am preparing to set up a conference between you and the people who distribute it from Canada."[12] Circulation grew quickly to around 40,000; copies passed from hand to hand in the ghettoes of America's major cities and traveled down the back roads of Mississippi with organizers of SNCC.[13] "In June of 1964," the mayor of Greenwood, Mississippi, complained, "Sam Block, Willie Peacock, and other SNCC workers from Greenwood were arrested in Columbus, Mississippi on a traffic charge and in their automobile the arresting officers found a large number of copies of 'The Crusader' which was obviously being distributed by them." The White Citizens' Council called the newsletter "absolute proof" that the 1964 Mississippi Summer Project in particular and the black freedom movement in general were part of an international Communist conspiracy. Later that year, when SNCC began to veer away from nonviolence, several members cited Williams approvingly in the fierce internal debates.[14]

As young black activists across the South began to reject even the tactical pretense of nonviolence, the influence of Robert Williams continued to spread. By the spring of 1962, "the example of the North Carolina militant," August Meier and Elliott Rudwick observe, had generated "a profound effect" within CORE.[15] "We don't talk about nonviolence anymore," two CORE field secretaries admitted in 1962. While official CORE ideology continued to stress nonviolence, local organizers did not; in fact, many found armed self-defense natural and necessary. "We cannot tell someone not to defend his property and the lives of his family," one CORE organizer wrote in the fall of 1963, "and let me tell you, those 15–20 shotguns guarding our meetings are very reassuring."[16]

Not only within CORE but across the movement, traditions of armed resistance worked hand in hand with nonviolent direct action and voter registration campaigns. "I believe very strongly in the same principles that you believe in," Slater King, president of the Albany Movement, wrote to Williams from Georgia in 1963.[17] "Armed self-defense is a fact of life in black communities—north and south—despite the pronouncements of the 'leadership,' " a North Carolina activist wrote to Williams in 1965.[18]

Long before Stokely Carmichael and Willie Ricks led the chants of "Black Power" that riveted national media attention in the summer of 1966, most elements of that ambiguous slogan already were in place; many of them, in fact, were woven into the very fabric of African American culture in the South. The press and many others described Black Power as a reversal in the movement, but it was as much a revival as a reversal.

In 1964 black veterans in Jonesboro, Louisiana, organized the Deacons for Defense and Justice, a self-defense organization that soon claimed between fifty and sixty chapters in five Southern states. Though these figures were vastly inflated to intimidate the Ku Klux Klan and the police, the legend of the Deacons encouraged similar groups to spring up across the South. "We had to arm ourselves because we got tired of the women, the children being harassed by white night-riders," Deacon spokesperson Charles Sims told an interviewer.[19] Few activists objected. "Your doctrine of self-defense set the stage for the acceptance of the Deacons For Defense and Justice," Lawrence Henry wrote to Williams in the spring of 1966. "As quiet as it is being kept, the Black man is swinging away from King and adopting your tit-for-tat philosophy."[20]

His dramatic confrontation with white supremacy made Williams a legend among radicals in the United States and a folk hero in Cuba. "They gave us an apartment and they gave us two guards, they assigned us a Cadillac, had the chauffeur drive us all over the countryside, wherever I wanted to go," Williams said.[21] North American visitors to Cuba noted his stature among the people of the island: "Met Robert Williams and his family," one tourist wrote home to Detroit. "The people everywhere recognize and cheer him."[22] When Conrad Lynn visited Williams in Havana in 1962, the attorney was "dumbfounded" by the extent to which Cubans in the street responded to Williams. "I was thoroughly unprepared for it,"

Lynn wrote later. "North Carolina wanted Williams in jail, but in Cuba he seemed to be the most popular person next to Castro."[23] They sat up far into the night at the Hotel Riviera, but the only thing Williams really wanted to talk about was the possibility of returning home. "Make sure and push the subpoenas," Williams wrote to his attorney a couple of weeks later. "Remember that I am fighting for return to the US. I feel this is a very important time for me to be there."[24]

Not only did Williams long to return to the South despite the kidnapping charges against him, but he quickly got into political trouble in Cuba. He had been on the island less than nine months when an FBI informant told Hoover that Williams "has stubbed his toes with the Communist Party of Cuba" because of his "criticism of [the] Communist Party for barring Negroes from leadership" and that he "may not be able to regain his footing."[25] The trouble, Mabel Williams said, was that "Rob never stopped being Rob." When they toured the Cuban Foreign Ministry and saw that the staff was all white, she recalled, "Rob told them that 'it looks like Mississippi in here.' I thought they would shoot him for sure."[26] When government officials called him to the office of the Cuban Institute for Friendship with Foreigners to complain that he had been critical of their agency, Williams was blunt: "I lived in the South of the United States," Williams told them. "And a lot of people are afraid to speak in the South. I have always said what I wanted to say and I have even defied death. I want you to know that I am not afraid to speak in Cuba, either."[27]

Not merely his defiant personality, however, but his political perspective created problems for Williams in Cuba. The position of Soviet-oriented Communist parties around the world with respect to race was, as black Communist Party USA official James Jackson wrote in 1963, that "the freedom struggle of the Negro people cannot be in conflict with, but conforms to, the interest of the working class as a whole."[28] In other words, as Williams put it, "it wasn't really a race problem, it was a class problem. The white workers didn't believe in racial discrimination," the Communists insisted, but instead "were dupes of the monopoly capitalists."

There could be no separate black revolt in the United States, the head of Cuban security told Williams, because white workers must be the primary revolutionary force due to their numbers. After black and white workers had made the revolution in the United States, he said, the American people would reject white supremacy. Williams replied, "What American people? You keep talking about [white] workers and farmers. You know, when I left Monroe they had about 5000 workers and farmers howling after me like mad dogs out in the streets. How am I supposed to unite with them?"

When one black radical wrote to Williams seeking to make ties with revolutionary Cuba, Williams pushed indigenous African American insurgency instead: "I think it should be more Nat Turner than whitey's Marxism-Leninism." To Mae Mallory, who had once had her own problems with Communists in Harlem and was now serving a prison sentence on the kidnapping charges that Williams had fled, the exile wrote, "I am not going to become another James Jackson to put a new set of crackers on top who are using Marxism to maintain world-wide white supremacy."[29]

If Williams found Stalinist politics disagreeable, he found Stalinist aesthetics repugnant. North Americans from the Communist Party USA and Cuban Communists who took a doctrinaire, Soviet-oriented position tried to interfere with Radio Free Dixie. Jazz, for example, was "imperialist music and degenerate," they argued, and Williams should not broadcast the culture of the imperialist Yankee to the north. "Jazz was actually the music of the black people in the United States," Williams insisted; it "went back to the spirituals, the blues, folk songs. All of this music was tied up in the tragic experience of the black man in America." Black music "originated from slaves, and I had never known imperialist slaves," Williams said. For a while his arguments prevailed. "Fidel told them, 'Look, we've given him the time, he can do what he wants with it, he knows more about America than we do.' "[30]

His relationships with Castro and Che Guevara protected Williams only for a time. As the Soviet strings on the Cuban revolution grew shorter and shorter, Williams resisted the increasing pressure to make his own politics conform to the Soviet line. Black nationalism, the Cuban Communists argued, would alienate the all-important white working class. Martin Luther King Jr., some argued ignorantly, others cynically, was winning the support of white workers in the United States and hence represented the best hope for unification of the working class across racial lines. "The Russian line is to love the white yankee and kiss his ass," Williams wrote to Mae Mallory. "I don't need amateurs to advise me in this." Cuban Communists and the increasingly influential Communist Party USA expatriates "are only interested in Martin Luther King and the cracker workers in the USA."[31]

In anguish, Williams wrote to Harry Haywood, the influential black Communist who had been expelled from the Communist Party USA in 1959 for similar apostasies: "I have never been a communist, but I once had great sympathy for them," Williams told Haywood. "I find many of [the Cuban Communists and Communist Party USA members in Cuba] to be very notorious racists. Any Afro-American who believes in self-defense and labors militantly for human rights is branded a black racist and considered ripe for liquidation," Williams said. "I am under constant attack by the [Communist Party USA]. They have been trying to cut off my facilities here in Cuba. One would think I am Hitler and Wall Street combined."[32]

Party bureaucrats eventually managed to diminish the wattage of Williams's broadcast so that it would hardly reach anyone in the United States. "Gus Hall's boys down here are getting worse than the crackers in Monroe," Williams complained to Julian Mayfield in 1964, referring to the Communist Party USA leader. "Things are about to the stage when I had to leave Monroe in a hurry."[33] "I had a choice of remaining in Cuba," Williams told a television interviewer several years later, "but I don't see any difference in being a socialist Uncle Tom than being an Uncle Tom in capitalist and racist America. I am not cut out to be an Uncle Tom no matter who it's for."[34]

Williams had visited both the People's Republic of China and North Vietnam in 1963, and as his situation became more precarious in Cuba, he and Mabel decided to send their sons, Johnny and Bobby, to school in China the following year.[35] "In fact," Sidney Rittenberg, an American expatriate close to Mao who met Williams in China, recalled, "Mao invited Robert Williams and his family to come live as honored guests in China." Though Castro would not permit Williams to leave, Rittenberg explained, "a stratagem was hatched under which North Vietnam invited Williams to come and broadcast to the American troops fighting in South Vietnam. Fidel could not refuse a request from the embattled Vietnamese, particularly when this would have been part of Cuba's support for the Vietnamese war effort."[36] Williams offered "to go there and stay for about six months and help him set up a propaganda system for broadcasting to the troops— black troops in South Vietnam. They said yes," Williams recounted, "and so this is how I was able to get out of Cuba." The Williamses left Cuba and joined their two young sons in Beijing in 1965.[37]

"I am out of Cuba permanently," Williams wrote to Conrad Lynn. "The Cuban Revolution is turning very reactionary as far as our people are concerned."[38] Though Williams "never really planned to live in Vietnam," Rittenberg explained, the notorious exile traveled to Hanoi to produce antiwar propaganda and spent hours talking to Premier Ho Chi Minh, whom he found to be "very jolly, very humble." The legendary revolution-ary leader impressed Williams at the first dinner by seating their waiter for dessert and serving cake to everyone himself. Ho also introduced Williams to a young man, living as a guest in his palace, who had been horribly dis-figured by American napalm. Ho and Williams swapped Harlem stories; Ho recounted his visits to Harlem in the 1920s as a merchant seaman and claimed that he had heard Marcus Garvey speak there and had been so inspired that he "emptied his pockets" into the collection plate. Fasci-nated, Williams found a sympathetic ear for his disillusionment with the U.S. government, with Cuban Communists, and with white leftists in general. Ho had been shocked after World War II when the United States chose to support French colonialism rather than Vietnamese national-ism, he told Williams. He was astounded even more, Ho explained, when French communists declined to support their comrades in Vietnam—on racial grounds, the North Vietnamese leader believed.[39]

Williams's experiences in Vietnam left him with a passionate new depth of commitment to stopping the Vietnam War, a political priority that he shared with the increasingly radical young insurgents of the freedom movement in the United States. In fact, Williams met Diane Nash of SNCC in Hanoi during another visit in 1966. On April 27, 1965, Williams sent a batch of telegrams to freedom movement leaders including James Forman of SNCC and James Farmer of CORE: "Racial terrorists exterminating colored humanity of Vietnam. Decency and conscience requires all free-dom fighters to join the battle for peace." That same day, Martin Luther King Jr. received another of Williams's patented political taunts: "As non-violent advocate and winner of the Nobel Peace Prize," he told the minis-ter, "decent people of the world await your resolute condemnation of racist America's savage slaughter of the colored humanity of Vietnam." In fact, King was under similar pressure from Stanley Levison, Bayard Rus-tin, and others on the left and had already begun to make public state-ments calling for a negotiated peace in Vietnam, though it would be two years before King denounced the war in terms that Williams could respect fully. Williams always believed, though he had no concrete evidence, that King's opposition to the Vietnam War led to his assassination.[40]

Settling in China, Williams was "lionized and feted by top Peking lead-ers," according to CIA intelligence reports. The Williams family "came to Beijing and were given a royal reception," Sidney Rittenberg confirmed. The distinguished fugitives "were given a spacious apartment in a villa that had once been an Italian Embassy building," Rittenberg recalled. "They had special cooks and other attendants. Robert Williams had a chauffeured limousine at his disposal day and night. Anything they wanted was theirs for the asking." Williams "met and talked with Mao, Zhou Enlai, and other Chinese leaders," Rittenberg said, "had long talks with them and was treated as a very special and honored guest." Even so, Rittenberg insisted, the Williamses were "very decent, courteous people, always modest," who asked very little for themselves and "did their best to fit in."[41]

The Chinese government gave Robert and Mabel an extensive tour of the country as though Williams were a visiting head of state. A state-produced full-length documentary film, *Robert Williams in China*, used his journey as a narrative device to showcase China's industrial development. Though his ideological differences with the Chinese were not unlike those he had with the Cubans, "the Chinese allowed me to produce my propaganda without interference and they never asked me to change my way of thinking," Williams said.[42]

The Crusader still made its way to the United States every month, thanks to his new benefactors. "On October 1, China's National Day," Williams wrote to an activist friend in Boston, "I was allowed to stand beside Chairman Mao on the Tien an Mien, as a representative of oppressed Afro-Americans and deliver an uncensored speech to one and a half million people." Williams could not resist pointing out to a friend that John Lewis of SNCC, who had been forced by white liberal allies to cut the more critical language from his speech at the Lincoln Memorial in 1963, "could not do this at the March on Washington."[43] China was hardly an oasis of freedom, however. Even if the Chinese leadership chose, for the moment, to permit Williams to write and speak unhampered, China's own dissidents had no such liberty. Where once Williams had denounced U.S. and Cuban racial discrimination almost in the same breath, it seemed that he could no longer summon the political clarity that had been his trademark.

What Williams also could not do from China was participate in the growing Black Power phase of the movement that he had done so much to inspire. His lack of proximity, however, did not seem to limit his appeal, as persistent endorsements from Malcolm X suggested. "They are giving some kind of benefit for you," one of his Harlem friends wrote to him. "Malcolm X told the people about it the other night at Adam Clayton Powell's church."[44] In 1964 Malcolm openly referred to Williams as "a very good friend of mine," though he also believed that Williams had "made some mistakes" by permitting "all the civil rights groups [to] unite against him. They allowed themselves to be used by the government against him."

Malcolm acknowledged the Monroe leader's decisive influence at a critical juncture in the freedom struggle: "Robert Williams was just a couple of years ahead of his time; but he laid a good groundwork, and he will be given credit in history for the stand that he took prematurely."[45]

After Malcolm's assassination the following year, Williams's appeal among black nationalists and the young expanded still further. "As I am certain you realize," Richard Gibson, editor of Now! magazine in New York, wrote to Williams in 1965, "Malcolm's removal from the scene makes you the senior spokesman for Afro-American militants." The Baltimore *Afro-American* featured Williams the following April in a lengthy article by Ralph Matthews titled "The Fugitive: Robert Williams—Can He Win the Unity Sought by Malcolm X?" *Life* magazine reported in 1966 that Williams's "picture is prominently displayed in extremist haunts in the big city ghettos."[46]

Even though Williams was abroad, two of the most influential black nationalist groups named him president-in-exile: the Revolutionary Action Movement (RAM) and the Republic of New Africa (RNA). RAM was organized primarily in Detroit, Philadelphia, and Cleveland in 1963 by adherents of Robert Williams, led by college student Max Stanford, who later changed his name to Akbar Muhammed Ahmed. In the spring of 1964 the Afro-American Student Movement held a conference on black nationalism at Fisk University in Nashville. Out of that conference, Muhammed recounts, organizers for RAM "went into the South to work with SNCC," whose field staff generally were receptive to armed self-defense and black nationalist politics.[47] RAM remained largely an underground group that, though it only had a few dozen devoted members, the CIA believed to be "the most dangerous of all the Black Power organizations." Many individuals secretly loyal to RAM belonged to other major civil rights groups. In 1966, U.S. Senator Frank Lausche of Ohio called RAM "a national conspiracy executed by experts" and charged that police in Cleveland, Chicago, and Brooklyn had broken up firebombing and sniping schools run by RAM.[48] Attorney General Nicholas Katzenbach sought to downplay any panic about Robert Williams's influence on RAM: "We are, of course, investigating these things," he said, "but I wouldn't want to create the impression that the activities of these juvenile gangs have been masterminded by Williams out of Cuba."[49] Williams sent RAM leaders small sums of money from time to time—he wrote checks in similar amounts to Fanny Lou Hamer of SNCC and to the Deacons for Defense and Justice—but remained largely a figurehead. "They asked me to become chairman of it," Williams explained, "because I was known among the youth of the ghetto and to have my endorsement helps them in recruiting."[50]

The RNA, too, found Williams a useful symbolic leader. In 1968 two hundred black nationalists met in Detroit to found the RNA and chose Williams as their first president. The RNA proposed that five Southern states be ceded to the descendants of the enslaved persons brought to this continent from Africa. Georgia, Louisiana, Mississippi, Alabama, and South Carolina, they proposed, would make up the Republic of New Africa, with $200 billion in federal reparations as seed money. Life-size cardboard posters of Robert Williams often were displayed at RNA meetings; although Williams was the president-in-exile, Milton and Richard Henry, two brothers from Detroit, led the organization. The RNA recruited several hundred members and remained influential among black radicals for several years, but internal divisions and gun battles with police hastened the organization's downfall. "I really didn't play any role in the Republic of New Africa, with the exception of letting them use my name," Robert Williams said later.[51]

Probably the most famous expression of the Black Power movement was the Black Panther Party for Self-Defense, founded by Huey P. Newton and Bobby Seale in Oakland, California in 1966. Historian Clayborne Carson has called the Black Panthers "the most widely known black militant political organization of the late 1960s" and names Williams as one of two central influences—the other being Malcolm X—on the Panthers.[52] Newton himself wrote that "reading *Negroes with Guns* by Robert Williams had a great influence on the kind of party we developed." Seale, who had been affiliated with RAM for two years before the founding of the Panthers, also acknowledged the importance of Williams's impact on their thinking.[53] Then-exiled Panther leader Eldridge Cleaver told an interviewer in 1970 that three men had influenced him more than anyone else: "Malcolm X, Huey P. Newton, and Robert Williams."[54] The CIA exaggerated slightly when it reported in 1969 that Williams "has long been the ideological leader of the Black Panther Party." It is closer to the truth to say that the Panthers were "a logical development" from the philosophy of Williams, as Reginald Major asserted in his 1971 *A Panther Is a Black Cat*.[55] "Despite his overseas activities," the CIA reported in 1969, "Williams has managed to becoming an outstanding figure, possibly the outstanding figure, in the black extremist movement in the United States."[56]

Like the Black Power movement itself, as Williams got farther from his roots in the South, he sometimes drifted into apocalyptic visions of black revolution. Though he had been one of the best organizers in the black freedom movement, his isolation from a local constituency made him vulnerable to the same frustrations, delusions, and "illusory revolutionary rhetoric," as Clayborne Carson terms it, that plagued the movement as a whole in the last half of the 1960s. Williams's 1967 essay "The Potential of a Minority Revolution," for example, depicted a scenario in which black saboteurs and guerilla enclaves could bring down the U.S. government. Those who took such words at face value often fared badly. "Despite their bravado—or perhaps because of it," Carson observes, "the Panthers and other self-styled black revolutionaries were brutally suppressed through covert and often illegal FBI 'counterintelligence' programmes and deadly raids by local police forces."[57]

Williams sometimes felt his anger at white supremacy so deeply that he could hardly perceive the consequences, but even his apocalyptic tendencies reflected long-standing elements of African American culture. "It's like Sampson who was blinded, brutalized and beaten," Williams explained, referring to an old gospel song, "Sampson and Delilah." Captured by the Philistines and chained in the temple, Sampson knows "he is going to die, with this feeling where they're making sport of him, and it made no difference that he got killed, because he had already been completely emasculated, he had been humiliated. So he pushed the pillars down and brought down the whole building."[58]

If Williams had had his way, however, he would not have brought the whole building down but, rather, would have moved back into it and remodeled. The exile remained lonely and impatient to come home. Often he explored ways to return to America, even though he realized that the trumped-up charges of kidnapping and the bitterly polarized political environment would probably lead to an extended prison sentence. "I have lost the will to roam / The road that was never home," he ended one of his poems from China.

"Don't be hasty, whatever you decide to do," a friend wrote to him. "Let's get some idea of Nixon's operation first." In the late 1960s, when President Richard Nixon and his mercurial national security adviser, Henry Kissinger, sought to open diplomatic relations with China, Williams saw both a threat to his safe asylum and an opportunity to return to the United States. On one hand, Williams said, "I knew eventually [China] would become closer to the U.S. and when they came closer I knew it would deny me a base of operations." If relations improved, in other words, the Chinese might not want a harsh critic of its new ally hurling his diatribes from

Chinese soil. On the other hand, Williams saw his position as a unique opportunity. China had been caught up in the tumult of the Cultural Revolution for several years and remained a mystery to outsiders. "I didn't really have any faith in the U.S. government," Williams recalled, "but I just knew that I'd be the only American coming in who had the kind of contact with the Chinese government that I'd had. They would want to know what I know."[59]

The story of Robert Williams's years abroad—in Cuba in the years following the Cuban Revolution, in North Vietnam during the Vietnam War, in China during the Cultural Revolution, to say nothing of his travels in Africa—would make an interesting book in itself. But such a work would be more about the many-sided international complexities of the Cold War than about Williams himself or the African American freedom struggle.

A hard truth for all who admire Williams's courage and leadership in the freedom movement is that, snared in exile, he became less a player than a pawn in the Cold War. From Monroe, Williams could sometimes harness the tectonic forces of the Cold War for his own purposes, much the same way that Martin Luther King Jr. used the Cold War to force the president of the United States to lean on white business leaders in Birmingham, Alabama. After he left Monroe in 1961, Williams surfed the political currents of his time with great skill but considerable frustration, until he finally saw a chance to ride them home again.

Williams wanted to return home, he wrote to Mae Mallory in 1967, but had "no illusions about doing big things" upon his return. No doubt Williams realized that federal agents would read every word that he wrote to someone like Mallory. "I am sure you recall that I have never craved leadership or the limelight," he said. "I have no intention of taking America by storm." In 1968 Williams again pondered his return to the United States, this time in a letter to journalist Robert Carl Cohen. Cohen and Williams were collaborating on an autobiography of Williams that Cohen published as his own work after Williams withdrew from the project. "A lot of people will be surprised after my arrival," Williams wrote, "not to find me fighting for leadership the way many others are doing."[60]

Certainly the CIA would be surprised. In an internal memorandum dated August 28, 1969, agents observed, "Williams has been a powerful and influential, if behind-the-scenes, figure in the most powerful of the black militant groups in this country; and it would seem that he may well be emerging as the over-all acknowledged Black Militant leader of the future." The report made careful review of the political landscape in the

Black Power movement. "Recent months have witnessed an apparent diminution in the leadership of Stokely Carmichael, H. Rap Brown, Eldridge Cleaver, and other black leaders," CIA analysts noted, "and one wonders if Williams may be about to claim the center of the Black Power stage, with the aid of his 'inside' helpers."[61]

The leaders of the Black Panther Party appeared to have similar concerns about Williams's potential impact on the movement. When he heard that Williams might be coming home, Masai Hewitt, Panther minister of education, contacted Williams through Cohen in order to instruct Williams on the correct ideological positions that he should take upon his arrival. The Panthers "felt that you should know that they are against the attack on white racism per se," Cohen wrote to Williams on April 13, 1969, "and feel that the enemy is the capitalist system which uses racism to perpetuate itself." Needless to say, this line of thought held no startling revelations for Williams. "Brother Masai says that [Williams's remarks upon his arrival] should have two basic points: (1) Revolution in the mother country (USA) and (2) Wars of liberation in the black colonies." It was particularly crucial that Williams "must denounce Karenga and the other Cultural Nationalists as reactionaries and racists," Cohen informed Williams, and say nothing that might "divide the working class." Williams's perspective, they informed him, "has been affected by your isolation" because "only middle-class people who can afford to buy expensive air tickets have been able to visit you."

Williams was both amused and confused. The Panthers "are in error if they say they have been unable to confer with me," he replied soon afterward. "Isn't Stokely [Carmichael] their Prime Minister? I talked to him here [in Beijing] and to Bobby Seale and Mrs. [Kathleen] Cleaver by telephone when I was in Africa. In fact," Williams continued, they "asked me to be Foreign Minister of the Panthers." It was not Williams who was out of touch, he argued. "I don't know what 'white proletariat' they have found to unite with," Williams wrote back to Cohen. "If they can produce one, though, I will be glad to join them in uniting with it." Williams would not take dictation from the young militants, even though he admired their ardor. He told Cohen to inform the Panthers that "I'll state my case when I get there."[62]

By late spring of 1969, Williams decided that international political realities now made it possible for him to come home. Williams wrote to Cohen that "Mabel and the boys should be arriving in Detroit in the next three or four weeks. I will probably be in the States the last of August or the first of September."

Before he left China permanently, Williams had a chance to meet with Mao once more and enjoyed a long, thoughtful conversation with Premier Zhou Enlai about the possibility of diplomatic relations between China and the United States. Though the premier warned that Williams could easily be assassinated in the United States, he hoped that the returning exile might "be able to work for better understanding and peaceful relations between the American people and the Chinese people," Williams wrote later.[63]

Williams flew first to Africa and then to London on Trans World Airlines in early September as "Robert Franklin," but when the FBI informed British authorities of the real identity of their passenger, the airline refused to fly him any farther. In fact, the British government locked the famous fugitive in Pentonville Prison for six days until Williams's hunger strike, demonstrations outside, and U.S. State Department intervention pressured them to relent. Williams flew into Detroit, Michigan, on September 12, 1969, as the sole passenger, apart from his attorney, Milton Henry, on a 142-seat TWA Boeing 707. Williams walked down the ramp like a free man, and gave a raised-fist salute to several hundred black citizens who cheered for him before the FBI placed him under arrest.

Williams was released on bond immediately. Jesse Helms, his old nemesis from Monroe, flew into a rage. "The commercial airline that scheduled a special $20,000 flight from London to return the black militant Robert Williams to the United States," Helms charged in a scathing editorial, "has made it clear that it did so only at the urging of high officials of the U.S. government." Helms was right.[64]

At the press conference when Williams landed in Detroit, Williams's hair was shorter and his rhetoric milder than many expected. "An Afro hair style may be unnecessary for the man who established his revolutionary credentials long before Black Power became the shorthand of militancy," the New York Times speculated. Mabel Williams, "described as a well-educated woman who had been his political aide," the Times continued, "was self-effacing" at the press conference. "She wore a Western-style dress and her hair was styled in a way that made it evident it had been straightened." In a political atmosphere in which caustic self-promotion had become the norm, "the stocky, bearded, 44-year-old seemed at times almost embarrassed by his status," the reporter said. Two days later, at a press conference called by the RNA, the Times observed, "Mr. Williams appeared, in some instances, to contradict the often strident militancy of some spokesmen for the Republic." Robert Maynard of the *Washington Post* noted that Williams "took gentle exception to the emotional appeals of some black nationalists."[65]

It remains unclear whether secret negotiations may have preceded Williams's trip home. It is entirely possible that Williams simply weighed his chances and acted on his own. Still under a kidnapping indictment, he stayed with his family in Detroit, where both of his brothers lived. Soon after his return to the United States, Williams received a letter from Paul H. Kreisburg, the director of the Office of Asian Communist Affairs, who explained what Williams already knew, that "the United States seeks to improve understanding and reduce tensions between the people of China and the United States" and that the State Department "would be most interested in hearing from you your experiences and observations during your stay in China and . . . your views of Peking's attitudes towards the U.S."[66] Through Allen S. Whiting, a former State Department official, scholar of international relations, and advocate of normalization of relations between China and the United States, Williams obtained a Ford Foundation-sponsored post at the Center for Chinese Studies at the University of Michigan. "Rob spent the year briefing the China experts at the State Department about how to approach the Chinese and the pitfalls to avoid," Gwendolyn Midlo Hall, an activist, scholar, and longtime Williams family friend wrote. "I briefed Whiting and Whiting briefed [Henry] Kissinger," Williams explained. This was an early part of the process that led to ping-pong diplomacy, Kissinger's secret trip to China in 1971, and eventual diplomatic relations between the United States and the People's Republic of China.[67]

If the State Department was glad to talk with Williams, that did not mean that the entire federal apparatus welcomed him home. J. Walter Yeagley, the Nixon administration's assistant attorney general in the Internal Security Division of the Justice Department, wrote to his counterpart in the Criminal Division: "Williams could be the person to fill the role of national leader of the black extremists. We should offset attempts by him to assume such a position."[68]

Williams was glad to be home, but he declined to push himself to the fore of the black freedom movement. He found the movement fragmented, dogmatic, and isolated from most of its potential constituents. The COINTELPRO operation, the FBI's effort to disrupt and divide the black movement, often by illegal means, clearly continued to take its toll,

Williams knew, although the name of the operation would not be revealed for several more years. Sometimes it was hard, Williams recalled, to tell the infiltrators from the idiots. Williams complained of "too much bickering, too much conflict among our people," and blamed "the new 'militancy' which too often condemns the so-called 'Uncle Tom' without trying to win him over," he told an interviewer for the *Black Scholar* in 1970. "The 'Uncle Tom' today may be the militant tomorrow," Williams reminded the movement. "This is no time for superficial divisions among us."[69]

Williams remained a black nationalist, but he stood out amid all the posturing and podium-pounding as an eclectic and flexible black nationalist. In an unfashionable move, Williams denounced racial separatism, calling for a "progressive black nationalism" that looked for allies, not apostates. "To limit one's scope of perception simply to black and white is to become a victim of stupidity," he declared. "Those who wrap themselves in the raiment of self-righteous political sages and arrogantly proclaim themselves the true believers and saints of purity," Williams said, "are the antithesis of social progress and transformation."[70]

Two months after he returned, Williams resigned from both RAM and the RNA, claiming that he wished them well but was intent on avoiding extradition to North Carolina.[71] Privately, there were deeper differences. "I had always considered myself an American patriot," he explained. "They didn't see it that way. I always stressed that I believed in the Constitution of the United States and that I thought it was the greatest document in the world. The problem is [the government and many citizens] didn't respect it." He was not interested in a politics of cultural style and vacant declarations. Many of the so-called militants, he wrote to Mae Mallory, "are just out to scare the ofays and play a cowboy game."[72]

In a 1970 interview, Williams contrasted the young militants of the Black Power movement with his own group in Monroe, dismissing much of the chaos that he had helped to inspire. "They have a lot of young teenagers who might have looked at 'The Battle of Algiers' or something," he argued, "and they get combat boots and berets and they grab a gun and go out and say 'Off the Pig.'" Williams sharply distinguished the Black Panthers' approach from the struggle in Monroe. "We had veterans who had been trained to use military equipment," he said. "We have people working in the houses of officials and we knew what was going on all the time." The Monroe NAACP chapter deterred rather than provoked violence, he argued. "We always tried to avoid a fight when we could, fighting is the last resort," Williams said. The young firebrands of Black Power "think a weapon is the first alternative," but, he emphasized, "a weapon is the last alternative." Williams affectionately criticized the young militants, whom he observed loudly proclaiming their willingness to use violence without actually having the military capacity to defend themselves. He also noted their lack of either mature leadership or coherent strategy. White terrorists in Union County, North Carolina, "knew if they attacked us, that a lot of people were going to get killed," he recalled. "But they also knew that we were the kind of people who could avoid a real showdown that would cost a lot of lives." The main point, Williams stressed, was that the terrorists understood "that it wasn't just going to be black lives anymore, but their lives."[73]

Though admirers flocked to pay him homage, Williams soon left Detroit and Ann Arbor. Neither the academy nor the Black Power movement had much to entice him at this point in his life. His legend had been intoxicating and his poster had been popular, but a man is not a poster. Williams wanted a quiet place where he and his family could recover a life of their own. After a year at the University of Michigan, he left his post at the Center for Chinese Studies and moved with his family to the small community of Baldwin in western Michigan, where they bought a modest home and planted flowers while the FBI watched.

"Many of us in the Republic of New Africa were very disappointed and felt used," Milton Henry said later. "He just sort of withdrew, went up north and lived in the woods." Robert's son John Chalmers Williams, who has devoted his life to working with inner-city youth in Detroit, described his father's withdrawal as a survival strategy. "The black leaders our youth know most about—Malcolm X, Martin Luther King, Medgar Evers—died young. The message is like, if you choose to follow these people's path, this is what happens to you in America," John Williams explained. "My dad chose to live."[74]

It was not a life of wealth and glamour. Working from a speaker's bureau in Boston, Robert Williams sometimes lectured at colleges and universities. He also spoke without charge at prisons, where he told inmates how Malcolm X had turned his prison cell into a college classroom and why it was important for black men to elevate their lives and their people. Mabel Williams became a social worker, first working with disadvantaged young families in Baldwin and then spending the last fifteen years of her career as project director of St. Ann's Lake County Senior Meals and Human Services Programs. The couple remained activists and NAACP members. Late in Robert Williams's life, the local Catholic priest,

Father Joseph Fix, still called him "the conscience of this community." Returning to family ties and local activism, Robert Williams spent the final quarter-century of his life in the small, trout-fishing village he and Mabel had decided to call home.[75]

After the State of North Carolina dropped the last of the charges against him in 1976, Robert Williams returned to Monroe each summer to visit friends and family. In 1995 Robert and Mabel rode in the lead convertible in the annual Winchester Avenue High School reunion parade. "It feels good to be home among old friends and classmates," he said. "It feels good to receive this warm welcome." As grand marshal of the parade, Robert Williams cruised down Main Street, where sixty years earlier he had watched a hulking white police officer beat a black woman. He toured streets where he had once faced down the Ku Klux Klan, and he waved at the crowd in the courthouse square, which had once echoed with gunfire and the roar of white mobs. "Civil Rights Activist Gets Hero's Welcome," the *Charlotte Observer*'s headlines announced. "We should have done it a long time ago," the head of the alumni association told reporters. The local black community raised several thousand dollars as a gift to Williams, hoping that he would use the money to move back to Monroe. Williams had often spoken of returning to Monroe, but as it turned out, there was not time.[76]

On a golden September afternoon back in Baldwin, Robert Williams, a few friends, and his family gathered around the table to hold hands and say a prayer before they feasted on crab cakes, shrimp, collard greens, mashed potatoes, summer squash, and biscuits. Everyone present knew that he was quite ill, but that seemed to cast no damper on the occasion. Williams beamed with pride about the autobiography that he had completed only a few days earlier. Everyone told family stories and laughed long and loud. After supper, one of the guests asked Williams, only half-joking, where he thought the city of Monroe would erect the inevitable Robert F. Williams monument.

Williams threw back his head, roared with mirth, and told one of his favorite stories. "Let me tell you how these monuments work," he said. "A black woman is driving down the street with her five-year-old son on the seat beside her. They pass Jimmie Lee Jackson High School and the boy asks, 'Mama, who is Jimmie Lee Jackson?' She tells him, 'Well, son, he was a black man who stood up for justice, but the white folks killed him.'" Williams grinned. "Then the woman takes a left on Martin Luther King Drive, and the boy says, 'Mama, who is Martin Luther King?' She tells him,

'Well, son, he was a black man who stood up for justice, but the white folks killed him.'" Williams squinted a weary smile that threatened to break into laughter. "Pretty soon," he chuckled, "that little boy starts to get the idea! And that's why there ain't gonna be no Robert Williams monument. I am fixing to die out here in my lovely little cottage in the woods, an old man surrounded by my family." Williams beamed with glee. "You start building monuments to a black man like me," he said, "and that little fellow might get the wrong idea. We can't let that happen."

Holding hands with Mabel, his wife of forty-nine years, his family at his bedside, Robert Williams died of Hodgkin's disease on October 15, 1996, at the age of seventy-one.

A week later, Rosa Parks climbed slowly into a church pulpit in Monroe, North Carolina. Her own refusal to move from a bus seat in Montgomery forty years earlier remained the most enduring symbol of nonviolence in the African American freedom struggle. A vast crowd packed the Central Methodist Church, black men and women who had fought alongside Robert Williams, and children who had only heard tales of a proud black man who struggled for his freedom and theirs. Beneath Parks lay the broad body of Robert F. Williams, clad in a gray suit given to him by Mao Zedong and draped with a red, black, and green Pan-African flag. Rosa Parks was glad, she told the congregation, finally to attend the funeral of a heroic black leader who had escaped the assassin's bullet and lived a long and happy life. She declared to the hundreds assembled that she and those who had marched with Martin Luther King Jr. in Alabama "always admired Robert Williams for his courage and his commitment to freedom. The work that he did should go down in history and never be forgotten."[77]

Her presence in that pulpit, nearly inexplicable when viewed through the traditional narrative of the civil rights movement, demonstrates in almost poetic fashion that historians should reexamine the relationship between civil rights and Black Power. Our vision of the postwar African American freedom movement prior to 1965 as one characterized solely and inevitably by nonviolent civil rights protest obscures the full complexity of racial politics. It idealizes black history, downplays the oppression of Jim Crow society, and even understates the achievements of African American resistance. Worse still, our cinematic civil rights movement blurs the racial dilemmas that follow us into the twenty-first century.

While it is clear that Robert Williams made a significant contribution to the African American freedom movement, his life unveils even more than he was able to achieve. The story of Robert F. Williams illustrates that the civil rights movement and the Black Power movement, often portrayed in very different terms, grew out of the same soil, confronted the same predicaments, and reflected the same quest for African American freedom. In fact, virtually all of the elements that we associate with Black Power were already present in the small towns and rural communities of the South where the civil rights movement was born. The story of Robert F. Williams reveals that independent black political action, black cultural pride, and what Williams called armed self-reliance operated side by side in the South, in uneasy partnership with legal efforts and nonviolent protest.

The life of Robert Williams underlines many aspects of the ongoing black freedom struggle: the decisive racial significance of World War II, the impact of the Cold War on the black freedom struggle, the centrality of questions of sexuality and gender in racial politics, and the historical presence of a revolutionary Caribbean. But foremost his life testifies to the extent to which, throughout World War II and the postwar years, there existed among African Americans an indigenous current of militancy, a current that included the willingness to defend home and community by force. This facet of African American life lived in tension and in tandem with the compelling moral example of nonviolent direct action. No doubt those who began to chant "Black Power" in the mid-1960s felt that slogan with an urgency specific to their immediate circumstances. But then, as now, many aspects of its meaning endure as legacies from earlier African American struggles. Above the desk where Williams completed his memoirs just before his death, there still hangs an ancient rifle—a gift, he said, from his grandmother.

Notes

INTRODUCTION

1. Lillian Smith, *Killers of the Dream*, 11.
2. "Trouble in Mind" was a well-known blues song composed by Richard Jones, published in 1926, and originally recorded by Bertha "Chippie" Hill. It is based on a slave spiritual of the same title. See Barlow, "*Looking Up at Down,*" 142–43. Complete lyrics may be found in Gates and McKay, *Norton Anthology of African American Literature*, 29. The story here is drawn from Robert F. Williams, "While God Lay Sleeping," 2–6.
3. Furguson, *Hard Right*, 30.
4. *Crusader* 9, no. 3 (December 1967): 3; Robert F. Williams, interview with Mosby, 1–2; Robert F. Williams, "While God Lay Sleeping," 5–6. For other accounts of the incident, see Robert F. Williams, interview with Cohen, 4–5; Robert F. Williams, interview with Banchero, 5; Robert F. Williams, interview with author, March 10, 1993; Cohen, *Black Crusader*, 21–22. The events described here reflect a persistent pattern in stories about Officer Helms. See, for example, Juan Williams, "Carolina Gothic," *Washington Post*, October 28, 1990. See also Furguson, *Hard Right*, 39–40; Mary C. Wilson, interview.
5. Rosa Parks, eulogy for Robert F. Williams, November 22, 1996, Central Methodist Church, Monroe, N.C., author's notes; videotape in Williams Family Collection.

CHAPTER ONE

1. Robert F. Williams, interview with Cohen, 61–62; memo, September 8, 1961, Robert Franklin Williams file, Federal Bureau of Investigation (hereafter cited as RFW/FBI); Robert F. Williams, interview with Mosby, 1. The U.S. Census of 1930, vol. 3, pt. 2, table 11, 349, indicates that 2,051 of the 3,238 Negro farmers in Union County were sharecroppers or day laborers. According to U.S. Bureau of the Census, *Farm Tenancy in the United States*, 53, 70.7 percent of North Carolina's Negro farmers were sharecroppers or tenant farmers.
2. Shute, interview with Durrill, 33.
3. *Monroe Enquirer*, May 7, 1956.
4. *Monroe Enquirer-Journal*, "Monroe Historical Edition," September 1974.
5. *Monroe Enquirer*, May 7, 1956; Furguson, *Hard Right*, 35–36.
6. Furguson, *Hard Right*, 31.
7. "Remember When," *Monroe Enquirer*, February 24, 1958.

8. *Monroe Enquirer*, September 12, 1960. This news story appeared when Judge James E. Griffin ended the long-standing custom by ordering that all citizens must now "appear in open court at the designated time."

9. Shute, *His Honor the Heretic*, 12–13.

10. Furguson, *Hard Right*, 31; Robert F. Williams, interview with Cohen, 60–61. See also "Monroe and Union County," magazine section of the *Monroe Journal*, October 23, 1952, 3.

11. Walden, "History of Monroe and Union County," 15.

12. Stack and Beasley, *Monroe and Union County*, 10, 27.

13. Daniel, *Breaking the Land*, 15–20.

14. "Monroe and Union County," 15, reports that 30,000 of the 42,000 residents of Union County worked in agriculture in 1925. The first quote is from Belton, interview with Banchero. The second quote is from Hall et al., *Like a Family*, 41.

15. Hall et al., *Like a Family*, xi.

16. U.S. Census of 1930, vol. 3, pt. 2, table 20, 385, shows 647 cotton mill workers. Twelve black men and two black women are also listed as cotton mill employees; these were almost certainly janitorial or loading dock workers who did not come into direct contact with white millworkers.

17. Hall et al., *Like a Family*, 183–236; Salmond, *Gastonia 1929*, 10, 46, 75.

18. Lee Overman to O. Max Gardner, September 26, 1929, box 13, Gardner Papers; Salmond, *Gastonia 1929*, 67, 113. For the racial dynamics of white working-class identity, see Roediger, *Wages of Whiteness*.

19. Robert F. Williams, interview with Cohen, 1, 24–25; John Herman Williams, interview with author, June 25, 1998.

20. Robert F. Williams, interview with Cohen, 26–27; John Herman Williams, interview with Banchero, 1994, 1; Hall, interview.

21. Robert F. Williams, interview with Cohen, 8–9.

22. John Herman Williams Collection; *Crusader* 1, no. 4 (July 18, 1959): 2; Cherry, interview.

23. Robert F. Williams, interview with Cohen, 8–9.

24. Henry Elwood Harris, "The History of Our Family Reunion," 1989, Williams Family Collection, 1; *Crusader* 1, no. 4 (July 18, 1959): 2; John Herman Williams, interview with author, October 15, 1997. The name "Tomblin" as recorded here may well be a misspelling of the name "Tomberlin," which is very common in Monroe today.

25. *Crusader* 1, no. 1 (June 26, 1959): 3.

26. Robert F. Williams, "While God Lay Sleeping," 11; John Herman Williams, interview with Banchero, 1994, 1–2.

27. Walden, "History of Monroe and Union County," 15; Blythe, *William Henry Belk*, 22. Even Walden, whose "History of Monroe and Union County" is otherwise proudly celebratory, concedes that "the stories extant about slavery in Union County do not seem to uphold the paternalistic view to any large extent." But he indicates that most white residents of the county do not agree with his assessment.

28. *Crusader* 1, no. 2 (July 4, 1959): 3; B. S. Tillinghast, letter to the editor, *Charlotte Observer*, January 28, 1959. For a fascinating discussion in this vein, see Nell Irvin Painter, "Soul Murder and Slavery: Toward a Fully Loaded Cost Accounting," in Kerber, Kessler-Harris, and Sklar, eds., *U.S. History as Women's History* (Chapel Hill: UNC Press, 1995).

29. At the courthouse, for example, one may buy a portrait of Old City Hall.

30. For this aspect of paternalism, see Genovese, Roll, Jordan, Roll, 41. "A slaveholding community did not intervene against a brutal master because of moral outrage alone; it intervened to protect its interests."

31. Walden, "History of Monroe and Union County," 15–17; Monroe Enquirer-Journal, "Monroe Historical Edition," September 1974. Charlotte Observer, "Union Observer," February 3, 1991. See also Shute, interview with Ammons, 10–12.

32. Shute, His Honor the Heretic, 11.

33. Crusader 1, no. 4 (July 18, 1959): 2.

34. Gavins, "Meaning of Freedom," 187, 191.

35. Robert F. Williams, interview with Cohen, 53; S. E. Williams, "Application Blank No. 15," and photograph of Sikes Williams, John Herman Williams Collection.

36. Escott, "White Republicanism and Ku Klux Klan Terror," 5, 12, 22. See also David S. Cecelski, "Abraham Galloway: Wilmington's Lost Prophet and the Origins of Black Radicalism in the American South," in Cecelski and Tyson, Democracy Betrayed, 43–72.

37. Monroe Enquirer, June 22, 29, 1875, June 26, August 28, 1876.

38. Quoted in Escott, "White Republicanism and Ku Klux Klan Terror," 21, 27

39. Monroe Enquirer, August 24, 1875, March 13, August 28, September 4, 1876, December 3, 1877.

40. Escott, "White Republicanism and Ku Klux Klan Terror," 30–31.

41. George P. Rawick, ed., The American Slave: A Compositive Autobiography, vol. 14, North Carolina Narratives, pt. 1 (1941; reprint, Westport, Conn.: Greenwood, 1974), 180–81. Coverson also noted that the Klan was especially hard on light-skinned former slaves who appeared to have white relatives. See also Crow, Escott, and Hatley, History of African Americans in North Carolina, 89.

42. Escott, Slavery Remembered, 157.

43. Escott, Many Excellent People, 155. For election returns, see "The Vote in Union County," Monroe Enquirer, November 13, 1876.

44. For the election of 1876, see Woodward, Reunion and Reaction. The quote from the Charlotte Democrat may be found in Olsen, Reconstruction and Redemption in the South, 194.

45. Monroe Enquirer, November 13, 1876.

46. Crow, "Cracking the Solid South," 335–37; V. C. Austin, "To the Colored Voters of Union County," campaign poster from Black History File. The poster notes that 1896 was "the first chance you have had to vote in twenty years."

47. Monroe Enquirer, July 21, 1877, February 11, 1878. Interestingly, the North Carolina Conference of the AME Zion Church passed a statewide resolution in 1878 thanking many white persons in Monroe for help in rebuilding the church. One of these persons, V. C. Austin, later became a "fusionist" political ally of blacks in Monroe.

48. Wayne Durrill, "Producing Poverty," 779–81; Monroe Enquirer, October 2, 20, 1881.

49. A. B. Smyer, "To the Editor," Monroe Enquirer, October 29, 1881.

50. Charlotte Messenger, June 30, 1883.

51. V. C. Austin, "To the Colored Voters of Union County," campaign poster from Black History File. Austin was a state senator.

52. Crusader 1, no. 4 (July 18, 1959): 2; John Herman Williams, interview with author, October 20, 1996.

53. Robert F. Williams, interview with Cohen, 11, 50–51; Robert F. Williams, interview with author, March 10, 1993. There are no known copies of the *People's Voice*, but its existence and its politics are confirmed not only by Williams family sources but by references in the local white newspapers. See "Monroe Historical Edition," *Monroe Enquirer-Journal*, September 1974.

54. Crow, "Cracking the Solid South," 339; Stack and Beasley, *Monroe and Union County*, 14–20.

55. John Hope Franklin, foreword to Cecelski and Tyson, *Democracy Betrayed*, xi.

56. Stack and Beasley, *Monroe and Union County*, 14–20, 66.

57. The quote is from Kousser, *Shaping of Southern Politics*, 76. On the Wilmington violence and politics of disfranchisement in North Carolina, see Cecelski and Tyson, *Democracy Betrayed*. See also H. Leon Prather, *"We Have Taken a City": The Wilmington Racial Massacre and Coup of 1898* (Cranbury, N.J.: Associated University Presses, 1984); Helen G. Edmonds, *The Negro and Fusion Politics in North Carolina, 1894–1901* (Chapel Hill: University of North Carolina Press, 1951).

58. Reprinted in Charlotte, N.C., *People's Paper*, August 11, 1899.

59. Escott, *Many Excellent People*, 259–60.

60. *Monroe Enquirer*, September 13, 1910; Escott, *Many Excellent People*, 260.

61. *Crusader* 1, no. 4 (July 18, 1959): 2.

62. Sullivan, *Days of Hope*, 14.

63. Robert F. Williams, interview with Cohen, 1–2, 32.

64. Robert F. Williams, "While God Lay Sleeping," 12–13; Robert F. Williams, interview with Cohen, 35–36.

65. Robert F. Williams, interview with Cohen, 18–19.

66. Ibid., 13–14, 1–2, 5–6; Robert F. Williams, interview with Mosby, 1.

67. Robert F. Williams, interview with Cohen, 20–21.

68. Robert F. Williams, "While God Lay Sleeping," 14–17.

69. W. E. B. Du Bois, "Fifty Years After," preface to the Jubilee Edition of *The Souls of Black Folk* (Blue Heron Press, 1953), reprinted in *The Souls of Black Folk* (New York: Faucett, 1961), xiv; Shute, interview with Durrill, 34.

70. *Monroe Enquirer*, July 19, 1956, July 7, September 1, 1955.

71. Haley, *Charles N. Hunter*, 214–15, 284.

72. Myers, "When Violence Met Violence," 10–11; Martin and House, *Public Letters and Papers of Thomas Walter Bickett*, 189–92.

73. Earl Lewis is quoted in Kelley, " 'We Are Not What We Seem,' " 79. See Timothy B. Tyson, "Renegade For Justice," *Charlotte Observer*, May 13, 1995; Mabel R. Williams, interview with author, March 20, 1997; *Crusader* 1, no. 52 (June 25, 1960): 5–6.

74. Robert F. Williams, interview with Cohen, 120–21; Myers, "When Violence Met Violence," 9. On the use of racial epithets, see, for example, an article by T. B. Laney in the *Monroe Enquirer* on January 25, 1925, in which Laney repeatedly used the word "nigger" to describe "Blind Jack" McNair, a local African American, and made fun of McNair's supposed sexual enthusiasm and purported intellectual limits. This type of language and "humor" abounded in Monroe's newspapers into the 1960s. See, for example, *Monroe Enquirer*, March 16, 1959, in which the editors describe a local man as a "fool nigger" in the same issue in which they denounce Robert Williams for "intemperate speech." (Williams is quoted in

Banchero, "Native Son Wants to Come Home"). A version of this article appeared in the *Charlotte Observer*, February 22, 1995.

75. Chalmers, *Hooded Americanism*, 3, 93, 96–97.
76. *Monroe Journal*, October 31, 1922.
77. Gavins, "NAACP in North Carolina," 106–7, 110. Gavins counts twenty-five black men lynched between 1900 and 1918 and thirty-seven lynchings between 1920 and 1943, all listed in NAACP records. These figures leave out two years in the heyday of lynching, of course, and readers should also bear in mind that lynchings frequently went unrecorded. The quotations are from the *Monroe Journal*, September 22, 1922.
78. Robert F. Williams, interview with Cohen, 32; Shute, interview with Durrill, 71.
79. *Crusader* 1, no. 52 (June 25, 1960): 5–6. Violence was not necessarily always a whites-only affair; left without any hope of legal recourse, black citizens sometimes struck back with whatever weapons could be had. In 1935, the *Monroe Enquirer* reported, a white family "became violently ill and six negroes were charged with placing arsenic in their well bucket." See "25 Years Ago This Week," *Monroe Enquirer*, December 5, 1960. It is possible, however, that this is but another case where blacks were victims, since well-poisoning was a common but improbable white paranoia.
80. Furguson, *Hard Right*, 38–39. For a sensitive scholarly description of racial etiquette in the piedmont during the Jim Crow era, see Brewton Berry, *Almost White*, 74–76. The best single work on the period is Litwack, *Trouble in Mind*.
81. Robert F. Williams, interview with Cohen, 16, 105–10; Mabel Williams to Timothy Tyson, December 4, 1998, in author's possession.
82. Barlow, "*Looking Up at Down*," 79–110.
83. Robert F. Williams, "While God Lay Sleeping," 19–21. See Tera Hunter's brilliant chapter on black vernacular dance in *To 'Joy My Freedom*, 168–86. See also Kelley, " 'We Are Not What We Seem.' "
84. John Herman Williams, interview with author, March 21, 1997; Robert F. Williams, interview with Cohen, 11–12.
85. Robert F. Williams, interview with Cohen, 11–12.
86. "Someday, I'm Going Back South," *Daily Worker* (Detroit ed.), April 9, 1949.
87. "The History of Our Family Reunion," Williams Family Collection; *Crusader* 1, no. 4 (July 18, 1959): 2.

CHAPTER TWO

1. Robert F. Williams, "While God Lay Sleeping," 27.
2. Robert F. Williams, interview with Cohen, 175–76.
3. A. Philip Randolph, "Call to Negro Americans," July 1, 1941, office file 93, Roosevelt Papers; Lewis Killian, unpaginated introduction to Garfinkel, *When Negroes March*.
4. Jervis Anderson, *A. Philip Randolph*, 242; Wynn, *The Afro-American and the Second World War*, 44. Randolph also found it convenient to exclude whites because it helped him to avoid participation by most communists.
5. See Sitkoff, "Racial Militancy and Interracial Violence," 661–81. Sitkoff argues that all-black militancy provoked "the wartime violence which summoned forth

the modern civil rights movement" but later gave way to "liberal interracialism, which all too easily accepted the appearance of racial peace for the reality of racial justice." There is much truth to this, especially in Sitkoff's largely undeveloped point that during World War II the radical position preceded the accommodationist phase, ostensibly reversing the familiar narrative arc "from civil rights to Black Power." In fact, wartime black activists mixed nonviolent direct action and armed self-defense, witnessed both landmark litigation and widespread rioting, and organized wholesale defiance of segregation laws alongside quiet lobbying for incremental amelioration. Sitkoff and others, neglecting the full complexity of American racial politics, framed wartime activism as moving from militancy to accommodation, much as historians would later jump to describe the postwar freedom movement as shifting from civil rights to Black Power, which neglected the continual and ongoing presence of many of the aspects of the freedom struggle—self-defense, cultural pride, and independent black political action, for example—which became associated with Black Power.

6. Leach, "Meaning of the Meeting," 10.
7. See Kapur, *Raising Up a Prophet*, 101–23.
8. Wynn, *The Afro-American and the Second World War*, 47.
9. *Chicago Daily Tribune*, July 5, 1943; *Philadelphia Tribune*, July 10, 1943.
10. Dower, *War without Mercy*.
11. *Philadelphia Tribune*, July 10, 1943.
12. Roy Wilkins, "The Negro Wants Full Equality," in Logan, *What the Negro Wants*, 115.
13. White, *A Man Called White*, 260. See also Dower, *War without Mercy*, 5, 175, 208, 244.
14. Wynn, *The Afro-American and the Second World War*, 113; Sullivan, *Days of Hope*, 141.
15. A. Philip Randolph, "A Reply to My Critics: Randolph Blasts Courier as 'Bitter Voice of Defeatism,'" *Chicago Defender*, June 12, 1943.
16. Sitkoff, "Racial Militancy and Interracial Violence," 662.
17. Payne, *I've Got the Light of Freedom*, 88–89.
18. Sitkoff, "African American Militancy in the World War II South," 77.
19. Sitkoff, "Racial Militancy and Interracial Violence," 662.
20. See Pauli Murray, "A Blueprint for First Class Citizenship," *Crisis* 51 (November 1944): 358–59. There were widespread rumors that groups of young black men in North Carolina sat down at drugstore lunch counters, demanded service, and were arrested by the police. See Odum, *Race and Rumors of Race*, 93.
21. Dr. C. T. Smith to Nell Battle Lewis, November 26, 1944, Lewis Papers.
22. Roy Wilkins, "It's Our Country, Too," *Saturday Evening Post*, December 14, 1940, 61.
23. Eagles, *Jonathan Daniels*, 89.
24. Madison S. Jones Jr. to Lucille Black, February 19, 1942, box C136, group 2, National Association for the Advancement of Colored People Papers (hereafter cited as NAACP Papers).
25. Clipping of the masthead from the *Carolina Times*, n.d., box 82, Broughton Papers.
26. Bruce Cameron to J. Melville Broughton, August 11, 1943, box 82, Broughton Papers.
27. Chafe, *Unfinished Journey*, 22.
28. Odum, *Race and Rumors of Race*, 97, 100, 103; Eagles, *Jonathan Daniels*, 113–14.
29. Frank Daniels to Jonathan Daniels, August 5, 1942, Daniels Papers. See also Odum, *Race and Rumors of Race*, 72, 74, 80. For the FBI's explanation, see Hill,

RACON, 278. This shift in employment simply reflected a sharply altered wartime labor market. H. R. Miller, an African American tailor in Greenville, wrote to Governor Broughton on June 8, 1943, and informed him that state unemployment agents were purging black seasonal tobacco workers from the unemployment rolls unfairly in an effort to make them accept domestic jobs. This injustice, he said, was not driving black women into domestic work, but instead "the Negro women are making an exodus to Newport-News, Norfolk, Washington, and Baltimore, canning factories in Maryland and to the truck farms of Pennsylvania." The entire tobacco labor force, he wrote, was "leaving here in droves." See box 82, Broughton Papers.

30. Jonathan Daniels to Lester B. Granger, August 14, 1942, Daniels Papers.
31. Frank Daniels to Jonathan Daniels, August 25, 1942, ibid.
32. Odum, Race and Rumors of Race, 6–7.
33. Lawson, Black Ballots, 66.
34. News Journal and Durham Messenger, July 15, 1943. Zoot suits were a potent symbol of racial identity and political dissidence. "By March 1942, because fabric rationing regulations instituted by the War Department forbade the wearing of zoot suits," Robin D. G. Kelley writes, "wearing the suit (which had to be purchased through informal networks) was seen by white servicemen as a pernicious act of anti-Americanism—a view compounded by the fact that most zoot suiters were able-bodied men who refused to enlist or found ways to dodge the draft." See "The Riddle of the Zoot: Malcolm Little and Black Cultural Politics during World War II," in Kelley, Race Rebels, 161–81.
35. Carolina Times, July 3, May 1, 1943.
36. E. R. Williams to Andrew J. Turner, June 23, 1945, box C138, group 2, NAACP Papers.
37. Petition to J. Melville Broughton, July 27, 1943, and Herbert B. Taylor to J. Melville Broughton, n.d., box 82, Broughton Papers.
38. Walden, "History of Monroe and Union County," 24; Shute, interview with Durrill, 48.
39. Monroe Journal September 10, 1943.
40. Shute, interview with Durrill, 48.
41. Union County Memorial Hospital Staff to Dr. Joseph J. Coombs, North Carolina Board of Medical Examiners, October 11, 1961, box 111, Sanford Papers.
42. Morrow, Forty Years a Guinea Pig, 37–38.
43. Odum, Race and Rumors of Race. While the quotes in the text are from pp. 30–31 and 54–55, Odum's survey finds the idea of interracial sexuality at the center of racial conflict across the region; for a few examples of "sex-caste" tension in North Carolina alone, see also pp. 27–28, 54–57, 61–62, 64–65, 117. The Raleigh News and Observer, June 5, 1945, reported that a black man was sentenced to two years on the chain gang for "assault on a female" and "forcible trespass" for making "improper advances" to a white woman over the telephone. The man was accused of trying to persuade a white woman to go on a date with him.
44. War Department memo, "Subject: Commingling of Whites and Negroes at Chapel Hill, N.C.," August 19, 1944, Roosevelt Papers. I am grateful to Christina Greene for sharing these and other documents.
45. Wynn, The Afro-American and the Second World War, 96.

46. David L. Cohn, "How the South Feels," *Atlantic Monthly*, January 1944, 50.

47. Egerton, *Speak Now against the Day*, 324. See also MacGregor, *Integration of the Armed Forces*, 22–23.

48. J. Melville Broughton to Margaret McCulloch, October 2, 1943, box 82, Broughton Papers.

49. J. Melville Broughton, "John Merrick: Pioneer and Builder," text of a speech given in Wilmington, North Carolina, July 11, 1943, ibid., 3.

50. Logan, *What the Negro Wants*, 329.

51. Ibid., 66–69, 233. Logan argues on p. 28 that "mixed schools, mixed employment, even social mingling in the more liberal parts of the United States have resulted in very few mixed marriages." F. D. Patterson states on p. 260 that "the argument that the common use of restaurants and public facilities by Negroes and whites will lead inevitably to race admixture has much evidence to the contrary." Langston Hughes, on p. 306, exclaims, "Why [white Southerners] think simple civil rights would force a Southerner's daughter to marry a Negro in spite of herself, I have never been able to understand." Sterling Brown, on page 326, states flatly that "Negroes have long recognized [the sexual issue] as the hub of the argument opposing change in their status," but assures white readers that "intermarriage is hardly a goal that Negroes are contending for openly or yearning for secretly."

52. Rev. B. W. Moneur, pastor of the local AME Zion Church, quoted in *Monroe Journal*, January 8, 1943.

53. James E. Shepard, "Race Relationships in North Carolina," February 17, 1944, box 82, Broughton Papers. In an interesting response to the broadcast, sociologist E. Franklin Frazier of Howard University wrote to Shepard and accused him of supporting "the ignorant and barbarous elements of the South" by "engaging in the old game of southern Negro leaders who have pretended that the Negro feels and believes that he is different from other people and is, therefore, unfit to associate with whites. . . . I believe in *Social Equality*." See E. Franklin Frazier to James E. Shepard, February 19, 1944, ibid.

54. Crow, Escott, and Hatley, *History of African Americans in North Carolina*, 147.

55. Robert F. Williams, interview with Cohen, 37. Again, here Williams's experience is typical; according to Franklin, *From Slavery to Freedom*, 438, more than 58,000 African Americans were enrolled in similar pre-employment courses by December 1942.

56. RFW/FBI, a brief account of the clash at the NYA camp marks the first entry in the file; Robert F. Williams, interview with Banchero. My thanks to Stephanie Banchero for sharing this and other documents with me. Williams's own recollections roughly correspond to the account that opens his FBI subject file.

57. Robert F. Williams, interview with Cohen, 38.

58. Wynn, *The Afro-American and the Second World War*, 29.

59. Stanley Winborne to J. Melville Broughton, June 17, 1943, box 82, Broughton Papers; chap. 147, section 3537, *Laws of the State of North Carolina*.

60. Motley, *Invisible Soldier*, 320–21.

61. Stanley Winborne to J. Melville Broughton, June 17, 1943, box 82, Broughton Papers; *Oxford Public Ledger*, May 2, 5, 1944, in Hays Collection, 22:139.

62. Jean B. Anderson, *Durham County*, 254; *Durham Morning Herald*, April 4, 1943;

Carolina Times, April 10, 1943; Stanley Winborne to J. Melville Broughton, June 17, 1943, box 82, Broughton Papers.

63. Robert F. Williams, "While God Lay Sleeping," 35.

64. Robert F. Williams, interview with Cohen, 44, 552–53; John Herman Williams, interview with Banchero, ca. 1995. For Hughes's poem, "Beaumont to Detroit, 1943," see *Common Ground*, Fall 1943, 104. On Conant Gardens, see Thomas J. Sugrue, *Origins of the Urban Crisis: Race and Inequality in Postwar Detroit* (Princeton: Princeton University Press, 1996), 41.

65. Payne, *I've Got the Light of Freedom*, 79–81.

66. Hill, RACON, 115, 117. See also Capeci, *Detroit and the "Good War,"* 70.

67. Hill, RACON, 120, 122, 132.

68. Robert F. Williams, interview with Cohen, 165, 552–53.

69. Sitkoff, "Racial Militancy and Interracial Violence," 673; Hill, RACON, 131.

70. Shogan and Craig, *Detroit Race Riot*, 34–35.

71. Robert F. Williams, interview with Cohen, 44; for a full account of what happened at Belle Isle that day, see Shogan and Craig, *Detroit Race Riot*, 34–43. See also Capeci and Wilkerson, *Layered Violence*.

72. Robert F. Williams, interview with Cohen, 44–45; Edward Williams, interview.

73. Shogan and Craig, *Detroit Race Riot*, 40.

74. Robert F. Williams, interview with Cohen, 44–45. Williams's account of what happened on the Jefferson Street bridge from Belle Isle meshes perfectly with other historical accounts. See, for example, Shogan and Craig, *Detroit Race Riot*, 39, 41; see also Capeci and Wilkerson, *Layered Violence*, 4–6.

75. Shogan and Craig, *Detroit Race Riot*, 43; Capeci and Wilkerson, *Layered Violence*, 87, 90. An excellent short account of the Detroit riot of 1943 may be found in Shapiro, *White Violence and Black Response*, 311–30, 337.

76. Broussard, *Black San Francisco*, 134.

77. Robert F. Williams, "While God Lay Sleeping," 36; Robert F. Williams, interview with Cohen, 41.

78. Robert F. Williams, "While God Lay Sleeping," 39; Robert F. Williams, interview with Cohen, 74.

79. Robert F. Williams, "While God Lay Sleeping," 40.

80. *Monroe Journal*, August 6, 1943.

81. *Monroe Enquirer*, December 24, 1942. According to *Population and Economy of Monroe, North Carolina*, table 14, p. 47, the war appeared to mark a historic watershed for women's labor; in the decade between 1940 and 1950, the percentage of Union County women employed outside the home increased by 73.5 percent, a rate of increase that slowed to only 59.9 from 1950 to 1960.

82. Robert F. Williams, "While God Lay Sleeping," 40; *Monroe Enquirer*, July 28, 1960; Robert F. Williams, interview with author, September 2, 1996.

83. *Monroe Enquirer*, March 5, 1943.

84. Walden, "History of Monroe and Union County," 68.

85. Shute, interview with Durrill, 48. See also *Monroe Enquirer*, October 19, 1942. The explosive inflation of the housing market, in fact, tempted local landlords to evict old tenants and take in new ones at more than twice the rent, a common violation of Office of Price Administration guidelines in Monroe. See *Monroe Enquirer*, December 17, 1942.

86. *Monroe Enquirer*, December 21, October 29, 1942.

87. "Camp Sutton, N.C. Racial Tensions," Daniels Papers, 1–2.

88. *Monroe Journal*, August 3, 1943.

89. "Camp Sutton, N.C. Racial Tensions," Daniels Papers, 1–2; Robert F. Williams, "While God Lay Sleeping," 40–41.

90. "Camp Sutton, N.C. Racial Tensions," Daniels Papers, 2.

91. Robert F. Williams, "While God Lay Sleeping," 42–49.

92. Union County, Record of Military Discharges, 7:97; Robert F. Williams, interview with Cohen, 75–76.

93. Robert F. Williams, "While God Lay Sleeping," 49–50.

94. Ibid., 51; Robert F. Williams, interview with Cohen, 129–30, 91–96. A poster of this description may be found in Dower, *War without Mercy*, 189.

95. Robert F. Williams, interview with Cohen, 169–72.

96. Robert F. Williams, "While God Lay Sleeping," 55; Robert F. Williams, interview with Cohen, 174, 127.

97. Union County, Record of Military Discharges, 7:99; memorandum, August 8, 1961, RFW/FBI.

98. Captain Grant Reynolds, quoted in the *Pittsburgh Courier*, July 22, 1944.

99. O. E. Clanton to J. Melville Broughton, September 1944, box 82, Broughton Papers.

100. Robert F. Williams, interview with Mosby, 18; Dittmer, *Local People*, 1–9.

CHAPTER THREE

1. Robert F. Williams, interview with Cohen, 143–45; *Monroe Enquirer*, June 31, 1946, and March 31, 1947; Barksdale, "Indigenous Civil Rights Movement," 42–43; McDow, interview.

2. McDow, interview; Woodrow Wilson, interview; Winfield, interview with Barksdale; Robert F. Williams, interview with Mosby.

3. Moon, *Balance of Power*, 237–44.

4. David Levering Lewis, "The Origins and Causes of the Civil Rights Movement," in Charles W. Eagles, *Civil Rights Movement in America*, 6.

5. Kluger, *Simple Justice*, 234–37.

6. Egerton, *Speak Now against the Day*, 573, 380; Juan Williams, *Thurgood Marshall*, 112.

7. Lawson, *Black Ballots*, 103, 107, 340.

8. "Progress Report on the Employment of Colored Persons in the Department of State," March 31, 1953, U.S. Department of State, in box A617, group 2, NAACP Papers. See Carol Elaine Anderson, "Eyes Off the Prize," esp. 1–55.

9. Dudziak, "Desegregation as a Cold War Imperative," 95; White, *A Man Called White*, 358–59.

10. Deton J. Brooks Jr. to W. E. B. Du Bois, October 13, 1947, box A637, group 2, NAACP Papers.

11. *To Secure These Rights*, 147.

12. Dudziak, "Desegregation as a Cold War Imperative," 111–12.

13. *Southern Patriot* 12, no. 3 (February 1954): 4.

14. Woodward, *Strange Career of Jim Crow*, 132.
15. *New York Times*, May 14, 1958.
16. Robert F. Williams, interview with Cohen, 191.
17. Sullivan, *Days of Hope*, 197; Egerton, *Speak Now against the Day*, 361–62. The exact number—as many as five—was in dispute because of Public Safety Commissioner Eugene "Bull" Connor's control over information.
18. Dittmer, *Local People*, 1–2; see also Payne, *I've Got the Light of Freedom*, 47.
19. Sullivan, *Days of Hope*, 202.
20. Dittmer, *Local People*, 1–9; see also Egerton, *Speak Now against the Day*, 598.
21. Sullivan, *Days of Hope*, 213.
22. Egerton, *Speak Now against the Day*, 366–69.
23. Ibid., 373–74; Sullivan, *Days of Hope*, 219–20.
24. Barksdale, "Indigenous Civil Rights Movement," 47–48; Robert F. Williams, "While God Lay Sleeping," 64.
25. Robert F. Williams, "While God Lay Sleeping," 64–65; Robert F. Williams, interview with Cohen, 98.
26. Mabel R. Williams, interview with Salaam.
27. Robert F. Williams, interview with Cohen, 147–50; Mabel R. Williams, interview with Salaam.
28. Mabel R. Williams, interview with Salaam; Mabel R. Williams, interview with author, July 24, 1997; memo to Director FBI, March 27, 1972, RFW/FBI.
29. Robert F. Williams, interview with Cohen, 147–50; Mabel R. Williams, interview with Salaam; memo to Director FBI, March 27, 1972, RFW/FBI. The FBI file gives the date of the marriage as June 20, 1947, but both Mabel and Robert Williams report it as June 19, which seems more reliable.
30. Cohen, *Black Crusader*, 48.
31. Mabel R. Williams, interview with Salaam.
32. Ibid.
33. Barksdale, "Indigenous Civil Rights Movement," 46–47; *Monroe Enquirer*, July 18, 1946; Rorie, interview with Barksdale.
34. Barksdale, "Indigenous Civil Rights Movement," 39–40.
35. Myers, "When Violence Met Violence," 11; Robert F. Williams, interview with Mosby.
36. Barksdale, "Indigenous Civil Rights Movement," 51–52; Belton, interview with Barksdale. Barksdale makes the excellent point that, unlike eastern North Carolina and the Deep South, Union County did not have enough black citizens to threaten the established political order in a fundamental way and hence did not face extreme opposition. Nonetheless, this expansion of the black electorate does serve as an indication of rising independent black political activity in the postwar era.
37. Kendrick, interview.
38. *News and Observer*, August 3, 1946; Wade, *Fiery Cross*, 276–77.
39. See Glenda Elizabeth Gilmore, "Murder, Memory, and the Flight of the Incubus," in Cecelski and Tyson, *Democracy Betrayed*, 73–93.
40. J. B. Benton, "Criminal Attacks Feature Biggest Local News of Week," *Review*, clipping in box 67, Cherry Papers. For examples of letters from white citizens that demonstrate these fears, see C. C. Stone to Governor Cherry, June 12, 1947; "Dear Gov." from "White Folks," n.d.; Mrs. R. P. Barber to Governor Cherry, May 29,

1947; Mrs. Robert B. Outland to Governor Cherry, June 4, 1947; Mr. and Mrs. J. H. Whitehurst to Governor Cherry, June 12, 1947; anonymous to Governor Cherry, March 1, 1948; David D. Markham Jr., Arvin V. Thornburg, and N. H. Godwin to Governor Cherry, June 5, 1947, all in ibid., with many similar letters.

41. Mr. and Mrs. J. H. Whitehurst to Governor Cherry, June 12, 1947, ibid.

42. Mrs. Frank Outland to Governor Cherry, n.d., also published in the *Murfreesboro News*, June 3, 1947, letter and clipping in box 67, Cherry Papers.

43. Mrs. R. P. Baker to Governor Cherry, May 29, 1947, box 67, Cherry Papers.

44. Mrs. Robert B. Outland, June 4, 1947, ibid.

45. Franklin H. Williams to Thurgood Marshall, February 10, 1948, box A406, group 2, NAACP Papers.

46. Walter White, "Lynchers of Law," May 23, 1947, box A406, ibid.

47. Leslie S. Perry to Roy Wilkins, May 23, 1947, box A64, ibid.

48. Lester Jones, "Special Report," May 26, 1947, box 67, Cherry Papers.

49. *To Secure These Rights*, 23, 100, 147–48.

50. Burran, "Racial Violence in the South," 275.

51. Gavins, "NAACP in North Carolina," 112.

52. John Powell, "The Klan Un-Klandestine," *Nation*, September 29, 1951, 254–56; *Time*, February 25, 1952, 28, and August 11, 1952, 21; Wade, *Fiery Cross*, 290–91.

53. Robert F. Williams, interview with Cohen, 552–53, 152–53, 176, 157, 165.

54. *Daily Worker* (Detroit ed.), April 9, 1949.

55. Mabel R. Williams, interview with Salaam.

56. Robert F. Williams, interview with Cohen, 157; Mabel R. Williams, interview with author, July 24, 1997.

57. Memorandum, May 7, 1959, RFW/FBI.

58. Freeland, *Truman Doctrine*. See also Robert Griffith, "American Politics and the Origins of 'McCarthyism,' " in Griffith and Theoharis, *The Spectre*, 16, and Athan Theoharis, "Truman and the Red Scare," in Thomas Reeves, *McCarthyism*, 77–87.

59. Athan Theoharis, "The Politics of Scholarship: Liberals, Anti-Communism, and McCarthyism," in Griffith and Theoharis, *The Spectre*, 278.

60. Sullivan, *Days of Hope*, 260–63; *Monroe Journal*, July 26, 1949.

61. Robert F. Williams, interview with Cohen, 160.

62. Branch, *Parting the Waters*, 209–10.

63. Caute, *Great Fear*, 168. An excellent recent work on domestic anticommunism during the 1940s and 1950s is Schrecker, *Many Are the Crimes*.

64. Robert F. Williams, interview with Cohen, 158, 179.

65. Robert F. Williams, "While God Lay Sleeping," 66.

66. Robert F. Williams, interview with Cohen, 194–95. For extensive information on Professor Herman George Canady, see G. James Fleming and Christian E. Burckel, eds., *Who's Who in Colored America: An Illustrated Biographical Directory of Notable Living Persons of African Descent in the United States*, 7th ed. (Yonkers-on-Hudson, N.Y.: Christian E. Burckel and Associates, 1950). See also "Biographical Notes on Herman G. Canady, Professor and Head of the Department of Psychology," Drain-Jordan Library, West Virginia State University, Institute, W.Va.

67. Robert F. Williams, "N. Carolina College Youth Calls for a Militant Student Generation," *Freedom* 2, no. 6 (June 1952): 5; West Virginia State College, *Quill* 1, no. 5 (May 1950): 4–5.

68. Robert F. Williams, interview with Cohen, 200; Robert F. Williams, "While God Lay Sleeping," 69.

69. Egerton, *Speak Now against the Day*, 557–60. For a sensitive and intelligent auto-biographical account, see Scales and Nickson, *Cause at Heart*.

70. Robert F. Williams, interview with Cohen, 204–5.

71. Pleasants and Burns, *Frank Porter Graham and the 1950 Senate Race*; the quote is from p. 270. See also Egerton, *Speak Now against the Day*, 511, 531; *Monroe Enquirer* June 2, 1955. The quote from Louis Austin is from his editorial in the *Carolina Times*, July 1, 1950.

72. Robert F. Williams, "N. Carolina College Youth Calls for a Militant Student Generation," *Freedom* 2, no. 6 (June 1952): 5; Robert F. Williams, interview with Cohen, 207.

73. Robert F. Williams, "While God Lay Sleeping," 69.

74. See *Caswell Messenger*, June 7, July 19, November 22, 1951; Robert L. Carter to North Carolina State Conference of Branches, January 9, 1952, and to Kelly M. Alexander, March 18, 1953, box 6, Kelly Alexander Papers; *Crusader* 9, no. 3 (December 1967): 2.

75. Robert F. Williams, "N. Carolina College Youth Calls for a Militant Student Generation," *Freedom* 2, no. 6 (June 1952): 5.

76. U.S. Senate, *Testimony of Robert F. Williams*, pt. 3, 211–12. The poems from Hughes are designated as "exhibit no. 43." The originals may be found in the Robert F. Williams Papers.

77. Robert F. Williams, "Go Awaken My People," *Militant* 17, no. 15 (April 13, 1953), copy in box 2, Committee to Combat Racial Injustice Papers (hereafter cited as CCRI Papers); Robert F. Williams, interview with Cohen, 207.

78. Robert F. Williams, interview with Cohen, 214–30; Mabel R. Williams, interview with Salaam. For the Jefferson School and others like it, see Caute, *Great Fear*, 174–75. According to Caute, the institutions were "nominally autonomous" but "in practice rigorously controlled by the Party." Founded in 1944, the Jefferson School enrolled more than 45,000 students from 1944 to 1948, but it soon came under serious pressure from the FBI and the Subversive Activities Control Board and closed in 1955. Though it is impossible to trace Robert Williams through school records—the Jefferson School deliberately stopped maintaining records of its students the year Williams attended—Williams told FBI agents in 1955 that he had only attended class at Jefferson one evening, found the instruction "inferior," and never went back. The rest of his several accounts over time support this contention.

79. RFW/FBI; Robert F. Williams, interview with Cohen, 237–41.

80. Robert F. Williams, "While God Lay Sleeping," 71; Robert F. Williams, interview with Cohen, 237–41.

81. Robert F. Williams, "While God Lay Sleeping," 71–88; Robert F. Williams, interview with Banchero, 19; U.S. Naval Intelligence, San Diego, Calif., Investigation Report, "21 Jan–28 April 1955, Intermittently," RFW/FBI; Robert F. Williams, interview with Mosby; Robert F. Williams, interview with Cohen, 242–64; John Herman Williams, interview with Banchero, [February 1995]; John Herman Williams, interview with author, June 7, 1998.

82. Carson et al., *Eyes on the Prize Civil Rights Reader*, 36; *Southern Patriot* 18, no. 11 (January 1960): 3.

83. Carson et al., *Eyes on the Prize Civil Rights Reader*, 36; Egerton, *Speak Now against the Day*, 609–10.

84. *Monroe Enquirer*, June 23, 1955, August 13, 1956; I. Beverly Lake, "Gradual Integration in North Carolina," TV editorial transcript, WRAL-TV, Raleigh, September 20, 1957, box 1, London Collection.

85. Davidson, *Best of Enemies*, 83–84; Luther H. Hodges to Bignall Jones, Record Publishing and Supply Company, Warrenton, N.C., May 5, 1955, box 21, Hodges Papers.

86. Luther H. Hodges, "Radio and TV Address," August 8, 1955, box 39, Hodges Papers.

87. *Monroe Enquirer*, August 18, 1955; Paul Green to Harry Golden, August 21, 1955, box 24, series 2.1, Golden Papers.

88. Chafe, *Civilities and Civil Rights*, 51–60; Douglas, *Reading, Writing, and Race*, 32–33.

89. Southern Regional Council, "Report on Charlotte, Greensboro, and Winston-Salem, North Carolina," September 4, 1957, box A105, group 3, NAACP Papers.

90. *Charlotte Observer*, August 16, 1956; *Monroe Enquirer*, August 13, 1956; "Ku Klux Klan Revival," [1957], box 131, Fred Alexander Papers, 3.

91. *Monroe Enquirer*, September 8, 1955.

92. Chafe, *Civilities and Civil Rights*, 54–60; Douglas, *Reading, Writing, and Race*, 26, 44–45.

93. Stack and Beasley, *Monroe and Union County*, 94–97; Shute, interview with Durrill; *Monroe Enquirer*, August 18, 1955.

94. See, for example, *Charlotte News*, June 20, 1954. Williams wrote, "How is it that a nation that professes to be democratic and flashes its constitution before the world to prove it, searches out its aristocracy for candidates less likely to uphold its democratic constitution and the human dignity of its people?"

95. Robert F. Williams, interview with Cohen, 111–14; Robert F. Williams, interview with Banchero, 24–26. Sometimes Shute was credited with the letters; sometimes white citizens blamed far-flung conspiracies. See, for example, John Briggs to Bill Sharpe, cc to Luther Hodges, February 23, 1959, box 423, Hodges Papers: Briggs, investigating Williams on behalf of Governor Hodges, refers to Williams as "Monroe NAACP head and prolific author of 'Letters to the Editor' which local citizens acquainted with Williams literary style suggest are ghostwritten out of town."

96. FBI teletype, October 11, 1956, RFW/FBI; Robert F. Williams, "While God Lay Sleeping," 89. For the FBI's role in creating such blacklists, see Schrecker, *Many Are the Crimes*, 211.

97. Myers, "When Violence Met Violence," 17; Robert F. Williams interview with Banchero, 24.

98. Robert F. Williams, interview with Cohen, 112–13; Robert F. Williams, "Col. Jim Crow's Last Stand: Sermon Delivered at All Souls Chapel Unitarian Fellowship, Monroe NC," March 25, 1956, box 3, Robert F. Williams Papers.

99. Myers, "When Violence Met Violence," 61–62.

100. Lott T. Rogers, City Manager, "Memorandum: For Personnel File, Subject: First Colored Policeman," June 27, 1955, Union County Courthouse, Monroe, N.C.; *Monroe Enquirer*, June 23, 1955; Gray, interview.

101. *Monroe Enquirer*, December 22, 1958; Myers, "When Violence Met Violence," 14–15; Rorie, interview with Banchero.

102. *Monroe Enquirer*, September 10, 1956, reported that the Ku Klux Klan "is becoming active in this area." Anti-Defamation League of B'Nai B'Rith, "The North Carolina Ku Klux Klan Revival," [1957], box 131, Fred Alexander Papers, dates the Klan upsurge from an October 19, 1956, rally at Shannon, North Carolina, and indicates that the majority of subsequent rallies have been near Monroe; one, near Salisbury, was attended by 6,000 whites. The Charleston *News and Courier*, September 21, 1956, reported that a Klan rally near Union, South Carolina—not far from Monroe—drew between 12,000 and 15,000 participants. For information on James "Catfish" Cole, see Cole Papers.

103. Henry Lee Moon to Roy Wilkins, November 29, 1957, box A92, group 3, NAACP Papers; *Southern Patriot* 15, no. 1 (January 1957): 1.

104. Charles McLean to Gloster Current, November 30, 1953, NAACP State Correspondence, 1953, Kelly Alexander Papers; Belton, interview with Banchero; Rushing, interview with Banchero; Robert F. Williams, interview with Cohen, 270–79; Robert F. Williams, interview with Mosby.

105. McDow, interview; Winfield, interview with Barksdale; Woodrow Wilson, interview; Byrd, interview.

106. Robert F. Williams, interview with Mosby; Robert F. Williams, interview with Cohen, 278–79; Robert F. Williams, *Negroes with Guns*, 51.

107. Robert F. Williams to NAACP, March 11, 1957, box 113A, group 3, NAACP Papers.

108. Robert F. Williams, "While God Lay Sleeping," 92.

109. Cherry, interview; see also Stephanie Banchero's excellent article, "Robert F. Williams: Hero or Renegade?" *Charlotte Observer*, February 25, 1995; Mabel R. Williams, interview with Braden.

110. Robert F. Williams, *Negroes with Guns*, 51; Robert F. Williams, interview with Banchero, 20; Mayfield, "Challenge to Negro Leadership," 298.

111. "Total Memberships Received from Branches in North Carolina," October 31, 1959, 2, box C113, and typescript of telephone conversation between Conrad Lynn and Charles A. McLean, June 16, 1959, box A333, both in group 3, NAACP Papers; Robert F. Williams, interview with Mosby; *Monroe Enquirer*, February 6, 1958.

112. Dr. A. E. Perry, Union County Council on Human Relations, to "Dear Fellow Citizen," April 11, 1957, Banchero Papers; *Monroe Journal*, clipping, n.d. [February 1956], box 26, Boyte Family Papers; Harry Golden to Burton Wolfe, August 30, 1961, Robert Williams File, Golden Papers.

113. Dr. A. E. Perry, "To the Parks and Recreation Committee," July 19, 1957, Banchero Papers; "Minutes of the Board of Aldermen," printed in *Monroe Enquirer*, October 14, 1935; "Visit Monroe–Union County." Dr. Perry did not exaggerate in his claim that drownings of black children were routine. For a sample of reports of drowning deaths among African American children in the area, see *Monroe Enquirer*, June 18, 21, 1951, June 21, 1956, March 27, 1961; *Jet*, October 31, 1957, 10–12; *Charlotte Observer*, May 11, 26, July 19, 24, 31, 1958. These reports, which by no means constitute a comprehensive study, represent the deaths of a dozen black children, most of which occurred within a two-year period.

114. Dr. A. E. Perry to Parks and Recreation Commission, Monroe, N.C., July 23, 1957, Banchero Papers.

115. Mabel R. Williams, interview with author, March 10, 1993; Dr. A. E. Perry, J. W. McDow, Matthew Williams, W. B. Nivens, "A Report," July 1957, Banchero Papers.

116. Robert F. Williams statement, June 26, 1969, typescript in RFW/FBI; *Crusader* 1, no. 2 (July 4, 1959): 2; Dr. A. E. Perry, J. W. McDow, Matthew Williams, W. B. Nivens, "A Report," July 1957, and Jack Elam, city attorney, Greensboro, N.C., to J. E. Hinkel, city manager, Monroe, N.C., November 28, 1960, Banchero Papers.

117. *Monroe Enquirer*, December 30, 1957; Robert F. Williams, *Negroes with Guns*, 53; Robert F. Williams, interview with Mosby; Robert Williams statement, June 11, 1961, typescript in RFW/FBI; Robert F. Williams to Kelly Alexander, July 31, 1957, Kelly Alexander Papers.

118. Harry Golden, "Monroe, North Carolina, and the 'Kissing Case,'" *Carolina Israelite*, January–February 1959, 2, and January 1955, 9; Harry Golden to Kelly Alexander, December 18, 1958, box A92, group 3, NAACP Papers.

119. *Monroe Enquirer*, November 11, 1957, clipping in box C113, group 3, NAACP Papers.

120. Southern Regional Council, "Report on Charlotte, Greensboro, and Winston-Salem, North Carolina," September 4, 1957, box A105, ibid., 11. The report concludes that textile unemployment in the area near Monroe "may be of great significance in the event that interracial tensions are precipitated."

121. Southern Regional Council, "North Carolina Ku Klux Klan Revival," appendix, 1957, box 131, Fred Alexander Papers, 4. For Chief Mauney's admission that he led Klan caravans in his squad car, see *Charlotte Observer*, May 12, 1959; see also *Norfolk Journal and Guide*, October 12, 1957.

122. *Southern Patriot* 18, no. 11 (January 1960): 3.

123. Harry G. Boyte to Truman Nelson, August 23, 1962, box 26, Boyte Family Papers.

124. Robert F. Williams, interview with Cohen, 50. See also Harry Golden to Burton Wolfe, August 30, 1961, Robert Williams File, Golden Papers.

125. Robert F. Williams, interview with Cohen, 273–74; Mabel Williams, "Looking Back," *Crusader* 1, no. 9 (August 22, 1959): 5.

126. Union County Memorial Hospital Staff to Dr. Joseph J. Combs, North Carolina Board of Medical Examiners, October 7, 1961, box 111, Sanford Papers.

127. *Monroe Enquirer*, September 1, 1955; *Jet*, October 31, 1957, 13–14; Robert F. Williams, interview with Cohen, 54–55.

128. Winfield, interview with Barksdale.

129. Robert F. Williams, interview with Cohen, 288–89.

130. Robert F. Williams, *Negroes with Guns*, 51; Robert F. Williams, interview with Mosby; Mabel R. Williams, interview with Banchero, 2.

131. *Norfolk Journal and Guide*, October 12, 1957; Winfield, interview with Barksdale; McDow, interview; Woodrow Wilson, interview; Robert F. Williams, *Negroes with Guns*, 57; Robert F. Williams, "While God Lay Sleeping," 104. For other accounts of the shootout, see Barksdale, "Indigenous Civil Rights Movement," 135–37; see also Myers, "When Violence Met Violence," 20.

132. "Outlaw A Menace," *Monroe Journal*, October 6, 1957; Article III, "Parades, Cavalcades, and Caravans," passed October 7, 1957, in *Code of the City of Monroe*, 473–75.

133. Winfield, interview with Barksdale; Banchero, "Native Son Wants to Come Home," 5.

CHAPTER FOUR

1. Robert L. Carter to Roy Wilkins, January 30, 1959, box A333, group 3, NAACP Papers, 1–2; "State's Witness Tells of Abortion," *Charlotte News*, n.d., clipping in box 26, Boyte Family Papers; *Monroe Enquirer*, December 1, 1958.
2. *Monroe Enquirer*, December 1, 1958; Forman, *Making of Black Revolutionaries*, 168.
3. Dr. Albert E. Perry Jr. to Roy Wilkins, January 14, 1959, box A92, group 3, NAACP Papers.
4. Winfield, interview with Barksdale; Robert F. Williams, interview with Mosby, 18.
5. *Crusader* 2, no. 8 (September 3, 1960): 3.
6. Robert F. Williams, interview with Mosby.
7. "Is North Carolina Leader a Marked Man?," *Jet*, October 31, 1957, 10–11.
8. Chester Davis, "Press in North Gives Distorted Versions"; *News and Observer*, November 11, 1958; *Monroe Enquirer*, December 1, 1958; Luther H. Hodges to Charles Pemberton, December 2, 1958, box 423, Hodges Papers. An administrative assistant to the governor told a critic that "the two Negro boys in question were charged with, and proved, molesting a young girl." See Robert E. Giles to Jerome Tannenbaum, November 20, 1958, box 423, Hodges Papers.
9. *Carolina Times*, December 20, 27, 1958.
10. J. Hampton Price to Luther H. Hodges, November 26, 1958, box 423, Hodges Papers; Roy Wilkins, "Memorandum To: NAACP Branch Presidents RE: North Carolina 'Kissing Case,'" January 16, 1959, 1, box C113, and Gloster B. Current to Roy Wilkins, December 23, 1958, box A92, both in group 3, NAACP Papers; James Hanover Grissom Thompson, interview; ; Weissman, "Kissing Case," 47; *Carolina Times*, January 10, 1959; *News and Observer*, January 1, 1959; *Time*, January 26, 1959, 22; *Charlotte Observer*, January 12, 1959.
11. Even the ages of the children changed from story to story in predictable patterns; accounts hostile to the boys often made them older and the "victim" younger, while in friendly accounts the gap between the children's ages sometimes narrowed.
12. Weissman, "Kissing Case," 47.
13. Quoted in Whitfield, *Death in the Delta*, 11.
14. John Dollard's classic, *Caste and Class in a Southern Town*, 134–72, defines this arrangement as part of the "sexual gain" for white men. It is not surprising that scholarship in the field in the six decades since has passed Dollard, but his analysis is still remarkably sophisticated.
15. For example, Arthur Miller, a twenty-one-year-old African American man accused of raping a seventeen-year-old black woman, was sentenced to ninety days for "assault on a female" and immediately became Mecklenburg County's first work release prisoner. See *Charlotte Observer*, May 16, 1958, and November 19, 1959. When black attorney James Walker entered the voting registrar's office in Halifax County, North Carolina, and allegedly shook his finger at the white woman registrar as he insisted that she permit Louise Lassiter, an African American woman, to register to vote, he also was charged with "assault on a female." Attorney Walker served considerably more time in jail for allegedly pointing his finger at a white woman than did Miller, the alleged rapist of a black teenager. See *Southern Patriot* 15, no. 4 (April 1957): 4, and 17, no. 2 (February 1959): 2.

16. Jacquelyn Dowd Hall, "Mind That Burns in Each Body," 64; Jacquelyn Dowd Hall, *Revolt against Chivalry*, 155.
17. Wendell Berry, *Hidden Wound*, 58–61.
18. Weissman, "Kissing Case," 47.
19. Gloster B. Current to Roy Wilkins, December 23, 1958, box A92, group 3, NAACP Papers; *Charlotte Observer*, January 12, 1959; *Carolina Times*, January 10, 1959; *Monroe Enquirer*, November 20, 1958; Evelyn Thompson, interview, 9–10.
20. *Charlotte Observer*, January 12, 1959. Although Mayor Fred Wilson denied that he had heard about a possible lynching, he said in the next breath that he thought that the boys should not be where the girl's parent could reach them.
21. James Hanover Grissom Thompson, interview, 11–12; *Southern Patriot* 17, no. 1 (January 1959): 3.
22. James Hanover Grissom Thompson, interview; Evelyn Thompson, interview, 2–3, 9–10; J. Hampton Price to Luther H. Hodges, November 26, 1958, box 423, Hodges Papers.
23. Conrad Lynn, "Attorney Bares Real Inside Story of N.C. Kissing Case," *Chicago Defender*, January 17, 1959.
24. Robert F. Williams to George Weissman, December 17, 1959, box 1, CCRI Papers; Chester Davis, "Communist Front Shouts 'Kissing Case' to World"; Writ of Habeas Corpus and Petition, Superior Court, Mecklenburg County, N.C., January 6, 1959, In the Matter of James Hanover Thompson and David Ezell Simpson, Case Nos. 192 and 193, Mola Papers; James Hanover Grissom Thompson, interview, 13–15.
25. *Monroe Enquirer*, November 20, 1958; Cohen, *Black Crusader*, 111–12; Gloster Current to Roy Wilkins, December 23, 1958, box A92, group 3, NAACP Papers; Robert F. Williams, interview with author, May 13, 1993.
26. *Monroe Enquirer*, November 20, 1958, quotes extensively from the *New York Post* article by Ted Poston; see also Weissman, "Kissing Case," 47; "Transcript of Statements Made by Attorney Conrad Lynn during interview on the 'Frank Ford Show,' Radio Station WPEN, Philadelphia, Pennsylvania, on June 20, 1959, from 12:40 until 1:35 A.M.," box A92, group 3, NAACP Papers.
27. *Carolina Times*, February 7, 1959. About a year earlier, for example, police officers in Statesville, North Carolina, a small town sixty miles north of Monroe, had stopped a carload of young people at 2:30 on the morning of November 13, 1957. Inside they found Judith and Martha Lamberth, white teenaged sisters, and two twenty-year-old black men. At eight o'clock the following evening, Statesville's chief of police escorted the entire Lamberth family to the county line only minutes before a mob of some 600 white citizens, some in Klan robes, descended upon the Lamberth home. Screaming angry taunts, the furious mob smashed the windows of the house and torched a large cross in the front yard. Although there were police officers present, they did not arrest anyone in the mob. In downtown Statesville, however, police arrested fourteen African Americans for disorderly conduct that night because they were "shouting insulting remarks," and they arrested another black man for carrying a concealed weapon. The community hovered on the edge of racial cataclysm; black and white ministers broadcast appeals for peace over the local radio station, while Klan motorcades patrolled the streets. Police officials told reporters that the Lamberth family had "decided to move away" from States-

ville. See *New York Times*, November 17, 1957; *News and Observer*, November 17, December 5, 1957; *Statesville Record and Landmark*, November 14, 16, 18, 25, December 3, 11, 1957.

For black men, the price for crossing the color line in matters of the heart could be considerably higher than mere banishment. In Williamston, North Carolina, an agricultural community similar to Monroe, Joseph Cross, a twenty-one-year-old junior at all-black North Carolina Agricultural and Technical College in Greensboro, had returned home to see his parents on September 7, 1957, and was leaving the following day for fall term. According to Sheriff Raymond Rawls, Polly Roberson, a local white waitress, complained that Cross asked her for a date over the telephone. What happened next remains a matter of dispute. Willis Williams, a local black man, swore that Sheriff Rawls and several deputies had kidnapped Joe Cross from his front yard.

According to the white sheriff, however, he had instructed the waitress to arrange a meeting with Cross in order to "set a trap." Hiding in the back seat of Roberson's car, he claimed, Sheriff Rawls and his deputy, Dallas Holiday, accompanied the waitress to the rendezvous on a dirt road at the edge of town. When Cross stepped from his vehicle, the sheriff and his deputy jumped out of Roberson's car with guns drawn. Holiday testified that he shot Cross in self-defense after the young man drew a knife. Even Holiday admitted that there had been no knife—the deputy speculated in court that it may have been the gleam of a belt buckle that he mistook for a knife blade. In any event, whether Cross had been lured to the country road by subterfuge or dragged there by force, the deputy shot the unarmed black man four times, killing him. Local rumor held that the two men then castrated the body. A jury comprised entirely of white men from the community acquitted Deputy Holiday of murder in less than fifteen minutes. The judge prohibited protest of the verdict, threatening to jail anyone who participated in any "demonstrations in this courtroom, in this courthouse, or on the streets." See David Carter, "New Inheritance." See also *News and Observer*, December 11, 1957; *Carolina Times*, December 14, 1957.

While bizarre, the Williamston incident was not unique in the South in the 1950s. Gus Foster, a seventeen-year-old African American man in Montgomery, Alabama, telephoned a white woman to ask her for a date in the summer of 1958. While the woman kept Foster on the line, local police traced the call to a telephone booth outside a drive-in. A carload of white officers rushed to the telephone booth and shot Foster several times, killing him. A local judge ruled the killing justifiable homicide. See *Charlotte Observer*, August 29, 1958.

28. Cash, *Mind of the South*, 119.

29. " 'Rape . . . The States': Civil Rights Report Inspires Complaint," *Charlotte Observer*, September 5, 1959; Egerton, *Speak Now against the Day*, 477.

30. Lilla Bull, letter to the editor, *Charlotte Observer*, July 10, 1959.

31. Angela Davis, "Racism and Contemporary Literature on Rape." The Austin quote is from *Carolina Times*, May 9, 1959. In Burlington, North Carolina, in the spring of 1959, Jesse Graves, an African American man accused of raping a white woman, narrowly escaped death when, according to newspaper accounts, he "was hustled away from an angry mob" by police. "Officers were forced to act swiftly," stated the *Charlotte Observer*, "when a crowd of some 100 persons swarmed around Graves

following his capture." Many in the crowd had guns and "despite officers' efforts to restrain them some fired shots at Graves." Although a dozen police officers witnessed the shooting, no one in the mob was charged in the incident. See *Charlotte Observer*, May 20, 21, 1959. Although lynching had become rare in the late 1950s, it remained a real threat to African American men accused of defiling white womanhood. See also Smead, *Blood Justice*.

32. Cash, *Mind of the South*, 116–20.

33. Chester Davis, "Communist Front Shouts 'Kissing Case' to World"; John Briggs to Bill Sharpe, cc to Luther H. Hodges, February 23, 1959, box 423, Hodges Papers.

34. Mrs. Grady W. Scott to Luther H. Hodges, December 24, 1958, box 423, Hodges Papers.

35. For the specific case of Governor Hodges and his evocation of the fear of miscegenation, see "Radio and TV Address, August 8, 1955," box 39, Hodges Papers. See Chafe, *Civilities and Civil Rights*, 48–60, for an account of both North Carolina's response to the *Brown* decision and Luther Hodges's leadership of opposition to school desegregation.

36. Bignall Jones, the publisher of the *Warren Record*, Warrenton, N.C., April 2, 1955, in an editorial titled "Only One Way to Maintain Schools," took the same position as Governor Hodges with regard to *Brown*—that "voluntary segregation" must be adopted in order to evade the Supreme Court ruling, lest the white majority simply force the closing of the entire public school system. What Jones and Hodges defined as "voluntary," however, is somewhat curious. "The white people of North Carolina control the state economically and politically," the publisher stated flatly, "and they will control it for many years to come. That fact may as well be faced once and for all. The white people are determined that there shall be no mixed schools in this state. Before they allow this to happen they will pull down the pillars of the temple." This was precisely the argument put forward by Hodges. Jones mailed a copy of his editorial to the governor. The clipping is in box 21, Hodges Papers.

37. Quoted in Whitfield, *Death in the Delta*, 11.

38. Dykeman and Stokely, "Inquiry into the Southern Tensions." See also *U.S. News and World Report*, September 19, 1958, 77–90.

39. Quoted in Spickard, *Mixed Blood*, 268.

40. *Monroe Enquirer*, October 30, 1958.

41. Chafe, *Civilities and Civil Rights*, 54–60; Douglas, *Reading, Writing, and Race*, 26, 44–45; Mrs. W. W. Rogers to the editor, *Charlotte Observer*, February 2, 1959.

42. M. Wilson to Luther H. Hodges, November 30, 1958, box 423, Hodges Papers; Gloster B. Current to Roy Wilkins, December 23, 1958, box A92, group 3, NAACP Papers; James Hanover Grissom Thompson, interview, 14.

43. Conrad Lynn, "Attorney Bares Real Inside Story of North Carolina Kissing Case," *Chicago Defender*, January 17, 1959; James Hanover Grissom Thompson, interview, 14.

44. J. Hampton Price to Luther H. Hodges, November 26, 1958, box 423, Hodges Papers.

45. *Monroe Enquirer*, September 1, 1955.

46. *Carolina Times*, January 17, 1959.

47. J. Hampton Price to Luther H. Hodges, November 26, 1958, box 423, Hodges Papers.

48. Chester Davis, "Communist Front Shouts 'Kissing Case' to World."

49. Roy Wilkins, "Memorandum To: NAACP Branch Presidents RE: North Carolina 'Kissing Case,'" January 16, 1958, 2, box C113, and "Transcript of Statements Made by Attorney Conrad Lynn during Interview on the 'Frank Ford Show,' Radio Station WPEN, Philadelphia, Pennsylvania, on June 20, 1959, from 12:30 until 1:35 A.M.," box A92, both in group 3, NAACP Papers.

50. News and Observer, November 14, 1958; Roy Wilkins, "Memorandum To: NAACP Branch Presidents RE: North Carolina 'Kissing Case,'" January 16, 1958, box C113, group 3, NAACP Papers, 1; M. Wilson to Luther H. Hodges, November 30, 1958, box 423, Hodges Papers.

51. Statement by Blaine M. Madison, Commissioner, Board of Corrections and Training, January 2, 1959, and Luther H. Hodges to Dr. Arthur Robinson, February 6, 1959, box 423, Hodges Papers.

52. J. Hampton Price to Luther H. Hodges, November 30, 1958, ibid.

53. Writ of Habeas Corpus and Petition, Superior Court, Mecklenburg County, N.C., January 6, 1959, In the Matter of James Hanover Thompson and David Ezell Simpson, Case Nos. 192 and 193, Mola Papers. These documents confirm that Thompson and Simpson were "sentenced to a term in said reformatory until they reach the age of 21 unless released prior thereto by reason of good conduct."

54. Winfield, interview with Barksdale; Charlotte Observer, October 24, 1959; Union County Medical Society to Dr. Joseph A. Combs, North Carolina Board of Medical Examiners, October 7, 1961, box 111, Sanford Papers; "The Perry Case," box 92, group 3, NAACP Papers.

CHAPTER FIVE

1. "Jail Kissing Case Kissed Off by Judge," Charlotte Observer, November 12, 1958; News and Observer, November 4, 13, 1958.

2. Branch, Parting the Waters, 141.

3. Ibid., 691.

4. Ibid., 791.

5. Robert F. Williams, Negroes with Guns, 41.

6. Wayne Addison Clark, "Analysis of the Relationship between Anti-Communism and Segregationist Thought in the Deep South," 2. See also Sullivan, Days of Hope.

7. A. M. Secrest, a native of Monroe and editor of the Cheraw, S.C., Chronicle, published an editorial on the kissing case that was reprinted in the Monroe Enquirer on December 11, 1958.

8. Monroe Enquirer, November 8, 1954.

9. Hodges, Businessman in the Statehouse, 23.

10. Charlotte Observer, October 14, 1958.

11. Ibid., October 18, 1958.

12. These data come from a Gallup Poll published in ibid., March 15, 1959.

13. Dallek, Lone Star Rising, 518.

14. *Charlotte Observer*, October 21, 1958, and November 29, 1959. Russell was quoted by syndicated columnist David Lawrence, *Charlotte Observer*, February 21, 1960.

15. *Business Week*, November 2, 1957, 80, stated that Hodges was widely considered a strong vice-presidential possibility for 1960. The *Charlotte Observer*, May 2, 1958, reported that Adlai Stevenson had met with Hodges in Chicago the previous day and that Stevenson reported that he had heard Hodges's name mentioned "several times" for the nomination. "Anyone would be highly honored by a position of that kind," Hodges told reporters, later implying that his name on the ticket might forestall a third-party effort by Southerners. See *News and Observer*, January 16, 1959; *Charlotte Observer*, May 1, 2, 1958, September 6, 1959, January 18, February 5, 1960.

16. *Newsweek*, September 26, 1960, 43. A Gallup Poll that appeared in the spring of 1959 found that one Southern voter in three "today says that he would not vote for his party's nominee if the nominee happened to be Catholic." The poll found that anti-Catholic sentiment was stronger in North Carolina than in the Deep South; this also had been true in 1928, when Catholic Al Smith headed the Democratic ticket and, unlike the states of the Deep South, North Carolina went heavily Republican. See *Charlotte Observer*, May 4, 1959. In Hot Springs, Arkansas, at the 1960 annual conference of Southern governors, Hodges circulated a telegram of support for Kennedy. He was the only governor willing to sign, although after the first televised Kennedy-Nixon debate, Hodges was able to recruit nine of his peers to join him. See Tom Wicker, *One of Us* (New York: Random House, 1991), 230.

17. The *Monroe Enquirer* noted on May 15, 1958, that "Governor Hodges is approaching a crossroads. If he is interested in making a serious bid for the vice presidential nomination, people who analyze the national political situation say that it will be necessary for Hodges to liberalize his views on segregation and civil rights. If he plans to run for the United States Senate it will be best to cling to his past position."

18. *Charlotte Observer*, January 1, 1959. The North Carolina Research Institute reported in the summer of 1954 that the state had the lowest manufacturing wages in the nation with an average weekly paycheck of $48.34, as compared with a national average of $71.69. See *Monroe Enquirer*, July 23, 1954.

19. *Charlotte Observer*, October 14, 1959; *Business Week*, November 2, 1957, 72.

20. *Reader's Digest*, December 1957, 177; *Charlotte Observer*, March 20, 1960, and December 10, 1958.

21. *Reader's Digest*, December 1960, 177–80; *Charlotte Observer*, November 7, 1959.

22. The Voice of America broadcast is quoted in the *Charlotte Observer*, December 22, 1958.

23. F. D. Bluford to Luther H. Hodges, November 5, 1955; North Carolina A&T Student Council to Luther H. Hodges, November 6, 1955; Cadet Frank D. Willingham, Corps Commander, and five other officers of the A&T Army–Air Force ROTC to Luther H. Hodges, November 8, 1955; Luther H. Hodges handwritten note to secretary Margaret Y. Birrell, n.d.; Luther H. Hodges to M. A. Arnold, November 14, 1955; Luther H. Hodges to J. N. Vann, November 16, 1955, all in box 20, Hodges Papers.

24. Chafe, *Civilities and Civil Rights*, 52; for the "Dixie" duet with Orval Faubus, which they sang atop Stone Mountain of Georgia, see *Charlotte Observer*, October 14, 1959.

25. *Business Week*, November 2, 1957, 78.

26. The *Time* story was reprinted in full in the *Monroe Enquirer*, February 9, 1959. It appeared in the international edition of the magazine and was published all over the world. Lynn, interview, 4–5.

27. Both Williams and sources hostile to him report essentially the same story here. See *Winston-Salem Journal and Sentinel*, February 8, 1959; *Monroe Enquirer*, January 15, 1959; Mayfield, "Challenge to Negro Leadership," 301. See also *New York Post*, November 3, 10, 1958.

28. *Monroe Enquirer*, November 2, 1958; Chester Davis, "Communist Front Shouts 'Kissing Case' to World."

29. For the sake of comparison, we may examine the case of two African American boys, seven and eleven years old, in Raleigh, North Carolina, who in 1958 were charged with thirty-two offenses, including twenty-seven burglaries and five cases of property damage. Both lived in broken homes; in one instance, the mother and four children lived solely on her $97.00 relief check. Unlike Hanover Thompson and Fuzzy Simpson, the two boys were left in the custody of their mothers. The telling difference in the cases is that the many offenses in the above case did not include violations of time-honored sex and race taboos. See *News and Observer*, March 13, 1958.

30. Robert F. Williams, interview with Cohen, 306–7. See also Robert F. Williams, "While God Lay Sleeping," 107.

31. Hawkins, interview, 1.

32. Robert F. Williams, *Negroes with Guns*, 59; Robert F. Williams, interview with Cohen, 306–7; Robert F. Williams, "While God Lay Sleeping," 108; John A. Morsell to E. Frederic Morrow, January 13, 1959, box A92, group 3, NAACP Papers.

33. Hawkins, interview, 1.

34. Morris, *Origins of the Civil Rights Movement*, 14.

35. Fairclough, *To Redeem the Soul of America*, 18–19, 22–23; Morris, *Origins of the Civil Rights Movement*, 40–76.

36. Patrick Jones, " 'Communist Front Shouts "Kissing Case" to World,' " 36–42. The quote is from Lynn, *There Is a Fountain*, 77.

37. Claude DeBruce, "On the Negro Question," *SWP Discussion Bulletin*, July 1956, 1–5, box 1, Socialist Workers Party Papers.

38. Patrick Jones, " 'Communist Front Shouts "Kissing Case" to World,' " 42.

39. Lynn, *There Is a Fountain*, 108–14.

40. Ibid., 144–45.

41. Mrs. M. Wilson to Luther H. Hodges, November 30, 1958, box 423, Hodges Papers. At first I assumed—and perhaps the writer intended for Hodges to assume—that the author was Mary Wilson, wife of Henry Hall Wilson, a prominent local Democrat. Mary Wilson, however, denied writing the letter, and longtime friends pointed out that it was not her handwriting. Three decades later, no one could imagine who the author could be; in a town as small as Monroe, this seems rather odd. It may be likely, then, that the author wrote under an assumed name. Certainly she had reason to be fearful of reprisal, regardless of her prominence in the community. While we are clearly led to believe that the author is a white woman from an affluent family, it is possible that black citizens, knowing that their views did not matter to the governor, faked the letter as a way of making themselves heard.

42. George Weissman to E. D. Nixon, December 16, 1958, box 1, CCRI Papers. See also Weissman, "Kissing Case," 17.

43. Governor Luther H. Hodges to Attorney General Malcolm B. Seawell, January 7, 1959, Mola Papers; see also Conrad Lynn, "The War against Children," Golden Papers, 3.

44. Lynn, *There Is a Fountain*, 146.

45. George Weissman to the Reverend C. K. Steele, December 16, 1958, box 1, CCRI Papers.

46. Lynn, *There Is a Fountain*, 147.

47. *Monroe Enquirer*, December 11, 1958; George Weissman to E. D. Nixon, December 16, 1958, box 1, CCRI Papers.

48. Robert F. Williams, interview with Cohen, 562–63; Tom Kerry, "Committee to Combat Racial Injustice," December 19, 1958, reel 9, frame 85, Socialist Workers Party Papers.

49. Louis E. Austin, "The High Cost of Justice in the South," *Carolina Times*, December 6, 1958.

50. George Weissman to the Reverend C. K. Steele, December 16, 1958, box 1, CCRI Papers; Tom Kerry, "Committee to Combat Racial Injustice," December 19, 1958, reel 9, frame 85, Socialist Workers Party Papers.

51. Klarman, "How *Brown* Changed Race Relations," 84, 89.

52. Fairclough, *To Redeem the Soul of America*, 48.

53. George Weissman to E. D. Nixon, December 16, 1958, box 1, CCRI Papers.

54. George Weissman to Anne Braden, March 2, 1959, box 49, Braden Papers; George Weissman to Carl Braden, December 22, 1958, and to E. D. Nixon, December 16, 1958, and Arthur Lobman to E. D. Nixon, December 20, 1958, all in box 1, CCRI Papers; Patrick Jones, " 'Communist Front Shouts "Kissing Case" to World,' " 43–52.

55. Payne, *I've Got the Light of Freedom*, 77–102.

56. George Weissman to Anne Braden, March 2, 1959, box 49, Braden Papers. It is interesting to consider what might have happened if the call had come a few months later—after Baker had lost faith in the SCLC but before she had become midwife to SNCC in 1960.

57. Branch, *Parting the Waters*, 203.

58. John White, "Nixon *Was* the One: Edgar Daniel Nixon, the MIA, and the Montgomery Bus Boycott," in Ward and Badger, *Making of Martin Luther King Jr.*, 45–63.

59. George Weissman to E. D. Nixon, December 16, 1958, box 1, CCRI Papers.

60. E. D. Nixon to George Weissman, December 20, 1958, ibid.

61. Branch, *Parting the Waters*, 198, 602.

62. George Weissman to Carl Braden, December 22, 1958; George Weissman to the Reverend C. K. Steele, December 16, 1958; Arthur Lobman to E. D. Nixon, December 20, 1958; George Weissman to E. D. Nixon, December 16, 1958, all in box 1, CCRI Papers. See also Patrick Jones, " 'Communist Front Shouts "Kissing Case" to World,' " 47, 51. Shuttlesworth was an important movement leader in Birmingham who would play a decisive role in the SCLC's 1963 campaign there. Frazier, author of the sociological classic *Black Bourgeoisie*, was an illustrious African American scholar. Mailer was a well-known novelist, though not yet the towering figure in American letters that he would become.

63. George Weissman to Louis E. Austin, December 16, 1958, box 1, CCRI Papers; *Monroe Enquirer*, February 16, 1959.

64. Joyce Egginton, "American Scene," *London News-Chronicle*, December 15, 1958, and January 13, 1960; Robert F. Williams, *Negroes with Guns*, 59–61; Mayfield, "Challenge to Negro Leadership," 301. Wilson is quoted in *Charlotte News*, October 3, 1981.

65. Joyce Egginton, "American Scene," *London News-Chronicle*, December 15, 1958; *Monroe Enquirer*, November 20, 1958. *News and Observer*, January 16, 1959, reported that "Italy's Communist press is splashing its front pages with the story of two American Negro boys sent to reform school after kissing a 6-year-old white girl." Thousands of letters to Governor Luther Hodges from readers of publications in these countries may be found in box 423, Hodges Papers.

66. Morrow, *Forty Years a Guinea Pig*, 37–38; Branch, *Parting the Waters*, 181.

67. *Carolina Times*, December 27, 1958; *News and Observer*, March 29, 1958; Morrow, *Black Man in the White House* (New York: McFadden, 1963), 198. Two months earlier, the White House had intervened in a similar "local matter" in which Jimmy Wilson, a fifty-five-year-old black man in Alabama, had been sentenced to die in the electric chair for the unarmed robbery of $1.96 from a white woman. Though prosecutors had not charged Wilson with any sexual crime, they argued in court that the robbery represented a sexual assault on "white womanhood." The death sentence stirred a storm of protest and inspired thousands of letters, telegrams, and telephone calls from across the globe to Governor "Big Jim" Folsom in Montgomery. Folsom was persuaded to commute Wilson's sentence to life imprisonment after the international outcry prompted a telegram from Secretary of State Dulles suggesting that the case was causing some concern as to U.S. relations with other nations. See *Charlotte Observer*, September 30, 1958. The comparison between these two cases originated not here but inside the public relations effort launched by Governor Hodges in early 1959 in response to the Monroe incident. One of the architects of the campaign wrote to another that "in the '$1.96 robbery' case in Alabama, which drew the usual protests from overseas, it might have been pointed out that armed assault is a crime whether the victim has $1.96 or $1 million." (Wilson was not armed.) He contrasted the failure to make this point to the Monroe case in which, "as any fair-minded person can see, the authorities were trying to protect the young hoodlums." See John Briggs to Bill Sharpe, cc to Luther H. Hodges, February 23, 1959, box 423, Hodges Papers.

68. USIA officials in the Netherlands estimated that between 11,000 and 12,000 persons had sent letters or signed petitions of protest to that one embassy, but because many such entreaties had been forwarded to Washington, "the exact number of petitions and signatories is probably far in excess of that reported herein." See Basil L. Whitener to Luther H. Hodges, March 2, 1959, box 423, Hodges Papers. See also Mayfield, "Challenge to Negro Leadership," 301; Robert E. Giles, administrative assistant, to President William C. Friday, February 6, 1959, box 423, Hodges Papers.

69. Chester Davis, "Press in North Gives Distorted Versions"; *Monroe Enquirer*, February 9, 1959, reprinted the *Time* story in full. The information on Clare Boothe Luce comes from Branch, *Parting the Waters*, 203.

70. "Statement from J. Hampton Price, Judge of the Juvenile Court, Union County

North Carolina," to Luther H. Hodges, November 26, 1958; Luther H. Hodges to Irene Drake Rodwell, January 7, 1959, states that "it is the general policy . . . not to make public detailed information on juvenile cases. The fact that this procedure was initially followed in this case played into the hands of some irresponsible people who wanted to exploit it. In response to that it became necessary to make public the facts concerning the case, as well as the facts concerning the home and family situation of the two boys" (see box 423, Hodges Papers). Chester Davis, in the Winston-Salem *Journal and Sentinel*, February 8, 1959, asserts that white officials "refused to discuss the case with the press. Lynn and Williams were by no means so reticent. As a result, the stories, and there were many of them—tended to carry the precise twist desired by Lynn and Williams." The *News* editorial was reprinted in the *Monroe Enquirer*, January 29, 1959.

71. *News and Observer*, November 26, 1957.

72. William Jefferson Jones, "Identity, Militancy, and Organization," 23. I am grateful to Jones for sharing this excellent paper with me.

73. Juan Williams, *Thurgood Marshall*, 168–69.

74. Reginald Hawkins to Kelly Alexander, May 12, 1959, box 1, Hawkins Papers.

75. Chester Davis, "Communist Front Shouts 'Kissing Case' to World."

76. Gloster B. Current to Roy Wilkins, December 23, 1958, box A92, NAACP Papers.

77. Robert F. Williams to George Weissman, December 17, 1958, box 1, CCRI Papers.

78. Gaillard, *Dream Long Deferred*, 18–21; Hill, interview.

79. Kelly Alexander to Roy Wilkins, December 26, 1958, "A Report of Activities of the N.C. State Conference of Branches in Reference to the Case of David Simpson and James Thompson of Monroe, N.C.," N.C. State Conference Papers, box A92, group 3, NAACP Papers; Patrick Jones, "'Communist Front Shouts "Kissing Case" to World,'" 63.

80. "Monroe Man Racial Group Head—Robert F. Williams Making Speaking Tour in North," *Monroe Enquirer*, December 29, 1958; George Weissman to Carl Braden, December 31, 1958, box 1, CCRI Papers.

81. George Weissman to Carl Braden, March 14, 1959, box 49, Braden Papers; for the letters of protest, see box 423, Hodges Papers; *Monroe Enquirer*, March 2, 1959.

82. Kelly M. Alexander to Roy Wilkins, December 26, 1958, and Roy Wilkins to Conrad Lynn, December 30, 1958, both in box A92, group 3, NAACP Papers; *Amsterdam News*, January 17, 1959.

83. *Monroe Enquirer*, December 1, 1958; Robert E. Giles to Jerome Tannenbaum, November 20, 1958, and Luther H. Hodges to Charles Pemberton, December 2, 1958, box 423, Hodges Papers.

84. *Monroe Enquirer*, February 9, 1959.

85. Luther H. Hodges to Fannie Padwe, December 2, 1958, and to James Piaser, February 9, 1959, box 423, Hodges Papers; *Charlotte Observer*, January 16, 1959; *News and Observer*, January 16, 1959.

86. *Charlotte Observer*, January 19, 1959. While this broadside may seem to have the ring of truth today, in the shadow of Rupert Murdoch's legacy to American journalism, this was not the case in 1959.

87. This editorial, which originally appeared in the *Fayetteville Observer*, was reprinted in the *News and Observer*, January 21, 1959.

88. *Journal and Sentinel*, February 8, 1959; *News and Observer*, January 11, 1959.

89. Statement by Blaine M. Madison, Commissioner, Board of Corrections and Training, January 2, 1959, box 423, Hodges Papers.

90. See, for example, Chafe, *Civilities and Civil Rights*, 49–60, and Bartley, *Rise of Massive Resistance*, 23, 142–43.

91. *Daily Worker*, January 11, 1959.

92. George Weissman to Carl Braden, January 21, 1959, box 1, CCRI Papers; Robert F. Williams, interview with Cohen, 334–36.

93. Robert F. Williams to George Weissman, December 17, 1958, box 1, CCRI Papers; *Southern Patriot* 17, no. 1 (January 1959): 3; *Charlotte Observer*, February 9, 1959.

94. Robert F. Williams to George Weissman, December 17, 1958, box 1, CCRI Papers; Governor Luther H. Hodges to Attorney General Malcolm B. Seawell, January 7, 1959, box 423, Hodges Papers.

95. *Monroe Enquirer*, February 16, 1959; Charles McLean, "Supplementary Report on the Relocation of Mrs. Thompson and Mrs. Simpson," March 11, 1959, box A92, group 3, NAACP Papers.

96. George Weissman to Carl Braden, January 21, 1959, box 1, CCRI Papers. Weissman quotes Williams in his letter.

97. *News and Observer*, January 11, 1959; *Charlotte Observer*, January 9, 10, 1959; *Monroe Enquirer*, January 12, 1959.

98. *Charlotte Observer*, October 17, 1958.

99. Gloster Current to Roy Wilkins, January 13, 1959, N.C. State Conference Papers, group 3, NAACP Papers.

100. Anson County, North Carolina Superior Court, January Criminal Term 1959, in the Matter of the Petition of Robert F. Williams, Petitioner, for a Writ of Habeas Corpus to Inquire into the Detention of Hanover Thompson and David E. Simpson, Against P. R. Brown, as Superintendent of Morrison Training School for Boys, Respondent, transcript in box 2, CCRI Papers (hereafter referred to as Hearing Transcript), 6–13.

101. Ibid., 16–19.

102. Ginger, " 'In Enemy Territory.' " For a personal account, see Braden, *Wall Between*.

103. Hearing Transcript, 20–60; *Gaffney Ledger*, January 15, 1959.

104. Ted Poston, "Families of 'Kiss' Boys Get New Home," *New York Post*, January 19, 1959.

105. Hearing Transcript, 34–68.

106. *New York Post*, January 13, 1959.

107. Robert F. Williams to George Weissman, January 16, 1959, box 1, CCRI Papers.

108. George Weissman to Carl Braden, February 19, 1959, ibid.; *Monroe Enquirer*, February 26, 1959; *Charlotte Observer*, January 28, 1959.

109. George Weissman to Carl Braden, February 19, 1958, box 49, Braden Papers; *Carolina Times*, February 14, 1959; *Monroe Enquirer*, March 12, 1959.

110. George Weissman to Carl Braden, March 14, 1959, box 49, Braden Papers; *Monroe Enquirer*, May 7, 1959.

111. *News and Observer*, January 21, 1959; *Monroe Enquirer*, January 17, 1959.

112. O. L. Richardson to Luther H. Hodges, n.d., but received in early 1959, box 423, Hodges Papers.

113. John Briggs to Bill Sharpe, cc to Luther H. Hodges, February 23, 1959; Bill Sharpe to Luther H. Hodges, February 12, 1959; Luther H. Hodges to Bill Sharpe, February 19, 1959, all in ibid.

114. Luther H. Hodges to Reed Surratt, executive editor of the Winston-Salem *Journal and Sentinel*, February 12, 1959, ibid.; Chester Davis, "Communist Front Shouts 'Kissing Case' to World."

115. George Weissman to Louis E. Austin, February 19, 1959, and Evelyn Thompson and Jennie Simpson to CCRI, both in box 1, CCRI Papers.

116. Chester Davis, "Communist Front Shouts 'Kissing Case' to World."

117. Chester Davis to Carl Braden, March 16, 28, 1959, box 49, Braden Papers.

118. Luther Hodges to Reed Surratt, February 12, 1959; John Briggs to Bill Sharpe, cc to Luther H. Hodges, received February 16, 1959; Luther H. Hodges to Bill Sharpe, February 19, 1959, all in box 423, Hodges Papers.

119. George Weissman to Louis E. Austin, February 19, 1959, box 1, CCRI Papers.

120. CCRI press release, February 14, 1959, box A92, group 3, NAACP Papers; *New York Times*, February 14, 1959; *Monroe Enquirer*, February 16, 1959.

121. Lynn, *There Is a Fountain*, 156. Robert Williams did confirm this explanation, in a general way, in *Negroes with Guns*, 58–60. But there is no corroborating evidence that Roosevelt called Eisenhower, or that Eisenhower called Hodges, or that any such action caused Hodges to relent.

122. Harry Golden to Burton Wolfe, August 30, 1961, and Kelly Alexander to *Commentary*, April 7, 1961, both in pt. 2, box 2, Golden Papers; *New York Post*, February 14, 1959.

123. *Monroe Enquirer*, February 12, 1959.

124. Roy Wilkins, "To Branches, Youth Councils, and College Chapters," February 26, 1959, box A92, group 3, NAACP Papers.

125. Harold B. Williams to Gloster Current, March 17, 1959, ibid.; *Monroe Enquirer*, February 26, 1959.

126. George Weissman to Carl Braden, February 19, 1959, box 1, CCRI Papers (emphasis in original).

CHAPTER SIX

1. Julian Mayfield to Richard Gibson, July 27, 1967, box 1, Robert F. Williams Papers.

2. "Cole Threat to Indians Reported," *Greensboro Daily News*, n.d., and "Klan Case Near Charge to Jury," Pembroke, N.C., *Robesonian*, n.d., both in box 5, Cole Papers.

3. James W. Cole, "An Invitation for You to Meet James W. Cole," box 2, Cole Papers.

4. Julian Mayfield to Richard Gibson, July 27, 1967, box 1, Robert F. Williams Papers. Gardner was not a Lumbee woman but was from eastern North Carolina. The fact that she was apparently involved with an African American man seems to have upset many white men in the area, judging from the regularity with which Cole referred to her relationship in his speeches.

5. *Gaffney Ledger*, February 4, 1958.

6. "Klobbered Klan," *News and Observer*, April 19, 1964, in box 5, Cole Papers.

7. It appears that press coverage was confined to "Citizens Fire Back at Klan," *Norfolk Journal and Guide*, October 12, 1957, and "Is North Carolina NAACP Leader a Marked Man?," *Jet*, October 31, 1957, 10–11. Both periodicals are aimed at black audiences and are published outside North Carolina, so it is not surprising that the Lumbee leader had not heard about events in Monroe.

8. *Carolina Israelite*, January–February 1958, 9.

9. Hy Gardner, *New York Herald Tribune*, and Max Lerner, *New York Post*, quoted in *Carolina Israelite*, January–February 1958, 1; "editorially speaking," *New Mexican*, January 21, 1958, in box 5, Cole Papers.

10. *News and Observer*, January 27, 1958; editorial, *Chapel Hill News Leader*, reprinted in *News and Observer*, January 30, 1958.

11. Robert F. Williams, *Negroes with Guns*, 57–58. The Lumbees drew upon a tribal tradition of armed resistance that was at least a century old, extending back to the Henry Berry Lowery gang in the nineteenth century. See Evans, *To Die Game*. See also Deborah Montgomerie, "Coming to Terms: Ngai Tahu, Robeson County Indians and the Garden River Band of Objibwa, 1840–1940, Three Studies of Colonialism in Action" (Ph.D. diss., Duke University, 1993), 313–34.

12. Governor Luther Hodges, press release, January 28, 1958, box 423, Hodges Papers; see also *Monroe Enquirer*, February 3, 1958.

13. *Monroe Enquirer*, March 17, 1958.

14. J. B. Stoner to James William Cole, August 15, 1959; Webster and Mary Sanford to James William Cole, May 21, 1959; Charlie Rea to James Williams Cole, November 19, 1959, and March 27, 1960, all in box 1, Cole Papers.

15. *Carolina Israelite*, January–February 1958, 1 (capital letters in the original). For a similar argument from the same geographical area but much earlier, see Merrell, "Racial Education of the Catawba Indians," 373–82.

16. Carolyn Cole, "Dear Fellow Patriot," April 3, 1959, box 1, Cole Papers.

17. Anthropologist Claude Levi-Strauss's observation that men often use women as "verbs" with which to communicate status and power speaks to this point. See Jacquelyn Dowd Hall, "Mind That Burns in Each Body," 64–69.

18. *Charlotte Observer*, September 11, 12, 1959.

19. Robert F. Williams, interview with Mosby; *Crusader* 1, no. 1 (June 26, 1959): 1.

20. Robert F. Williams to Slater King, December 17, 1963, box 1, Robert F. Williams Papers.

21. *Crusader* 2, no. 30 (May 29, 1961): 3.

22. Though her work here is specific to an earlier context, a crucially instructive source is Jacquelyn Dowd Hall, *Revolt against Chivalry*.

23. Robert F. Williams, interview with Mosby.

24. *Crusader* 1, no. 13 (September 19, 1959): 3.

25. Ibid., no. 52 (June 25, 1960): 5–6. This may refer to the lynching of Anthony Crawford in 1916. See Litwack, *Trouble in Mind*, 309–11.

26. Ibid., no. 2 (July 4, 1959): 3.

27. Ibid., no. 16 (October 10, 1959): 4.

28. Reed, *Enduring South*, chap. 5, "To Live—and Die—in Dixie: Southern Violence"; Cash, *Mind of the South*; Sheldon Hackney, "Southern Violence," in Graham and Gurr, *History of Violence in America*, 502–27; Brown, *Southern Honor*.

29. *Charlotte Observer*, October 19, 1958.

30. *Crusader* 2, no. 10 (September 24, 1960): 5.

31. These placards appear fairly often in the iconography of the freedom movement. See, for example, Kasher, *Civil Rights Movement*, 228–29.

32. See Smead, *Blood Justice*. The quote is from *London News-Chronicle*, January 15, 1960.

33. *Southern Patriot* 18, no. 11 (January 1960): 3. Williams's comments originally appeared in *Liberation* magazine in September 1959.

34. Dittmer, *Local People*, 85.

35. *Pittsburgh Courier*, June 20, 1959.

36. "Four Armed White Men Are Arrested in Kidnapping, Rape of Negro Coed," *Washington Post*, May 3, 1959.

37. *New York Times*, May 7, 1959; *Pittsburgh Courier*, June 20, 1959; *Charlotte Observer*, May 3, 4, June 12, 1959; *Washington Post*, May 3, 1959; Woodard, "Summer of African-American Discontent," 6; "Tallahassee Rape Case," box A91, group 3, NAACP Papers. See McGuire, "Rape, Race, and Revolt."

38. "Negroes Boycott Classes; Protest Assault of Coed," *State*, May 5, 1959. On the question of violence and nonviolence in the student response to the rape case, see Robert M. White, "The Tallahassee Sit-ins and CORE: A Nonviolent Revolutionary Submovement" (Ph.D. diss., Florida State University, 1964), 66–68.

39. The best work on the sit-in movement is Chafe, *Civilities and Civil Rights*.

40. See Whitfield, *Death in the Delta*.

41. Lomax, *Negro Revolt*, 112–16.

42. *Carolina Times*, July 20, 1957; *Gaffney Ledger*, July 20, 1957. On the larger pattern of sit-ins in the late 1950s, see Morris, *Origins of the Civil Rights Movement*, 188–89, 198. The quote from Baldwin is on p. 88.

43. Robert F. Williams, "N. Carolina College Youth Calls for a Militant Student Generation," *Freedom* 2, no. 6 (June 1952): 5; Sellers with Terrell, *River of No Return*, 19. The best book on SNCC remains Carson, *In Struggle*.

44. Walter F. Anderson to Hugh Cannon, September 14, 1961, and State Bureau of Investigation Report, interrogation of Howard Williams, Albert Rorie, and J. D. Blount, September 14, 1961, box 111, Sanford Papers, both reveal the presence of at least one machine gun and a "grease gun" submachine gun. *Monroe Enquirer*, August 31, 1961, states that fifty-eight sticks of dynamite were found at Williams's house and that police confiscated "a small arsenal of weapons, including automatic rifles."

45. "Maid Claims She Was Kicked Down Stairs," *Monroe Enquirer*, January 26, March 9, 1959; *New York Post*, January 27, May 7, 1959; *Crusader* 4, no. 7 (April 1963): 4; *Carolina Times*, February 7, 1959.

46. *New York Post*, January 27, 1959; *Carolina Times*, January 31, 1959.

47. Albert E. Perry Jr., M.D., to George Weissman, February 12, 1959; George Weissman to Walter Nivens, February 17, 1959; George Weissman to Carl Braden, February 19, 1959, all in box 1, CCRI Papers. See also *Carolina Times*, January 31, 1959.

48. *New York Age*, May 16, 1959; *Carolina Times*, February 7, 1959.

49. State Bureau of Investigation Director Walter F. Anderson to Oscar L. Richardson, Attorney at Law, Monroe, N.C., April 1, 1959, "RE: State v. B. F. Shaw," Mola Papers. See also O. L. Richardson to Luther H. Hodges, n.d., box 423, Hodges Papers.

50. Memo dated May 6, 1959, RFW/FBI.

51. *Monroe Enquirer*, March 9, 1959; State Bureau of Investigation Director Walter F. Anderson to Oscar L. Richardson, Attorney at Law, Monroe, N.C., April 1, 1959, "RE: State v. B. F. Shaw," Mola Papers.

52. *Monroe Enquirer*, May 7, 1959; *New York Post*, May 7, 1959.

53. Ted Poston, " 'Equal Protection of the Law' in a Carolina Town," *New York Post*, November 11, 1958; *Daily Worker*, January 25, 1959.

54. Robert F. Williams, interview with Mosby; "Telephone Conversation between Mr. Wilkins in New York and Mr. Robert Williams in Monroe, North Carolina, May 6, 1959, at 11:04 A.M.," box A333, group 3, NAACP Papers, 3.

55. George Weissman to Carl Braden, December 22, 1959, box 1, CCRI Papers.

56. *Monroe Enquirer*, March 9, 1959; George Weissman to Walter Nivens, February 17, 1959, box 1, CCRI Papers.

57. *Crusader* 4, no. 7 (April 1963): 4.

58. "Referral from May 11 Board Meeting," box A92, group 3, NAACP Papers, 2; *New York Post*, May 7, 1959; *Crusader* 9, no. 3 (December 1967): 3; *Southern Patriot* 18, no. 11 (January 1960): 3.

59. U.S. Senate, *Testimony of Robert F. Williams*, pt. 2, 89–90; *Crusader* 9, no. 3 (December 1967): 3; Robert F. Williams, interview with Mosby; *Southern Patriot* 18, no. 11 (January 1960): 3; *New York Post*, May 7, 1959; *Monroe Enquirer*, May 7, 1959.

60. Robert F. Williams, interview with Mosby; U.S. Senate, *Testimony of Robert F. Williams*, pt. 2, 89–90.

61. "Text of telegram from NAACP Executive Secretary Roy Wilkins to Robert Williams, president of branch in Monroe, North Carolina, May 6, 1959," and "Rec'd via phone from UPI—May 6, 1959," both in box A333, group 3, NAACP Papers. See also "N.A.A.C.P. Leader Urges Violence," *New York Times*, May 7, 1959; "Year in Review," *Carolina Times*, January 5, 1960.

62. "Year in Review," *Carolina Times*, January 5, 1960.

63. *New York Times*, May 7, 1959; Jackson, Miss., *State-Times*, May 6, 1959; *News and Courier*, May 7, 1959, clipping in box A333, group 3, NAACP Papers.

64. Wilkins, *Standing Fast*, 265.

65. "Telephone Conversation between Mr. Wilkins in New York and Mr. Robert Williams in Monroe, North Carolina, May 6, 1959, at 11:04 A.M.," box A333, group 3, NAACP Papers.

66. "Text of telegram from NAACP Executive Secretary Roy Wilkins to Robert Williams, president of branch in Monroe, North Carolina, May 6, 1959," ibid.

67. Lomax, *Negro Revolt*, 130–31.

68. Telegram from Robert F. Williams to Roy Wilkins, May 7, 1959, box A333, group 3, NAACP Papers.

69. "Roy Wilkins, Executive Secretary, Complainant, Against Robert F. Williams, Respondent, Brief for Respondent," ibid., 1–2.

70. *New York Times*, May 7, 1959.

71. Roy Wilkins to P. L. Prattis, "Personal, Not for Publication," May 28, 1959, box A333, group 3, NAACP Papers.

72. Payne, *I've Got the Light of Freedom*, 49–50.

73. Kluger, *Simple Justice*, 3.

74. Juan Williams, *Thurgood Marshall*, 248–49.

75. Payne, *I've Got the Light of Freedom*, 44.

76. Daisy Bates to Thurgood Marshall, August 3, 1959, box 2, Bates Papers.

77. William Jefferson Jones, "Identity, Militancy, and Organization," 10–11.

78. Carl Braden to George Weissman, October 30, 1959, box 49, Braden Papers; *Carolina Times*, May 9, 1959.

79. *Durham Morning Herald*, May 8, 1959.

80. *Afro-American*, May 30, 1959; *Arkansas State Press*, May 23, 1959.

81. Western Union telegrams from all over the country, dated May 7 to May 10, 1959, in support of Roy Wilkins's suspension of Robert Williams, box A333, group 3, NAACP Papers.

82. Mrs. E. A. Johnson to Roy Wilkins, Western Union telegram, May 9, 1959, ibid.

83. Kelly Alexander to Daisy Bates, May 21, 1959, box 19, Kelly Alexander Papers.

84. Thurgood Marshall, Federal Bureau of Investigation Subject File, no. 100-111437, SAC New York to Director, June 5, 1959. My thanks to Alex Charns for providing me with copies of these FBI files, which he obtained under the Freedom of Information Act.

85. Juan Williams, in his biography of Marshall, defends Marshall's depiction of Robert Williams as part of a Communist conspiracy against the NAACP. Robert Williams's "infatuation with Communists" began with the kissing case, Juan Williams states, and Conrad Lynn (who had actually been expelled by the Communist Party decades earlier) was "a civil rights attorney with Communist ties." Robert Williams's later flight to Cuba and China "seemed to validate Marshall's tips to the FBI," according to Juan Williams. In fact, the journalist apparently just repeats Marshall's false charges. There is no evidence in either the text or the notes of his biography to substantiate these claims. Given Robert Williams's subsequent clashes with the Communist Party and his pronounced black nationalism, it is doubtful that he allied himself with the party. In any case, there is no evidence in the historical record to support these charges, and considerable evidence contravenes them. See Juan Williams, *Thurgood Marshall*, 280–83 and nn. 7–9, 423–24.

86. Ben Stocking, "Report Shows Marshall's Secret FBI Ties," *News and Observer*, December 3, 1996.

87. Brooklyn Branch to Roy Wilkins, May 8, 1959, and Flint, Mich., Branch, "Resolution to the National Board, National Association for the Advancement of Colored People," May 24, 1959, both in box 2, CCRI Papers.

88. Charles J. Adams to Roy Wilkins, May 8, 1959, box A333, group 3, NAACP Papers.

89. James Benjamine, Esq., to NAACP, May 7, 1959, ibid.

90. N. L. Gregg to Kelly Alexander, May 19, 1959, box 19, Kelly Alexander Papers.

91. John McCray, "There's Nothing New about It," *Afro-American*, May 23, 1959.

92. *Amsterdam News*, June 6, 1959. My thanks to Steve Estes for this clipping.

93. Daisy Bates, untitled speech, 1959, box 3, Bates Papers.

94. Daisy Bates to Roy Wilkins, July 29, 1959, box 19, Kelly Alexander Papers. Apparently Wilkins was not altogether faithful in making his payments. In this letter, Bates tells Wilkins that "it is becoming increasingly unpleasant for me to constantly bring to the organization our financial plight." She then reminds Wilkins that "you promised that the organization would supplement our income at $600 per month until December 31, 1959. On May 19 your communication stated that the board authorized advertising for May, June, and July."

95. Kelly Alexander to Daisy Bates, May 21, 1959, box 19, Kelly Alexander Papers. The emphasis is mine.

96. Egerton, *Speak Now against the Day*, 232.

97. "Referral from May 11 Board Meeting—The Matter of Mr. Robert F. Williams' suspension as president from the Monroe, N.C. Branch," box A92, and Robert F.

Williams Defense Committee press release, May 27, 1959, 3, box A333, both in group 3, NAACP Papers.

98. *Carolina Times*, June 13, 1959.
99. Robert F. Williams, interview with Mosby.
100. *New York Times*, May 12, 1959.
101. Lomax, *Negro Revolt*, 112; Roy Wilkins to P. L. Prattis, May 28, 1959, box A333, group 3, NAACP Papers, 2.
102. Conrad Lynn to Earl Dickerson, Esq., and to Robert F. Williams, June 29, 1959, both in box 1, Robert F. Williams Papers.
103. Garrow, *Bearing the Cross*, 78, 91, 166.
104. John Morsell, "Coordinating the Assault on Segregation: A Preliminary Statement," n.d., box 6, Bates Papers. The figure of "51 years" suggests that it was written in late 1959 or early 1960.
105. Branch, *Parting the Waters*, 190.
106. Lomax, *Negro Revolt*, 113.
107. *New York Times*, July 14, 1959.
108. *The Single Issue in the Robert Williams Case*, box A333, group 3, NAACP Papers.
109. Lomax, *Negro Revolt*, 114; *New York Times*, July 18, 1959. Ironically, Jackie Robinson deserted the NAACP a few years later to protest what he called "the clique of the Old Guard." See Tygiel, *Baseball's Great Experiment*, 340.
110. *Pittsburgh Courier*, July 25, 1959; *Crusader* 1, no. 5 (July 25, 1959): 1; Lomax, *Negro Revolt*, 114.
111. *Charlotte Observer*, July 18, 1959; *Crisis*, August–September 1959, 410; Lomax, *Negro Revolt*, 14; Juan Williams, *Thurgood Marshall*, 282.
112. Bates, *Long Shadow of Little Rock*, 162. See also *Afro-American*, July 18, 1959.
113. Western Union telegram, July 8, 1959, to U.S. Attorney General, Department of Justice, Washington, D.C., box 2, Bates Papers.
114. Robert F. Williams to Daisy Bates, August 17, 1959, box 2, Bates Papers.

CHAPTER SEVEN

1. Mallory, interview, 2–4, 10–11. It seems possible, too, that Mallory was like many other working-class blacks in Harlem who were, Mark Naison writes, "so uncomfortable around whites that they found Party branch life a great strain." See Naison, *Communists in Harlem*, 281.
2. Smith and Sinclair, *Harlem Cultural/Political Movements*, 61–62.
3. Mallory, interview, 19–20.
4. Ibid., 17.
5. Fairclough, *To Redeem the Soul of America*, 21.
6. See Klarman, "How Brown Changed Race Relations," 82. See also Bartley, *Rise of Massive Resistance*.
7. McCoy, interview. Payne, *I've Got the Light of Freedom*, 217–18, makes this same point very persuasively: "Legislation serves our need to render history understandable by giving us convenient benchmarks, and we may therefore be tempted to exaggerate its significance. The bill is taken to be a great watershed. The bill itself, though, may have been less important than the willingness of [local black

activists] to insist that it be enforced. That insistence, I would argue, is the crucial break with the past, not the legislation itself."

8. The best single work on Black Power is Van Deburg, *New Day in Babylon*.

9. Myers, "When Violence Met Violence," 44–45.

10. Robert F. Williams, *Negroes with Guns*, 40.

11. Cruse, in *Crisis of the Negro Intellectual*, 382–401, found fault with Robert Williams for being insufficiently ideological and demonstrating "deeply ingrained protest pragmaticism." For his chapter on Williams, Cruse consulted only a single issue of *The Crusader*—one from 1964, when Williams had been in exile for almost three years and had begun to lose his moorings—and two interviews by other people. Unable to examine Williams's political activism in any detail, Cruse found it easy to dismiss Williams as only an integrationist with a gun, who had "devised a concept of revolution that not a single Marxist theorist in America would swallow." Given the political achievements of Marxist theorists and their adherents over the three decades since Cruse issued his assessment, however, it may be time to reconsider the kind of provisional and eclectic homegrown radicalism that black Southerners developed in the late 1950s and early 1960s. Charles Payne provides a brilliant, detailed historical analysis of this indigenous radicalism in *I've Got the Light of Freedom*. For a brief, persuasive, and engaging theoretical analysis in this vein, see Clayborne Carson, "Rethinking African-American Political Thought in the Post-Revolutionary Era," in Ward and Badger, *Making of Martin Luther King Jr.*, 115–27.

12. Robert F. Williams, foreword to "Radio Free Dixie" manuscript, box 1, Robert F. Williams Papers, 1.

13. Robert F. Williams, interview with Mosby, 76–78.

14. Mabel Williams, "The Birth of the Crusader," *Crusader* 1, no. 53 (July 2, 1960): 1.

15. "From Charlotte to Director," July 31, 1959, RFW/FBI.

16. Mabel Williams, "The Birth of the Crusader," *Crusader* 1, no. 53 (July 2, 1960): 1.

17. "From Charlotte to Director," July 31, 1959, RFW/FBI.

18. *Crusader* 1, no. 5 (July 25, 1959): 2. Capital letters in the original.

19. Cyril V. Briggs, "Declaration of War on the Ku Klux Klan," *Crusader*, January 1921, quoted in Shapiro, *White Violence and Black Response*, 208–9 and 495 n. Williams told historian Robert A. Hill, "Many years ago I heard of Cyril V. Briggs and his *Crusader* . . . but not being aware of his approval or disapproval of my use of the name I changed it by adding 'Weekly Newsletter.' " See Robert A. Hill's introduction to Cyril V. Briggs, ed., *The Crusader*, vol. 1 (New York: Garland, 1987), xlviii. Hill may, however, overstate Briggs's importance to Williams when he claims that "Robert F. Williams, the leader of the militant NAACP chapter in Monroe, North Carolina . . . emulated the concept of black self-defense pioneered by the African Black Brotherhood in 1919." Williams clearly knew about Briggs, but his grandfather Sikes Williams, to name only the most obvious influence, was a far more important model. The larger truth, of course, is that black self-defense, in both the 1920s and the 1950s, grew out of the ongoing traditions and unavoidable realities of African American life and history.

20. *Crusader* 1, no. 9 (August 22, 1959): 9.

21. Ibid., no. 1 (June 26, 1959): 2–4.

22. Ibid., no. 13 (September 19, 1959): 3.

23. Ibid., no. 11 (September 5, 1959): 5.

24. Ibid., no. 5 (July 25, 1959): 3.

25. Ibid., no. 2 (July 4, 1959): 4.

26. Ibid., no. 7 (August 8, 1959): 3.

27. Mabel R. Williams, interview with Anne Braden. See also "Total Memberships Received from Branches in North Carolina, January 1–October 1, 1959," box C113, and typescript summary of telephone conversation between Conrad Lynn and Charles A. McLean, June 16, 1959, box A333, group 3, NAACP Papers.

28. *Crusader* 1, no. 53 (July 2, 1960): 1–2. According to the *Monroe Enquirer*, July 20, 1961, the newsletter had a circulation of about 2,000 at that time.

29. Robert F. Williams, foreword to "Radio Free Dixie" manuscript, box 1, Robert F. Williams Papers, 2–3.

30. Azalea Johnson, "Did You Know?," *Crusader* 1, no. 2 (July 4, 1959): 4.

31. Ibid., no. 1 (June 26, 1959): 1.

32. Cruse, *Rebellion or Revolution*, 15.

33. *Crusader* 1, no. 12 (September 12, 1959): 3.

34. Ibid., 2, no. 23 (February 4, 1961): 5.

35. Ibid., no. 10 (September 24, 1960): 8.

36. Ibid., 1, no. 41 (April 9, 1960): 2–3.

37. Ibid., no. 14 (September 26, 1959): 6.

38. Ibid., no. 16 (October 10, 1959): 4.

39. Ibid., no. 2 (July 4, 1959): 1.

40. Ibid., 2, no. 21 (December 31, 1960): 3, 4.

41. Harry G. Boyte, "Education and the Unfinished Task of Democracy," [1961], conference paper, box 26, Boyte Family Papers.

42. Harry G. Boyte to Truman Nelson, August 23, 1962, ibid.

43. Janet Boyte, "White Rebel of SCLC."

44. Rogers lived in Harlem, and activists there considered his book "the handbook of the nationalist." It is interesting that the influence of black intellectuals in Harlem reached as far away as Monroe and then back again, when Robert Williams became an influential political presence in Harlem. See Smith and Sinclair, *Harlem Cultural/Political Movements*, 18, 45.

45. *Crusader* 2, no. 7 (August 27, 1960): 7.

46. Quoted in Lawrence W. Levine, "Marcus Garvey and the Politics of Revitalization," in Franklin, *Black Leaders of the Twentieth Century*, 105.

47. *Crusader* 1, no. 3 (July 11, 1959): 4.

48. Ibid., 2, no. 6 (August 20, 1960): 6.

49. Ibid., no. 13 (July 2, 1960): 3. See Raboteau, *Slave Religion*.

50. Ibid., 1, no. 41 (April 9, 1960): 7.

51. Ibid., 2, no. 6 (August 20, 1960): 5, and vol. 1, no. 42 (April 16, 1960): 5.

52. Ibid., 2, no. 16 (November 5, 1960): 5.

53. Ibid., 1, no. 47 (May 21, 1960): 5, and vol. 2, no. 27 (April 15, 1961): 2, 6.

54. Ibid., 2, no. 12 (October 8, 1960): 3.

55. Ibid., no. 6 (August 20, 1960): 6.

56. *Monroe Enquirer*, September 8, 1960.

57. *Crusader*, 2, no. 8 (September 3, 1960): 1–2.

58. Ibid., 1, no. 50 (June 11, 1960): 6.

59. *Monroe Enquirer*, August 18, 1960.

60. *Charlotte Observer*, August 22, 1960, clipping in Mola Papers; *Crusader* 2, no. 7 (August 27, 1960): 2.

61. Robert F. Williams, interview with Cohen, 658; *Crusader* 2, no. 15 (October 29, 1960): 3.

62. *Crusader* 2, no. 19 (December 10, 1960): 6.

63. Mr. and Mrs. Artis Ward to Robert F. Williams, July 2, 1963, box 1, Robert F. Williams Papers.

64. Lynn, interview; *Crusader* 2, no. 22 (January 21, 1961): 8.

65. Mallory, interview, 17–18; Muhammed Ahmad [Max Stanford], "Queen Mother Moore," in Buhle, Buhle, and Georgakas, *Encyclopedia of the American Left*, 486–87.

66. Robert F. Williams, interview with Mosby; Mallory, interview, 18.

67. Robert F. Williams to George Weissman, February 1, 1960, box 1, CCRI Papers.

68. Smith and Sinclair, *Harlem Cultural/Political Movements*, 46.

69. Cruse, *Crisis of the Negro Intellectual*, 358–59. Cruse argues that "Robert Williams himself was never a nationalist, but an avowed integrationist, a fact that later created much propaganda confusion." Here Cruse is perhaps excessively rigid in his insistence that everyone in the freedom struggle fit into his categories. It is not necessary, in my view, for black nationalists to eschew support for integration; one can believe, for example, that black ethnicity is an appropriate cultural and political engine and still believe that persons of that ethnicity should be able to enjoy the same privileges as anyone else and to make alliances with others who respect their views, whatever their color. Cruse portrayed Williams's worldview as insufficiently ideological and systematic, but in retrospect this seems a strength rather than a weakness.

70. *Crusader* 2, no. 19 (December 10, 1960): 6. Needless to say, Robert Williams did not report here that Mayfield and Clarke had brought weapons, but merely expressed thanks for the large load of clothing. Both Williams and Mayfield, however, noted the weapons in later accounts.

71. Robert F. Williams, interview with Mosby, 143.

72. Mayfield, interview, 41; Mayfield, "Challenge to Negro Leadership," 302.

73. Mayfield, "Tales from the Lido." I am grateful to Kevin Gaines for sharing these materials. Though it is speculation, Amiri Baraka [then LeRoi Jones] is a "famous black writer" who supported Williams and in 1959–60 had "rejected Martin Luther King's philosophy" and wrote "A Poem Some People Will Have to Understand," the last line of which is "Will the machinegunners step forward?" See Baraka, *Autobiography of LeRoi Jones*, 237. In an interview, Baraka neither confirmed nor denied having supplied the machine guns. See Baraka, interview with author. An anonymous but reliable source interview confirms that he did.

74. Robert F. Williams, interview with Cohen, 382–83. Historian Andrew Myers supports Williams on the point, stating flatly that Malcolm X's 116th Street temple "donated money for the purchase of arms." See Myers, "When Violence Met Violence," 26. Williams's FBI file indicates clearly that the bureau found Williams's relationship with Malcolm X alarming. See Director to Charlotte SAC, June 18, 1959, RFW/FBI. See also Gallen, *Malcolm X as They Knew Him*, 164–65.

75. FBI memo from Director to Charlotte SAC, June 18, 1959, "Security-NOI," RFW/FBI; Robert F. Williams, interview with Mosby, 252.

76. Robert F. Williams to George Weissman, February 1, 1960, box 1, CCRI Papers; Myers, "When Violence Met Violence," 26.

77. Robert F. Williams, *Negroes with Guns*, 120.

78. Ibid., 117.

79. Myers, "When Violence Met Violence," 44–45; Robert F. Williams, *Negroes with Guns*, 121.

80. Robert F. Williams, *Negroes with Guns*, 117–18.

81. *Crusader* 2, no. 33 (June 26, 1961): 5.

82. Patrick Jones, " 'Communist Front Shouts "Kissing Case" to World,' " 44.

83. Carey McWilliams to Robert F. Williams, July 23, 1959, box 1, Robert F. Williams Papers.

84. Slim Brundage to the editor, *Crusader* 1, no. 49 (June 4, 1960): 2.

85. Ibid., no. 41 (April 9, 1960): 9.

86. Ibid., 2, no. 17 (November 12, 1960): 8.

87. Robert F. Williams, *Negroes with Guns*, 111.

88. *Crusader* 2, no. 12 (October 8, 1960): 1, and no. 16 (November 5, 1960): 8.

89. Robert F. Williams, foreword to "Radio Free Dixie" manuscript, box 1, Robert F. Williams Papers, 1.

90. Memo from Director to Charlotte SAC, September 18, 1961, RFW/FBI.

91. FBI teletype, October 11, 1956, RFW/FBI; Robert F. Williams, interview with Cohen, 303–4; John Herman Williams and Edward Williams, interviews with Banchero.

92. Harry G. Boyte, "Education and the Unfinished Task of Democracy," [1961], conference paper, box 26, Boyte Family Papers.

93. Eskew, *But for Birmingham*, 19, 30.

94. Reddick, *Crusader without Violence*.

95. *Southern Patriot* 18, no. 11 (January 1960): 3.

96. Carl Braden to George Weissman, October 30, 1959, box 49, Braden Papers.

97. Eskew, *But for Birmingham*, 32, 48.

98. Garrow, *Bearing the Cross*, 254, 260–62; Branch, *Parting the Waters*, 765, 793–802.

99. *Southern Patriot* 21, no. 6 (June 1963): 3.

100. Ibid., 18, no. 11 (January 1960): 3.

101. Logan, *Betrayal of the Negro*. For Ida B. Wells's statement, see Giddings, *When and Where I Enter*, 20.

102. "Bad Nigger with a Winchester: Colored Editors Declare for Armed Resistance to Lynch Law," *Washington Post*, August 10, 1901. I am grateful to Ted Frantz for sharing this clipping with me. On W. E. B. Du Bois's preparation for armed self-defense, see Litwack, *Trouble in Mind*, 317. On Robert Moton's preparation for self-defense, see White, *A Man Called White*, 70.

103. Kelley, *Hammer and Hoe*, 45, 229. See also Carson, *In Struggle*, 162–64.

104. *Eagle Eye: The Woman's Voice*, August 20, 1955, 1.

105. "Statement of Dr. T. R. M. Howard," [1955], box A422, group 2, NAACP Papers.

106. Stewart Burns, *Daybreak of Freedom*, 22. See Lynd, *Nonviolence in America*.

107. *Fundhi: The Story of Ella Baker*, directed by Joanne Grant (Songtalk Publishing, 1980).

108. King, *Freedom Song*, 318.

109. Raboteau, *Slave Religion*. See also Charles Joyner, *Down by the Riverside: A South Carolina Slave Community* (Urbana: University of Illinois Press, 1984).

110. Kapur, *Raising Up a Prophet*, 163–64.

111. Robert F. Williams, interview with Mosby, 170–71.

112. Jervis Anderson, *Bayard Rustin*, 111–29, 183–98; Dan Georgakas, "David Dellinger," in Buhle, Buhle, and Georgakas, *Encyclopedia of the American Left*, 191.

113. *Crusader* 1, no. 15 (October 3, 1959). Memo, October 17, 1961, RFW/FBI, 9, reports the debate at Community Church and another one at the Libertarian Center on October 23, 1959, titled "Should Negroes Meet Violence with Violence?" Robert F. Williams was to debate on the affirmative team. See George Weissman to Carl Braden, October 20, 1959, box 49, Braden Papers.

114. *Liberation*, September, October 1959. The two essays appear side by side in the *Southern Patriot* 18, no. 11 (January 1960): 3, with an excellent commentary by editor Anne Braden. Abbreviated versions may be found in Carson et al., *Eyes on the Prize Civil Rights Reader*, 110–13. The account that follows draws on all of these sources.

115. Jervis Anderson, *Bayard Rustin*, 194.

116. Julian Bond to Timothy B. Tyson, September 5, 1997 (in possession of the author).

117. *Southern Patriot* 18, no. 11 (January 1960): 3, and 21, no. 2 (February 1963): 2.

118. Chafe, *Civilities and Civil Rights*, 71–72. This work remains the definitive treatment of the Greensboro sit-ins, one of the best local studies of the black freedom struggle and the most important work on racial politics in North Carolina.

119. The best work on SNCC remains Carson, *In Struggle*.

120. Barksdale, "Indigenous Civil Rights Movement," 326–27; *Charlotte Observer*, March 2, 1960; Robert F. Williams, *Negroes with Guns*, 67; *Monroe Enquirer*, January 2, 1961.

121. May, interview.

122. Clipping from *Charlotte Observer*, group 3, box A92, NAACP Papers.

123. Criminal Record #75CR9796. See also Myers, "When Violence Met Violence," 27.

124. *Charlotte Observer*, March 9, 1960; *Crusader* 1, no. 41 (April 9, 1960): 3.

125. *Crusader* 2, no. 31 (June 5, 1961): 3.

126. Ibid., 3, no. 4 (July 31, 1961): 7; Secrest, interview.

127. *Charlotte Observer*, March 22, 1960; *Crusader* 1, no. 46 (May 14, 1960): 1–2.

128. *Crusader* 1, no. 46 (May 14, 1960): 1–2.

129. See, for example, Branch, *Parting the Waters*, 370–80, and the section of photographs in the center of the book; Moody, *Coming of Age in Mississippi*, 264–67.

130. Robert F. Williams, *Negroes with Guns*, 68; May, interview.

CHAPTER EIGHT

1. Plummer, *Rising Wind*, 290–91; Drew Pearson, syndicated column, [September 1960], clipping in Williams Family Collection.

2. *Monroe Enquirer*, May 24, 1956.

3. Gosse, *Where the Boys Are*, 46.

4. Pérez, *Cuba and the United States*, 221–25; Schlesinger, *A Thousand Days*, 165.

5. Gosse, *Where the Boys Are*, 110–11; Schlesinger, *A Thousand Days*, 207.

6. Julian Mayfield, "Dear Friend," July 10, 1961, reel 15, frame 151, Du Bois Papers.

7. Gosse, *Where the Boys Are*, 110–11, 120–21, 170 n. 61; Plummer, *Rising Wind*, 287;

Welch, *Response to Revolution*, 127–28; Mayfield, "Author Says Cuba Has Solution to Race Problem"; Robert F. Williams, *Negroes with Guns*, 68–69.

8. Gosse, *Where the Boys Are*, 111–17; Wyden, *Bay of Pigs*, 26–29.

9. Gosse, *Where the Boys Are*, 6–7, 131–32, 148; Welch, *Response to Revolution*, 128; Plummer, *Rising Wind*, 288; Robert F. Williams, interview with Mosby.

10. Gosse, *Where the Boys Are*, 138–41; Robert F. Williams, interview with Cohen, 176–77.

11. LeRoi Jones, "Cuba Libre," 19; *Crusader* 1, no. 50 (June 11, 1960): 7–8; Robert F. Williams, interview with Mosby, 177; Robert F. Williams to Berta Green, June 28, 1960, quoted in Gosse, *Where the Boys Are*, 170 n. 64.

12. Baraka, interview with author; Mayfield, "Challenge to Negro Leadership," 300; *Crusader* 2, no. 8 (September 3, 1960): 3.

13. *Crusader* 1, no. 52 (June 25, 1960): 2; 2, no. 2 (July 9, 1960): 1; 2, no. 23 (February 4, 1961): 1.

14. *Crusader* 1, no. 52 (June 25, 1960): 1–2; memorandum, October 17, 1961, RFW/FBI, reported that the *Chicago Defender*, June 22, 1960, had printed these remarks by Robert Williams.

15. *Crusader* 1, no. 51 (June 18, 1960): 7–8.

16. Robert F. Williams, interview with Cohen, 406.

17. Robert F. Williams, "While God Lay Sleeping," 127; Carlos Moore, *Castro, the Blacks, and Africa*, 62, 387 n. 23.

18. Clarke, "Journey to the Sierra Maestra," 32–35.

19. William J. Harris, introduction to *The LeRoi Jones/Amiri Baraka Reader*, xvii.

20. Baraka, interview with author; Amiri Baraka, interview with Kim Benston, 1977, in Reilly, *Conversations with Amiri Baraka*, 108–9. Baraka also details the importance of Robert Williams to his political transformation in LeRoi Jones, "Cuba Libre," 13.

21. Baraka, *Autobiography of LeRoi Jones*, 241–44; LeRoi Jones, "Cuba Libre," 13; Clarke, "Journey to the Sierra Maestra," 33.

22. Mayfield, "Tales from the Lido"; Mayfield, interview, 40. My thanks to Kevin Gaines for sharing a copy of the Mayfield autobiography.

23. *Monroe Enquirer*, July 18, 1960; LeRoi Jones, "Cuba Libre," 19, 25, 32; Baraka, interview with author; *Crusader* 2, no. 8 (September 3, 1960): 2.

24. *Monroe Enquirer*, August 1, 1960.

25. Mabel R. Williams, interview with author, June 6, 1998.

26. Baraka, *Autobiography of LeRoi Jones*, 245.

27. Robert F. Williams, "While God Lay Sleeping," 128; Baraka, interview with author.

28. Clarke, "Journey to the Sierra Maestra," 34; *Crusader* 2, no. 3 (July 30, 1960): 1.

29. Cruse, *Crisis of the Negro Intellectual*, 356–57; LeRoi Jones, "Cuba Libre," 43–62; Clarke, "Journey to the Sierra Maestra," 35.

30. Robert F. Williams, "While God Lay Sleeping," 127.

31. *Crusader* 2, no. 3 (July 30, 1960): 1, and no. 5 (August 13, 1960): 2.

32. Lynn, *There Is a Fountain*, 167; Baraka, *Autobiography of LeRoi Jones*, 246.

33. Amiri Baraka, interview with Kim Benston, 1977, in Reilly, *Conversations with Amiri Baraka*, 108–9; Robert F. Williams, foreword to "Radio Free Dixie" manuscript, box 1, Robert F. Williams Papers, 1.

34. *Crusader* 1, no. 50 (June 11, 1960): 1.

35. Ibid., 2, no. 5 (August 13, 1960): 2.

36. *Monroe Enquirer*, September 22, 1960; Mealy, *Fidel and Malcolm X*, 33–35. Teresa Casuso, a member of the Cuban delegation who later defected, claimed that Castro calculated the move to Harlem all along. Other persons in a position to know attributed the idea to Richard Gibson or others within the Fair Play for Cuba Committee circle of activists. On balance, these accounts are more in keeping with the evidence. Whatever the origin of the idea, Conrad Lynn was correct to term it "a master stroke" of propaganda. See Casuso, *Cuba and Castro*, 237, 240–41; Mealy, *Fidel and Malcolm X*, 33–36; Lynn, *There Is a Fountain*, 168–69; Carlos Moore, *Castro, the Blacks, and Africa*, 78–79; Plummer, *Rising Wind*, 288–97.

37. Mealy, *Fidel and Malcolm X*, 21–22, 41–44, 48–49.

38. "Senator Sam Ervin Says," *Monroe Enquirer*, September 29, 1960.

39. Plummer, *Rising Wind*, 290–91; Gosse, *Where the Boys Are*, 150; Carlos Moore, *Castro, the Blacks, and Africa*, 79–80; Mealy, *Fidel and Malcolm X*, 50; Lynn, *There Is a Fountain*, 168–69.

40. Drew Pearson, syndicated column, September 1960, clipping in Williams Family Collection; Carlos Moore, *Castro, the Blacks, and Africa*, 80; Gosse, *Where the Boys Are*, 150; Plummer, *Rising Wind*, 293–95.

41. Gosse, *Where the Boys Are*, 145–47, 152; Robert F. Williams, interview with Cohen, 627.

42. Richard Gibson to Lyle Stuart, March 13, 1971, box 1, Cohen Papers.

43. Baraka, interview with author; Mabel R. Williams, interview with author, March 27, 1998.

44. *Fair Play* 2, no. 5 (October 25, 1960): 3; *Crusader* 2, no. 12 (October 8, 1960): 2; Gosse, *Where the Boys Are*, 148–49.

45. *Fair Play* 2, no. 10 (February 4, 1961): 1; Baraka, interview with author.

46. Smith and Sinclair, *Harlem Cultural/Political Movements*, 15.

47. *Crusader* 2, no. 26 (April 8, 1961): 3, 8.

48. James Baldwin, "East River, Downtown: A Postscript to a Letter from Harlem," in Baldwin, *Nobody Knows My Name*, 67; Lynn, *There Is a Fountain*, 163; Baraka, *Autobiography of LeRoi Jones*, 267.

49. Plummer, *Rising Wind*, 302–3.

50. James Baldwin, "East River, Downtown: Postscript to a Letter from Harlem," in Baldwin, *Nobody Knows My Name*, 68.

51. *Fair Play* 2, no. 10 (February 4, 1961): 1; *Student Council* 2, no. 2 (February 11, 1961): 4.

52. *Student Council* 2, no. 4 (March 24, 1961): 1, and no. 5 (May 22, 1961): 4; *Crusader* 2, no. 26 (April 8, 1961): 4.

53. Gosse, *Where the Boys Are*, 6; *Student Council* 2, no. 5 (May 22, 1961): 4.

54. Gosse, *Where the Boys Are*, 1; *Crusader* 2, no. 30 (May 29, 1961): 8.

55. *Monroe Enquirer*, April 10, 1961; Robert F. Williams, *Negroes with Guns*, 70. The correspondence between Williams and Current appears in both places.

56. Schlesinger, *A Thousand Days*, 267–68; Gosse, *Where the Boys Are*, 216–22.

57. Schlesinger, *A Thousand Days*, 273; *Crusader* 2, no. 28 (April 22, 1961): 6.

58. Carlos Moore, *Castro, the Blacks, and Africa*, 112–14.

59. Wyden, *Bay of Pigs*, 189–90. I. F. Stone, the independent leftist journalist, shrewdly noted that Stevenson's misguided tales "could not hide the truth from the Cubans; they knew they had not been bombed by planes from their own airfields. The false

story—and this is the important point—was designed to hide the truth from the American press and the American public." In short, the Kennedy administration had misled Stevenson, apparently because they thought he would lie more effectively if he believed the lies himself. The ambassador later told colleagues that he had been "deliberately tricked" by his own government. See Stone, In a Time of Torment, 390. The commentary was published first in I. F. Stone's Weekly on May 3, 1961, and the emphasis is in the original. See also Richard Reeves, President Kennedy, 109.

60. "Cuba—A Declaration of Conscience by Afro-Americans," Afro-American, April 22, 1961. Reprinted in Mealy, Fidel and Malcolm X, 79–80.

61. Carlos Moore, Castro, the Blacks, and Africa, 113.

62. Hilty, Brother Protector, 442.

63. News and Observer, May 19, 1961; Crusader 2, no. 30 (May 29, 1961): 8; Monroe Enquirer, May 18, 1961. See also Cohen, Black Crusader, 151–55. Cohen's account, while lively, is not notable for its strict adherence to the facts, and I do not draw on it here except for the quote from the NAACP official, which Williams confirmed in a telephone conversation.

CHAPTER NINE

1. Meier and Rudwick, CORE, 135.
2. Hilty, Brother Protector, 317; Branch, Parting the Waters, 413.
3. Moses Newson, "Mob Attacks Bus with Fire Bombs," Afro-American, May 20, 1961.
4. Peck, Freedom Ride, 124–26; Branch, Parting the Waters, 417–18.
5. "FBI-Klan Link Revealed," Dallas Morning News, August 20, 1978; Branch, Parting the Waters, 420–32.
6. "Will Ride Again," Pittsburgh Courier, May 27, 1961.
7. Branch, Parting the Waters, 445–50.
8. Ibid., 459–65.
9. Forman, Making of Black Revolutionaries, 147–48; Branch, Parting the Waters, 467–68.
10. Robert F. Williams to Martin Luther King Jr., May 20, 1961, quoted in Walker, "History of the Southern Christian Leadership Conference," 97–98; Robert F. Williams, "A Disappointing King," Crusader 2, no. 31 (June 5, 1961): 2–3.
11. Branch, Parting the Waters, 477.
12. New York Times, June 30, 1961.
13. Hilty, Brother Protector, 327–28.
14. Robert F. Williams, foreword to "Radio Free Dixie" manuscript, box 1, Robert F. Williams Papers, 2; George Beasley Jr., "Notes by the Wayside," Monroe Journal, June 27, 1961, clipping in box 111, Sanford Papers.
15. Monroe Enquirer, June 8, 1961.
16. Chafe, Civilities and Civil Rights, 103.
17. Sanford, interview.
18. Kelly Alexander and Charles McLean, "Annual Report, North Carolina State Conference, NAACP, 1961 Branch Activities," box C113, NAACP Papers.
19. Crusader 2, no. 32 (June 19, 1961): 2–3; A. W. Welch, Captain, Troop D, to David T. Lambert, Colonel, June 6, 1961, and David T. Lambert, Colonel, to Hugh Cannon, Office of the Governor, June 7, 1961, box 111, Sanford Papers.

20. Lynn, *There Is a Fountain*, 163–64; *Crusader* 2, no. 33 (June 26, 1961): 2.

21. *Crusader* 2, no. 32 (June 19, 1961): 5; C. Raymond Williams, Enforcement Division, to Hugh Cannon, Office of the Governor, June 26, 1961, box 111, Sanford Papers; *Monroe Enquirer*, June 22, 1961.

22. *Charlotte Observer*, June 25, 1961, clipping in box 111, Sanford Papers; *Crusader* 2, no. 33 (June 26, 1961): 3.

23. *Crusader* 2, no. 33 (June 26, 1961): 5.

24. Memorandum, including a lengthy statement given by Robert F. Williams, June 26, 1961, RFW/FBI; *Charlotte Observer*, June 24, 1961; Myers, "When Violence Met Violence," 28–29.

25. Robert F. Williams, "While God Lay Sleeping," 134–36.

26. Ibid., 136; *Charlotte Observer*, June 24, 1961, clipping in box 111, Sanford Papers; Myers, "When Violence Met Violence," 28–29; *Crusader* 3, no. 2 (July 17, 1961): 7.

27. Memo dated June 30, 1961, including statement by Robert F. Williams, June 26, 1961, RFW/FBI.

28. C. Raymond Williams, Director, State Highway Patrol Enforcement Division, to Hugh Cannon, Office of the Governor, June 26, 1961, box 111, Sanford Papers; memo dated June 30, 1961, RFW/FBI, contains both the statement by Robert Williams given June 26, 1961, and reports from FBI interviews with Police Chief Mauney and newspaper accounts.

29. Robert F. Williams, "While God Lay Sleeping," 137.

30. C. L. Teague to C. Raymond Williams, State Highway Patrol, June 30, 1961, box 111, Sanford Papers; Robert F. Williams, *Negroes with Guns*, 45.

31. C. Raymond Williams, Director, Enforcement Division, to Hugh Cannon, Office of the Governor, June 26, 1961, box 111, Sanford Papers.

32. Robert F. Williams, *Negroes with Guns*, 45–46; Robert F. Williams, "While God Lay Sleeping," 138–39. J. D. Blount, who was in the car, confirmed this story in all its details in an interview with the author at Williams's funeral in Monroe on October 22, 1996.

33. Robert F. Williams, "While God Lay Sleeping," 139; C. Raymond Williams, Director, Enforcement Division, to Hugh Cannon, Office of the Governor, June 26, 1961, box 111, Sanford Papers.

34. FBI teletype, June 26, 1961, RFW/FBI.

35. Memo, June 30, 1961, including statement by Robert F. Williams given June 26, 1961, 4:00 P.M., RFW/FBI.

36. Memorandum, June 30, 1961, RFW/FBI, 10–11.

37. *Charlotte News*, October 3, 1961; Myers, "When Violence Met Violence," 33–34.

38. *Monroe Journal*, June 27, 1961.

39. C. Raymond Williams, Director, Enforcement Division, to Hugh Cannon, Office of the Governor, June 26, 28, 1961, box 111, Sanford Papers.

40. Sanford, interview; Governor Terry Sanford to J. R. Larkins, July 20, 1961, box 112, and J. R. Larkins to Hugh Cannon, "Report on Union County and Monroe Race Situation," July 7, 1961, box 113, Sanford Papers, 1–7; *Crusader* 4, no. 5 (January 1963): 4.

41. Mabel R. Williams, interview with Salaam; Myers, "When Violence Met Violence," 30; *Crusader* 3, no. 4 (August 7, 1961): 1–2; Charlotte SAC to Director, teletype,

July 30, 1961, RFW/FBI; C. L. Teague to C. Raymond Williams, June 30, 1961, cc to Hugh Cannon, Office of the Governor, box 111, Sanford Papers.

42. *Crusader* 3, no. 1 (July 10, 1961): 3–4, 7; no. 4 (August 7, 1961): 6; no. 4 (July 31, 1961): 3. For the early August attack on Williams's house, see Walter F. Anderson to Hugh Cannon, September 14, 1961, including excerpts from the interrogation of Albert Rorie, September 5, 1961, box 111, Sanford Papers, 3; Robert F. Williams, interview with Mosby; Charlotte SAC to Director, August 8, 1961, RFW/FBI.

43. *Crusader* 3, no. 3 (July 24, 1961): 3; emphasis added.

CHAPTER TEN

1. Forman, *Making of Black Revolutionaries*, 146–48.
2. James Forman to David Ray, Vice President of the National Freedom Council, and Anne Braden, Field Secretary of the Southern Conference Educational Fund, August 5, 1961, box 56, Braden Papers.
3. Jefferson is quoted in Boles, *South through Time*, 176. For slave arson, see Genovese, *Roll, Jordan, Roll*, 613–15. For the persistence of arson as black protest in the post-Emancipation South, see Albert C. Smith, " 'Southern Violence' Reconsidered." For the persistence of arson as black protest during World War II, see Timothy B. Tyson, "Wars for Democracy: Racial Militancy and Interracial Violence in North Carolina during World War II," in Cecelski and Tyson, *Democracy Betrayed*, 253–75. For the persistence of arson as black protest in North Carolina during the postwar black freedom movement, see Tyson, "Burning for Freedom."
4. *Monroe Enquirer*, July 27, 31, August 3, 7, 10, 1961; *Crusader* 3, no. 6 (August 21, 1961): 4. Responsibility for these fires remains far from clear. "I introduced the Molotov cocktail to the struggle," Williams boasted ten years later (see Robert F. Williams, interview with Mosby). Pressed on this point, however, Williams stated that he had only referred to the fact that his sentries were armed with gasoline bombs that could throw up a wall of flame in case of massive Ku Klux Klan attacks (see Robert F. Williams, interview with author, March 23, 1993). It was true that the guards sometimes kept firebombs handy. Under interrogation by the police in 1961, seventeen-year-old Jay Vann Covington "stated that he had seen molotov cocktails in the grass behind Robert Williams' house." Covington also claimed not to know who had started the fires but acknowledged that "he had heard some people say that he [himself] had been doing it." During the same investigation, Albert Rorie "stated that he had heard some people say they had seen Jay Van Covington running up the street away from a warehouse the night of one of the fires." Rorie said he "had never seen Jay Vann Covington make any of these gasoline bombs although he had seen Robert Williams make them." Rorie upheld Williams's description of the role of the firebombs, noting that Williams "was expecting a visit from the Ku Klux Klan" and had instructed the youths to throw the firebombs "under the cars if the mob came by his house" (see Walter F. Anderson, State Bureau of Investigation, to Hugh Cannon, Office of the Governor, September 14, 1961, box 111, Sanford Papers, 3–7). Robert Williams's son John Williams claimed that his father had admonished the young men around him that he did not want to know who had done it, but that if they knew who was burning

the buildings, to tell them to stop because it was hurting the cause (see John Chalmers Williams, interview with author). By 1961 Big Jesse Helms had retired from the police department and had become fire chief.

5. James Forman to David Ray, Vice President of the National Freedom Council, and Anne Braden, Field Secretary of the Southern Conference Educational Fund, August 5, 1961, box 56, Braden Papers.

6. Paul Brooks to Nashville Christian Leadership Conference, August 19, 1961, box 1, Robert F. Williams Papers, lists the names of the Freedom Riders: Ed Bromberg, Larry Hunter, Paul Dietrich, Ed Kale, Ken Shilman, David Morton, Price Chatham, John Lowery, Richard Griswold, Joe McDonald, Frederick Leonard, Leroy Right, Charles Butler, Dan Thompson, William Mahoney, and Heath Rush; Janet Boyte, "White Rebel of SCLC"; Trillin, "Monroe, North Carolina, October 1969"; *Monroe Enquirer*, August 31, 1961; Burke Marshall, notes from conversation with Gordon Carey et al., alphabetical file, box 2, Kennedy Papers; Hinkel, interview.

7. Paul Brooks to Nashville Christian Leadership Conference, August 19, 1961, box 1, Robert F. Williams Papers; *Charlotte Observer*, August 16, 1961, in clipping file, Banchero Papers; Gene Gratz to Harry Golden, September 14, 196[1], pt. 2, box 2, Golden Papers; "The Freedom Riders Speak," *Crusader* 3, no. 6 (August 21, 1961): 3; *Southern Patriot* 19, no. 8 (October 1961): 2.

8. *Crusader* 3, no. 6 (August 21, 1961): 1; Robert F. Williams, "While God Lay Sleeping," 160–61.

9. *Crusader* 4, no. 7 (April 1963): 1–2, and 3, no. 6 (August 21, 1961): 1; Robert F. Williams, cable to William Worthy, October 3, 1961, box 1, Robert F. Williams Papers; Robert F. Williams, interview with Mosby.

10. Robert F. Williams, foreword to "Radio Free Dixie" manuscript, box 1, Robert F. Williams Papers; *Crusader* 3, no. 6 (August 21, 1961): 3; Robert F. Williams, "While God Lay Sleeping," 160–62; Robert F. Williams, interview with Mosby; Forman, *Making of Black Revolutionaries*, 187–88.

11. "English Girl Involves Self in Monroe's Race Violence," *Monroe Enquirer*, August 31, 1961; Lever, "Monroe Doctrine."

12. Mayfield, "Tales from the Lido," 3.

13. *Monroe Enquirer*, August 21, 1961.

14. Myers, "When Violence Met Violence," 33–34; Banchero, "Native Son Wants to Come Home"; Robert F. Williams, *Negroes with Guns*, 80; *Monroe Enquirer*, August 24, 1961. For the attack on Prentice Robinson, see Forman, *Making of Black Revolutionaries*, 188–89; Lever, "Monroe Doctrine"; Robert F. Williams, interview with Mosby; Robert F. Williams, "While God Lay Sleeping," 164.

15. Myers, "When Violence Met Violence," 33–34; Lynn, interview, 6; Robert F. Williams, interview with Mosby, 131–33; Julian Mayfield, "The Monroe Kidnapping," box 3, Robert F. Williams Papers, 2.

16. For city vehicles fogging the demonstrators with insecticide, see Myers, "When Violence Met Violence," 34; J. W. Rushing, city police captain, interview with Myers; Robert F. Williams, *Negroes with Guns*, 80; Cohen, *Black Crusader*, 174; Robert F. Williams, interview with Mosby; Lever, "Monroe Doctrine." For the air-rifle attack on Ed Bromberg, see Lowery, "Should Violence Be Met with Violence?"; Julian Mayfield, "The Monroe Kidnapping," box 3, Robert F. Williams Papers, 2; Forman, *Making of Black Revolutionaries*, 189.

17. C. Raymond Williams, Director, Enforcement Division, State Highway Patrol, to Edward Scheidt, Commissioner, Department of Motor Vehicles, August 28, 1961, box 113, Sanford Papers.

18. Lowery, "Should Violence Be Met with Violence?," 8; Forman, *Making of Black Revolutionaries*, 191–92; Lever, "Monroe Doctrine"; Robert F. Williams, interview with Mosby, 131–33; Julian Mayfield, "What Happened in Monroe, North Carolina," Detroit Committee to Aid the Monroe Defendants, [1961], box 3, Robert F. Williams Papers, 2.

19. Helms, "Viewpoint," reprinted in *Monroe Enquirer*, September 22, 1969; Furguson, *Hard Right*, 77; Robert F. Williams, interview with author, March 23, 1993. On Helms's defense of the Ku Klux Klan against what he viewed as unfair media coverage, see Furguson, *Hard Right*, 218–19.

20. Banchero, "Native Son Wants to Come Home," 20; Robert F. Williams, interview with Mosby, 128–29; Forman, *Making of Black Revolutionaries*, 192.

21. Forman, *Making of Black Revolutionaries*, 192; *Monroe Enquirer*, August 28, 1961; Lowery, "Should Violence Be Met with Violence?," 8.

22. Lowery, "Should Violence Be Met with Violence?," 8; "Union Observer," *Charlotte Observer*, February 3, 1991, estimates the crowd at 5,000; *Charlotte News*, August 29, 1961, clipping from London Collection, reported that "last night's violence . . . saw an estimated 5,000 persons jam the central business district . . . hundreds in cars which jammed the four-lane streets which box in the Union County Courthouse." The *Monroe Enquirer-Journal*, August 27, 1989, called the crowd "an estimated 2,000." Woodrow Wilson told reporters for the *Charlotte News*, October 3, 1981, "There were at least 4,000 or 5,000 white people downtown." Forman, *Making of Black Revolutionaries*, 193, estimated the crowd to be "at least three thousand people."

23. Myers, "When Violence Met Violence," 35–37; Lever, "Monroe Doctrine"; *Charlotte News*, October 3, 1981; Woodrow Wilson, interview; Forman, *Making of Black Revolutionaries*, 193–98; U.S. Government Memorandum, "Racial Situation, Monroe, North Carolina," August 28, 1961, RFW/FBI.

24. Lowery, "Should Violence Be Met with Violence?," 8; *Jet*, September 14, 1961, 17; *Monroe Enquirer*, August 28, 1961.

25. Mayfield, "Tales from the Lido," 33; Julian Mayfield, "The Monroe Kidnapping," box 3, Robert F. Williams Papers; C. Raymond Williams, Director, Enforcement Division, State Highway Patrol, to Edward Scheidt, Commissioner, Department of Motor Vehicles, August 28, 1961, box 113, Sanford Papers.

26. Shirley Rutherford to Roy Wilkins, February 14, 1962, box A92, group 3, NAACP Papers; *Charlotte Observer*, September 1, 1961; *Monroe Enquirer*, March 24, 1958, September 28, November 2, 1961; *News and Observer*, August 31, 1961; Julian Mayfield, "What Happened in Monroe, North Carolina," Detroit Committee to Aid the Monroe Defendants, [1961], box 3, Robert F. Williams Papers. Stack was released from jail, but a few weeks later Monroe authorities committed him to the state hospital for the criminally insane.

27. Mallory, interview, 20; Walter F. Anderson to Hugh Cannon, September 14, 1961, including an SBI report on the interrogations of Albert Rorie, September 5, 1961, and Jimmy Covington, September 6, 1961, box 111, Sanford Papers; Robert F.

Williams, interview with Mosby, 142; Myers, "When Violence Met Violence," 38; *Monroe Enquirer*, November 6, 1961.

28. C. Raymond Williams, Director, Enforcement Division, State Highway Patrol, to Edward Scheidt, Commissioner, Department of Motor Vehicles, August 28, 1961, box 113, Sanford Papers; *Charlotte News*, October 3, 1981; *News and Observer*, August 29, 1961; *Monroe Journal*, n.d. [ca. August 30, 1961], clipping in London Collection; Harry G. Boyte to Truman Nelson, August 23, 1962, box 26, Boyte Family Papers. For the attack on the Shute home, see also Albert E. Perry to Robert F. Williams, c/o Havana Radio, October 5, 1961, box 1, Robert F. Williams Papers. Dr. Perry writes, "Ray Shute has changed his phone and cannot be reached. Fifteen shots were fired into his house that night. He is scared as hell, too."

29. *Monroe Journal*, n.d. [late August 1961], clipping in box 20, London Collection; Lowery, "Should Violence Be Met with Violence?," 9; Robert F. Williams, interview with Cohen, 57. See also Walter F. Anderson to Hugh Cannon, September 14, 1961, including an SBI report on the interrogation of Marvin Reape, September 7, 1961, box 111, Sanford Papers, 15.

30. Myers, "When Violence Met Violence," 38–39. The details here are drawn from SBI reports on the interrogations of Howard Williams, Jimmy Covington, and Jonathon Dean Blount, all of which may be found in Walter F. Anderson to Hugh Cannon, September 14, 1961, box 111, Sanford Papers, 5–10.

31. Lowery, "Should Violence Be Met with Violence?," 9.

32. Janet Boyte, "White Rebel of SCLC"; Sanford, interview; 5:30 P.M., 28 Aug 61, telephone logs, box 9, Marshall Papers.

33. Sanford, interview.

34. *Monroe Journal*, n.d. [ca. late August 1961], clipping in box 20, London Collection; Robert F. Williams, interview with Cohen, 57.

35. C. Raymond Williams, Director, Enforcement Division, State Highway Patrol, to Edward Scheidt, Commissioner, Department of Motor Vehicles, August 28, 1961, box 113, Sanford Papers; Lowery, "Should Violence Be Met with Violence?," 9; Robert F. Williams, interview with Mosby, 149–50.

36. Lowery, "Should Violence Be Met with Violence?," 9; Stegall, interview.

37. According to Deputy Sheriff Cliff Dutton's report, "The Stegalls stated that they were leaving Monroe about 6:00 P.M. and due to traffic congestion, it was necessary for them to take back streets to get back on the highway. . . . They became lost and were traveling in colored section of town in an effort to get back on the highway. They were stopped and surrounded by approximately 200 colored people as they proceeded down a street in Monroe. They advised that practically all of the colored people were armed." See C. Raymond Williams, Director, Enforcement Division, State Highway Patrol, to Edward Scheidt, Commissioner, Department of Motor Vehicles, August 28, 1961, box 113, Sanford Papers. See also Lowery, "Should Violence Be Met with Violence?," 9; Robert F. Williams, interview with Mosby, 149–50; Stegall, interview.

38. Robert F. Williams, interview with Mosby; for the threats to kill the Stegalls, see also Walter F. Anderson, State Bureau of Investigation, to Hugh Cannon, Office of the Governor, September 6, 1961, including transcript of Howard Williams interrogation, box 111, Sanford Papers. See also Myers, "When Violence Met Violence," 39.

39. Dwayne Walls, "She Begged for Freedom 'But They Wouldn't Listen,'" *Charlotte Observer*, August 29, 1961; Robert F. Williams, interview with Mosby, 151.

40. *Southern Patriot* 22, no. 3 (March 1964): 4; Mabel R. Williams, telephone interview with author, January 23, 1998; Woodrow Wilson, quoted in *Charlotte News*, October 3, 1981; Stegall, interview.

41. "Text of Letter By Robert F. Williams," n.d. [ca. October 1961], box 1, Robert F. Williams Papers; "Testimony of Robert F. Williams," CR# 75CR9794, Union County Courthouse, Monroe, N.C.; Robert F. Williams written testimony, *State of North Carolina v. Richard Crowder, et al.,* [1962], box 3, Robert F. Williams Papers; Mallory, interview.

42. C. Raymond Williams, Director, Enforcement Division, State Highway Patrol, to Edward Scheidt, Commissioner, Department of Motor Vehicles, August 28, 1961, box 113, Sanford Papers; Mallory, interview, 21; Forman, *Making of Black Revolutionaries,* 201.

43. *Monroe Enquirer,* August 31, 1961; Stegall, interview. For a careful but slightly different evaluation of the alleged kidnapping, see Myers, "When Violence Met Violence," 39.

44. C. Raymond Williams, Director, Enforcement Division, State Highway Patrol, to Edward Scheidt, Commissioner, Department of Motor Vehicles, August 28, 1961, box 113, and Walter F. Anderson, State Bureau of Investigation, to Hugh Cannon, Office of the Governor, September 14, 1961, including transcript of Howard Williams interrogation, September 6, 1961, box 111, Sanford Papers; Robert F. Williams, interview with Mosby, 148.

45. Robert F. Williams, "While God Lay Sleeping," 182; Robert F. Williams, interview with Banchero; Robert F. Williams, *Negroes with Guns,* 88; also Robert F. Williams written testimony, *State of North Carolina v. Richard Crowder, et al.,* [1962], box 3, and "Text of Letter by Robert F. Williams," n.d. [ca. October 1961], and Robert F. Williams to "Doc," October 5, 1961, box 1, all in Robert F. Williams Papers.

46. For tales of Fidel Castro's helicopters, see Robert F. Williams, interview with Cohen, 478; see also notes from anonymous source interviews with the author, Monroe, N.C., November 22, 1996; Janet Boyte, "White Rebel of SCLC"; Robert F. Williams, "While God Lay Sleeping," 183–87; Mayfield, "Tales from the Lido," 35–37.

47. Robert F. Williams, interview with Cohen, 455–58; Mayfield, "Tales from the Lido," 36–37.

48. Robert F. Williams, interview with Cohen, 455–58; Robert F. Williams, "While God Lay Sleeping," 184.

49. "Amid a national manhunt by the FBI at the direction of Attorney General Robert Kennedy," Gosse writes, Williams "was spirited north to Canada by members of the SWP also active in Fair Play, and eventually made his way to Cuba via the U.S. and Mexico." This overstates the point and accepts speculation as fact; some of the people who helped Williams hide and escape were SWP members, but others were not. While Mexico was the usual route to Cuba during this period, Williams actually flew from Nova Scotia straight to Havana. See Gosse, *Where the Boys Are,* 154.

50. Mayfield, "Tales from the Lido," 38.

51. Robert F. Williams, "While God Lay Sleeping," 184; Worthy, "Visit from the FBI"; Myers, "When Violence Met Violence," 42, 61–63.

52. Radiogram, September 1, 1961, RFW/FBI; for the weapons located during the search of the black community in Monroe, see Doc [Dr. Albert E. Perry] to Mr. William Robert Worthy [Robert F. Williams], October 5, 1961, box 1, Robert F. Williams Papers; *Monroe Enquirer*, August 31, 1961; *Charlotte Observer*, August 29, 1961; Walter F. Anderson to Hugh Cannon, September 14, 1961, box 111, Sanford Papers.

53. Charlotte SAC to Director, FBI teletype, September 11, 1961, and Charlotte Field Office Report, "ROBERT FRANKLIN WILLIAMS," October 6, 1961, RFW/FBI; Doc [Dr. Albert E. Perry] to William Robert Worthy [Robert F. Williams], October 5, 1961, box 1, Robert F. Williams Papers; Charlotte SAC to Director, FBI teletype, September 11, 1961, RFW/FBI.

54. Radiogram, September 1, 1961, RFW/FBI; Shirley Graham Du Bois, *His Day Is Marching On*, 327–28.

55. Robert F. Williams, "While God Lay Sleeping," 185.

56. Worthy, "FBI in Cold War and Peace."

57. Robert F. Williams, "While God Lay Sleeping," 185–87.

58. *New York Times*, September 30, 1961.

59. J. Edgar Hoover to Kenneth O'Donnell, September 29, 1961, RFW/FBI.

60. "Radio Free Dixie," January 21, 1966, and September 11, 1964, audiotapes in box 9, Robert F. Williams Papers. See also Robert F. Williams, "Speech from Radio Free Dixie," in Van Deburg, *Modern Black Nationalism*, 94–97; "Radio Free Dixie" folder, series 1486, Johns Committee Papers. I am grateful to Alex Lichtenstein for calling my attention to the Johns Committee Papers.

CONCLUSION

1. Charlotte field office report, June 6, 1963, RFW/FBI, 7; also Hank Weiner, Des Moines, Wash., to Robert F. Williams, July 24, 1966; Joseph H. Boatwright, Basking Ridge, N.J., to Radio Free Dixie, February 5, 1966; Alan O. Campbell to Robert F. Williams, October 5, 1964; David Rattray to Robert F. Williams, September 24, 1963; and Conrad Lynn to Mabel Williams, January 30, 1963, all in box 1, Robert F. Williams Papers.

2. Robert F. Williams, interview with Cohen, 622–23.

3. "Radio Free Dixie" audiotapes, box 9, Robert F. Williams Papers; transcripts of "Radio Free Dixie," August 7, 1964, series 1486, carton 18, Johns Committee Papers. The Reverend Albert B. Cleage's editorials were taken from *Illustrated News* in Detroit. For his theological legacy to the Black Power movement, see Cleage, *Black Messiah*.

4. "Richard" at NOW! magazine to Robert F. Williams, September 5, 1966; Anne and Vernel Olsen to Robert and Mabel Williams, September 12, 1962; Robert F. Williams to "Leroi," ca. 1963; William Worthy to Robert F. Williams, September 21, 1961, attached draft article, all in box 1, Robert F. Williams Papers.

5. Transcript of "Radio Free Dixie," August 7, 1964, series 1486, carton 18, Johns Committee Papers; Robert F. Williams, interview with Cohen, 622–23.

6. Marc Schliefer to Carl Marzani, March 9, 1963; Ken Greaves, KPFA Radio, Berkeley, Calif., to Robert F. Williams, August 19, 1963; Robert Perkins, Los Angeles,

Calif., to Robert F. Williams, December 15, 1962, all in box 1, Robert F. Williams Papers.

7. Robert F. Williams, *Negroes with Guns*, 39–40, 120; *Detroit Free Press*, August 12, 1969, clipping attached to Detroit SAC to Director, September 30, 1969, RFW/FBI. For Williams's influence on Newton, see Horowitz, *Destructive Generation*, 146. Horowitz, a harsh and vituperative critic of Newton, describes Williams's book as the single most important intellectual influence on Newton. Hugh Pearson, a critic who shows far more sympathy, confirms in *Shadow of the Panther*, 28, that *Negroes with Guns* "fascinate[d]" Newton. Gilbert Moore, an uncritical admirer of Newton, traces the Black Panther leader's political awareness to his discovery of Robert Williams. See Gilbert Moore, *Special Rage*, 4. See also Newton, *Revolutionary Suicide*, 112.

8. Anne Leslie, "Exciting in Form, Ugly in Content" (Los Angeles) *People's World*, July 3, 1965. "LIVE is only running out of bookings now," author Frank Greenwood wrote to Robert Williams six months after the review. "We appeared in Watts and really shook up and inspired the brothers out there. . . . The reception was something else, Bob. My folks are ready, man! And particularly the young ones. . . . We did a free show for Watts and Venice teenagers at the center and afterwards they got up en masse and applauded!" See Frank Greenwood to Robert F. Williams, December 1, 1965, box 1, Robert F. Williams Papers. *The Crusader* was popular in Watts, though it is absurd to blame Williams for the Watts riot, as many right-wing observers did. See Horne, *Fire This Time*, 265, 268.

9. "Bill" to Robert F. Williams, April 29, 1962, and Gary Green to Robert F. Williams, n.d., box 1, Robert F. Williams Papers.

10. Stuart R. Schram, *The Political Thought of Mao Tse Tung* (New York: Praeger, 1969), 409–12. This was originally published in *Hung-ch'i*, no. 16 (1963): 1–2. See also Robert F. Williams, interview with Cohen, 665.

11. Robert F. Williams, "While God Lay Sleeping," 189.

12. Robert F. Williams to "Max," n.d., box 1, Robert F. Williams Papers.

13. For circulation information on *The Crusader*, see U.S. Senate, *Testimony of Robert F. Williams*, pt. 2, 90. See also Robert F. Williams, interview with Cohen, 623–24. For evidence of the extent of the newsletter's distribution in the Mississippi movement, see Supplemental Correlation Summary, April 19, 1969, bureau memorandum, June 23, 1964, RFW/FBI, and copies of *The Crusader* 5, no. 3 (March–April 1964), attached to it.

14. See untitled report, [summer 1964], Robert F. Williams file, Mississippi State Sovereignty Commission Papers. See also speech by Rep. William M. Colmer, October 3, 1964, *Congressional Record*, October 22, 1964. See also notes attached to a copy of *The Crusader* found in box 135, Johnson Family Papers; see also *Shreveport Councilor*, September 30, 1964, in Robert Williams file, Mississippi State Sovereignty Commission Papers. My thanks to Elizabeth A. Corris for locating these materials for me. For transcripts of SNCC deliberations in which Williams was cited, see Lyons, *Memories of the Southern Civil Rights Movement*, 147.

15. Meier and Rudwick, *CORE*, 202–4.

16. Bell, *CORE and the Strategy of Nonviolence*, 57; Meier and Rudwick, *CORE*, 263–64; see also Fairclough, *Race and Democracy*, 342.

17. Slater King to Robert F. Williams, November 10, 1963, box 1, Robert F. Williams Papers.

18. Clyde Appleton to Robert F. Williams, September 20, 1965, ibid.

19. Hill, "Deacons," 47–63; Fairclough, *Race and Democracy*, 342, 345, 357–59. See also Charles R. Sims, interview with William Price, *National Guardian*, August 20, 1965, reprinted in Aptheker, *Documentary History of the Negro People*, 373–79.

20. Lawrence Henry to Robert F. Williams, March 31, 1966, box 1, Robert F. Williams Papers.

21. Robert F. Williams, interview with Mosby, 180–81.

22. Helen Travis to "Hi, friends," February 28, 1962, attached to Michigan State Police Complaint Report, March 13, 1962, RFW/FBI.

23. Lynn, *There Is a Fountain*, 174.

24. Robert F. Williams to Conrad Lynn, February 27, 1962, box 1, Robert F. Williams Papers.

25. Memorandum from A. B. Eddy to Mr. Evans, May 14, 1962, RFW/FBI.

26. Mabel R. Williams, interview with Banchero, 2.

27. Robert F. Williams, interview with Cohen, 576–77; Robert F. Williams, "While God Lay Sleeping," 191–93.

28. Jackson, "Democratic Uprising of the Negro People," 19.

29. Robert F. Williams, "While God Lay Sleeping," 195–96; Robert F. Williams, interview with Cohen, 513; Robert F. Williams to "Brother Sherman," n.d., and to Mae Mallory, n.d., box 1, Robert F. Williams Papers.

30. Robert F. Williams, interview with Cohen, 516–17, 580–83; Robert F. Williams, interview with Mosby, 198.

31. Robert F. Williams to Mae Mallory, n.d., box 1, Robert F. Williams Papers.

32. Robert F. Williams to "Harry," n.d., ibid.

33. Robert F. Williams, interview with Cohen, 845–51; Robert F. Williams to Julian Mayfield, n.d. [1964], Robert F. Williams Papers.

34. Transcript, "Television Interview in the Hotel Kilamanjaro," July 20, 1968, box 1, Cohen Papers, 26.

35. Myers, "When Violence Met Violence," 69.

36. Rittenberg, "Recollections of Robert F. Williams," 1.

37. Robert F. Williams, interview with Mosby, 211.

38. CIA report, "Robert Franklin Williams," August 28, 1969, RFW/FBI; Robert F. Williams to Conrad Lynn, September 29, 1966, box 1, Robert F. Williams Papers. For copies of Williams's antiwar propaganda, see Robert Williams, *Listen, Brother*, a pamphlet in the Robert F. Williams Papers.

39. Rittenberg, "Recollections of Robert F. Williams," 2; Robert F. Williams, interview with Cohen, 312; Robert F. Williams, interview with Mosby, 196; Mabel Williams to Timothy Tyson, December 4, 1998, in author's possession. For Ho's experience with the French Communist Party, see Stanley Karnow, *Vietnam: A History* (New York: Viking, 1983), 152, 154.

40. Robert F. Williams, telegrams to James Farmer; James Forman; Senators Wayne Morse, Ernest Gruening, and Paul Douglas; the War Resisters League; Women's Strike for Peace; the Organization of Afro-American Unity; and Martin Luther King Jr., SCLC, April 27, 1965, box 1, Robert F. Williams Papers. Diane Nash Bevel spent about a month in Vietnam with a small group of American women in 1966. See Halberstam, *The Children*, 629. For King's evolving position on the Vietnam War, see Garrow, *Bearing the Cross*, 394, 422, 425, 428–30, 436–40, 443–46, 449–

50, 453, 455, 458–59, 461, 469–70, 472, 485, 502, 538, 539, 541–47, 549–61, 564–66, 572–73, 575–78, 592, 595, 604, 697–98 n. 20, 708 n. 16.

41. CIA report, "Robert Franklin Williams," August 28, 1969, RFW/FBI; Rittenberg, "Recollections of Robert F. Williams," 2–4.

42. *Robert Williams in China*, videotape in possession of the author; copies are available at the Bentley Historical Library, Ann Arbor, Mich., and the Wilson Library, University of North Carolina, Chapel Hill. See also Robert F. Williams to Paul Ramos, November 10, 1966, box 1, Robert F. Williams Papers.

43. Robert F. Williams to Paul Ramos, November 10, 1966, box 1, Robert F. Williams Papers.

44. Monroe S. Frederick III, to Robert F. Williams, n.d. [1964], ibid.

45. Gallen, *Malcolm X as They Knew Him*, 164–65.

46. Richard Gibson to Robert F. Williams, March 5, 1965, box 1, Robert F. Williams Papers; Ralph Matthews, "The Fugitive: Robert Williams—Can He Win the Unity Sought by Malcolm X?," *Afro-American*, April 20, 1966, clipping in RFW/FBI; Sackett, "Plotting a War on Whitey."

47. *Southern Patriot* 22, no. 5 (May 1964): 3; Sales, *From Civil Rights to Black Liberation*, 99–100, 130, writes, "RAM had direct ties to Robert Williams, then exiled in Cuba and the nationalist wing of the southern student movement and its northern support groups. RAM also had a grounding in Marxist-Leninist ideology which gave to its variant of Black nationalism a particularly leftist character."

48. CIA report, "Revolutionary Action Movement," August 8, 1968, copy in RFW/FBI; Robert F. Williams, interview with Cohen, 4A3-14-15; "The Role of RAM and the Militant Marxists: Hints—and Denials—of Conspiracy in Race Riots," *National Observer*, August 1, 1966, 3, clipping in Robert F. Williams file, Mississippi State Sovereignty Commission Papers.

49. Myers, "When Violence Met Violence," 70–71.

50. CIA report, "Revolutionary Action Movement," August 8, 1968, copy in RFW/FBI; Robert F. Williams, interview with Cohen, 14–15; Robert F. Williams, interview with Mosby, 252.

51. Investigative Report, "Republic of New Africa," December 7, 1971, Office of the Attorney General, State of Mississippi, Robert Williams File, Mississippi State Sovereignty Commission Papers; Van Deburg, *New Day in Babylon*, 144–49; Robert F. Williams, interview with Mosby, 248.

52. Sackett, "Plotting a War on Whitey"; Clayborne Carson, "The Black Panther Party," in Buhle, Buhle, and Georgakas, *Encyclopedia of the American Left*, 96.

53. Newton, *Revolutionary Suicide*, 112; Hampton and Fayer, *Voices of Freedom*, 356.

54. Lee Lockwood, ed., *Conversation with Eldridge Cleaver* (New York: Dell, 1970), 89.

55. CIA report, "Robert Franklin Williams," August 28, 1969, RFW/FBI; Major, *A Panther Is a Black Cat*, 63–64.

56. This claim is probably an exaggeration, though its degree of validity reflects not only Williams's appeal among increasingly radical black youth but also, as the report noted, "the apparent diminution in the leadership of Stokely Carmichael, H. Rap Brown, Eldridge Cleaver, and other black leaders; one wonders if Williams is about to claim the center of the Black Power stage." See CIA report, "Robert Franklin Williams," August 28, 1969, RFW/FBI, 2.

57. *Crusader* 9, no. 2 (September–October 1967): 1; Clayborne Carson, "Rethinking

African-American Political Thought in the Post-Revolutionary Era," in Ward and Badger, *Making of Martin Luther King Jr.*, 121–22.

58. Robert F. Williams, interview with Cohen, 4A4-22.

59. Robert Carl Cohen to Robert F. Williams, February 4, 1969, box 1, Cohen Papers; Robert F. Williams, interview with Banchero, 2; *Monroe-Journal*, August 27, 1989, 1-D.

60. Robert F. Williams to Mae Mallory, September 15, 1967, box 1, Robert F. Williams Papers; Robert F. Williams to Robert Carl Cohen, April 26, 1969, box 1, Cohen Papers, 3. See Cohen, *Black Crusader*.

61. CIA report, "Robert Franklin Williams," August 28, 1969, RFW/FBI, 2.

62. Robert Carl Cohen to Robert F. Williams, April 13, 1969, and Robert F. Williams to Robert Carl Cohen, April 26, 1969, box 1, Cohen Papers.

63. Robert F. Williams, "While God Lay Sleeping," 265–67.

64. Helms, "Viewpoint." J. H. Gale, U.S. Government Memorandum to Mr. DeLoach, September 22, 1969, RFW/FBI, states, "The State Department has worked out with TWA arrangements for the return of Williams to the United States." J. Walter Yeagley, Assistant Attorney General, Internal Security Division, memorandum, September 10, 1969, RFW/FBI, states, "It is our understanding that at the request of the British authorities in facilitating Williams' onward travel, the State Department advised TWA that it would appreciate such assistance in effecting Williams' onward travel under such safety precautions as TWA deemed necessary."

65. *New York Times*, September 13, 1969; Myers, "When Violence Met Violence," 75–76.

66. Paul H. Kreisburg, Department of State, to Robert F. Williams, December 22, 1969, RFW/FBI.

67. Gwendolyn Midlo Hall, "Tribute to Robert F. Williams"; Robert F. Williams, interview with Mosby.

68. J. Walter Yeagley, Assistant Attorney General, Internal Security Division, to Will R. Wilson, Assistant Attorney General, Criminal Division, August 8, 1969, RFW/FBI.

69. Robert F. Williams interview, *Black Scholar*, May 1970, 11.

70. Ibid.

71. Myers, "When Violence Met Violence," 76–77.

72. Robert F. Williams, interview with Banchero, 18; Robert F. Williams to Mae Mallory, n.d., box 1, Robert F. Williams Papers.

73. Robert F. Williams, interview with Mosby, 107.

74. James Bock, "A New Debate over Nonviolence," *Baltimore Sun-Journal*, March 2, 1997.

75. Father Joseph Fix, eulogy for Robert F. Williams, October 22, 1996, Central Methodist Church, Monroe, N.C., author's notes; videotape in Williams Family Collection.

76. Stephanie Banchero, "Civil Rights Activist Gets Hero's Welcome," *Charlotte Observer*, August 20, 1995; Becky Fischer, "Civil Rights Activist Returns for Winchester Reunion," *Enquirer-Journal*, August 20, 1995.

77. Rosa Parks, eulogy for Robert F. Williams, November 22, 1996, Central Methodist Church, Monroe, N.C., author's notes; videotape in Williams Family Collection.

Bibliography

MANUSCRIPT SOURCES

Fred Alexander Papers. Special Collections. J. Murray Atkins Library. University of North Carolina, Charlotte.

Kelly Alexander Papers. Special Collections. J. Murray Atkins Library. University of North Carolina, Charlotte.

Stephanie Banchero Papers. Madison, Wisc. In possession of the author.

Daisy Bates Papers. State Historical Society of Wisconsin. University of Wisconsin, Madison.

Black History File. Heritage Room. Union County Courthouse. Monroe, N.C.

Boyte Family Papers. Special Collections. Perkins Library. Duke University, Durham, N.C.

Carl and Anne Braden Papers. State Historical Society of Wisconsin. University of Wisconsin, Madison.

Governor J. Melville Broughton Papers. North Carolina Division of Archives and History. Raleigh.

Ralph Johnson Bunche Oral History Collection. Moorland-Spingarn Research Center. Howard University, Washington, D.C.

Cherokee County. South Carolina Criminal Court Records. No. 18737, *State of South Carolina v. James R. McCullough and James E. Painter, Jr.*, December 6, 1957. Gaffney, S.C.

Governor R. Gregg Cherry Papers. North Carolina Division of Archives and History. Raleigh.

Robert Carl Cohen Papers. State Historical Society of Wisconsin. University of Wisconsin, Madison.

James William Cole Papers. East Carolina Manuscript Collection. J. Y. Joyner Library. East Carolina University, Greenville, N.C.

Committee to Combat Racial Injustice Papers. State Historical Society of Wisconsin. University of Wisconsin, Madison.

Jonathan Daniels Papers. Southern Historical Collection. Louis Round Wilson Library. University of North Carolina, Chapel Hill.

W. E. B. Du Bois Papers, microfilm. Amistad Research Center. Tulane University, New Orleans, La.

Duke University Oral History Collection. Special Collections. Perkins Library. Duke University, Durham, N.C.

Governor O. Max Gardner Papers. North Carolina Division of Archives and History. Raleigh.

Harry Golden Papers. Special Collections. J. Murray Atkins Library. University of North Carolina, Charlotte.

Reginald Hawkins Papers. Special Collections. J. Murray Atkins Library. University of North Carolina, Charlotte.

Hays Collection. Richard B. Thornton Public Library. Oxford, N.C.

Governor Luther H. Hodges Papers. North Carolina Division of Archives and History. Raleigh.

Johns Committee Papers. Florida State Archives. Tallahassee.

John F. Kennedy Papers. John F. Kennedy Library. Boston, Mass.

Johnson Family Papers. University of Southern Mississippi. Manuscript Collections. Hattiesburg, Miss.

Nell Battle Lewis Papers. North Carolina Division of Archives and History. Raleigh.

Isaac S. London Collection. North Carolina Division of Archives and History. Raleigh.

Burke Marshall Papers. John F. Kennedy Library. Boston, Mass.

Julian Mayfield Papers. Schomburg Center for Research in Black Culture. New York Public Library. New York.

Mississippi State Sovereignty Commission Papers. Jackson.

Laura Mola Papers. Madison, Wisc. In possession of the author.

Reverend John B. Morris Papers. South Carolinia Library. University of South Carolina, Columbia.

National Association for the Advancement of Colored People Papers. Library of Congress. Washington, D.C.

North Carolina Collection. Durham County Public Library. Durham, N.C.

North Carolina Collection. Louis Round Wilson Library. University of North Carolina, Chapel Hill.

Franklin Delano Roosevelt Papers. Franklin Delano Roosevelt Library. Hyde Park, N.Y.

Governor Terry Sanford Papers. North Carolina Division of Archives and History. Raleigh.

Governor Kerr Scott Papers. North Carolina Division of Archives and History. Raleigh.

Socialist Workers Party Papers. State Historical Society of Wisconsin. University of Wisconsin, Madison.

Southern Christian Leadership Conference Papers. Martin Luther King Jr. Center for Nonviolent Social Change. Atlanta, Ga.

Southern Historical Collection. Louis Round Wilson Library. University of North Carolina, Chapel Hill.

John Herman Williams Collection. Detroit, Mich.

Robert and Mabel Williams Family Collection. Baldwin, Mich.

Robert Franklin Williams Papers. Bentley Historical Library. University of Michigan, Ann Arbor.

INTERVIEW SOURCES

Interviews are by the author and privately held unless otherwise noted.

Baraka, Amiri. Madison, Wisc., April 9, 1998. Notes and audiotape.

Bazemore, P. E. Duke University Oral History Collection. Special Collections. Perkins Library. Duke University, Durham, N.C.

Belton, Edward. Interview with Marcellus Chandler Barksdale. April 30, 1977. Box 9, Duke University Oral History Collection. Special Collections. Perkins Library. Duke University, Durham, N.C.

———. Interview with Stephanie Banchero. [1995]. Transcript. Stephanie Banchero Papers. Madison, Wisc.

Black, Robert. Interview with Lane Windham. Greensboro, N.C., [1993]. Privately held.

Blount, J. D. Monroe, N.C. October 22, 1996.

Byrd, Walter. Interview with Stephanie Banchero. Monroe, N.C., [1995]. Transcript. Stephanie Banchero Papers. Madison, Wisc.

Cavers, Reverend Walter. Charlotte, N.C., [1994].

Cherry, Annie Bell. Interview with Stephanie Banchero. Monroe, N.C., [1995]. Transcript. Stephanie Banchero Papers. Madison, Wisc.

Gray, Elgie. Interview with Stephanie Banchero. [1995]. Stephanie Banchero Papers. Madison, Wisc.

Hall, Gwendolyn Midlo. New Orleans, La., [1994].

Hawkins, Reginald. Interview with Stephanie Banchero. Charlotte, N.C., [1996]. Transcript. Stephanie Banchero Papers. Madison, Wisc.

Hill, Herbert. September 18, 1995.

Hinkel, James. Interview with Stephanie Banchero. [1996]. Stephanie Banchero Papers. Madison, Wisc.

Hodges, Governor Luther H. Southern Historical Collection. Louis Round Wilson Library. University of North Carolina, Chapel Hill.

Kendrick, Virginia. Interview with Stephanie Banchero. Monroe, N.C., [1996]. Transcript. Stephanie Banchero Papers. Madison, Wisc.

Lynn, Conrad. Interview with Malaika Lumumba. May 11, 1970. Transcript. Ralph Johnson Bunche Oral History Collection. Moorland-Spingarn Research Center. Howard University, Washington, D.C.

McCoy, James Edward. Oxford, N.C., June 11, 1991.

McDonald, Julias Crowder. Monroe, N.C.

McDow, J. W. Monroe, N.C., September 17, 1993.

Mallory, Mae. [1970]. Transcript. Ralph Johnson Bunche Oral History Collection. Moorland-Spingarn Research Center. Howard University, Washington, D.C.

May, W. R. Monroe, N.C., May 26, 1994.

Mayfield, Julian. Transcript. Ralph Johnson Bunche Oral History Collection. Moorland-Spingarn Research Center. Howard University, Washington, D.C.

Rorie, Magdalene Gillespie. Interview with Marcellus Chandler Barksdale. May 1, 1977. Box 9, Duke University Oral History Collection. Special Collections. Perkins Library. Duke University, Durham, N.C.

———. Interview with Stephanie Banchero. [1995]. Transcript. Stephanie Banchero Papers. Madison, Wisc.

Ross, Dean. Gaffney, S.C., [1993].

Rushing, J. W. Interview with Andrew Myers. Notes. [1993]. In possession of Andrew Myers, Columbia, S.C.

Rushing, James. Interview with Stephanie Banchero. Monroe, N.C., [1995]. Transcript. Stephanie Banchero Papers. Madison, Wisc.

Sanders, Dr. James H., Jr. Brevard, N.C., [1993].

Sanford, Senator Terry. Durham, N.C., July 22, 1993. Audiotape.

Secrest, Andrew McDowd. Chapel Hill, N.C., [1993].

Shute, J. Raymond. Interview with J. Ammons. "Monroe Symposium," #4007, B-54-2, Southern Oral History Collection.

——. Interview with Wayne Durrill. June 25, 1982. Transcript. Southern Historical Collection. Louis Round Wilson Library. University of North Carolina, Chapel Hill.

Stegall, Mrs. C. Bruce. Interview with Algernon Watt. *London Daily Telegram* [1962]. Audiotape in possession of the author.

Thompson, Evelyn. Interview with Oprah Winfrey. "The Oprah Winfrey Show," April 2, 1993. Transcript.

Thompson, James Hanover Grissom. Durham, N.C., May 13, 1993.

Wallace, Max. Gaffney, N.C., [1993].

Williams, Edward. Interview with Stephanie Banchero. [1995]. Stephanie Banchero Papers. Madison, Wisc.

Williams, John Herman. Detroit, Mich., October 20, 1996; March 21, October 15, 1997; June 7, 25, 1998.

——. Interview with Stephanie Banchero. 1994; [February 1995]. Transcript. Stephanie Banchero Papers, Madison, Wisc.

Williams, John Chalmers. Detroit, Mich., November 15, 1996.

Williams, Mabel Robinson. Baldwin, Mich., March 10, 1993; July 24, 1997; January 23, March 20, 27, June 6, 1998.

——. Interview with Anne Braden. [1959]. Notes in box 56, Carl and Anne Braden Papers. State Historical Society of Wisconsin. University of Wisconsin, Madison.

——. Interview with Kalamu ya Salaam. New Orleans, La., March 23, 1997. Audiotape and transcript in possession of the author.

——. Interview with Stephanie Banchero. [1994]. Transcript. Stephanie Banchero Papers, Madison, Wisc.

Williams, Robert Franklin. Baldwin, Mich., March 10, 23, May 13, 1993; September 2, 1996.

——. Interview with Robert Carl Cohen. 1968. Transcript. Box 1, Robert Carl Cohen Papers. State Historical Society of Wisconsin. University of Wisconsin, Madison.

——. Interview with Stephanie Banchero. [1995]. Transcript. Stephanie Banchero Papers, Madison, Wisc.

——. Interview with Thomas Mosby. [1970]. Transcript. Ralph Bunche Oral History Collection. Moorland-Spingarn Research Center. Howard University, Washington, D.C.

Wilson, Mary C. Monroe, N.C., September 17, 1991.

Wilson, Woodrow. Interview with Marcellus Chandler Barksdale. [1976]. Box 9, tape 21, Duke University Oral History Collection. Special Collections. Perkins Library. Duke University, Durham, N.C.

Winfield, B. J. Interview with Marcellus Chandler Barksdale. [1976]. Box 9, Duke University Oral History Collection. Special Collections. Perkins Library. Duke University, Durham, N.C.

——. Interview with Stephanie Banchero. [1995]. Transcript. Stephanie Banchero Papers, Madison, Wisc.

Clark, Walter, ed. *State Records of North Carolina.* Vol. 11. Goldsboro, N.C., 1907.
Code of the City of Monroe, 1958. North Carolina Collection. Louis Round Wilson
    Library. University of North Carolina, Chapel Hill.
Criminal Record #75CR9796. March 11, 1960. Union County Courthouse. Monroe, N.C.
Laws of the State of North Carolina. North Carolina Collection. Louis Round Wilson
    Library. University of North Carolina, Chapel Hill.
Marshall, Thurgood. Federal Bureau of Investigation Subject File, no. 100-111437.
Population and Economy of Monroe, North Carolina. North Carolina Collection. Louis
    Round Wilson Library. University of North Carolina, Chapel Hill.
To Secure These Rights: The Report of the President's Committee on Civil Rights. New York:
    Simon and Schuster, 1947.
Union County, North Carolina. Record of Military Discharges. Union County Public
    Library.
U.S. Bureau of the Census. *Census of the United States, 1920: Farm Tenancy in the United
    States.* Washington, D.C.: Government Printing Office, 1924.
——. Eighth Census of the United States, Population Schedules, North Carolina.
    Volume 4, Slave Schedules, Union County. Union County Public Library. Monroe, N.C.
——. U.S. Census of 1930. Vol. 3.
——. U.S. Census of Housing, 1960.
——. U.S. Census of the Population, 1960.
U.S. Senate. *Hearings before the Subcommittee to Investigate the Administration of the Internal
    Security Act and Other Internal Security Laws of the Committee on the Judiciary, Testimony of
    Robert F. Williams.* 91st Cong., 2d sess., pt. 1., February 16, 1970; pt. 2, March 24,
    1970; pt. 3, March 25, 1970.
Williams, Robert Franklin. Federal Bureau of Investigation Subject File. Obtained
    under the Freedom of Information Act, Baldwin, Mich.

PAMPHLETS

Braden, Anne. *House Un-American Activities Committee: Bulwark of Segregation.* Los
    Angeles: National Committee to Abolish the House Un-American Activities
    Committee, 1963. In possession of the author.
Conference on Race Relations. North Carolina College for Negroes, July 10, 11, 12, 1944,
    Durham, N.C. North Carolina Collection at the Durham County Public Library.
Cousins, Ralph E., Larry A. Jackson, and John B. Morris, eds. *South Carolinians Speak: A
    Moderate Approach to Race Relations.* Dillon, S.C., 1957. In possession of the author.
Laney, T. B. *Biographies.* Monroe, N.C., 1925. North Carolina Collection. Louis Round
    Wilson Library. University of North Carolina, Chapel Hill.
Nelson, Truman. *People with Strength in Monroe, North Carolina.* New York: Committee to
    Aid the Monroe Defendants, 1963.
The Peachoid. Board of Public Works, Gaffney, S.C., ca. 1982.
"Visit Monroe–Union County." Monroe–Union County Chamber of Commerce, 1961.
    North Carolina Collection. Louis Round Wilson Library. University of North
    Carolina, Chapel Hill.

PERIODICALS

Afro-American (Baltimore, Md.)
Amsterdam News (New York, N.Y.)
Arkansas State Press
Atlanta Constitution
Atlantic Monthly
Bee (Danville, Va.)
Business Week
Carolina Israelite (Charlotte, N.C.)
Carolina Times (Durham, N.C.)
Carolinian (Raleigh, N.C.)
Caswell Messenger
Chapel Hill Weekly
Charlotte Messenger
Charlotte News
Charlotte Observer
Chicago Defender
Chronicle (Cheraw, S.C.)
Commentary
Common Ground
Crisis (New York, N.Y.)
Crusader (Monroe, N.C.; Havana and
    Peking)
Daily Worker (New York, N.Y.)
Dallas Morning News
Detroit Free Press
Durham Morning Herald
Fair Play
Fayetteville Observer
Freedom (New York, N.Y.)
Freedomways
Gaffney Ledger
Greensboro Daily News
Independent (Anderson, S.C.)
Jet
Journal and Sentinel (Winston-Salem, N.C.)
Liberation

London News-Chronicle
Michigan Chronicle (University of
    Michigan, Ann Arbor)
Michigan Daily (Detroit)
Militant
Monroe Enquirer
Monroe Journal
Nation
News and Courier (Charleston, S.C.)
News and Observer (Raleigh, N.C.)
New South
Newsweek
New York Age
New York Post
New York Times
Norfolk Journal and Guide
Oxford Public Ledger
People's Paper (Charlotte, N.C.)
Philadelphia Tribune
Pittsburgh Courier
Political Affairs
Quill (Charleston, W.Va.)
Reader's Digest
Realist
Robesonian (Pembroke, N.C.)
Saturday Evening Post
Southern Patriot
Spectator (London)
State (Columbia, S.C.)
State-Times (Jackson, Miss.)
Student Council
Time
Union Daily Times
U.S. News and World Report
Warren Record (Warrenton, N.C.)
Washington Post

BOOKS

Adams, Frank. James A. Dombrowski: An American Heretic, 1897–1983. Knoxville:
    University of Tennessee Press, 1993.
Alexander, Edward Porter, ed. The Journal of John Fontaine: An Irish Huguenot Son in Spain
    and Virginia. Williamsburg: William and Mary Press, 1972.

Anderson, Jean B. *Durham County: A History of Durham County, North Carolina*. Durham: Duke University Press, 1990.

Anderson, Jervis. *A. Philip Randolph*. New York: Harcourt Brace Jovanovich, 1973.

———. *Bayard Rustin: Troubles I've Seen*. New York: HarperCollins, 1996.

Aptheker, Herbert. *A Documentary History of the Negro People in the United States*. Vol. 7, *From the Alabama Protests to the Death of Martin Luther King Jr.* New York: Citadel Press, 1994.

Baldwin, James. *Nobody Knows My Name*. New York: Dell, 1961.

Baraka, Amiri. *The Autobiography of LeRoi Jones*. Chicago: Lawrence Hill Books, 1997.

Barlow, Perry. "Looking Up at Down": The Emergence of Blues Culture. Philadelphia: Temple University Press, 1989.

Barnard, Hollinger F., ed. *Outside the Magic Circle: The Autobiography of Virginia Durr*. New York: Simon and Schuster, 1987.

Bartley, Numan. *The Rise of Massive Resistance: Race Relations in the South during the 1950s*. Baton Rouge: Louisiana State University Press, 1969.

Bates, Daisy. *The Long Shadow of Little Rock*. New York: David McKay, 1962.

Bell, Inge Powell. *CORE and the Strategy of Nonviolence*. New York: Random House, 1968.

Berry, Brewton. *Almost White*. New York: Macmillan, 1963.

Berry, Wendell. *The Hidden Wound*. San Francisco: North Point Press, 1989.

Blythe, LeGette. *William Henry Belk: Merchant of the South*. Chapel Hill: University of North Carolina Press, 1958.

Boles, John B. *The South through Time: A History of an American Region*. Englewood Cliffs, N.J.: Prentice Hall, 1995.

Braden, Anne. *The Wall Between*. New York: Monthly Review Press, 1959.

Branch, Taylor. *Parting the Waters: America in the King Years, 1954–1963*. New York: Simon and Schuster, 1988.

Broussard, Albert. *Black San Francisco: The Struggle for Racial Equality in the West, 1900–1954*. Lawrence: University of Kansas Press, 1993.

Brown, Bertram Wyatt. *Southern Honor: Ethics and Behavior in the Old South*. New York: Oxford University Press, 1982.

Buhle, Mari Jo, Paul Buhle, and Dan Georgakas, eds. *The Encyclopedia of the American Left*. Urbana: University of Illinois Press, 1992.

Burns, Stewart, ed. *Daybreak of Freedom: The Montgomery Bus Boycott*. Chapel Hill: University of North Carolina Press, 1997.

Butler, Lindley S., and Alan D. Watson, eds. *The North Carolina Experience: An Interpretive and Documentary History*. Chapel Hill: University of North Carolina Press, 1984.

Capeci, Dominic. *Detroit and the "Good War": The Wartime Letters of Mayor Edward Jeffries and Friends*. Lexington: University Press of Kentucky, 1996.

Capeci, Dominic, and Martha Wilkerson. *Layered Violence: The Detroit Rioters of 1943*. Jackson: University Press of Mississippi, 1991.

Carson, Clayborne. *In Struggle: SNCC and the Black Awakening of the 1960s*. Cambridge: Harvard University Press, 1981.

Carson, Clayborne, David J. Garrow, Gerald Gill, Vincent Harding, and Darlene Clark Hine, eds. *The Eyes on the Prize Civil Rights Reader*. New York: Penguin, 1991.

Carter, Dan T. *Scottsboro: A Tragedy of the American South*. Baton Rouge: Louisiana State University Press, 1979.

Cash, Wilbur J. *The Mind of the South*. New York: Knopf, 1941.

Casuso, Teresa. *Cuba and Castro*. New York: Random House, 1961.

Caute, David. *The Great Fear: The Anti-Communist Purge under Truman and Eisenhower*. New York: Simon and Schuster, 1978.

Cecelski, David S. *Along Freedom Road: Hyde County, North Carolina, and the Fate of Black Schools in the South*. Chapel Hill: University of North Carolina Press, 1994.

Cecelski, David S., and Timothy B. Tyson, eds. *Democracy Betrayed: The Wilmington Race Riot of 1898 and Its Legacy*. Chapel Hill: University of North Carolina Press, 1998.

Chafe, William H. *Civilities and Civil Rights: Greensboro, North Carolina, and the Black Struggle for Freedom*. New York: Oxford University Press, 1980.

——. *The Paradox of Change: American Women in the Twentieth Century*. New York: Oxford University Press, 1991.

——. *The Unfinished Journey*. New York: Oxford University Press, 1986.

Chalmers, David M. *Hooded Americanism: The History of the Ku Klux Klan*. 3d ed. Durham: Duke University Press, 1981.

Chapin, Kim. *Fast as White Lightning: The Story of Stock Car Racing*. New York: Dial Press, 1981.

Charles, Allen D. *The Narrative History of Union County, South Carolina*. Spartanburg, S.C.: Reprint Company, 1987.

Clark, Thomas D. *The Emerging South*. New York: Oxford University Press, 1961.

Cleage, Albert B., Jr. *The Black Messiah*. New York: Sheed and Ward, 1969.

Cohen, Robert Carl. *Black Crusader*. New York: Lyle Stuart, 1972.

Couch, W. T., ed. *Culture in the South*. Chapel Hill: University of North Carolina Press, 1934.

Cronon, E. David. *Black Moses: The Story of Marcus Garvey*. Madison: University of Wisconsin Press, 1966.

Crow, Jeffrey J., Paul D. Escott, and Flora Hatley. *A History of African Americans in North Carolina*. Raleigh: Division of Archives and History, North Carolina Department of Cultural Resources, 1992.

Cruse, Harold. *The Crisis of the Negro Intellectual*. New York: William Morrow, 1967.

——. *Rebellion or Revolution*. New York: William Morrow, 1968.

Dallek, Robert. *Lone Star Rising: Lyndon Johnson and His Times, 1908–1960*. New York: Oxford University Press, 1981.

Daniel, Pete. *Breaking the Land: The Transformation of Cotton, Tobacco, and Rice Cultures since 1880*. Urbana: University of Illinois Press, 1985.

——. *Standing at the Crossroads: Southern Life in the Twentieth Century*. New York: Hill and Wang, 1986.

Davidson, Osha Gray. *The Best of Enemies: Race and Redemption in the New South*. New York: Scribner's, 1996.

Dittmer, John. *Local People: The Struggle for Civil Rights in Mississippi*. Urbana: University of Illinois Press, 1994.

Dollard, John. *Caste and Class in a Southern Town*. New Haven: Yale University Press, 1937.

Douglas, Davison M. *Reading, Writing, and Race: The Desegregation of the Charlotte Schools*. Chapel Hill: University of North Carolina Press, 1995.

Dower, John. *War without Mercy: Race and Power in the Pacific War*. New York: Pantheon, 1986.

Duberman, Martin Bauml. *Paul Robeson: A Biography*. New York: Ballantine, 1989.

Du Bois, Shirley Graham. *His Day Is Marching On: A Memoir of W. E. B. Du Bois*. New York: Lippincott, 1971.

Du Bois, W. E. B. *The Souls of Black Folk*. 1903. Reprint, New York: Vintage, 1990.

Eagles, Charles. *Jonathan Daniels: The Evolution of a Southern Liberal*. Knoxville: University of Tennessee Press, 1982.

———, ed. *The Civil Rights Movement in America*. Jackson: University Press of Mississippi, 1986.

Egerton, John. *Speak Now against the Day: The Generation before the Civil Rights Movement in the South*. New York: Knopf, 1994.

Escott, Paul D. *Many Excellent People: Power and Privilege in North Carolina, 1850–1900*. Chapel Hill: University of North Carolina Press, 1985.

———. *Slavery Remembered: A Record of Twentieth-Century Slave Narratives*. Chapel Hill: University of North Carolina Press, 1979.

Eskew, Glenn T. *But for Birmingham: The Local and National Movements in the Civil Rights Struggle*. Chapel Hill: University of North Carolina Press, 1997.

Evans, William McKee. *To Die Game: The Story of the Lowery Band, Guerrillas of Reconstruction*. Baton Rouge: Louisiana State University Press, 1971.

Fairclough, Adam. *Race and Democracy: The Civil Rights Struggle in Louisiana, 1915–1972*. Athens: University of Georgia Press, 1995.

———. *To Redeem the Soul of America: The Southern Christian Leadership Conference and Martin Luther King Jr.* Athens: University of Georgia Press, 1987.

Forman, James. *The Making of Black Revolutionaries*. 1972. Reprint, Seattle: University of Washington Press, 1997.

Franklin, John Hope. *Black Leaders of the Twentieth Century*. Urbana: University of Illinois Press, 1982.

———. *The Color Line: Legacy for the Twenty-first Century*. Columbia: University of Missouri Press, 1993.

———. *From Slavery to Freedom*. 6th ed. New York: Knopf, 1991.

Freeland, Richard M. *The Truman Doctrine and the Origins of McCarthyism*. New York: New York University Press, 1985.

Furguson, Ernest. *Hard Right: The Rise of Jesse Helms*. New York: Norton, 1986.

Gaillard, Frye. *The Dream Long Deferred*. Chapel Hill: University of North Carolina Press, 1988.

Gallen, David, ed. *Malcolm X as They Knew Him*. New York: Carroll and Graf, 1994.

Garfinkel, Herbert. *When Negroes March: The March on Washington Movement in the Organizational Politics for FEPC*. New York: Atheneum, 1973.

Garrow, David. *Bearing the Cross: Martin Luther King Jr. and the Southern Christian Leadership Conference*. New York: William Morrow, 1986.

Gates, Henry Louis, and Nellie Y. McKay, eds. *The Norton Anthology of African American Literature*. New York: Norton, 1997.

Genovese, Eugene. *Roll, Jordan, Roll: The World the Slaves Made*. New York: Vintage, 1976.

Giddings, Paula. *When and Where I Enter: The Impact of Black Women on Race and Sex in America*. New York: William Morrow, 1984.

Gilmore, Glenda Elizabeth. *Gender and Jim Crow: Women and the Politics of White Supremacy in North Carolina, 1896–1920*. Chapel Hill: University of North Carolina Press, 1996.

Goodwyn, Lawrence. *Democratic Promise: The Populist Moment in America*. New York: Oxford University Press, 1976.

Gosse, Van. *Where the Boys Are: Cold War America and the Making of a New Left*. New York: Verso, 1993.

Graham, Hugh Davis, and Ted Robert Gurr. *The History of Violence in America: Historical and Comparative Perspectives*. New York: Praeger, 1969.

Griffith, Robert, and Athan Theoharis. *The Spectre: Original Essays on the Cold War and the Origins of McCarthyism*. New York: New Viewpoints, 1974.

Hacker, Andrew. *Two Nations: Black and White, Separate, Hostile, and Unequal*. New York: Scribner's, 1992.

Halberstam, David. *The Children*. New York: Random House, 1998.

Haley, John H. *Charles N. Hunter and Race Relations in North Carolina*. Chapel Hill: University of North Carolina Press, 1987.

Hall, Jacquelyn Dowd. *Revolt against Chivalry: Jessie Daniel Ames and the Women's Campaign against Lynching*. 1979. Rev. ed., New York: Columbia University Press, 1993.

Hall, Jacquelyn Dowd, James Leloudis, Robert Korstad, Mary Murphy, Lu Ann Jones, and Christopher B. Daly. *Like a Family: The Making of a Southern Cotton Mill World*. Chapel Hill: University of North Carolina Press, 1987.

Hampton, Henry, and Steve Fayer, eds. *Voices of Freedom: An Oral History of the Civil Rights Movement from the 1950s through the 1980s*. New York: Bantam, 1990.

Harris, William J., ed. *The LeRoi Jones/Amiri Baraka Reader*. New York: Thunder's Mouth Press, 1991.

Hill, Robert A., ed. *The FBI's RACON: Racial Conditions in the United States during World War II*. Boston: Northeastern University Press, 1995.

Hilty, David. *Robert Kennedy: Brother Protector*. Philadelphia: Temple University Press, 1997.

Hine, Darlene Clark, ed. *Black Women in United States History*. New York: Carlson, 1990.

Hodges, Luther H. *Businessman in the Statehouse: Six Years as Governor of North Carolina*. Chapel Hill: University of North Carolina Press, 1962.

Hodgson, Godfrey. *America in Our Time*. New York: Vintage, 1976.

Horne, Gerald. *Fire This Time: The Watts Uprising and the 1960s*. Charlottesville: University Press of Virginia, 1995.

Horowitz, David. *Destructive Generation: Second Thoughts about the Sixties*. New York: Summit, 1989.

Huckaby, Elizabeth. *Crisis at Central High: Little Rock, 1957–58*. Baton Rouge: Louisiana State University Press, 1980.

Hunter, Tera W. *To 'Joy My Freedom: Southern Black Women's Lives and Labors after the Civil War*. Cambridge: Harvard University Press, 1997.

Hurston, Zora Neale. *I Love Myself When I Am Laughing . . . and Then Again When I Am Looking Mean and Impressive*. New York: Feminist Press of the City University of New York, 1979.

———. *Mules and Men*. 1935. Reprint, New York: Harper and Row, 1990.

Irons, Peter. *The Courage of Their Convictions*. New York: Free Press, 1988.

Jones, LeRoi [now Amiri Baraka]. *Home: Social Essays by LeRoi Jones*. New York: William Morrow, 1966.

Jordan, Winthrop. *White over Black: American Attitudes toward the Negro, 1550–1812*. New York: Pelican, 1969.

Kapur, Sudarshan. *Raising Up a Prophet: The African American Encounter with Gandhi.* Boston: Beacon Press, 1992.

Kasher, Steven. *The Civil Rights Movement: A Photographic History, 1954–1968.* New York: Abbeville Press, 1996.

Kelley, Robin D. G. *Hammer and Hoe: Alabama Communists during the Great Depression.* Chapel Hill: University of North Carolina Press, 1990.

———. *Race Rebels: Culture, Politics, and the Black Working Class.* New York: Free Press, 1994.

Key, V. O., Jr. *Southern Politics.* New York: Knopf, 1949.

King, Mary. *Freedom Song.* New York: William Morrow, 1987.

Kluger, Richard. *Simple Justice.* New York: Knopf, 1976.

Kousser, J. Morgan. *The Shaping of Southern Politics: Suffrage Restriction and the Establishment of the One-Party South.* New Haven: Yale University Press, 1974.

Lawson, Steven F. *Black Ballots: Voting Rights in the South, 1944–1969.* New York: Columbia University Press, 1976.

Lee, Ulysses. *The Employment of Negro Troops.* Washington, D.C.: Center of Military History, 1990.

Lefler, Hugh Talmadge, and Albert Ray Newsome. *North Carolina: The History of a Southern State.* Chapel Hill: University of North Carolina Press, 1973.

Lerner, Gerda. *Black Women in White America: A Documentary History.* New York: Pantheon, 1972.

———. *The Grimké Sisters.* Boston: Houghton Mifflin, 1967.

Litwack, Leon. *Trouble in Mind: Black Southerners in the Age of Jim Crow.* New York: Knopf, 1998.

Logan, Rayford Whittingham. *The Betrayal of the Negro, from Rutherford B. Hayes to Woodrow Wilson.* New York: Da Capo, 1997. Originally published in 1954 as *The Negro in American Life and Thought: The Nadir, 1887–1901.*

———, ed. *What the Negro Wants.* Chapel Hill: University of North Carolina Press, 1944.

Lomax, Louis E. *The Negro Revolt.* New York: Signet, 1962.

Lynd, Staughton. *Nonviolence in America: A Documentary History.* New York: Bobbs-Merrill, 1966.

Lynn, Conrad. *There Is a Fountain: The Autobiography of a Civil Rights Lawyer.* Westport, Conn.: Lawrence Hill, 1979.

Lyons, Danny. *Memories of the Southern Civil Rights Movement.* Chapel Hill: University of North Carolina Press, 1992.

MacGregor, Morris J., Jr. *The Integration of the Armed Forces, 1940–1965.* Washington, D.C.: Center for Military History, 1989.

McMillen, Neil, ed. *Remaking Dixie: The Impact of World War II on the American South.* Jackson: University Press of Mississippi, 1997.

Major, Reginald. *A Panther Is a Black Cat.* New York, 1971.

Martin, Santford, and R. B. House, eds. *Public Letters and Papers of Thomas Walter Bickett, Governor of North Carolina, 1917–1921.* Raleigh: Edwards and Broughton, 1923.

Mealy, Rosemary. *Fidel and Malcolm X: Memories of a Meeting.* Melbourne: Ocean, 1993.

Meier, August, and Elliot Rudwick. *CORE: A Study in the Civil Rights Movement, 1942–68.* Urbana: University of Illinois Press, 1975.

Merrell, James H. *The Indians' New World: Catawbas and Their Neighbors from European Contact through the Era of Removal.* Chapel Hill: University of North Carolina Press, 1989.

Moody, Anne. *Coming of Age in Mississippi*. New York: Dell, 1968.

Moon, Henry Lee. *Balance of Power: The Negro Vote*. Garden City: Doubleday, 1949.

Moore, Carlos. *Castro, the Blacks, and Africa*. Los Angeles: Center for Afro-American Studies, 1988.

Moore, Gilbert. *A Special Rage*. New York, 1971.

Morris, Aldon D. *The Origins of the Civil Rights Movement: Black Communities Organizing for Change*. New York: Free Press, 1984.

Morrow, E. Frederic. *Black Man in the White House*. New York: McFadden, 1963.

———. *Forty Years a Guinea Pig: A Black Man's View from the Top*. New York: Pilgrim, 1980.

Motley, Mary Penick. *The Invisible Soldier: The Experience of the Black Soldier, World War Two*. Detroit: Wayne State University Press, 1975.

Muse, Benjamin. *Ten Years of Prelude: The Story of Integration since the Supreme Court's 1954 Decision*. New York: Viking, 1964.

Naison, Mark. *Communists in Harlem during the Depression*. New York: Grove Press, 1983.

Newton, Huey P. *Revolutionary Suicide*. New York: Harcourt Brace Jovanovich, 1973. Reprint, New York: Writers and Readers, 1995.

Odum, Howard W. *Race and Rumors of Race: Challenge to American Crisis*. Chapel Hill: University of North Carolina Press, 1943.

Olsen, Otto. *Reconstruction and Redemption in the New South*. Baton Rouge: Louisiana State University Press, 1980.

O'Reilly, Kenneth. *"Racial Matters": The FBI's Secret File on Black America*. New York: Free Press, 1989.

Payne, Charles. *I've Got the Light of Freedom: The Organizing Tradition and the Mississippi Freedom Struggle*. Berkeley: University of California Press, 1995.

Pearson, Hugh. *Shadow of the Panther: Huey Newton and the Price of Black Power in America*. Reading, Mass.: Addison-Wesley, 1994.

Peck, James. *Freedom Ride*. New York: Simon and Schuster, 1962.

Percy, William Alexander. *Lanterns on the Levee: Recollections of a Planter's Son*. Baton Rouge: Louisiana State University Press, 1984.

Pérez, Louis A., Jr. *Cuba and the United States: Ties of Singular Intimacy*. Athens: University of Georgia Press, 1990.

Peters, William. *The Southern Temper*. Garden City: Doubleday, 1959.

Pleasants, Julian M., and Augustus M. Burns III. *Frank Porter Graham and the 1950 Senate Race in North Carolina*. Chapel Hill: University of North Carolina Press, 1990.

Plummer, Brenda Gayle. *Rising Wind: Black Americans and U.S. Foreign Affairs, 1935–1960*. Chapel Hill: University of North Carolina Press, 1996.

Potter, Lou. *Liberators: Fighting on Two Fronts in World War II*. New York: Harcourt Brace Jovanovich, 1992.

Quint, Howard. *Profile in Black and White: A Frank Portrait of South Carolina*. Washington, D.C.: Public Affairs Press, 1958.

Raboteau, Albert. *Slave Religion*. New York: Oxford University Press, 1978.

Ransome, Roger, and Richard Sutch. *One Kind of Freedom: The Economic Consequences of Emancipation*. Cambridge: Cambridge University Press, 1977.

Reddick, L. C. *Crusader without Violence*. New York: Harper and Brothers, 1959.

Redwine, John M. *Union County, 1842–1953*. Monroe, N.C.: Cory Press, 1954. North Carolina Collection, Louis Round Wilson Library, University of North Carolina, Chapel Hill.

Reed, John Shelton. *The Enduring South: Subcultural Persistence in Mass Society*. Chapel Hill: University of North Carolina Press, 1976.

Reeves, Richard. *President Kennedy*. New York: Simon and Schuster, 1993.

Reeves, Thomas, ed. *McCarthyism*. Malabar, Fla.: Krieger Publishing, 1982.

Reilly, Charles, ed. *Conversations with Amiri Baraka*. Jackson: University Press of Mississippi, 1994.

Robinson, Armstead L., and Patricia Sullivan, eds. *New Directions in Civil Rights Studies*. Charlottesville: University Press of Virginia, 1991.

Roediger, David. *The Wages of Whiteness: Race and the Making of the American Working Class*. London: Verso, 1991.

Sales, William W., Jr. *From Civil Rights to Black Liberation: Malcolm X and the Organization of Afro-American Unity*. Boston: South End Press, 1994.

Salmond, John A. *Gastonia 1929: The Story of the Loray Mill Strike*. Chapel Hill: University of North Carolina Press, 1995.

Scales, Junious Irving, and Richard Nickson. *Cause at Heart: A Former Communist Remembers*. Athens: University of Georgia Press, 1987.

Schlesinger, Arthur M., Jr. *A Thousand Days*. Greenwich: Faucett, 1965.

Schrecker, Ellen. *Many Are the Crimes: McCarthyism in America*. New York: Little, Brown, 1998.

Scott, Anne Firor. *The Southern Lady: From Pedestal to Politics, 1830–1930*. Chicago: University of Chicago Press, 1970.

Scott, James C. *Domination and the Arts of Resistance: Hidden Transcripts*. New Haven: Yale University Press, 1990.

Sellers, Cleveland, with Robert Terrell. *The River of No Return: The Autobiography of a Black Militant and the Life and Death of SNCC*. 1973. Reprint, Jackson: University Press of Mississippi, 1990.

Shapiro, Herbert. *White Violence and Black Response: From Reconstruction to Montgomery*. Amherst: University of Massachusetts Press, 1988.

Shogan, Robert, and Tom Craig. *The Detroit Race Riot: A Study in Violence*. New York: Da Capo, 1976.

Shute, J. Raymond. *His Honor the Heretic*. Self-published memoir, n.d. North Carolina Collection, Louis Round Wilson Library, University of North Carolina, Chapel Hill.

Smead, Howard. *Blood Justice: The Lynching of Mack Charles Parker*. New York: Oxford University Press, 1986.

Smith, Kleytus, and Abiola Sinclair. *The Harlem Cultural/Political Movements, 1960–1970*. New York: Gumbs and Thomas, 1975.

Smith, Lillian. *Killers of the Dream*. 1949. Reprint, New York: Norton, 1961.

Sosna, Morton. *In Search of the Silent South: Southern Liberals and the Race Issue*. New York: Columbia University Press, 1977.

Spickard, Paul R. *Mixed Blood: Intermarriage and Ethnic Identity in Twentieth Century America*. Madison: University of Wisconsin Press, 1989.

Stack, [Amos Morehead], and [Roland Fowler] Beasley. *Sketches of Monroe and Union County*. Charlotte: News and Times Print, 1902. North Carolina Collection, Louis Round Wilson Library, University of North Carolina, Chapel Hill.

Stone, I. F. *In a Time of Torment, 1961–1967*. Boston: Little, Brown, 1989.

Sullivan, Patricia. *Days of Hope: Race and Democracy in the New Deal Era*. Chapel Hill: University of North Carolina Press, 1996.

Trillin, Calvin. U.S. Journal. New York: Dutton, 1971.

Tygiel, Jules. Baseball's Great Experiment: Jackie Robinson and His Legacy. New York: Oxford University Press, 1983.

Van Deburg, William L. Modern Black Nationalism: From Marcus Garvey to Louis Farrakhan. New York: New York University Press, 1997.

———. New Day in Babylon: The Black Power Movement and American Culture, 1965–1975. Chicago: University of Chicago Press, 1992.

Wade, Wynn Craig. The Fiery Cross: The Ku Klux Klan in America. New York: Simon and Schuster, 1987.

Ward, Brian, and Tony Badger, eds. The Making of Martin Luther King Jr. and the Civil Rights Movement. New York: New York University Press, 1997.

Weisbrot, Robert. Freedom Bound: A History of America's Civil Rights Movement. New York: Norton, 1990.

Welch, Richard E., Jr. Response to Revolution: The United States and the Cuban Revolution, 1959–1961. Chapel Hill: University of North Carolina Press, 1985.

White, Walter. A Man Called White. New York: Viking, 1948.

Whitfield, Stephen J. The Culture of the Cold War. Baltimore: Johns Hopkins University Press, 1991.

———. A Death in the Delta: The Story of Emmett Till. Baltimore: Johns Hopkins University Press, 1991.

Wilkins, Roy. Standing Fast: The Autobiography of Roy Wilkins. New York: Penguin, 1982.

Williams, Juan. Thurgood Marshall: American Revolutionary. New York: Times Books, 1998.

Williams, Robert F. Negroes with Guns. New York: Marzani and Munsell, 1962.

Wood, Peter H. Black Majority: Negroes in Colonial South Carolina from 1670 through the Stono Rebellion. New York: Oxford University Press, 1975.

Woodward, C. Vann. Reunion and Reaction: The Compromise of 1877 and the End of Reconstruction. Garden City: Doubleday, 1956.

———. The Strange Career of Jim Crow. 2d rev. ed. New York: Oxford University Press, 1966.

Wyden, Peter. Bay of Pigs. New York: Simon and Schuster, 1979.

Wynn, Neil. The Afro-American and the Second World War. New York: Holmes and Meirer, 1976.

ARTICLES

Barksdale, Marcellus Chandler. "Robert F. Williams and the Indigenous Civil Rights Movement in Monroe, North Carolina, 1961." Journal of Negro History 69, no. 2 (Spring 1984): 73–89.

Burns, Augustus M., III. "Graduate Education for Blacks in North Carolina, 1930–1951." Journal of Southern History 46, no. 2 (May 1980): 195–218.

Carter, Dan T. "From the Old South to the New: Another Look at the Theme of Change and Continuity." In From the Old South to the New: Essays in the Traditional South, edited by Walter B. Fraser and Winfred B. Moore Jr., 25–43. Westport, Conn.: Greenwood Press, 1981.

Clarke, John Hendrik. "Journey to the Sierra Maestra." Freedomways 1, no. 1 (Spring 1961): 32–35.

Craven, Bruce. "The Truth about Jackson's Birthplace." *North Carolina Booklet* 9, no. 4 (April 1910): 233.

Crow, Jeffrey J. "Cracking the Solid South: Populism and the Fusionist Interlude." In *The North Carolina Experience: An Interpretive and Documentary History*, edited by Lindley S. Butler and Alan D. Watson, 333–54. Chapel Hill: University of North Carolina Press, 1984.

Dalfiume, Richard M. "The 'Forgotten Years' of the Negro Revolution." *Journal of American History* 55, no. 1 (June 1968): 90–106.

Davis, Angela. "Racism and Contemporary Literature on Rape." *Freedomways* 16, no. 1 (1976): 32.

Davis, Chester. "Communist Front Shouts 'Kissing Case' to World." Winston-Salem *Journal and Sentinel*, February 8, 1959, 1.

———. "Press in North Gives Distorted Versions" Winston-Salem *Journal and Sentinel*, February 8, 1959, 1.

Dudziak, Mary. "Desegregation as a Cold War Imperative." *Stanford Law Review* 41 (November 1988): 61–120.

Durrill, Wayne. "Producing Poverty: Local Government and Economic Development in a New South County, 1874–1884." *Journal of American History* 71, no. 4 (March 1985): 764–81.

Dykeman, Wilma, and James Stokely. "Inquiry into the Southern Tensions." *New York Times Magazine*, October 13, 1957, V-20.

Escott, Paul. "White Republicanism and Ku Klux Klan Terror: The North Carolina Piedmont during Reconstruction." In *Race, Class, and Politics in Southern History: Essays in Honor of Robert F. Durden*, edited by Jeffrey J. Crow, Paul D. Escott, and Charles L. Flynn Jr., 3–34. Baton Rouge: Louisiana State University Press, 1989.

Gavins, Raymond. "The Meaning of Freedom: Black North Carolina in the Nadir, 1880–1900." In *Race, Class, and Politics in Southern History: Essays in Honor of Robert F. Durden*, edited by Jeffrey J. Crow, Paul D. Escott, and Charles L. Flynn Jr., 175–215. Baton Rouge: Louisiana State University Press, 1989.

———. "The NAACP in North Carolina during the Age of Segregation." In *New Directions in Civil Rights Studies*, edited by Armstead L. Robinson and Patricia Sullivan, 105–25. Charlottesville: University Press of Virginia, 1991.

Hall, Jacquelyn Dowd. "The Mind That Burns in Each Body." *Southern Exposure*, November/December 1984, 64–69.

Helms, Jesse, Jr. "Viewpoint: An Editorial Expression of the Voice of Free Enterprise in Raleigh-Durham." No. 2173, September 16, 1969, WRAL-TV, Raleigh, N.C. North Carolina Collection, Louis Round Wilson Library, University of North Carolina, Chapel Hill.

Higginbotham, A. Leon. "An Open Letter to Justice Clarence Thomas from a Federal Judicial Colleague." In *Race-ing Justice, En-Gendering Power: Essays on Anita Hill, Clarence Thomas, and the Construction of Social Reality*, edited by Toni Morrison, 3–37. New York: Pantheon, 1992.

Jackson, James E. "Democratic Uprising of the Negro People." *Political Affairs* 42, no. 11 (October 1963): 17–21.

Jones, LeRoi. "Cuba Libre." In *Home: Social Essays by LeRoi Jones*, 11–62. New York: William Morrow, 1966).

Kelley, Robin D. G. " 'We Are Not What We Seem': Rethinking Black Working-Class

Opposition in the Jim Crow South." *Journal of American History* 80, no. 1 (June 1993): 75–112.

Klarman, Michael. "How Brown Changed Race Relations: The Backlash Thesis." *Journal of American History* 81, no. 1 (June 1994): 81–118.

Korstad, Robert, and Nelson Lichtenstein. "Opportunities Found and Lost: Labor, Radicals, and the Early Civil Rights Movement." *Journal of American History* 75, no. 3 (December 1988): 787–811.

Lever, Constance. "Monroe Doctrine." *Spectator*, September 15, 1961, 346.

Lowery, John. "Should Violence Be Met with Violence?" *Realist*, no. 32 (March 1962): 7–9.

Mayfield, Julian. "Author Says Cuba Has Solution to Race Problem." *Fair Play* 5, no. 1 (October 25, 1960): 1.

———. "Challenge to Negro Leadership: The Case of Robert Williams." *Commentary* 31 (April 1961): 297–305.

Maynor, Joe. "His Name Was Papa and to Jesse Helms He Was Always Right." *Conservative Digest*, May 1981, 6.

Merrell, James. "The Racial Education of the Catawba Indians." *Journal of Southern History* 50, no. 3 (August 1984): 363–84.

Poe, Clarence. "Indians, Slaves, and Tories: Our Eighteenth Century Legislation Regarding Them." *North Carolina Booklet* 9, no. 1 (July 1909): 6.

Sackett, Russell. "Plotting a War on Whitey." *Life*, June 10, 1966, 100.

Sitkoff, Harvard. "African American Militancy in the World War II South: Another Perspective." in Neil McMillen, ed., *Remaking Dixie: The Impact of World War II on the American South*, edited by Neil McMillen, 70–92. Jackson: University Press of Mississippi, 1997).

———. "Racial Militancy and Interracial Violence in the Second World War." *Journal of American History* 58, no. 3 (1971): 663–83.

Smith, Albert C. " 'Southern Violence' Reconsidered: Arson as Protest in Black-Belt Georgia, 1880–1910." *Journal of Southern History* 51, no. 4 (November 1985): 527–64.

Trillin, Calvin. "Monroe, North Carolina, October 1969: Historical Note." In *U.S. Journal*. New York: Dutton, 1971. Reprint of article in the *New Yorker*, May 17, 1969, 89–96.

Weissman, George. "The Kissing Case." *Nation*, January 17, 1959, 46–49.

Worthy, William. "The FBI in Cold War and Peace." *Realist*, no. 31 (February 1962): 1.

———. "A Visit from the FBI." *Realist*, no. 32 (March 1962): 10.

UNPUBLISHED WORKS

Anderson, Carol Elaine. "Eyes Off the Prize: African-Americans, the United Nations, and the Struggle for Human Rights, 1944–1952." Ph.D. diss., Ohio State University, 1995.

Banchero, Stephanie. "Native Son Wants to Come Home." February 22, 1995. Draft article. *Charlotte Observer* files. Stephanie Banchero Papers. Madison, Wisc. In possession of the author.

Barksdale, Marcellus Chandler. "The Indigenous Civil Rights Movement and Cultural

Change in North Carolina, 1946–1965: Weldon, Chapel Hill, and Monroe." Ph.D. diss., Duke University, 1977.

Bostick, Tanisha R. "The Results of One Act of Defiance: Booker T. Spicely's Story." Paper, Duke University, 1994. In possession of the author.

Boyte, Janet. "White Rebel of SCLC." Ca. 1963. Draft manuscript. Box 26, Boyte Family Papers. Special Collections. Perkins Library. Duke University, Durham, N.C.

Burran, James Albert. "Racial Violence in the South during World War II." Ph.D. diss., University of Tennessee, 1977.

Carter, David, "New Inheritance: A History of the Williamston Freedom Movement." M.A. thesis, Duke University, 1995.

Clark, Wayne Addison. "Analysis of the Relationship between Anti-Communism and Segregationist Thought in the Deep South, 1948–1964." Ph.D. diss., University of Wisconsin, Madison, 1976.

Gerth, Shawn. "Dr. Albert E. Perry and the Civil Rights Movement in Monroe, North Carolina." Paper, Duke University, 1994. In possession of the author.

Ginger, Daniel. " 'In Enemy Territory': A Story of Racial Integration in the Cold War South." Senior thesis, University of Wisconsin, Madison, 1996. In possession of the author.

Hall, Gwendolyn Midlo. "A Tribute to Robert F. Williams: A Towering Figure in the Civil Rights Movement." October 27, 1996. Typescript in possession of author.

Hill, Lance E. "The Deacons for Defense and Justice: Armed Self-Defense and the Civil Rights Movement." Ph.D. diss., Tulane University, 1997.

Hunt, Jo. "Beans and Potatoes: Booker T. Spicely and the Bus Driver's Daughter." Paper, Duke University, 1994. In possession of the author.

Jones, Patrick. " 'Communist Front Shouts "Kissing Case" to World': The Committee to Combat Racial Injustice and the Politics of Race and Gender during the Cold War." M.A. thesis, University of Wisconsin, Madison, 1996.

Jones, William Jefferson. "Identity, Militancy, and Organization: Robert F. Williams and the NAACP in North Carolina, 1949–1959." Seminar paper, University of North Carolina, Chapel Hill, 1995. In possession of the author.

Leach, D'Etta. "The Meaning of the Meeting: The Southern Win-the-War Rally." Seminar paper, University of North Carolina, Chapel Hill, 1991. In possession of the author.

McGuire, Danielle. "Race, Rape, and Resistance: The Tallahassee Story." M.A. thesis, University of Wisconsin, Madison, 1999.

Master, Kathleen J. "The Leering Case." Paper, Duke University, 1994. In possession of the author.

Mayfield, Julian. "Tales from the Lido." [1975?]. Autobiography. Julian Mayfield Papers. Schomburg Center for Research in Black Culture. New York Public Library, New York.

Myers, Andrew. "When Violence Met Violence: Facts and Images of Robert F. Williams and the Black Freedom Struggle in Monroe, North Carolina." M.A. thesis, University of Virginia, 1993.

Rittenberg, Sidney. "Recollections of Robert F. Williams." May 4, 1997. Typescript in possession of the author.

Secrest, Andrew M. "In Black and White: Press Opinion and Race Relations in South Carolina, 1954–1964." Ph.D. diss., Duke University, 1971.

Tyson, Timothy B. "Burning for Freedom: White Terror and Black Power in Oxford, North Carolina." M.A. thesis, Duke University, 1990.

Walden, H. Nelson. "A History of Monroe and Union County, North Carolina." M.A. thesis, Appalachian State University, 1963. North Carolina Collection. Louis Round Wilson Library. University of North Carolina, Chapel Hill.

Walker, Eugene P. "A History of the Southern Christian Leadership Conference, 1955–1965: The Evolution of a Southern Strategy for Social Change." Ph.D. diss., Duke University, 1978.

Williams, Robert F. "While God Lay Sleeping: The Autobiography of Robert F. Williams." 1996. Typescript in possession of the author.

Windham, Lane. "Green Hands: A History of Local Ten of the Food, Tobacco, and Agricultural Allied Workers of America in Greenville, North Carolina, 1946." Honors thesis, Duke University, 1994.

Woodard, Kimberly R. "The Summer of African-American Discontent." Paper, Duke University, 1994. In possession of the author.

Acknowledgments

Several years ago I interrupted an idyllic family picnic beside Lake Mendota to squander a delightful summer evening at work on *Radio Free Dixie*. No one was happy about this, least of all Sam, our then three-year-old son. Furrowing his brow with undisguised belligerence, he blurted, "Why can't you write a *shorter* book about Wobert, Dad? Like about *nine pages!*" Now that I have completed the manuscript and Sam is old enough to read it, I am ashamed to admit that we will all be lucky if I can keep even the acknowledgments under nine pages. But I remain grateful for the suggestion.

The unconventional length of these acknowledgments reflects my unusual good fortune; it's not that I don't know any better, but simply that I owe a lot. My first thanks must go to Robert F. Williams and his entire family, without whom this book never could have been written. Robert died before I completed this book, but he supported my efforts without fail. He instructed his kin to help me and bluntly insisted that they must not compromise my scholarly independence in any way. Despite knowing that there would be parts of the book they would not like, the Williams family opened their homes and their hearts to me. Mabel R. Williams has inspired me with her loving spirit and selfless devotion to human dignity. I am thankful for the many times she dug up documents, verified facts, and faced my endless questions. John Herman Williams cheerfully provided photographs from his collection and graced me with his friendship. John Chalmers Williams was consistently helpful. Edward "Pete" Williams corrected errors of fact in Chapter 2. The entire Williams family has been gracious beyond any reasonable expectation. I hope that the renewed attention that this book may bring to their family tradition of struggle repays them in some small measure for my many intrusions.

No apprentice ever found more generous masters than I did in the Department of History at Duke University. William H. Chafe, my dissertation adviser, furnished a dazzling role model of personal integrity and zest for life. His intuitive coaching, unfaltering patience, and literary flair shaped my life and this book. John Herd Thompson, beloved friend and treasured mentor, tutored me in the historian's craft; shared editing, groceries, whisky, and coffee; and taught me the meaning of collegiality. Lawrence Goodwyn's generosity of spirit and his vision of democracy kept me in graduate school during those first years when I daily threatened to flee. Vivian Jackson was a reliable source of assistance and good humor. Sydney Nathans and Peter Wood were inspiring teachers and supportive friends. Raymond Gavins and Julius Scott grounded me in the basics of African American historiography. John Hope Franklin inspired me by his tireless service to our country and our calling and encouraged me with his friendship. Anne Scott and Jack Cell took time to provide encouragement and insight even though my work fell outside their many duties. Janet Ewald loaned me her office. Cynthia Herrup, bless her heart, gave me excellent emergency advice when I had lost my clothes at the last minute and had to attend three job interviews dressed like Jethro Bodine. Dott Sapp told me several dozen dirty jokes. Genna Golnick, Grace Guyer, Keith Knight, and Thelma Kithcart were always helpful. James Applewhite, one of the South's great poets, showed me the way to go home. When I think of Duke, I fall back on Thoreau's magnificent phrase: "I grew in those years like corn in the night."

Our roots in North Carolina are only one of the ties that bind me to David S. Cecelski, without whose friendship and assistance this book would not have been possible. David seasoned every page of this manuscript with his literary gifts and historical insights. David twice flew to Wisconsin to edit the entire manuscript, working fourteen or fifteen hours at a sitting with nothing but steaks, ribs, barbecue, crab cakes, smoked chicken, mashed potatoes and gravy, collard greens, butterbeans, sweet potato biscuits, beer, bourbon, and seven-dollar cigars to sustain him. Any lingering flaws in this book are entirely his fault, every single one of them.

None of Radio Free Dixie's weaknesses, however, can be attributed to the many other scholars who have helped me with this work. John Dittmer read this manuscript twice and offered warm encouragement and priceless comments. His pathbreaking Local People: The Civil Rights Struggle in Mississippi appeared at a decisive moment and confirmed my hesitant sense of this project's promise. Glenda Elizabeth Gilmore's Gender and Jim Crow: Women and the Politics of White Supremacy in North Carolina, 1896–1920 influenced me greatly; she also took time out from her many labors at Yale to read this manuscript and sharpen its focus. Patricia Sullivan, whose Days of Hope: Race and Democracy in the New Deal Era pointed me toward the origins of the freedom movement, read the entire manuscript and furnished an invaluable critique. The discerning reader will see the mark of Charles Payne's I've Got the Light of Freedom: The Organizing Tradition and the Mississippi Freedom Struggle throughout these pages. Charles, too, presented telling criticisms of a paper that outlined Radio Free Dixie's major themes. Christopher Strain's comments were extremely helpful. Joel Williamson read two early chapters of this book when I was in graduate school and told me to roll on, which I appreciated. Marcellus Chandler Barksdale, whose dissertation on the civil rights movement in North Carolina broke first ground on the story of Robert F. Williams, sent me a copy of his fine 1984 article on Monroe in the Journal of Negro History. I am also grateful to Professor Barksdale for making his excellent interviews from Monroe available to scholars in the Duke University Oral History Collection. Adam Fairclough, David Garrow, Kalamu ya Salaam, and Gerald Horne each made insightful comments on an article that helped me to frame this work, and Kalamu brought his literary craft and historical judgments to the entire manuscript. Gwendolyn Midlo Hall, a brilliant historian, veteran activist, and dear friend to the Williams family, read the manuscript and provided good counsel and good company. Kevin Gaines, Alex Lichtenstein, Ted Frantz, and Christina Greene sent me important documents for which I am grateful.

It was my good fortune soon after I finished my dissertation to attract the attention of David Perry of the University of North Carolina Press. His faith, his patience, his talent, and his humor helped make this process a pleasure. UNC Press is among a small handful of the finest institutions the South has ever produced—SNCC, Sun Records, Highlander Folk School, Wilber's Barbecue, and Manuel's Tavern spring to mind—and I am proud to be associated with the folks there.

Financial support for *Radio Free Dixie* came from the Department of History at Duke University, which provided me with full funding for my doctoral studies; the Graduate School at Duke University, which awarded me the Mattie J. Russell Instructorship of Southern History; the Graduate School Research Council at the University of Wisconsin at Madison, which furnished me three summers of salary support; and the Hilldale Undergraduate/Faculty Research Fellowship, which gave two of my students, Jennifer Olsen and David Boxer, awards that provided their faculty sponsor with research funds. I am grateful to all of them.

A number of people who did not actually read this work nonetheless deserve my thanks and more. Joy Burwell Averett and Ben Averett of Oxford, North Carolina, taught me to love words, work hard, and live free. Joy died in the midst of this project and I still mourn her loss, but she lives forever in my heart. Thad Stem, Oxford's poet laureate, made me yearn to be a writer soon after I first learned to make marks on paper. Frank Adams, one of the finest minds of the South, introduced me to the best political traditions of our homeland. Fred Chappell, James Clotfelter, Janet Varner Gunn, James Thompson, and Janet Wall transformed a twenty-four-year-old probationary freshman at the University of North Carolina at Greensboro and after two years packed me off to Emory University. In Atlanta, the spellbinding stories and infectious laughter of Dan T. Carter inspired me to write history and saved me from law school. Fraser Harbutt's lively lectures on the Cold War and warm encouragement of my writing motivated me. The intellectual seeds that Allen Tullos planted sprouted in due season.

A community of friends, classmates, and political allies in North Carolina nurtured me. Nick Biddle taught me about love, death, history, and politics. Herman Bennett and I may have acted like kindergartners, but even our critics must concede that we played well with others. Lane Windham found my best self and helped me to hold on to it through terrible loss and ineffable joy. Christina Greene kept me laughing. Rhonda Mawhood Lee was friend, counselor, and sometimes ambassador to my family. Donna Dickinson and Don Boyle confirmed my long-standing conviction that it is best to ride all the rides. Colonel David E. Johnson helped me hold my ground. Patrick Wilkinson was a peach. Melody Ivins graced these pages with her magic pen and brightened my life with her kindness. Deb Baldwin, Chuck Bolton, Tim Borstelman, Martha Jane Brazy, David Carter, Vera Cecelski, Lorna Chafe, Jim Conway, Matthew Countryman, Mary Ellen Curtin, Ann Farnsworth-Olvear, Kirsten Fischer, Nell Goodwyn, Laura Hansen, Haken Heimer, Lynn Holland, Janet Irons, Karen Irr, Wayne Lee, Gretchen Lemke-Santangelo, Carolyn Lesjak, Beth Loveland, George Loveland, Jodi-beth McCain, Larry Malley, Jennifer Morgan, Margaret Nelson, John Ott, Connie Pearcy, Miriam Peskowitz, Dirk Philipsen, Alice Poffinberger, Rick Roderick, Susan Saenger, Jill Schlessinger, Miriam Shadis, Katrin Thompson, George Waldrep, John Waters, Bob White, and Howard Wolfson all earned my enduring gratitude.

If old friends and colleagues in North Carolina helped me launch this project, new friends and colleagues at the University of Wisconsin at Madison proved indispensable to its completion. In particular, Craig Werner, one of the most brilliant and generous people I have known, served as relentless coach, tireless editor, and crucial adviser. He listened to my stories many times over, lent his immense literary gifts to each chapter of this book—typically, he would return a much-improved chapter to me within hours—badgered me when it was necessary, and bought me a beer when my spirits sagged and when they didn't. It is simply impossible to imagine finishing this book without his assistance. Steve Kantrowitz stood by me until both the book and the "merest nib-nub" of bourbon were finished. Nellie McKay, fine scholar and exemplary teacher, nurtured me with her generosity and friendship. Richard Ralston, chair of the Department of Afro-American Studies, defended me against enemies foreign and domestic. William L. Van Deburg has been a patient and invaluable mentor. Jean Comstock has been a gift from heaven. Herbert Hill saved me from errors of fact and interpretation and sustained me with his friendship. Sandra Adell helped me to obtain priceless information for which I am grateful. Donia Allen, Jean Boydston, Suzanne Dezan, Colleen Dunlavy, Barbara Forrest, Linda Gordon, Carla Hasse, Stanlie James, Lynn Keller, Joy Newmann, Ronald Radano, Meryl Schwartz, Freida High W. Tesfagiorgis, Michael Thornton, and Franklin Wilson have all helped to support me in ways both scholarly and personal.

The members of Bookclub Number 6—Dick Cates, Jeff Dreyfuss, John Frey, Steve Kantrowitz, Tom Leiterman, Tim Size, and Michael Weiden—endured my endless whining about this book for several years. After all that, they were kind enough to read the entire manuscript prior to publication. I thank them from the bottom of my heart. They liked this book and understood it, and that is good enough for me.

My students at Duke University and here at the University of Wisconsin-Madison have given me inspiration, friendship, and sometimes decisive assistance. Tanisha Bostick and Jo Hunt at Duke uncovered evidential gold mines about World War II in North Carolina that contributed considerably to Chapter 2, and I am grateful to them for sharing their findings. Jo even cut my hair during the long months when I scarcely left the Carr Building. Shawn Gerth, Kathleen Master, and Kimberly Woodard all wrote papers that helped build paragraphs in this book. Katherine Mellen began as my student and soon became my dear friend and brilliant colleague; I will always be proud of her and grateful for her friendship. Danielle McGuire performed many hours of patient research for this book, helped keep its author in good spirits, and made a fine index for it; I am grateful to her on all counts. Patrick Jones wrote an excellent master's thesis on the CCRI that helped me to understand things I had been studying for five years. Alison Stocking proofread this book and signed on as a sister. Neelum Wadhwani is a gem. Don Baylor remains the king of gumbo. Torsten Evans has no game. Michael Biddick, Vanessa Bliss, Molly Cooley, Liz Corris, Ben Doherty, Jay Driskell, Jon Effron, Jessica Engel, Dan Ginger, Heather Goodwin, Shanna Greene, Andrea Tillman Jackson, Amanda Klonsky, Trina Mikonowitz, David Sarnowsky, Stephanie Sauve, Lauren Schmidt, Rita Soenksen, Gretchen Vrieze, and Melvina Johnson Young, among many others, taught me much and made me proud.

After many a long night of labor, the weary author made his way home by way of Madison's Harmony Bar, where the best jukebox in the country and the merciful attentions of Alison Mader, who puts the tender in bartender, helped ease his troubled mind. For all these blessings and the timeless wisdom of the blues, I am grateful.

One of the great blues poets of the South, B. B. King, sings, "Nobody loves me but my mother / And she could be jiving, too." In my case, she is clearly not jiving. My parents, Martha and Vernon Tyson, have stood by me, sometimes for no apparent reason. This project would not have been possible without their steadfast love. My father, a scholar in his own right and the best damn preacher who ever beat on the Book, blessed my life with his love for language, his wisdom, and his commitment to racial justice and redeeming love. He also read many drafts of this manuscript, offered excellent editorial suggestions, accompanied me to several archives, and found important historical materials, to say nothing of lunch. All hail to the sisteren, Boo, Julie, Lorí, and T., who blanketed us with love and stood by us through the storms. My brother, Vern Tyson, has been blood on blood and a staunch friend besides. When I was far from home, lonely and poor, Jane and Vern sent chocolate chip cookies and birthday checks. The Morgans of Corapeake (and I mean all twenty-three of them) were generous and kind and resisted the temptation to ask whether this scribbling would ever amount to anything. My nephew, Jason Ward, was an able research assistant. My father-in-law, Sam Morgan, remains a source of inspiration by his example. And bees may buzz as brazenly as they please, but can make no honey sweeter than my mother-in-law, D. Morgan. Many of y'all who have mothers-in-law think I am just saying that, but she knows I am not.

As always, I drew my deepest strength from family. My son, Sam Tyson, as noted above, made editorial suggestions, played basketball with me, and endured my absences as best he could. Hope Tyson, a writer herself now, comforted her father and kept him going. When her brother Sam demanded to know why we had to drive all the way to Michigan to see Robert and Mabel Williams, Hope wheeled around in her seat and exclaimed, "Because they're *freedom fighters*, silly!" I always appreciated how clearly she understood her father's work. My children's clarity about justice and mercy is a wellspring of hope to me, and I love them always.

The mother of these angels, Perri Anne Morgan, is a brilliant woman whose one large blind spot it has been my privilege to occupy. This book has cost her a great deal, well beyond her brilliant editing, and I am sorry about that. But she has been my friend for twenty-five years and was a soldier for racial justice the day that I met her; at fourteen, Perri had already piped up in Parker's United Methodist Church in Corapeake, North Carolina, right there in front of God, to tell the preacher exactly why he was wrong to let the church sponsor an all-white softball league. Perri believed in this book because she knew what nonviolence had and had not meant in the rural South. Perri and I have stuck by each other for a long time, and I can scarcely express my gratitude and respect. But I dedicate this book to her, with all my love, borrowing these lines once more from Edna St. Vincent Millay:

> Love in the open hand, no thing but that,
> Ungemmed, unhidden, wishing not to hurt,
> As one should bring you cowslips in a hat,
> Swung from the hand or apples in her skirt,
> I bring you, calling out as children do:
> "Look what I have!—And these are all for you!"

TIMOTHY B. TYSON
Madison, Wisconsin

Index

Abolitionists, 13, 263

Accommodation, 8, 12, 27, 122, 194, 258. See also Racial etiquette

Acheson, Dean, 52

Africa, 14, 15, 69, 145, 191, 195, 196–97, 235, 237, 241

African American: intelligentsia, 213, 226–27, 242, 343 (n. 44); soldiers, 2, 34, 37, 38, 43–45, 73, 294; veterans, 2, 9, 27, 29, 48–62 passim, 80–82, 88, 116, 119, 141, 268, 275, 291

—churches, 14, 197–98, 200; ministers in, 8, 14, 36, 60, 86, 198. See also Afro-Christianity

—freedom movement, 2–3, 80–82, 110–11, 115–18, 136, 144–45, 152–53, 157–59, 190–92, 207–19, 296–308; and Black Power, 3, 27–28, 191–213 passim, 289–308 passim, 313 (n. 5); class conflict within, 80–81, 112, 122, 126, 160–62, 194–97, 210–11; and Cold War, 2–3, 51–53, 59–61, 64, 68, 103–4, 117–20, 128, 132–34, 145, 155–56, 162, 226, 241–42, 247–48, 285, 300; in Monroe, 80–89, 98–99, 141, 191–203 passim, 217–19, 251–81 passim; nationally, 103, 115–16, 144–45, 161–62, 190–92, 213–17, 240–50 passim, 289–91; origins of, 3, 25, 50–51, 57, 67, 77–79, 116, 157–58; and World War II, 3, 26–59 passim

—manhood. See Manhood

—middle class. See Middle class

—press, 15, 16, 29, 30, 152, 193, 211; Afro-American (Baltimore, Md.), 154, 157, 211, 221–22, 234, 242, 263, 297; Amsterdam News (New York, N.Y.), 123, 158; Arkansas State Press, 154; Atlanta Age, 211; Carolina Times (Durham, N.C.), 30, 33, 36, 67, 92, 100, 115, 133, 149, 154; Chicago Defender, 223, 226; Columbia Lighthouse and Informer, 157; Crisis (New York, N.Y.), 29, 193; Ebony, 222; Freedom (New York, N.Y.), 68–69; Jet, 91, 216; Pittsburgh Courier, 234. See also Crusader

—resistance. See Armed resistance

—women, 1–2, 9, 19, 20, 88, 94, 148–49, 195; and armed resistance, 25, 71, 91–92, 141, 147–49, 153, 158, 160, 190, 211–12, 216, 237, 259–60, 276, 279; and domestic work, 22, 30, 31, 81, 141, 161, 201, 314 (n. 99); and rape by white men, 10, 61, 97, 140–41, 143–49, 150, 163, 325 (n. 15)

See also Culture: African American

African Black Brotherhood, 194

Afro-American. See African American—press: Afro-American

Afro-American Press Association, 211

Afro-Christianity, 8, 15, 114, 192, 200, 212, 213. See also African American—churches

Afro-Cubans, 222, 235, 285

Ahmed, Akbar Muhammed. See Stanford, Max

Alabama, 33, 46, 121, 245, 246

Alabama Christian Movement for Human Rights, 111

Albany, Ga., 210, 288

Albany Movement, 291

Alexander, Kelley, 85, 109, 110, 121–23, 125–26, 133, 135, 154, 157, 249, 258

American Friends Service Committee, 207

American Labor Party, 70

Amsterdam News. See African American—press: *Amsterdam News*

Anderson, Jerry, 269

Anderson, Marian, 224

Anderson, Walter, 147

Angelou, Maya, 242

Anniston, Ala., 245

Anticolonialism, 51, 191, 196, 207, 237

Anticommunism: and Cuba, 222–23, 225, 229, 236, 238–43, 265; and NAACP, 120–21, 155–56, 162, 222, 239–40; and white supremacy, 7, 59, 64, 66–68, 77, 79, 85–86, 104, 105, 111, 115, 120, 121, 124, 128–34, 189–90, 207, 229, 247–48, 252, 265, 271, 285, 290; of Robert Williams, 292–94. *See also* Cold War

A Panther is a Black Cat, 298

Apartheid, 195, 267

Aptheker, Herbert, 195

Arkansas State Press. See African American—press: *Arkansas State Press*

Armed resistance: and American culture, 198, 214; and idea of "armed self-reliance," 87, 153, 191, 205–7, 214, 266, 308; instances of, 2, 50, 53, 54, 60, 80, 86–89, 96, 138–63 passim, 191–219 passim, 229, 245–308 passim; and manhood, 141–43, 158–59, 163–64; and NAACP members, 157, 164; by Native Americans, 137–40, 154, 157; during Reconstruction, 13, 16, 25; and Southern black culture, 3, 86–87, 152–53, 157–58, 180, 192, 195, 198, 209–13, 215–16, 245–46, 249–50; and Williams family, 16, 18, 25, 40–41, 50, 57, 71, 86, 209; during World War II, 32–48 passim

—advocated by: Daisy Bates, 153, 159, 165; J. A. Delaine, 153; W. E. B. Du Bois, 211; Florida A&M students, 144; N. L. Gregg, 157; King, 212, 215–16; Thurgood Marshall, 153; Amzie Moore, 153; NAACP membership, 157, 164; Ida B. Wells, 211; Walter White, 54

See also African American—women: and armed resistance

Armfield, Elmsley, 18

Arson, 14, 74, 263, 351 (n. 4). *See also* Armed resistance

Atlanta, Ga., 18, 208, 262

Atlanta Age. See African American—press: *Atlanta Age*

Austin, Louis, 30, 36, 67, 92, 96, 100, 115, 116, 118, 133, 134, 153–54

Aycock, Charles B., 17

Bailey, N.C., 61

Baker, Ella, 29, 30, 39, 115, 116, 217, 262

Baldwin, James, 145, 206, 223, 225, 227, 237, 238

Baldwin, Mich., 305, 306

"Ballad of Monroe," 290

Baraka, Amiri (LeRoi Jones), 204, 224–42 passim, 250, 288, 344 (n. 4)

Barber, Chalmers, 56

Barnett, Ross, 247

Bass, Cora, 209

Bates, Daisy, 153, 154, 155, 159, 164–65, 243

Bates, L. C., 154

Batista, Fulgencio, 220, 221, 227

Bay of Pigs, 239, 240, 241, 242, 247, 248, 348 (n. 59)

Beal, Fred, 7

Beasley, Roland, 44

Beijing, 294. *See also* China

Belgium, 119

Belk, William Henry, 10–11

Belk family, 55, 56

Belle Isle Amusement Park, 40–42

Belton, Edward, 58, 78, 80

Belzoni, Miss., 154

Benjamine, James, 157

Bennett, Charles, 225

Berry, Wendell, 94–95

Bickett, Thomas, 6, 21

Biddle Institute, 12

Bilbo, Theodore, 29, 58

Birdsong, T. S., 247

Birmingham, Ala., 33, 46, 53, 103, 111, 153, 210, 245, 290, 300

Black Arts Movement, 227

Black churches. *See* African American—churches

Black nationalism, 27–28, 65, 143, 190, 194, 196–97, 199, 203, 204–5, 206, 207; revived in late 1950s, 235–37, 250–51; revived in mid-1960s, 288, 297, 298, 299; Robert Williams's variant of, 205–7, 289, 303–5

Black Panther Party for Self Defense, 289, 298, 299, 301, 304

Black Power, 3, 27–28, 69, 191–92, 196–97, 199, 208, 250, 291, 296–308 passim

Block, Sam, 290

Blount, J. D., 254

Blues, 1, 23–24, 38, 50, 69, 195, 288, 293. *See also* Culture: music

Bluford, F. D., 107

Bohemia, 224

Bond, Julian, 216

Bosque, Juan Almeida, 222, 231, 234, 285

Boston University, 213

Boswell, William Jean, 68

"Bourbons," 16. *See also* Democratic Party

Boynton v. Virginia, 244

Boyte, Harry, 86, 198–99, 209, 264, 276, 282

Boyte, Janet, 264, 277

Braden, Anne, 81, 117, 128, 195, 210, 211, 216–17, 265

Braden, Carl, 116, 117, 128, 129, 133, 134, 148, 153, 210, 214

Bradshaw, F. F., 35

Branch, Taylor, 64, 116, 244

Briggs, Cyril V., 194, 342 (n. 19)

Bromberg, Ed, 269

Brooks, Paul, 246, 262, 263, 264, 265

Brotherhood of Sleeping Car Porters, 27, 116

Broughton, J. Melville, 31, 33, 37, 48

Brown, Eugene, 249

Brown, H. Rap, 301

Brown, John, 284

Brown, P. R., 130, 134

Brown, Sterling, 36

Brown v. Board of Education, 51, 52, 73–74, 78, 87, 115, 127, 144, 153, 215; white resistance to decision, 74, 98–99, 191, 214

Brundage, Slim, 207

Burlington, N.C., 64

Bush, Godwin, 60–61

Business Week, 108

Byrd, Walter, 80

Cameron, Bruce, 30–31

Camp Butner, N.C., 37

Camp Crowder, Mo., 46, 47

Camp Pendleton, Calif., 72

Camp Sutton, N.C., 34, 43–45, 56, 87

Canada, 119, 284

Canady, Herman, 65

Cannon, Hugh, 257

Carmichael, Stokely, 211, 237, 291, 301

Carolina Times. *See* African American—press: *Carolina Times*

Carson, Clayborne, 298, 299

Cash, W. J., 97

Castro, Fidel, 2, 220–42 passim, 252, 282, 285, 293, 294, 348 (n. 36)

Caswell County, N.C., 68

Caswell Messenger, 68

Center for Chinese Studies, 303, 305

Central High School (Little Rock, Ark.), 153, 159

Central Intelligence Agency, 222, 225, 239, 288, 295, 300

Central Methodist Church (Monroe, N.C.), 307

Central Prison (Raleigh, N.C.), 50

Chafe, William H., 75, 108

Chapel Hill, N.C., 35

Chapel Hill News Leader, 139

Charleston, S.C., 152, 207

Charlotte, N.C., 6, 12, 15, 23, 30, 64, 67, 69, 109, 122, 125, 126

Charlotte Democrat, 14

Charlotte News, 24, 76–77
Charlotte Observer, 124, 218, 252, 253, 265, 306
Charns, Alex, 156
Chatham, Price, 264
Chelstrom, Winifred, 238
Cherry, Annie Bell, 9, 81
Cherry, R. Gregg, 60
Chicago, Ill., 122, 131, 150
Chicago Daily News, 135
Chicago Defender. See African America—press: Chicago Defender
Childress, Alice, 225, 227
China, 119, 294, 296, 299–303
Christianity. See Afro-Christianity
Civil Rights Act of 1964, 191
Civil Rights Commission, 97
Civil rights movement. See African American—freedom movement
Civil War, 6, 12, 158
Clarendon County, S.C., 153
Clark, David, 7
Clark, Ed, 227
Clarke, John Hendrick, 204, 206, 223, 225, 227, 230, 233, 235, 242
Clay, Frank, 79
Cleage, Albert B., 288
Cleaver, Eldridge, 298, 301
Cleaver, Kathleen, 301
Cleveland, Ohio, 122, 131
Cobb, Charles, 212
Codero, Ana Livia, 227
Cohen, Robert Carl, 300, 301
Cohn, David L., 35
COINTELPRO, 299, 303
Cold War, 107, 220–48 passim, 254, 285–86, 299–302, 308; enables Robert Williams to return to United States, 300–302; fuels right wing resurgence, 59–62, 64, 66–68, 104–5, 121, 124, 222, 248, 290; gives African Americans unprecedented political leverage, 3, 51–53, 59–60, 67–68, 103–4, 117–20, 145, 225, 245, 247
Cole, James "Catfish," 79, 86, 88, 137–39, 140

Coleman, Ornette, 288
College students: and African American freedom struggle, 29–30, 69, 107, 143–45, 192, 217, 262, 297
Colonization, 17
Colored Methodist Episcopal Church, 56. See also African American—churches
Columbia, S.C., 207
Columbia Lighthouse and Informer. See African American—press: Columbia Lighthouse and Informer
Columbus, Miss., 290
Committee on Civil Rights, 52, 61
Committee to Combat Racial Injustice (CCRI), 111, 115, 116, 117, 122–34 passim, 147, 155, 210
Communism, 7, 37, 39, 59, 64, 76, 77, 271. See also Anticommunism
Communist Manifesto, 39, 66
Communist Party, 39, 40, 66, 68, 70, 111, 121, 133, 147, 189, 235, 283, 292, 293, 294
Communist Party of Cuba, 292
Conant Gardens neighborhood, 38
Concord, N.C., 45
Congress of Industrial Organizations, 39, 62. See also United Automobile Workers
Congress of Racial Equality, 28, 29, 112, 144, 208, 244, 247, 262, 264, 290, 291
Connor, Eugene "Bull," 103, 245
Conservatives. See Democratic Party
Cooks, Carlos, 204
Cooke, Sam, 286
Coordinating Committee for Southern Relief, 206
Coverson, Mandy, 13
Covington, Jay Vann, 254, 255
Cox, Frances, 82
Crawford, Andrew, 142
Creft, H. H., Jr., 201
Creft, Hubert, 7
Crisis. See African American—press: Crisis
Crisis of the Negro Intellectual, 204
Cross, Joseph, 326 (n. 27)

Cross, Lonnie, 206
Crowder, Richard, 252, 254, 255, 266, 276, 281
Crowder, Roy, 89
Crusader, 141, 194–239 passim, 250, 259, 266, 290; in China, 296; in Cuba, 290; family, 203, 204, 224; influence on freedom movement, 210; and King, 246, 247; mission of, 208, 209
Crusaders Association for Relief and Enlightenment (C.A.R.E), 203
Crusader without Violence, 210
Cruse, Harold, 196–97, 204, 207, 225, 227, 230
Cuba, 2, 221–41 passim, 254, 285, 293–94; and African American freedom movement, 222–24, 227, 230; and racial politics, 222–26, 228, 234–35, 241, 247–48, 265, 286
Cuban Foreign Ministry, 292
Cuban Revolution, 207, 221–35 passim
Culture: African American, 1, 8–9, 38–39, 50, 69–70, 116, 192, 194–95, 204, 212, 213, 224–25, 308; music, 1, 4, 23–24, 38, 50, 69, 101, 114, 195, 224, 285–86, 288, 289, 293, 299
Current, Gloster, 122, 127, 129, 239–40, 243

Dadeville, Ala., 211
Daily Worker, 25, 40, 62
Daniels, Frank, 31, 32
Daniels, Jonathan, 32, 45, 74
Daniels, Josephus, 16, 22
Davidson, Osha Gray, 74
Davis, Chester, 100, 132–34
Davis, Edmund, 14
Davis, Edward "Pork Chop," 204
Davis, John W., 65
Davis, Ossie, 204, 242, 250
Davis, Sammy, Jr., 131, 137
Deacons for Defense and Justice, 291, 297
DeBruce, Claude, 111–12
Decatur, Miss., 53
Dee, Ruby, 204

De Gaulle, Charles, 247
Delaine, J. A., 153
Dellinger, David, 213, 216
Dellums, C. C., 27–28
Democratic Party, 66–67, 105–6, 124, 131; and white supremacy campaign, 13–17, 32
Desegregation, 98–99, 115, 153, 190, 191, 201, 202, 244; and Freedom Rides, 192, 244–49, 262, 264, 267; and Monroe swimming pool campaign, 82–87, 251–60; resistance to, 73, 74, 75, 98, 214, 215, 328 (nn. 35, 36); and sexual politics, 6, 10, 34, 35, 61–62, 67, 75, 79, 98, 99; and sit-in movement, 144, 145, 192, 217, 218, 219, 249. *See also* African American—freedom movement; *Brown v. Board of Education*; Integration
Detroit, Mich., 29, 37–42, 62, 122, 238; Riot of 1943, 26, 40–42
Detroit Free Press, 289
Dies, Martin, 64
Dietrich, Paul, 269
Diggs, Charles, 73
Disfranchisement, 13–17, 22, 25, 51
Dittmer, John, 48
"Dixiecrats," 97, 105. *See also* Democratic Party
Domestic service. *See* African American—women: and domestic work
Douglass, Frederick, 66
Du Bois, Shirley Graham, 204, 242, 284
Du Bois, W. E. B, 20, 36, 52, 97, 121, 211, 242, 284
Durham, N.C., 36, 38, 53, 64, 66, 92, 145
Durham Committee on Negro Affairs, 249
Durham County, N.C., 61
Durham Morning Herald, 154
Durr, Virginia, 33, 117
Dutton, Cliff, 280

Earle, Willie, 59–60
East Flat Rock, N.C., 79
Eastland, James, 64, 107, 121

Ebony. See African American—press:
  Ebony
Eckford, Elizabeth, 159
Economic intimidation, 79–80, 158, 159,
  199
Education, 21, 99, 201. *See also Brown v.*
  Board of Education
Egginton, Joyce, 118
Eisenhower, Dwight D., 73, 110, 115, 119,
  120, 135, 222, 225, 241, 248
Eisenhower, Mamie, 120
Eleanor Clubs, 59. *See also* Rumors;
  World War II
Electoral politics, 12–18, 21–22, 51, 53,
  58, 64, 67, 104–8, 127, 248–49; in
  1948, 62, 64; in 1960, 240; and sex,
  58–59, 248; and violence, 22–23, 51,
  53–54, 58, 191, 288, 291
Elizabeth Baptist Church, 4, 8, 82
Elliott, Jake, 252, 255, 273
Emancipation, 12, 73
Emergency Civil Liberties Union, 112
Enfield, N.C., 13
Ervin, Sam, 234
Erwin, N.C., 33
Evers, Medgar, 53, 143, 153, 305
Executive Order 8802, 27

Fairclough, Adam, 191
Fair Employment Practices Commission,
  27
Fair Play for Cuba Committee, 221,
  223–24, 226, 233, 234–39, 283, 284
Farmer, J. C., 61
Farmer, James, 28, 247
Farrakhan, Louis, 288
Faubus, Orval, 106, 108, 222
Fayetteville Observer, 124
Federal Bureau of Investigation, 2, 31,
  35, 36–37, 39, 60, 63, 64, 68, 245,
  253–54, 256, 299; and campaign
  against Robert Williams, 131–32, 155,
  193, 208–9, 283–85, 287, 292, 302
Federal Employee Loyalty Program, 64
Fellowship of Reconciliation, 112, 212
Fifteenth Amendment, 151

First Baptist Church (Monroe, N.C.), 104
First Baptist Church (Montgomery, Ala.),
  245, 271
Fix, Joseph, 306
Florida A&M University, 9, 143, 144
Folsom, Jim, 138, 333 (n. 67)
Forest Club, 41
Forman, James, 262–65, 270, 272, 273
Fort Bragg, N.C., 46
Foster, Gus, 326 (n. 27)
Foster, Larry, 109
Fourteenth Amendment, 98, 151, 163
Frazier, E. Franklin, 117
Freedom. See African American—press:
  Freedom
Freedom jazz, 286. *See also* Culture:
  music
Freedom Riders, 192, 244–49, 262, 264;
  in Monroe, 265–75 passim
Freeman, Sidney, 277
Free Will Baptist Church, 79
Fusion between Populists and Republi-
  cans, 15–17, 58

Gamble's Drug Store, 217
Gandhi, Mohandas, 28, 208, 212–13,
  215, 244, 246, 266
Gardner, Ava, 137
Garrow, David, 161
Garvey, Marcus, 3, 196, 197, 199, 295
Gastonia, N.C., 7, 102
Gender politics, 2, 3, 138–65 passim,
  243, 308. *See also* African American—
  women; Manhood; Rape; Sexuality;
  White womanhood
George, Henry, 44
Georgia, 58, 207
GI bill, 65, 70
Gibson, Richard, 223, 224, 226, 234,
  235, 236, 242, 288, 297
Ginsberg, Allen, 234
Golden, Harry, 83, 85, 108, 110, 118, 125,
  135, 140
Gospel music, 1, 23, 50, 195, 299
Graham, Frank Porter, 35, 66, 67
Graham, Shirley, 204, 242, 284

Granger, Lester B., 32
Gray, Don, 253
Gray, Elgie, 78
Greater King Solomon Baptist Church (Detroit, Mich.), 238
Green, Berta, 235, 236
Green, Paul, 75
Green Ray plantation, 10
Greensboro, N.C.: sit-ins, 29–30, 144, 192, 217
Greensboro Register, 13
Greenville, S.C., 33, 207
Greenwood, Frank, 289
Greenwood, Miss., 290
Gregg, N. L., 157
Griffin, Bynum, 253
Griffin, D. S., 257
Griffin, J. Emmett, 147, 310 (n. 8)
Grifton, N.C., 33
Griswold, Richard, 269, 274
Guevara, Ernesto "Che," 231, 293
Gulledge, Frank, 146

Haddad, Ed, 223
Hall, Gwendolyn Midlo, 303
Hamer, Fanny Lou, 297
Hamilton, Thomas, 61–62
Hancock, Gordon B., 36
Hanoi, 2, 294–95
Hansberry, Lorraine, 69
Harlem, 2, 48, 70, 190, 203, 204, 233, 234, 250
Harlem Mothers, 190
Harlem Writers Guild Workshop, 233
Harris Funeral Home, 50, 53, 80
Harvard University, 221, 240, 248
Havana, 220–32 passim, 285, 286, 291
Hawkins, Reginald, 109, 121, 258
Haywood, Harry, 211, 293–94
Heath, Lura, 5
Helms, Coke, 5
Helms, Jerry, 255, 275
Helms, Jesse (senator), 1, 5, 67, 75–76, 220, 271, 302
Helms, Jesse A., 1, 48, 55, 149, 263, 269, 309 (n. 4)

Hendersonville, N.C., 61
Henry, Lawrence, 291
Henry, Milton, 298, 302, 305
Henry, Patrick, 198
Henry, Richard, 298
Hewitt, Masai, 301
Hicks, Calvin, 237, 250, 251
Highlander Folk School, 207
Hinkel, James, 265
Hitler, Adolf, 24–38 passim, 214
Ho Chi Minh, 2, 294–95
Hodges, Luther H., 74–76, 86, 92, 97–98, 104–8, 110, 113, 138, 146, 148, 330 (n. 15); and kissing case, 110, 113, 123–25, 127, 131, 132, 135
Hodges, Martha Blakeney, 104
Hoffman, N.C., 100, 101, 113
Holiday, Dallas, 326 (n. 27)
Holmes County, Miss., 212
Holt Street Baptist Church, 103
Honeycutt, Susanna, 10
Hoover, J. Edgar, 45, 70, 156, 193, 205, 208, 209, 292
Hotel Theresa (Harlem), 233, 234, 237
House, Gladys, 41
House, Ray, 23
House Un-American Activities Committee, 128–29
Houston, Frank, 254
Howard, T. R. M., 212
Howard University, 29, 265
Hughes, Langston, 38, 69, 225, 227, 234, 286

If We Must Live, 289
India, 28, 214
Industrialization, 105
Ingram, Mack, 68
Integration, 197, 200, 204, 210. See also Desegregation
Interracial sex. See Sexuality

Jackson, James, 292, 293
Jackson, Miss., 212, 247, 264
Jackson, N.C., 60
Jacksonville, Fla., 208, 250

James, C. L. R., 111
Jazz, 195, 285, 286, 288, 293
Jefferson, Thomas, 198, 262
Jefferson School of Social Science, 70, 321 (n. 78)
Jerome, Thomas J., 16
Jet. See African American—press: Jet
Jim Crow. See Segregation
John Birch Society, 248
John Dewey Society, 238
Johnson, Ethel Azalea, 21–22, 81, 141–42, 155, 193–207 passim, 218, 251, 252, 260
Johnson, Lyndon, 106
Johnson C. Smith College, 67, 69, 70, 87
Johnston, Walter, 127, 130, 148
Jones, Charles M., 35
Jones, Doland, 217–18
Jones, E. Stanley, 28
Jones, LeRoi. See Baraka, Amiri
Jones, Lester, 60
Jonesboro, La., 291
Jones Drug Store, 217, 218, 219
Jordan, Cull, 275
Journal and Sentinel (Winston-Salem, N.C.), 124, 133, 134
Journey of Reconciliation, 112, 213, 244. See also Nonviolent direct action
Joyner, James Y., 21
Justice Department, 52, 86, 244, 248, 252, 256, 264, 277, 285, 303

Kale, Ed, 265
Karenga, Ron, 301
Katzenbach, Nicholas, 297
Kennedy, John F., 103, 105, 236–48 passim, 256, 285
Kennedy, Robert F., 247, 253
Kenya, 153
Kenyatta, Jomo, 153
Keziah, Don, 252
Khrushchev, Nikita, 220, 234, 247
Killens, John Oliver, 204, 227, 233, 227
Kilpatrick, James J., 98
King, Martin Luther, Jr., 2, 3, 116, 117, 191, 192, 208, 210, 211, 213, 228, 245–46, 282, 293; and armed resistance, 211, 212, 215–16; criticism of, 241, 247, 250, 262, 266, 289; and debate with Robert Williams, 163, 164, 214–16; and international politics, 103, 120, 245, 246, 295, 300
King, Slater, 291
Kissing case, 92–140 passim, 193, 235, 236, 238, 333 (n. 67); and anticommunism, 128, 129, 132, 134; and international politics, 103, 108, 118, 119, 120, 123, 333 (n. 68); and NAACP, 109–10, 121, 122, 123, 125, 126; and sexual politics, 118, 119, 121, 123, 124, 133, 136, 140; trial, 128, 129, 130, 135; white reaction to, 96–98, 124, 125, 134; and white womanhood, 123, 124, 133
Kissinger, Henry, 299, 303
Kreisburg, Paul H., 303
Ku Klux Klan, 2, 38, 44, 49, 50, 58, 61, 75, 76, 121, 127, 129, 137, 323 (n. 102), 326 (n. 27); armed resistance to, 89, 137, 138, 140, 153, 154; and Democratic Party, 13, 14, 16; and kissing case, 96, 99; and Lumbee Indians, 136, 137, 138, 139, 153, 154, 157; in Monroe, 22, 49–50, 80, 86–89, 136, 138, 214, 229, 245, 247, 250, 256, 257, 274, 281; in 1920s, 194, 211; rebirth of, 61, 75, 76; during Reconstruction, 2, 13, 14, 16, 22, 38, 44, 49, 50, 58; Robert Williams's shootout with, 85, 86, 89, 256, 257, 275

Labor, 6–7, 27, 38–43, 50, 57, 62–63, 131, 250–51, 266; and women, 43, 146. See also African American—women: and domestic work
Lake, I. Beverly, 74, 75, 127, 248
Lambert, Judith, 326 (n. 27)
Lambert, Martha, 326 (n. 27)
Larkins, John R., 258–59
Lassiter, Louise, 325 (n. 15)
Lausche, Frank, 297
Lautier, Louis, 154
Leadbelly (Huddie Ledbetter), 288

Lee, George, 154
Left, 116, 132, 206–7, 210, 234, 239, 240, 285, 289, 295
Lenin, Vladimir, 66
Lever, Constance, 267, 268, 269, 272
Levison, Stanley, 295
Lewis, David L., 51
Lewis, John, 296
Lewis, Nell Battle, 7
Liberation, 214, 216
Liberation Committee for Africa, 237
Life, 138, 221, 297
Lincoln, Abby, 237, 288
Lincoln, Abraham, 12, 228, 234
Little Rock, Ark., 115, 153, 154, 159, 225
Logan, Rayford Whittingham, 36, 211
Lomax, Louis, 144, 160, 162, 164
London News-Chronicle, 118, 119, 122
Look, 144
Losado, Manuel Pineira, 226
Los Angeles, Calif., 72, 203, 238, 287
Louis, Joe, 223
Louisville, Ky., 128, 129
Louisville Courier-Journal, 128
Lowery, John, 265, 269, 270, 272, 274, 276, 277, 279
Lowndes County, Ala., 211
Luce, Clare Boothe, 120
Luce, Henry R., 120
Lumbee Indians, 137–40, 154, 157
Lumumba, Patrice, 237
Lunes de Revolucion, 225, 227
Lynching, 14, 18, 22, 47, 50, 54, 57, 59, 60, 149, 196, 211, 213, 214, 255, 313 (n. 77); of Andrew Crawford, 142; of Mack Charles Parker, 143, 145, 152, 163; of Emmett Till, 144. See also Violence: by mobs
Lynd, Staughton, 212
Lynn, Conrad, 112–35 passim, 161, 203, 206, 231–32, 234, 237, 242, 244, 250, 287, 288, 291, 294

McCarthy, Joseph, 189
McCarthyism, 156. See also Anticommunism

McCoy, James Edward, 191
McCray, John, 157–58
McDonald, Joseph, 265
McDow, J. W., 50, 80, 81, 84, 114, 242, 260, 266, 275, 282–83
McKissick, Floyd, 61
McLean, Charles, 79, 126
McLeod, Malcolm, 138
McNair, "Blind Jack," 312 (n. 74)
Macon, Ga., 189, 207
McWilliams, Carey, 207
Madison, Blaine M., 100, 101, 125, 134–35
Madison Square Garden, 28
Mahoney, William, 265
Mailer, Norman, 117, 223
Major, Reginald, 298
Malcolm X, 2, 145, 204, 205, 220, 233, 234, 237, 296, 297, 298, 305, 344 (n. 74)
Mallory, Willie Mae, 189, 190, 193, 203, 204, 237, 250, 268, 275, 278, 279, 280, 282, 293, 300, 304
Mangum, W. W., 49
Manhood, 2, 36, 61, 94, 139–49 passim, 158, 159, 163–64, 198, 206, 214, 215, 243, 277, 291
Mao Zedong, 2, 3, 290, 294, 296, 302, 307
March on Washington (1963), 296
March on Washington Movement (MOWM), 27, 28, 213
Marine Corps, U.S., 71, 72
Marshall, Burke, 264, 277
Marshall, Thurgood, 51, 60, 121, 153, 155, 156
Marshville, N.C., 57, 195, 250
Marx, Karl, 7
Marxism, 39, 71, 111, 238; view of race and class, 42, 70–71, 111, 232, 292–94, 301. See also Communism; Communist Party; Left; Socialist Workers Party
Marzani and Munsell, 289
Matthews, Ralph, 297
Mauney, A. A., 86, 88, 91, 99, 229, 252, 253, 254, 256, 259, 270, 275, 280, 281

Maxton, N.C., 137–39, 154
May, W. R., 217–18
Mayfield, Curtis, 286
Mayfield, Julian, 147, 204–5, 221, 223, 224, 225, 227–28, 235, 242, 250, 254, 268, 274, 281–83, 294
Maynard, Robert, 242, 303
Medlin, John, 11
Medlin, Lewis, 147, 148
Meharry Medical School, 87
Meier, August, 290
Memphis, Tenn., 211
Messenger, 15
Michaux, Louis, 204
Michigan, 51, 131, 238
Middle class, 38, 79, 80, 81, 126, 196, 210, 223
Migration, 26, 40, 50, 53, 62
Militant, 69, 207
Mills, C. Wright, 234, 240
Miscegenation, 6, 10, 13, 34, 35, 61, 62, 67, 68, 74, 75, 79, 98. *See also* Gender politics; Sexuality: and racial politics
Mississippi, 94, 237, 246–47, 290
Mississippi Highway Patrol, 247
Mississippi Summer Project, 290
Mitchell, Clarence, 243
Mobley, Ora Mae, 203, 250
Mobs. *See* Violence: by mobs
Monroe, Ga., 54
Monroe, N.C., 1–25 passim, 108; and African American freedom movement, 80–89, 98–99, 141, 191–203 passim, 217–19, 251–81 passim; arson in, 14, 74, 263, 351 (n. 4); and Camp Sutton, 34, 38, 43–44, 45, 56, 87; demographics of, 4, 5, 21, 205; Ku Klux Klan in, 22, 49–50, 80, 86–89, 136, 138, 214, 229, 245, 247, 250, 256, 257, 274, 281; and Newtown, 4, 18, 20, 23, 54, 56, 114, 270–71, 276, 278, 282; during Reconstruction, 12–17, 25; and swimming pool campaign, 82–87, 251–60; and white resistance to African American freedom movement, 21, 22, 74–75, 86–87, 113, 120, 121, 123–25,

226, 248–61 passim, 268–78 passim; during World War II, 34, 43–45
Monroe Chamber of Commerce, 6
Monroe Country Club, 83, 201, 202, 251, 254
Monroe Enquirer, 12, 13, 17, 21, 43, 74, 75, 76, 79, 85, 99, 114, 123, 131, 146, 202, 229, 233, 248, 264, 267, 268, 272
Monroe Journal, 22, 44, 63, 89, 247, 257, 275, 276
Monroe Nonviolent Action Committee, 266, 267, 268, 269, 271, 272
Monroe Police Department, 256
Monroe–Union County Civic League, 58
Montgomery, Bennie, 36, 37, 46, 49–50, 53
Montgomery, Ala., 191, 245–47, 250
Montgomery Bus Boycott, 3, 78, 103, 111, 115, 116, 144, 161, 210, 212, 213, 215, 307
Montgomery Improvement Association, 111, 117
Moody, Ralph, 127, 129
Moore, Amzie, 153
Moore, Audley "Queen Mother," 203
Moore, Carlos, 226, 234, 237, 242
Morgan v. Virginia, 112
Morrison, Harvey, 84
Morrison Training School for Negroes, 100, 125, 129, 130, 134
Morrow, E. Fredric, 119
Morrow, John Samuel, 119
Morsell, John, 110, 161
Moses, Bob, 153, 212
Moton, Robert, 211
Murray, Pauli, 29, 30, 159–60
Murrow, Edward R., 221
Music. *See* Blues; Culture: music; Gospel music; Jazz
Muste, A. J., 213, 216
Myrdal, Gunnar, 93

Nash, Diane, 245, 246, 295, 358 (n. 40)
Nashville, Tenn., 245, 262, 297
Nasser, Gamal Abdel, 220, 234
Nation, 114, 207, 223

National Association for the Advancement of Colored People (NAACP), 2, 29, 52, 61, 73, 74, 76, 143–45, 149, 190, 191, 193, 202, 205, 207, 208, 210, 216, 234, 238, 265, 305; and anticommunism, 155, 156, 162, 222, 249; campaign against Robert Williams, 150–55, 192, 194, 258; class tensions in, 80–82, 122, 126, 150, 160, 161, 162, 239–40, 243, and Cold War, 59, 60; and kissing case, 90, 91, 96, 100, 109–26 passim, 131–35, 203; and Mack Ingram case, 68; Monroe chapter of, 58, 78–88 passim, 137, 141–42, 146–47, 195, 204, 206, 251, 260, 266, 276, 281, 304; national office of, 110, 151, 153, 160, 163, 239; veterans in, 53–54; in World War II, 48, 50

National Freedom Council, 264

National Memorial African Bookstore, 204

National Review, 98

National Rifle Association, 128

National Textile Workers Union, 7

National Youth Administration, 36, 37, 49

Nation of Islam, 143, 205, 207, 208, 251, 288

Native Americans. See Lumbee Indians

Negroes With Guns, 289, 298, 357 (n. 7)

Nehru, Jawaharlal, 214, 220, 234

Nelson, Truman, 206

New Deal, 251

New Left. See Left

New Rochelle, N.Y., 131

News (Lancaster, S.C.), 120

News and Courier (Charleston, S.C.), 150

News and Observer (Raleigh, N.C.), 7, 16, 22, 31, 32, 58, 74, 102, 124, 127, 139

Newton, Huey, 298, 357 (n. 7)

New York Citizen-Call, 233

New York City, 2, 68, 111, 122, 129, 160, 189, 203, 204, 233, 234, 250. See also Harlem

New York Herald Tribune, 138

New York Post, 96, 108–9, 110, 112, 124, 130, 135, 147, 242, 260

New York Times, 70, 149, 153, 223, 225, 234, 238, 302

Nivens, M. S., 255

Nivens, W. B., 84

Nixon, Angela, 93

Nixon, E. D., 111, 116, 117

Nixon, Richard, 52, 105, 240, 299, 303

Nonviolent Action Group, 265

Nonviolent direct action, 143–45, 154, 164, 177–79, 190–92, 198–99, 206, 244–51, 262–73 passim, 307–8; abandoned by movement, 290–91, 296–99; and armed resistance, 3, 188, 307–8; and Cold War, 103–4; controversy over, 144–65 passim, 174, 192, 198–99, 209–10, 213–19; and Journey of Reconciliation, 112, 213, 244; and manhood, 143, 158–59, 164, 206; resisted by NAACP national office, 115, 144, 161–62, 164; and Southern black culture, 192, 211–15, 307–8; success of, 191–92, 217; violence critical to success of, 115, 191, 257; during World War II, 28–30

—and Robert Williams: critiqued by, 24, 141, 149, 151, 163–65, 198, 206, 213–17, 241, 243, 250, 262, 265–66, 289, 295; practiced by, 30, 84–85, 207, 217, 219, 251–58; praised by, 78, 213–14, 216, 289

North Carolina: anticommunism in, 12, 64–68, 76, 85–86, 121, 132–34, 146–47, 247; Ku Klux Klan in, 13–14, 22, 50, 58, 61–62, 79, 86, 88–89, 96, 137–40, 214, 229, 247, 250; labor struggles in, 6–7; liberals in, 82–87, 96–97, 248; and paternalism, 10–11, 44, 55–56, 107; and politics, 15–17, 30–32, 107–8, 121, 127, 146–47, 217–19, 247–49; racial violence in, 1–2, 11, 13–14, 16, 30–64 passim, 74, 79, 86–96 passim, 112, 140, 191, 214, 249–61 passim, 268–81; and reaction to Brown decision, 74–77, 79–80; slavery in, 6, 9–11; during World War II, 30–38, 43–45, 48

North Carolina Agricultural and Technical College, 29–30, 107, 217, 326 (n. 27)

North Carolina College for Negroes, 36, 66

North Carolina Council on Human Relations, 249

North Carolina NAACP Youth Council, 144

North Carolina State Bureau of Investigation, 68, 146, 147

North Carolina State Highway Patrol, 60, 254, 257, 260, 269

North Carolina State Utilities Board, 37

North Carolina Supreme Court, 16, 68, 101, 219

Nova Scotia, 284

O'Donnell, Kenneth, 285

Odum, Howard, 31–35

Office of Asian Communist Affairs, 303

Ohio Sentinel, 223

Olsen, Anne, 284, 288, 290

Olsen, Vernal, 284, 288, 290

100 Amazing Facts about the Negro, 199

Only in America, 118

Overton, L. Joseph, 234

Oxendine, Simeon, 138

Oxford, N.C., 191

Paar, Jack, 221

Pacifism, 24, 212–16, 266

Packinghouse Workers Hall, 131, 238

Pan-Africanism, 3, 237, 307. *See also* Black nationalism

Parchman Farm Penitentiary, 264

Parker, Mack Charles, 143, 145, 152, 154, 163, 214

Parks, Rosa, 3, 307

Parrish, Robert, 249

Paternalism, 10, 11, 55, 106, 107, 279, 311 (n. 30)

Patriarchy, 94, 142. *See also* Gender politics

Payne, Charles, 39, 116, 153

Peachland, S.C., 195

Peacock, Willie, 290

Pearsall Plan, 75, 76

Pearson, Drew, 220, 234, 235

Penn Station, 222

Pentonville Prison, 302

People's Voice, 16, 312 (n. 53)

Perry, Albert E., 34, 80–92 passim, 110, 114, 117, 129, 141, 145, 146, 266, 282, 284; and abortion case, 90–92, 115, 118, 133, 216; trial of, 101

Perry, Bertha, 87, 88, 91, 118

Perry, Booker T., 50, 55, 77, 82

Philadelphia Tribune, 223

Pickle Meadows, Nev., 73

Picott, Rosa Lee, 33

Pittsburgh Courier. See African American—press: *Pittsburgh Courier*

Pledger, W. A., 211

Pless, J. Will, 102

Police brutality, 1, 18, 29, 33, 34, 42, 44, 78, 95, 99, 299, 326 (n. 27)

Polk, Miss Sis, 23

Polk County, N.C., 61

Polkton, N.C., 195

Poplarville, Miss., 143, 152, 154, 163

Populism, 15. *See also* Fusion between Populists and Republicans

Port Chicago, Calif., 42

Poston, Ted, 108–9, 112, 130, 147, 260

Powell, Adam Clayton, 73, 204, 221, 296

Prattis, P. L., 152

Pravda, 103, 238

Press. *See* African American—press; names of specific newspapers and magazines

Price, J. Hampton, 96, 99–102, 113, 128, 129, 130, 134

Progressive Party, 62

Protection of womanhood, 61, 94, 139–49 passim, 198, 206, 214, 215, 243, 277, 291

Race and Rumors of Race: Challenge to American Cities, 34

Race riots, 26, 38, 40–42, 211, 288, 289–90
Racial epithets, 312 (n. 74)
Racial etiquette, 20, 27, 49, 92, 94, 99, 113, 194
Racial violence. *See* Violence: by mobs
Radio Free Dixie, 285, 287, 288, 293
Radio stations: KPFA, 288; Radio Havana, 2; WBAI, 288; WFMO, 79; WLIB, 189
Raines, William, 29–30
Randolph, A. Phillip, 27, 28, 213
Rankin, John, 52, 64
Rape, Lilly Mae, 90–92
Rape, 60, 61, 124, 140, 143, 160, 163, 196; against African American women by white men, 10, 61, 97, 140–50 passim, 163, 325 (n. 15); attitudes regarding, in the South, 22, 34, 58, 59, 68, 92, 94, 97; in Tallahassee, Fla., 143, 150
Rawls, Raymond, 326 (n. 27)
Reader's Digest, 106
Reape, Harold, 276, 281
Reconstruction, 12–16, 25, 31, 58, 107, 119, 158; and African American armed resistance, 13, 16, 211; and Democratic Party, 12–16, 22, 32, 51; and fusion between Populists and Republicans, 15, 16, 17, 58, 164
Reddick, L. D., 210
Redfern, Geraldine, 254
Redfern, Lillian, 254
"Redshirts," 16
Reed, J. C., 147
Reed, Mary Ruth, 147, 148
Register (Greensboro, N.C.), 13
Republican Party, 12–14, 105. *See also* Fusion between Populists and Republicans
Republic of New Africa, 297, 298, 302–5
Resistance. *See* African American—freedom movement; Armed resistance
Reston, James, 238
Revolución, 224
Revolutionary Action Movement, 290, 297, 298, 304, 359 (n. 47)

Reynolds, Grant, 48
Richardson, Boyce, 18
Richardson, O. L., 131–32, 146, 148
Richardson Creek, 45
Rich Square, N.C., 59–61
Ricks, Willie, 291
Rittenberg, Sidney, 294, 295–96
Roa, Raul, 234, 241
Roberson, Polly, 327 (n. 27)
Robertson, A. Willis, 121
Robert Williams in China, 296
Robeson, Paul, 68, 240
Robeson County, N.C., 137–40
Robinson, David, 55
Robinson, Emma Perry, 55
Robinson, Jackie, 163, 164, 234, 341 (n. 109)
Robinson, Mabel Ola. *See* Williams, Mabel
Robinson, Prentice, 269
Rock and roll, 239, 285–86
Rockefeller, Nelson, 162
Rocky Mount, N.C., 30, 37, 59
Roddy, Cad, 66
Roddy, Sam, 24
Rogers, J. A., 199
Roosevelt, Eleanor, 31, 120, 135
Roosevelt, Franklin D., 27, 32
Roper, N.C., 153
Rorie, Albert, 252, 253, 275, 276
Rorie, Magdalena Gillespie, 79
Royal Canadian Mounted Police, 284
Royster, Vermont, 105
Rudwick, Elliott, 290
Rumors, 31–32, 282, 284, 314 (n. 29)
Rush, Heath, 273, 274
Rushing, George, Sr., 195
Rushing, J. W., 273, 275
Rushing, James, 57–58, 80
Rusk, Dean, 241
Russell, Richard, 105
Rustin, Bayard, 28, 213, 216, 295
Rutherford County, N.C., 13

Sagner, Alan, 223
Saint Ann's Lake County Senior Meals and Human Services Program, 305

Saint Luke's Lutheran Church (Monroe, N.C.), 272

Salisbury, N.C., 86

"Sampson and Delilah," 299

Sanford, Terry, 127, 248–49, 258, 277

San Francisco, Calif., 42, 238

Saris, Stephanns, 120

Savannah, Ga., 207–8

Scales, Junius, 66

Schlesinger, Arthur M., Jr., 221, 240

Schliefer, Marc, 289

Seaboard Air Line Railway, 4, 18–19, 43, 56, 263

Seale, Bobby, 298, 301

Seawell, Malcolm, 126–29

Secrest, A. M., 218

Secrest Drug Store, 10, 218

Seeger, Pete, 290

Segregation, 20–23, 26, 27, 37, 43, 44, 54, 67, 74, 94, 118, 224, 232, 242; African American resistance to, 21, 37, 53, 74–76, 195, 197, 200–202, 217–19, 251–58; in Monroe, 6, 21–23, 82–85, 113–14, 195, 197, 201, 251–60; in the North, 71; and social order in the South, 21, 94–95

Self-defense. *See* Armed resistance

Sellers, Cleveland, 145

Sexuality, 3, 6–7, 19, 20, 34–36, 44, 47, 58–62, 92, 93, 102, 158, 159, 244, 248, 272, 273; and kissing case, 92–95, 97, 99, 109; and racial politics, 67–68, 74–75, 85, 97–98, 118, 119, 121, 140, 143–44, 148, 158–59, 163–64, 244, 248, 272–73, 308, 315 (n. 43), 316 (n. 51), 325 (nn. 14, 15), 326 (n. 27), 327 (n. 31)

Sexual violence. *See* Rape

Sharecroppers, 4, 6, 15, 49, 57–58, 68, 211, 309 (n. 1)

Share Croppers' Union, 211

Shaw, Brodus F., 145, 147, 148

Shaw University, 217

Shepard, James, 36

Shilman, Kenneth, 264, 274

Shores, Arthur, 153

Shure, John, 120, 124

Shute, J. Raymond, 4–5, 11, 21, 22, 34, 43, 261, 276; and defense of Albert Perry, 92; on desegregation, 76, 77; in Union County Council of Human Relations, 82, 87, 96

Shuttlesworth, Fred, 117

Simmons, Furnifold, 17

Simone, Nina, 286

Simpson, Bunyan, 21

Simpson, David Ezell "Fuzzy," 92–93, 95–96, 99, 100, 101, 102, 113, 119, 123, 129–30, 133

Simpson, Jennie, 100, 126, 130, 133

Single Issue in the Robert Williams Case, 163

Sit-in movement, 144, 145, 192, 217, 218, 219, 249. *See also* Greensboro, N.C.: sit-ins; Nonviolent direct action

16th Street Baptist Church (Birmingham, Ala.) bombing, 290

Slavery, 15, 67; legacy of, 7, 9–12, 46, 212; resistance during, 31, 195, 211, 212, 351 (n. 3); in Union County, 310 (n. 27)

Smiley, Glenn, 212

Smith, Lillian, 1

Smith, Willis, 66–67

Smith Act, 66, 132

Smith v. Allwright, 51

Smyer, A. B., 14

Snipes, Maceo, 54

"Social equality," 13, 34–36, 44, 67

Socialist Party, 284

Socialist Workers Party, 39, 69, 111–12, 114–15, 132, 203–4, 207, 208, 235, 239, 283

Soul music, 285–86

South Carolina, 6, 59–60, 157, 207

Southern Christian Leadership Conference (SCLC), 103, 115, 116, 162, 191, 198, 208, 209, 210, 213, 262, 264, 267

Southern Conference Educational Fund, 81, 117, 210, 264

Southern Negro Youth Congress, 66

Southern Patriot, 79, 210, 216

Southern Textile Bulletin, 7

Soviet Union, 51, 64, 103, 119, 120, 220, 234, 242, 285

Spirituals, 39, 50, 224, 286, 288, 293. *See also* Afro-Christianity; Culture: music

Stack, Floyd, 274

Stack, Howard J., 274–75

Stanford, Max, 290, 297

State Department, U.S., 51, 124, 135

Statesville, N.C., 326 (n. 27)

State Times (Jackson, Miss.), 150

Steele, C. K., 111, 114, 116, 117

Stegall, Charles Bruce, 278–81, 354 (n. 37)

Stegall, Mabel, 278–81, 354 (n. 37)

Stevenson, Adlai, 105, 241–42

Stimson, Henry, 35

Stitt, Ella Belle, 10, 11, 142, 195

Stone, I. F., 234

Stone Mountain, Ga., 58, 330 (n. 24)

Stoner, J. B., 139

Strand, Willie, 256

Student Nonviolent Coordinating Committee (SNCC), 145, 153, 192, 211, 216, 217, 247, 262, 265, 288, 290, 295, 296, 297

Sullivan, Ed, 221

Sullivan, L. B., 245

Supreme Court, U.S., 51, 52, 244

Surratt, Reed, 134

Sutton, Frank, 34

Sutton, Sissy, 93, 95, 100

Taber, Robert, 223, 235, 236

Tabor City, N.C., 61

Tallahassee, Fla., 111, 143–45, 150, 160, 163–64

Talmadge, Eugene, 29, 58

Taylor, Herbert, 33

Taylor Gospel Singers, 195

Textile industry, 6, 7, 86

Thomas, Claude, 6

Thomas, Darling, 16

Thompson, Daniel, 269, 270

Thompson, Evelyn, 95, 96, 100, 108, 126, 130, 133, 134

Thompson, Hanover, 92–96, 99–101, 108, 112–13, 118–19, 123–31, 133–35

Thompson, Mary Lou, 108

Thurmond, Strom, 97

Tiananmen Square, 2, 296

Till, Emmett, 94, 97, 98, 144, 154

Time, 108, 120

Times-Mercury, 17

Tomblin, Daniel, 10

Toronto Globe and Mail, 284

Trans World Airlines, 302

Trinity, N.C., 249–50

Trotskyists, 207, 236, 238. *See also* Socialist Workers Party

Truman, Harry S., 52, 61, 64, 222

Tubman, Harriet, 195

Turnbow, Hartman, 212

Turner, Joe, 288

Turner, Nat, 293

Tuskegee Institute, 122, 211

Ulacia, Gabino, 222

Umstead, William, 105

Underground Railroad, 195, 283

Union County, N.C., 15–16, 21, 58, 137, 232, 319 (n. 36); demographics of, 4, 6, 310 (n. 14), 317 (n. 81); slavery in, 7, 10–11, 12, 13, 310 (n. 27). *See also* Monroe, N.C.

Union County Civic League, 84

Union County Council on Human Relations, 82–84, 87, 96

Union County Employment Security Commission, 146

Union County Industrial Development Commission, 197

Union County Memorial Hospital, 22, 90

Union Supply, 263

Unitarian fellowship, 77, 82, 128, 261

United Automobile Workers of America, 39, 62; Local 600, 29, 42, 40, 62

United Nations, 51–52, 233, 237, 238, 241

United Press International, 61, 149, 153, 202

United States Information Agency, 107, 120, 124
University of British Columbia, 238
University of Colorado, 238, 248
University of Michigan, 238, 303, 305
University of Minnesota, 238, 239
University of North Carolina, 31, 35, 61–62, 66–67, 75, 120, 160
University of Washington, 238
U.S. Naval Intelligence, 73
U.S. News and World Report, 132

Vesey, Denmark, 152, 195
Veterans. See African American: veterans
Veterans Administration, 54, 56
Veterans of Foreign Wars, 138
Vietnam, 294, 295
Violence: in African American communities, 142; against white dissenters, 5, 13, 16, 22, 23, 64, 128; by mobs, 13, 14, 16, 18, 40–42, 44, 49, 53, 54, 61, 95, 142, 143, 158, 211, 213, 244–45, 249–56, 272–76, 326 (n. 27)
—against African Americans, 11, 53–54, 61, 74, 79, 86, 88–89, 94, 96, 142, 165, 199, 214, 244–81 passim; and manhood, 1–2, 140–43, 206; by police, 1–2, 18, 33, 34, 38, 42, 44, 45, 53, 95, 99; during Reconstruction, 13, 14, 16, 17, 25, 32, 73, 158; sexualized, 1–2, 140–41, 143–44, 145–49, 158–59, 163–64, 214; during World War II, 26, 30, 33, 34, 37–38, 40–42, 44–45. See also Lynching
Voice of America, 52, 107
Voter registration, 12, 14, 51, 58, 288, 291
Voting Rights Act of 1965, 191

Waddell, Alfred, 16
Wadesboro, N.C., 127–30, 195
Walker, James, 325 (n. 15)
Wallace, Henry, 62, 64
War Department, U.S., 35, 37, 44, 45
Waring, Thomas, 150
Warren, Robert Penn, 121

Washington, Booker T., 200, 211
Washington, D.C., 9, 30
Watt, Daniel, 237, 242
Watts riot, 288–90
Weissman, George, 93, 112–36 passim, 148, 153, 204, 205, 210, 214
Wells, Ida B., 211
West Virginia State College, 65–66
What the Negro Wants, 36
While God Lay Sleeping, 2
White, Georgia Davis, 145, 146, 148
White, Walter, 50, 52, 54, 60
White Citizens' Council, 5, 121, 158, 222, 290
White supremacy, 7, 12–14, 20–23, 25, 44, 67, 92, 201, 208, 214, 222, 255; and anticommunism, 7, 59, 64, 66–68, 76–77, 85–86, 104, 222, 225, 229, 238, 271, 285; internalized by African Americans, 27–28, 65, 93, 99, 200, 306–7; and religion, 21, 62, 200. See also White Supremacy Campaign of 1898
White Supremacy Campaign of 1898, 16–17, 21, 25, 32. See also Wilmington, N.C.
Whiteville, N.C., 61
White womanhood, 94, 97, 123, 138, 148, 327 (n. 31), 333 (n. 67)
Whiting, Allen S., 303
Wilkins, Roy, 31, 60, 91, 123, 192, 193, 243, 249; and campaign against Robert Williams, 150–64 passim
Williams, Charlie, 8–9, 26, 57, 62
Williams, Edward "Pete," 38, 41, 209
Williams, Ellen Isabel, 9–10, 12, 15, 24–25, 63, 142, 164, 308
Williams, Emma Carter, 1, 4, 7, 8, 9, 26, 45–46, 56, 63
Williams, Estelle, 70
Williams, Howard, 276
Williams, John Chalmers, 66, 67, 142, 259, 276, 294, 305
Williams, John Herman, 10, 38, 46, 209
Williams, John L., 4, 8, 17, 18, 19, 45–46, 56–57, 271

Williams, Mabel, 82, 84, 87, 134, 142, 252, 268, 282–85, 296, 302; and armed resistance, 57, 71, 87–88, 91–92, 141, 203, 229, 236, 259–60, 307; and *Crusader*, 193–98, 290; early life of, 43, 55–57, 66, 67; later life of, 302–8; marriage to Robert Williams, 56–57, 62–63, 65–67, 70, 98, 99, 305–7; and Radio Free Dixie, 285–88, 292, and women's activism, 81, 141, 195

Williams, Robert: in Baldwin, Mich., 305–6; and Baraka, 204, 227–32, 236, 288; and Daisy Bates, 159, 164–65, 243; and black nationalism, 65, 194, 196–97, 199, 203–7, 235–36, 297, 304; and Black Power movement, 3, 197, 250, 296, 297–305, 357 (n. 7); and Castro, 220–21, 223–24, 226, 231, 232–35; childhood and youth, 1–26 passim, 37; in China, 294–96, 299, 302; on Cold War, 64, 104, 135–36, 145, 225, 240–42; college education of, 65–70; death of, 2, 3, 306, 307; escapes from Monroe, 282–85; and Ho Chi Minh, 294–95; and Hughes, 38, 69, 225, 227, 234, 286, 288; and interracialism, 15, 17, 76–78, 82–87, 197, 202, 207, 304; and King, 161, 163, 192, 213–16, 246–47, 250, 262, 266, 282, 289; as local organizer, 80–89, 136, 145–49, 191–203, 217–19, 251–84 passim; and Malcolm X, 2, 145, 205–7, 220, 237, 296–97, 298, 344 (n. 74); and manhood, 141–43, 148–49, 158–59, 164, 206; and Mao Zedong, 2, 294, 296, 302; and Thurgood Marshall, 155–56; and Marxism, 7, 39–40, 42, 62, 66, 70–71, 111–12, 114–15, 207, 292–94; military service of, 26–27, 46–48, 71–73; returns to Monroe, 306; and school desegregation, 98–99; significance of, 2–3, 209–10, 264, 285–86, 297–302, 307–8; and Southern roots of Black Power, 1–3, 15–17, 25, 38–40, 47, 50, 53, 191–213 passim,

250–51, 262, 264, 287–91, 297–98; in Vietnam, 294–95; and Wilkins, 109–10, 123, 150–52, 159–64, 193, 243; and Charlie Williams (uncle), 8–9, 57; and Ellen Isabel Williams (grandmother), 9–10, 12, 24–25, 308; and Emma Carter Williams (mother), 1, 4, 7–9, 23, 45–46; and John L. Williams (father), 17–19, 56–57; and Mabel Williams (wife), 55–57, 62–63, 66, 70–73, 84, 98–99, 285–86, 302, 305–7; during World War II, 26–27, 36–43, 45–48; as a writer, 2, 47, 62, 65–66, 68–70, 72, 77, 267. *See also* Armed resistance; Cuba; Nonviolent direct action

Williams, Robert, Jr., 142, 276, 294

Williams, Sikes, 12, 15–16, 17, 25, 67, 164, 308

Wilmington, N.C., 16, 30–31

Wilson, Fred, 78, 96, 99, 118, 127–28, 257, 269, 275, 277

Wilson, Mary, 331 (n. 41)

Wilson, Woodrow, 80, 88, 260, 264, 268, 273, 279

Winchell, Walter, 106

Winchester Avenue High School (Monroe, N.C.), 54, 56, 65, 306

Winfield, B. J., 80, 88, 89, 91, 101

Wingate, N.C., 195

Winston-Salem, N.C., 48, 140

Wolfe, Fred, 21

Womanhood. *See* White womanhood

Women. *See* African American—women; Gender politics; Sexuality; White womanhood

Woolworth's Department Store, 217

Works Progress Administration, 83, 251, 258

World War II, 3, 26–51 passim, 61, 76, 116, 137, 222, 223, 235, 291, 295; and African American freedom movement, 3, 26–59 passim, 313 (n. 5); African American soldiers in, 2, 34, 37, 38, 43–45, 73; and armed struggle, 32–48 passim, 313 (n. 78); and racial poli-

tics, 31, 32, 34, 35, 43, 47, 48, 50, 52,
68, 119, 213, 308, 321, 333 (n. 67); veterans of, 2, 9, 27, 29, 48–62 passim,
80–82, 88, 116, 119, 291; and violence
against African Americans, 26–45
passim
Worthy, William, 222, 223, 235, 237,
242, 266, 283, 288

WRAL-TV, 5, 271
Wright, Sarah Elizabeth, 227, 233

Yale University, 238
Yeagley, J. Walter, 303
Young Americans for Freedom, 238, 239

Zhou Enlai, 296, 302